EUROPE TRAVELBOOK™

THE GUIDE TO PREMIER DESTINATIONS

2002 EDITION

AAA

President & CEO: Robert Darbelnet
Executive Vice President, Publishing & Administration: Rick Rinner
Managing Director, Travel Information: Bob Hopkins

Director, Product Development: Bill Wood
Director, Sales & Marketing: John Coerper
Director, Purchasing & Corporate Services: Becky Barrett
Director, Business Development: Gary Sisco
Director, Tourism Information Development (TID): Michael Petrone
Director, Travel Information: Jeff Zimmerman
Director, Publishing Operations: Susan Sears
Director, GIS/Cartography: Jan Coyne
Director, Publishing/GIS Systems & Development: Ramin Kalhor

Managing Editor, Product Development: Margaret Cavanaugh
Development Editor: Greg Weekes

AAA Travel Store & e-store Manager: Sharon Edwards

Manager, Product Support: Linda Indolfi
Manager, Electronic Media Design: Mike McCrary

Published by AAA Publishing, 1000 AAA Drive, Heathrow, Florida 32746

The *AAA Europe TravelBook – The Guide to Premier Destinations* was created and produced for AAA Publishing by AA Publishing, Basingstoke, England.

Written by Des Hannigan, Sally Roy and Nia Williams
2002 edition verified by Colin Follett
Page make-up by Anton Graphics Ltd.

Cover photos
Main photo: Venetia, Italy
© Joe Cornish/Stone Images
Cover inset: Greece
© Will & Demi McIntyre/Stone Images
Spine: Neuschwanstein, Germany

ISBN 1-56251-680-9

Cataloging-in-Publication Data is on file with the Library of Congress.

Color separations by Leo Reprographic Ltd., Hong Kong

Printed and bound in Italy by Fratelli Spada SpA

View from beneath the Eiffel Tower in Paris, France

Foreword

Welcome to the 2002 edition of the AAA Europe TravelBook!

If you are thinking about going to Europe, this book will help make your trip truly memorable and enjoyable. Although every traveler has a personal favorite European destination, for this book we've selected places that have special appeal, particularly if you're a first- or second-time visitor. Experience world capitals that have delighted visitors for centuries: the broad 18th-century boulevards, wonderful museums and superb food of Paris; London, where tradition and royal pageantry are juxtaposed with a lively arts scene; Prague's medieval grandeur, vibrantly emerging after decades of suppression; Rome, cradle of one of the world's great civilizations; and Vienna, with a magnificent opera house that is still a focus for world-renowned music.

But not all Europeans reside in big cities. Odense, in Denmark, welcomes visitors to the charming museum that was the birthplace of famed storyteller Hans Christian Andersen. York, in England, has an atmospheric old center, the "Shambles," with ancient cobbled streets, leaning half-timbered shops and pubs, and the mighty towers of the grand York Minster cathedral. And for centuries the city of Santiago de Compostela, in Spain, has welcomed Christian pilgrims from the far corners of Europe to its monumental cathedral built around the reputed grave of St. James; pilgrims still come, drawn by the myth and beauty of this holy place.

This book will not only whet your travel appetite with lively text and striking photographs; it also provides a wealth of practical information that will enable both seasoned and novice travelers to get the most out of their trip. Included are tips about what you will need to bring and about getting around once you're there, maps to help you find your way, detailed descriptions of what to see, suggestions for where to stay and eat, and insider advice from specialist authors to increase your enjoyment of the fascinating cultures that make up Europe.

EUROPE TRAVELBOOK™

THE GUIDE TO PREMIER DESTINATIONS

CONTENTS

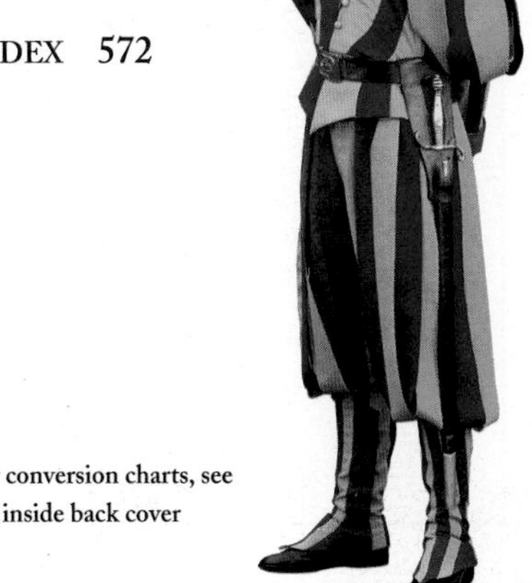

For conversion charts, see the inside back cover

Map of Europe

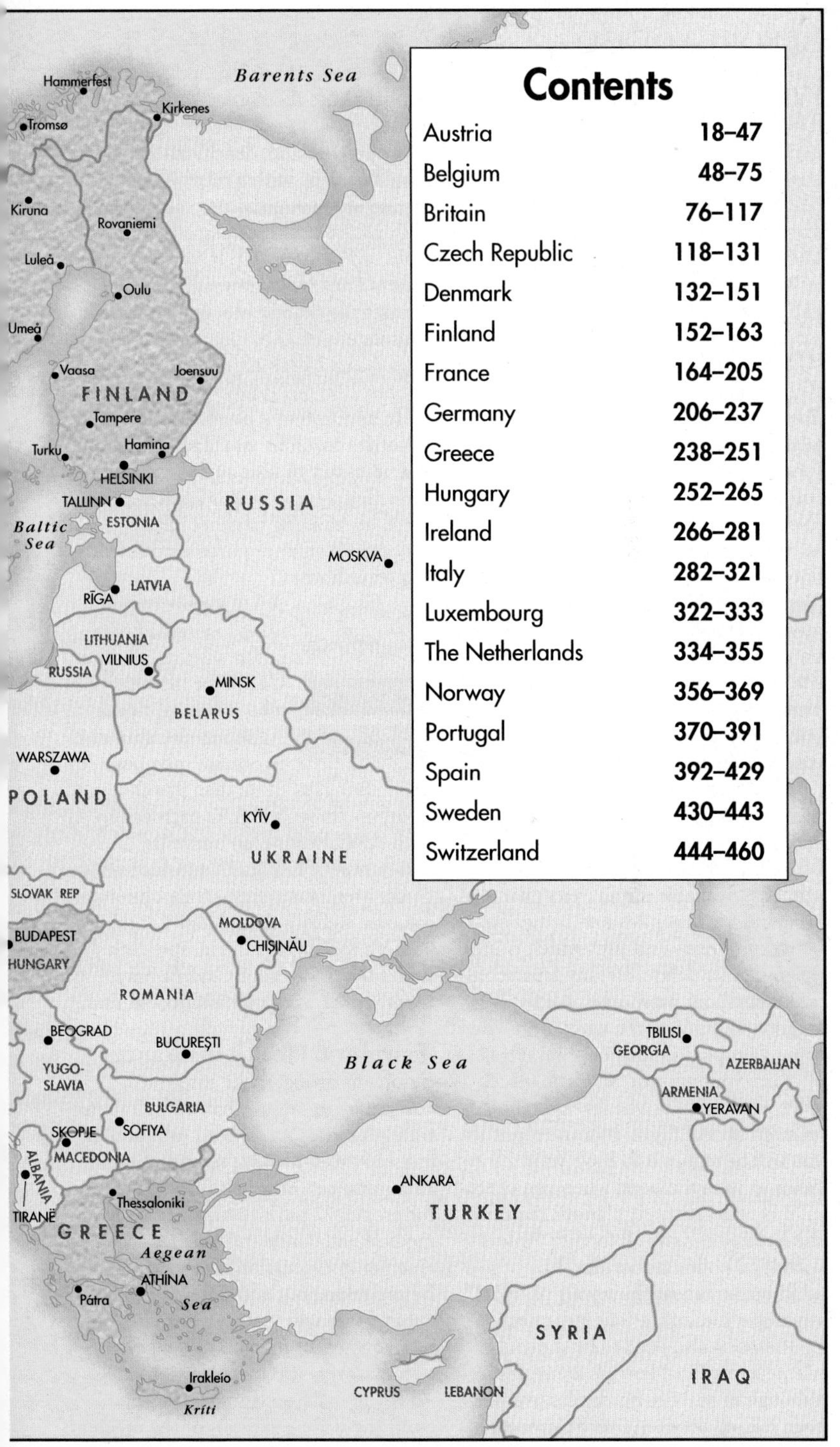
Barents Sea
Hammerfest
Tromsø
Kirkenes
Kiruna
Rovaniemi
Luleå
Oulu
Umeå
Vaasa
Joensuu
FINLAND
Tampere
Turku
Hamina
HELSINKI
TALLINN
ESTONIA
Baltic Sea
RUSSIA
MOSKVA
RĪGA
LATVIA
LITHUANIA
VILNIUS
RUSSIA
MINSK
BELARUS
WARSZAWA
POLAND
KYÏV
UKRAINE
SLOVAK REP
BUDAPEST
HUNGARY
MOLDOVA
CHIŞINĂU
ROMANIA
BEOGRAD
BUCUREŞTI
YUGO-SLAVIA
Black Sea
TBILISI
GEORGIA
AZERBAIJAN
ARMENIA
YERAVAN
BULGARIA
SOFIYA
SKOPJE
MACEDONIA
ALBANIA
TIRANË
Thessaloniki
ANKARA
TURKEY
GREECE
Aegean Sea
ATHÍNA
Pátra
SYRIA
IRAQ
Irakleío
Kríti
CYPRUS
LEBANON

Contents

BEFORE YOU GO

Passports and Visas

The most important document you'll need to arrange before you travel is a passport. Passport application forms can be obtained by contacting any Federal, state or probate court or post office, library or county or municipal office authorized to accept passport applications. U.S. passport agencies have Offices in major cities; check the Yellow Pages (U.S. Government, State Department, Bureau of Consular Affairs, Office of Passport Services) for the one nearest you. You also can request an application form by calling the National Passport Information Center at (888) 362-8668. (Note: There is a $4.95 credit card charge to contact the center by phone.) Phone lines are open Mon.–Fri. 8:30–5 (Eastern Time). Comprehensive passport information and application forms are available on the U.S. Department of State Internet site at www.travel.state.gov. Travel warnings, consular information sheets, public announcements and publications information also can be accessed.

Each person traveling must have a passport; apply early, since processing can take several months from the time of application until it arrives. Rush service is available for an extra charge. Demand for new passports is highest between January and July, which could mean further delays. Before departure, make sure your passport is valid at least six months prior to the expiration date; some European countries require this.

Keep your passport in a safe place, since you'll need it whenever you board an international flight. In some countries, you will be required to leave your passport with the hotel when you check in; this is to satisfy regulations requiring the hotel to register all foreign visitors with local police authorities. In addition, you must show your passport whenever you cash a traveler's check.

Passports also need to be shown whenever national borders are crossed, although in practice border controls have been relaxed between many European Union (E.U.) member countries. In Geneva, the city transportation system crosses national borders and the airport also straddles the border, so you'll need a passport simply to get around.

Photocopy the identification page; leave one copy with a relative or friend in case of emergency, and carry one with you in case your passport is lost or stolen while traveling. If this occurs, inform local police immediately and contact the nearest U.S. embassy or consulate. The U.S. Department of State has a 24-hour traveler's hotline; phone (202) 647-5225.

In addition to a passport, some countries require a visa. Travel visas are not necessary to visit any of the countries covered in this book, but if you'll be traveling to other nations, check their entry requirements before you leave home.

AAA members will want to visit aaa.com before visiting Europe. Check for merchants who will accept your AAA membership card to obtain "member only" savings at more than 9,000 locations through AAA's partnership with ARC Europe, an umbrella association of European automobile clubs. Members visiting their club's aaa.com website should look for the "Search for Savings in Europe" link under the Show Your Card & Save (or Member Savings/Benefits) section.

Travel and Health Insurance

Before departing, make sure you are covered by insurance that will reimburse travel expenses if you need to cancel or cut short your trip due to unforeseen circumstances. You'll also need coverage for property loss or theft, emergency medical and dental treatment, and emergency evacuation if necessary. Before taking out additional insurance, check to see whether your current homeowners or medical coverage already covers you for travel abroad.

If you make a claim, your insurance company will need proof of the incident or expenditure. Keep copies of any police report and related documents, or doctor or hospital bills or statements, to submit with your insurance claim.

Weather and When To Go

The European continent occupies a far more northerly location than its overall moderate climate would suggest. Lisbon and Athens are at about the same latitude as Washington, D.C., and Helsinki, Oslo and Stockholm lie as far north as Anchorage, Alaska. Different factors affect the weather at any given destination. One of the most prominent is the warming influence of the Gulf Stream, which affects all countries with an Atlantic coastline, from Spain and Portugal north through the British Isles into Scandinavia. The North and Baltic seas also affect temperatures and precipitation of the coastal areas they border, causing unpredictable weather.

Another definer is altitude, and Europe's great mountain ranges affect local temperatures and rainfall as well. The Pyrenees divide the Iberian Peninsula and France, while the Alps form an immense natural barrier across Austria, Switzerland and northern Italy south into France, where they descend to the Mediterranean Sea at Monaco. This entire region is popular with winter skiers, while summer visitors can expect clouds, mist and cool temperatures. The Apennines cut down the boot of Italy, also creating somewhat changeable conditions. But settled weather in the mountainous areas is grand indeed, with fresh air and crisp blue skies accentuating the views of craggy peaks and villages nestled in deep valleys.

Destinations bordering the Mediterranean are ideal for summer vacations, with mostly sunny skies, warm temperatures and little rain. The flip side can be the heat – especially in southern Spain and Greece – so protect yourself from overexposure to the sun and carry drinking water for any extended outdoor excursions. Winters in the Mediterranean region are cool and rainy, although temperatures are not usually severe and snow is rare in coastal areas.

Summer also is the main vacation season in central Europe, which has warm, generally dry summers and cold winters with plenty of snow at higher elevations. The weather in spring is generally more unpredictable than in the fall.

The British Isles – infamous for damp, dreary weather – can actually have weeks of dry conditions in summer, although that is the exception rather than the rule. It's best to come prepared for rain; a collapsible umbrella should be an essential traveling companion. British winters are indeed rainy, although temperatures are rarely extremely cold. Snow is uncommon except in the higher elevations of northern England and Scotland.

Scandinavia also has widely varying weather, as well as overall lower temperatures. Daytime highs in the summer months rarely exceed 75 degrees Fahrenheit, and the coastal locations of Copenhagen, Oslo, Stockholm and Helsinki increase the probability of unsettled conditions. Winters are uniformly severe, with significant snowfall the rule.

European school vacations are another factor in planning when to schedule your trip. Schools in most countries are in session from September until early July, making May and June good months to visit.

What To Pack

Your main objective should be to travel as lightly as possible. Layers of clothing can be peeled off as the day warms up, with something waterproof to wear on top if necessary. Pack an umbrella, and a hat or other headgear to protect against the cold in winter or the sun in summer. Casual dress is acceptable in European cities, with the exception of churches – visitors will not be welcome wearing shorts or a scanty top.

Break in your shoes before you leave home. Shoes with soft, substantial soles are not only ideal for walking but can ease the difficulty of maneuvering the cobbled streets that characterize many old city centers.

Electrical appliances will require an adapter that changes the shape of the plug prongs, as well as an electrical voltage converter that will allow a normal 110-volt American appliance to take 220- to 240-volt European current. Two-in-one adapter/converters are available at some hardware stores.

Bring a first-aid kit with plenty of bandages, sunblock, insect repellent and over-the-counter remedies for minor ailments. Include written prescriptions for prescription medicines in case you need more or need to show the prescription to customs officials. Tissues will come in handy, as local restrooms in some areas will likely be below U.S. standards. European hotel rooms provide the usual array of towels but often no washcloth, so pack one just in case.

The offerings at open-air markets, bakeries and delicatessens are great for an impromptu picnic to go. Bring a knife for cutting bread and a spoon for small cartons of salad or other edibles (utensils aren't provided). Always pack the knife in your stowed luggage for plane trips so that airport security officials don't construe it as a weapon.

WHILE YOU ARE THERE

Emergencies

For emergency information pertaining to each of the countries covered in this book, refer to the Essential Information section, pages 462–537.

Health

Take sensible precautions during hot weather. Wear a hat, sunglasses and sunblock, especially if you are on or near the water. Drink plenty of fluids, and remember that alcoholic beverages and the caffeine in coffee, tea and some sodas have a dehydrating effect. Slow down or take a break in the shade if you suddenly feel tired or ill.

The tap water in northern Europe is generally safe to drink, although its high mineral content can cause minor upsets if you're not used to it. Bottled water is an inexpensive and widely available alternative. If you're in an area where the tap water is unsafe, it's best to avoid ice cubes and salads with ingredients that are likely to have been washed in water.

Pharmacists are a good first source for dealing with minor health problems; a pharmacist will be able to direct you to a doctor if necessary. For advice pertaining to specific topics, see the "Health" subheading under individual countries in Essential Information.

Language

Traveling is always more enjoyable if you can converse a bit in the local language. "Yes," "no," "please" and "thank you," accompanied by a pleasant smile and polite manner, will go far toward oiling social wheels. Refer to the "Useful Words and Phrases" subheading under individual countries in Essential Information for a helpful list.

The areas where English is most likely to be spoken are Scandinavia, the "Benelux" countries of Belgium, the Netherlands and Luxembourg, and Germany, Austria and Switzerland. In Britain and Ireland you may encounter strong regional accents, as well as unfamiliar words and expressions.

To some Europeans – particularly the French and the British – good manners are a social necessity. "Please" and "thank you" should be part of every request in Britain; in France, anyone you don't know personally (including the staff in stores and restaurants) should be addressed as "monsieur" ("sir"), "madame" ("madam") or "mademoiselle" ("miss").

If you're really stuck with communications, remember that hotel receptionists usually speak English, and are invariably helpful and friendly; you can ask them to phone for taxis and arrange for cleaning and similar personal services.

Media

Room televisions in the larger hotels have satellite or cable connections and broadcast BBC channels, the British Sky network or CNN. On the radio you may be able to pick up

Voice of America, Radio Canada or BBC broadcasts.

In larger cities, American newspapers (usually previous-day editions) and magazines are widely available; the most common are *USA Today*, the international edition of the *New York Herald Tribune* and *Time* magazine. They can be purchased at airports and central train stations, as well as at newsstands, tobacconists and "stationers," shops that also sell books and stationery.

Money and Valuables

Having some of your funds in local currency is a necessity, but only carry what you'll need for a day or two. If it's lost or stolen you almost certainly won't get it back, and if you have to convert a large amount back to dollars or to another foreign currency you'll pay again for exchange charges. Customs restrictions may apply if you need to carry large amounts of currency. For additional information see the "Money" subheading under individual countries in Essential Information.

Currency exchange facilities are widely available in Europe. There are exchange offices at airports and central train stations, in the central business districts in cities, and at seaports and other international border crossing points. They are often open extended hours in summer and during vacations. Most hotel reception desks also will exchange currency. Exchange rates are normally displayed; local newspapers and the international editions of U. S. newspapers also provide the current rate of exchange. A commission is charged for each transaction. Although it is likely to be a little higher at hotels, it may be worth paying extra for the convenience.

Traveler's checks are reliable and safe. Keep a record of the check numbers you redeem, and carry numbers and receipts in a separate place in case you need to produce them in the event of loss. Be prepared to show your passport each time you cash in a check or offer one in payment. If you're going to be spending time in just one or two countries you may want to obtain traveler's checks in the local currency. You can use them for purchases in stores, although you'll still need to show your passport.

Credit cards, increasingly accepted in Europe, are an easy and trouble-free method of payment. American Express, MasterCard and VISA are the most widely accepted; check with your credit card company before departure if you have any doubt about its validity abroad. Keep a record of your card number in a separate place, and note the international phone number to report card losses in case yours is misplaced or stolen. You also can get cash advances with your credit card from an ATM, usually at favorable exchange rates.

Leave valuable jewelry at home; small items are easily lost or mislaid, and ostentatious displays mark you as a prospective target for theft. Make sure your luggage is lockable and labeled both outside and inside. Never leave your bags unattended. Train stations normally provide lockers or check desks where you can leave a heavy bag while sightseeing. If you're traveling by car, keep your doors locked in slow-moving traffic or when driving through busy urban areas, and put everything in the trunk while the car is parked.

If the worst happens and you do have belongings stolen, report the incident to the police immediately and get a written police report or statement to provide to your insurance company as evidence for your claim.

Personal Safety

Most of the rules for personal safety constitute common sense. Keep valuables (passport, money, checks, credit cards) hidden when you're on the move; a money belt or neck purse worn inside clothing is the safest option. Put money in different places so that if one bag is lost you have another source of funds. Fanny packs and pockets are not safe places to carry valuables. Any bag you'll be carrying with you during the day should have a secure fastener, with a sturdy strap that goes over your neck and crosses your body – not simply over the shoulder. This helps ensure that bulkier items (cameras, binoculars, etc.) will be safe from pickpockets and petty thieves in crowded urban areas or on buses or trains.

The big tourist attractions are prime territory for pickpockets, as are buses, trains, subways, markets and airports. Be on guard for people who "accidentally" bump into you, or watch while you use an ATM. In large cities, be on the lookout for gangs of youngsters who create a commotion and then steal bags from tourists while their attention is distracted.

People begging in the street can be quite persistent; walk quickly away without responding or making eye contact. Contact a police officer if anyone becomes particularly aggressive; police on city streets throughout Europe are usually very approachable and often speak a little English. In general, avoid walking alone after dark. In southern European city centers during the summer, however, you'll almost certainly encounter throngs of locals out walking and shopping late into the evening, refreshed by a few hours of afternoon siesta.

Phone Service

You can make international calls from most European telephones; for specific information see "Telephones" under individual countries in the Essential Information section. To place a call to another country, first dial the international code, then the country code, then the area code (usually minus any initial zero) and the local number. Sometimes you'll need to wait for another dial tone after dialing the international code. In some countries the telecommunications infrastructure is fairly fragile, and it may take two or three tries before you get through.

The easiest and least expensive way to make an international call is to use a calling card. Dialing the appropriate access number (numbers differ according to country) will connect you with an English-speaking operator who can place a collect call or a call credited to your card. To obtain a card and a list of country access numbers, contact your telephone service provider. If you use a pay phone, you may need to insert a coin in the local currency to get an outside line to make the call.

The convenience of making a phone call from your hotel room will be offset by the hefty surcharges tacked onto the bill. It's always less expensive to use the pay phone in the lobby; ask the hotel staff for assistance if you can't figure out how the phone works.

Some cell phones may be adaptable for use in Europe, but the operating frequencies are different; check with your service provider. Fax machines are available in the central business centers of cities and at some hotels. If you can't do without e-mail, cybercafés are popping up in major cities throughout Europe – handy places to stop for coffee and a bite to eat, as well as using the computers to send e-mail and check your favorite websites.

If you're staying in one country for a few days, it may be worthwhile to obtain a local prepaid telephone card, which can be used with phones that accept them. They can normally be purchased at small stores called "tobacconists" that also sell cigarettes, candy, snacks, magazines and sometimes postage stamps.

Travelers with Disabilities

Facilities for disabled visitors in northern and central European countries are generally very good, but old castles, palaces and cathedrals may not be adapted for special access. The Mediterranean countries, Czech Republic and Hungary are improving, but if you need help it is advisable to check in advance with local tourist offices. The old central cores of European cities are often difficult to change or adapt to make them suitable for those with special needs. Expect steps and stairways in city centers (some stairways have no handrails), in addition to cobbled and uneven street and sidewalk surfaces.

Almost all of the old buildings in Europe – including those that house hotels and such attractions as museums and castles – are likely to contain stairways, narrow halls and doorways, and other access irregularities. Make certain that accessibility standards meet your requirements when reserving accommodations.

Often hotels will be able to provide a room with adequate access if they know your needs in advance. Call ahead to attractions and restaurants as well to ascertain the nature of their facilities. Motorized carts at airports will whisk you to and from arrival and departure gates.

GETTING AROUND

City Transportation

A good first stop when you arrive at your destination is either a central public transportation information center or the tourist information office (see the Essential Information boxes in the introduction to each featured city). Spend time here and obtain information on how to get around the city, including transportation maps and detailed city maps. You also may be able to purchase travel tickets for public transportation, including those valid for multiple rides or more than one day; they will save you money and the inconvenience of having to buy a new ticket for every journey.

There are a variety of public transportation options in Europe:

- Subways are underground trains that tunnel beneath city centers, occasionally emerging to ground level in less congested suburban areas, or to cross rivers.
- Buses operate along designated routes in city centers; double-decked buses are common for carrying larger numbers of passengers. Some cities have special sightseeing buses in summer, with an open-topped deck for better views. Long-distance buses are commonly known as "coaches" in Britain and Ireland.
- Trams are vehicles that travel on rails set into the street surface. They are often powered by overhead electric cables that run along the route. If you are walking or in a car, be especially careful of trams; they always have the right of way, and because they run quietly can appear with little warning.
- Trolley buses run on tires, but are powered by overhead electric cables running above the route. Like trams, they have right of way in traffic and run quietly.
- Funiculars are passenger cars that ascend and descend steep hills or cliffs on a track set into the ground, typically on slopes leading down to a beach but also in some cities, such as Lisbon or Barcelona, where there are steep inclines.
- Cable cars are suspended from cables attached to the top of the cars. They are common at ski resorts, and also in some cities.
- Rack railways are a feature in Switzerland, where trains that need to negotiate steep mountains connect with a cog system between the rails that provides extra power up the slopes.

In many continental European countries, the procedure is to buy a travel ticket at a ticket office or booth and then validate it by pushing it into a special machine, either at the stop or on the vehicle, which will give the ticket a date and time stamp validating it for the appropriate journey or time period. If you buy a tourist ticket that is valid for a number of days, you will usually need to validate it only once before you first use it.

Between Cities

Trains Most countries in Europe have a national train system, with trains operating across national borders. Service is generally efficient, although local routes with frequent stops can be slow. If your entire trip is going to be by train it may be well worth obtaining a Eurail pass from your travel agent in the United States before you go (note that they are not on sale in Europe).

Passes are valid for periods from a few days to three months. In addition, many national rail systems have their own passes for travel within a country; these also are available from travel agents in the United States and Canada, and also in Europe.

Tickets for most trains are available either in advance or just before travel. For special trains (some express trains – for instance, in Spain; overnight sleeper trains; the Orient Express; or the Eurostar trains between Britain and France that travel through the tunnel beneath the English Channel) you may need to buy tickets a few days in advance to be sure of getting a seat. This is especially the case during busy vacation times.

Information about main city train stations is in the Essential Information box for each city.

Airlines Most countries have a national airline as well as independent operators that operate internationally, based on hub cities within the country. Additionally, smaller airlines serve smaller destinations, usually functioning within the country. Schedules, fares and availability are subject to frequent change. If you have a specific itinerary in mind, your travel agent is the best place to start for flight information.

You are most likely to have the best choice of flights and better prices if you reserve your tickets well in advance. Big airports in major cities – in Paris, London and Rome, for example – will have the largest choice of flights, but also are the busiest. It can be a good idea to begin your trip at a smaller destination, where the number of travelers will be fewer and the pace less frantic.

Ferries Services transport individual passengers as well as cars, and in some cases trains (the cars of the train actually travel on the boat). Ferry companies offering longer-distance journeys of two or three days have very comfortable ships, and they promote these services as "mini-cruises" that can make a relaxing interlude between busy city sightseeing sessions.

Ferries operate regularly in the Scandinavian archipelago and along the Norwegian fjords; among the Scottish islands; between Britain and Ireland, Scandinavia, Germany, the Netherlands, Belgium, France and Spain; and throughout the islands and coastal ports of the Mediterranean countries and islands.

Generally speaking, transfers from ports to city centers are less straightforward than from airports and train stations. If you intend to carry a lot of luggage, it may be advisable to ask tourist information offices about this when planning your trip.

European Customs and Immigration

Each country has its own customs import regulations; see the Essential Information section beginning on page 461. For the purposes of customs and duty-free allowances, the countries of the European Union are considered as one customs area, and there are no limits on goods for personal use when traveling between member countries. However, customs restrictions do apply when traveling between E.U. countries and non-E.U. countries. The E.U. member countries include all the countries in this book, with the

AAA Travel Agencies

AAA Travel Agencies offer various services to help simplify the logistics of international travel planning, especially for the first-time visitor. They can make airline reservations, book accommodations, set up escorted tours and independent travel packages, offer passport and visa assistance, arrange for car rentals and an official International Driving Permit, and provide fee-free American Express traveler's checks. AAA members also are eligible for discounts on selected hotels and motels and receive exclusive savings on cruising vacations.

exception of Norway, Switzerland, the Czech Republic and Hungary.

At the immigration barrier in E.U. countries, travelers are separated into two lanes – one for E.U. citizens and one for non-E.U. citizens. Border controls between E.U. countries are gradually being relaxed. You will probably pass through an immigration desk when arriving in a new country by plane or train, but road barrier checkpoints within the E.U. have largely disappeared in recent years. Border controls remain between the E.U. and the rest of Europe, however.

DRIVING IN EUROPE

European Automobile Clubs

For the benefit of members traveling abroad, AAA maintains reciprocal agreements with motoring clubs in Europe. Presentation of your valid AAA membership card at participating motoring clubs allows you to receive services they provide to their own members. Operating philosophies and facilities differ from country to country, however, so service may not be the same as back home. AAA members will need to visit their local club to obtain information about services that can be expected from a specific European motoring club.

Refer to the Essential Information pages for each country for motoring club contact details, as well as documentation requirements and information concerning driving regulations.

Car Rental

If you intend to drive across national borders tell the rental company, as this will affect both the rate and the type of insurance documentation required. British and Irish rental agencies may require several days' notice to supply a car available for travel to continental Europe. Most car rental companies in Europe will not rent to an individual under 21.

To rent a car you will need a valid U.S. driver's license and preferably an International Driving Permit, and you will probably be asked to show your passport. Depending on which rental company you use, you may be required to produce an additional credit card or further proof of identity for renting premium or luxury cars.

European cars are generally small and have manual transmissions. Local rental companies rarely offer vehicles equipped with air conditioning. Rates vary, but a AAA travel agent should be able to give you an accurate estimate. Reciprocal arrangements with European motoring clubs may not apply if you are driving a rental car (see the Driving section under Essential Information for each country). Be sure to inquire about local taxes; in France, taxes increase rental rates by up to one-third. Find out exactly what insurance coverage is included, and check whether you need a collision damage waiver (CDW) – you might already be covered through your personal car insurance policy or credit card company. A CDW may not cover certain types of damage; for example, in Greece damage to the underside of a car caused by a rough road may not be covered.

AAA Travel Agencies can reserve a car for you before you leave, provide prepayment arrangements, or reserve a car for you for specified dates and destinations. Rates are lower if reservations are made in the United States prior to your departure, and guaranteed in U.S. dollars if you prepay; reserve well in advance. If you plan to travel through several countries, make certain that the rental company has been informed, and that you have the necessary documents.

Hertz Affordable Europe offers discounts to AAA members guaranteed in U.S. dollars, with 24-hour emergency roadside assistance, free unlimited mileage, computerized driving directions and English-speaking staff at 2,500 locations throughout Europe. For reservations contact Hertz, (800) 654-3080, or a AAA Travel Agency.

Green Card

If you drive a car in Europe you will need a Green Card (sometimes called an International Insurance Certificate) to prove that you have liability insurance. Car rental agencies will provide this with the vehicle; most companies include it in the rental price.

A Green Card also is advised for motorists taking their own vehicle overseas; for additional information contact your automobile insurer.

International Driving Permit (IDP)

An International Driving Permit is a document containing your photograph and confirming that you hold a valid driver's license in your own country. It has a standard translation in several languages and is a useful document to carry if you plan to drive in Europe, even if it is not specifically required by the country. The permit is available from AAA Travel Agencies.

Driving Regulations

Driving in busy European cities can be a daunting prospect if you're not used to the signs, driving habits and local regulations. If you are renting a car, be sure to get as much information from the rental company as possible. They will usually be able to provide a chart of common road signs and an area road map.If you are visiting a city by car, park outside the city center, preferably close to a public transportation link, and proceed to the center by public transportation.

Check parking signs where you leave your car: insure there are no restrictions, that you pay for and display a parking sticker if necessary, and check closing times if you use a multistory parking garage. Because of congestion in city centers, parking regulations are strictly enforced.

Specific driving regulations for each country are provided in the Essential Information section. In some countries, police can levy on-the-spot fines for serious offenses – including speeding and driving while drunk.

RETURNING TO THE UNITED STATES

Confirming Return Travel

If you are flying, it is advisable to contact the airport the day before leaving to be sure flight details are unchanged. Some carriers require you to reconfirm flights after an extended stopover of more than a few days; check the information that was supplied with your ticket. Allow plenty of time to get to the airport for check-in and clearing security.

Tax-free Shopping

Some major stores offer "tax-free shopping" to tourists. Although specific procedures differ slightly between countries, this enables you to make purchases and have them either sent to the airport of your departing flight, or directly to your home address. Such shopping saves the (often substantial) sales tax, but these items are still subject to any applicable U.S. import duty, plus postage and handling charges.

U.S. Customs

During your flight or voyage returning to the United States, you will be required to complete a customs declaration. You are allowed $400 worth of personal goods and gifts (including items purchased in duty-free shops); keep sales slips and have them ready for inspection. The duty-free exemption can include 100 cigars and 200 cigarettes, as well as one liter of wine, beer or liquor if you are 21 or over. (Tobacco products of Cuban origin are prohibited unless they were acquired in Cuba.) Any purchases in excess of the $400 exemption will be subject to duty. There is no restriction on the importing or exporting of currency.

For more information contact your local customs office, listed in the U.S. Government section (Treasury Department) of the telephone directory. Contact U.S. Customs Headquarters, 1300 Pennsylvania N.W., Washington, DC 20229, phone (202) 354-1000 (www.customs.gov) for a copy of their brochure *Know Before You Go*, which gives details of customs requirements.

Premier Destinations

"In whichever country of Europe one dwells, one feels that the other countries are near..."

From *The American Commonwealth*
by British politician and writer James Bryce

AUSTRIA

"THE country is wonderful. Mountains holding up cups of snow to the fiery sun..."

English novelist George Meredith, praising the Alps in a letter to Frederick A. Maxe, July 1861

Opposite: Snow-capped mountains dwarf a village and pastureland in the Leogang area of Austria

Austria

Small yet beautiful, Austria has unrivaled Alpine scenery, some of Europe's finest baroque architecture, a long tradition of music and culture, and a reputation for the warmth and hospitality of its people. Straddling the center of Europe, the country has exerted a critical influence on the region's history through the centuries, becoming a major player in world politics. Today, despite loss of territory and power after two world wars, Austria retains its status as the crossroads of modern Europe. The year-round grandeur of the mountains draws visitors from all over the world, while the combination of efficiency and charm makes Austria one of Europe's easiest and most beguiling tourist destinations.

The Land

Austria is the most mountainous country in Europe, with more than 70 percent of the land occupied by the Alps and Alpine valleys. This section of the eastern Alps is characterized by massive mountain chains with sheer rock faces and jagged ridges broken by deep valleys. The Tyrol region, bordering the Swiss and Italian Alps in western Austria, is renowned for its stunning scenery and is a popular skiing and hiking area. Below the tree line the mountains are heavily forested, giving way to lush Alpine meadows, grazed in summer by gentle-faced cattle and carpeted with vivid wildflowers.

Picturesque villages sit amid the pastures and along the valley bottoms, each with distinctive churches, clusters of traditional shuttered houses and wooden farm buildings. The Danube (Donau) river dominates northeastern

MORE TOP DESTINATIONS IN AUSTRIA

• Baden E2 • Bad Ischl C2 • Eisenstadt E2 • Eisriesenwelt C2 • Graz D2 • Grossglockner Hochalpenstrasse C1 • Hallstatt C2 • Kitzbühel B2 • Maria Saal D1 • Melk D3 • Mondsee C2 • Ötztal A2 • Riegersburg E2 • Salzkammergut C2 • St. Anton A2 • Stein D3 • Wachau D3 • Zillertal B2

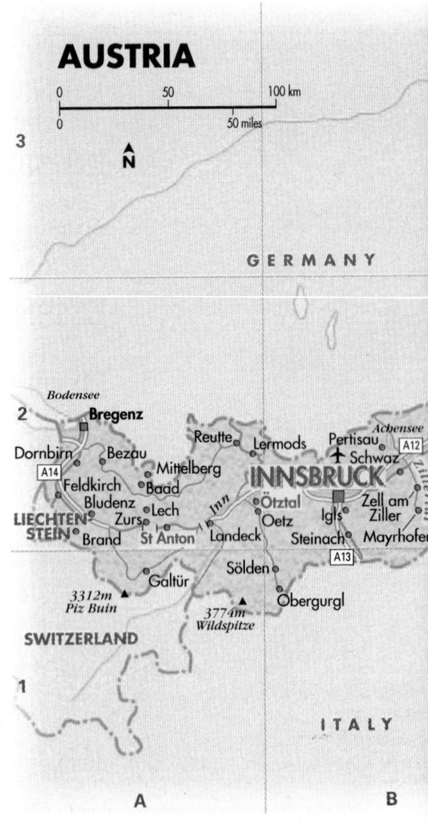

Austria, and most of the country's people inhabit the rolling terrain around the river. The flat fields of the Vienna basin are intensely cultivated, producing grain, fruit and vines.

The Habsburg Legacy

Throughout six centuries of Habsburg rule, Austria dominated the politics of much of Europe. The Habsburg Empire spread from Spain to Hungary, with sons and daughters of the ruling families marrying into other European ruling houses and thus furthering its influence. Vienna, with its grandiose architecture, splendidly illustrates Austrian prestige, and the entire country is rich in buildings from the days of the empire.

The Viennese Court sent administrators and army officials into the provinces; they brought along Viennese customs, attitudes and manners, as did the nobility who spent time both in the capital and on their country estates. The high-handed approach of these outsiders throughout the provinces has left a legacy of mistrust of the Viennese still discernible today. Historically, too, because of the terrain, the different areas of Austria were immensely varied, each valley having its own dialect, dress, habits and way of life.

Crossroads of Europe

At the end of World War II, Austria was divided into four zones of occupation, with the Allied powers occupying most of the western half. With the help of the Marshall Aid after

The architecture and setting of the Old Town make Innsbruck a popular holiday destination

World War II, this area was able to industrialize more efficiently than the Soviet-occupied zone, and the east-west divide continued even after the Second Republic was founded in 1955 and independence was regained.

Present-day Austria shares a boundary with eight other European countries: Germany, Italy, the Czech Republic, Hungary, Slovak Republic, Slovenia, Switzerland and Lichtenstein. Its 8 million inhabitants live in nine provinces, each with its own very distinctive characteristics.

More than half the working population is employed in the service sector: education, tourism, administration and health. Traditional agriculture only continues thanks to large subsidies, and now employs less than 10 percent of the workforce. The vast majority of Austrians speak German or a German dialect. Austria was unaffected by the Protestant Reformation and is still a deeply Catholic country. Its glorious baroque churches are packed for Sunday Mass.

Proud Traditions

Despite sharing a common language, Austrians are very different from their German neighbors – more lighthearted, less prone to take themselves seriously and generally more relaxed in their approach to life. They see themselves, correctly, as hospitable and cordial, thus defining the term *Gemütlichkeit*. This manifests itself in an easy friendliness to everyone, and it's one of the first things visitors notice. Every region sees itself as the best, and people proudly wear regional dress and enjoy traditional music and festivals. So when you encounter people wearing *Lederhosen* (leather pants) and *Dirndl* (bodiced dresses), it's for their benefit, not yours.

There's an elegance and ease to much Austrian life; cafés buzz with the chatter of people, *Bierkellern* (taverns) are packed with young and old, and streets are full of strolling crowds. Manners are conservative, even old-fashioned; this is a country where children open doors and give up seats for adults, and every stranger is greeted with an amicable "*Grüss Gott.*"

Environmental Issues

It's not only the tree-clad mountain slopes and verdant valleys that make Austria green; this is one of the most environmentally aware countries in Europe. Austria banned all nuclear power in the 1970s, and since then its green policy has made giant strides.

Heavy investment in public transportation has dramatically lessened the use of cars. This is a huge benefit to visitors, making travel in Austria, with its seamless connections between different forms of public transportation, very easy. Despite the Alpine terrain, Austrians cycle a lot, and every town has bike routes and parks. Recycling is a way of life; there are many different types of garbage cans, each clearly labeled for the appropriate trash.

Sauerkraut and Strudel

Austrians take food seriously and waiters are genuinely interested to know whether you've enjoyed a meal and alarmingly downcast if you can't cope with the vast portions served. Mealtimes are closer to American schedules than elsewhere, with lunch around noon and dinner any time after 6.

Each region has its own specialties, but the emphasis everywhere is on heavy soups, plenty of meat, *Knödel* (dumplings) and noodles, and cream, cream, cream. The latter appears in sauces, soups, coffee and whipped mounds decorating just about every dessert. Sauerkraut (pickled cabbage) frequently accompanies main courses, along with piles of potatoes, and salads are drenched in creamy dressings.

Austrians indulge their passion for coffee and cakes between meals, and you should certainly sample *Apfelstrudel* (apple strudel) and *Sachertorte*, a wickedly rich frosted chocolate cake oozing apricot jam. There are many different types of beer, and some excellent wines. You should also try *Schnapps*, a strong fruit or herb-based liqueur, drunk as a digestive aid. Coffee is the national drink, with cafés often serving as many as 20 or more different variations; hot chocolate is good, too. And on the healthy side, there are outstanding fruit and vegetable juices.

Summer and Winter

Austria offers visitors as much in the winter as in the summer. For Europeans, the Austrian Alps have been a favorite skiing destination for many years, with impeccably organized facilities, trails ranging from gentle slopes to world-class black runs, and wonderful après-ski dining and nightlife.

Summer sees the Alpine pastures at their best, and the whole country is crisscrossed with hiking trails through glorious mountain scenery. It's in summer, too, that the cities come alive, with strolling crowds, colorful flowers and a plethora of music and folk festivals. Spring starts late, so it's best to plan a visit in June or later.

In early spring and again in autumn, you may experience the dreaded *Föhn* wind in western Austria; this is a fierce, warm, dry wind from the south that is notorious for making people generally tired and grumpy, so be prepared.

The traditional *Loden* jacket and *Dirndl* skirt, worn at festival time

TIMELINE

15 BC to AD 50	Romans establish frontier provinces along the Danube and found legionary fortress of Carnuntum.
500–700	After final withdrawal of Romans, Alamanni and Bavarian tribes settle lower Alpine regions.
966	Austmark, established as a bulwark against attacks from the east, is first referred to as Ostarrichi.
1278	Founding of Habsburg Dynasty, beginning 640 years of power.
1493–1519	Foundations of the Habsburg world empire laid by marriage contracts of Maximilian I.
1699	Conquest of Hungary; Habsburgs gain hereditary right to the Hungarian throne in the male line.
1805	Napoleon defeats the Austrians at Battle of Austerlitz; end of Holy Roman Empire.
1814–15	Congress of Vienna restructures the political map of Europe.
1914	Assassination of heir to Austrian throne at Sarejevo leads to outbreak of World War I; Austria fights on losing side.
1919	Dissolution of Austro-Hungarian monarchy; loss of territories.
1938	Hitler incorporates Austria into the German Reich.
1939–45	World War II; Austrians fight in German army; following defeat, Austria is divided into four zones of occupation.
1955	Full sovereignty and founding of Second Republic; Austria is admitted to the United Nations.
1986	Kurt Waldheim is elected president.
1995	Austria joins European Community.
1999	Austria enters European Monetary Union.

THE LAST OF THE KNIGHTS

Maximilian I ruled from 1493 until 1519; these years saw the establishment of his family, the Habsburgs, as hereditary emperors of the Holy Roman Empire and rulers of Austria and far beyond, a dynasty that continued until 1918. Maximilian, through two strategic marriages, gained control over Burgundy (a region in northern France) and the Low Countries. He married his son into the Spanish royal family, giving the Habsburgs rights over Spain, Naples and Spanish America and thus laying the foundations for the vast empire that was to come. Maximilian reformed the governmental administration, patronized the arts, loved hunting and jousting, and was known as "the last of the knights" who led Austria from the Middle Ages to the bright light of the Renaissance and the empire.

Stop at a sidewalk café on the Graben to absorb the atmosphere of Vienna

Survival Guide

- Always return greetings; hospitality is Austria's most important national characteristic, and people expect a reply to their welcoming *"Grüss Gott,"* meaning "God's greeting."
- For the opera men should wear a jacket and tie; women, a dress, suit or smart pants.
- When going into churches, remember that it's disrespectful to show bare shoulders or upper arms.
- Take an umbrella; it can rain heavily, anywhere, at any time of year.
- For a day in the mountains, remember that the temperature drops as you gain altitude. Take warm clothes so you can layer, and if you're hiking, wear suitable footwear, and bring water and food.
- Austrians are very litter-conscious and streets are immaculately clean; do your part to leave them that way.
- It's considered polite to stand in line when waiting for a bus or at an attraction, and to defer to the elderly.
- Bedding in Austria consists of a large, puffy feather quilt in a cotton cover. This will be folded on your bed, waiting to be opened up at bedtime.
- Austrians eat and drink with gusto, and spirits as well as the noise level rise during the evening. Drunkeness, however, is considered uncouth.
- All cafés, bars and restaurants have coat hooks and umbrella stands, and it's considered more respectful to leave coats and umbrellas there rather than on your chair.
- It's acceptable to spend up to an hour lingering over one or two drinks in a café.
- Public restrooms are free, numerous and spotless; you'll find them in virtually all public buildings, and you can also use bathrooms in cafés and restaurants.
- Always cross the street at official crossings and wait for the green man signal. It's illegal, though seldom prosecuted, to cross anywhere else.

VIENNA

For much of the 20th century, Vienna (Wien) had an air of fading grandeur, a city whose days of imperial glory had truly passed. But in the 1980s Vienna began to redefine itself, and continues to do so. The population has since increased for the first time since 1919; a vibrant youth culture has emerged; and the imperial architecture of the 18th and 19th centuries has been joined by exciting modern designs, such as the huge museum quarter being built on the site of the emperor's former stables. At the beginning of the 21st century Vienna seems to be shaking off its torpor and styling itself, once again, as a dynamic European cultural center.

Finding Your Way

Between 1857 and 1865 Emperor Franz Josef I had the bastions surrounding Vienna's Old Town (Innere Stadt) demolished, and laid out a vast boulevard known as the Ring. Within the Old Town and the Ring are Vienna's most important sights, including St. Stephen's Cathedral (Stephansdom, see page 32) and the Imperial Palace (Hofburg, see page 29).

It's possible to take in the main sights on foot, but the "Hopper" buses are a flexible alternative, allowing you to hop on or off anywhere along their route. There are also trams and underground (U-Bahn) trains running through and around the area. A more expensive option is to hire a horse-drawn carriage (*Fiaker*) at Stephansplatz, Heldenplatz or Albertinaplatz. Be sure to agree on the price and length of trip before you begin your journey.

The Third Man

One of Vienna's favorite parks is the Prater, situated on the former imperial hunting grounds. It was opened to the public in 1766, and its attractions now include racing tracks, a fairground and a Ferris wheel built in 1896. This is where Joseph Cotten and Orson Welles had their confrontation high over the city in the 1949 film *The Third Man*.

An outer ring road, the Gürtel (belt), links the city with major freeways. East of Vienna, the Danube river and the Danube canal cut through some 23 districts, and on the southern outskirts are the Vienna Woods (Wienerwald). Maps showing walking routes through the woods are available from the efficient information center at the corner of Albertinaplatz and Maysedergasse.

Architecture

Wandering Vienna's streets is a treat for lovers of architecture. Styles range from the Gothic pointed arches of St. Stephen's Cathedral and the neo-Gothic arcades of the New City Hall (Neues Rathaus) to the baroque of the 17th and 18th centuries.

Imperial 19th-century majesty is typified in buildings lining the Ring

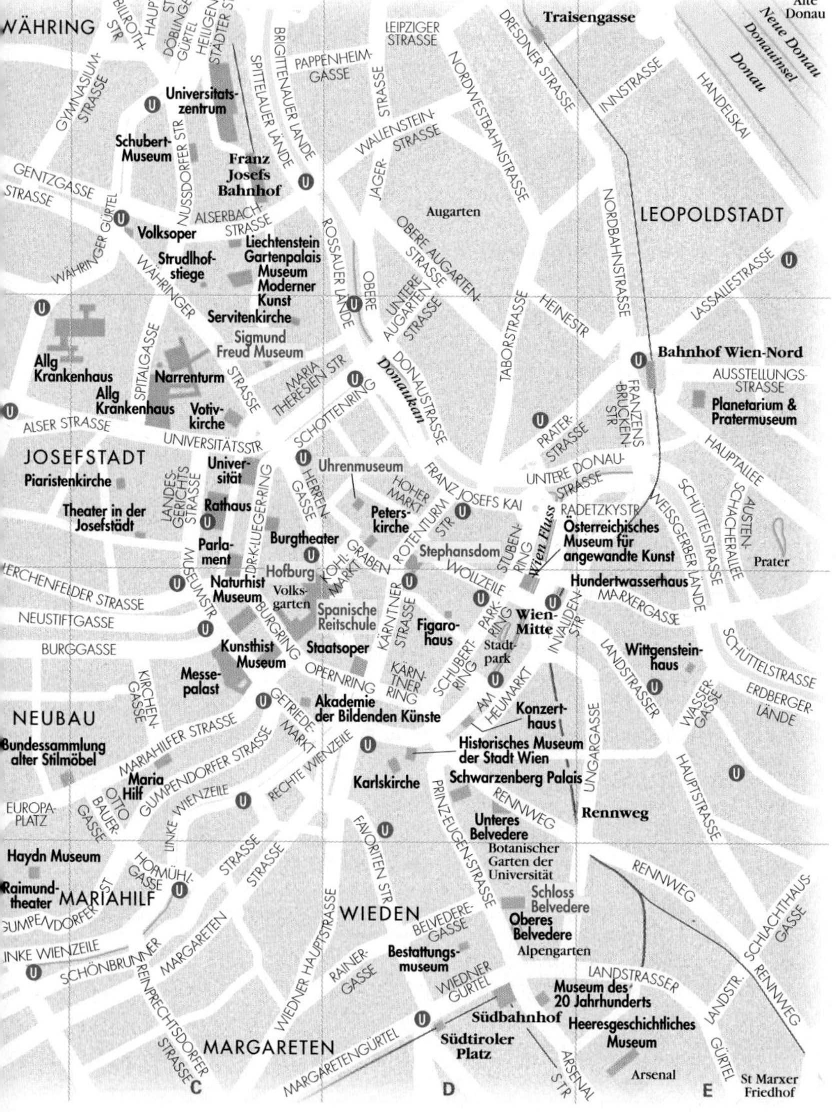

and also in the art nouveau edifices, known here as the "Secession" style because its practitioners seceded from the staid Association of Fine Artists in 1897. They went on to set up their own exhibitions in the Secession Building on Friedrichstrasse.

There also are modern styles, such as the shining glass curves of the 1900 Haas-Haus by Hans Hollein, opposite St. Stephen's; and a postmodern housing block by Friedensreich Hundertwasser, a Hansel-and-Gretel building of colored mosaics, in Kegelgasse.

Viennese Music

Vienna is proud of its long history as a center of classical music, and celebrates with a busy schedule of concerts, balls and café concerts. On the grand end of the scale is a series of annual balls, reaching its peak with February's Opera Ball at the State Opera (Staatsoper).

The city's classical music venues are worth seeing just for their extravagant decoration. The main sights are the State Opera (on Opernring); the Konzerthaus (on Lothringerstrasse); the Musikverein (at Karlsplatz); and the Imperial Palace's Royal Chapel (Burgkapelle) where the Vienna Boys' Choir still sings at Sunday Mass.

Viennese Shopping

Expect high prices; you can get items of similar quality for up to a third less just over the border in Germany. Clothes are especially expensive – the best options are chain stores such as Humanic, in the mall at Vösendorf on the southern edge of the city (to get there, take the bus from the Oper/Karlsplatz station).

Porcelain and glassware have been produced in Vienna for more than 200 years. Several outlets on Kärntner Strasse (near the central Stephansplatz) sell good examples, including J & L Lobmeyr, which has an exhibition of its early work on the top floor. The Old Town has plenty of window-shopping potential, and stores usually stay open until 7:30 one evening a week (either Thursday or Friday).

ESSENTIAL INFORMATION

TOURIST INFORMATION
Wiener Tourismusverband (Vienna Tourist Board)

- Obere Augartenstrasse 40, A-1025, Vienna ☎ 01 21114 222; fax 01 216 8492 www.info.wien.at
- corner Albertinaplatz/Maysedergasse
- Vienna International Airport

URBAN TRANSPORTATION

Vienna has a network of subway (U-Bahn) lines, trams (Strassenbahn) and buses. U-Bahn lines 1, 2 and 4 meet at central Oper/Karlsplatz. Subways are marked with a U on the city map. A rapid transit railroad, the S-Bahn (Schnellbahn), travels into the city center from the suburbs. Hopper buses 1A, 2A and 3A stop near major Old Town sights. Pick up transportation maps at the Opern Passage/ Karlsplatz U-Bahn information counter (☎ 01 79 09 10-5). Taxis can be ordered: ☎ 01 31 30-0, 01 40 10-0 or 01 60 16-0.

AIRPORT INFORMATION

Vienna International Airport (☎ 01 7007 22233; 24 hours) is a 20-minute bus ride from the City Air Terminal, in the city center. Shuttle buses run regularly between the two sites (☎ 01 93000 2300) plus from the airport to Südbahnhof and Westbahnhof railroad stations. There also are S-Bahn trains from the airport to the city center.

CLIMATE – average highs and lows for the month

JAN.	FEB.	MAR.	APR.	MAY	JUN.	JUL.	AUG.	SEP.	OCT.	NOV.	DEC.
2°C	3°C	9°C	14°C	19°C	22°C	25°C	24°C	20°C	14°C	7°C	4°C
36°F	37°F	48°F	57°F	66°F	72°F	77°F	75°F	68°F	57°F	45°F	39°F
-3°C	-2°C	2°C	5°C	9°C	13°C	15°C	15°C	12°C	6°C	2°C	-1°C
27°F	28°F	36°F	41°F	48°F	55°F	59°F	59°F	54°F	43°F	36°F	30°F

CITY SIGHTS

Key to symbols

map coordinates refer to the Vienna map on pages 26–27; sights below are highlighted in yellow on the map.

address or location · telephone number · opening times · nearest subway · nearest bus or tram route · restaurant or café on site or nearby · admission charge: $$$ more than S70, $$ S30 to S70, $ less than S30 · other relevant information

HOFBURG

Kaiserappartements C2 · Michaelerplatz (entrance: beneath Michaelerkuppel cupola) · 01 533 7570 · Daily 9–4:30 · Augustinerkeller Restaurant, see page 540 · U-Bahn: Herrengasse, Stephansplatz or Volkstheater · 48A, 57A; tram D, J, 1, 2, 46, 49 · $$$

Schatzkammer · Schweizerhof · 01 533 7931 · Wed.–Mon. 10–6 · Augustinerkeller Restaurant, see page 540 · U-Bahn: Herrengasse, Stephansplatz or Volkstheater · 48A, 57A; tram D, J, 1, 2, 46, 49 · $$$

Blue and gold domes top the magnificent Hofburg (Imperial Palace), which took more than six centuries to build. The original fortress, built in 1275, made way for the Schweizerhof (Swiss Courtyard), whose Schweizertor (Swiss Gate) went up in the 16th century. Other sections were added in rich baroque style during the 17th and 18th centuries, including the gorgeously decorated Hofbibliothek (Library) and the Reitschule (Riding School), where white Lipizzaner horses are put through their paces for visitors (see page 32). The Kaiserappartements (State Apartments) were built in the 19th century, and new sections were added on as recently as 1913 to create today's enormous complex of 18 wings, 2,600 rooms and 19 courtyards. Tours take you through the State Apartments where Habsburg trappings are on display, including the imperial crowns in the Schatzkammer (Treasuries) and gleaming silver tableware in the Silberkammer (Court Silver Depot).

KIRCHE AM STEINHOF

Off the map · Baumgartner Höhe 1, Penzing · 01 91060 11204 · Mon.–Fri. 8–3 · 47A, 48A · $$ · Entrance only by guided tour Sat. at 3

Huge copper angels guard the portico of the eccentric, domed Kirche am Steinhof (Steinhof Church), built in 1907 for people suffering from mental illness. Its white interior is full of light; colored glass, and windows by Secessionist artist Kolo Moser brighten the vault and side altars. Short benches have plenty of space in between so that patients taken ill could be helped out. Running water was provided in the stoop (entranceway) to lessen the risk of infection. A ceiling under the cupola gives the effect of a starry sky.

Spanning 600 years of architectural history, the Imperial Palace stands in its own lovely gardens

Neptune's Fountain stands proudly in the formal gardens of the impressive Schönbrunn Palace

SCHLOSS BELVEDERE

D1 Rennweg 6A (Unteres Belvedere), Prinz-Eugen-Strasse 27 (Oberes Belvedere) 01 79557 261 Palace: Tue.–Sun. 10–6; Apr. 1–late Oct.; 10–5, rest of year. Alpine Gardens (at Oberes Belvedere): daily 10–6; Apr.–Jul. (closed in bad weather) Im Palais Schwarzenberg, see page 540 Tram 71 (Lower); bus 13A, tram D, O, 18 (Upper) $$ Tours daily at 11 a.m.

The spectacularly baroque Schloss Belvedere (Belvedere Palace) was built for Austrian general and prince Eugene of Savoy, who led his army to many victories over the French. Begun in 1714, building was in two phases: the Unteres Belvedere (Lower Belvedere), where Eugene's military triumphs are celebrated in a ceiling fresco; and the Oberes Belvedere (Upper Belvedere), which housed his collection of paintings and later became the Imperial Picture Gallery. Archduke Franz Ferdinand, whose assassination sparked the events leading to World War I, lived here for 20 years until his death. The Belvedere is now devoted wholly to art, with Austrian baroque paintings on view in the lower palace, and medieval works in the Orangerie (Orangery); the Upper Belvedere has superb 19th- and 20th-century paintings, including *The Kiss* by Gustav Klimt and *Death and the Maiden* by Egon Schiele.

SCHLOSS SCHÖNBRUNN

A1 Schönbrunner Schlossstrasse 01 81113 239 (palace); 01 8773 244 (coach collection); 01 8779 2940 (zoo); 01 8775 087 406 Palace: daily 8:30–7, Jul.–Aug.; 8:30–5, Apr.–Jun. and Sep.–Oct.; 8:30–4:30, rest of year. Coach collection: daily 9–6, Apr.–Oct.; Tue.–Sun. 10–4, rest of year. Zoo: daily 9–6:30, May–Sep.; 9–6, in Apr.; 9–5:30, Mar. and Oct.; 9–5, in Feb.; 9–4:30, rest of year. Palm house: daily 9:30–5:30, May–Sep.; 9:30–4:30, rest of year Tyrolean Restaurant in grounds Schönbrunn 10A; tram 10, 58 Audio-guided tours $$$

The imposing size and symmetry of the Schloss Schönbrunn (Schönbrunn Palace), the imperial summer getaway, successfully made the point that the Habsburgs were very wealthy and very powerful. There are no fewer than 1,400 rooms: the original, 1695 plan was to show that the Austrians would not be outdone by the French monarchs' glorious palace of Versailles. But the first design was not finished, and between 1744 and 1749 court architect Nikolaus Pacassi came up with a new version. He was responsible for the geometric splendor of the long building that overlooks a former hunting park, now laid out with ornamental gardens and fountains. In the park beyond there's a zoo and a glass-and-iron palm house. Inside the palace there is a coach collection (to the right of the entrance) and dazzling displays of Indian and Persian miniatures, Japanese and Italian art, 18th-century porcelain and furnishings, and frescoes and painted landscapes.

SIGMUND FREUD MUSEUM

C3 Berggasse 19 01 319 1596 Daily 9–6, Jul.–Sep.; 9–5, rest of year U-Bahn: Schottentor–Universität 40A; tram D, 37, 38, 40, 41, 42 $$

He has many critics and his methods have been denounced by some as bogus, but there's no denying that Sigmund Freud had a profound effect on American and European psyches in the 20th century. He is widely credited with inventing psychoanalysis – pioneering theories of free association, dream interpretation, the Oedipus complex, and the influence of infant sexuality on adult development. His ideas have filtered through art, literature, film,

Beethoven's house on Probusgasse – he was drawn to the musical city of Vienna when he was only 20

City of Composers

Many 17th- and 18th-century Habsburg rulers were music lovers and musicians: Leopold I was a composer, Charles VI was a violinist, and Maria Theresa played the double bass. Royal patronage drew some of the world's greatest composers to Vienna, including Beethoven and Brahms; Mozart gave his first public concert at age six in Schönbrunn's Hall of Mirrors.

The waltz is inextricably linked to Vienna thanks to Johann Strauss, the "Waltz King," and every New Year's Day the Vienna Philharmonic Orchestra plays his waltzes to a billion television viewers around the world. A gilded statue of Strauss, affectionately known as "Schoni," with jaunty moustache and playing his violin, stands in City Park (Stadtpark).

In 1498 Emperor Maximilian I engaged 12 young male choristers to sing with the court orchestra. Over the following centuries some of Austria's greatest composers served their apprenticeships with the choir, including Franz Schubert and Joseph Haydn. Schubert and Haydn would have been dressed in full imperial military uniforms, like the rest of the choir. The current naval-style dress wasn't implemented until 1919.

The elaborate and gilded Musikverein was built in the 19th century as a concert venue for the city's Society of the Friends of Music. (It's here that the Vienna Philharmonic performs its New Year concert.) In 1913 the hall was the scene of a brawl between conservatives and radicals of musical taste, at a concert performed by Arnold Schönberg.

Schönberg changed the face of modern musical composition by abandoning the standard eight-tone scale familiar to the Western ear and devising a complex 12-tone system. Together with his former pupils Alban Berg and Anton von Webern, he formed the Second Viennese School of Music and continued to compose according to his new scale, despite the hostile response of the Vienna audience.

education, social policy and even everyday conversation ("the ego," a "Freudian slip"). He grew up in Vienna's Jewish community, and enjoyed the city's social life, playing cards at the Café Landtmann on the Ringstrasse (which is still in business), and walking daily along the boulevard. He rented an apartment on Berggasse street, where some of his original writings, photographs, books and furniture, and oddities that he gathered on his travels, and personal effects such as his hat and walking stick are on display.

SPANISCHE REITSCHULE

D2 Josefsplatz 01 535 0186 Performances: Sun. at 10:45 a.m. and some evenings, mid-Feb. to Jun. 30 and late Aug.–early Nov. Training: Mon.–Fri. 10–noon; closed holidays U-Bahn: Herrengasse, Stephansplatz or Volkstheater 48A, 57A; tram D, J, 1, 2, 46, 49 $$$

In a glittering white arena of the Imperial Palace the white Lipizzaner horses of the Spanische Reitschule (Spanish Riding School) strut to the gavotte, quadrille and waltz and show off the leaping, rearing and trotting of the high school (*haute école*) of dressage. Originally the horses were brought from Spain and bred at a 16th-century stud farm at Lipica, Slovenia (hence their name) – not to go into show business, but to fight to the death. Those high-kicked hooves would be lethal at close range.

Full performances, complete with music and uniformed riders, are booked well in advance, but tickets for the less glamorous morning training sessions can be purchased at Josefsplatz 2, Gate 2.

St. Stephen's Cathedral towers above shoppers and sightseers in Stephansplatz

STEPHANSDOM

D3 Stephansplatz 01 51552 3767 Daily 6 a.m.–10 p.m. Do & Co Im Haas-Haus, see page 540 Stephansplatz Guided tours: Mon.–Sat. at 10:30 and 3, Sun. at 3 (also Sat. at 7 p.m., Jun.–Sep.)

Stephansdom (St. Stephen's Cathedral) is an unmistakable landmark, with its black, yellow and green tiled roof and the 446-foot Gothic South Tower, known to locals as "Steffle," or "Little Steve." Relics of earlier churches are incorporated into the building, including the Giant's Door and the Tower of Heathens, supposedly the site of a pagan shrine. Inside, St. Stephen the Martyr is represented on a baroque 17th-century altar painting by Tobias Pock. The catacombs house an ossuary – a storage place for bones – where the remains of plague victims were kept.

UHRENMUSEUM

D3 Schulhof 2 01 5332 265 Tue.–Sun. 9–4:30 U-Bahn: Herrengasse or Stephansplatz $$

In 1917 Vienna's city councilors set up a museum devoted to timepieces through the ages in Obizzi Palace. The little palace was once the home of Count Ernst Rüdiger von Starhemberg, who defended Vienna against the 1683 Turkish siege; it is tucked into a side street by the Am Hof Church. The Uhrenmuseum (Clock Museum) has more than 3,000 fascinating items on display, including an onion clock, a sand clock and an astronomical clock whose hand takes 20,904 years to complete one circuit.

VIENNESE FLAVORS

A quiet corner to pause and sample Vienna's culinary delights

Coffeehouses and pastry shops (*Konditoreien*) are two pretty good reasons for visiting Vienna. At the turn of the 20th century, artists, musicians and writers gathered in cafés to swap ideas, work, read or just sit, and some of their old haunts are still going strong. Stop by Bräunerhof (Stallburggasse 2, ☎ 01 512 38 93); Central (Herrengasse 4 ☎ 01 533 37 63-26); or the grand old Imperial (Kärnter Ring 16, ☎ 01 501 10-3890), in the former city mansion of the Duke of Württemberg. Customers are generally left alone to linger in the grandiose surroundings, sipping one of the many coffee drinks.

On average, Austrians drink about 423 pints of coffee a year, and the menu usually offers dozens of varieties. *Mocca* is black coffee; a *Kleiner* or *Grosser Brauner* has a little milk, a *Melange* has more; a *Fiaker* is mocca with rum or brandy; and an *Einspänner* is a mocca with whipped cream. The *café-Konditorei*, or pastry-shop-cum-café, is a showcase for Vienna's pastry makers. Here you'll find irresistible cakes and pastries, and often a light lunch menu.

Wine made from the most recent grape harvest is known here as *Heuriger*, and this is also the name for the Viennese taverns that serve it. These *Heurigen* stand in their own vineyards in the Vienna Woods, and serve food – usually roast meat, cheese and salad – to soak up the wine. A small band is likely to be playing rousing folk music, and in summer there are often long tables and benches set outside. A bunch of fir twigs is traditionally hung outside the tavern door to show that it's open.

Viennese cooking is plain, simple and filling. It's collectively known as *Beisl* – a Yiddish word introduced by traditionally Jewish tavern owners. Dishes might include boiled beef (*Tafelspitz*), steak with crispy onions (*Zwiebelrostbraten*), chopped calves' heart and lungs in sauce (*Beuschel*) and – perhaps the best-known export – *Wiener Schnitzel*, a fried veal cutlet coated with egg and breadcrumbs. For dessert the popular choice is *Strudel*, fruit-filled baked dough with raisins and cinnamon (a perfect choice with a Viennese coffee).

INNSBRUCK

Strategically and beautifully situated on the Inn river, in the heart of the Alps, Innsbruck stands at a great European crossroads. The 19th-century construction of the east-west railroad through the Arlberg valley, in combination with the city's historic control of the north-south trade route through the Brenner Pass, placed it firmly on the trans-European map. Today, travelers from across Europe pass this way, and Innsbruck, with its excellent tourist facilities, is well worth more than a brief stop en route.

Innsbruck Through Time

Innsbruck has had a checkered past. By the 12th century a fortified town was growing up beside the bridge over the Inn river, near the site of an old Roman garrison. By the 1360s, when the Habsburgs had acquired the Tyrol region, the settlement had outgrown its original fortifying walls. Under Maximilian I, Emperor of the Germans from 1507 to 1519, Innsbruck was the Habsburg empire's administrative and cultural center.

The next 100 years encompassed a golden age that continued through the reign of Empress Maria Theresa from 1717 to 1780. When Napoleon conquered the Tyrol in the 1790s Innsbruck became part of Bavaria, but was handed back to Austria in 1814. The city became part of Italy following World War I and suffered much damage during World War II. But since then Innsbruck has prospered, and today it is a university city as well as a popular tourist destination.

Exploring Innsbruck

The center of Innsbruck is small, and it's likely your hotel will be within easy walking distance of the historic Old Town (Altstadt), a pedestrianized maze of picturesque streets. Attractions outside the city are served both by regular local buses and

A spectacular view across Innsbruck from the Stadtturm, the 187-foot-high Town Tower

special tourist shuttles that take you right to where the action is. It's worth buying the Innsbruck Card, which gives you free entry to many museums and other attractions, free use of public transportation and three mountain cable car systems, the latter otherwise very expensive. It's valid for one, two or three days and obtainable at the tourist office.

A Rich Culture

Because of its long history, Innsbruck is richly endowed with some marvelous buildings, churches and museums. The Old Town is a tiny area packed with handsome houses and narrow arcaded streets. Outside this ancient core you'll find splendid Renaissance, baroque and rococo architecture. Many of these fine buildings house Innsbruck's museums, some devoted to history and the arts, others offering insights into such subjects as Tyrolean railroads, bells and hunting. The cathedral and churches are packed with artistic treasures.

Landmarks along the 17th- and 18th-century street, Maria-Theresien-Strasse, include a column topped by a statue of the Virgin (the Annasäule), and a resplendent arch, the Triumphforte, built in 1765. Nowadays, six bridges span the Inn river – originally called the Innbrücke – from which the city gets its name, leading to the riverfront houses of the Mariahilf neighborhood. This area is also home to a botanic garden.

You can stroll beside the river, with mountains towering in the background, to the Hofgarten – a colorful garden first laid out by Archduke Ferdinand II in the 16th century. To the east of the city center, overlooking the Inn valley, is Ferdinand's palace, Schloss Ambras.

Mountain Scenery

Dramatic mountains encircle Innsbruck, their lower slopes scattered with picturesque villages. The surrounding countryside offers year-round opportunities for fresh air and exercise against a backdrop of some of Europe's loveliest upland scenery. The best way to experience this landscape is on foot, and the tourist office arranges free guided walks outside the city; they'll even provide you with free use of boots and a backpack. You can swim, ride, play golf, go rafting or summer skiing, or just enjoy the Alps from the comfort of

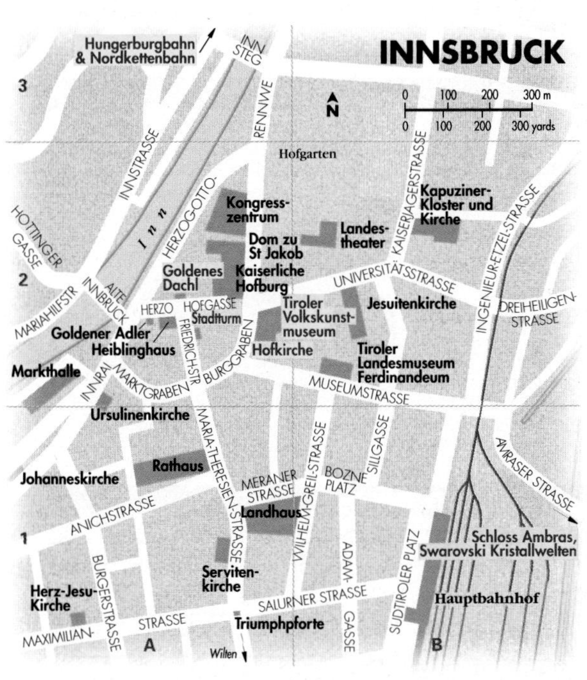

a sightseeing airplane flight. Winter brings the skiing season, when sports fans flock to Innsbruck from all over the world and the city's architecture is particularly beautiful under a fresh blanket of snow.

Tyrolean Tastes

You can sample a wide range of Austrian and Tyrolean specialties at Innsbruck's restaurants, taverns and cafés (see page 541). The food is good and portions are generous, and you'll find the warm welcome that is so common all over Austria. In the summer, follow dinner with a cable car ride up the Seegrube mountain to enjoy a drink while watching the sparkling lights of the city far below, or take a lantern-lit hike to a party held in a hillside hut.

Year round you can take in a Tyrolean folklore evening, which includes traditional dances, yodeling and a performance on the alphorn; during the summer, *Schuhplatter* dancers and brass bands perform in the center of town. Innsbruck's casino offers a more sophisticated evening, and there's always a choice of classical music, and often opera.

Woodcarvings and *Christkindl*

Some of Innsbruck's most appealing stores are tucked away in the narrow streets of the Old Town, where you'll find ethnic Austrian souvenirs, clothes, knitwear, antiques and interior design pieces. Woodcarvings make ideal presents, as do dried-flower garlands and baskets – charming decorations for Christmas and Easter – and intricately made national costumes.

Maria-Theresien-Strasse has a range of department, home furnishing and linen stores. Excellent bookstores offer English-language illustrated books about Austria, as well as beautiful calendars that make good gifts. The atmospheric Christmas market *(Christkindl)* sets up in the Old Town, its stalls brimming with gifts, traditional decorations, cookies and tempting sweetmeats.

ESSENTIAL INFORMATION

TOURIST INFORMATION
Innsbruck Tourismus (Innsbruck Tourist Board)
• Burggraben 3 ☎ 0512 59850; fax 0512 59850-7; www.tiscover.com/innsbruck
• Hotel Information, Hauptbahnhof (Central Station) ☎ 0512 583766; fax 0512 583767

URBAN TRANSPORTATION
Many of Innsbruck's main sights are grouped together within walking distance in and around the Old Town (Altstadt); use the excellent tram and bus service for venturing farther afield. You can buy a day-use ticket, book of tickets or weekly transportation card from the tourist information office and some tobacconists. Validate your ticket when boarding, and press the illuminated button near the door to open the doors when you want to get off. Local bus drivers are particularly helpful. There are taxi stands throughout the city center, or you can call a taxi (☎ 0512 1718, 0512 5311, 0512 202070 or 0512 24411).

AIRPORT INFORMATION
Innsbruck Airport (☎ 0512 22525-0), with domestic and some European flights, is 2 miles west of the city center. Bus F runs throughout the day to the central railroad station and the city center, or you can pick up a taxi outside the terminal.

CLIMATE – average highs and lows for the month

JAN.	FEB.	MAR.	APR.	MAY	JUN.	JUL.	AUG.	SEP.	OCT.	NOV.	DEC.
1°C	4°C	10°C	15°C	20°C	23°C	25°C	24°C	20°C	14°C	8°C	2°C
34°F	39°F	50°F	59°F	68°F	73°F	77°F	75°F	68°F	57°F	46°F	36°F
-7°C	-4°C	0°C	4°C	8°C	11°C	13°C	12°C	9°C	4°C	0°C	-4°C
19°F	25°F	32°F	39°F	46°F	52°F	55°F	54°F	48°F	39°F	32°F	25°F

CITY SIGHTS

Key to symbols

map coordinates refer to the Innsbruck map on page 35; sights below are highlighted in yellow on the map.

address or location telephone number opening times nearest subway nearest bus or tram route restaurant or café on site or nearby admission charge: $$$ more than S70, $$ S30 to S70, $ less than S30 other relevant information

GOLDENES DACHL

A2 Herzog-Friedrich-Strasse 15 0512 581111 Daily 10–6, May–Sep.; Tue.–Sun. 10–12:30 and 2–5, rest of year 0, K, L, N; tram 1, 3, 6 $$

Innsbruck's Goldenes Dachl (Golden Roof) is, in fact, an oriel (bay) window, added onto the front of the previous ducal palace to commemorate Emperor Maximilian I's marriage to Bianca Maria Sforza of Milan in 1494. Beautifully decorated with reliefs of the Emperor, it is roofed with more than 2,700 gilt copper tiles – hence its name. From here, Maximilian watched festivities in the square below. An informative audiovisual show and small museum will fill you in on Maximilian's life and times.

HOFKIRCHE

A2 Universitätsstrasse 2 0512 584302 Mon.–Sat. 9–5:30, Jul.–Aug.; 9–5, rest of year 0, K, L, N; tram 1, 3, 6 $

The Hofkirche (Court Church) of Innsbruck is one of Europe's least known but most impressive monuments. Built in the late Gothic style between 1555 and 1565, this three-aisled structure houses the tomb (now empty) of Maximilian I, among the finest existing works of German Renaissance sculpture. Twenty-eight larger-than-life-size bronze statues surround Maximilian's black marble sarcophagus, decorated with 24 reliefs showing scenes from the Emperor's life. These represent Maximilian's ancestors and contemporaries, and were created by the best artists of the time. Albrecht Dürer was responsible for several, including the figure of the legendary King Arthur of England, considered the finest statue anywhere of a Renaissance knight. Elsewhere in the church you can see bronze saints and busts of Roman emperors, all figures destined for Maximilian's unfinished sarcophagus.

The Golden Roof recalls 15th-century Innsbruck

HUNGERBURGBAHN AND NORDKETTENBAHN

Hungerburgbahn Off the map Rennweg 41 0512 292250 Daily 8:10–6:10, Jul.–Sep.; 8:25–5:40, Apr.–Jun. and in Oct.; 8:25–5:10, rest of year Cafés and restaurants at top and bottom of car J, D, E, 4; tram 1 $$

Nordkettenbahn Off the map Höhenstrasse 145 0512 293344 Daily 8:25–5:30, Jul.–Sep.; 8:40–5:30, Apr.–Jun. and in Oct.; 8:55–4:40, rest of year (also every Fri. until 11:30 p.m.) Cafés and restaurants at top and bottom of car J, N, D, E, 4; tram 1; Hungerburgbahn $$$ (reduced price Fri. evening)

These two connecting mountain transportation systems will take you effortlessly up the Nordkette to 6,250-foot Seegrube; from here you can go even higher, to 7,657-foot Hafelekar. The Hungerburgbahn is a steep funicular, built around 1900 to link lower and upper

Ride the funicular for dramatic views of Innsbruck and the surrounding mountains

Innsbruck; it's a fun ride to a pretty area with pleasant woodland walks and attractive outdoor cafés. From here, the Nordkettenbahn cable car runs up Hungerburg mountain over precipitous slopes to the Seegrube station, with ever-widening views over Innsbruck, the valley and the high Alpine peaks. A wonderful panorama of mountains awaits you at the top.

SCHLOSS AMBRAS

Off the map · Schlossstrasse 20 · 0512 348446 · Daily 10–5, Apr.–Oct.; Wed.–Mon. 2–5, rest of year · Restaurant and café · K or tram 1, 3, 6, then special shuttle from Maria-Theresien-Strasse (Altes Landhaus) · $$$

Schloss Ambras (Ambras Castle) lies outside Innsbruck, a beautiful 16th-century conversion of a medieval castle standing in a landscaped garden above the Inn valley. It was the home of Archduke Ferdinand from 1563 to 1595; an avid collector and patron of the arts, he built the superb Spanish Hall, with its colorful frescoes and beautiful ceiling, and amassed a collection of curiosities. They are displayed in the Wunderkammer (Wonder-room), a sort of early museum that offers great insight into the Renaissance mind. The castle also contains a fine armory and large portrait gallery, dedicated to the imperial Habsburg family, although most visitors find Ferdinand's wife's bathroom far more interesting. It is a perfect and rare example of a 16th-century bathroom, complete with sunken copper bath.

STADTTURM

A2 · Herzog-Friedrich-Strasse 21 · 0512 561500-3 · Daily 10–6, Jun.–Aug.; 10–5, Mar.–May and Sep.–Oct.; 10–4, rest of year · O, L, K, N; tram 1, 3, 6 · $$

For a bird's-eye view of Innsbruck, climb (there's no elevator) the 187-foot-high Stadtturm (Town Tower), built in 1440 as a watchtower. The bulbous cupola was added in the 16th century.

SWAROVSKI KRISTALLWELTEN

Off the map · Kristallweltenstrasse 1, Wattens · 05224 510800 · Daily 9–6 · Restaurant and café · Bus transfer every half hour from the Innsbruck railroad station · $$

One of the Innsbruck area's most visited attractions, Swarovski Kristallwelten (Swarovski Crystal Worlds) in Wattens, 9 miles east of Innsbruck, has to be experienced to be believed. This multimedia theme park centers around the magic of crystal and features moving walls, sculptures and sparkling crystals in underground caverns. You enter through the Giant, a leafy face on the side of a hill with glowing eyes and a water-filled mouth, to experience truly imaginative sights, sounds and smells.

TIROLER VOLKSKUNST-MUSEUM

B2 · Universitätsstrasse 2 · 0512 584302 · Mon.–Sat. 9–5, Sun. 9–noon · O, L, K, N; tram 1, 3, 6 · $$

The appealing Tiroler Volkskunst-museum (Museum of Tyrolean Folk Art) is a great introduction to the traditional way of life in the Tyrol. This large museum, with exhibits excellently labeled in English, has fascinating displays on every aspect of rural life, as well as complete Gothic and Renaissance house interiors. Don't miss the models of farmhouses or the charming Christmas nativity scenes, where Jesus' birth is depicted in busy Alpine villages.

Spectacular descent in the Tyrol – snowboarding is gaining in popularity

WINTER SPORTS IN INNSBRUCK

Innsbruck and its surrounding villages offer superb skiing amid beautiful Alpine landscapes. Winter sports enthusiasts will find something for every taste, and some excellent all-inclusive deals can be arranged through the Innsbruck tourist office.

Skiing

You can ski at spots throughout the Innsbruck area as well as at surrounding resorts such as Kitzbühel and Arlberg-St. Anton. There are some 322 miles of well-maintained downhill runs served by 210 lifts. Every skill level is catered to, from gentle runs of hard-packed snow for families and beginners to extreme slopes and off-run skiing for experts. Special areas are designated for snowboarding and carving, and for the truly tough and experienced back-country skier there are superb high-altitude itineraries.

Cross-country skiing on the downhill runs is very popular in Europe, and 12 different cross-country areas are accessible, offering 310 miles of tracks. Ski and snowboard schools operate daily, and ski guides can be hired on a daily basis. Several areas have snowmaking equipment to supplement early winter snow. Access to the slopes is by a combination of bus, funicular, cable car, chairlifts and surface lifts, which operate daily 8:30–4. Free buses take skiers from the city center to their chosen ski area and collect them at the end of the day; these buses also run to Kitzbühel and St. Anton. Innsbruck's season runs from early December through March.

Winter Fun

There are plenty of other activities besides hitting the slopes. With its Olympic facilities, Innsbruck offers skating and curling, or you can take a piloted bobsled ride down the Olympic run. Dog- and horse-drawn sleigh rides give you a chance to appreciate the winter beauty of the mountains, and tobogganing and winter walking provide a gentler pace. Various events are organized throughout the season, culminating on New Year's Day with torchlit celebrations in the Old Town and on the mountains.

i Information on ski packages is available from the tourist information office (✉ Innsbruck Tourismus, A-6021 Innsbruck, Burggraben 3, Austria ☎ 0512 59850; fax 0512 59850-7)

SALZBURG

The little city of Salzburg, stretching along the Salzach river and tucked beneath Mönchsberg hill, is a delightful combination of medieval, Renaissance and baroque architecture, the birthplace of Wolfgang Amadeus Mozart and the gateway to some of Austria's most

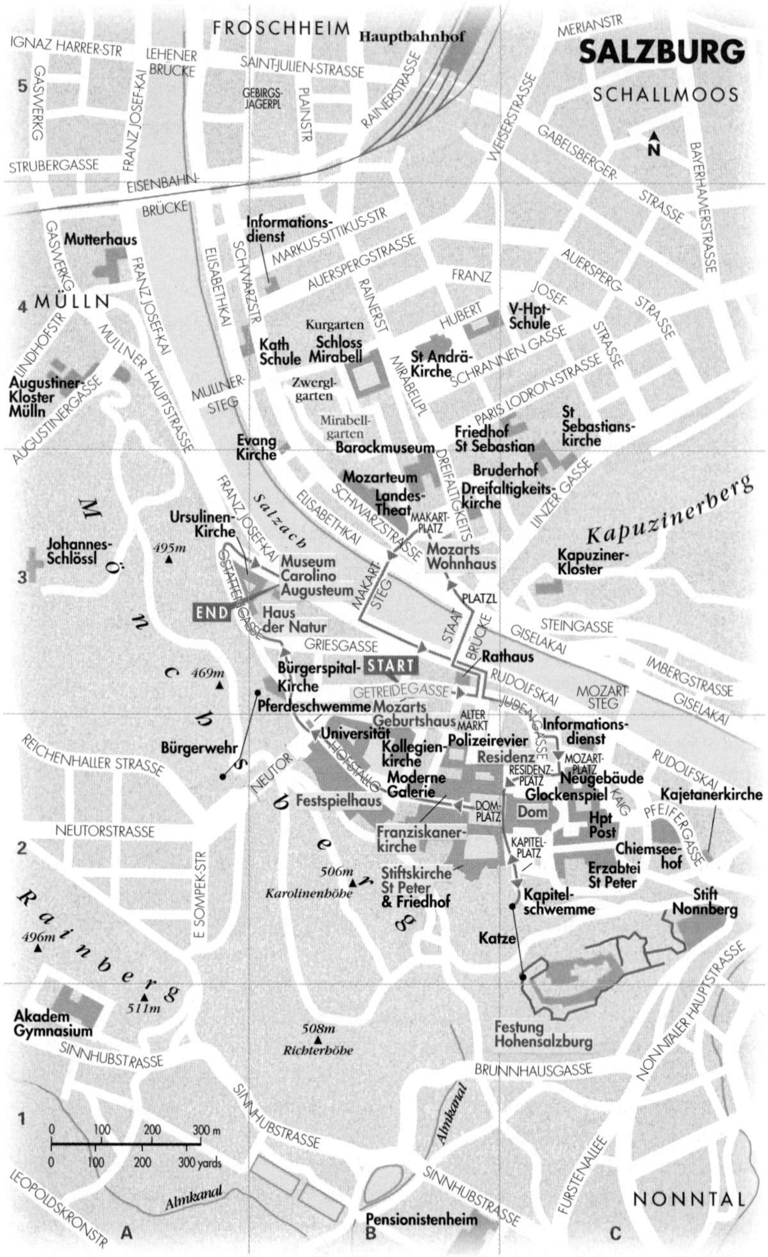

splendid landscapes. Add to this friendly people, a relaxed way of life and one of the world's greatest music festivals, and it's easy to see why Salzburg is popular year-round with tourists. For fans of the movie *The Sound of Music,* there's the added bonus that the city was home to the von Trapp family; movie locations are scattered around the city and are easy to visit.

Mozart's Footsteps

Many visitors simply enjoy Salzburg's beauty, atmosphere and charm although others come for specific reasons – to study the superb baroque architecture, listen to music or tread in Mozart's footsteps. Others flock here to follow *The Sound of Music* trail, and various tour companies run trips with English guides that take you to sites associated with the film.

For classical music lovers, festivals are the main draw (see page 42); the city is packed during festival season and it's hard to find accommodations. Salzburg's charming cityscape, however, can be enjoyed any time of year; late spring and autumn are good times to visit, but whenever you come it will probably rain: Salzburg has a reputation for being the country's wettest city.

Getting Your Bearings

Salzburg is an easy city to negotiate. The historic center on both banks of the Salzach river is pedestrianized; you can walk from end to end in roughly half an hour, though you'll want to spend longer enjoying the medieval streets and spacious baroque squares. Most of what you'll want to see is concentrated here, with a few sights across the river.

The tourist offices sell the Salzburg Plus Card, which is good for free admission to many museums and attractions, offers discounts at other attractions and on services, and provides free access to public transportation. The card is valid for 24, 48 or 72 hours. The Salzburg Plus – All-inclusive Card includes excellent deals for accommodations, dining and cultural events, particularly useful if you're traveling with children.

Various companies will take you on city tours or farther afield to see the landscape of the Salzkammergut, one of the loveliest parts of Austria. There are fascinating walking tours around Salzburg, concentrating on different aspects of the city; or if you just want to sit back and relax, you can take a trip in a horse-drawn carriage (*Fiaker*); pick one up on the Residenzplatz.

Cosmopolitan Cuisine

You'll eat extremely well in Salzburg, which has dozens of restaurants, inns, taverns and cafés where you can enjoy anything from local and regional specialties to Japanese sushi. Traditional cooking is hearty and filling; plates of meat with solid dumplings, soups and spicy *Gulasch* (meat stew).The local specialty is *Salzburger Nockerl* (an egg dessert), and a variety of drinks and open wines (available by the glass) are offered.

Make a point of lingering an hour or so in one of Salzburg's traditional cafés, which specialize in coffee and cream cakes served in elegant surroundings. Many cafés and restaurants have summertime beer gardens, some beautifully situated.

Salzburg Souvenirs

Salzburg is filled with tempting stores, many of them lining the Getreidegasse (see page 44) and its surrounding streets, although there's a good cluster on the left bank of the river. The exquisite traditional women's clothes are appealing buys, but keep in mind that what looks lovely here might not look so good back home. Also look for attractive wooden carvings, delicate porcelain and crystal, and bright china and linens, all with an Austrian theme, as well as big European designer names. Don't forget Austria's well-organized tax-free shopping service.

Music and Marionettes

Although classical music is the heart of Salzburg's entertainment scene, it's not the only attraction. Year-round, there are concerts at citywide venues; enjoy a traditional dinner in the Festung Hohensalzburg (Hohensalzburg Fortress, see page 43), followed by a Mozart serenade from musicians in period dress. The main festival season runs from late July through August, but there's something happening almost every month, including an autumn jazz festival and fairs in September and the weeks before Christmas. Experience a visit to the city's casino, and children aren't the only ones who will love a performance at the Marionette Theater.

Austrian Cafés

There's no better way to get the feel of the country than by spending an hour or so in a café, a quintessential Austrian experience. Café decor ranges from chandelier-hung baroque splendor to wood-paneled coziness, but the basic elements are always similar: excellent service, a vast range of coffees, and a wide choice of feather-light cream cakes and pastries, all indulged in by well-dressed locals chatting or reading the newspapers. Reading materials are provided by the establishment and hung on wooden poles. Cafés often serve beer and wine, and some offer savory snacks. Many have summertime terraces, the perfect place to write your postcards and rest your feet.

ESSENTIAL INFORMATION

TOURIST INFORMATION

- Mozartplatz 5 ☎ 0662 889 87-330
- Hauptbahnhof: Bahnsteig 2a ☎ 0662 889 87-340
- Salzburg-Mitte: Münchner Bundesstrasse 1 ☎ 0662 889 87-350 (Easter–Oct. 31)
- Flughafen: Ankunftshalle, Innsbrucker Bundesstrasse 95 ☎ 0662 8580-7911; www.salzburginfo.at

URBAN TRANSPORTATION

Salzburg's small central core makes it possible to walk to everything you'll want to see. There are, however, good bus and trolley bus services covering the whole city. Buy your ticket before boarding, either at the machines at the main bus stops or from any tobacconist, and remember to validate it as soon as you board the bus. Validation machines are marked "Entwerter." There is no need to punch them again if you change buses. To open the doors from either outside or inside the bus you must press the illuminated button beside the door. There are several taxi stands outside the historic center, or you can call Funktaxi (☎ 0662 17 15) or Salzburger Funktaxi (☎ 0662 874 400). If you are driving to Salzburg, do not try to bring your car into the city center, where parking is an enormous problem. There are large, supervised parking lots outside the city where cars can safely be left, then take a shuttle bus service to the city center.

AIRPORT INFORMATION

Salzburg's W. A. Mozart Airport (☎ 0662 85 80-251), with domestic and some European flights, is about 4 miles west of the city center. Bus 77 runs every 15 minutes throughout the day to the railroad station, and there is a taxi stand outside the terminal.

CLIMATE – average highs and lows for the month

JAN.	FEB.	MAR.	APR.	MAY	JUN.	JUL.	AUG.	SEP.	OCT.	NOV.	DEC.
2°C	4°C	10°C	14°C	19°C	22°C	24°C	24°C	20°C	14°C	7°C	2°C
36°F	39°F	50°F	57°F	66°F	72°F	75°F	75°F	68°F	57°F	45°F	36°F
-5°C	-4°C	-2°C	2°C	8°C	12°C	13°C	13°C	9°C	4°C	-2°C	-3°C
23°F	25°F	28°F	36°F	46°F	54°F	55°F	55°F	48°F	39°F	28°F	27°F

City Sights

Key to symbols

map coordinates refer to the Salzburg map on page 40; sights below are highlighted in yellow on the map.

address or location telephone number opening times nearest bus, tram, or funicular route restaurant or café on site or nearby admission charge: $$$ more than S70, $$ S30 to S70, $ less than S30 other relevant information

Dom

C2 Domplatz Cathedral excavations: 0662 845 295; Museum 0662 844 189 Cathedral excavations: Mon.–Sat. 11–5, May–Oct. Museum: Mon.–Sat. 10–5, Sun. 1–5, May–Oct. 5, 6, 51, 55 Cathedral excavations $; Museum $$

The ornate facade of the Dom (Cathedral), the first truly Italian-style church to be built north of the Alps, dominates the Domplatz, its four huge marble statues giving an indication of the interior splendors. There's been a cathedral here since the eighth century; today's structure is the third to occupy the site. It was built between 1614 and 1628, badly damaged during World War II, and completely restored by 1959. The huge interior, accommodating 10,000 people, is a riot of stucco, marble and gilding, the simple 14th-century font providing a serene contrast. You can visit the crypt to see the foundations of the medieval cathedral and the remains of the original Roman church, while the museum has superb treasures such as an eighth-century cross.

Festspielhaus

B2 Hofstallgasse 0662 849 097 Guided tours daily at 9:30, 2 and 3:30, Jul.–Aug.; at 2 and 3:30, Jun. and Sep.; at 2, Jan.–May and Oct. 1–Dec. 20 1, 5, 6, 51, 55 $$/$$$ Entry is only with a guided tour; tour times are subject to change if rehearsals are in progress. Check before you visit

Even if you're not musically inclined, Salzburg's Festspielhäuser (Festival Theaters), are well worth visiting. They stand on the site of the old court stables, the winter riding school that was converted to form the Kleines Festspielhaus (Little Theater). The Grosses Festspielhaus (Large Theater), built in the 1950s, runs right into Mönchsberg hill; vast amounts of rock were removed during its construction. The only way to see the theaters, unless you attend a performance, is by guided tour; this will give you a chance to experience the superb acoustics of the 2,000-seat Large Theater, said to be among the best in the world.

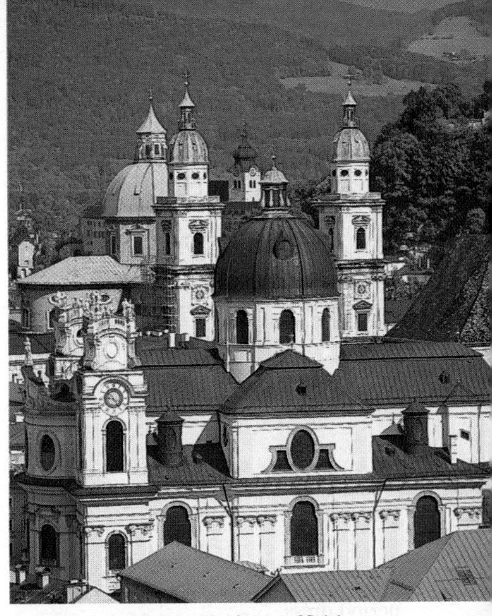

An architectural delight, the domes of Salzburg nestle beneath a grand mountain backdrop

Festung Hohensalzburg

C1 Mönchsberg 34 0662 842 430-11 Grounds: daily 8:30–7, mid-Jun. to mid-Sep.; 9–6, mid-Mar. to mid-Jun.; 9–5, rest of year. Interior: daily 9–6, mid-Jun. to mid-Sep.; 9:30–5:30, mid-Mar. to mid-Jun.; 9:30–5, rest of year. Rainer Museum: daily, May 1 to mid-Oct. Café and restaurant (see pages 42 and 542) in fortress Festungbahn funicular: daily 9–9, May–Sep.; 9–5, rest of year Grounds $$; interior $$. Includes funicular

The massive Festung Hohensalzburg (Hohensalzburg Fortress) dominates Salzburg from Mönchsberg hill. This rambling fortress was built, altered and extended between 1077 and 1681 by Salzburg's ruling archbishops. Walk up or take the funicular to wander through the courtyards and admire the views before joining one of the guided tours, the only way to visit the interior. You'll see winding passages and ornate state rooms, including the Golden Room with its gilded tracery, and the Golden Hall, with a superb gold and blue coffered ceiling. The Rainer Museum displays instruments of medieval torture, weapons and coats of arms.

Medieval Getreidegasse, with its attractive buildings and enticing stores

FRANZISKANERKIRCHE

B2 Sigmund-Haffner Gasse Daily 6:30 a.m.–7:30 p.m. 5, 6, 51, 55

A few steps from the cathedral stands the Franziskanerkirche (Franciscan Church), a peaceful and lofty building dedicated to the Virgin that was Salzburg's parish church until 1635. The nave, with its Romanesque details, is the oldest part, its dimness set off by the airy Gothic choir, built in the 15th century. Be sure to go behind the altar to admire the ring of baroque chapels that encircle it.

GETREIDEGASSE

B3 Getreidegasse 5, 6, 51, 55

The medieval street known as the Getreidegasse runs through the center of old Salzburg and is lined with stores, each with a distinctive wrought-iron sign hanging above. Most of the houses date from the 15th through the 18th centuries and were built by prosperous burghers for their businesses and families. Passages run through the buildings to connect with picturesque courtyards and squares; these are called *Durchhäuser*, meaning "through the houses." Crowds throng the street and its continuation, the Judengasse, and there's no better place to soak up Salzburg's unique atmosphere.

HAUS DER NATUR

B3 Museumsplatz 5 0662 842 653 Daily 9–5 Café in museum 49, 60, 80, 81, 95 $$

A few hours in Salzburg's Haus der Natur (Natural History Museum) provides a splendid antidote to an excess of fine architecture and Mozart. Popular with families, the museum's 80 rooms house a wide range of scientific and nature displays, including a reptile zoo, European animal exhibits and an excellent aquarium complete with great white sharks. Children of all ages will enjoy the space discovery hall, with its dioramas, models and mock-up of a future space city.

MIRABELLGARTEN

B4 Mirabellplatz Daily 6:30 a.m.–dusk 1, 5, 6, 51, 55

The beautiful Mirabellgarten (Mirabell Garden) spreads around the Schloss Mirabell (Mirabell Castle), built in 1606 by Archbishop Wolf Dietrich as a home for his mistress, Salome Alt. The terraces, gardens, lawns and flower beds around the house are a splendid example of baroque garden design, where trees, shrubs and flowers contrast with statues and fountains to create a truly civilized landscape. Concerts are held in the castle's Marble Hall, one of the loveliest places to hear Mozart's music.

MOZARTS GEBURTSHAUS

B2 Getreidegasse 9 0662 844 313 Daily 9–7, Jul.–Aug.; 9–6, rest of year Café on ground floor of museum 5, 6, 51, 55 $$/$$$ Guided tours

Wolfgang Amadeus Mozart was born in a modest middle-class apartment in the heart of Salzburg on January 27, 1756. These rooms are among Salzburg's most visited sights, a place of pilgrimage for music lovers from all over the world. Climb the stairs to enter the Mozarts Geburtshaus (Mozart's Birthplace), today a simple museum containing family portraits and mementos of the composer, including his first violin. The next-door flat has been filled with period furniture to give an idea of the appearance of 18th-century living

Mozart and the Salzburg Festival

Although Mozart spent much of his adult life in Vienna, his name is inextricably linked with his birthplace, Salzburg. Considered by many to be the world's greatest composer, Mozart's spiritual legacy to his native city is one of the world's greatest music festivals, the Salzburg Festival, and a year-round program of musical events.

Mozart

Wolfgang Amadeus Mozart was born in Salzburg in 1756, the son of a respected court musician, himself a fine violinist whose treatise on violin technique is still respected. The boy soon showed signs of genius, playing a variety of instruments by sight and ear and starting to compose at an early age. Mozart's father touted his talented son all around the European courts, keeping a stern eye on his behavior, spending and morals, and thus storing up trouble for the pair's future relationship.

Eventually, the small-town atmosphere of Salzburg, with its reliance on the bishops for employment, proved too stifling, and Mozart moved to Vienna, where he married Constanze. He composed prodigiously and was capable of writing scores as if by divine dictation, while chatting to his friends. Unfortunately, Mozart's genius did not extend to managing his finances; weighed down by money worries and stress, he died in 1791 and was buried in a pauper's grave.

The Salzburg Festival

The Salzburg Festival is held annually during the last week of July and most of August. Established in 1920 by Max Reinhardt, Richard Strauss and other Austrian musicians, this music festival attracts audiences and renowned performers from all over the world. Its main venues are the Festival Theaters complex (see page 43), but performances are held in buildings all over the city. The program always includes Mozart operas and orchestral works, but many other composers are featured, as well as plays – in particular *Everyman*, which is traditionally performed outside in the Domplatz.

If you want to attend the festival it is essential to book far ahead; the deadline is in January, when you should also have your accommodations reserved as well.

Salzburg Ticket Service ✉ Salzburg information, Mozartplatz 5, A-5020 Salzburg, Austria ☎ 0662 840 310; fax 0662 842 476

Mozart's Birthplace, on the third-floor apartment in Getreidegasse

quarters, where each room opens from its adjoining room and communal wooden balconies overlook a courtyard. One floor down, you can study stage sets and costumes from festival productions of Mozart's works while listening to his sublime music.

Mozart-Wohnhaus

B3 Makartplatz 8 0662 874 227-40 Daily 9–7, Jul.–Aug.; 9–6, rest of year 15, 27, 51 $$ Guided and self-guided tours

In 1773 the Mozart family left their modest flat in Getreidegasse and moved across the river to Makartplatz to occupy a far more spacious and elegant apartment, now the Mozart-Wohnhaus (Mozart's House). The building was badly damaged in World War II and was finally renovated and reopened for the 240th anniversary of Mozart's birth in 1996. The result is a superb state-of-the-art museum with evocative displays of Mozart memorabilia.

A true picture of the composer emerges – a man who loved games and jokes, who had an earthy sense of humor and a difficult relationship with his father. Here are scribbled letters, musical manuscripts, instruments and books, all brought to life through an English-language commentary. Two rooms are devoted to audiovisual programs about Mozart's early life and his travels through Europe, which, given 18th-century roads, were impressive.

Museum Carolino Augusteum

B3 Main Building: Museumsplatz 1. Toy Museum: Bürgerspitalplatz 2 Main Building: 0662 841 134-0. Toy Museum: 0662 847 560 Main Building: daily 9–5 (also Thu. 5–8). Toy Museum: Tue.–Sun. 9–5 49, 60, 80, 81, 95 $$ (each museum) Reduced combination ticket available for both buildings

Salzburg's primary museum has collections housed in two buildings – the Haupthaus (Main Building) covers classical antiquities and art; the Spielzeugmuseum and Musikinstrumente (Toy Museum and Musical Instruments) has a charming collection of toys, dolls and musical instruments. You can trace Salzburg's history from Roman times and admire some lovely 17th-century paneled rooms. Among the highlights is a beautiful Celtic ewer. The toys and dolls, some 300 years old, include splendid train sets and puppet theaters.

Residenz

B2–C2 Residenzplatz 1 Palace: 0662 8042-2690. Art Gallery: 0662 840 451 Palace: daily 10–5 (closed 2 weeks for Easter). Art Gallery: daily 10–5 Apr.–Sep.; Thu.–Tue. 10–5, rest of year 5, 6, 49, 51, 55 Palace $$$, Art Gallery $$

The Residenzplatz is the triumphant architectural landmark of the inner city, splendidly adorned with an ebullient baroque fountain (the largest in northern Europe) complete with horses and dolphins and topped by a conch-blowing triton. Opposite rises the Residenz (Archbishop's Palace), built in the early 1600s around three courtyards. See the impressive baroque interiors on an audio-guided tour that leads through rooms of sugary magnificence, decorated with stucco, gilding, marble and astonishing painted ceilings. Nothing gives a better sense of the scale of grandeur and luxury enjoyed by Salzburg's prince bishops. The palace also contains an art gallery. Concerts are held in the state rooms.

Stiftskirche St. Peter

B2 St. Peter-Bezirk 0 62 844 578-0 Church: daily 8–7. Catacombs: Tue.–Sun. 10:30–5, May–Sep.; Wed.–Thu. 10:30–3:30, Fri.–Sun. 10:30–4, rest of year Stiftskeller St.Peter, see page 542 5, 51 ,55 Catacombs $

The lovely Stiftskirche St. Peter (St. Peter's Church) was built between 1131 and 1143 but altered to its present rococo appearance in the 17th and 18th centuries. A simple Romanesque west door leads into a sumptuous interior, resplendent with 16 marble altars in its side chapels and decorated with green and pink molding and golden cherubs. See the monument to Mozart's beloved sister Nannerl before leaving the church to explore the charming old Friedhof (cemetery), with its flower-bedecked graves and monuments.

A Day in Salzburg

Although several companies offer a variety of tours in and around Salzburg, the city is small enough to find your way around easily, so it makes sense to plan your own day's sightseeing.

A Mozart Morning

After a hearty Austrian breakfast, spend the morning concentrating on Wolfang Amadeus Mozart, Salzburg's most famous son. His father, employed as a musician in the city, lived in a house on Getreidegasse, where Mozart was born in 1756. After visiting the house and its museum you may be ready for a cup of coffee; head for the Café Tomaselli in the Alter Markt. It was here that Mozart's widow came with her second husband to write the composer's biography in 1820.

Next, cross the Staatsbrücke and walk along the river to Mozart's House (Mozart-Wohnhaus) on Makartplatz, a far grander house where Mozart's family lived between 1773 and 1780 in a spacious apartment. Nearby you'll find the Mozarteum, the music conservatory that holds the Mozart archives. The hut on the grounds is the Little Magic Flute House (Zauberflötenhäuschen) which once stood in Vienna. Here, Mozart dashed off the opera in less than five months.

An Afternoon in the Altstadt

Back across the river, have lunch and then spend the afternoon exploring the Old Town (Altstadt). Most sights are clustered around the trio of lovely squares known as the Residenzplatz, the Domplatz and the Mozartplatz. Behind the cathedral (Dom, see page 43), take the funicular up to the fortress of Hohensalzburg (see page 43).

After this, visit the fine Museum Carolino Augusteum. En route, stop at the Pferdeschwemme (literally, "horse-swim"), a frescoed fountain-cum-pool where horses once were led down sloping ramps to be washed. Leave time to enjoy the stores along Getreidegasse and in the alleys leading off it, where you'll find every imaginable Austrian souvenir.

A Salzburg Evening

No Salzburg visit would be complete without some music; many visitors enjoy special Mozart evenings, with dinner followed by a performance of the composer's works played by costumed musicians. Then wander back through the atmospheric streets to your hotel with music ringing in your ears. For the walk route, see the city map on page 40.

Take a *Fiaker* (horse-drawn carriage) for a leisurely view of old Salzburg

Breathtaking in evening light, Salzburg's medieval fortress towers over the city

MUSEE
MUSEUM

BELGIUM

"THE buildings, streets, squares, all are picturesque; the houses, green, blue, pink, yellow, with richest ornaments..."

From English poet Dorothy Wordsworth's *Journal*, July 14, 1820

Opposite: The Carpet of Flowers festival takes place biennially in Brussels' Grand-Place

BELGIUM

Belgium is a young country in terms of "old" Europe. Its name derives from a prehistoric tribe, the Belgae, but there is no racial or cultural link with such a distant past. The country has been in the melting pot of European history for centuries and only achieved true national identity in 1830. Yet nowhere else on the Continent will you be so close to such a powerful sense of European history.

Influential Neighbors

The Belgium of today is a nation born out of a divided Europe, a remarkable survivor in spite of the differences in politics, territory and language that remain within its own borders. Too often it is seen as the administrative focus of the European Union, a country preoccupied with international politics and commerce. Geographically, it is tiny (about the size of Maryland) relative to the size of Europe's larger nations. The Netherlands lies to its north, Germany to its east, France to its south and Luxembourg, an independent Grand Duchy linked historically to Belgium, adjoins it on the southeast.

The northwestern coastline of Belgium faces Britain across the narrow neck of the English Channel. The influences and interests of all of these countries have impacted on Belgium and, in the case of France and the Netherlands, have radically shaped the country's north-south linguistic and cultural divide.

Landscape of History

Apart from the canals in the north, Belgium has no outstanding landscape features that define it in the way that Norway is defined by its fjords, Greece by its islands, Switzerland by its Alps or Britain by its surrounding seas. Yet Belgium has a very special, very powerful identity expressed through historic cities and a peerless artistic legacy. You will be seduced by medieval Bruges and old Brussels; feel a sense of history in Ghent, Antwerp and regional cities such as Leuven and Mechelen; and be enchanted by the castles in the Ardenne

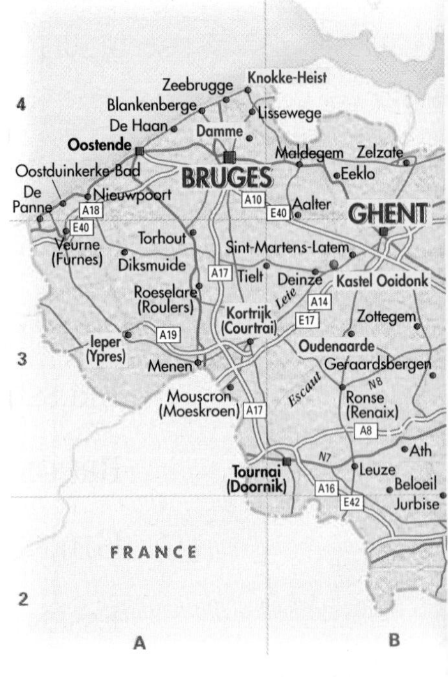

MORE TOP DESTINATIONS IN BELGIUM

• Alden Biesen D3
• Antwerpen C4
• Damme A4 • Ieper A3
• Kastel Ooidonk B3
• Knokke-Heist A4 • Kortrijk A3
• Leuven C3 • Mechelen C3
• Oudenaarde B3
• La Roche-en-Ardenne D2
• Villers-la-Ville C3

region. The dazzling works of art of early Flemish Masters and medieval painters will fascinate you: prepare yourself for Jan van Eyck, Hans Memling and Peter Paul Rubens, as well as the Brueghels, Anthony van Dyck and Jacob Jordaens.

Belgium is about the landscape of history rather than of scenery. Yet outside the cities and towns, beyond the busy network of main roads, lies a quietly charming countryside of fruitful farms, serene waterways and flower-filled meadows. On the immediate outskirts of Brussels is the Forêt de Soignes, a superb beech forest that is an oasis of peace and reflection. In the Haspengouw region to the west of Brussels are several historic castles, such as the stately Gaasbeek with its formal gardens and the 13th-century, moated Alden Biesen. A more somber yet compelling aspect of Belgium is enshrined in the poem *In Flanders Fields.* Throughout Europe's turbulent history

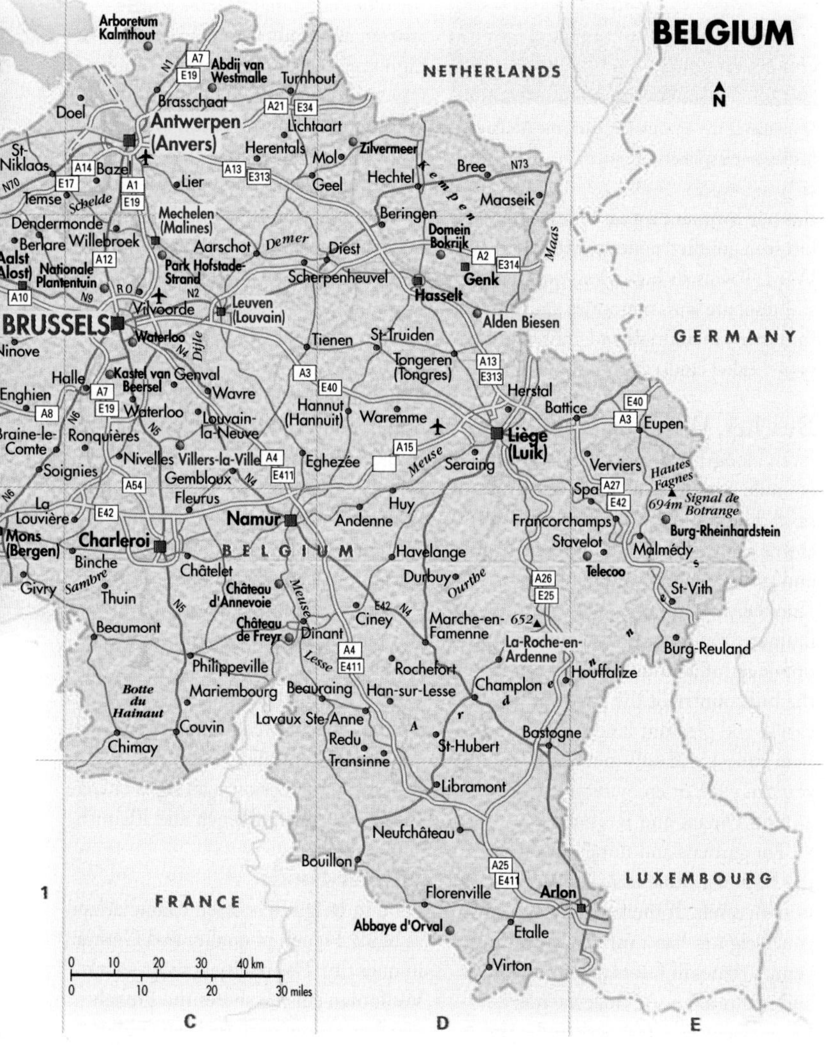

Dominating the surrounding park, the Atomium has become a symbol of Brussels

this northwestern corner of the Continent has seen conflict, none so bitter as World War I. Towns such as Mons and Ieper still resonate with memories and you will find many memorials and graves in the now-healed landscape.

Beaches, Woodlands and Parks

Even along Belgium's relatively short 60-mile coastline there are attractive sand dunes, beaches and resorts, lively towns such as Oostende, and exclusive and stylish places like De Haan or Knokke. And though there may be no dramatic mountains, the southern provinces of Namur and Liège embrace the hill country of the Ardennes, a varied and pleasant landscape of woods, river valleys and soft moorland where you can walk or enjoy bicycle rides around Dinant and Rochefort.

For gardens and floral displays, try the National Botanical Garden at Meise, near Brussels. If theme parks appeal to you, Belgium has a variety of exciting venues that will fascinate children and adults alike. At Bellewaerde, near Ieper, is a large safari park and a vivid flower garden; just outside Bruges, at Boudewijnpark, is Europe's largest dolphinarium.

Exploring Belgium

Public transportation in Belgium is universally efficient, but the railroad network is by far the best way to travel. It is well integrated with systems in neighboring countries, and trains are frequent. Inter-city trains are fast and comfortable; local trains tend to be slower, and you may feel that some of the older equipment seems a little spartan and drab. Overall, however, the high standards that distinguish rail travel throughout northern Europe prevail. City transportation systems are also well run. Trams are a northern European institution, and the larger cities in Belgium have good tram and bus services. Brussels and Antwerp have well organized subway systems that visitors will find useful.

Renting a car will give you independence, but driving in Belgium is a challenge due mainly to the small size of the country and, in part, to its congested urban nature.The road system is excellent, but because distances between built-up areas can be short, you are frequently faced with busy intersections. Traffic in Brussels and in the larger cities is hectic, and navigation can be complicated for visitors because road signs are in French and Flemish. Out on the road, along the east-west dividing line between French-speaking and Flemish-speaking Belgium, destination names on road signs change suddenly between French and Flemish.

Diverse Foods

Food in Belgium is often characterized as being French in quality and German in quantity. The reality is more subtle. Wallonian cuisine shares the French penchant for wine-based sauces, but

Scene of one of the most famous battles in history, Waterloo lies 12 miles south of Brussels

traditional Belgian cuisine focuses particularly on beef and pork, and specializes in seafood in the west and game in the Ardennes.

In most good hotels you will find the generous buffet breakfasts that are an international staple, comprising a variety of cereals, cheeses and hams, along with fish and smoked meats. For lunch and dinner, be adventurous. Try *maatjes*, raw herring swallowed whole, but not quite the raw experience it seems. Or settle for *mosselen*, Belgian mussels in a variety of tangy sauces. For a truly filling meal, try *waterzooi*, a traditional Flemish stew of fresh vegetables with rabbit, chicken or fish, or *paling in 't groen*, freshwater eels in a green herb sauce. And do not miss Ardennes pâté or the region's excellent specialty smoked ham.

In spring look for asparagus with a butter-based sauce, chopped boiled egg and chopped ham. This goes nicely with one of Belgium's many excellent beers, which tend to be rich, mellow and smooth. In the Flemish and the Liège regions of Belgium the specialty is *jenever*, a grain spirit.

For those with a sweet tooth, Belgium's famous *chocolatiers* will be irresistible. The specialties are individually made pralines with liqueur or cream fillings, and truffles with the utterly indulgent ingredients of butter, cream and sugar. *Gaufres*, tasty waffles, are a Belgian treat that you can buy from street vendors.

Traditional Courtesy

Throughout Belgium, visitors will find the local people unfailingly helpful. This is a conservative country with a strongly Roman Catholic religious tradition, aspects that make people courteous yet reserved. The language divide (see page 54) lends a certain rivalry to relations between Flemings and Walloons, yet such cultural diversity seems to make most Belgians amenable to and interested in visitors. The people may seem busy and preoccupied, but they will respond politely and matter-of-factly if you ask for advice or information about their country, which is, after all, a distillation of the most significant aspects of old and new Europe.

TIMELINE

57 BC	Romans in northern Europe conquer Iron Age Belgae tribe territory, part of land now occupied by present-day Belgium.
AD 751	Carolingian Dynasty is formed; during reign of Charlemagne, Holy Roman Emperor, the Low Countries prosper.
1419	Central government established at Bruges; the city becomes a center of the cloth trade and a focus of early Flemish painters.
1519	Charles V of Spain is crowned Holy Roman Emperor; the Netherlands comes under Spanish control.
1581	The Netherlands divides into United Provinces of the Netherlands and Spanish Netherlands (Belgium).
1713	War of Spanish Succession ends; Austria controls Belgium.
1815	Congress of Vienna; Belgium and the United Provinces of the Netherlands form the Kingdom of the Netherlands, ruled from the Hague by the Dutch William of Orange.
1839	Belgian independence recognized by the (Dutch) Netherlands.
1914–18	Most of Belgium is occupied by Germany.
1940–44	Belgium again occupied by Germany.
1957	European Economic Community (now the European Union) establishes its headquarters in Brussels.
1967	NATO sets up headquarters in Brussels.
1993	Belgium signs the Maastricht Treaty, establishing the European Union.
2000	Belgium (along with the Netherlands) hosts Euro 2000, the European Football (soccer) Championships; Brussels designated a European City of Culture.
2002	Bruges designated Cultural Capital of Europe.

LANGUAGE DIVIDE

There is a dramatic linguistic divide between north and south Belgium, a legacy of the country's formation from a southern French-influenced area and a northern Flemish-influenced area. In northern Belgium the dominant language is Flemish, a German-based language similar to Dutch. In southern Belgium, in the area known as Wallonia, the prevailing language is a French dialect. Brussels lies within the Flemish half of Belgium and is officially bilingual, but within the city French is the dominant language.

Be careful in comparing Flemish too closely with Dutch. Brugeans (residents of Bruges) will tell you that theirs is a far subtler language, with more lyrical twists and turns. And Ghentenaars (residents of Ghent) will tell you that they speak better Flemish than Brugeans; if you visit more remote rural districts you will find even more robust regional differences.

SURVIVAL GUIDE

- Flemish and French are both spoken in Brussels, where even street signs are in both languages. You can try out your French in Brussels and Wallonia and your Flemish in Ghent, Bruges and in the north; but to use either language in the wrong area may elicit a frosty reaction. Many Belgians speak English to a greater or lesser degree, and this is often the wisest option, wherever you are.
- You will usually find that the Flemish and French proper names have similarities; for example, Bruges is Bruges (French) and Brugge (Flemish), Louvain is Louvain (French) and Leuven (Flemish). But there are problematic differences. For example, Ghent is Gand (French) but Gent (Flemish), and Mechelen is Malines (French) but Mechelen (Flemish). If in doubt, especially when checking train or bus destinations, confirm the destination with an English-speaking official.
- There are a few public restrooms in Belgian cities, but they are often not clean. Railroad and bus stations, restaurants and the bigger cafés have public bathrooms with attendants. You are expected to pay about 10 francs to use restrooms.
- In restaurants, the *menu* usually signifies the dish of the day. If you want to choose from a selection of dishes, ask for the *kaart* (Flemish) or the *carte* (French).
- In the rue des Bouchers area of Brussels, you may find that prominently displayed *menus* at reasonable prices become suddenly replaced as soon as you are seated. You may be repeatedly offered house specialties at inflated prices. If this is not what you want, move on to another restaurant.

Sample one of the 400 Belgian beers at a sidewalk café in the historic Grand-Place

- For a quick snack, there are numerous fast food outlets, stalls and, in large shopping precincts, café counter service. Apart from the universal hamburgers and french fries, there is usually a big selection of *broodjes*, baguettes crammed with mouthwatering fillings. Seasoned and smoked sausages are sold from street vendors in the northern areas of Belgium. *Gaufres*, tasty, vanilla-flavored waffles, are another treat, bought fresh from street stalls and spread with jam.
- Beer brewing is a Belgian specialty, and there are hundreds of different Belgian brews. Try a *bière* with your meal at a restaurant. It is perfectly in keeping with the cuisine, which incorporates beer in many dishes. The best Belgian beers can be as fine as wine.

BRUSSELS

Brussels (Bruxelles) takes most people by surprise. The city's name is so closely associated with the modern trappings of the European Union (E.U.) that for many it is synonymous with modern high-rise buildings and the world of suited bureaucrats. The real Brussels has a far more colorful and resonant life. It is an exciting, modern city, yet rich in beautiful medieval and art nouveau buildings, outstanding museums and galleries, and a cultural life vibrantly international in character.

Life in the City

You may feel intimidated at first by the hectic pace of the busy streets, but Brussels is genuine "old Europe" at heart – open, friendly and welcoming. Life between the busy boulevards is engagingly relaxed. There is a wonderful

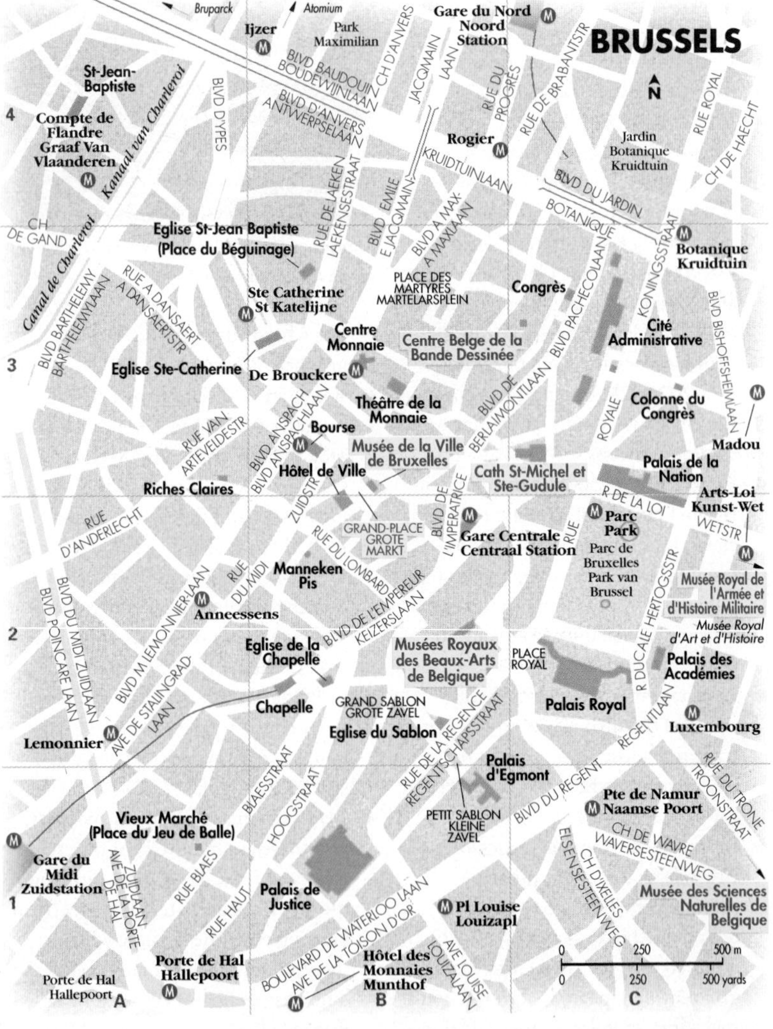

variety about Brussels, a sense of its being several urban "villages" within a whole.

The heart of the city lies within a barrier of encircling main roads known as the *petit ring*. You should be able to reach the inner city's finest features easily, and you should have no difficulty finding your way around; another option is to join one of the many guided tours. For areas outside the *petit ring* use the city's subway system, one of the easiest ways of getting around the larger area of Brussels.

Medieval Townscape

Historic Brussels is celebrated by the breathtaking Grand-Place (Grote Markt, see pages 59 and 61), the best-preserved medieval townscape in Europe. North of here you will find the rue des Bouchers area, where narrow cobbled streets are lined with competing restaurants more reminiscent of Mediterranean cities. Nearby are the elegant, glass-roofed shopping malls of the 19th-century Galeries St. Hubert.

A short distance west of Grand-Place, along rue au Beurre, is the massive neoclassical Bourse, the city's stock exchange, its front facing busy boulevard Anspach. Nearby is rue Neuve, a lively shopping street. Head west from boulevard Anspach and discover Brussels' very old heartland of place St.-Géry, with its covered market, and place Ste.-Cathérine and place du Béguinage, old cobbled squares with slightly worn but still splendid baroque churches. Between St.-Géry and Ste.-Cathérine lies rue Antoine Dansaert, a street featuring chic clothing stores.

Sightseeing and Shopping

Outside the center there are other atmospheric and stylish areas: Le Sablon, near the southern edge of the *petit ring*, is convenient to the Royal Museums of Fine Arts of Belgium (Musées Royaux des Beaux-Arts de Belgique, see page 60) or a passing glance at the Royal Palace and the Palace of Justice. The place de Grand Sablon, a pleasant leafy square, is the center of Brussels' antique trade, and there are also some fine restaurants, cafés and stores here. Just south of Le Sablon is the busy and fashionable shopping street of avenue Louise.

There is so much to see in Brussels that you'll need to use your time efficiently to visit as many of the superb attractions as possible. Branch out beyond the *petit ring* to places like Heysel, 4 miles north of Grand-Place. Here stands the Atomium, a vast model of a metal crystal, its steel spheres gleaming in the sun. At its foot the popular Mini-Europe presents scaled-down versions of Europe's most famous buildings. Visit the Parc du Cinquantenaire, Leopold II's 1880 celebration of the Golden Jubilee of the Belgian State. The park has a central

Petit Julien

South of Grand-Place on rue du Chène (reached via rue Charles-Buls and Stoofstraat) stands the famous *Manneken-Pis*, a bronze fountain statuette of a naked little boy happily urinating. *Petit Julien*, as he is properly called, dates from 1619 and has long been an irreverent and endearing symbol of "carefree" Brussels.

Banners fly at a colorful Belgian pageant

avenue, named after John F. Kennedy, that leads to a triumphal arch linking monumental halls. Several major museums are located here.

Cuisine and Culture

Make sure you enjoy classic Brussels cuisine at superb gourmet restaurants such as Comme Chez Soi (see page 543); or try a less pricey local *geuze* or *kriek* beer in any one of the café bars in and around Grand-Place and rue Marché aux Herbes. Sample Brussels' mussels, of course, but also enjoy *anguilles au vert,* freshwater eels in sauce, or *waterzooi,* fish or chicken stew with vegetables and creamy sauce, and spoil yourself with Belgian chocolate.

Enjoy great music in the superb national opera house, Théâtre de la Monnaie, or in one of the lively rock and jazz venues. There are also colorful street theaters, annual festivals and puppet theater events for kids.

ESSENTIAL INFORMATION

TOURIST INFORMATION

Tourist and Information Office-Brussels (TIB)

• Hôtel de Ville, Grand-Place ☎ 02 513 8940; fax 02 513 8320; www.tib.be
• Brussels International Airport ☎ 02 720 5161
• Hall TGV/Thalys, Gare du Midi/Zuidstation (South Station)

URBAN TRANSPORTATION

Brussels has three railroad stations: the Gare du Nord/Noordstation (Brussels North), Gare Centrale/Centraal Station (Brussels Central) and Gare du Midi/Zuidstation (Brussels South). Eurostar service from London's Waterloo train station (2 hours, 40 minutes) arrives at Brussels South, as does the TGV/Thalys train (1 hour, 20 minutes) from Paris. There are subway (metro) stops at all three stations. Subway stations are marked on the map as "M." For rail information call ☎ 02 555 2525. Brussels has several public transportation options, including subways, buses and an underground tram (same ticket for all), as well as a decent taxi service. The three subway lines with several stations are conveniently placed near major attractions. Underground trams run between Gare du Nord and Gare du Midi. For general information on city transportation call ☎ 02 515 2000. Licensed taxis have a light on their roofs and can be hailed in the street or from a taxi stand. They are metered; rates double when traveling outside the city. There are taxi stands at Grand-Place and at Brussels Gare Centrale.

AIRPORT INFORMATION

Brussels International Airport is located at Zaventem, 8 miles northeast of the city. There is an Airport City Express train that runs to all of Brussels' main stations at 20-minute intervals (journey time 30 minutes), from 5:24 a.m.–11:46 p.m. from the airport and 5:40 a.m.–11:10 p.m. from the city. There is a Tourist and Information Office in the arrival hall. Accommodations can be reserved here, and you can obtain information about Brussels and northern Belgium. For general flight information call ☎ 0900 70000.

CLIMATE – average highs and lows for the month

JAN.	FEB.	MAR.	APR.	MAY	JUN.	JUL.	AUG.	SEP.	OCT.	NOV.	DEC.
4°C	6°C	10°C	13°C	18°C	22°C	22°C	22°C	20°C	15°C	9°C	5°C
39°F	43°F	50°F	55°F	64°F	72°F	72°F	72°F	68°F	59°F	48°F	41°F
-1°C	0°C	2°C	5°C	8°C	11°C	12°C	12°C	10°C	7°C	3°C	0°C
30°F	32°F	36°ºF	41°F	46°F	52°F	54°F	54°F	50°F	45°F	37°F	32°F

City Sights

Key to symbols
map coordinates refer to the Brussels map on page 56; sights below are highlighted in yellow on the map. address or location telephone number opening times nearest subway nearest bus or tram route restaurant or café on site or nearby admission charge: $$$ more than 150BF, $$ 80BF–150BF, $ less than 80BF other relevant information

Cathédrale St.-Michel et Ste.-Gudule

C3 Parvis Ste.-Gudule 02 217 8345 Daily 8–6 Gare Centrale Free; entrance to crypt $

The Cathédrale St.-Michel et Ste.-Gudule (Cathedral of St. Michael and St. Gudula) occupies an elevated site above bland modern buildings and passing traffic. Work on the cathedral began in the 13th century. Architecturally, the building is a lesson in the various forms of Brabantine Gothic that evolved over the 300 years it took to complete the work. Inside the church, baroque style is lavishly celebrated by giant figures of the apostles, while Renaissance influence shines from the exceptional stained glass of the 16th-century west window. The Romanesque remains of an 11th-century church can be seen down in the crypt.

Centre Belge de la Bande Dessinée

C3 rue des Sables 20 02 219 1980 Tue.–Sun. 10–6 Museum restaurant Gare Centrale 29, 38, 63, 71; tram 23, 55, 81, 92 $$$ Reading room Tue.–Sun. 10–6

The rather plainly named Centre Belge de la Bande Dessinée (Belgian Center for Comic Strip Art) encompasses a dazzling celebration of the strip cartoon, the *bande dessinée.* The strip cartoon is closely associated with Belgium, not least in the shape of Hergé's (Georges Rémi's) famous character Tin Tin, created in 1929. The form has strong design links to art nouveau and it is an added delight that the museum building was designed in 1906 as a fabric shop by Victor Horta, the most distinguished of art nouveau architects.

Guild House, Grand-Place

Grand-Place

B2–B3 Grand-Place La Rose Blanche, see page 543 Bourse Tram 23, 52, 56, 81 Location of numerous events throughout the year. Daily flower market, songbird market on Sundays, summer concerts, biennial Carpet of Flowers. Annual medieval festival, the *Ommegang*, in early July. Lively Planting of the Maytree procession on Aug. 9

Brussels' Grand-Place is an extravaganza of medieval architecture, as displayed in the numerous guild houses that complement the Place's monumental Hôtel de Ville (Town Hall, see page 61). Opposite stands the splendid La Maison du Roi (The King's House), which is the location of the City of Brussels Museum. There is an information center on the first floor of the Town Hall. Many events and festivals are held in the square. The spectacular *Ommegang* is an annual costume parade during the first week of July in which the Grand-Place is transformed into a stunning medieval stage.

Tin Tin's space rocket from "Destination Moon"

Musée Royal de l'Armée et d'Histoire Militaire

Off the map ✉ parc du Cinquantenaire 3 (Autoworld at number 11) ☎ Museum 02 737 7811; Autoworld 02 736 4165 Museum: Tue.–Sun. 9:30–5. Autoworld: Daily 10–6, Apr.–Sep.; 10–5, rest of year Museum café Merode 20, 28, 36, 61, 80; tram 81, 82 Museum $$; Autoworld $$$

The entire gamut of military artifacts is displayed at the Musée Royal de l'Armée et d'Histoire Militaire (Royal Museum of the Army and Military History), and a visit is a campaign in its own right. The main museum features display after display of military uniforms, artifacts and weaponry. The glass-roofed Hall of the Air has dozens of aircraft, including an 80-seater Caravelle frozen in mid-flight above your head.

Across the courtyard from the museum is Autoworld, with a remarkable collection of more than 950 vehicles, including elegant landaus, broughams and calèches of past centuries to the opulence of the 20th-century Lincoln and the Hispano Suiza.

Musée des Sciences Naturelles de Belgique

Off the map ✉ rue Vautier 29 (entry: chaussée de Wavre 260) ☎ 02 627 4227 or 02 627 4238 (24-hour recorded information) Tue.–Fri. 9:30–4:45, Sat.–Sun. 10–6 Museum café Train: Quartier Léopold. Subway: Maelbeek or Troon/Trône 34, 80 $$ Guided tours and workshops

The delightful Musée des Sciences Naturelles de Belgique (Museum of Natural Sciences in Belgium) is a haven of individuality in the modern European Union district. The main hall is a riot of dinosaur skeletons and reconstructions of Tyrannosaurus Rex and other prehistoric animals that roar and sway convincingly.

Several floors hold general biological exhibitions, including an Antarctica tunnel with sound effects to go with its polar bears, walruses, and penguins. "Of Men and Mammoths" traces human evolution and features Neanderthal remains discovered at Spy near Namur. There are no English-language labels except for part of the Antarctica section, but the exhibits speak volumes in themselves, not least to totally enthralled youngsters.

Musée de la Ville de Bruxelles

B3 ✉ rue du Poivre 1 (entrance from Grand-Place) ☎ 02 279 4350 Mon.–Thu. 10–12:30 and 1:30–5, Sat.–Sun. 10–1, Apr.–Oct.; Mon.–Thu. 10–12:30 and 1:30–4, Sat.–Sun. 10–1, rest of year Bourse Tram 23, 52, 56, 81 $$

The Musée de la Ville de Bruxelles (City of Brussels Museum) is a local celebration of Brussels and has very little information in English. It deserves a visit, however, because of its porcelain, pottery and Brussels' tapestries' collections, as well as its paintings, including Pieter Breughel the elder's splendid *The Marriage Procession.*

The museum is located on Grand-Place in the handsome building known as the King's House (Maison du Roi). On the top floor there is an entertaining display of some of the 600 costumes in the "wardrobe" of the Manneken-Pis (see page 57) that have been donated by heads of state and others since 1698.

Musées Royaux des Beaux-Arts de Belgique

B2 ✉ Museum of Ancient Art: rue de la Régence 3; Museum of Modern Art: place Royal 1–2 ☎ 02 508 3211 Tue.–Sun. 10–5 Museum café Gare Centrale 20, 38, 60, 71, 95, 96; tram 92, 93, 94 $$ (includes both museums)

The Musées Royaux des Beaux-Arts de Belgique (Royal Museums of Fine Arts of Belgium) are housed in the former court of Charles Lorraine. The entrance fee includes both the Musée d'Art Ancien (Museum of Ancient Art) and the Musée d'Art Moderne (Museum of Modern Art); the two are linked by an underground passage.

The complex contains one of the most comprehensive and exciting collections of paintings in Europe, covering the 14th century to the present day. Pieter Breughel, Pablo Picasso and Auguste Rodin are only a few of the leading names of Flemish and Western art represented here.

You'll enjoy this stunning feast of art even more if you rent the audio program (available in many languages) for the Ancient Art section. It's not available for the superb Modern Art section.

GRAND-PLACE

Grandiose gables on the guild houses in Grand-Place recall the wealth of their creators

The late medieval Grand-Place, or Grote Markt in Flemish, is one of the most glorious sights of urban Europe. A first glimpse of Grand-Place, whether by day or floodlit at night, should stop even the most jaded in their tracks. These are buildings that seem wrought from nature, yet their symmetry and elegance is ravishing. Any debate about the competing merits of traditional or Modernist architecture melts away in the face of such adventurous style. Even the fast-food stores, bars and cafés that have taken over the ground-floor premises shrink into insignificance.

What you see in Grand-Place today are some of the finest examples of Dutch Renaissance and Gothic architecture, most of which are 17th-century replacements of older wooden-framed guild houses. The originals were destroyed in 1695 during a devastating bombardment of Brussels by the troops of a spiteful Louis XIV. The citizens rebuilt the heart of their city in a bold act of defiance. The Town Hall (Hôtel de Ville) is the focus of Grand-Place. Its soaring tower dominates the Brussels skyline; its carved facade is crammed with dukes, duchesses, monks, saints and sinners.

The guild houses, which make up the other sides of the square, are named and represented by gilded statues, bas-reliefs, motifs and classical orders. They are a riot of exquisite forms and symbols. Look for No. 7, Le Renard (The Fox), the Drapers' guild house; and No. 6, Cornet (Horn), the guild house of the Boatmen.

Opposite the Town Hall is The King's House (La Maison du Roi), known also as the Bread House (Broodhuis) and home to the City of Brussels Museum (Musée de la Ville de Bruxelles). On the east side of Grand-Place is the restored facade of the house of the Dukes of Brabant, six individual houses united by the cool elegance of a single Renaissance facade.

Finally, in the southeast corner to the left of the Town Hall, is No. 10, L'Arbre d'Or (The Golden Tree). This is the headquarters of the Brewers' Guild, the Knights of the Mash Staff, and also houses a Brewery Museum. Next door is Le Cygne (The Swan), complete with a graceful swan motif and rounding off the magnificent Grand-Place with a flourish.

BRUGES

In Bruges (Brugge), the survival of exquisite medieval buildings provides a vivid architectural record of 16th-century Europe. Yet that survival is the result of a commercial decline that lasted for nearly 400 years. By the early 16th century, the Zwin river, which linked Bruges and its elegant canals to the North Sea, could not be navigated because of silting; the successful cloth trade had declined, and local and foreign traders moved their businesses to the flourishing port of Antwerp. There was no wealth with which to modernize the venerable townscape. We can thank the rough handling of history for a city that now delights with the completeness of its medieval street plan and its ornate buildings.

Finding Your Way

If you arrive at Bruges railroad station you will find a small tourist information office on Stationsplein, outside the station to the right. It is only a short bus

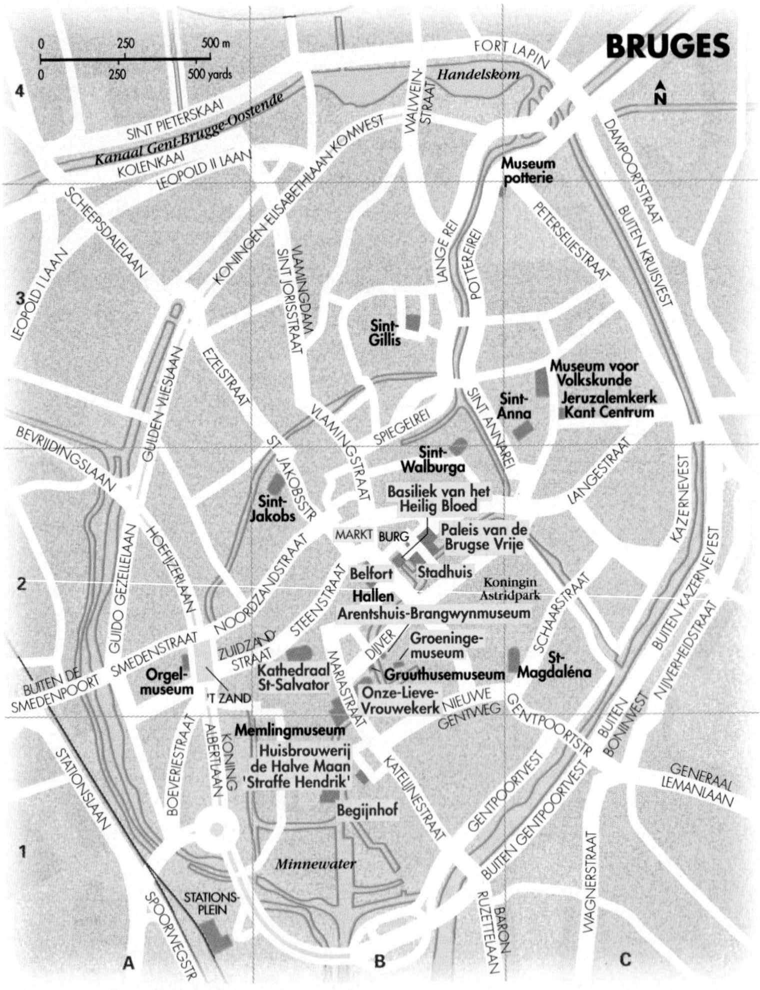

"The Venice of the north" – take a leisurely boat trip on one of Bruges' canals

ride from Stationsplein to Bruges' grand central square, the Markt (see page 67), where the city begins. A short walk along Breidelstraat, the street that begins at the southeast corner of the Markt, is the Burg (see pages 68–69), the historic heart of Bruges.

You can enjoy Bruges through guided tours, on foot, by bicycle, by bus or by canal boat. Trips on the famous horse-drawn carriages and trams of Bruges are enjoyable, but expensive. The city is an easy and rewarding place to explore on your own, however.

A City of Canals

A few steps south of the Burg, along the narrow alley known as Blind Donkey Street (Blinde Ezelstraat) will bring you to the colonnaded fish market, a lively scene Tuesday to Saturday mornings. From here proceed right, to Huidenvettersplein and then along Rosary Quay (Rozenhoed-kaai) to the canalside Dijver. Dijver has splendid museums and an exquisite complex of buildings, made up of the Gruuthusemuseum of decorative art and the Church of Our Lady (Onze-Lieve-Vrouwekerk, see page 67), which are centered around St. Boniface Bridge, an enduring image of medieval Bruges.

Explore the city's ancient walls and surviving gates, and take an early morning stroll along the old central canals from Jan Van Eyckplein just north of the Markt. Even more than the canals of Amsterdam, the canals of Bruges have a style that is truly reminiscent of Venice.

Cosmopolitan Tastes

Amid this historical splendor, modern Bruges has its own delights. The city's social life is centered on a huge open area known as 't Zand. The inner side is lined with sidewalk cafés and bars, and there is a market on Saturday mornings. Between 't Zand and the Markt lie

Lace

Bruges has long been famous for its lace. Lace making in Flanders originated in the 16th century, when lace makers specialized in bobbin lace, a method that used weaving and plaiting with thread-loaded bobbins, with the threads pinned to the pattern. The other great lace-making center was Italy, where needlepoint lace originated, a method of embroidering with buttonhole and other stitches.

Intricate work of the lace maker on Wollestraat

Bruges' busiest streets, Noordzandstraat and Zuidzandstraat, the latter leading into the shopping area of Steenstraat, with connecting squares and narrow streets harboring cafés and bistros. Eating out in Bruges is a diner's delight. You will find every type of international restaurant, but try Belgian specialties such as *kalfsblanket*, veal ragout, or *lapin à la gueuze*, rabbit cooked in *gueuze* beer.

Lace, Chocolate and Music

Between Noordzandstraat and Zuidzandstraat lies Zilverpand, a complex of 50 stores, many of them stylish fashion boutiques. If you like lace, do not miss the Gruuthuse lace shop on the Dijver for authentic work, or the many lace shops on Wollestraat, the street running south from the Markt. For antiques and craft shops, Mariastraat running south from Simon Stevinplein on Steenstraat is the place; and for mouth-watering *chocolatiers*, try Pralinette at Wollestraat 31B (see box, page 542), or Godiva at Zuidzandstraat 36.

At night, Bruges lights up spectacularly. The buildings in the Markt and elsewhere are illuminated, and there is plenty to do. Find out what's happening at Cultuurcentrum in St. Jakobsstraat, a venue for theater and music, or catch one of the summer concerts in the Town Hall.

ESSENTIAL INFORMATION

TOURIST INFORMATION
Toerisme Brugge
• Burg 11 ☎ 050 448 686; fax 050 448 600; www.brugge.be
• Toerisme Brugge, Stationsplein, Bruges railroad station

URBAN TRANSPORTATION
Bruges railroad station lies just over a mile southwest of the Markt. The station is small, well kept and has standard facilities. For information call ☎ 050 382 406 or 050 382 382. There is also an efficient bus service that caters to the city and its environs. Call ☎ 059 565 353 for information. If you'd prefer to take a taxi, cab stands are at the Markt (☎ 050 334 444) and at Stationsplein (☎ 050 384 660).

AIRPORT INFORMATION
Bruges does not have an airport; the nearest one is Brussels International Airport at Zaventem (see page 58). For flight information call ☎ 0900 70000. Train connections for Bruges are made at Brussels' Nord/Noord (North), Centrale/Centraal (Central) and Midi/Zuid (South) stations.

CLIMATE – average highs and lows for the month

JAN.	FEB.	MAR.	APR.	MAY	JUN.	JUL.	AUG.	SEP.	OCT.	NOV.	DEC.
5°C	6°C	8°C	11°C	15°C	18°C	19°C	20°C	18°C	15°C	10°C	6°C
41°F	43°F	46°F	52°F	59°F	64°F	66°F	68°F	64°F	59°F	50°F	43°F
1°C	2°C	3°C	5°C	9°C	11°C	12°C	12°C	11°C	8°C	4°C	2°C
34°F	36°F	37°F	41°F	48°F	52°F	54°F	54°F	52°F	46°F	39°F	36°F

City Sights

Key to symbols

map coordinates refer to the Bruges map on page 62; sights below are highlighted in yellow on the map. address or location telephone number opening times nearest bus route restaurant or café on site or nearby admission charge: $$$ more than 150BF, $$ 80BF–150BF, $ less than 80BF other relevant information

Arentshuis – Brangwynmuseum

B2 Dijver 16 050 448 763 Wed.–Mon. 9:30–5, Apr.–Sep.; 9:30–12:30 and 2–5, rest of year Marieke van Brugghe, see page 543 1 $$

The genteel and charming Arentshuis – Brangwynmuseum (Arents House, also known as the Brangwyn Museum) occupies an 18th-century town house on the Dijver. It contains collections of impressive lace work, and has a fascinating exhibit on its upper floor of paintings by Sir Frank Brangwyn, the Bruges-born son of Welsh parents and a great painter and designer.

All labeling is in Flemish, but an excellent English-language booklet explaining the lace exhibits is on sale at the entrance. The needlepoint and bobbin work displayed includes exquisite examples of Binche, Valenciennes, Chantilly and Bruges lace. The lace maker's life is portrayed through paintings and work tools.

Basiliek van het Heilig Bloed

B2 Burg 10 050 336 792 Daily 9:30–noon and 2–6, Apr.–Sep.; 10–noon and 2–4, rest of year. Closed Wed. afternoon Tom Pouce, see page 543 1 Churches free; Museum $

The Basiliek van het Heilig Bloed (Basilica of the Holy Blood, see pages 68–69) has been a place of pilgrimage for many centuries, and is one of the major sights of Bruges. The basilica consists of two chapels, one above the other, and the treasury is a small museum displaying religious objects.

Begijnhof

B1 Wingaardstraat 050 330 011 Beguinage: Daily sunrise–sunset. Beguine's House: Daily 10–noon and 1:45–5:30 (Sun. until 6), Apr.–Sep.; daily 10:30–noon and 1:45–5, Mar. and Oct.–Nov.; Wed.–Thu. and Sat.–Sun. 2:45–4:15, Fri. 1:45–6, rest of year. Church: Daily 6–noon and 3–6 1 Beguinage free; Beguine's House $

The Begijnhof (Beguinage) complex, a wonderful testimony to a more sedate spiritual age, has retained its tranquil atmosphere even though huge numbers of people visit it. It was founded in 1245 to accommodate pious single women, many of them lace makers, who lived reclusive lives. These inhabitants, known as Beguines, abandoned the complex in the 1920s, but Benedictine nuns later settled in the Beguinage and still live here today. The 17th-century cottages surround a peaceful square. You can visit the Begijnhuisje (Beguine's House), a museum house that has old-style furnishings and a delightful little cloister. The Begijnhof Church of St. Elizabeth has a simple grace.

Springtime at the Beguinage – a haven of peace and serenity

A detail from *The King Drinks* by Jacob Jordaens (1593–1678) on display in the Groeningemuseum

BELFORT

B2 Markt 050 448 711 Daily 9:30–5, Apr.–Sep.; 9:30–12:30 and 1:30–5, rest of year 1–10, 13, 15, 16 $$ Carillon recitals Mon., Wed. and Sat. 9–10 a.m., Sun. 2:15–3, mid-Jun. through Sep. 30; Wed. and Sat.–Sun. 2:15–3, rest of year

Bruges' famous Belfort (Belfry) dominates the Markt. You can reach the top of the 289-foot tower by climbing the 366 steps. Ascending it is a challenge but every step will be memorable. You may marvel at the vast number of bricks and the tons of mortar holding everything together, including the 27 tons that the 47-bell carillon weighs. Just below the belfry is the chamber containing the clock mechanism and copper carillon drum. The bells ring out at each quarter hour. You have time to watch the ingenious system whir and click into life, like some great mechanical beast, before the final short climb to the belfry to enjoy the melodic, and surprisingly muted, peals and to take in the stunning view.

GROENINGEMUSEUM

B2 Dijver 12 050 448 711 Wed.–Mon. 9:30–5, Apr.–Sep.; 9:30–12:30 and 2–5, rest of year Marieke van Brughe, see page 543 1 $$$ Audio guide available

The Groeningemuseum, also called the City Museum of Fine Arts, is housed in a former Augustinian monastery on the Dijver and contains Bruges' superb civic collection of 15th- to 20th-century Belgian and Dutch paintings. There are exceptional works here, including Jan van Eyck's *The Madonna with Canon Joris van der Paele*, the works of Pieter Pourbus and Hans Memling, and *The Last Judgement* by Hieronymus Bosch, a painting that demands close attention.

HUISBROUWERIJ DE HALVE MAAN 'STRAFFE HENDRIK'

B1 Walplein 26 050 332 697 Guided tours daily 10–5, Apr.–Sep.; only at 11 and 3, rest of year 1 $$

For relief from Bruges' cultural and artistic delights, step into the Huisbrouwerij De Halve Maan 'Straffe Hendrik' (The Half Man 'Strong Henry' Brewery), where the local Strong Henry beer has been brewed since 1546 (the present building dates from 1856). Even the air of the brewery is so aromatic that it might make your head spin, although a visit to the roof will clear it. There is a guided tour of the brewery museum and a complimentary drink of beer at the attractive bar to finish. Tours begin when there are at least 15 visitors.

KATHEDRAAL ST.-SALVATOR

B2 Zuidzandstraat 050 866 188 Cathedral: Mon.–Fri. 10–11:30 and 2:30–5, Sat. 10–11:30 and 2:30–4, Apr.–Sep.; Mon.–Fri. 10–11:30 and 2:30–4:30, Sat. 10–11:30 and 2:30–4, rest of year. Museum: Mon.–Sat. 10–11:30 and 2–5, Sun. 3–5, Apr.–Sep.; Mon.–Sat. 2–5, rest of year 1–5, 13, 89 Cathedral free; museum $ Major concerts held in cathedral

Bruges' great churches reflect sober Flemish Protestantism rather than Latin exuberance, not least in their rather stark interiors. But the Kathedraal St.-Salvator (St. Saviour's Cathedral) has many enriching features to counteract its Gothic vastness. The high altar and the 15th-century choir stalls add a richly decorative note; the rood loft, beneath the organ case, contains a superb baroque sculpture of God the Father in white marble by Arthur Quellin the Younger. Visit the Cathedral Museum; among its crowning glories is the vivid realism of Dirk Bouts' 15th-century triptych *The Martyrdom of St. Hippolytus*.

The opulent mausoleum of Charles the Bold in the Church of Our Lady

Markt

B2 Markt Most buses Horse-drawn carriage trips and mini-bus tours start from the Markt

The Markt (Market Square) is the bustling heart of Bruges. The majestic Gothic buildings of the Provinciaal Hof, seat of the government of West Flanders, and the adjoining Central Post Office dominate the east side of the square, where the covered Waterhalles dock once stood. The Belfry stands on the south side. The crow-stepped gables of a row of old guild houses, now painted in bright colors, catch the sun on the north side of the square. They stand behind a statue of Jan Breydel and Pieter de Coninck, Flemish heroes who led a 1302 uprising against French overlordship. The east side of the Markt has a mix of handsome buildings, including the 15th-century Maison Bouchoute and the Craenenburg House (now the Café Craenenburg) flanking the entrance to Sint Amandstraat.

Onze-Lieve-Vrouwekerk

B2 Mariastraat 050 345 314 Mon.–Fri., 10–11:30 and 2:30–5, Sat. 10–11:30 and 2:30–4, Apr.–Sep.; Mon.–Fri. 10–11:30 and 2:30–4:30, Sat. 10–11:30 and 2:30–4, rest of year. No sightseeing during services Marieke van Brughe, see page 543 1 Church free; choir $

The exquisite Gothic gloom of the Onze-Lieve-Vrouwekerk (Church of Our Lady) is emphasized by mournful piped music. Prepare to repent. Notices everywhere exhorting *stilte* (silence) will keep you suitably hushed. Even Michelangelo's masterful sculpture the *Madonna and Child* seems constrained within the cold prison of its marble altar. Yet the church's powerful sense of sanctity and its outstanding works of sacred art overpower the initial feeling of gloominess. The pulpit, designed by Bruges artist Jan Antoon Garemijn, is a marvelous rococo extravaganza that will cheer you on your way to the choir and the magnificent, gilded Renaissance mausoleums of Mary of Burgundy and Charles the Bold.

Paleis van de Brugse Vrije

B2 Burg 11A 050 448 686 Daily 9:30–12:30 and 1:15–5, Apr.–Sep.; 9:30–12:30 and 2–5, rest of year Tom Pouce, see page 543 1 $$ (courtyard free)

The Paleis van de Brugse Vrije (Palace of the Liberty of Bruges) is a neo-classical style 18th-century building. One wing houses Old Recorders' House, a 16th-century building once used to hold public records.

Stadhuis

B2 Burg 12 050 448 711 Daily 9:30–5, Apr.–Sep.; 9:30–12:30 and 2–5, rest of year Tom Pouce, see page 543 All buses to the Markt Gothic Hall $

The Stadhuis (Town Hall) of Bruges stands in the Burg (see pages 68–69) and dates from the late 13th century. It has been rebuilt over the years and has a superb carved facade. Inside is the splendid Council Chamber, also known as the Gothic Hall.

A MEDIEVAL EXPERIENCE: THE BURG

The Burg is medieval Bruges at its most tangible. Once it was a jealously guarded enclave, walled and with locked gates. The northern side of this outstanding architectural complex once contained the 10th-century Romanesque Church of St. Donation, demolished in 1799. A scale model of the church under the trees on the square, the Burgplein, is a reminder of a lost final flourish to the Burg. Also on the northern side, on Breydelstraat, is the handsome baroque facade of the Provost's House of St. Donation.

On the east side of the Burg is the Palace of the Liberty of Bruges (Paleis van de Brugse Vrije). This was once the ruling seat of the Bruges Vrije, a territorial precinct of Flanders. The building now houses the Bruges tourist information center in one wing. The other wing harbors a magnificent Renaissance chimney piece created in honor of Charles V, Count of Flanders and Holy Roman Emperor. The lower section is in black marble with an alabaster frieze depicting the biblical story of Suzanna and the Elders. The main section is in exquisitely carved wood and depicts the Emperor and fellow members of the Habsburg family, the male contingent endowed with startling Habsburgian codpieces.

To the right of the palace across narrow Blind Donkey Street (Blinde Ezelstraat) is the Town Hall of Bruges (Stadhuis). This exquisite building dates from the late 13th century but has been rebuilt and renovated over the centuries. The turreted, Gothic facade is a lyrical evocation of the mason's craft. Inside is the Council Chamber, the Gothic Hall (Gotische Zaal), with

Procession of the Holy Blood

historical wall paintings and a handsome chimney piece. Its glorious vaulted ceiling is all gilded wooden arches with slender ribs and hanging keystones. Fortunate couples are married here.

To the right of the Town Hall in the southwest corner of the Burg is the most medieval building of all, the Basilica of the Holy Blood (Basiliek van het Heilig Bloed). In the building is a sacred vial said to contain drops of Christ's blood, brought to Bruges in 1150 from the Holy Land by Diederik von den Elzas, count of Flanders. The Holy Blood is still deeply venerated. Each Ascension Day in May or June, the relic is the focus of the most important event in West Flanders, the Procession of the Holy Blood (Heilig-Bloedprocessie), a theatrical costume pageant depicting religious events.

There is something strangely compelling about the Basilica of the Holy Blood. It has a medieval

Medieval elegance in lights – an evening meal in the atmospheric Burg after a long day of sightseeing

authenticity that is irresistible, even to the ungodly. The building contains an upper and lower chapel. You enter the lower chapel through a modest doorway and it is as if you are stepping straight into the Middle Ages.

The basilica dates from the 12th century and was built to house the relics of St. Basil. It has been partly restored, but is still one of the finest surviving examples of Romanesque architecture in Flanders. Squat pillars support the vaulted roof of the nave. Wall carvings are simple, almost primitive. The air is dense and exterior sounds are muffled and resonant; there are worn statues, slightly garish yet of great religious significance, in gloomy side chambers.

Gothic Mood

You re-emerge into the daylight, pass through an enchanting Gothic doorway in the ornate facade of the main chapel and then mount a wide staircase beneath shallow vaults. Here, the sweet odor of incense hangs in the air. The upper chapel is a breathtaking contrast to the somber Romanesque below the stairs. It is lavishly decorated in a late Gothic style that overlays original Romanesque themes. A rococo white marble altar, barrel roof, luminous stained glass, carved wood, and gold and silver artifacts all create a mood that is reminiscent of the heavy decoration of Orthodox churches.

There is a delightful spherical oak pulpit with disk canopy but without any visible access. The secret is a small door to the side of the Holy Blood altar, which opens on hidden stairs to the pulpit. The Holy Blood is contained within a crystal sheath with gold crown stoppers and is supported by gilded copper and silver angels.

Adjoining the upper church is a small museum with a few religious artifacts on display, including the gold and silver reliquary in which the Holy Blood is carried during processions.

GHENT

At first glance Ghent (Gent or Gand) seems slightly rough around the edges, a city lacking the sparkle of Luxembourg or the carefully preserved splendor of Bruges. Ghent has been an industrial and commercial center throughout its long history, and the fabric of the city has suffered because of this. But behind the urban realities of Ghent lies Belgium's "City of Flowers," along with some of the finest historical and cultural artifacts in Europe, and architecture that blends soaring towers with exquisitely decorative domestic buildings. Its citizens, the friendly Gentenaars, are shrewd, down to earth and personable. Many speak some

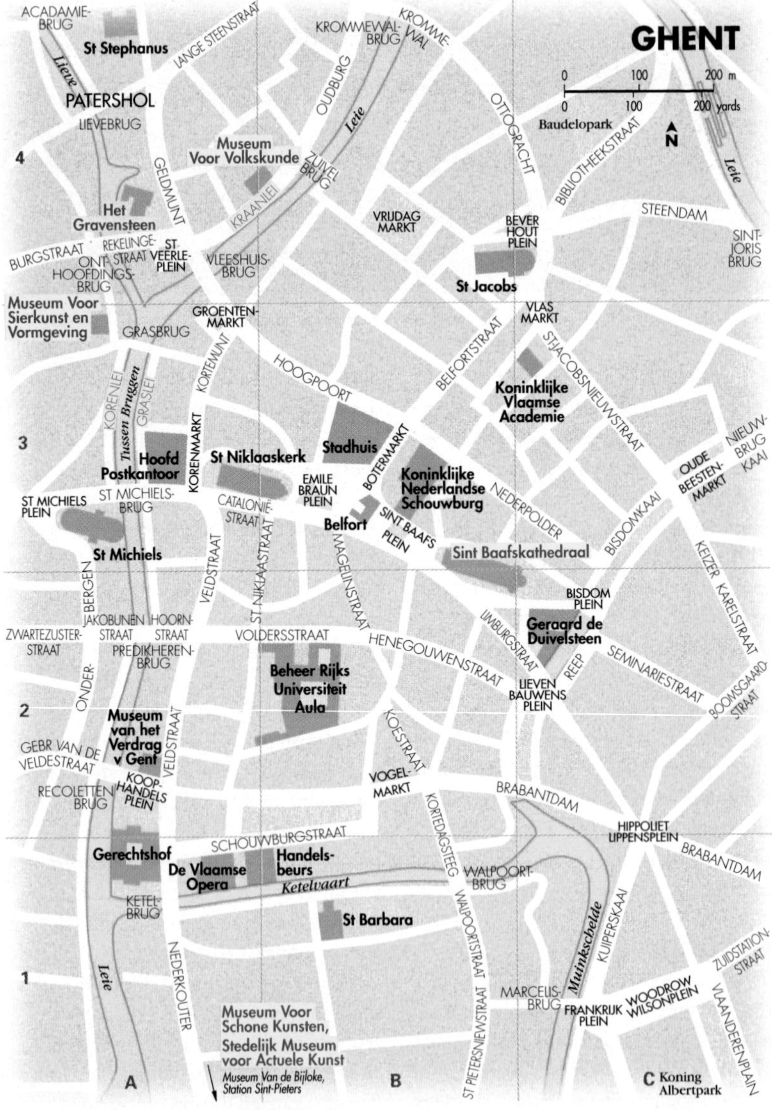

The towers of Ghent reflect the wealth of the city created during the 14th- and 15th-century cloth trade

English and are always ready to oblige the visitor with guidance and advice.

First Impressions

Ghent's main railroad station, St. Pieter's, lies just over a mile south of the city center. The station can be a sobering experience for the first-time visitor. It is a busy place and has reasonable facilities, but there is not much information for new arrivals. Head to the heart of the city and the helpful tourist information center in the crypt of the Belfry (Belfort) in Botermarkt, St. Baafsplein.

Trams leave regularly for Korenmarkt from a covered terminal on the east side of St. Pieter's Station (Sint Pietersstation). Ghent's trams run along extremely narrow streets, a mildly alarming experience at first; but they do so with great efficiency. Do not be surprised to see the driver stop, get out and adjust the wing mirror of a parked car so that the tram may squeeze past.

The great central squares are the best places to get a handle on Ghent. Here are the powerful Gothic churches of St. Baafskathedraal (see page 74) and St. Niklaaskerk. Civic buildings between them include the Belfry (Belfort), the Cloth Hall (Lakenhalle) and the Town Hall (Stadhuis), with their distinctive mix of architectural styles. Take the glass elevator to the top of the Belfort for superb views of this remarkable city of towers and steeples.

Old Ghent

For a taste of old Ghent, go west from St. Niklaaskerk, past the neo-Gothic, neo-Renaissance flamboyance of the 1910 former post office, to the bridge of St. Michielsbrug that spans the Leie river. Look back from the bridge for a breathtaking view of the skyline. North of the bridge is Tussen Bruggen, once a busy harbor and still lined by the gabled buildings of Graslei and Korenlei.

North of Graslei is Groentenmarkt, a tree-shaded square flanked by the sturdy 15th-century Meat Hall, which has little shops between deep bays where tripe stalls once stood. Today the Groentenmarkt is the scene of a daily fruit and vegetable market except on Sundays, when there's an open-air art forum. A few steps farther is the Sint

Veerleplein, with a monumental baroque archway to the old fish market and handsome gabled houses. These are all overshadowed by the brooding mass of Gravensteen, the Castle of the Counts (see opposite page).

Across the street, to the east of Gravensteen, is the side street of Kraanlei, a row of late medieval buildings lining a stretch of the Leie river. This is one of Ghent's finest streetscapes. From Kraanlei's far end, the Zuivelbrug (Zuivel Bridge) crosses the canal into the square of Vrijdagmart; the surrounding streets are crammed with stores to explore.

Shopping in Ghent

Ghent's main commercial and shopping area lies to the south of Korenmarkt and Botermarkt. The busy Veldstraat has stores of all types, but if you walk through the network of little streets just east of here, including Mageleinstraat, St. Niklaasstraat, Kortedagsteeg and Koestraat, you'll find numerous specialty shops. These include chic fashion salons, delicatessens, *chocolateries*, antiques and crafts shops, and a cheese shop and coffee shop that are second to none. At the heart of the area are Kouter and the Voglemarkt, famous flower markets at their colorful best on Sundays, a vivid indication of Ghent's fame as the "City of Flowers."

Night Lights

Eating out in Ghent is an essential experience. Try such local specialties as *Gentse hazenpeper* (jugged hare) or *Gentse waterzooi van riviervis* (freshwater fish stew). There are intimate restaurants in the Patershol area north of Kraanlei. Enjoy Ghent by night, when the main buildings are lit up and the shopping streets hum with life. Spend an evening at Koninklijke Nederlandse Schowburg (Royal Dutch Theater) on St. Baafsplein; at De Vlaamse Opera on Schouwburgstraat; or at the classical music venue De Bijloke on Jozef Kluyskensstraat.

ESSENTIAL INFORMATION

TOURIST INFORMATION
Toerisme Stad Gent
• Infokantoor (Inquiry Desk), Belfort (Belfry), Botermarkt 17A
☎ 09 266 5232; fax 09 225 6288; www.gent.be

URBAN TRANSPORTATION
Ghent railroad station (Sint Pietersstation) is 1 mile south of the city center. For information on train services phone ☎ 09 222 4444. Ghent's main bus and tram stations adjoin the railroad station. Most buses and trams also run from the Korenmarkt, outside the former post office. For information, call ☎ 09 210 9491. There are taxi stands at the Korenmarkt and outside St Pietersstation. To call a taxi, phone ☎ 09 222 2222, 09 223 2323 or 09 225 2525.

AIRPORT INFORMATION
Ghent does not have an airport. The nearest airport is Brussels International Airport at Zaventem (see page 58). For flight information, call ☎ 0900 70000. Train connections to Ghent can be made at Brussels' Nord/Noord (North), Centrale/Centraal (Central) and Midi/Zuid (South) stations. The trip from Brussels airport to Ghent takes about 30 minutes.

CLIMATE – average highs and lows for the month

JAN.	FEB.	MAR.	APR.	MAY	JUN.	JUL.	AUG.	SEP.	OCT.	NOV.	DEC.
5°C	6°C	9°C	11°C	17°C	21°C	22°C	22°C	20°C	15°C	9°C	5°C
41°F	43°F	48°F	52°F	63°F	70°F	72°F	72°F	68°F	59°F	48°F	41°F
0°C	1°C	2°C	5°C	8°C	11°C	12°C	12°C	11°C	7°C	4°C	2°C
32°F	34°F	36°F	41°F	46°F	52°F	54°F	54°F	52°F	45°F	39°F	36°F

CITY SIGHTS

Key to symbols

map coordinates refer to the Ghent map on page 70; sights below are highlighted in yellow on the map. address or location telephone number opening times nearest bus, trolley bus, or tram route restaurant or café on site or nearby admission charge: $$$ more than 150BF, $$ 80BF–150BF, $ less than 80BF other relevant information

GRASLEI EN KORENLEI

A3 Graslei en Korenlei 16, 18, 38; trolley bus 3

Graslei and Korenlei are the two wharves flanking the medieval harbor Tussen Bruggen (meaning "between the bridges") that lies to the north of the bridge of St. Michielsbrug. Their names relate to their role in the early grain trade; their flanking buildings were the trade and guild houses of the medieval period, carefully restored for the World Exhibition of 1913. The facades of these magnificent buildings offer an impression of Ghent in the days when the wharves were alive with the raucous, colorful world of medieval trade.

HET GRAVENSTEEN

A4 Sint Veerleplein 09 225 9306 Daily 9–6, Apr.–Sep.; 9–5 rest of year Tram 1, 10, 11, 13 $$$ (includes museum)

Magnificent Gravensteen (Castle of the Counts) has all the authentic menace of 12th-century feudalism. A visit to this well-restored building is irresistible, and merely passing through the shadowy, arched entrance feels like a commitment. The main castle is a series of intriguing rooms linked by winding staircases. In the upper rooms there are historical exhibitions, one of which, the Museum voor Gerechtsvoorwerpen (Museum of Court Paraphernalia), displays tools of torture and execution.

KRAANLEI

A4 Kraanlei De Hel, see page 544 Tram 1, 10, 11, 13

Kraanlei is one of Ghent's finest surviving

Medieval guild houses line the Leie

canal-side streets. Its name derives from a wooden crane that was used to unload cargo. Today the baroque facades of Kraanlei's buildings, with touches of Gothic, are splendid survivors of an exuberant age of prosperity and Flemish culture. The houses have stepped gables and pediments. Look for Ghent's version of Brussels' *Manneken Pis* (see page 57), perched above the door of a restaurant a few buildings from the beginning of the street. Halfway along is the Museum voor Volkskunde (Museum of Folklore, see page 74). Three of the finest facades are at the far end of Kraanlei and include the exquisite 17th-century house known as "The Flying Deer." A few steps north of Kraanlei takes you into the Patershol area, a warren of narrow cobbled streets lined with tall buildings. Once the factory workers' district, Patershol is being rejuvenated, with restaurants, art galleries and refurbished apartments.

MUSEUM VOOR SCHONE KUNSTEN

Off the map Nicolaas de Liemaeckereplein 3, Citadelpark 09 221 1703 Tue.–Sun. 9:30–5 5, 50, 70, 71, 90, 91 $$

The Museum voor Schone Kunsten (Museum of Fine Arts) is located in Ghent's attractive Citadelpark. The collection is exceptional and includes works by Flemish and other European masters, including Rogier van der Weyden, Frans Hals and Gustave Courbet. Of special note are works by Hieronymus Bosch, including the

Magnificent St. Bavo's Cathedral and Belfry

compelling *The Bearing of the Cross.* Other superb works include Pieter Breughel the Younger's *Wedding Feast.* Jef Lambeaux's monumental relief panel, *Human Passions*, will keep you occupied and amazed.

MUSEUM VOOR SIERKUNST EN VORMGEVING

A3 Jan Breydelstraat 5 09 267 9999 Tue.–Sun. 10–6 Tram 1, 3, 11, 12 $$

The Museum voor Sierkunst en Vormgeving (Museum of Decorative Arts and Design) is a Ghent experience not to be missed. Housed in the handsome old Hôtel de Coninck, and with a stunning contemporary extension, the museum exhibits Belgian decorative and applied art, crafts and design from the Renaissance to 20th-century art nouveau, art deco and contemporary work. The older part of the museum displays superb period interiors and has lucid explanations of baroque, rococo and classical styles. Look for the amazing "banana skin" armchair.

MUSEUM VOOR VOLKSKUNDE

A4–B4 Kraanlei 65 09 269 2350 Tue.–Sun. 10–12:30 and 1:30–5 De Hel, see page 544 Tram 1, 11, 12 $$ Puppet shows Wed. and Sat. (except Aug.) at 2:30

The intriguing Museum voor Volkskunde (Museum of Folklore) owes much of its charm to its location among the old buildings of the 14th-century Kinderen Alijns Hospitaal (Hospial of the Alijns Children), on the canal-side street of Kraanlei. Children will be thrilled with the museum's marionette theater and other delights. The collections are spread throughout a number of quaint little houses surrounding a central square. The domestic and commercial life of Ghent through the ages is exhaustively represented in excellent set-piece tableaux and displays. The museum's puppet theater company *'t Spelleke van de Folklore* is based here, and performances are staged regularly.

SINT BAAFSKATHEDRAAL

B3 Sint Baafsplein (entrance: Gandastraat) 09 225 1626 Cathedral: daily 8:30–6, Apr.–Oct.; 8:30–5, rest of year. Closed Sun. morning. Ghent Altar and Crypt: Mon.–Sat. 9:30–5, Sun. 1–5, Apr.–Oct.; Mon.–Sat. 10:30–4, Sun. 2–5, rest of year St.-Jorishof – Cour St.-Georges, see page 544 16, 17, 18, 19, 38; tram 12, 41 Cathedral free; altar and crypt $$ (includes audio guide)

The tall four-stage tower of Sint Baafskathedraal (St. Bavo's Cathedral) dominates the east end of Botermarkt. Externally, the cathedral is a stern mix of Gothic styles beneath a patina of city grime. Inside is one of the great art treasures of the world, the multi-paneled *Het Lam Gods* (*The Mystic Lamb*) known as the Ghent Altar (see opposite page). Other treasures include the rococo pulpit in Carrara marble and Danish oak, its staircases like twisted tree roots and the canopy a mass of writhing branches. The 12th-century Romanesque crypt of St. Baafs is full of religious artifacts and works of art.

STEDELIJK MUSEUM VOOR ACTUELE KUNST

Off the map Citadelpark 09 221 1703 Tue.–Sun. 10–6 Café in museum 5, 50, 70–74, 76–78, 90 $$$

Opposite the Museum of Fine Arts (see page 73) is the Stedelijk Museum voor Actuele Kunst (Municipal Museum of Contemporary Art). Belgium's finest contemporary (post-1945) art collection, it includes works by Andy Warhol.

De Aanbidding van het Lam Gods – The Adoration of the Mystic Lamb

The famous Ghent Altar, *Het Lam Gods* (*The Mystic Lamb*), lives up to your highest expectations. Whatever else you do in Ghent, a visit to Sint Baafskathedraal and a view of the altar should not be missed. This luminous, enthralling work has the kind of impact that can change lives and attitudes.

The Ghent Altar is a polyptych, a painting made up of many panels. It is allegedly the work of two 15th-century Flemish painters, the brothers Hubert and Jan van Eyck. There are doubts over whether or not Hubert van Eyck even existed, however. In any case, Jan van Eyck was unquestionably the most famous painter of his generation. He was a technical master who is credited with developing oil painting to such an extent that the paint he used has retained its vivid colors to this day, with a little help from restoration and refurbishment through the ages.

The Ghent Altar is composed of two rows of paintings, one above the other. The centerpiece in the upper row is of Christ the King, who is flanked by the Virgin Mary, St. John the Baptist, singing angels, a musician, and nude portraits of Adam and a pregnant Eve within the wing panels. The focus of the lower row is the Adoration of the Lamb of God. The flanking panels depict processions of the faithful, judges, knights, hermits and pilgrims. The painted wing panels fold over to enclose the central panels. All of this is presented in breath-taking color and luminosity against superbly detailed Flanders landscapes.

The altar has survived the dangerous meddling of history. Iconoclasts sought to destroy it. In the 1780s, Emperor Joseph II prudishly replaced the sensual nude figures of Adam and Eve with clothed versions. During World War II, German soldiers stole the work and hid it in a mine, from which it was liberated by American troops. Two panels were stolen in 1934; the thief demanded a ransom, but was refused. The panel depicting John the Baptist was later found wrapped in a blanket in Brussels Central railroad station. The panel of the Righteous Judges has never been traced and was replaced by a copy, painted by a Belgian artist, who incorporated his own likeness into one of the figures, a forgivable indulgence for any painter dreaming of immortality.

BRITAIN

"A LITTLE foggy island in the north-west corner of Europe..."

From *The Australians*, 1893, by Australian poet and essayist Francis Adams

Opposite: Colorful Tudor pond garden at London's Hampton Court Palace

Britain

BRITAIN
0 50 100 km
0 25 50 miles
N
Isle of Lewis
Outer Hebrides
N Uist
Isle of Skye
S Uist
Rum
Mull
Islay
Arran
Thurso
Orkney Islands
A882
Wick
A9
Ullapool
North West Highlands
Inverness
A96
A96
A90
A87
A82
A9
Spey
SCOTLAND
A93
Dee
Aberdeen
Deeside
Grampian Mountains
Fort William
A9
Pitlochry
A90
Glen Coe
A82
Oban
A83
Perth
A90
Dundee
St Andrews
NORTH SEA
The Trossachs
A9
A82
M90
M9
Stirling
Glasgow
M9
M8
M8
EDINBURGH
Berwick-upon-Tweed
M74
A702
Selkirk
Tweed
A1
A83
Ayr
A74(M)
Southern Uplands
A74
A7
Cheviot Hills
A77
Moffat
Dumfries
A74(M)
Newcastle-Upon-Tyne
A75
Stranraer
Carlisle
A69
Durham
Sunderland
A596
Penrith
Workington
A66
Lake District
M6
A66
A1(M)
Middlesbrough
Scotch
NORTHERN IRELAND
Isle of
Lerwick
Shetland Islands
Kirkwall
Thurso
Orkney Islands
6
5
4

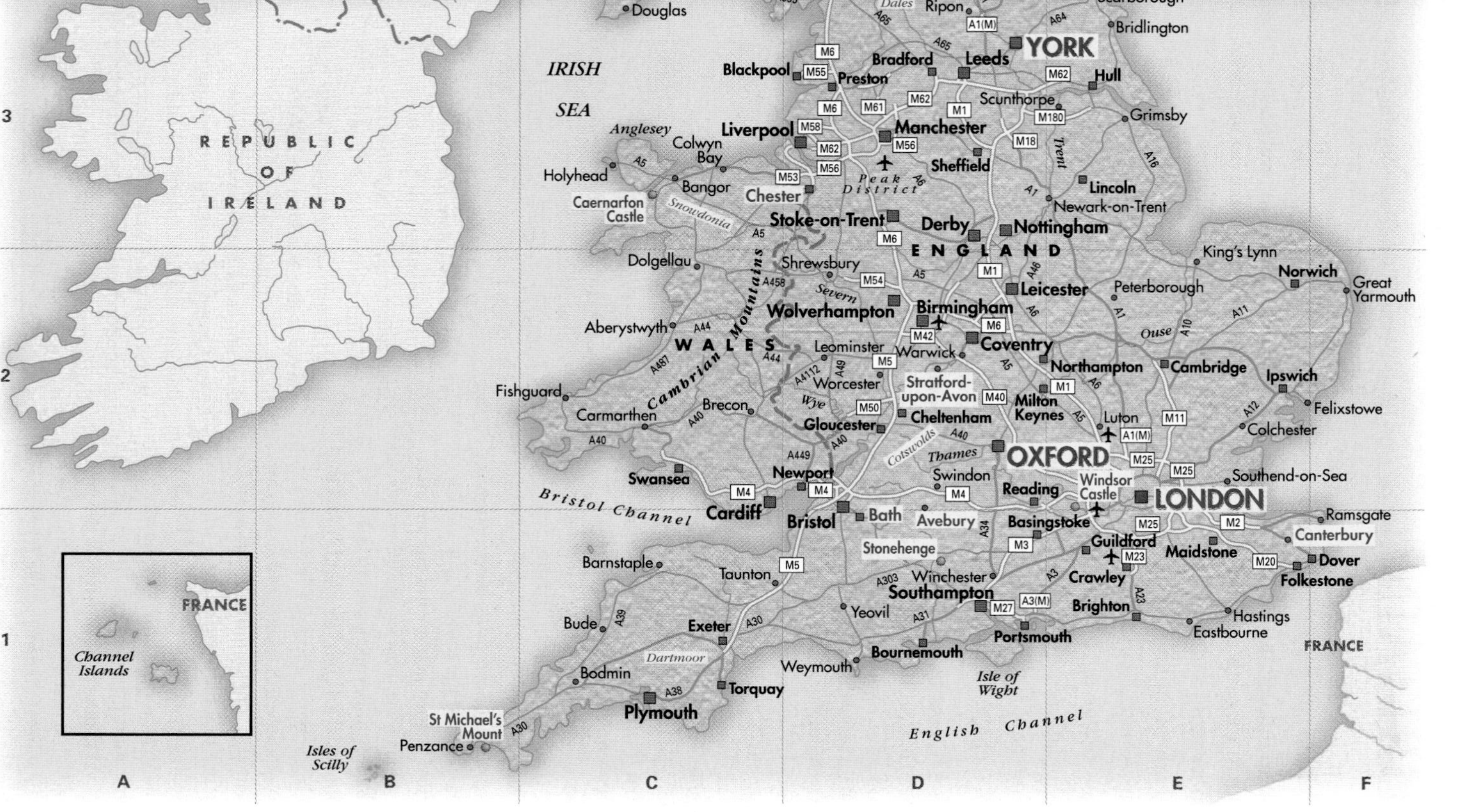
REPUBLIC
OF
IRELAND
IRISH
SEA
Douglas
Anglesey
Holyhead
Colwyn Bay
Bangor
Caernarfon Castle
Snowdonia
Dolgellau
Aberystwyth
WALES
Cambrian Mountains
Fishguard
Carmarthen
Brecon
Swansea
Cardiff
Newport
Bristol Channel
Blackpool
Preston
Liverpool
Chester
Stoke-on-Trent
Shrewsbury
Severn
Wolverhampton
Leominster
Worcester
Wye
Gloucester
Bradford
Leeds
YORK
Ripon
Dales
Bridlington
Hull
Scunthorpe
Grimsby
Manchester
Peak District
Sheffield
Trent
Lincoln
Newark-on-Trent
Derby
Nottingham
ENGLAND
Leicester
Birmingham
Coventry
Warwick
Stratford-upon-Avon
Cheltenham
Cotswolds
Thames
Swindon
Northampton
Milton Keynes
Luton
Peterborough
Ouse
King's Lynn
Norwich
Great Yarmouth
Cambridge
Ipswich
Felixstowe
Colchester
Southend-on-Sea
OXFORD
Reading
Windsor Castle
LONDON
Ramsgate
Canterbury
Dover
Folkestone
Maidstone
Guildford
Crawley
Brighton
Hastings
Eastbourne
FRANCE
Basingstoke
Bath
Avebury
Bristol
Stonehenge
Winchester
Southampton
Portsmouth
Isle of Wight
English Channel
Bournemouth
Weymouth
Yeovil
Taunton
Barnstaple
Bude
Exeter
Dartmoor
Torquay
Bodmin
Plymouth
St Michael's Mount
Penzance
Isles of Scilly
FRANCE
Channel Islands
A B C D E F
1 2 3

Britain

BRITAIN

Within this remarkable nation, an island barely 700 miles from north to south and less than 350 miles at its widest point, live nearly 60 million people. From this small island, a large percentage of the world's population inherited many of the linguistic and cultural influences that shaped their lives.

A Diverse Unity

England, Scotland and Wales – collectively known as Britain – each retain individual cultural characteristics. To complicate matters further for the visitor, there are distinct regions within regions, all reflecting the resilient and determined individuality that is typically British. If you spend any time traveling through Britain, you will find that the landscape and the customs of the people change dramatically, sometimes within only a few miles.

People have been arriving at all points around Britain's corrugated coastline for centuries, but London is the focus of the country as a whole. Here history, politics and culture meet in one of the most invigorating cities in the world. Beyond London lies provincial and rural England. You'll find a landscape of meadows, hedgerows and woods, its earth relentlessly farmed for centuries. The countryside has retained, in between the maze of roads and highways, a semblance of Old England, and in treasured corners the beauty of the past is preserved.

At Canterbury, in Kent, is the great cathedral that drew tens of thousands of medieval pilgrims to the relics of the revered Thomas à Becket, the great English churchman. These pilgrims inspired the country's first great poet, Geoffrey Chaucer, to write his *Canterbury Tales*, as vivid a picture of the medieval world as you will find.

Yet before Chaucer and before Canterbury, the earliest Britons had raised their own pagan equivalents to the Christian cathedrals. At Stonehenge, and perhaps more hauntingly at Avebury in Wiltshire, at the heart of southern England, are the standing stones and burial chambers of Britons who commanded England centuries before Romans, Danes, Anglo Saxons and Normans ever did.

Britain Explained

The name "Britain" (or "Great Britain") refers to the countries of England, Scotland and Wales located on the main island of Britain. To include Northern Ireland, the correct name is the "United Kingdom." The United Kingdom is the official unified entity, governed by the central parliament in London and (nominally) by Queen Elizabeth II.

However, political boundaries are becoming increasingly blurred by the European Union. Member countries are subject to E.U. rules and regulations, and regions are now being encouraged in their efforts at self-determination, with the result that Scotland and Wales – historically uneasy with what they saw as an English parliament (and Queen) in London – now have their own national assemblies and a degree of autonomy. But the legacy of London remains, and when the British talk about "this country" they usually mean Britain.

Sunrise over ancient Britain – Stonehenge is a reminder of the achievements of early inhabitants

Village Greens and Seaside

Throughout scores of picturesque villages in southern and western England, you will find the essence of the country where people still play cricket on village greens, dance around maypoles on May Day and sell jars of local honey at village festivals – weather permitting, of course.

Yet England also boasts great cities and historic towns that bustle with life. The great seaport of Bristol is one. The Georgian city of Bath, where golden Cotswold stone and the classical elegance of 18th-century fashion conspired to create one of the world's most astounding cityscapes, seems consumed with golden light in the summer sun.

Miles of coastline fringe the English Channel. On the southern coast are the cliffs of Beachy Head, famous resorts like Brighton and Bournemouth, as well as long stretches of green and peaceful coast that run westward past Dorset's limestone cliffs and the red cliffs of Devon to the golden beaches of Cornwall.

From Oxford to the Lakes

North and west of London, in the counties of Oxfordshire and Warwickshire, are such cities as Oxford, university town par excellence, matched only by its rival Cambridge in the fen country of eastern England. Here, too, you will find the Cotswold Hills and the historic town of Stratford-upon-Avon.

Progress through the cultural heart of England is not an idyllic rural journey by any means. Yet the cities of

MORE TOP DESTINATIONS IN BRITAIN

• Avebury D2 • Bath D1 • Caernarfon Castle C3 • Canterbury E1 • Chester D3 • Cotswolds D2 • Dartmoor C1 • Deeside D5 • Glen Coe C5 • Isle of Skye B6 • Lake District D4 • Snowdonia C3 • St. Andrews D5 • St. Michael's Mount B1 • Stratford-upon-Avon D2 • Stonehenge D1 • The Trossachs C5 • Windsor Castle E2 • Yorkshire Dales D3

Scottish piper in full regalia

Manchester, Leeds, Birmingham and Liverpool are vibrant and exciting places, while historic cities such as Chester, on the Welsh Borders, and York in the east have managed to preserve their medieval townscapes. Beyond this great sprawl an unspoiled England survives. Derbyshire's Peak District, the Yorkshire Dales, the exquisite Lake District of Cumbria and the lonely heights of Northumbria seem to appear like magic in the landscape.

Wild Wales

Wales is renowned as a land of poetry and song and as a part of Britain that seems older than time. In these green borderlands, the ruined castles of Norman Britain survive, relics of a time when England failed to entirely subdue the "wild Welsh." Strongholds of the Anglo Norman conquerors, such as Caernarfon Castle, are reminders of a later age of determined feudalism. But in the beautiful countryside of central Wales, on the rugged west coast and in the great mountains of Snowdonia, the spirit of the ancient Welsh lives on, the powerful identity of modern Wales a token of that endurance.

North to the Highlands

North of Cumbria and Northumberland, the Southern Uplands guard Scotland's borderland, once infamous for its violent robber clans. It was this raw border country that gave courage to heroic Scottish patriots like Robert Bruce and William Wallace as they pitted themselves against England's might. And across these hills in 1745 marched Charles Edward Stuart – Bonnie Prince Charlie, the last of a moribund royal line – supported by the cream of the Highland clans in a doomed final gesture of defiance by Scotland against English domination.

North of the Southern Uplands are the Central Lowlands of Scotland, with the capital city of Edinburgh to the east and Glasgow, the great powerhouse of old industrial Scotland, to the west. Edinburgh is the historic distillation of all things Scottish, the political and cultural focus of the nation from a time when poet Robert Burns and novelist Walter Scott graced fashionable 18th-century salons, to the vigorous and progressive Edinburgh Festival of today.

Across the Forth river (Firth of Forth) from Edinburgh lies the region of Fife, often referred to as the "Kingdom of Fife," home to the university town and golfing mecca of St. Andrews. To the north and west are the Scottish Highlands, Britain's most dramatic landscape, and some of the last great wilderness areas of Europe.

At the edge of the Highlands are the Trossachs, Scotland's equivalent to England's Lake District, steeped in the history of real-life characters like Rob Roy Macgregor, inspiration for the classic novels of Sir Walter Scott. Farther north are the mountains of Aberdeenshire. Here, on Royal Deeside, sits Balmoral Castle, traditional retreat of the Queen and her family. Scotland's most spectacular mountain country lies to the far west and north, at the Pass of Glen Coe, and then for more than 100 miles northward along the west coast to Kintail and Wester Ross. Out to sea is the Isle of Skye and the misty Hebrides, romantic islands at Britain's far western edge.

Seeing the Country

Britain's essence lies in its diversity and in the hidden corners between the most popular places. Traveling independently by train or bus is one way to explore off the beaten track, but you will need to plan carefully. Britain's long-distance bus network is generally good, but away from major cities and main roads service can vary greatly. Organized bus tours, on the other hand, will whisk you efficiently to all the major tourist sights. Traveling by car is another option; Britain is so diverse that you can drive for a few hours on a main highway and then veer off onto quieter byways.

London is a year-round destination, but outside the main summer season and major vacation periods, Britain's hidden corners are extremely quiet. May and June are good months to visit – the freshness of early June is invigorating in England's upland areas, northern Wales and the Scottish Highlands. Winter is another story, of course, but even in December and January Britain's larger cities are vibrant; London, Manchester, Liverpool, Edinburgh and Glasgow all pulse with British fashion and style.

Great classical music can be savored year-round in London, Manchester and Edinburgh. Attend world-class theater in Cardiff and Glasgow. Outstanding choirs fill England's cathedrals with truly heavenly music, and the open-air performances by Welsh and Cornish choirs are enchanting. Join the singing customers or listen to folk music at a neighborhood pub, or discover a colorful local festival or time-honored custom in a Devonshire hamlet or Yorkshire town.

The Taste of Britain

The same variety applies to shopping. The British were dismissed by Napoleon as a "nation of shopkeepers," but the intended slight is actually a compliment. The British engaged in trade the world over, and today that spirit of enterprise, curiosity, good business sense and eclectic style is maintained. Fashion salons rival those in France and Italy. Britain has some of the finest antique shops, art galleries and auction houses in Europe. Traditional and modern styles are blended to produce some colorful and out-of-the-ordinary clothing and craft items, and it is often in the provinces that the best examples are found.

Not so long ago, British food was seen as typically uninspired and overcooked. But British nouvelle cuisine is exciting yet still essentially British, the ingredients fresh and flavorful. British beer has rediscovered great traditions, too; every English county has a lively range of local ales to back up the standard brews. In Scotland, sample the best from the country's range of whiskeys and superb single malts.

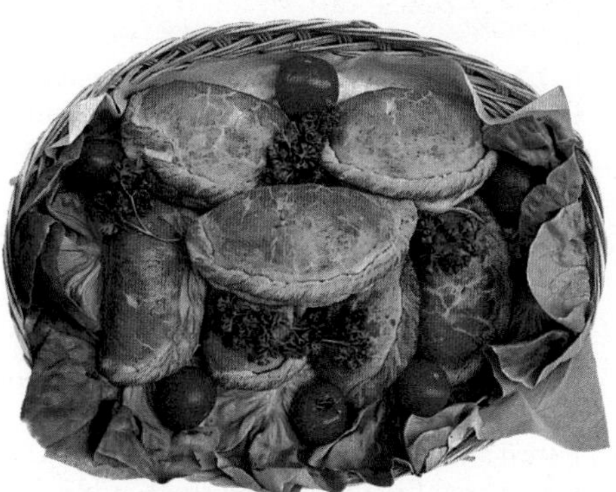

Cornish pasties – with tasty, savory fillings

TIMELINE

8000 BC	Mesolithic hunter-gatherers journey into southern Britain.
4000 BC	Neolithic "Stone Age" people settle in southern Britain.
circa 500 BC	Iron age culture develops in Britain.
55–54 BC	Julius Caesar makes expeditions to Britain.
AD 43	Roman conquest of Britain begins; first settlement of London by Romans.
circa 400	Roman army and administration withdraws from Britain.
1066	Battle of Hastings; Norman Conquest of Britain.
1314	Battle of Bannockburn, in which England suffers disastrous defeat at the hands of Scotland's Robert Bruce.
1534	Henry VIII appoints himself head of the Church in England; beginning of English Reformation.
1649	King Charles I executed; British Commonwealth established.
1707	Scotland and England unite by Act of Union.
1776	American colonies declare independence from Britain.
1815	Battle of Waterloo; Napoleon defeated by combined European force led by Duke of Wellington.
1914–18	Britain plays major part in World War I.
1939–44	World War II begins; Winston Churchill becomes Prime Minister of Britain; D-Day, Allied forces invade Normandy.
1945	War ends; Churchill loses in national elections.
1973	Britain joins European Community.
1999	Britain is part of NATO alliance in bombing campaign over Serbian ethnic cleansing in Kosovo.

PROTECTED BY SEA

Britain's island location has protected it from invasion over the centuries. The country has experienced two definitive "invasions," by the Romans in the first century and by the Normans in 1066. Others tried their best. The Danes, or Vikings, steadily occupied eastern England during the ninth century but were later repulsed. The Anglo Saxons did not invade in the sense of armed occupation, but rather by a slow and steady immigration and integration after Roman withdrawal left chaos and uncertainty within the country. In later centuries Britain developed a powerful military and naval force, and although almost constantly at war with various European powers during the medieval period was itself never invaded. In more recent times both Napoleon and Hitler tried and failed to conquer. The English Channel and the surrounding seas have been Britain's greatest strategic blessing.

Royal pageantry at the annual Trooping the Colour, a celebration of the Queen's "official" birthday, held in June at the Horse Guards Parade in central London

SURVIVAL GUIDE

- If visiting London, try to see one of the city's pageants, such as Trooping the Colour on Queen Elizabeth's birthday, or the Lord Mayor's Show in November. For something altogether informal, join the fun at the fantastic Notting Hill Carnival at the end of August.
- In York, be careful where pedestrian zones end and traffic begins. Also watch out for pickpockets on crowded streets.
- Try Britain's various regional foods. The national dish – fish and chips – can be found almost anywhere. In London, seek out genuine East End whelks. In Cornwall, look for Cornish pasties (savory pastry), a true hand-held meal. In Wales, sample Caerphilly cheese; in Yorkshire, try beef and Yorkshire pudding; and don't miss steak-and-kidney pie in any English country pub. In Scotland, tackle haggis, tatties (potatoes) and neeps (turnips), or kippers (smoked herring) – all accompanied by a thick and creamy regional beer or a good strong cup of tea.
- Be prepared for dramatic changes in the weather. They say that Britain has no climate, it just has weather. The truth is that the country is caught between the extremes of northern and southern Europe, while its island nature allows vast amounts of condensed Atlantic sea water to be deposited as wind-blown rain at regular intervals. Expect rain, and if it comes, enjoy it; or, like the British do, blame the government.
- Make sure you always know what county of England you are in, and try not to confuse counties, especially not Yorkshire and Lancashire. Never refer to Welsh or Scottish people as English.
- In southwest England especially, enjoy a cream tea. This grand traditional indulgence is fresh, fluffy scones (biscuits) spread with jam and clotted cream – a delicious thick cream. The cream – lots of it – is slathered on top of the jam.
- The strength of the summer sun can deceive in Britain, often because a wind may be blowing or there are passing clouds. Guard against sunburn even if there is a cool breeze.

LONDON

London is one of the world's great experiences, a city that is always exhilarating, sometimes bewildering, sometimes exhausting, but never disappointing. This financial, commercial and political center is also a year-round tourist city. The excitement is palpable. There is a feeling that something is always happening, that you are in the middle of one of a handful of truly great cities.

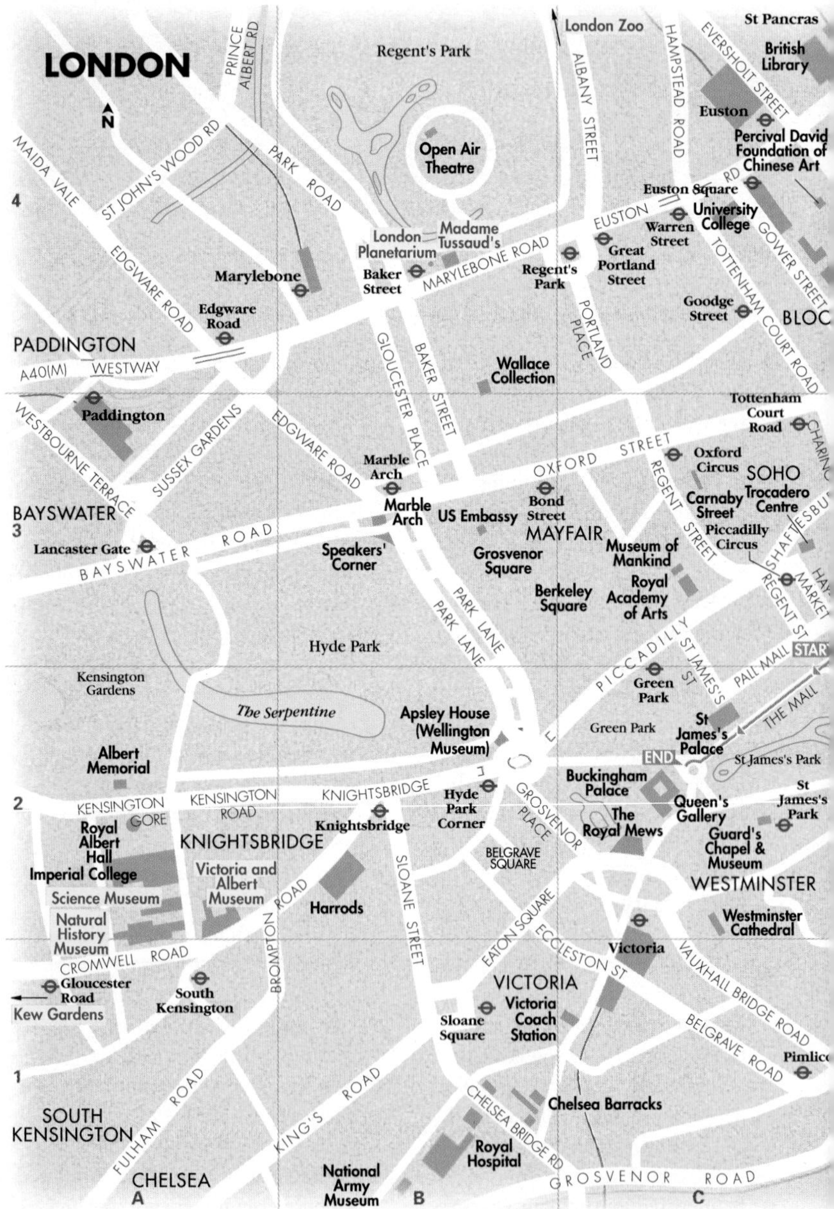

London needs to be taken very much on its terms; if you do so, you will enjoy it thoroughly. It is an expensive and sometimes stressful place; admission prices to major attractions are steep and the crowds of fellow visitors can be huge.

There are excellent guided tours, and bus tours are an easy way to sample all London (and beyond) has to offer. Exploring independently can be hugely rewarding, however, provided you plan well. Many of London's attractions are some distance apart, and if you set out

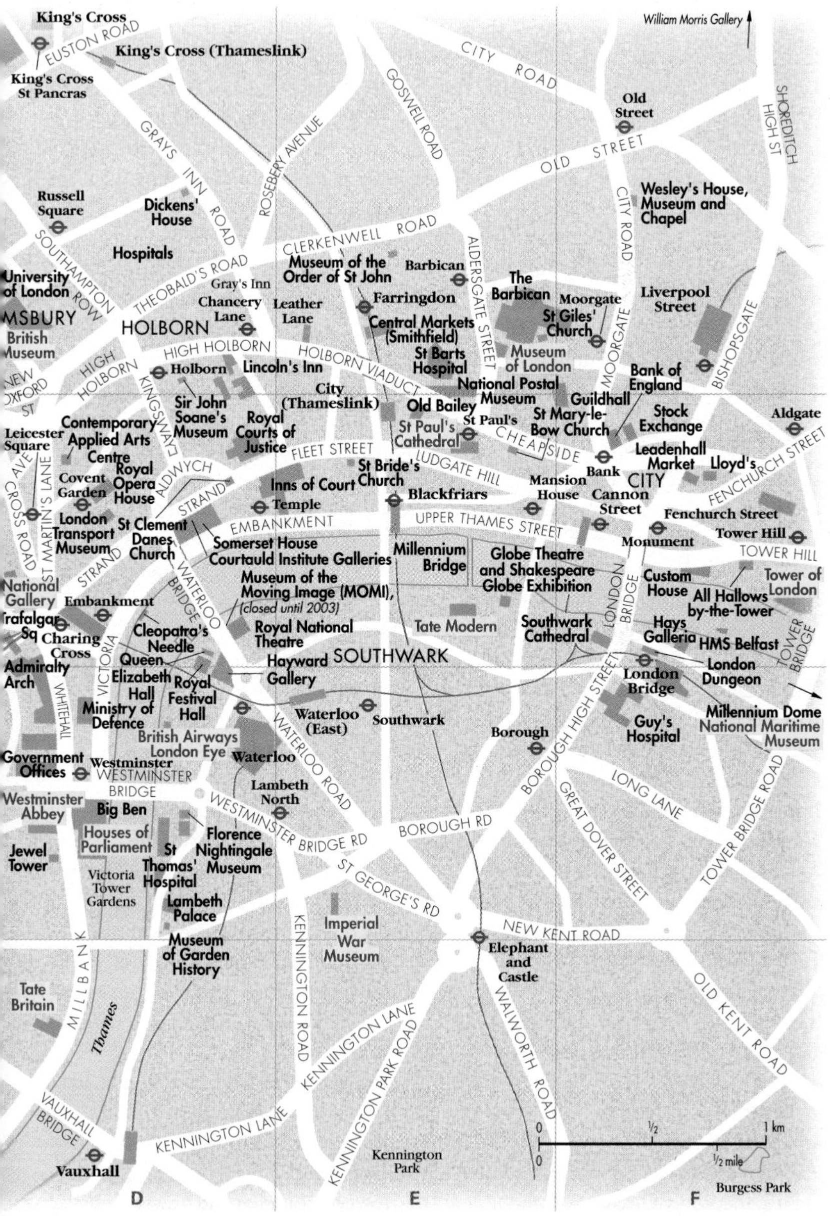

blindly determined to see everything you may end up frustrated and exhausted. Orient yourself by establishing two or three familiar focal points from which you can connect to other parts of the city.

Trafalgar Square to Big Ben

Trafalgar Square should be one of these focal points. It is the symbolic center of London; the towering pillar of Lord Nelson's column rises 172 feet into the London sky. At the base of the column are fountains and monumental guardian lions. All around the central square a constant throng of people is besieged by fluttering pigeons. Trafalgar Square is overlooked from the north by the National Gallery. At the southwest corner of the square is Admiralty Arch, through which you reach The Mall and progress toward Buckingham Palace.

Whitehall, London's "political" street, runs due south from Trafalgar Square. You'll see such landmarks as Big Ben, the clock tower of Westminster, as you walk past the Old Admiralty Building and the Horse Guards, where helmeted troopers in scarlet or blue sit immobile on their sleek, black, patient horses. Soon you pass the gates of Downing Street, where Britain's Prime Minister and Chancellor of the Exchequer have their homes. In the middle of the street is the Cenotaph, a stark and simple memorial to the dead of two world wars. Beyond the Cenotaph, Whitehall merges with Parliament Street and then meets Parliament Bridge Street. To the left is Westminster Bridge and the River Thames; to the right are the Houses of Parliament and Westminster Abbey.

Piccadilly Circus to Covent Garden

Another prime focus of central London is busy Piccadilly Circus, with the elegantly poised statue of Eros at its center. You can reach Piccadilly from Trafalgar Square by walking along Pall Mall from in front of the National Gallery and then turning right up Haymarket. From Piccadilly you can plunge into London's world of great shopping. To the north lies Soho, the long-established heart of late-night London, slightly risqué but full of character. Here are some of the capital's best theaters, cafés and restaurants, a multitude of offbeat and specialty stores, and a resident population that maintains the area's tradition of eccentricity, style and eclectic fashion.

Soho spills eastward through the rather small Chinatown area around Gerrard Street to reach another of London's focal points, Leicester Square, lined with movie theaters and restaurants. To the east, along Cranbourne and Garrick streets, is Covent Garden, one of London's liveliest and most entertaining venues, featuring stores, cafés, restaurants and a nonstop show of street entertainers.

Beyond the Center

Once familiar with central London, you can start to venture beyond the focal points. This is where the city's excellent subway network, the Tube (London Underground), comes in handy. London buses also supply excellent service, but if you can master the subway system you can reach just about everything worth seeing. Use of the subway does mean you lose some grip of how London lies above ground; sometimes it is more rewarding if you walk to your destination, provided it isn't too far.

Head east from Trafalgar Square, by subway or on foot, along the Strand, Fleet Street and Ludgate Hill, to St. Paul's Cathedral. Then proceed east to the Tower of London and Tower Bridge.

Or go west from Trafalgar Square, beyond Buckingham Palace, to the great green space of Hyde Park and fashionable Knightsbridge, where you will find Harrods department store. Here, too, are three great London museums: the Victoria and Albert, the Science Museum and the Natural History Museum.

Something for Everyone

To get the most out of London during a short stay, pick and choose carefully. Visit museums in which you have a particular interest. Tackle shopping the same way. Attend a performance at the National Theatre, at the South Bank Centre, or take in a West End show. Eat out in style if you can afford it, or enjoy the atmosphere at one of London's many traditional pubs.

You will find a fascinating mix of people; this is one of the most cosmopolitan cities in the world. There can be a sharp edge to Londoners, but you will never be short of advice or direction. And when in doubt, remember that London policemen are perhaps the most helpful and courteous citizens of all.

ESSENTIAL INFORMATION

TOURIST INFORMATION
London Tourist Board
- Victoria Station Forecourt
- Waterloo International Terminal (railroad station)
- Liverpool Street Underground Station
- Heathrow Airport, Terminals 1, 2 and 3
- Britain Visitor Centre, 1 Regent Street

Open to personal visits only. Recorded information: ☎ 09068 66 33 44 (toll call)
www.londontown.com

URBAN TRANSPORTATION
For schedule and fare information, contact National Rail Enquiries (☎ 08457 484950) 24 hours daily. The London Underground (subway) trains operate daily 5:30 a.m.–midnight and serve central London stations every 5–10 minutes. Lines are named and color-coded on an easy-to-follow map, posted in stations. Buy tickets from attended booths in station entrance halls or from machines. The symbol of the subway is a red circle crossed by a horizontal line – marked on the city map.
London's red buses cover central London and suburbs. Tickets are bought on board from the driver or an attendant. For information about the subway, buses, trams, riverboats, Docklands Light Railway and rail services in London, call London Travel Information ☎ 020 7222 1234 (24 hours daily).
London's cabs (formerly black, now in various colors) can be expensive if you are traveling alone. They are metered and are available for hire when the yellow light is on. Taxis can be flagged down in the street or ordered by calling ☎ 020 7272 5471 or 020 7272 0272.

AIRPORT INFORMATION
London is served by two major airports; Heathrow (☎ 08700 000123), 15 miles west of the city, and Gatwick (☎ 01293 535353), about 30 miles south. Services below operate during the day, daily 8–8; outside these times services will be less frequent.
From Heathrow, the Heathrow Express nonstop train goes to Paddington Station every 15 minutes; journey time is 15 minutes (20 minutes from Terminal 4). The subway's Piccadilly Line to central London departs every few minutes; journey time is around 50 minutes. Buses from the Heathrow bus terminal operate to various city destinations about every half hour, with journey time of about an hour; the schedule (which varies periodically) is available from the bus terminal. Taxis (expensive) are available 24 hours from passenger arrival areas; time to central London is about an hour.
From Gatwick, Gatwick Express and Connex trains go to London's Victoria Station every 15 to 30 minutes; journey time is 30 to 40 minutes. Thameslink trains go to King's Cross Station every 15 to 30 minutes; journey time is 50 minutes. Flightline buses travel to London's Victoria Coach Station hourly; journey time is 1 hour 15 minutes. Taxis operate from taxi stands at all of the London bus and railroad stations.

CLIMATE – average highs and lows for the month

JAN.	FEB.	MAR.	APR.	MAY	JUN.	JUL.	AUG.	SEP.	OCT.	NOV.	DEC.
6°C	6°C	10°C	13°C	16°C	20°C	21°C	21°C	18°C	14°C	10°C	7°C
43°F	43°F	50°F	55°F	61°F	68°F	70°F	70°F	64°F	57°F	50°F	45°F
2°C	2°C	3°C	5°C	8°C	11°C	13°C	13°C	11°C	7°C	5°C	3°C
36°F	36°F	37°F	41°F	46°F	52°F	55°F	55°F	52°F	45°F	41°F	37°F

The Houses of Parliament, a spectacular example of 19th-century Victorian Gothic Revival architecture

City Sights

Key to symbols

map coordinates refer to the London map on pages 86–87; sights below are highlighted in yellow on the map.

address or location telephone number opening times nearest subway nearest bus route riverboat restaurant or café on site or nearby admission charge: $$$ more than £6, $$ £2–£6, $ less than £2 other relevant information

British Airways London Eye

D2 County Hall 0870 5000 600 Daily 10–10, late May–early Sep.; 10-8, Apr. 1 to late May and early–late Sep.; 10–7, rest of year Embankment, Charing Cross, Waterloo, Westminster $$$

Built as part of the city's millennial celebrations, the London Eye is a superb feat of construction. Essentially a huge Ferris wheel, it slowly rotates, giving visitors a bird's-eye view across London from within 32 glassed capsules. At 450 feet high, it is the largest observation wheel in the world, dwarfing the Houses of Parliament across the Thames.

British Museum

D4 Great Russell Street 020 7323 8000 Museum: Daily 10–5:30 (also Thu.–Fri. 5:30–8:30). Great Court: Mon.–Sat. 9–9 (also Thu.–Sat. 9–11 p.m.), Sat. Sun. 9–6 Museum restaurant Holborn, Russell Square, Tottenham Court Road 7, 10, 14 Free ; possible charge for special exhibitions

The British Museum is a treasure house of global artifacts, many of them the riches of Britain's imperial past. There are more than 6 million exhibits, including the Elgin Marbles, magnificent fifth-century BC relief sculptures taken from the Parthenon in 1801 by Thomas Bruce, the Earl of Elgin, and still the subject of Greek demands for their return. Other highlights are the Rosetta Stone, key to the understanding of Egyptian hieroglyphics; the 2,000-year-old Lindow Man, whose preserved body was found in an English peat bog; the Mildenhall Treasure, a collection of Roman silver; and Anglo Saxon artifacts from a ship burial. A visit to the museum can be exhausting; be selective. Don't miss the Egyptian Galleries, the finest collection outside Egypt itself. The year 2000 saw the opening of the Great Court development, increasing the museum's public space by 50 percent. A massive glass roof now spans the central courtyard, making it the largest covered square in Europe. The area houses galleries, an education center, Compass (a multimedia information database) and, at its heart, the stunning Reading Room (once home to the British Library).

Houses of Parliament

D2 St. Margaret Street 020 7219 4272 (House of Commons), 020 7219 3107 (House of Lords) Mon.–Fri. (times vary; phone for details)

Westminster 3, 11, 12, 24, 53, 77A, 88, 109, 159, 184, 511 Free; tours $$

The Houses of Parliament, also known as the Palace of Westminster, are mainly to be admired from the outside. The present building replaced an older palace dating from the 11th century. Most of this earlier building burned down in 1834. The present structure's linear form is doubly enhanced by the vertical thrust of Victoria Tower and the clock tower known as Big Ben. Inside access is limited because of security reasons and because it is the workplace of British government. You can attend debates in the House of Lords and House of Commons on a first-come-first-served basis in a line for the "Strangers' Galleries" (public galleries) outside St. Stephen's Entrance. Tours of the Houses of Parliament are possible by applying to the Parliamentary Education Unit, Norman Shaw Building (North), London SW1A 2TT, U.K. (020 7219 4600) at least four weeks in advance, except between early August and late September when tickets ($$) can be purchased at the Houses of Parliament.

Imperial War Museum

E2 Lambeth Road 020 7416 5000 Daily 10–6 Museum restaurant Elephant and Castle or Lambeth North 3, 15, 59 $$

Two vast guns stand in front of the handsome Ionic portico of the Imperial War Museum, where the story of 20th-century conflict is documented. There is a cruel irony in the fact that the museum was formerly the infamous Bethlehem Royal Hospital, notorious asylum for the insane, and known as "Bedlam," a word well-suited to the horror of war. There are more than 50 historic aircraft, tanks, and other field weapons on display, but the most fascinating exhibits involve the human element through re-creations of World War I trench warfare and the London Blitz. The cruel lessons of conflict are not shirked, especially in the permanent exhibition on the Holocaust.

Kew Gardens

Off the map Kew Road, Richmond 020 8940 1171 Open daily at 9:30 a.m.; closing time varies seasonally Restaurant in gardens Kew Gardens $$

The Royal Botanical Gardens at Kew and their location away from central London are a delightful antidote for those suffering from city fatigue. The gardens date from 1759 and represent one of the finest collections of plants in the world, all contained within a 300-acre site. Wander at will through the world's hugely varied climatic environments. The vast Temperate House contains plants from every continent, and the architectural wonders are just as fascinating. Highlights include the Palm House, a billowing pavilion in glass and wrought iron that is a classic expression of creative 19th-century design. Scattered throughout the gardens are such interesting buildings as a 10-story pagoda and Kew Palace (due to reopen in 2003), the latter built in 1631 by a Dutch merchant and used as a country retreat by George III, and a superb example of classical brickwork.

London Zoo

Off the map Regent's Park 020 7722 3333 Daily 10–5:30, Mar.–Sep.; 10–4, rest of year Restaurant at zoo Camden Town or Regent's Park C2, 274 $$$

London Zoo is irresistible for children but a treat for all. In keeping with contemporary attitudes, the zoo has a strong conservation ethic and is working hard toward transforming the captive-animal emphasis of old-fashioned zoos. There are daily events and programs, including feeding time, "Animals in Action" and the Children's Zoo, where kids can handle docile animals. The spectacular Snowdon Aviary is a highlight, as is the Penguin Pool with its spiral ramp.

Madame Tussaud's and the London Planetarium

Madame Tussaud's B4 Marylebone Road 0870 400 3000 Mon.–Fri. 10–5:30, Sat.–Sun. 9:30–5:30. Opening time earlier during school holidays Café Baker Street 13, 18, 27, 30, 74, 82, 113, 139, 159, 274 $$$. Combination ticket with London Planetarium available Book ahead by credit card to avoid the sometimes hour-long line.

London Planetarium B4 Marylebone Road Mon.–Fri. 12:20–5, Sat.–Sun. 10–5; daily 10–5 during school holidays Baker Street Bus 13, 18, 27, 30, 74, 82, 113, 139, 159, 274 $$$

A visit to Madame Tussaud's celebrated wax model museum could be described as blatant people-watching. The experience is expensive, but where else can you peer up the nose of a world leader or make faces at the rich and famous? Just about everyone is here: royalty, presidents, politicians, celebrities, stars, heroes and villains. You can tell those with charisma and those without, even in wax.

Exhibits such as The Garden Party and The Grand Hall cast new light on the phrase "rubbing shoulders with the rich and famous." The Chamber of Horrors has hideous charm, although perhaps not for the very young; the murderous are still menacing, even in effigy, and you'll watch them uneasily out of the corner of your eye. Other attractions include a quick trip through London history as glimpsed from a miniature city taxicab. The adjacent planetarium provides a relaxing half-hour's mocked-up stargazing and several space exhibits.

Museum of London

E4 150 London Wall 020 7600 3699 Mon.–Sat. 10–5:50, Sun. noon–5:50 Restaurant at museum Barbican or St. Paul's 4, 8, 25, 56, 100, 172, 501, 521 $$ (entrance ticket valid for free return within one year) Free admission after 4:30; last admission at 5:30

To really get a handle on London and its utterly fascinating history, visit this rewarding and enjoyable museum. The story of the city from prehistoric times to the present is told through set piece galleries focusing on important periods. The Roman section is superb; its reconstructed rooms, one with a fabulous mosaic floor, and its sculptures are particularly special highlights. Another highlight is the Lord Mayor's State Coach from the 1750s, a glittering golden extravaganza that is still used during the Lord Mayor's Show each November. Numerous displays, special exhibitions, reconstructions and events add to this special London experience.

National Gallery

D3 Trafalgar Square 020 7747 2885 Daily 10–6 (also Wed. 6–9) Restaurant and café in gallery Charing Cross or Leicester Square 3, 6, 9, 11, 12, 13, 15, 23, 24, 29, 53, X53, 77A, 88, 91, 109, 139, 159, 176 Free (donation suggested for tours) The National Gallery stages temporary exhibitions of major artists, for which there is usually an admission charge

London's National Gallery contains one of the finest collections of Western art in the world. You may find most of the world here on a busy day, but "the National" seems able to absorb the crowds. The collection is displayed chronologically in four wings: the Sainsbury Wing (1260–1510), West Wing (1510–1600), North Wing (1600–1700) and East Wing (1700–1900). You will need a floor plan to navigate. Portable CD players are available (free); the Gallery Guide Soundtrack provides guidance and commentaries. There are also daily guided tours.

Among the highlights not to miss are: the Leonardo da Vinci cartoon *The Virgin and Child with St. Anne and John the Baptist;* da Vinci's accompanying *Virgin of the Rocks;* Sandro Botticelli's *Venus and Mars;* Titian's vivid and agile *Bacchus and Ariadne;* Jan van Eyck's *The Arnolfini Marriage;* Diego Velázquez's sensual *The Toilet of Venus;* Rembrandt's haunting *Self Portrait;* and Vincent van Gogh's *Sunflowers*.

Head for the North Wing's octagonal Room 15, where glorious works by the great landscape painters Claude Lorrain and J. M. W. Turner are displayed. And where else would you find a room such as Room 34, the Sackler Room, where you are surrounded by the works of English masters such as Thomas Gainsborough, Sir Joshua Reynolds and John Constable?

National Maritime Museum

Off the map Romney Road, Greenwich 020 8858 4422 or 020 8312 6565 (24-hour recorded information) Daily 10–5 (last entry at 4:30) Café in museum Docklands Light Railway:

Covent Garden Through Time

London is an ever-changing city and, over the years, has evolved from surprising origins. A classic example of London's fascinating development is Covent Garden, today a lively focus of entertainment, dining and shopping. The area gets its name from being the medieval-era "Garden of the Convent," when vegetables were grown for the kitchens at Westminster Abbey.

During the 17th century it was laid out as the finest square in London, complete with the Church of St. Paul and arcaded houses. The architect was Inigo Jones, who planned it in Italianate style, with the square known as the piazza. Then the owner of Covent Garden, the Earl of Bedford, decided to hold a market in the square. Commerce overcame culture; some of the buildings were erected – first the older fruit and vegetable market and then the floral market. The Opera House was added later.

In 1974 the market moved to new premises and the piazza market halls were renovated and filled with stores, cafés and restaurants that have transformed the old "Garden of the Convent" into a major leisure area.

Covent Garden Today

From Covent Garden subway station, turn right and walk southeast, past Evelyn and Crabtree (renowned for bath oils and soaps) on your right, into the heart of Covent Garden. This is an excellent place to browse and wander at your leisure. There are fashion boutiques for all tastes. These line the cobbled piazza, tastefully blending in with the Italianate architecture and elegant columns. Under the glass-and-iron roof of the renovated market building set in the middle of the square, you'll find stalls selling crafts, jewelry and clothing. There is a small branch of the much-loved London toy shop, Hamleys, on the northern side of the central market. In front of St. Paul's Church, on the western side of the market, street performers often entertain the crowds with comedy or magic tricks. It all adds to the exciting bustle of this area.

If you walk back toward the Covent Garden subway and head two blocks north, you will find yourself in the maze of small streets that intersect with Neal Street. Neal's Yard has a bohemian air, and there are some good places to buy vegetarian food or eat a light meal. Neal's Yard Dairy sells some of the best cheese in the country – it's all British or Irish made.

Back to traditional roots – selling flowers in the "Garden of the Convent"

Classical facade of St. Paul's Cathedral

Cutty Sark Riverboat to Greenwich Pier from Westminster, Waterloo, Embankment or Tower Piers $; senior citizens and under 17 free

A visit to the world's largest maritime museum offers insight into Britain's past maritime expertise. The Nelson Gallery celebrates the great admiral, with his bullet-pierced coat from the Battle of Trafalgar adding drama. In the glass-roofed Neptune Court is the gilded state barge created for Frederick, Prince of Wales in 1732. Themed galleries tell of early explorers, the age of ocean liners, naval costumes and the British Empire. Children can try their hands at things nautical in the All Hands and Bridge galleries, while all ages can test their knowledge in the Search Station zone.

Natural History Museum

A2 Cromwell Road (Life Galleries entrance), Exhibition Road (Earth Galleries entrance) 020 7942 5000 Mon.–Sat. 10–5:50, Sun. 11–5:50; last admission at 5:30 Cafés in museum South Kensington 14, 49, 70, 74, 345, C1 $$$; Mon.–Fri. free after 4:30, Sat.–Sun. free after 5

The Natural History Museum shouldn't be missed and is a great favorite with children. It's housed in a self-consciously Gothic revival building of great style, and you may feel you have stumbled into someone's rather grand house as you roam the rooms and halls of the Life Galleries. There are a reputed 68 million objects on display, from the tiniest of preserved insects to a reconstructed blue whale. The Dinosaur Gallery features an animatronic tableau of three vicious deinonychi (extinct, elephant-like animals) and a huge, lifelike Tyrannosaurus rex. This is not quite Disney, but the main exhibits tell the dinosaur story through a mix of science and entertaining effect. The Earth Galleries deal with the world beneath our feet and are every bit as fascinating.

St. Paul's Cathedral

E3 Ludgate Hill 020 7246 8348 Mon.–Sat. 8:30–4 (crypt and ambulatory 8:45–4, galleries 9:30–4) Restaurant at cathedral St. Paul's 11, 15, 23 Cathedral and crypt $$, if galleries included $$$

St. Paul's Cathedral is one of Sir Christopher Wren's greatest achievements, but its location, now crowded by indifferent buildings, robs it of some grandeur. However, the twin towers and baroque elements of its facade and the crowning glory of its dome are still breathtaking. The airy, bright interior is full of stately monuments, memorials and statues. You can descend to the crypt or ascend heavenward up 530 steps, first to the famous Whispering Gallery, where you can whisper your thoughts for everyone else to hear, and then to the Golden Gallery for superb views over London.

Science Museum

A2 Exhibition Road 0870 870 4868 Daily 10–6 Café in museum South Kensington 14, 74 $$$

Every aspect of science and technology is covered in this vast collection, and you will find everything from atoms to the *Apollo 10* command module. The museum's official guidebook will help you find your way around the seven floors. On display are George Stephenson's early locomotive, the *Rocket,* and Charles Babbage's enormous prototype computer. The huge Flight Galleries contain ranks of aircraft, and the East Hall's great steam

The Tower of London recalls some of the most dramatic times of British history over 900 years

engines from the Industrial Revolution hiss and revolve. Many of the exhibits have a hands-on element. Check for any special events or demonstrations on the day you visit. The Wellcome Wing, opened in June 2000, is a groundbreaking complex of up-to-the-minute exhibits that give visitors the chance to interact with and explore current scientific issues.

TATE BRITAIN

D1 Millbank (also entrance: Atterbury Street) 020 7887 8000 or 020 7887 8008 (24-hour recorded information) Daily 10–5:50 Restaurant and café in gallery Pimlico 2, 3, 36, 77A, 88, 159, 185, 507, C10; shuttle bus Riverboat from Tate Modern Free; special exhibitions $$$ Guided tours (free), events, talks and films

Tate Britain exhibits the world's greatest collection of British art from 1500 to the present in lively, thematic displays. Works by artists as diverse as Barbara Hepworth, William Hogarth and Damien Hirst are on display. The Turner Collection in the Clore Gallery comprises 300 paintings and watercolors by J.M.W. Turner.

TATE MODERN

D1 Bankside (entrances: river walkway or Holland Street) 020 7887 8000 or 020 7887 8008 (24-hour recorded information) Daily 10–6 (also Fri.–Sat. 6–10 p.m.) Cafés in gallery Southwark or Blackfriars 45, 63, 100, 344, 381; shuttle bus Riverboat from Tate Britain Free; special exhibitions $$$ Guided tours ($), events, talks and films

Housed in the former Bankside Power Station, on the south bank of the River Thames with a good view of St. Paul's Cathedral on the opposite bank, the Tate Modern opened in 2000. Britain's national museum of modern art features an international collection from 1900 to the present. Proclaimed as a gallery for the 21st century, it includes works by major figures such as Salvador Dalí, Pablo Picasso, Henri Matisse, Edvard Munch, Piet Mondrian, Jackson Pollock, Andy Warhol and Roy Lichtenstein. Works featuring differing styles are shown alongside each other in a series of themed rooms. Adventurous and often controversial conceptual works and installations also are a feature.

You can approach the Tate Modern in style from north of the river. A spectacular millennium project, a pedestrian-only bridge complete with sculptures, slices straight across the Thames between Peter's Hill, below St. Paul's, and Bankside. The two Tate galleries also are linked by shuttle bus and boat services.

The simple memorial to World War I victims lies beneath the soaring arches of Westminster Abbey

Tower of London

F3 Tower Hill 020 7709 0765
Mon.–Sat. 9–5, Sun. 10–5, Mar.–Oct.; Tue.–Sat. 9–4, Sun.–Mon. 10–4, rest of year Restaurant and café at Tower Tower Hill 15, 25, 42, 78, 100, D1 $$$

There are crowds of visitors at the Tower most of the year, and you may find yourself being marched through some of the sections, especially the Crown Jewels exhibition, where moving walkways do the walking for you. It is an astonishing place all the same, steeped in history. Many of the nation's most daring personalities ended up here, as prisoners or as reluctant "guests"; or, like Henry VIII's wives Anne Boleyn and Catherine Howard, on a final trip to the executioner's block. Tours conducted by the Yeoman Warders, or "Beefeaters," give an excellent introduction, after which you can wander at will to ponder the Bloody Tower, Traitors' Gate, the Tower Ravens and the execution site at Tower Green.

Victoria and Albert Museum

A2 Cromwell Road 020 7942 2000 or 0870 442 0808 (24-hour recorded information) Daily 10–5:45 (also Wed. and selected Fri. 5:45–10) Restaurant and cafés at museum South Kensington 14, 74, C1 $ (additional charge for exhibitions); free after 4:30 Free guided tours

The "V&A," as it is affectionately known, is recognized as being the world's greatest repository of applied and decorative art, containing a ravishing collection of jewelry, silverware, glass, ceramics, textiles, dress, furniture, sculpture, paintings, books, prints and photographs from all over the world. Decide what you want to see amid the 7 miles of corridors, galleries and stairs. The European Galleries alone are a day's work. The Sculpture Galleries; the Asian and Near Eastern Galleries; the Ceramics, Glass and Jewellery Galleries; and the superb art collection are all worth seeing. Take a guided tour for an informative overview; or arm yourself with a floor plan from the information desks, and launch forth.

Westminster Abbey

D2 Dean's Yard 020 7222 5152
Mon.–Fri. 9–4:45 (also Wed. 6–7:45 p.m.), Sat. 9–2:45; last admission 1 hour before closing. Nave and cloisters: daily 8–6. Abbey Museum: daily 10:30–4. Westminster or St. James' Park 3, 11, 12, 88, 159 $$

Westminster Abbey has been the ceremonial site of almost every British coronation, from William the Conqueror in 1066 to Queen Elizabeth II in 1953. Monarchs buried here include Henry VII, Elizabeth I and Mary, Queen of Scots. The abbey is full of monuments and memorials to famous people.

Despite the crowds of visitors, there is serenity within the venerable walls, and the architectural features are thrilling. The present abbey dates, in part, from the 13th century and is a powerful expression of English Gothic style, with distinctive French elements.

Henry VII's chapel, designed in Late Perpendicular style, has a style of airy elegance that represents Gothic at its finest. Tiered sculptures line the walls, and the lofty roof is hung with exquisite fan vaulting. The Tomb of the Unknown Warrior commemorates the hundreds of thousands of British servicemen killed in World War I. In the south transept is Poets' Corner, resting place of Chaucer, Robert Browning and Alfred Tennyson, among others. Also worth seeing are the abbey's Cloisters, the Chapter House and the Abbey Museum.

Looking from St. James's Park to the exuberant Victoria Monument and Buckingham Palace beyond

A Royal Stroll

Royal London begins at Admiralty Arch, at the southwest corner of Trafalgar Square. The arch dates from 1911 and was erected as part of a general celebration of Queen Victoria's life and reign. Beyond the arch is The Mall, a broad open avenue that runs southwest, directly toward Buckingham Palace. It was first laid out by Charles II in the 1660s as part of St. James's Park. It is open to traffic, but as soon as you pass beneath Admiralty Arch the city's character becomes less frantic.

Keep to the sidewalk on the left of the avenue and you'll soon pass a statue of the seafarer Captain James Cook. St. James's Park spreads out to the left – a great sweep of open lawns, trees and gardens with a lake at its heart. The right (north) side of The Mall is lined with stately buildings. First is Carlton House Terrace, broken halfway by the Duke of York's Steps that lead up to the Duke of York's Column. At St. James's Palace, sentries guard the Tudor Tower. Next to the palace is Clarence House, the London home of the Queen Mother.

On your way to the large open area in front of Buckingham Palace is Lancaster House (a building now used by the government). In front of the palace is the spectacular bronze and marble Victoria Monument, erected in 1911 and constructed with more than 2,300 tons of marble. A marble Queen Victoria stares frostily from the east side. The exuberant bronze winged Victory crowns the monument.

Beyond the monument and behind a barricade of railings and gates stands Buckingham Palace, a heavy-handed building rather than a fairy-tale one. The "royal standard" (the Queen's flag) flies when the Queen is in residence. The Changing of the Guard takes place daily at 11:30 a.m. from April to early July, and on alternate days the rest of the year (weather permitting). The crowds pressed against the railing can be large, and the experience may well rob you of a more relaxed stroll down The Mall.

Eighteen of Buckingham Palace's state rooms are open from the second week in August until the end of September, when the royal family are not in residence. The Royal Mews are worth a visit for their state carriages and splendid horses. For the walking route, see the city map on pages 86–87.

Horse Guards ride along The Mall

EDINBURGH

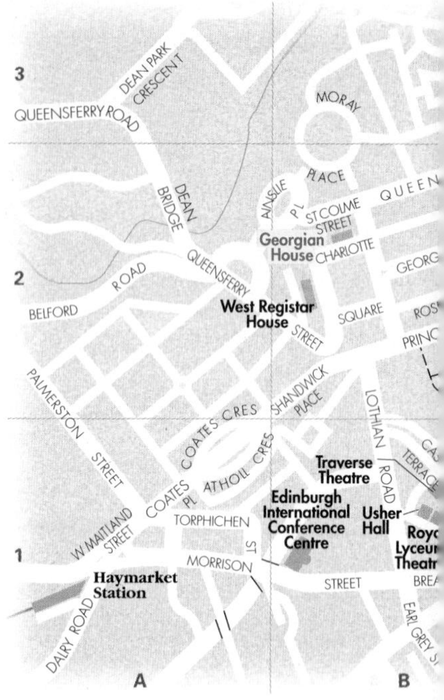

Edinburgh is Scotland in microcosm. In this vibrant capital city, buildings do not overpower the spectacular landscape of hills and crags that march across the southeastern horizon. Yet Edinburgh's buildings – from the old houses of the Royal Mile to the elegant Georgian terraces and crescents of the New Town – are outstanding complements to the city's natural setting. Few other capitals seem to reflect the history and culture of their country so potently.

Edinburgh's famous castle sits high on a craggy promontory, Castle Rock, made inaccessible on three sides by steep cliffs and with a long descending ridge on its fourth side. The city's layout is linear, a pattern set by Castle Rock and Castle Ridge, down which the Royal Mile descends to the Palace of Holyroodhouse. North of the Royal Mile lies a shallow valley once covered by swampy Nor' Loch, and now occupied by the lovely Princes Street Gardens, with Waverley Station, the city's main railroad station, at their eastern end. Above the gardens and to the north is Edinburgh's main thoroughfare, Princes Street, its south side uncluttered by buildings and thus serving as a splendid place from which to view the castle and Old Edinburgh.

First Impressions

Most visitors arrive by train at Waverley Station. From the station you emerge onto Waverley Bridge and get an

Greyfriars Bobby

This Skye terrier's devotion to his dead master is enshrined in Edinburgh folklore. The famous Greyfriars Bobby was a trained police dog who worked with his master, Constable John Gray, guarding livestock at Edinburgh's city market, the Grassmarket, during the 1850s. When Gray died at age 45 he was buried in Greyfriars churchyard, and his devoted terrier took up what became a 14-year vigil by his grave. Bobby was cared for and beloved by everyone in the neighborhood. Just inside the church gate is Bobby's Bothy, a gift kiosk. Nearby, a statue of Greyfriars Bobby stands at the junction of Candlemaker Row and the George IV Bridge.

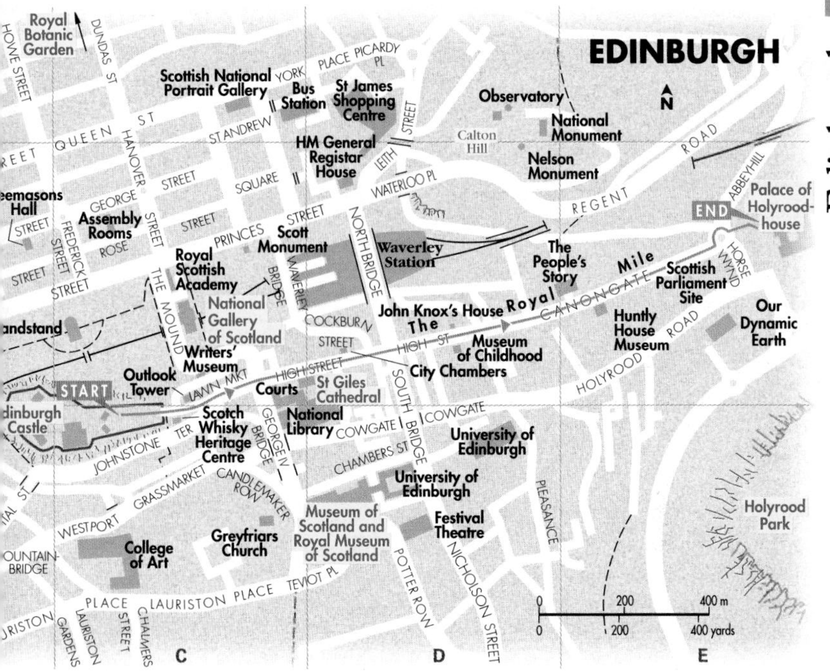

immediate first impression of the city's visual drama. The castle and the dark soaring back walls of the buildings that enclose the Royal Mile rise to the south like extensions of the cliffs of Castle Rock. To the north is Princes Street. Here, the Sir Walter Scott Monument, a towering Gothic steeple, dominates one view; the bulk of the North British Hotel, itself castle-like, dominates the other. At night all of these buildings are spectacularly illuminated.

From Waverley Bridge you can take an instant Guide Friday open-top bus tour that will introduce you to the city. Details about city transportation are available from the Edinburgh Traveline office, which is diagonally opposite the south end of Waverley Bridge, at the corner of Cockburn and Market streets. Next door is The Hub, Edinburgh's Festival Centre. You can also find out about various other guided tours from the Edinburgh tourist information center on Princes Street, only a minute or so from Waverley Station. They include historical walking tours and highly entertaining Ghost or Witchery tours that take you through the Old Town's maze of historic lanes and courtyards.

Two Edinburghs

Exploring the city on your own is straightforward. Old Edinburgh is the southern part, encompassed by the castle and the Royal Mile; beyond them are the areas of Southside, the Grassmarket and Canongate. To the south of the Royal Mile you will find the Royal Museum, the new Museum of Scotland (see page 102) and the Festival Theatre, a venue presenting fine drama and opera. Edinburgh Castle and the Royal Mile are Old Edinburgh's main attractions. You can easily spend an entire day here, and amid the souvenir shops and tourist spots there is a potent sense of history embodied by the splendid clutter of tall old sandstone buildings. Also take time for a walk in Holyrood Park, a green world of spectacular craggy hills, lochs and glens that is a genuine slice of Highland Scotland.

North of Waverley Bridge is Edinburgh's New Town, where Old Edinburgh expanded during the 18th century as part of a typically Georgian exercise in town planning. Above Princes Street is George Street, with handsome Charlotte Square and St. Andrew Square at either end. The elegance and unity of Georgian architecture – an exhilerating contrast to the equally splendid Royal Mile – can be appreciated at such locations as Queen Street Gardens, the Royal Circus (a circular residential street), Great King Street and Drummond Place – all north of George Street – as well as around Moray Place, west of Queen Street Gardens.

Life in Edinburgh

George Street and Princes Street, and the short connecting streets between them, are Edinburgh's main shopping streets. On Princes Street you will find an Edinburgh institution, Jenners, a department store that sells luxury items and has a wonderful food hall. This street also has branches of House of Fraser, Debenhams, Next and Gap.

Edinburgh is crowded during the summer, but the cultural feast of the Edinburgh Festival, in the second half of August and early September, is well worth taking in. There also are good alternatives outside the festival season – modern Scottish drama at the Traverse Theatre, or musical performances at Usher Hall.

Stylish Edinburgh restaurants offer distinctive Scottish dishes like wild salmon, Aberdeen Angus beef, or game such as grouse. Local residents are friendly and down to earth, always willing to help visitors. Traditional Scottish reticence is replaced here by a style that reflects sophistication without pretension, and by pride in the city's internationalism. And with a historic return to the Royal Mile by Scotland's recently formed governing body, the Scottish Parliament, Edinburgh enters a new millennium with renewed stature and optimism.

ESSENTIAL INFORMATION

TOURIST INFORMATION
Edinburgh and Scotland Information Centre
• 3 Princes Street ☎ 0131 473 3800; fax 0131 473 3881; www.edinburgh.org
• Edinburgh International Airport, walk-in visitors only.

URBAN TRANSPORTATION
The main train station for visitors is Waverley Station on Princes Street, (☎ 08457 484 950). A good bus network services Edinburgh. For information contact Lothian Buses (☎ 0131 555 6363) or First Edinburgh (☎ 0131 663 9233). Taxis can be hailed on the street; there are also stands at Waverley Station and on Waverley Bridge. For information call Central Radio Taxis (☎ 0131 229 2468) or City Cabs (☎ 0131 228 1211).

AIRPORT INFORMATION
Edinburgh International Airport at Turnhouse, is 8 miles west of the city center. There's a tourist office in the main concourse, and buses run every 6 minutes daytime, every 20 minutes evening, to and from Waverley Station. Taxis also serve the airport. For airport information call ☎ 0131 333 1000.

CLIMATE – average highs and lows for the month

JAN.	FEB.	MAR.	APR.	MAY	JUN.	JUL.	AUG.	SEP.	OCT.	NOV.	DEC.
5°C	6°C	7°C	10°C	13°C	16°C	18°C	17°C	15°C	12°C	9°C	6°C
42°F	43°F	45°F	50°F	55°F	61°F	64°F	63°F	59°F	54°F	48°F	43°F
1°C	1°C	2°C	4°C	6°C	9°C	11°C	11°C	9°C	6°C	4°C	2°C
34°F	34°F	36°F	39°F	43°F	48°F	52°F	52°F	48°F	43°F	39°F	36°F

Dramatically perched on a volcanic crag, Edinburgh Castle dates back to the 12th century

City Sights

Key to symbols

map coordinates refer to the Edinburgh map on pages 98–99; sights below are highlighted in yellow on the map.

address or location telephone number

opening times nearest bus route

restaurant or café on site or nearby

admission charge: $$$ more than £6, $$ £2–£6, $ less than £2 other relevant information

Calton Hill

Calton Hill D2–D3 Waterloo Place 26, X85, X86 Free

Nelson Monument 0131 556 2716 Mon. 1–6, Tue.–Sat. 10–6, Apr.–Sep.; Mon.–Sat. 10–3, rest of year $$

Calton Hill, at the east end of Princes Street, is crowned with neoclassical buildings that have earned Edinburgh the nickname "The Athens of the North," but their dark stonework hardly matches the bare, bright brilliance of the Parthenon or the Temple of the Winds. There are great views of Princes Street, Edinburgh Castle and Arthur's Seat from this hilltop, as well as distant panoramas of the Forth river and the hills beyond. You can also climb the 143 steps of the tall monument to Admiral Horatio Nelson for an even better view from its top. Note: This site should be avoided at dusk and after dark.

Edinburgh Castle

B1–C1 Castlehill 0131 225 9846 Daily 9:30–6, Apr.–Sep.; 9:30–5, rest of year Restaurant at castle 1, 6 $$$ Last admission 45 minutes before closing

You can tackle Scotland's most visited attraction in several ways. There are official guided tours, which are entertaining and informative. A self-guiding audio tour is a good option that helps focus the mind amid inevitable crowds. Brace yourself for the One O' Clock Gun, a 25-pounder that blasts off a single blank charge from the Half Moon battery at 1 p.m. daily, except Sunday. Castle highlights are the 12th-century St. Margaret's Chapel; the Stone of Scone; the Vaults, where the mighty 500-year-old siege gun, Mons Meg, stands in grim splendor like some huge black beast; and the Great Hall, with its glorious hammer beam roof and masses of weaponry. The Honours of the Kingdom exhibition is an evocative journey through history that culminates with a display of Scotland's luminous Crown Jewels.

Hikers enjoy the view of Edinburgh from Arthur's Seat in Holyrood Park, 822 feet above the city

Georgian House

B2 7 Charlotte Square 0131 225 2160 or 0131 226 3318 Mon.–Sat. 10–5, Sun. 2–5, Mar.–Oct. 124 $$ Last admission 30 minutes before closing

The Georgian House is the showplace of New Town's Charlotte Square and one of the most prestigious addresses in Scotland. Once home of the chief of the Lamont clan, the upper floor of the building is the present residence of the Moderator of the General Assembly, the leader of the Church of Scotland. The lower floors, full of delectable furnishings and fine paintings, are open to the public. The basement houses the original wine cellar and kitchen.

Holyrood Park

E1 Queen's Drive 1, 6 Free

Few cities are blessed with such a marvelous open space as Holyrood Park, or Queen's Park, as it is also known. The park is dominated by the dramatic Salisbury Crags and by Arthur's Seat, a high, rounded hill. You can enter the park from the bottom of the Royal Mile (see pages 104–105), just beyond Holyrood House. The park's high ground is encircled by a public road, the Queen's Drive, but the area is better enjoyed on foot. A broad, slanting path slices up the slopes below Salisbury Crags. It takes you high above the city, and the views are outstanding. Arthur's Seat can also be climbed, but it is a challenging hike. You can keep to the low ground of the park and still enjoy the splendid sights.

Museum of Scotland and Royal Museum of Scotland

D1 Chambers Street Royal Museum: 0131 247 4219; Museum of Scotland: 0131 247 4422; both museums: 0131 225 7534 (24-hour recorded information) Mon.–Sat. 10–5 (also Tue. 5–8), Sun. noon–5 Restaurant and café at museums 40, 41, 42, 46 $$ (for access to both museums); free Tue. 4:30–8 (both museums) Free guided tours

The story of Scotland from ancient times to the 20th century is vividly presented in these adjoining museums. The long-established Royal Museum is a splendid 19th-century building enclosing a vast space framed by elegant ironwork, with galleries rising through several floors. Here are traditional displays covering the natural world, science and industry and the decorative arts. The Royal Museum has been merged with an adventurous new building, the Museum of Scotland, a dramatic modern design in golden stone. The complex contains several levels, each displaying a particular era of Scotland's history. Ask at the information desk for floor plans and advice on finding your way around the galleries, or take a guided tour.

National Gallery of Scotland

C2 The Mound 0131 624 6200 Mon.–Sat. 10–5, Sun. 2–5 3, 4, 11, 17, 21, 26, 33 Free; special exhibitions $

The National Gallery is a large, 19th-century neoclassical building with a good selection from all periods, including a splendid altarpiece, the *Trinity Panels*, by Hugo van der Goes, and the seductive *Venus Anadyomene*, by Titian. Most of the major names in 17th-century European art are represented; there are some fine landscapes by Claude Lorrain in Room 4, and Nicholas Poussin's *Seven Sacraments* is on view in the Octagon Room. In Room 11 there is a powerful work by Frederick Edwin Church, *Niagara Falls from the American Side*. Scottish painting is well represented by Gavin Hamilton and Allan Ramsay. Look for *Edinburgh Castle and the Nor' Loch,* by Alexander Nasmyth, for some idea of what Old Edinburgh looked like before the Nor' Loch was drained and supplanted by Princes Street Gardens. Sir Henry Raeburn's *The Rev. Robert Walker Skating on Duddingston Loch* and Sir George Harvey's *The Curlers* are wonderfully lively and very typical Scottish narrative works.

Palace of Holyroodhouse

E2 Canongate 0131 556 7371 Daily 9:30–6, Apr.–Oct.; 9:30–4:30, rest of year $$–$$$ Closed last week in Jun. and first week in July for state functions; last admission 45 minutes before closing

Ancient Holyroodhouse was part of the Abbey of Holyrood, but was built in its present form as a royal palace for King Charles II. The severe neoclassicism of the courtyard block reflects the distinctly English fashion of the time; nevertheless it exudes Scottish history. The State Apartments of Charles' palace are luxurious and grand, crammed with artifacts and paintings elegantly displayed beneath superb stucco ceilings. Deep in the Historical Apartments is the bedchamber of Mary, Queen of Scots and the adjoining closet where, in 1566, her secretary and confidante, David Rizzio, was stabbed to death by associates of the Queen's delinquent husband, Lord Darnley. You can view the palace by guided tour only, but you'll be in the hands of highly entertaining and knowledgeable staff.

Royal Botanic Garden

Off the map 20A Inverleith Row 0131 552 7171 Daily 9:30–7, Apr.–Aug.; 9:30–6, Mar. and Sep.; 9:30–5, Feb. and Oct.; 9:30–4, rest of year Café in garden 23, 27 Free

The Royal Botanic Garden is just north of the New Town. Its showpiece features are the rhododendrons, which are at their colorful best from late April to early June. Other attractions are the Glasshouse Experience, where orchids, palms and other exotics flourish in defiance of Scotland's less than tropical climate; the Chinese Collection; and a decidedly Scottish heather garden.

St. Giles Cathedral

D2 Parliament Square 0131 225 9442 (for guided tours) Mon.–Fri. 9–7, Sat.–Sun. 9–5, Easter–Sep. 30; Mon.–Sat. 9–5, Sun. 1–5, rest of year Restaurant in crypt Bus 1, 6 Free; donation requested for viewing Thistle Chapel

St. Giles Cathedral (or the High Kirk of St. Giles) is the seat of Scotland's Presbyterian religion and a powerful feature of the Royal Mile (see pages 104–105). The Kirk is an uneasy mix of medieval Gothic and Georgian Gothic, the latter grafted on in the early 19th century; the interior reflects an enthusiastic Victorian restoration. There are some superb external features, including the 19th-century west door and the late medieval tower and spire, a dramatic sight on Edinburgh's skyline. Inside, St. Giles has many fine features and memorials. A 20th-century addition is the Thistle Chapel, built in 1911 as a private chapel for the Knights of the Most Holy Order of the Thistle. Richly carved stonework enlivens the interior of the chapel, and the lierne vaulting of the roof, with its carved bosses, is outstanding. Look carefully near the entrance door for the tiny bagpipe-playing angel.

Stroll Down the Royal Mile

Edinburgh's Royal Mile is the epitome of Old Edinburgh. Made up of four linked streets – Castlehill, Lawnmarket, High Street and Canongate – it descends the sloping back of a long, steep-sided ridge from Edinburgh Castle (see page 101) at the west end to the Palace of Holyroodhouse (see page 103) at the east end. On either side of the Royal Mile are tall buildings, riddled with courtyards and passageways known as "closes" and separated by narrow streets known as "wynds", all of it a delight to explore. All the way down the Royal Mile historic buildings punctuate the general streetscape, and there are numerous stores, cafés, restaurants and pubs.

The start of the atmospheric Royal Mile, marked by tall, narrow sandstone buildings

You can begin a relaxed descent of the Royal Mile from the entrance to the Castle Esplanade, starting with Castle Hill. Attractions beckon from either side. On the left is the Old Town Weaving Company, with its masses of tartan cloth and working mill. On the right is the Scotch Whisky Heritage Centre. Next on the left and well worth a visit is the fascinating Outlook Tower, a camera obscura where moving images of the surrounding area are projected onto a white viewing table. The street is narrow here but opens up just past the powerful Highland Tolbooth, a handsome Gothic building with the tallest spire in Edinburgh. It is now The Hub, Edinburgh's Festival Centre, home of the Edinburgh International Festival and a focus of the city's cultural life. At this point, the Royal Mile becomes the much wider Lawnmarket, once the city's linen market.

Keep to the left side of the street, where steps rise from street level to the pavement. There are several stores here selling woolen and tartan goods. Soon you come to Gladstone's Land, a 17th-century merchant's house now restored by the National Trust for Scotland. The house's Painted Chamber is stunning. Just a bit farther is the entrance to Lady Stair's Close. A narrow alleyway leads to an open square and to Lady Stair's House, now the Writers' Museum, a quiet little corner housing memorabilia associated with Scotland's finest writers, including Robert Burns, Robert Louis Stevenson and Sir Walter Scott. The spiral stairs have an uneven step halfway up, a common trick in medieval houses aimed at tripping an intruder in the dark.

The Lawnmarket reaches a junction with Bank Street and the street called George IV Bridge, where the Royal Mile becomes High Street. Here you will find a remarkable concentration of historic buildings. On the east corner with Bank Street is the High Court, with a bronze statue of Scottish philosopher David Hume in front of it. Next to the High Court is Edinburgh City Chambers, with an arcaded entrance screen.

At the foot of the Royal Mile on the fringe of Old Edinburgh, Holyroodhouse is the official Scottish residence of Queen Elizabeth II

Opposite is St. Giles Cathedral (see page 103). Behind St. Giles is Parliament Square and the old Parliament House, seat of the Scottish Parliament until the union with England in 1707.

High Street then descends gently to a junction with North and South Bridge Street. Stay on the north side of High Street, past the entrances to various passageways, and look for Chalmer's Court. Go through the entrance and down the steps to the preserved apse of the 15th-century Trinity College Church, home to the fascinating Brass Rubbing Centre.

On the other side of High Street opposite Chalmer's Court is the entertaining Museum of Childhood. Farther down High Street, just before the junction with Jeffrey Street and St. Mary's Street, is the John Knox House, a celebration of the 16th-century religious reformer who brought the Protestant Reformation to Scotland with more than a whiff of fire and brimstone. Beyond Jeffrey Street the Royal Mile becomes Canongate and narrows once more. Halfway down Canongate is the old Tolbooth, with its wonderful clock and conical-roofed towers. Canongate Tolbooth was once a courtroom and jail and is now the Peoples Story Museum, an exhibition of Edinburgh life. Just opposite is Huntly House Museum, a late 16th-century building now beautifully restored and containing an excellent collection of Edinburgh artifacts.

Diagonally opposite Huntly House is the 17th-century Canongate Kirk and Kirkyard, which has a wonderfully bright interior. The church has close royal connections; the royal family worship here when they are in residence at nearby Holyroodhouse, and the royal coat of arms can be seen on one of the church benches, or pews. A short distance past the church the Royal Mile reaches its junction with Abbey Hill and Horse Wynd, where it becomes Abbey Street and ends its progress through Scottish history at the gates of the Palace of Holyroodhouse. For the walking route, see the city map on pages 98–99.

With the spires of Christ Church and Merton College in the background, a rowing "eight" carries on Oxford student sporting traditions

OXFORD

Oxford, 56 miles northwest of London, is a typical English market town at heart. It is located within a hollow amid low hills at the gentle confluence of the River Thames and River Cherwell. What makes Oxford exceptional is its university, the oldest in the English-speaking world, an institution that is represented not by a single campus but by 39 independent colleges that are scattered throughout the city. They represent elegant seats of learning, but are also blessed with beautiful buildings.

The history of Oxford is said to have begun with the founding of a priory by the Saxon St. Frideswide, near where the River Thames and River Cherwell meet. Christ Church Cathedral supplanted the priory, and in time wealth from the medieval wool trade led to the founding of other religious houses, where learning was revered. Scholars were drawn to Oxford, and from these beginnings the university evolved.

Unless you're a student, Oxford is more of a journey through history and great architecture than through academia. For the visitor, the experience may seem faintly voyeuristic. You visit the colleges, picking your way through elegant quadrangles, chapels, arched passageways, gardens, and libraries, and at times you may feel you are intruding on a select world of academic privilege and of cultural paradigms.

Yet the physical integration of Oxford's colleges with the realities of Oxford as a city dispel any sense of intrusion. This is a living, vibrant place that retains its own identity and commercial life. Take a ride on a Guide Friday open-top bus to see the principal sights, leaving the bus where and when you like, or take a guided walking tour of historic Oxford or of the colleges. Stroll by the Thames or take a river cruise.

Oxford's Colleges

This is a small city, and you can walk around central Oxford in under an hour, but it is the density and complexity of colleges and great buildings that is so absorbing. The heart of the university lies between High Street and Broad Street and is enclosed by the colleges of Brasenose, All Souls, Hertford and Exeter. The Church of St. Mary the Virgin (see page 110) is on High Street. Behind St. Mary's is Radcliffe Square, which has the elegant 18th-century Renaissance rotunda of the Radcliffe Camera (chamber) at its heart. On the east side of the square is All Souls College. On the west side is Brasenose College, named after a traditional brass "mask" door knocker and a treasured college possession; a replica can be seen on the great oak doors.

From Radcliffe Square you can walk into the Schools Quadrangle of the Bodleian Library, with its superb Jacobean entrance tower and decorative inner walls. Through the arch on the north side of the quadrangle is the Sheldonian Theatre, where the *Encaenia* (the ceremony to confer honorary degrees) and the degree ceremony for Oxford graduates are held.

The Radcliffe Square area is the heart of the university, but try to visit some of the colleges when their grounds are open to the public. Include Christ Church (see page 109), the largest and most famous of the colleges, and do not miss nearby Merton College, reputedly the oldest of them all and certainly one of the finest, with its delightful gardens, ancient quadrangle, medieval library and chapel. Adjoining Merton Street, cobbled and quiet, is one of the finest parts of the city. Merton counts among its alumni 14th-century religious reformer John Wycliffe, poet T. S. Eliot and actor-singer Kris Kristofferson. Then head east toward Magdalen (pronounced "Maudlin") and its superb tower, Cloister Quad, gardens and riverside walks. Magdalen alumni include playwright Oscar Wilde and actor Dudley Moore.

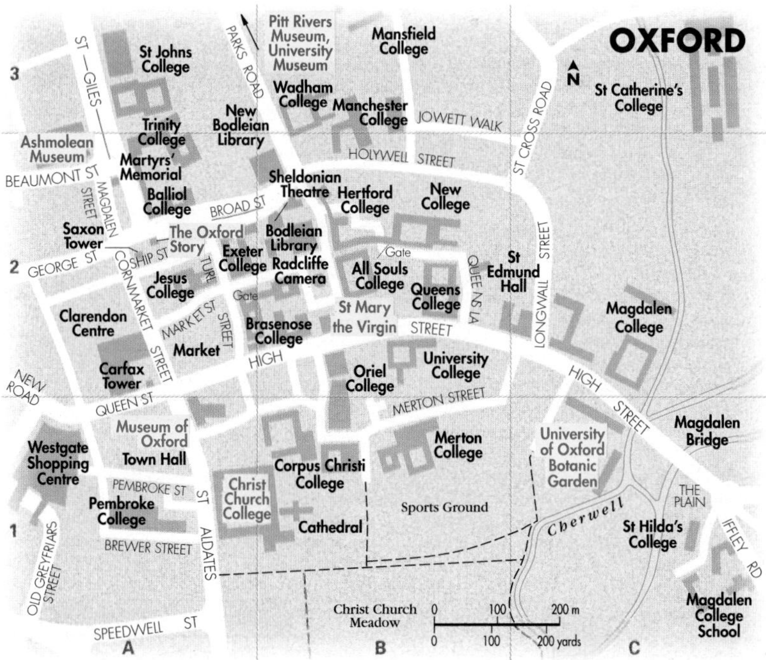

The Market Town

Oxford itself is famous for automobile manufacturing, and is the home of the Morris Oxford and the T-series MG sports car. They were produced at Oxford Cowley factories, built up by William Richard Morris, later Viscount Nuffield, a self-made man who founded Oxford's Nuffield College among his numerous charitable acts. Visit the Museum of Oxford and discover the history of the city, and take in the Pitt Rivers Museum and the University Museum of Natural History. Climb to the top of Carfax Tower for great views of Oxford.

The streets radiating from Carfax constitute Oxford's main shopping area. Cornmarket has a range of well-known stores. Off Cornmarket's east side is Golden Cross, where Shakespeare's plays are said to have been performed. Just beyond is the celebrated covered market, with excellent food stalls and other outlets.

Oxford's university population and townspeople exhibit a fascinating contrast of lifestyles. In medieval times this duality led to occasional bloody battles, but although today's students are noted for their often boisterous post-exam antics, Oxford is an eminently civilized place where the traditions of "town and gown" rest easily side by side.

The Original Alice

The children's books *Alice in Wonderland* and *Alice Through The Looking Glass* were inspired by Oxford life. Charles Ludwidge Dodgson, a lecturer and ordained deacon at Christ Church College, wrote the books during the latter part of the 19th century. Dodgson formed an intense friendship with Alice Liddell, the young daughter of the dean of Christ Church. He entertained her and her sisters with his stories of Wonderland, and they were later published under the pseudonym Lewis Carroll. Alice's Shop, ✉ 83 St. Aldates, ☎ 01865 723793, sells Alice memorabilia.

ESSENTIAL INFORMATION

TOURIST INFORMATION

Oxford Tourist Information Centre
• The Old School, Gloucester Green
☎ 01865 726871; fax 01865 240261
www.oxford.gov.uk

URBAN TRANSPORTATION

Oxford railroad station (✉ Botley Road) offers regular train connections to and from London. Central Oxford is a 10-minute walk from the station. Local bus services in and around the city are frequent. Two companies provide all local services: the Oxford Bus Company (☎ 01865 785400) and Stagecoach Oxford (☎ 01865 772250 24 hours). Taxi stands are located at the railroad station, Carfax and the Gloucester Green bus station. Call 001 Taxis (☎ 01865 240000 for information).

AIRPORT INFORMATION

London's Heathrow and Gatwick airports (see page 89) have bus connections to and from Oxford; buses depart every half hour, daily 24 hours. For information call Oxford Express (☎ 01865 785400). Birmingham Airport has daily rail (☎ 08457 484950) and bus (☎ 08705 808080) connections to and from Oxford.

CLIMATE – average highs and lows for the month

JAN.	FEB.	MAR.	APR.	MAY	JUN.	JUL.	AUG.	SEP.	OCT.	NOV.	DEC.
7°C	7°C	10°C	13°C	16°C	16°C	21°C	18°C	18°C	14°C	10°C	8°C
45°F	45°F	50°F	55°F	61°F	61°F	70°F	64°F	64°F	57°F	50°F	46°F
3°C	3°C	4°C	5°C	8°C	10°C	13°C	13°C	11°C	8°C	6°C	4°C
37°F	37°F	39°F	41°F	46°F	50°F	55°F	55°F	52°F	46°F	43°F	39°F

CITY SIGHTS

Key to symbols
map coordinates refer to the Oxford map on page 107; sights below are highlighted in yellow on the map. address or location telephone number opening times nearest bus route restaurant or café on site or nearby admission charge: $$$ more than £6, $$ £2–£6, $ less than £2 other relevant information

ASHMOLEAN MUSEUM

A3 Beaumont Street 01865 278000 Tue.–Sat. 10–5, Sun. 2–5 Café 61 Free; tours $ Tours Sat. at 11 a.m.

The Ashmolean is a fascinating museum of grand oddities and elegant art, housed in an equally grand and elegant neoclassical building dating from the 1840s. The oldest museum in Britain, the Ashmolean's collection is extensive and includes much medieval material; Greek, Roman and Egyptian artifacts; and fine Asian porcelain. The upper floor has a dazzling collection of Italian Renaissance paintings, including works by Michelangelo and Raphael.

CHRIST CHURCH COLLEGE

A1–B1 St. Aldates College: 01865 276150; Cathedral: 01865 276154; Picture Gallery: 01865 276172 College: Mon.–Sat. 9:30–5:30, Sun. 11:30–5:30. Picture Gallery: Mon.–Sat. 10:30–1 and 2–5:30, Sun. 2–5:30, Easter–Sep. 30; Mon.–Sat. 10:30–1 and 2–4:30, Sun. 2–4:30, rest of year 2, 4, 13, 15, 22 College and Cathedral $$, Picture Gallery $ May close unexpectedly at any time and for several weeks at a time

Oxford's largest college, Christ Church, is the most visited of all the university's colleges. Entry is gained through a turnstile by the War Memorial Gardens in the street known as St. Aldates, where college "bulldogs," immaculately dressed custodians in bowler hats, cheerfully order you around.

The present cathedral, known familiarly as "The House," dates from the late 12th century. Among its many fine features are exquisite stained-glass windows. Tom Quad is Christ Church's glorious central quadrangle; Mercury Pond, with Mercury Fountain at its center, adds an elegant accent. The figure of Mercury sports tiny patches of well-watered moss and often sprouts neckties and other "dress" donated by students. The entrance to Tom Quad and to Christ Church is the mighty gate tower, Tom Tower, that holds a massive seven-ton bell, Great Tom. Visit Christ Church's vaulted Great Hall, the Picture Gallery and Canterbury and Peckwater quadrangles.

Above: Porcelain figures in the Ashmolean

MUSEUM OF OXFORD

A1 St. Aldates 01865 252761 Tue.–Sat. 10–4 (also Sat. 4–5), Sun. noon–4 2, 13, 15, 22 $$

The Museum of Oxford, housed in the Town Hall gives an excellent account of Oxford's history from the earliest times. Everyone who played a part in the making of Oxford is here, from prehistory through the Roman, Saxon and Norman periods to the present day. The museum's well-arranged exhibits and organized layout make a visit very rewarding. The realities of town life, from both sides of the track, are depicted through 19th-century house interiors from residential and working class districts.

THE OXFORD STORY

A2 6 Broad Street 01865 728822 Daily 9–6, Jul.–Aug.; daily 9:30–5, Apr.–Jun. and Sep.–Oct.; Mon.–Fri.10–4:30, Sat.–Sun. 10–5, rest of year 2, 60 $$

For those who have visited York's Viking City of Jorvik, The Oxford Story's mobile "desks" will be familiar transportation through the varied tableaux and sound effects of this enjoyable attraction. You enter from Broad Street, watch a video introduction and then climb into old-fashioned school desks that travel gently up a steep ramp, gliding past displays about the university, its history and the personalities associated with it, accompanied by persuasive commentary.

Pitt Rivers Museum

Off the map · Parks Road (enter from interior of the University Museum) · 01865 270927 · Mon.–Sat. 1–4:30, Sun. 2–4:30 · 2, 60 · Free · Audio-guided tours

This fascinating museum is a marvelous example of 19th-century museum culture. It displays the often wildly eccentric collection of Lieutenant General Augustus Henry Lane Fox Pitt Rivers, who served throughout the British Empire and gathered a great many artifacts along the way. The collection reflects the general's intense interest in tribal cultures and is an invaluable comment on the human condition worldwide. Ritual masks, shrunken heads and weird magical objects are just part of the huge collection. Children will love it all.

St. Mary the Virgin

B2 · High Street · 01865 279111 · Daily 9–7, Jul.–Aug.; 9–5, rest of year · Café in adjoining Old Convocation House · 2, 4, 13, 15, 22 · Church free; tower $

St. Mary the Virgin is both the parish church of Oxford and the university's church. It is a splendid building that forms the southern side of Radcliffe Square. The early 14th-century tower rises above all of Oxford's dreaming spires, domes and cupolas. The south porch, facing High Street, is a splendid baroque extravagance, a daring 17th-century addition that trumpeted Italian influence with its twisted columns and heavily decorated segmental arch. The interior of the church is filled with monuments and wall tablets. You can plod up the tower as far as the base of the spire for fine views over Oxford, in the company of grinning gargoyles and fellow visitors. The climb is narrow and steep, and the up and down flow of people can cause traffic jams.

Dramatic wrought-iron arches over dinosaur skeletons at the University Museum

University Museum

Off the map · Parks Road · 01865 272950 · Daily noon–5 · 2, 60 · Free

The University Museum is housed in an inspirational 19th-century building in Italianate Gothic style, its facade embellished with marvelous carvings. The interior is a single open space, surrounded by an ambulatory and forested with slender iron columns that support a wrought-iron vault and glass roof. The exhibits range from large dinosaur skeletons to minerals and fossils. Visitors can access the Pitt Rivers Museum from the rear of the University Museum.

University of Oxford Botanic Garden

C1 · Rose Lane · 01865 276920 · Garden: daily 9–5, Apr.–Sep.; 9–4:30, rest of year. Greenhouses: daily 10–4:30, Apr.–Sep.; 10–4, rest of year · Apr.–Aug. $$; rest of year, free · Last admission at 4:15

The University of Oxford Botanic Garden was founded as a "physic garden" in 1621 and is Britain's oldest botanic garden. In imitation of the herbal gardens of mainland Europe, it has evolved into a delightful enclave with a collection of more than 8,000 plants. The River Cherwell and Magdalen College's handsome tower enhance the setting, and the original layout survives today. South of the main garden is the New Garden, a less geometrically designed display created in the 1940s. There also are splendid greenhouses.

Anne Hathaway's cottage, just west of Stratford, the childhood home of William Shakespeare's wife

Shakespeare's Stratford-upon-Avon

Stratford-upon-Avon was the birthplace of William Shakespeare and today the town is something of a shrine to the poet-playwright, its numerous Tudor and Jacobean half-timbered houses enhancing the Shakespearean theme. Shakespeare's Birthplace on Henley Street has been restored with late 16th-century furnishings and is full of fascinating memorabilia. Another fine old building is the Elizabethan Harvard House, which, although having no connection to Shakespeare, is interesting as the birthplace of John Harvard, who founded Harvard College in Massachusets.

After an intriguing life, Shakespeare died in 1616 at the early age of 52 in a house called New Place in Stratford. The original house was demolished by the owner in 1759 because he found visitors a nuisance. The foundations remain and are adjoined by the Elizabethan Garden and Nash's House, the superbly restored 17th-century home of Thomas Nash, husband of Shakespeare's granddaughter, Elizabeth Hall.

Another famous Stratford building is Holy Trinity Church, located on the banks of the River Avon. Here you will see the remarkable alabaster bust of Shakespeare, modeled on a wax impression of the playwright's face at his death. Nearby is Shakespeare's tomb and those of his wife, Anne Hathaway, and his daughter, Susanna. On the banks of the River Avon to the north of the church is the Memorial Theatre, where the Royal Shakespeare Company performs the Bard's plays.

Arrange day trips to Stratford at the Oxford tourist office or through Cotswold Roaming.

Tourist Information Centre ✉ The Old School, Gloucester Green, Oxford OX1 2DA ☎ 01865 726871; fax 01865 240261

Cotswold Roaming ✉ Box 784, Headington, Oxford OX3 9YS ☎ 01865 308300; fax 01865 763232

Walk along the city walls for a view of York Minster, Britain's largest medieval cathedral

YORK

Two thousand years of English history are written across the face of York. Within the old city's walls, and within sight and sound of the magnificent York Minster cathedral, narrow, cobbled streets, ancient remains, medieval buildings, historic churches, and award-winning museums sit happily alongside modern stores, restaurants and hotels.

York is a small town at heart. It began life as a riverside encampment established by an ancient British tribe, the Brigantes. In turn, Brigantes were usurped in AD 71 by Roman invaders who made York their empire's northern European capital. Anglo Saxons, who established York as a center of early Christianity, followed the Romans. In AD 867, the settlement was captured by the Danes – the plundering Vikings of romantic history.

In subsequent centuries York fell under the control of the Normans, who laid the first substantial foundations of the present minster and built the original city walls. During the 16th and 17th centuries, religious and dynastic struggles kept the city in the national forefront, at a time when poverty, plague and famine often made ordinary life harsh and terrible. The more enterprising world of the 18th and 19th centuries and the emergence of York as the railroad capital of northern England made the city a fashionable commercial center, one that was only lightly touched by the more brutal aspects of the Industrial Revolution. Today visitors walk on hallowed ground that has supported more than 2,000 years of human achievement, as well as misery.

Sightseeing in York

Many parts of central York are pedestrian-only, and though crowds may throng the narrow streets, people have precedence over vehicles. In the nicest areas of old York there is no stream of roaring traffic pinning you to the sidewalk. You go with the flow, but there is no rush-hour element even during the busiest times of day.

York's flavor can be captured via a Guide Friday open-top double-decker bus or in a horse-drawn carriage. The inner city can be explored on one of numerous city tours, led by local experts. Or you can take a "ghost walk," complete with an entertaining guide and actors making impromptu, phantom appearances in dark alleys. Leisurely daytime guided walks take in the city walls and ancient streets.

You could also explore on your own. Central York is not large, and you're never far from the next fascinating building, museum or attraction. Few houses in York rise above two or three stories, and the sun finds its way into hidden corners, lighting the upper parts of old buildings. Take time as you stroll to appreciate the colorful facades and architectural features, like Stonegate's little red devil above the corner with Coffee Yard Lane.

The many different people who colonized York left an engaging but confusing legacy of local words. The word "bar" means gate and refers to the magnificent stone gateways, such as Bootham Bar and Monk Bar, that punctuate the city walls. On the other hand, the Viking word "gate," as in Stonegate and Petergate, means street.

Walk part of the city walls for a superb overview of York. Try the section from Monk Bar (location of the fascinating Richard III Museum), at the north end of Goodramgate, to Bootham Bar at the west end of High

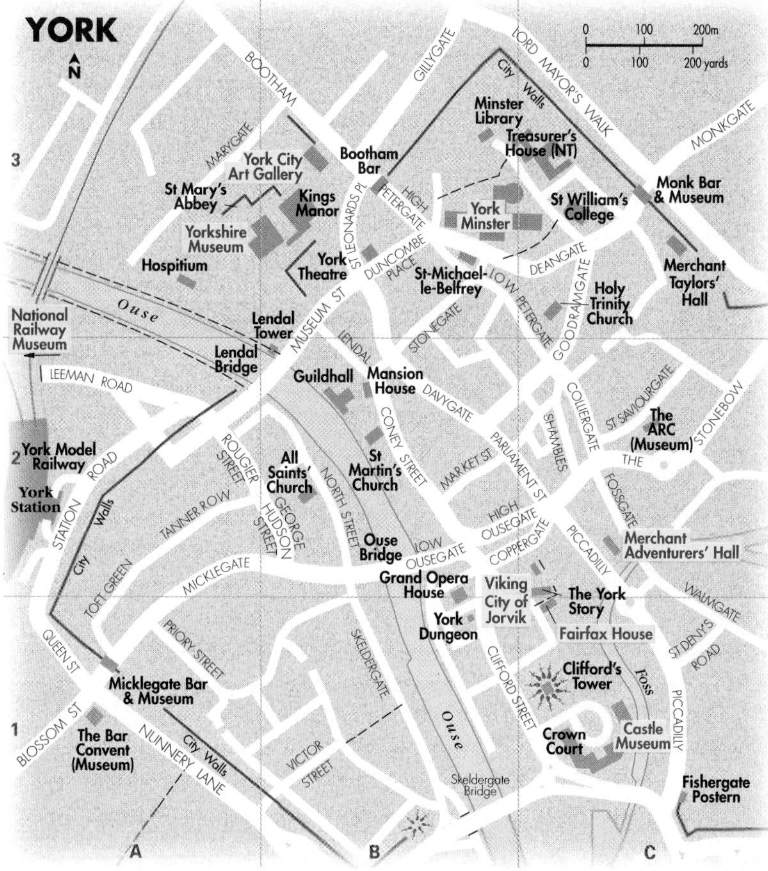

Petergate. The views of York Minster along this stretch are outstanding.

Visit such main attractions as York Minster and the Viking City of Jorvik, but do not neglect other sights like the hands-on Archaeological Resource Centre in St. Saviourgate and The York Dungeon on Clifford Street, both great fun for children. Enjoy the talented street entertainers, and check out the many festivals and events staged each year in and around the city.

Minster

The Old English word "Minster" was used in medieval England as a variant of the word "monastery." It was sometimes applied to describe the church attached to a monastery, which was used for worship by the monks. Through time the word became associated with certain cathedral churches, like York Minster.

Shopping in Old York

Shopping in York is fun. Streets such as Stonegate and the Shambles are overflowing with specialty stores, including antique shops, art and craft galleries, bookstores, jewelers, tea blenders and boutiques. Every major chain store is represented in the main shopping areas of Coney Street, St. Mary's Square and Parliament Street.

A huge variety of eateries will tempt you, from traditional English tea and coffee houses – such as Betty's in St. Helen's Square and Taylor's Tea Rooms and Coffee Shop in Stonegate – to dozens of restaurants. Authentic English pubs include Stonegate's Ye Old Starre Inne and the 15th-century Black Swan, on Peasholme Green.

York is essentially English at heart, but its northern regional identity makes it very different from London and southern England. Expect friendliness and helpfulness from locals, but be prepared for that matter-of-fact approach for which Yorkshire people are famous. You will be given facts rather than fiction and guidance rather than gossip to help you get the best out of the heartland of historic England.

ESSENTIAL INFORMATION

TOURIST INFORMATION
York Tourism Bureau
• 20 George Hudson Street
☎ 01904 554455; fax 01904 554460
www.york-tourism.co.uk
• De Grey Rooms, Exhibition Square
☎ 01904 621756
• York railroad station, Station Road
☎ 01904 621756

URBAN TRANSPORTATION
York railroad station (☎ 08457 484950) is the main terminal, with frequent service to and from major cities. Local service is run by Great North Eastern Railways (☎ 08457 225225), whose "First Stop York" program offers savings on attractions, restaurants, pubs and theaters (mid-Sep. to mid-May). There are taxi stands at York railroad station (☎ 01904 623332) and at Duncombe Place, near York Minster.

AIRPORT INFORMATION
Leeds-Bradford Airport is an hour's drive from York; for information call ☎ 0113 250 9696. Manchester Airport, 56 miles southwest by road, has direct train services to York; for information call ☎ 0161 489 3000.

CLIMATE – average highs and lows for the month

JAN.	FEB.	MAR.	APR.	MAY	JUN.	JUL.	AUG.	SEP.	OCT.	NOV.	DEC.
6°C	7°C	9°C	13°C	16°C	19°C	21°C	20°C	18°C	14°C	9°C	7°C
43°F	45°F	48°F	55°F	61°F	66°F	70°F	68°F	64°F	57°F	48°F	45°F
0°C	1°C	2°C	4°C	7°C	10°C	12°C	11°C	10°C	7°C	4°C	2°C
32°F	34°F	36°F	39°F	45°F	50°F	54°F	52°F	50°F	45°F	39°F	36°F

City Sights

Key to symbols

map coordinates refer to the York map on page 113; sights below are highlighted in yellow on the map.

address or location telephone number

opening times nearest bus route

restaurant or caféon site or nearby

admission charge: $$$ more than £6, $$ £2–£6, $ less than £2 other relevant information

Castle Museum

C1 The Eye of York 01904 653611

Daily 9:30–5, Apr.–Oct.; 9:30–4:30, rest of year

Museum café $$

This museum is housed in two former prisons. Behind the handsome neoclassical facade of the building is an outstanding collection of exhibits illustrating the social history of York, and of Britain, over the past 400 years. Walkways lead past vivid reconstructions of complete Victorian and Edwardian streets, lined with old stores full of authentic contents. Allow several hours to enjoy the experience, which includes a visit to the condemned cell that once held legendary highwayman Dick Turpin.

Fairfax House

C1 Castlegate 01904 655543

Mon.–Thu. and Sat. 10–5, Sun. 1:30–5 $$

Guided tours Fri. only at 11 and 2

This elegant house was lavishly decorated by Viscount Fairfax in 1759, but was neglected in later years. It was bought in 1980 by the York Civic Trust, which carried out an inspired restoration. Today, Fairfax House is one of the finest examples of an 18th-century town house in England. Enjoy the sumptuous plasterwork ceilings, damask hangings, marble fireplaces and magnificent furnishings.

Merchant Adventurers' Hall

C2 Fossgate 01904 654818 Mon.–Sat. 9:30–5, Sun. noon–4, Apr.–Sep.; daily 9:30–3:30, rest of year The Blue Bicycle, see page 547 $$

The opulent salon in Fairfax House

This medieval Guild Hall is the finest of its kind to survive in Europe. Its brick and timber-framed exterior, the vast, open timber work of the Great Hall and the interior paneling effortlessly transport visitors from the present into a convincing medieval environment. The hall was built from 1357 to 1361 by a religious fraternity that evolved into a merchants' guild, which survives today as a charitable organization and guardian of this outstanding building.

National Railway Museum

Off the map Leeman Road 01904 621261

Daily 10–6 Museum restaurant and café

$$$ (under 17 and over 60 free)

For travel enthusiasts young and old, this atmospheric museum – the largest of its kind in the world – offers vivid insight into 200 years of transportation history. Displays of almost 50 steam, diesel and electric locomotives include a restoration of George Stephenson's famous 1829 *Rocket* and the wonderful *Mallard*, still operating and the fastest steam engine in the world.

Viking City of Jorvik

C2 Coppergate 01904 643211

Daily 9–5:30 $$$ Last admission at 5:15

This very popular attraction reveals the archeological remains of Viking York, or "Jorvik." Deep underground, you're shuttled back in time 1,000 years to a reconstructed Viking street complete with thatched houses, lifelike figures and the evocative sounds and smells of everyday life. Traveling in a "time capsule" back to the year AD 975, you "fly" across the Viking city to discover how the basic structure of modern York is remarkably similar to that of the Viking Age.

York City Art Gallery

B3 Exhibition Square 01904 551861 Daily 10–5 $$ Last admission at 4:30

The excellent collection in this small, friendly and informative gallery provides an overview of European art from the Italian Renaissance to the contemporary scene. There are a number of paintings by York artist William Etty, who had a liking for exuberant nudes. There also is a collection by leading 20th-century potters such as Bernard Leach and Shoji Hamada.

York Minster

B3 Minster Yard 01904 557216 Daily 7 a.m.–6:30 p.m., Apr.; 7 a.m.–7:30 p.m., May; 7 a.m.–8:30 p.m., Jun.–Aug.; 7 a.m.–8 p.m., Sep.; 7 a.m.–7 p.m., Oct.; 7–6, Nov.–Mar. Hours vary, particularly in summer when concerts and plays may restrict opening times; call for details Minster restaurant/café Entry to main building is free, but a donation is requested. Crypt, Chapter House, Treasury, Foundations Exhibition and tower $ Free tours (except Sun.) begin at 9:30 (10 in winter). Ask at the reception area or book by phone 10 days in advance.

York cathedral's present foundations were laid by the Normans in the 12th century. The Minster is a historical experience as well as a religious one; the walls are crowded with dramatic monuments and the architectural features are superb.

Past the broad introductory nave is the central crossing, where north and south transepts, nave and choir all meet below the soaring vaulted roof of the central tower, 200 feet above. The choir is full of intricate design and ornamentation. At the east end of the church you will find the Lady Chapel and the great East Window – as big as a tennis court and the largest medieval stained-glass window in the world.

Tower and spires of York Minster

Also visit the intriguing crypt where the pillars are from the original Norman church. In the Chapter House, look for the wickedly irreverent figures of priests and prelates scattered among the carvings above the encircling stalls. The Foundations Exhibition in the Minster's undercroft, or "basement," has displays of Roman and Norman remains.

Consider climbing the 275 spiral steps of the great 234-foot tower, but do so only if you're in good physical condition; it can prove to be a small Everest for some.

Yorkshire Museum

A3–B3 Museum Gardens 01904 629745 Daily 10–5 $$ Events and changing exhibitions at various times; opening times vary

This award-winning museum includes some of the finest Roman, Viking, Anglo Saxon and medieval artifacts in Europe. The grounds feature handsome gardens that contain York's oldest ruins – the Multiangular Tower, part of fourth-century Roman fortifications. Brightly feathered peacocks strut around the approach to the building.

A major exhibit is the luminous Middleham Jewel, a beautiful 15th-century sapphire set within a gold pendant. The museum building incorporates part of the ruins of medieval St. Mary's Abbey. This section, with its haunting reconstructions and medieval music, is a delight.

WALK THROUGH THE PAST

York's appeal stems largely from the survival of its central streets in their original form. While many cities and towns had their centers remodeled over the years, central York was spared wholesale change. Plans to demolish the city walls during the Victorian period were resisted, and within the precise boundaries of those restored walls the narrow streets and interlocking alleys and courtyards make up one of the best preserved late medieval cities in Europe.

Many of York's old houses are not the original buildings; they have been rebuilt or restored over time. But their styles are medieval, and so venerable is the layout of central York that when you walk down Stonegate you follow the exact line of the Roman approach road to the imperial encampment of AD 71.

The most famous of York's ancient thoroughfares is the Shambles, a narrow street overhung by timber-framed houses. Its name derives from the butchers' shops and slaughterhouses once located here. Today's the Shambles is a delight. It typifies York's medieval character, but in times past this would have been a filthy, raucous, rough-and-ready place that would horrify modern sensibilities. Today it can be enjoyed for its quaintness, free of medieval realities. Don't miss bustling Newgate Market (open daily) behind the Shambles, where – within the rules of modern hygiene and legality – some of the liveliness of medieval times still survives.

To get the most out of old York, explore the interlocking alleys that connect the center. Wander at will with a city map, which will show you the main landmarks, but investigate the twists and turns of the numerous passages leading off Stonegate, Petergate, Davygate and Church Street. They'll land you unexpectedly in the bustle of St. Helen's Square, with its handsome Mansion House and Guildhall, or in King's Square, where old gravestones make up part of the paving. Brimming with charming little shops, cafés and restaurants, old York exudes unforgettable character.

A rainy night in the Shambles, where medieval buildings overhang cobbled lanes

ORTVS
AVRORA

Czech Republic

"Not all the seductions of Vienna…nor the dominion of a German bureaucracy have broken the stubborn heart of the Czech…"

From *A History of Europe*, by English historian H. A. L. Fisher

Opposite: The 15th-century Astronomical Clock dominates the front of the Old Town Hall in Prague

Czech Republic

Since 1989, the Czechs have been embracing change and finding their footing as a new republic. In that year, the Velvet Revolution saw Czechoslovakia discard 40 years of Communist rule without firing a single shot. At the start of the 21st century, the country is coping with the difficulties and benefits of adapting to Western capitalism and establishing a new social, and economic order.

Bohemia and Moravia

Most visitors to the Czech Republic head straight for Prague, but there is plenty to enjoy in the country's diverse landscapes. Locked between Poland, Germany, Slovakia and Austria, the republic takes in two regions: Bohemia, itself surrounded by a ring of mountains, and the lowlands of Moravia. Both have suffered adversely from the effects of heavy industrialization – acid rain and deforestation among them – but both also have areas of real beauty.

In southern Bohemia, such medieval towns as České Budějovice (home of Budweiser beer) and Český Krumlov, with its great 13th-century castle, recall a time when kings and lords were eager to build in one of Europe's richest regions. To the west are famous spa

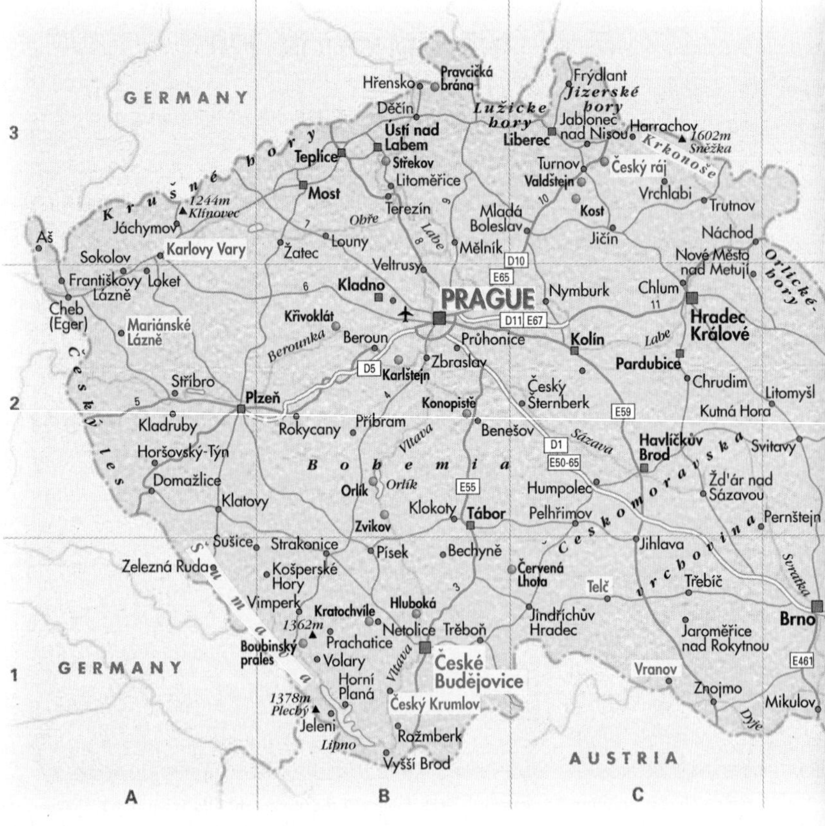

towns best known by their German names: Karlsbad (Karlovy Vary) and Marienbad (Mariánské Lázně).

In Moravia, wedged between the western uplands and the eastern White Carpathian mountains, the 19th-century city of Brno gives access to the Punkva Caves (Punkevní jeskyně).

Czech Culture

Despite the hijacking of the term "bohemian" by the West to mean "unconventional," the Czechs are generally rather reserved. Beyond this, though, is a friendliness and genuine interest in other cultures. Young Czechs often speak English, and are tuned in to Anglo-American pop culture.

Love of arts and literature is not confined to Prague. Václav Havel, the first post-Communist president, was better known among Czechs as a poet and playwright. Music has a special place in Czech life, too – from oompah-style brass bands to the classical tradition that produced such composers as Antonin Dvořák.

The face of the modern Czech Republic – President Václav Havel

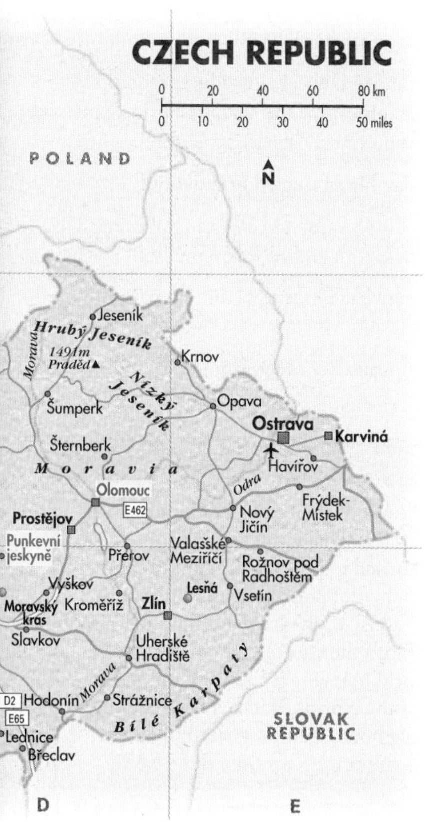

Overall, most people who travel around the Czech Republic will be struck by the diversity of this small nation. As the republic moves away from Communism towards capitalism, there is anxiety as well as hope. A visit to this society in transition between two worlds is sure to be rewarding.

MORE TOP DESTINATIONS IN THE CZECH REPUBLIC

• České Budějovice B1 • Český Krumlov B1 • Český ráj C3 • Karlovy Vary A3 • Krkonoše C3 • Mariánské Lázně A2 • Olomouc D2 • Punkevní jeskyně D1 • Šumava A1–B1 • Telč C1 • Vranov C1

TIMELINE

AD 700	The Přemysl Dynasty begins its 500-year rule of Bohemia.
929	Good King Wenceslas (Václav I) is assassinated by his brother and made the country's patron saint.
1346	Devout Charles IV, Holy Roman Emperor, is crowned king of Bohemia and ushers in its Golden Age.
1415	Religious reformer Jan Hus is burned at the stake in Constance; in Prague his supporters throw Catholic councilors from town hall windows and start the Hussite Wars.
1583	The Habsburg court moves to Prague.
1848	The Habsburgs suppress an uprising of Czech nationalism.
1914	Czechs are forced to fight for the Austrian Habsburgs in World War I, but thousands desert to the Russians.
1918	With the defeat of Austria-Hungary, the new state of Czechoslovakia is proclaimed.
1938	Czechoslovakia is forced to hand over Sudetenland to Hitler.
1945	Slovakia and the Czech lands are liberated by the Red Army; the Communist Party seizes power in 1948.
1968	The First Secretary, Alexander Dubček, introduces "socialism with a human face" in the reforms of the "Prague Spring"; in August, Soviet troops invade Czechoslovakia.
1989	"Velvet Revolution"; Václav Havel elected president of Czechoslovakia.
1993	Czechoslovakia splits into Czech and Slovak republics.
1997	Czech Republic becomes a NATO member and prepares to join the European Union.
2000	Prague designated a European City of Culture.

THE VELVET REVOLUTION

On November 17, 1989, a week after the fall of the Berlin Wall, there was an officially sanctioned demonstration in Prague to mark the Nazi suppression of Czech universities. It soon turned into a protest march against the authorities, and was forcefully put down by riot police. A rumor began that the police had killed one demonstrator. In fact, it wasn't true, but the story was enough to fuel public anger. People poured into the streets night after night, watched by television viewers across the world. Alexander Dubček was brought back from obscurity in Bratislava to address the crowds. Václav Havel headed a newly established Civic Forum, and on December 10 a new government was formed, with the Communists reduced to a minority. Less than three weeks later, Havel was installed as president.

Clean, fast and cheap – Prague's excellent subway system is a good way to get around

SURVIVAL GUIDE

- Czech pronunciation is difficult, but worth mastering if only for place names. Some Czechs – particularly young city dwellers – may speak a little English, and a grasp of German is also useful.
- The cuisine is heavily meat-based and dull – dumplings and pork are popular dishes. Coffee and cakes are a highlight, and the cafés (*kavárna*) are excellent. This is the home of light beer, and the products of Budějovice (Budweis) and Plzeň (Pilsen) are only the most famous among a multitude of local varieties.
- It's worth looking through bookstores, despite the language barrier, as the illustrated books are a treat. For souvenirs, take home Bohemian crystal, porcelain, lacework, ceramics and prints.
- Easter is a more important holiday in Orthodox churches than Christmas, and is marked by the bizarre fertility ritual of boys whipping girls' legs with birch twigs.
- At Christmas, neighborhood St. Nicholas figures walk the streets with an angel, giving candy to good children and coal to bad. Christmas dinner is traditionally carp – sold live at street stalls to be eaten on Christmas Eve with potato salad and schnitzel.
- Prague is even busier than usual in May and early June, when it hosts the International Music Festival: Reserve accommodations several weeks in advance for this period.
- Public transportation is an enjoyable way of seeing the republic. Almost every town has a railroad station (*nádraží*), and side trips are cheap. The fast trains (*rychlík*) stop at major cities; local trains (*osobní vlak*) are slow, stop everywhere and usually have only second-class carriages.
- The Czech Republic suffers from a shortage of hotels and hostels, although this is fast changing. Some of the Communist-era hotels still operate, and many have been overhauled. There's been a surge of new accommodations in converted buildings. A sign saying *Zimmer frei* ("rooms available") indicates bed and breakfast in a private home.

Prague

Nothing can prepare you for the beauty of Prague. Its title of "Golden City" barely conveys the color and elegance of its historic center: painted medieval facades glinting pink and green and silver in the sun; a jumble of rust-red rooftops; mellow stone, turquoise domes, steel-gray Gothic spires. Prague's buildings and streets span 1,000 years. Wandering the cobbled passageways and alleys thus becomes the highlight of any visit.

Compass Bearings

Central Prague is made up of four towns, joined together in 1784. On the west bank of the Vltava river are Hradčany and the Lesser Quarter (Malá Strana); on the east bank are the Old Town (Staré Město) and New Town (Nové Město). In the 19th century the Jewish ghetto, Josefov, was also incorporated into the Old Town. Beyond this core is a circle of suburbs, but the main historic sights are within the substantially traffic-free center.

Nerudova

A steep street climbs from Malostranské Square, near Prague Castle, in the Lesser Quarter. This street, Nerudova, was named after journalist and writer Jan Neruda. He wrote stories about daily life in 19th-century Prague, and was born at No. 47, near the top. Eighteenth-century houses line the street, identified by intricately crafted signs; numbers weren't introduced until the 1770s. Look for The Three Fiddles (No. 12), The Green Lobster (No. 43) and Neruda's home, The Two Suns.

Prague Castle

The two banks of the Vltava are connected by a series of 15 bridges, the oldest of which, the Charles Bridge (Karlův most), is a magnet for tourists, performers and vendors. On the West Bank, Hradčany, the area around Prague Castle and its hill, is the major

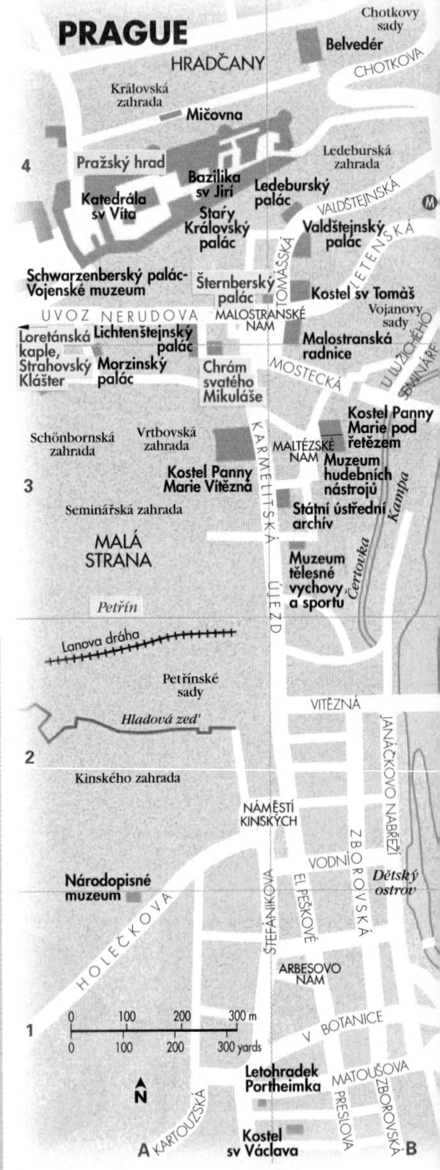

attraction. It includes (as well as the castle itself) Golden Lane (Zlatá ulička), with tiny houses originally occupied by the Emperor's gatekeepers; the Gothic Powder Tower (Prašná brána), where alchemists once struggled to make gold from base metals; and the palaces surrounding Hradčany Square.

Old and New Prague

Across the river in the Old Town is Old Town Square, perhaps the most popular with tourists. Here are the sprawling Old Town Hall (Staroměstská radnice, see page 130), the white Church of St. Nicholas (Chrám svatého Mikuláše, see page 127) and the dark towers of Týn

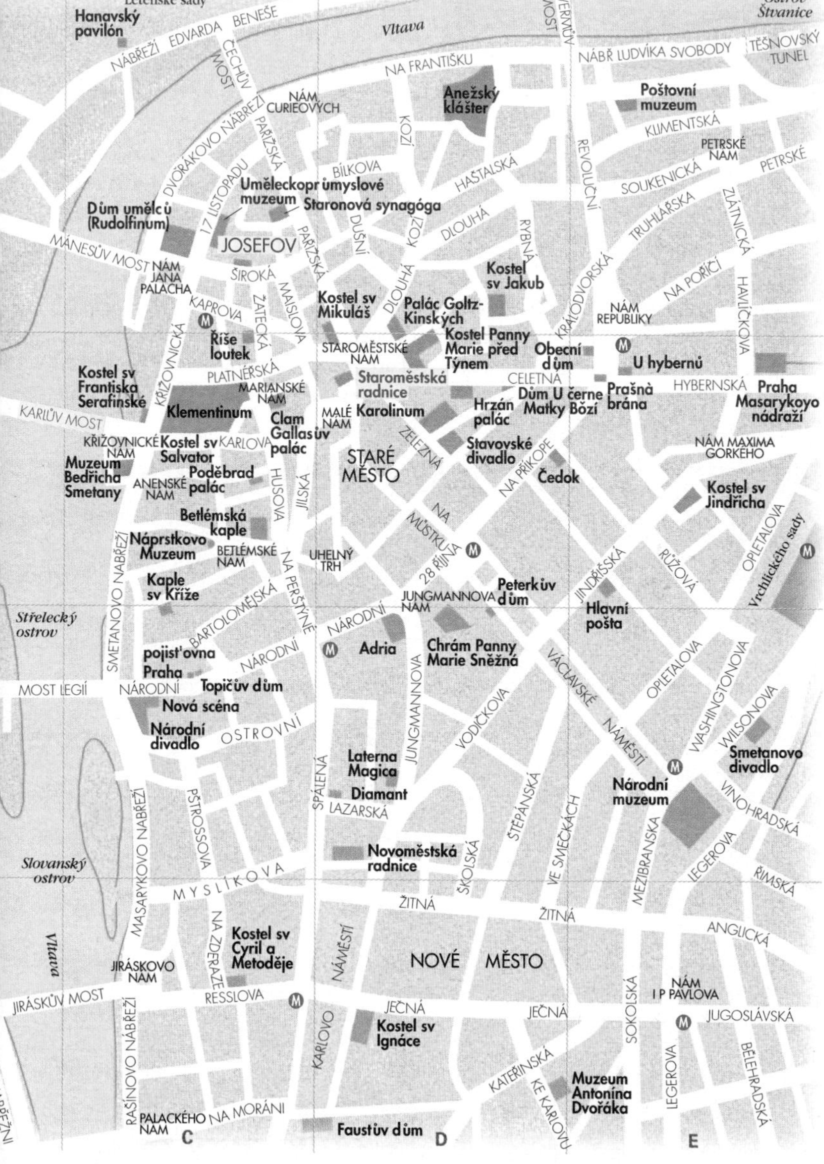

Prague Castle and the spires of St. Vitus' Cathedral

Church. This is where street artists perform. The hub of the New Town is Wenceslas Square, a busy boulevard renowned as the focus of protests during the Velvet Revolution.

Locals love their music – as Mozart found out, when he triumphed here after only moderate success in Vienna. Classical music seems to be everywhere in Prague, advertised in listings guides and on posters across the city. Tickets are reasonably priced and the performances are invariably superb.

Czech Beer and Puppets

Restaurants and cafés fill up quickly in Prague, but Czechs tend to eat early, so your chances of getting a table will improve by about 8 p.m. There's a wide range of options, from American and Italian to Lebanese and Japanese. Don't leave the city without tasting at least one Czech beer. Prague's own brews are Staropramen and U Fleků.

The best shopping is in the maze of arcades under the buildings of Wenceslas Square along the pedestrian-only street Na Příkopě and also along Národní třída. There are interesting craft shops on Karlova, near the Charles Bridge. Puppets make ideal gifts – they're works of art, not just playthings. For books, try Firma AMI, Obchod Vším Mažným at Nerudova ulice 45.

ESSENTIAL INFORMATION

TOURIST INFORMATION
Pražská informační služba (Prague Information Service)

- Staroměstská radnice (Old Town Hall), Staroměstské náměstí 1
- Na Příkopě 20
- Praha hlavní nádraží (Prague railroad station)
- Karlův most (Charles Bridge) – summer only
- ☎ Central information numbers: 187 or 02 54 44 44

www.prague-info.cz

URBAN TRANSPORTATION
Prague has three subway lines: A (green), B (yellow) and C (red). Stations are indicated by the letter "M" (marked in a red circle on the city map). Trains run frequently every day between 5 a.m. and midnight. Trams and buses are also frequent, (4:30 a.m. to midnight with some night services) but buses run mainly outside the city center. One ticket can be used for the subway, buses and trams. For bus information call ☎ 1034.
Taxis can be hailed on the street or located at taxi stands. A lit sign on the car shows that it's free. Make sure the taxi has a meter registering the fare.

AIRPORT INFORMATION
Praha-Ruzyně Airport, 10 miles west of the city, is a bus ride from the center. Airport bus number 119 runs to Dejvická and 179 to Nové Butovice subway stations; shuttle buses run to náměstí Republiky or V Celnici street. There also are shuttle services to the main hotels. Call for flight information (☎ 02 2011 3314 or 02 2011 3321), or call Czech Airlines (ČSA) ☎ 02 2010 4310.

CLIMATE – average highs and lows for the month

JAN.	FEB.	MAR.	APR.	MAY	JUN.	JUL.	AUG.	SEP.	OCT.	NOV.	DEC.
2°C	2°C	8°C	12°C	18°C	20°C	22°C	23°C	18°C	12°C	5°C	2°C
36°F	36°F	46°F	54°F	64°F	68°F	72°F	73°F	64°F	54°F	41°F	36°F
-4°C	-4°C	0°C	2°C	7°C	10°C	13°C	12°C	9°C	0°C	0°C	-2°C
25°F	25°F	32°F	36°F	45°F	50°F	55°F	54°F	48°F	32°F	32°F	28°F

City Sights

Key to symbols

map coordinates refer to the Prague map on pages 124–125; sights below are highlighted in yellow on the map.
address or location telephone number
opening times nearest subway nearest bus or tram route restaurant or café on site or nearby admission charge: $$$ more than 110Kč, $$ 70Kč–110Kč, $ less than 70Kč other relevant information

Chrám svatého Mikuláše

A3 Malostranké náměstí Daily 9–4. Tower: daily 10–6, Apr.–Oct.; Sat.–Sun. 10–5, rest of year Malostranská Tram 12, 22 $
Guided tours are available

Mozart played the 2,500-pipe organ here in 1787; he couldn't have chosen a more grandiose setting than the Chrám svatého Mikuláše (Church of St. Nicholas). It was constructed in the 18th century to celebrate Catholic counter-Reformation propaganda. It's a frenzy of decoration: pink-and-green mock-marble pillars; a 16,146-square-foot ceiling fresco; a copper statue of St. Nicholas; and huge sculptures of the four church fathers, including St. Cyric killing the devil.

Josefov

C4 Josefov 02 2481 9456 Jewish Museum sites: Sun.–Fri. 9–6, Apr.–Oct.; 9–4:30, rest of year. Closed Jewish holidays. Old-New Synagogue: Sun.–Thu. 9–6, Fri. 9–5, Apr.–Oct.; Sun.–Thu. 9–5, Fri. 9–2, rest of year Kosher Restaurace Shalom, see page 548 Tram 17, 18 Jewish Museum $$$; Old-New Synagogue $$$; Spanish Synagogue $

Walls went up around Prague's Jewish community in 1254, in keeping with a church law that Christians and Jews should live apart. But the walls did nothing to protect the inhabitants of the ghetto from centuries of persecution. In 1389, 3,000 were massacred in a pogrom, and at regular intervals, kings passed laws forcing Jews to wear particular clothes or colors to identify them.

Even in the face of such vicious discrimination, the ghetto developed as a center of learning, and some members were able to buy occasional privileges for the community from the imperial court. In 1784 Joseph II abolished residence restrictions (the area was later named after him). Over a century later, most of its slums were demolished.

Inside the dome of St. Nicholas' Church

In the confined space of the Stary zidovsky hrbitov (Old Jewish Cemetery), 100,000 people are buried. Crooked gravestones lean and overlap; pebbles and prayers are still left on them as tributes. At the entrance, the Old Gravediggers' Hall has an exhibition of drawings by children held here before being sent by the Nazis to Auschwitz concentration camp; about 15,000 children passed through. By the end of World War II, Prague's Jewish population had been virtually wiped out. A museum devoted to the Holocaust is housed in the Pinkasova synagoga (Pinkas Synagogue).

The oldest building is the 13th-century Staronová synagoga (Old-New Synagogue), where legend has it the clay man, or Golem, created by Rabbi Löw in 1580 to serve and guard the ghetto, is still kept in the attic. The Rabbi had to return his creation to clay after it ran rampant through the streets. This and other synagogues around the cemetery survived World War II because of Hitler's perverse plan to create a museum dedicated to a vanished race. The synagogues, still places of worship, collectively (apart from the Old-New Synagogue) form the Zidovske muzeum (Jewish Museum) and can all be visited on one ticket.

The 17th-century cloisters of the Loreta shrine

KARLŮV MOST

B3–C3 Staré Město/Malá Strana
Reykavík, see page 548 Tram 12, 22 to Malá Strana square

Karlův most (Charles Bridge) is more than just a river crossing. A walk across the 1,700-foot span takes you past more than 30 sculptures, plus countless courting couples, puppeteers, musicians, souvenir sellers and tourists, and offers a breathtaking view both of the river and of the city's domes and spires. It was the work of Petr Parléř, who also created much of St. Vitus' Cathedral, and was built in 1357 to link the Old Town with the Lesser Quarter. Known until 1870 as the Stone or Prague Bridge, it has 16 sandstone arches but was originally relatively plain. The first ornament, a bronze crucifix, was added in 1657. Over the following 60 years statues were erected, evenly spaced along the parapets; they include St. John of Nepomuk (with the spangled halo), who was thrown from the bridge in 1393 after taking the side of the church in a dispute with the king.

LORETÁNSKÁ KAPLE

Off the map Loretánské náměstí 7, Hradčany
02 2437 2362 Tue.–Sun. 9–12:15 and 1–4:30
U Ševce Matouše, see page 548 Tram 22 to Pohorelec $$

As part of their campaign to win worshipers back to Catholicism after the Reformation, the church made much of the cult of the Virgin Mary, and the ornate Loretánská kaple (Loreta Chapel) is one result. It was built in 1626 around a replica of Mary's house, supposedly flown by angels from Nazareth to Loreto in Italy, and it soon became a site of pilgrimage. Don't miss the painting of St. Starosta, who grew a beard to repel her suitor and was crucified by her infuriated father.

PETŘÍN

A3 Petřín Lookout Tower: Petřínské sady. Funicular railway: Újezd, Malá Strana Lookout Tower: daily 10–6, Jun.–Oct. Funicular: daily 9:15–8:45 (every 10–15 minutes) Tram 22 to Strahov
Tower $; Funicular $

Woods and orchards cover this hill on the city's western bank, and a funicular railway, the Lanová dráha na Petřín, takes passengers up and down. The carriages were installed in 1891, the same year that the Petřínská rozhledna (Petřín Lookout Tower) was constructed at the top, both great Czech achievements. Steps (299 of them) lead to the tower's viewing platform and a panorama of the city and the mountains far beyond.

PRAŽSKÝ HRAD

A4 Hradčany 02 2437 3368 Castle precincts: daily 5 a.m.–midnight, Apr.–Oct.; 5 a.m.–11 p.m., rest of year. Castle sights: daily 9–5, Apr.–Oct.; 9–4, rest of year. Castle gardens: daily 10–6, Apr.–Oct. U Ševce Matouše, see page 548; U Zlaté hrušky, see page 548 Tram 22 to Pražský hrad $$$

Looming over the city and the river, Pražský hrad (Prague Castle) has been a symbol of Czech authority since the first fortress was built on this high, rocky site in the ninth century. The name actually refers to a complex of palaces, courtyards, churches and streets, all spread across the hill known as Hradčany. A long flight of broad steps (usually lined with souvenir sellers) climbs

Franz Kafka's diminutive house on Golden Lane

KAFKA

Franz Kafka wrote two of the 20th century's most significant novels – *The Trial* and *The Castle* – but he died practically unknown, having made his friend, Max Brod, promise to destroy all his writings. It's only because Brod broke that promise that Kafka is read throughout the world today.

His tales of helpless individuals caught in the workings of massive bureaucracy were inspired by the overgrown Habsburg administration. They came to represent the menace and detachment of authority in general, and the term "Kafkaesque" was coined to describe a seemingly ordinary but surreal and dangerous world of systems with their own life and logic.

Kafka was born in Prague, and moved with his family from house to house around Old Town Square, where his father was a haberdasher. He studied law and worked as an insurance clerk, writing his stories by night. The city appears throughout his writings. *The Castle* was inspired by Prague Castle; his story *The Great Wall of China* was based on the "Hunger Wall" on Petřín Hill, built as part of a 14th-century job creation scheme and funded by money expropriated from Jews. Kafka rented a house on Golden Lane, but his health was always poor and he died of tuberculosis at the early age of 41. His grave can be seen at the Old Jewish Cemetery. He left behind a third, unfinished novel, *Amerika*, and many short stories.

The most famous, *Metamorphosis*, related the story of Gregor Samsa, who awakens to find himself transformed into a giant insect and to his family becomes an object first of horror, then of pity and eventually of contempt. The theme of a bewildered victim of inexplicable events is characteristic of Kafka's style.

The author also recorded his wanderings around Prague, his relationship with his father and with Felice Bauer (to whom he was twice engaged), and his tortured nights of writing in his diaries, which also were posthumously published.

The Communist regime subsequently suppressed Kafka's work, but he is now, finally, acknowledged and honored in the city he described as "a little old mother with sharp claws: she won't let go."

The Astronomical Clock on the Old Town Hall

to the castle itself, a mixture of styles spanning 450 years of restoration and guarded by a series of courtyards. At the entrance to the outer courtyard, two soldiers stand at attention under grotesque and threatening statues of the Titans. The guard is changed every hour, on the hour. In the second courtyard, entered through the 17th-century Matthias Gate, are the castle's art gallery and information center. Finally, you reach the courtyard of Katedrála sv Víta (St. Vitus' Cathedral), which took 600 years to complete, only consecrated in 1929. The royal palace, to the right, is a maze of rooms centered around the 15th-century Vladislav Hall, where mounted knights would trot down the Riders' Staircase to take part in indoor jousting matches. Nearby are the Chancellery of Bohemia offices.

STAROMĚSTSKÁ RADNICE

D3 Staroměstské náměstí 1 02 2448 1111 Tue.–Sun. 9–6, Mon. 11–6, Apr.–Oct.; Tue.–Sun. 9–5, Mon. 11–5, rest of year Reykavík, see page 548 Tram 17 to Staroměstské náměstí $ Guided tours offered by Prague Information Service (tourist office)

Since a merchants' house was earmarked by the city council in 1338, the Staroměstská radnice (Old Town Hall) has gradually expanded and taken over a whole row of houses. A tower and chapel were added; features range from the original carved facade to the 19th-century house known as "At the Cock." Its main attraction is the intricate Astronomical Clock high on one wall, which gives the time, month, season, zodiac signs, course of the sun and Christian holidays. On the hour a skeleton appears and chimes the bell, followed by the Twelve Apostles and other assorted characters, all parading from their little doors above the clock face.

ŠTERNBERSKÝ PALÁC

A4 Hradčanské náměstí 15 02 2051 4634–7 or 02 2051 4599 Tue.–Sun. 10–6 Kavárna ve Šternberskén Palačí, in the palace Tram 22 to Pražský hrad $

Tucked into an alley off Hradčany Square is Šternberský palác (Sternberg Palace), a town house built for Count Sternberg in 1698. It has an impressive collection of old masters. Highlights include *The Feast of the Rosary*, by German Renaissance painter and engraver Albrecht Dürer, and *Adam and Eve*, by painter, etcher and woodcut-designer Lucas Cranach Senior.

STRAHOVSKÝ KLÁŠTER

Off the map Strahovské nádvoří 1/132, Hradčany 02 2051 6671 Daily 9–noon and 1–5 Peklo ("Hell") restaurant in the cellars Tram 22 to Pohořelec $

The baroque spires of Strahovský klášter (Strahov Monastery) dominate the hilltop west of Hradčany: the monastery's name means "to watch over," and it has guarded this sight since the 12th century. Elaborately decorated library halls store more than 130,000 books and manuscripts; the oldest, the *Strahov Gospels*, is displayed at the entrance. The upper floor of the cloisters is now a gallery of artworks returned to the monks by former Communist rulers.

EXCURSION TO KUTNÁ HORA

The 14th-century Italian Court at Kutná Hora, built on the proceeds from mining

When silver and copper ore deposits were found on this hill 40 miles south-east of Prague, a town shot up virtually overnight, taking the appropriate name of Kutná Hora, or "Mining Mountain." That was in the late 13th century, and soon a royal mint was set up, hammering out the silver coin known as *Pražské groše* in its workshops. Also constructed was a royal palace known as the Italian Court, a reference to the Florentine advisers of King Wenceslas II (1278–1305). The town flourished on its mining proceeds, and even managed to recover after being taken over by one force after another during the Hussite Wars. But by the end of the 16th century the mountain was all mined out and the town fell into decay, suffering the final blow with a disastrous fire in 1770.

The handsome Cathedral of St. Barbara was paid for by miners and dedicated to their patron saint. For its design they turned to the prestigious architect of Prague's St. Vitus' Cathedral, Petr Parléř, who rose to the occasion with distinctive tent-like spires and flying buttresses. In the side chapel, frescoes show the coin makers and the miners at work.

Sculptures line Barbarská ulice, a street leading to an impressive 15th-century house built for a profiteer who ran an illegal private mining operation. It's now the Mining Museum, and behind it is the medieval mine itself, consisting of 820 feet of tunnels; a horse-drawn winch at the entrance drew out the bags of ore. The royal mint is gone (although it is still possible to make out its outline); parts of the Italian Court – including the chapel, adorned with art nouveau frescoes – can be visited.

About 2 miles north of the town, in Sedlec, is an ossuary (storehouse for bones) originally owned by Cistercian monks. During the 19th century its 40,000 human bones were put to artistic use by František Rint, who made them into chandeliers, bells and other disconcerting items.

Contact a tourist information office for details of public transportation to Kutná Hora and Sedlec.

Agencies organizing tours from Prague to Kutná Hora include:

Martin Tour ✉ Štěpánská 61, 110 00-Praha (Prague) 1 ☎ 02 2421 2473; fax 02 2422 5437

Jomys ✉ Na Morani 5, 120 00-Praha (Prague) 2 ☎ 02 2491 6485; fax 02 2492 2452

DENMARK

"*COPENHAGEN is the best-built city of the north.*"

From *Travels into Poland, Russia, Sweden, etc.* by English historian and travel writer William Coxe

Opposite: ***The Little Mermaid*, Copenhagen's most enduring symbol**

DENMARK

Denmark was the cradle of ancient Scandinavia. Talk of the first Vikings and you talk of Danes. It was from this fragmented mosaic of peninsulas and islands between mainland Europe and the Swedish-Norwegian landmass that those consummate seamen first struck out in search of plunder and new territory. Denmark is the smallest of the four Scandinavian nations, yet the Danes have made their country one of the most advanced and progressive in the world.

Danish Archipelago

The Kingdom of Denmark is just over 200 miles long, and the Jutland peninsula (the primary landmass) is only 75 miles wide. Nowhere in Denmark is much higher than 100 feet

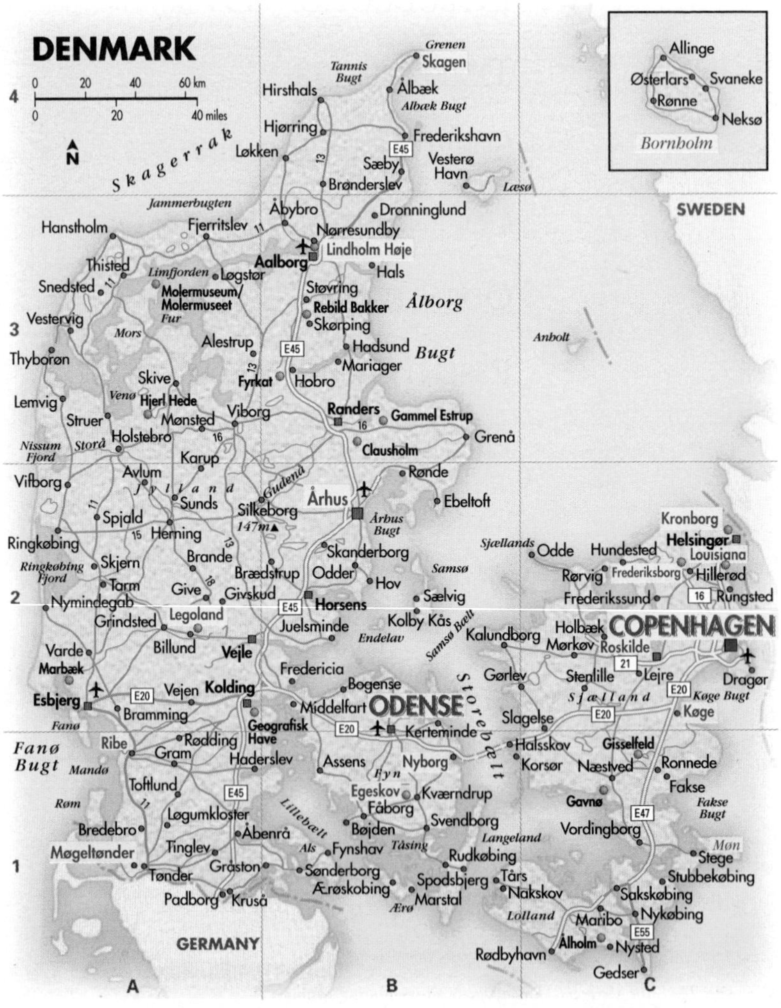

above sea level, and the country's highest point – Yding Skovhøj in central Jutland – is only 567 feet in elevation. Jutland's narrow southern border is with Germany; its west coast adjoins the North Sea.

East of Jutland, and with barely a sliver of water in between, is Denmark's second-largest island, Funen (Fyn). East of Funen is Zealand (Sjælland), the largest island, its northeastern edge a stone's throw from the Swedish coast, and home to the capital, Copenhagen (København). Zealand and Funen lie like natural fortresses across the Kattegat, the channel separating Denmark from Sweden. This strategic position across the entrance to the Baltic Sea has always placed the country at the maritime heart of northern Europe.

Attractive half-timbered houses in Rønne, on the Danish island of Bornholm

The Jutland Peninsula

Copenhagen is the magnet for visitors, but the rest of this disparate and fascinating country has much to offer. Far western Jutland has an invigorating coastal landscape of long, sandy beaches backed by broad dunes and moorland. This landscape is repeated in north Jutland beyond the dividing waters of the Limfjord and all the way to the Skagen peninsula, the birdlike beak of land that thrusts into the sea at Denmark's northern edge. In north Jutland, outside the city of Aalborg, are evocative traces of Scandinavia's Viking culture at Lindholm Høje, a remarkable Viking burial ground of nearly 700 graves, many marked by stones in the shape of long ships.

The heathland of the west coast of central Jutland gives way in the east to a fertile undulating countryside of small farms and woodland, interspersed with country towns and pretty villages. On the east coast is Århus, a sophisticated and historic university city and Denmark's second largest. Here you will find the mighty Århus Cathedral and the intriguing Den Gamle By, the Old Town and its dozens of restored, timber-framed buildings. South of Århus is a great stretch of woodland where you can enjoy peace and quiet along walking, bicycling and horseback riding trails. Southwest of Århus is the

MORE TOP DESTINATIONS IN DENMARK

• Århus B2 • Bornholm C4
• Egeskov B1 • Frederiksborg C2
• Køge C2 • Kronborg C2
• Legoland A2 • Lindholm Høje B3
• Louisiana C2 • Møgeltønder A1
• Møn C1 • Nyborg B1 • Ribe A1
• Roskilde C2 • Skagen B4

town of Billund and Denmark's famous Legoland, the country's most visited attraction outside of Copenhagen. Beyond all the plastic bricks is the farming country of south Jutland, with such fascinating towns and villages as the ancient settlement of Ribe, which has a handsome cathedral, cobbled streets and gabled houses. The little village of Møgeltønder, in the far southwest, has a superb frescoed church and charming thatched houses.

Country of Islands

Denmark is a world of islands. There are more than 400 of them scattered around the country's coasts and across the Kattegat and the Baltic Sea. About 100 islands are inhabited. Funen (Fyn) is hailed as the "Garden of Denmark" because of its rich alluvial soils, legacy of the glacial debris left by retreating ice sheets.

The capital of Funen is Odense, the birthplace of Hans Christian Andersen. Funen has a gentle rural nature overall, its lush farmland complemented by a pleasant southern coastline and by good beaches on the peaceful island of Langeland, off the southeast coast.

Funen is connected to Denmark's largest island, Zealand, by a typically Danish feat of remarkable engineering. The 11-mile-long Great Belt rail and road fixed link bridge island-hops, via the island of Sprogø, across the Great Belt (Storebælt) channel.

The ferry connection, used by visitors prior to 1998, was more romantic, but Scandinavian efficiency finally triumphed with a tunnel and bridge combination. A similar joint Danish-Swedish project, linking Copenhagen to Malmö across an artificial island built in the middle of the Øresund, was completed in July 2000, thus laying the foundations for a new cultural and economic region.

Historic Zealand

Copenhagen may dominate Zealand, but the whole island is a treasure house of Danish history. North Zealand has much to offer in terms of historic buildings: the lakeside setting of magnificent Frederiksborg Castle (Frederiksborg Slot); and Elsinore Castle (Kronborg Slot) at Helsingør, the awe-inspiring setting for Shakespeare's *Hamlet*, overlooking the Øresund and the Swedish coast.

Just west of Copenhagen is Roskilde, Denmark's medieval capital, with a splendid cathedral housing the decorated crypts of 38 Danish kings and queens. In southern Zealand is the city of Køge, whose medieval center survives; at Trelleborg, on the west coast where the new rail bridge slices across the Great Belt, are the remains of the finest Viking ring fort in Denmark. Finally, just off the south coast of Zealand are the islands of Møn, Falster and Lolland, all linked to the main islands by bridges. Of these, Møn is the most interesting because of its chalk cliffs, a startling contrast to Denmark's almost uniform flatness.

Exploring Denmark

Denmark is one of the most accessible European countries. Its compact size and the smooth transition from island to island that modern engineering has accomplished makes exploring various regions by car an easy option once you are clear of Copenhagen's urban center.

This compactness makes traveling by public transportation almost as convenient. Fast, comfortable trains can whisk you from Zealand to Funen, and then on to Jutland, in a few hours. The efficient and extensive rail network offers stiff competition to long-distance bus services in Denmark, although buses are less expensive than trains.

Legoland, where millions of tiny Lego bricks have been made into an amazing model world

Denmark's climate is typical of a maritime environment, and the low elevation means there are no great extremes of temperature. Summers are pleasantly mild, but there can be wet spells; in winter snow is likely at times, but much less so than in the other Scandinavian countries.

Denmark is different in other ways as well, yet in matters of food and drink it remains engagingly – and tastily – Scandinavian. Danes relish the same hearty sandwich feast, here called the *smørrebrød*, that you find in Norway and Sweden, complete with its garnished mixes of delicious meat and seafood. Beer is a Danish specialty, and the famous Danish breweries of Carlsberg and Tuborg produce some of the most popular brews in the world.

You will find that Danes are generally helpful and friendly. In rural areas and in provincial cities such as Odense, people are unfailingly so, but in Copenhagen there may be a sharper edge to people's attitudes. At times you may detect an apparent reserve on the part of Danish people. It is not a negative sentiment; the Danes are supremely accomplished, and beneath the reserve is a fierce national pride in their enduring country.

TIMELINE

4000 BC	Neolithic settlers begin developing a farming economy.
500 BC to AD 500	Iron Age people set up trading centers in Jutland and Funen.
AD 793	Danish Vikings raid England's east coast, plundering the monastery of Lindisfarne, and penetrate deep into mainland Europe along the northern rivers.
circa 925	Gorm the Old becomes first king of a united Denmark.
1167	Founding of Copenhagen by Absalon, Bishop of Roskilde.
1588	Christian IV becomes king of Denmark and promotes the construction of great Renaissance buildings, particularly in the city of Copenhagen.
1611–60	Periodic wars with Sweden.
1901	First democratically elected government takes power.
1914–18	Denmark is neutral during World War I.
1940	Denmark is invaded by the German army in spite of its declared neutrality; the Danish Resistance carries out a vigorous campaign against Germany.
1945	Denmark is liberated and begins a program of postwar reconstruction.
1949	Denmark joins NATO.
1993	Danish people vote to join the European Union.
1996	Copenhagen designated as a European City of Culture.
1998	Opening of the fixed link rail and road bridge across the Storebælt (Great Belt).
2000	Inauguration of the rail and road fixed link bridge across the Øresund.

A TALENTED ROYAL LADY

Denmark's current queen, Margrethe II, was born in 1940. She was the eldest daughter of King Frederik IX, who had no sons. After a favorable 1953 referendum, the Danish constitution, which allowed only for a male heir to the throne, was amended to enable female succession. Margrethe became queen at the age of 32, after Frederik's death in 1972. She is Denmark's first female monarch since the 15th century. Queen Margrethe qualified as an archeologist after studying at Copenhagen, Århus, Cambridge and Paris. She is a talented artist and illustrator, illustrating an edition of J. R. R. Tolkien's fantasy *Lord of the Rings* and designing stamps for the Danish postal service. The queen has also designed theatrical costumes and stage settings for the Danish Royal Theatre. An accomplished linguist, Queen Margrethe has translated the work of the French novelist Simone de Beauvoir, a task in which she worked with her husband, French-born Prince Henrik.

SURVIVAL GUIDE

- If you drive or cycle through Denmark, ask the tourist office for details about "The Marguerite Route," which is a series of linked routes (2,100 miles long) along quieter roads through the most scenic parts of the country. Signs display a daisy (marguerite) motif on a brown background. A free map indicates the route.
- If you are visiting Denmark on June 23, Midsummer Night *(Sankt Hans)* is a time of celebration, with bonfires throughout the country.
- In Denmark *morgenmad* is the word for breakfast, while *frokost* is lunch. *Smørrebrød,* the tasty Scandinavian open-faced sandwich, remains a lunchtime favorite; but try *frikadeller,* delicious fried meat or fish patties with salad and potatoes; or dip into the heftier *koldt bord*, a buffet-style selection. For main meals, enjoy *kogt torsk,* poached cod in mustard sauce, or old-fashioned *Hvid labskovs*, Danish stew.
- Delicious Danish pastries are called *wienerbrød* and come in a variety of shapes and tasty flavors. In every town and large village you will find a bakery selling pastries.
- Amber is a Danish specialty. The Amber Specialist shop on Strøget is the place to look in Copenhagen, but you will find distinctive amber jewelry in stores throughout the country. If you're shopping for a colorful Scandinavian sweater go to Sweater Market, one of the biggest outlets, in Copenhagen's Frederiksberggade.
- Denmark, like Sweden, is noted for its distinctive furnishing designs. The style known as "Danish Modern" is a classic merging of the functional with the aesthetic. Visit Illums Bolighus on Amagertorv in Copenhagen for some of the finest examples.
- Unlike the northern Scandinavian countries, Denmark has a more relaxed approach to the sale of liquor. You can buy wines, spirits and beers in grocery stores, and you may find that prices are lower than in Norway, Sweden or Finland.
- Soft drinks in ring-pull cans are currently banned because of their damaging potential to the environment and wildlife when discarded. Bottled drinks are therefore the norm and carry a hefty deposit, which will be refunded when empty bottles are returned to the place of purchase.
- Traditionally formal, Danes have become more relaxed about what to wear when eating out. Smart, casual clothes, especially during the summer months, are fine for dining at most restaurants.

Standing guard at the Amalienborg Palace

Copenhagen

COPENHAGEN

Copenhagen (København) is where the European experience becomes Scandinavian. This is a magnificent city, far more a "Wonderful Copenhagen" than even the Danny Kaye song implies. It is a city of towers and steeples that are elegant and sculptural, as well as monumental. It is a city that draws you in along

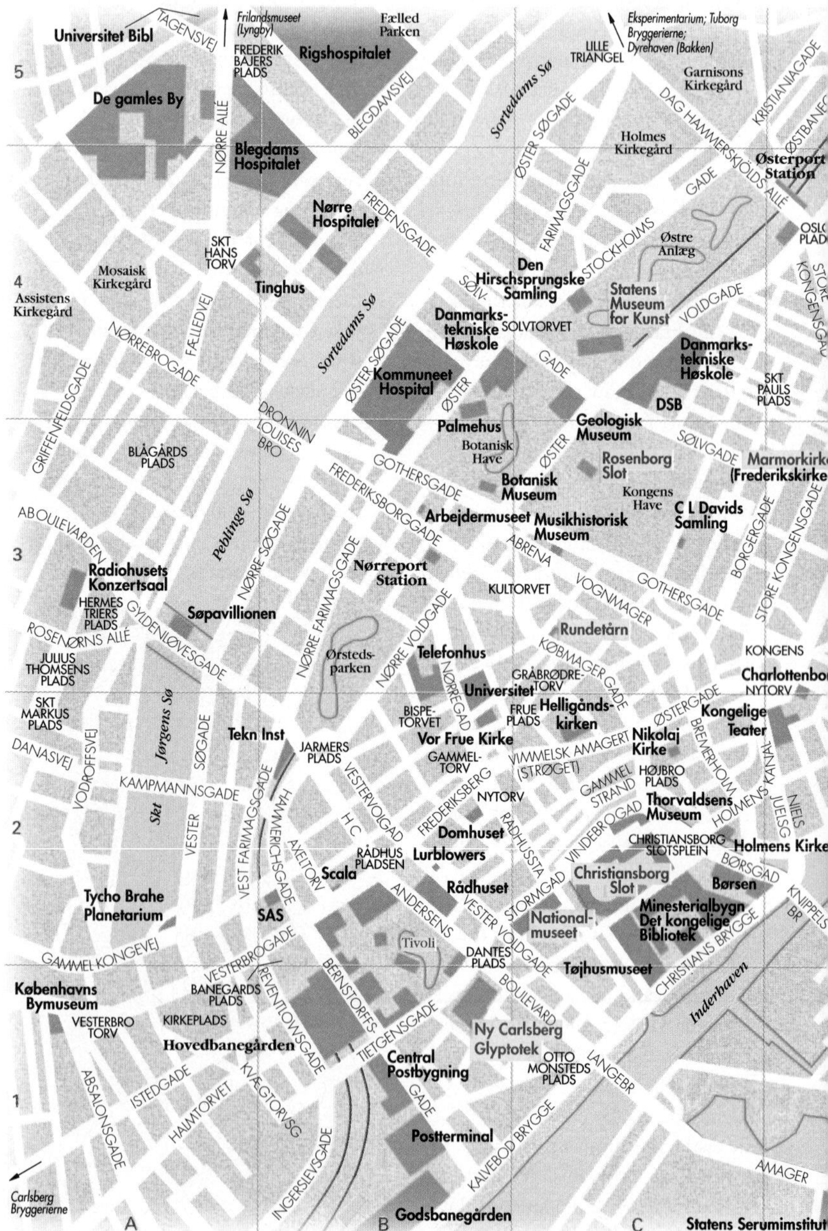

pedestrian-only streets that lead in and out of delightful squares. It is a city with museums and attractions, restaurants, cafés and entertainment that place it among the finest of European capitals.

Copenhagen originated, like so many other Scandinavian towns and cities, as a small fishing village, its occupants taking advantage of the sheltered waters around Slotsholmen Island, the island that is now home to the Danish National Parliament (Folketing), and the Christiansborg Palace (Christiansborg Slot). By the 12th century Slotsholmen had been fortified in keeping with the settlement's growing commercial status, a status signified by its name, Kømandshavn, the "port of the merchants," later amended to København. By the middle of the 15th century, Copenhagen was the recognized capital of Denmark.

The city's status was enhanced by the construction of many fine buildings during the reign of Christian IV of Denmark in the 17th century, and by the 19th century Copenhagen had emerged as a major European capital. Development continued during the 20th century, and at the start of the new millennium Copenhagen stood as a mature and hugely successful city.

First Impressions

The initial impression visitors have of Copenhagen is of a city overpowered by traffic. To reach the central City Hall Square (Rådhuspladsen) from Copenhagen's central railroad station (Hovedbanegården), visitors pass Tivoli and then negotiate busy downtown streets. Hans Christian Andersens Boulevard, a broad and howling stream of traffic, is as far removed from Andersen's fairy-tale world as can be imagined. Keep your eyes open for cyclists as well as cars. The broad expanse of City Hall Square, a relaxed, traffic-free environment, leads to a refreshing world of lively streets, colorful squares and hidden corners, where pedestrians are the priority.

There is a lot to see in Copenhagen. Some attractions, such as Rosenborg Castle and the National Museum for Fine Arts, are some distance from City Hall Square. Even the famous statue of *The Little Mermaid* is a long walk along the waterfront from the central parts of the city. Getting around is easy, however, if you take advantage of the various guided walking tours that are available. They include the service of authorized guides who attend to just about all your needs. Other sightseeing tours go by bus and by harbor or canal boats. The city's bus service is extremely efficient and comprehensive. Because of the city center's pedestrian-only status, however, exploring on your own here is a pleasure.

Strøget and Beyond

Start at City Hall Square. Look back across the rushing traffic and up at the Unibank building, where you will see a unique bronze weathervane featuring a girl who appears on her bicycle when the weather is fine, and with an umbrella when it rains.

The sequence of streets known collectively as Strøget begins at City Hall Square, at the narrow Frederiksberggade. Amid the stores and restaurants fascinating side streets lead to antique and specialty outlets; vistas suddenly reveal the city's impressively grand architecture and fashionable people.

City on the Water's Edge

At the far end of Strøget, cross the big, bustling square of New Royal Market (Kongens Nytorv) to reach New Harbor (Nyhavn), the old harbor inlet, now an area of fashionable restaurants. Visit Amalienborg Square and Amalienborg Palace, then head east to waterside Larsens Plads; from this square a pleasant walk north takes you to *The Little Mermaid*.

Nearby is the Museum of the Danish Resistance (Frihedsmuseet), an inspiring celebration of resistance against the Nazis. These attractions all spotlight Copenhagen's chief lure for visitors: its astonishing variety.

ESSENTIAL INFORMATION

TOURIST INFORMATION

Wonderful Copenhagen Tourist Office
• Bernstorffsgade 1 ☎ 70 22 24 42; fax 33 93 49 69; www.visitcopenhagen.dk

USE IT (Youth Information Center)
• Råhusstræde 13 ☎ 33 73 06 20; fax 33 73 06 49 www.useit.dk

URBAN TRANSPORTATION

Copenhagen's main railroad station is Hovedbanegården, on Bernstorffsgade. The station has modern facilities, including many stores, and is only a few minutes from the city center. Copenhagen has a very good network of bus routes. City buses leave from Rådhuspladsen. The first stage of a metro (subway) linking eastern and western parts of the city is scheduled to open in October 2002. For transport information call ☎ 36 45 45 45. Taxis have fixed rates. For service, call ☎ 35 35 35 35 or 32 51 51 51.

AIRPORT INFORMATION

Copenhagen Airport is at Kastrup, 6 miles south of the city center on the island of Amager. An Airport Express train runs from Hovedbanegården every 20 minutes, daily 5:30 a.m.– 11:30 p.m (journey time 12 minutes). Airport buses leave every 15 minutes from outside Hovedbanegården, on Bernstorffsgade. For airport information, call ☎ 32 47 47 47.

CLIMATE – Average highs and lows for the month

JAN.	FEB.	MAR.	APR.	MAY	JUN.	JUL.	AUG.	SEP.	OCT.	NOV.	DEC.
3°C	3°C	5°C	10°C	15°C	19°C	20°C	20°C	16°C	11°C	7°C	4°C
37°F	37°F	41°F	50°F	59°F	66°F	68°F	68°F	61°F	52°F	45°F	39°F
-2°C	-2°C	0°C	2°C	7°C	11°C	13°C	12°C	10°C	7°C	3°C	0°C
28°F	28°F	32°F	36°F	45°F	52°F	55°F	54°F	50°F	45°F	37°F	32°F

City Sights

Key to symbols

map coordinates refer to the Copenhagen map on pages 140–141; sights below are highlighted in yellow on the map.
address or location telephone number
opening times nearest train station: S (local), RE (regional) nearest bus route restaurant or café on site or nearby admission charge: $$$ more than DKr25, $$ DKr12–DKr25, $ less than DKr12
other relevant information

Amalienborg Plads

D3 Amalienborg Plads Palace: 33 12 21 86 Palace: daily 10–4, May–Oct.; Tue.–Sun. 11–4, rest of year S/RE Østerport 1, 6, 9, 10, 29, 650S Palace $$$

The royal heart of Copenhagen is the octagonal Amalienborg Plads (Amalienborg Square), with a statue of Frederick V at its center, rococo palaces on four sides, and broad avenues leading off the other four. The Danish royal family spends most of autumn and winter in the palaces, their very private presence gives the square a rather detached, lifeless atmosphere, except during the colorful changing of the guard, daily at noon when the Queen is in residence.

On the northwest corner of the square is Christian VIII's Palace (or Amalienborg Palace), containing a charming collection of royal memorabilia and a sequence of reconstructed rooms that illustrate the life of the royal Glücksburg family from the mid-19th to mid-20th centuries.

Christiansborg Slot

Christiansborg Slot C2 Prins Jørgens Gård 1 33 92 64 92 S/RE København H 1, 2, 5, 6, 8, 9, 10, 28, 29, 31 37, 550S, 650S 901, 90
Slotsholmen ruins 33 92 64 92 Daily 9:30–3:30, May–Sep.; Tue., Thu. and Sat.–Sun. 9:30–3:30, rest of year $$
De Kongelige Repræsentationslokaler 33 92 64 92 Guided tours daily at 11, 1 and 3, May–Sep.; Tue., Thu. and Sat.–Sun. at 11 and 3, rest of year $$$
Kongelige Stalde og Kareter 33 40 10 10 Fri.–Sun. 2–4, May–Sep.; Sat.–Sun. 2–4, rest of year $$
Teatermuseet 33 11 51 76 Sat.–Sun. noon–4, Wed. 2–4 $$
Tøjhusmuseet 33 11 60 37 Tue.–Sun. noon–4 $$$
Christiansborg Slotskirke 33 92 64 91 Daily noon–4, Easter and Jul. 1 to mid-Oct.; Sun. noon–4, rest of year Free

The monumental complex that makes up Christiansborg Slot (Christiansborg Palace) dominates the island of Slotsholmen. It presents a rather stern face to the city approaching across the encircling canal from Strøget and Højbro Plads (Højbro Square). A visit here may take you all day. The vast west wing houses the Danish Parliament, the Supreme Court and the Foreign Office, built between 1907 and 1916 to replace a more stylish building that burned down in 1884. Also here is the De Kongelige Repræsentationslokaler (Royal Reception Chambers), with lavishly decorated rooms, and grand Renaissance Hall.

Below the palace are the preserved ruins of Absalon's Fortress, the original Slotsholmen castle dating from 1167; and its successor, Copenhagen Castle. There are a number of other museums located around the central royal riding grounds, including the Kongelige Stalde og Kareter (Royal Stables and Museum of Royal Coaches), the Teatermuseet (Theater Museum) and the Tøjhusmuseet (Royal Arsenal Museum).

The Christiansborg Slotskirke (Christiansborg Palace Church), dating from 1826 but devastated by fire in 1992, reopened in 1997. It is used on royal and state occasions and may also be visited.

Den Lille Havfrue

Most visitors don't leave Copenhagen without seeing *The Little Mermaid* (*Den Lille Havfrue*), the most popular expression of Hans Christian Andersen's fairy-tale world. Some may find the experience disappointing. Designed in 1913, she languishes in rather stark isolation at the northern end of the city's waterfront. Sadly, vandals have damaged *The Little Mermaid* by sawing off her arm and her head on separate occasions. The original molds survive, however, making the Mermaid – in one sense – forever renewable.

The great marble dome of Marmorkirken

MARMORKIRKEN

D3 Frederiksgade 4 33 15 01 44 Mon.–Thu. 10–5 (also Wed. 5–6), Fri.–Sun. noon–5 1, 6, 9, 29 Free

Frederikskirken (Frederick's Church), known universally as Marmorkirken (Marble Church), seems out of place in a Copenhagen of slender, convoluted steeples and towers. The church was begun in 1749 as a final flourish to the nearby Amalienborg Palace, but was not completed until 1894. Modeled on St. Peter's in Rome, its dome measures 100 feet in diameter.

The nave is circular and is surrounded by a circular walkway, above which there is a whispering gallery with superb acoustics. Try whispering, and see how far the sound carries. The paneled frescoes on the inside of the dome are glowingly painted and gilded.

NATIONALMUSEET

C2 Ny Vestergade 10 33 13 44 11 Tue.–Sun. 10–5 Museum café 1, 2, 5, 6, 8, 10, 28, 29, 30, 32, 33, 550S, 650S $$$ (free on Wed.)

Copenhagen's Nationalmuseet (National Museum) is one of the finest of its kind in Europe. There is a lot to see and the experience can be tiring if you try to take in everything during one visit; use the floor plan to get your bearings. The museum has outstanding exhibits on Danish history, with such superb Bronze Age artifacts as burial remains in oak coffins, a golden sun chariot and the silver Gundestrip cauldron. Among Iron Age finds are the magnificent North Slesvig Golden Horns. Other artifacts include a collection of *lur,* the wonderful horn instruments that were used for ceremony and communication. Other major collections cover the Middle Ages and the Renaissance, Egyptian and classical antiquities, and human cultures. There is also a children's museum. The museum has a film theater.

NY CARLSBERG GLYPTOTEK

B1 Dantes Plads 7 33 41 81 41 Tue.–Sun. 10–4 Museum café 1, 2, 5, 6, 8, 10, 28, 29, 30, 32, 33, 550S, 650S $$$ (free on Wed. and Sun.)

A splendid winter garden with huge palm trees is the unexpected focal point of the Glyptotek, one of the country's finest art museums. Carl Jacobson, the owner of the Carlsberg breweries who founded the museum, was mostly interested in ancient art from the Mediterranean, and Danish and French art from the 19th-century onwards. Highlights of a visit to the Glyptotek are the Etruscan collection, one of the largest outside Italy, and French sculpture (including a superb collection of works by Rodin) and painting. The French collection, housed in a new, specially designed structure, includes paintings by the main Impressionists and 35 works by Paul Gauguin.

ROSENBORG SLOT

C3 Øster Voldgade 4a 33 15 32 86 Daily 10–5, Jul.–Sep.; daily 10–4, May–Jun.; daily 11–3, in Oct.; Tue.–Sun. 11–2, Jan.–Apr. and Nov. 1–Dec. 15. Treasury: Same opening hours as the palace Café/restaurant 5, 10, 14, 16, 31, 42, 43, 184, 185, 350S $$$

The early 17th-century Rosenborg Slot (Rosenborg Castle) is an outstanding example of Renaissance architecture and style; it stands at the edge of the lovely Kongens Have, the King's Gardens. The lavishly decorated rooms reflect the regal styles of Danish monarchs from Christian IV to Frederick IV. There are superb marbled ceilings, late 17th-century Dutch tapestries, gilded mirrors, silver lions that seem poised to leap, gold and enamelware, and beautiful ceiling paintings. The Royal Treasury is in the castle basement; here the Danish crown jewels and other royal treasures glow in the delicate light.

RUNDETÅRN

C3 Købmagergade 52a 33 73 03 73 Tower: Mon.–Sat. 10–8, Sun. noon–8, Jun.–Aug.; Mon.–Sat. 10–5, Sun. noon–5, rest of year. Observatory: Tue.–Wed. 7–10 p.m., Oct.–Mar. S/RE Nørreport 5, 14, 16, 31, 42, 43, 73E, 173E, 184, 185, 350S $$

The Rundetårn (Round Tower) is located on Købmagergade, one of the city's liveliest streets. A visit is a must for anyone who feels fit enough to trek up the covered and cobbled ramp that winds its way for 685 feet and through seven and a half turns to the top of the 115-foot landmark. Peter the Great of Russia is said to have ridden his horse up the ramp while the Czarina followed in a horse-drawn carriage. Today, everybody walks; keep to the outside for the easiest angle. From the top there are marvelous views of Copenhagen's red-tiled roofs and far-flung outskirts. The Round Tower dates from 1642 and was built by Christian IV as an observatory. It still functions as such and, by appointment in winter, the public has access to the astronomical telescope.

STATENS MUSEUM FOR KUNST

C4 Sølvgade 48–50 33 74 84 94 Tue.–Sun. 10–5 (also Wed. 5–8) Museum café 10, 14, 40, 42, 43, 72E, 150S, 184, 185 $$$ (free on Wed.) Audio guide available

Following the opening of a new extension in 1998, a huge number of works are now on display at the Statens Museum for Kunst (National Museum for Fine Arts). International and Danish art from the 14th century to 1900, shown in the old building, includes superb 17th-century Dutch paintings by Pieter Bruegel, Rembrandt, Jacob Jordaens and Jacob van Ruisdael; 19th-century Danish painting is represented by Golden-Age artists such as Christoffer Eckersberg and Christen Købke, and by the Skagen painters, Theodor Philipsen and the Funen Painters. Twentieth century art,

Fanciful facade at the ever-popular Tivoli

displayed in the new building, includes major works by Henri Matisse (*Odalisque*), Max Ernst, the Cobra Group (*Springtime* by Asger Jorn), Georges Braque and Pablo Picasso, and other contemporary works.

TIVOLI

B2 Vesterbrogade 3 33 15 10 01 Daily 11 a.m.–midnight (also Fri.–Sat. until 1 a.m.), mid-Jun. to mid-Aug.; 11–11 (also Wed.–Thu. until midnight and Fri.–Sat. until 1 a.m.), Easter to mid-Jun. and late Aug. to late Sep.; 11–9 (also Fri.–Sat. until 10 p.m.), late Nov. to Dec. 23 37 restaurants 1, 2, 6, 8, 10, 11, 12, 13, 14, 16, 28, 29, 30, 34, 40, 67, 68, 69, 150S, 250S, 550S, 650S $$$

Copenhagen's famous Tivoli is unmissable, except during the winter months when the gardens are closed. (They are open during the Christmas vacation season, however.) Located at the busy heart of the city, the 21-acre park is given over to conspicuous entertainment, a combination of flower gardens, lakes, theater, concert hall, carnival rides, amusements, food and drink, and above all people-watching. Children will adore it all. There is an entrance fee and separate charges for carnival rides and various indoor attractions. Tivoli is never dull; it is lit brilliantly at night, and there are fireworks shows on Wednesday, Friday and Saturday. You will enjoy it as much as the 5 million other annual visitors do.

ODENSE

Odense seems to radiate the persuasive charm of a story by its most famous son, Hans Christian Andersen. Even factory chimneys on the outskirts of the city are gaily painted and are thus less stark against the sky, and the surviving medieval buildings of the Old Town are enchanting. Above all, the city makes a refreshing change from the urban bustle of Copenhagen. Odense's wealth of museums and attractions are worthy of a city several times its size.

An important regional capital and university town, Odense retains its provincial charm, and is rightly celebrated as the birthplace of Hans Christian Andersen and Denmark's great composer Carl Nielsen.

The Modern City

You will relax as soon as you arrive at Odense's modern railroad station, on Østre Stationsvej. Street life is busy here and the traffic is just as heavy as in any city, but directly across the road is Kongens Have, the old Royal Park. The park provides a peaceful introduction to Odense and takes you pleasantly along tree-shaded paths past the Odense Theater and the Funen Art Museum into the heart of the city. The center of Odense is at Flakhaven, a pedestrian-only area in front of the redbrick Town Hall, the interior of which can be viewed on a guided tour. The friendly and helpful Odense Turist Bureau is to the left of the Town Hall.

All buses leave from central stops near the Town Hall, but you will have little need of public transportation in

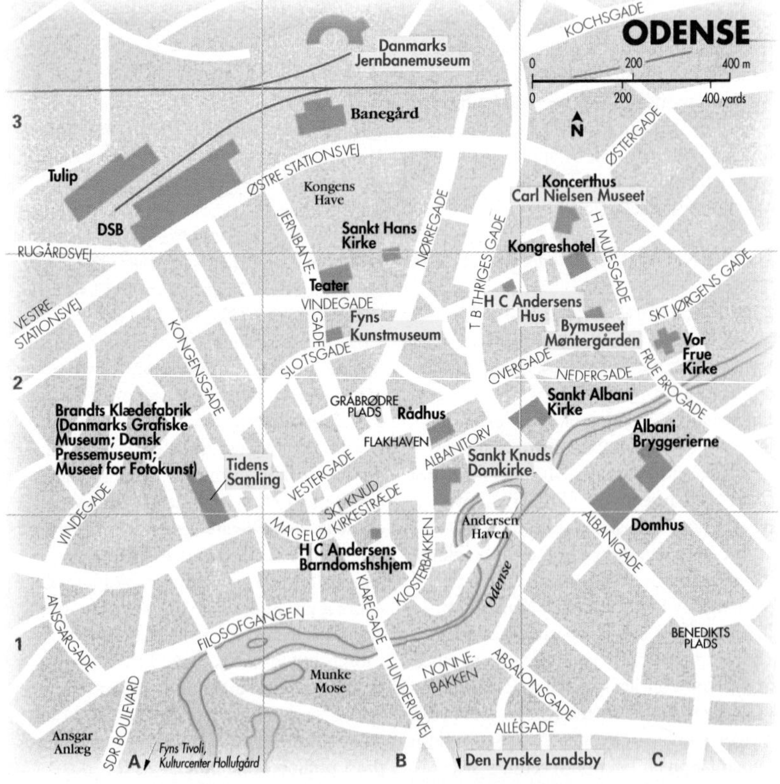

Odense unless you travel outside the city. Most attractions are a short walk from the center, and it is very easy to find your way around.

From Flakhaven turn left along the street Vestergade, which takes you into the pleasant, pedestrian-only heart of modern Odense. Here you will find a variety of stores, including top fashion boutiques. Visit Inspiration Zinck at Nos. 82–84 Vestergade for the best in Danish design and handicraft. Step down the adjoining street of Jernbanegade to Målet's bar and restaurant for a *smørrebrød*, Denmark's popular and delicious lunchtime snack, an open slice of rye bread heaped with sliced meat or fish and loaded with different garnishes.

The Old Town

Going east from the Town Hall takes you across the traffic-laden street Thomas B. Thriges Gade and into Odense's Old Town. Here in Hans Jensens Stræde is the Hans Christian Andersen House, amid a little complex of cobbled streets and doll-like houses that was once the poor quarter of the city. Nearby is the Carl Nielsen Museum, which adjoins the Odense Concert Hall. Charming as this area is, the best of Old Odense is a couple of streets away, where the medieval thoroughfares of Overgade and Nedergade retain many of their enchanting old buildings.

Pause at the entrance to Nedergade and look down the little side street leading down to the river. This is Paaskestræde, location of the Old Poor House, with its rippled red-tile roof and scalloped cornice above the first floor. Hans Christian Andersen went to school here, and the wording on the wall is his touching comment: "Here I went with my wooden shoes to the poor school."

The combination of old and new is what makes Odense such a delight. The city's human scale, its sense of healthy provincialism and its vigorous regional culture are all enhanced by the international cachet of Hans Christian Andersen and Carl Nielsen. What you will find refreshing is that the locals have retained a friendly, unaffected nature in the face of all this.

ESSENTIAL INFORMATION

TOURIST INFORMATION
Odense Turist Bureau (Odense Tourist Bureau)
• Rådhuset, Jernbanegade ☎ 66 12 75 20; fax 66 12 75 86; www.odenseturist.dk

URBAN TRANSPORTATION
Odense's railroad station (✉ Østre Stationsvej 27 ☎ 70 13 14 15) has modern facilities and is about a 10-minute walk from the city center. Odense's main attractions are within a small area of the city center, but if you need bus information, call ☎ 66 13 13 72, ext. 2929. For taxi service, call Odense Taxa ☎ 66 15 44 15 or Odense Mini Taxi ☎ 66 12 27 12.

AIRPORT INFORMATION
Odense Airport is located 7 miles west of the city. Mærsk Air operates connecting flights from Billund Airport. Airport buses arrive and depart from the Hans Christian Andersen Hotel (see page 549). For airport information, call ☎ 65 95 50 72; see page 142 for information on Copenhagen Airport.

CLIMATE – average highs and lows for the month

JAN.	FEB.	MAR.	APR.	MAY	JUN.	JUL.	AUG.	SEP.	OCT.	NOV.	DEC.
3°C	3°C	5°C	10°C	15°C	19°C	20°C	20°C	17°C	12°C	7°C	4°C
37°F	37°F	41°F	50°F	59°F	66°F	68°F	68°F	63°F	54°F	45°F	39°F
-2°C	-2°C	0°C	3°C	7°C	10°C	13°C	13°C	10°C	7°C	3°C	0°C
28°F	28°F	32°F	37°F	45°F	50°F	55°F	55°F	50°F	45°F	37°F	32°F

Windmill at the imaginative open-air museum of Funen Village, near Odense

City Sights

Key to symbols

map coordinates refer to the Odense map on page 146; sights below are highlighted in yellow on the map.

address or location telephone number opening times nearest bus route restaurant or café on site or nearby admission charge: $$$ more than DKr25, $$DKr12–DKr25, $ less than DKr12

other relevant information

Bymuseet Møntergården

C2 Overgade 48 66 14 88 14
Tue.–Sun. 10–4 $$

Housed in a marvelous old building – with redbrick, red-timber framing and a red-tiled roof – the Bymuseet Møntergården (City Museum Møntergården) tells the story of Odense's past through a number of clever and interesting exhibits. Behind the main building is a lovely yard with a huge tree in the center. On one side of the yard is a series of preserved domestic interiors from the 17th and 18th centuries and up to the 1950s. In keeping with Odense's charm, the museum has a wonderful air of quiet authenticity often absent in big-city institutions.

Carl Nielsen Museet

C3 Claus Bergs Gade 11 66 14 88 14
Tue.–Sun. noon–4, Jun.–Aug.; Thu.–Sun. noon–4, rest of year $$

Already blessed with Hans Christian Andersen, Odense also boasts Denmark's most famous composer, Carl August Nielsen, as another native son. Nielsen was born in 1865 at nearby Nørre Lyndelse and began his musical career as a trumpeter in a local band. Nielsen's most famous works are his six symphonies, including *Saul and David* and choral works such as *Spring of Funen*. The Carl Nielsen Museet is a restful place housed in an extension of the Odense Koncerthus. It tells the story of the composer's life through displays of artifacts. Pause at key points, don earphones and drift away listening to Nielsen's music. His wife, Anne Marie Broderson, was an accomplished sculptress, and there are displays of her work.

Danmarks Jernbanemuseum

B3 Dannebrogsgade 24 66 13 66 30 Daily 10–4 Museum café $$$

Danmarks Jernbanemuseum (Denmark's Railway Museum) is ideally located next to Odense railroad station. It is the biggest museum of its kind in Scandinavia and is a delight for everyone, not just locomotive enthusiasts. It features a reconstructed early 19th-century station and locomotives, including luxurious royal carriages. Add to this a model train section, trips on a mini train and a section on ferries and you might not get out of the station.

Den Fynske Landsby

Off the map Sejerskovvej 20 66 14 88 14 Daily 9:30–7, mid-Jun. to mid-Aug.; Tue.–Sun. 10–5, Apr. 1 to mid-Jun. and mid-Aug. to Oct. 31; Sun. and holidays 11–3, rest of year Museum café $$$

The open-air museum of Den Fynske Landsby (Funen Village) gives colorful insight into rural life on the island of Funen during the 18th and 19th centuries. The thatched, timber-framed buildings are arranged like a farming village complete with duck pond, smithy, water mill and windmill. Farming is carried on during the summer months, and harvesting, beer brewing and craftwork are conducted as part of village life. There are particularly imaginative tableaux detailing the lives of a poor and a well-off 19th-century villager.

Fyns Kunstmuseum

B2 Jernbanegade 13 66 14 88 14 Tue.–Sun. 10–4 $$$

The Fyns Kunstmuseum (Art Museum of Funen) is located in an elegant, classical building and contains a superb collection. The museum has a distinctive atmosphere of serenity that is missing from some major galleries. Most of the works are by Danish artists. Highlights include Jens Juel's vivid *The Open-Mouthed One* and P. S. Krøyer's *Italian Field Workers*, with its interesting preponderance of left-handed men – a little art puzzle. H. A. Brendekild's big painting *Finished*, with its prostrate worker in a vast, flat field, portrays the hard life of peasant workers in old Funen. By contrast, a real charmer is Gustava Emilie Grüner's *Group Portrait of the Family Leunbach*, with its cheerful, inviting faces. The museum also has some fine sculptures and a small collection of contemporary art.

Hans Christian Andersens Hus

Hans Christian Andersens Hus B2 Hans Jensens Stræde 37–45 66 14 88 14 Daily 9–7, mid-Jun. to Aug. 31; Tue.–Sun. 10–4, rest of year Den Grimme Ælling, see page 549 $$$

Fyrtøjet-et Kulturhus for Børn Hans Jensens Stræde 21 66 14 44 11 Tue.–Sat. 2–4 (also 11–2, late Feb., Easter and summer holidays) Den Grimme Ælling, see page 549 $$$

Odense can hardly do without its most famous son, but it says everything about the city's restrained style that it has not let the Andersen story overpower good taste. Hans Christian Andersens Hus (Hans Christian Andersen House) is located at the heart of a charming complex of old single-story houses, once the "poor quarter" of Odense, and somewhat like a fairy tale in its own way. The museum tells a thorough tale of Andersen's extraordinary life and the intensity of character that shaped his work. Attached to the museum is the utterly delightful Fyrtøjet-et Kulturhus for Børn (The Tinderbox – a Cultural Center for Children), where children can plunge straight into Andersen's enchanting world through play and adventure while adults marvel at the enduring magic of this great storyteller.

Sankt Knuds Domkirke

B2 Flakhaven 66 12 03 92 Mon.–Sat. 9–5, Sun. and holidays noon–3, Apr.–Oct.; Mon.–Sat. 10–4, Sun. and holidays noon–3, rest of year Free

The elegant Gothic style of Sankt Knuds Domkirke (St. Canute's Cathedral), Funen's cathedral, reflects the importance of early medieval Odense and the homage paid to King Knud (Canute), who – with his brother Benedikt (Benedict) – was slaughtered by Jutland farmers in a rather drastic protest against royal taxes. The church has some powerful artifacts, not the least its splendid rococo pulpit and its altarpiece, a dazzling wood triptych with exquisite carvings and gold leaf that is one of the finest pieces of religious art in northern Europe. Down the stairs, in the chilly crypt are two reliquaries containing the reputed skeletons of Knud and Benedikt, macabre but endearing in their gaunt way.

Tranquil scene at St. Canute's Cathedral

Tidens Samling

A2 Brandts Passage 29 65 91 19 42 Daily 10–5 Museum café $$$

For a museum with a difference, Tidens Samling (Time Collection) is hard to beat. It is located in a large loft area, where half the space is used for exhibitions that always have an imaginative, cultural or fashion theme. The second half houses the permanent Time Collection – a series of set-piece interiors from various periods between 1900 and 1970, each one crammed with authentic artifacts and furnishings.

The result is delightful – a unique look at changing domestic style. One of the many charming aspects of the Time Collection is that you can step into the displays, relax in the chairs, poke through the drawers, or do a bit of sock-mending. There is even a period-style coffee bar. Occasional fashion shows are done with absolute flair.

The Martyred King

The violent death of the 11th-century Danish King Knud (Canute), a descendant of Canute, one-time king of England, did Odense a favor. The king and his brother, Benedikt, were slaughtered in Odense's old Church of St. Alban's on July 10, 1086, by Jutland peasant farmers angered by excessive taxes the king levied to finance war with England. Fourteen years later Pope Paschalis II canonized the king as St. Knud the Holy. In an ironic twist, Benedictine monks from England settled in Odense and successfully promoted the town as a place of pilgrimage to the murdered ruler. The skeletons of Knud and Benedikt can still be seen in Sankt Knuds Domkirke.

Statue of the writer, on the boulevard that bears his name

The house where Andersen spent his formative years – now a museum

HANS CHRISTIAN ANDERSEN

Odense's most famous son left his native city at an early age. Yet Odense is still associated with Hans Christian Andersen. From humble beginnings – his mother was a washerwoman, his father a shoemaker – Andersen's astonishingly fertile imagination and creativity led him on extensive travels throughout Europe and established him as Denmark's major literary figure. He was born in 1805 in Odense, but it is not certain in which location. By the age of seven Andersen was inspired after visiting the theater in Odense; by 14 he was in Copenhagen, where he tried unsuccessfully to join the Royal Theater Company.

Andersen was a man of complex sensitivities whose relationships were profound and often difficult, although he was never short of friends and benefactors. He was essentially a poet and dramatist, and his early works reflect this. He had the urge to travel, typical of a lonely and introverted artist, and his first, self-published book was about a journey he made on foot through Denmark. In 1835 he published *Fairy Tales, Told for Children*. Plays, novels and travel accounts followed, along with a continuing output of the fairy tales that were to make his name.

Andersen's fairy tales were far more profound than mere fantasy, however charming. He was a powerful moralist, an intensely humane man who understood the human condition and injected into his stories remarkable life lessons. Famous tales such as *The Emperor's New Clothes, The Little Mermaid, The Ugly Duckling, The Tinder Box* and *The Nightingale* have entered the consciousness of generations of readers worldwide, for their literary elegance as much as their theatricality.

Andersen remained an intense and sometimes troubled man. He was a friend and associate of kings and of the famous. He never married, though he was deeply in love at times, not least with the Swedish singer Jenny Lind. He died at 70 in 1875. In the Denmark of his day Andersen was criticized and diminished for what was seen as his absorption with the wider European world. As always with genius, however, his work transcended time. In Odense the spirit of this remarkable man is vividly present, at the museum and also in quieter corners of the Old Town.

FINLAND

"THE appearance of the town is entirely modern, in some respects suggesting America rather than Europe."

An early reference to Helsinki, from *Russia with Tehran, Port Arthur and Peking* by German travel publisher Karl Baedeker

Opposite: Sauna house on a lake edge near Jyvaskyla, Finland

FINLAND

Finland, one of the world's great survivors, is a small nation that has had to contend with harsh nature and belligerent neighbors in an often hostile northern European world. For centuries Finland was trapped between the aggressive ambitions of Sweden and Russia, and then in the 20th century between the Eastern and Western protagonists of the Cold War. The country's emergence as a self-confident, modern nation, with its historic identity intact, is a celebration of steady nerve, political shrewdness and tenacity.

Land of Forests and Lakes

Finland is bordered on the east by Russia, on the northwest by Sweden and on the north by Norway. Most of Finland is less than 600 feet high, and over 70 percent of the country contains coniferous spruce and pine. The northern areas are covered with peat bog, and there are said to be more than 180,000 lakes. All of Finland is a seemingly endless blanket of trees, water and wide skies.

The main "lake district" of Saimaa in the east is a paradise of woodland and navigable rivers and lakes, punctuated by rugged cliffs and a glittering mosaic of islands and lakeside towns and villages. Apart from the special nature of the Finnish landscape, the main cities and towns – Helsinki, Turku, Tampere, Porvoo, Savonlinna, Oulu and Rovaniemi – have much to offer the visitor. They are as modern as any other European urban center, yet retain a deep-seated Finnish identity.

The striking Sibelius monument, located in Sibelius Park in Helsinki

The Islands and Lapland

The mirror image of the inland water world is Finland's coastal region. Off Finland's southwestern coast is the Saaristomeri archipelago, with its thousands of islands and little rock islets known as "skerries." Farther out lie the Åland Islands, stepping stones to Sweden. You can explore the archipelago by ferry or steamship, or stay on shore at the beaches of Yyteri, near Pori, on the coast to the north.

In northern Finland, in the great wilderness of Lapland, you can learn about the life and culture of the Sami people in Rovaniemi's Arctic Center (Arktikum). The adventurous can go white-water rafting on the Tornionjoki river, follow one of the numerous hiking routes or head into the mountains of the northwest, where Finland's highest peak, Haltitunturi, reaches 4,300 feet.

Traveling in Finland

Traveling by car is a good way to see rural Finland. There are excellent road systems around Helsinki and between the main towns, but in rural areas some roads may be only dirt tracks. Finland's

Sunset over Lake Kallavesi, in the lakeland region at the heart of Finland

state railroad, Valtion Rautatiet, serves the whole country (except the extreme north), with the most frequent service in the south. Bus service is also good, and the east-west network in central and southern Finland is especially efficient.

The Finnish climate is far more amiable than you might expect from such a northern country. In spite of being in the same latitude as Alaska and Siberia, Finland and the whole Scandinavian peninsula enjoy a much milder climate owing to the influence of the Gulf Stream. There can be very warm dry spells in summer.

The Finnish people have a well-developed sense of irony, which may emerge in the form of jovial self-disparagement, especially among the young. The Finns know when to keep quiet and may appear to be unwilling to talk very much. But throughout the country you will be welcomed, and helped, with courtesy and kindness.

MORE TOP DESTINATIONS IN FINLAND

• Åland A1 • Helvetinjärven Kansallispuisto A2 • Lapland B3 • Loviisa B1 • Porvoo B1 • Rauma A1 • Rovaniemi B3 • Saimaa B1 • Savonlinna B2 • Tampere A1 • Turku A1 • Vaasa A2

Timeline

4000 BC	Sami peoples move into northern Finland from the east.
1600 BC	Development of Iron Age culture and emergence of the Finno-Ugric language.
1100	Finland is occupied by four tribal elements: the Sami in the north, Karelians in the east, Tavastians in the central lakes and Finns in the southwest.
1249	Swedish Birger *Jarl* conducts a "Christian Crusade," thinly disguised as Swedish colonization of southwest Finland.
1290s	Invasions by Russia lead to Swedish–Russian conflicts.
1555	Finland is made a Swedish duchy; beginning of 250 years of Swedish influence.
1807	Czar Alexander I of Russia occupies Finland.
1917	Finland becomes an independent republic.
1939–44	Finland declares neutrality but Russia invades; Finland declares itself a "co-belligerent" with Germany in resisting Russian attacks; Britain declares war against Finland.
1992	The 1948 Treaty of Friendship, Cooperation and Mutual Assistance between Finland and Russia is dissolved.
1995	Finland becomes a member of the European Union.
2000	Helsinki is designated as a European City of Culture; Tarja Halonen becomes the first female president of Finland.

A Bridge Between East and West

Finland's 20th-century relationship with Russia has often been misunderstood. The term "Finlandization" was used disparagingly by some to describe the country's carefully orchestrated policy toward its giant neighbor, but Finland's sensitive geographic position dictated this policy. For centuries, Russia competed with Sweden for domination over Finland. After 1807, Russian influence prevailed. Finland's declaration of independence in 1917 led to an uneasy relationship between the two countries, and resulted in bitter conflict during World War II. After the war, Finland was forced to tread a careful path between the Cold War policies of East and West. The Finnish politician who did the most to maintain his country's identity under these circumstances was Urho K. Kekkonen, who was the country's president from 1956 to 1981. Kekkonen's pragmatism and his careful balancing act between East and West earned him much criticism from Western politicians. But Finland remained essentially a Scandinavian country while maintaining "friendly coexistence" with Russia. Finland's rapid emergence, post-Cold War, as a democratic, pluralist and modern society is a testament to the wisdom of Kekkonen's strategy. It is said that he frequently conducted discussions with visiting Russian politicians in the relaxation of a traditional sauna, where everyone feels happily equal.

Survival Guide

- For Finnish and international fashion in Helsinki, try Marimekko at Pohjois Esplanadi 2 and 31. For exclusive silkwear look for Marja Kurki's scarfs in Stockmann. For traditional jewelry and Finnish national clothing, you cannot beat Kalevala Koru, Unioninkatu 25.
- Driving with dimmed headlights in the daytime is compulsory in rural areas but not in towns, although it's a good idea to do so everywhere. When driving in rural Finland, look out for elk and reindeer on roads.
- You will find that consumer goods are generally more expensive in Finland than in the rest of Europe, although prices are coming down. Accommodations and eating out are also more expensive.
- Many hotels in Finland have saunas, but most are electrically heated. The traditional Finnish "smoke" sauna is heated by a wood-burning stove and is considered the real experience. For information on traditional saunas, contact the Finnish Sauna Society, ☎ 09 686 0560.
- In Helsinki, especially, you will find numerous "grill kiosks," little huts selling fast food in the form of hamburgers, french fries, meat-filled pies and grilled sausages (*grillimakkara*). The kiosks are good for daytime snacks, but late at night they often attract loud, drunken revelers.
- On the weekend between June 20 and 26 there are midsummer celebrations throughout the country. After the long, dark nights of winter, Finns celebrate Midsummer's Day with gusto.
- For lunchtime snacks there are the ubiquitous baguettes, often with tasty fillings. Also try such Finnish favorites as salted salmon or herring slices with new potatoes, or typical minced meat dishes such as *metsästäjänpihvi* (minced meat in mushroom sauce).
- There is a state monopoly on the sale of alcohol, apart from medium-strength beers, which can be bought in some grocery stores. Wine and spirits can be bought only in state-controlled outlets known as ALKO. Wine prices have come down but brandy and whisky remain pricey. Restaurants usually serve alcohol.
- Public restrooms in Finland are generally clean and modern. Signs are *Naiset* for ladies and *Michet* for men.

Sampling some local dishes in a Helsinki café

HELSINKI

Helsinki (sometimes referred to in Swedish as Helsingfors) will take your breath away. It does so quite literally in the frozen winter, but even then it can have days of glorious weather – blue skies and pure white panoramas. In summer, the city will delight you even more with its stunning architecture and its blue Baltic waters.

City of the Sea

As with Oslo, the best way to approach Helsinki is by sea. The Lutheran Cathedral (Tuomiokirkko) and the Uspenski Cathedral (Uspenskin Katedraali) stand out against the skyline behind the handsome row of waterfront buildings that include the 19th-century City Hall and Presidential Palace. In front of them is Market Square, crammed with vendors selling everything from fish to handicrafts.

You miss this introduction to the city if you arrive by plane, bus or train, but the 19th-century railroad station is a striking example of Helsinki's remarkable architecture. Bus and railroad stations are close to the heart of things and only a few streets from Senate Square and the bustle of Mannerheimintie, the city's main street.

Svensk-Finland

The form of Swedish spoken in Finland is *Svensk-Finland*, "Finland's Swedish." Today about six percent of Finnish residents speak Swedish exclusively. In most of Finland signs and street names are in Finnish and Swedish. Unless you are fluent in either language, you are best sticking to English, Finland's "second language."

Helsinki is an accessible city that is easy to explore independently. Trams and buses serve all parts of the city, but the subway system, *Metro*, is a single, mainly suburban service line of little help to visitors.

The heart of summertime Helsinki is the tree-lined Esplanade (Esplanadi) that runs west from Market Square and

South Harbor (Eteläsatama) to Mannerheimintie. There is a bandstand next to the renowned Kappeli restaurant (see page 550), where you can sample tasty Finnish specialties such as salmon soup (*lohikeitto*). The streets bordering the Esplanade have many stylish boutiques, such as Marimekko and Annikki Karvinen, as well as colorful cafés and restaurants. Stop for coffee and pastries at Café Kafka, in the Swedish Theater at the west end of the Esplanade.

Quiet Corners

For green spaces and seashore walks go south from the Esplanade, past the University Observatory and past the

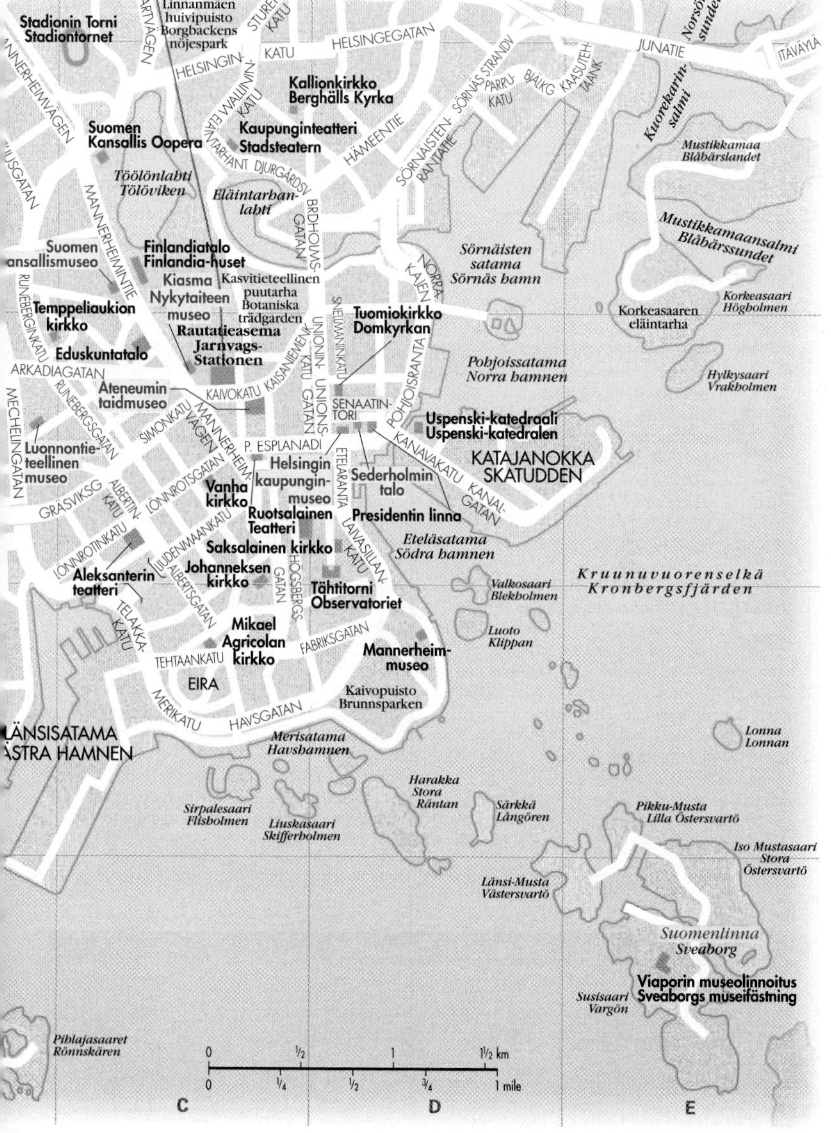

austere Russian Embassy, to reach Kaivopuisto Park. Beyond lies the seashore road of Ehrenströmintie, where moored yachts enhance the views of numerous islands. Or go north from the square in front of the railroad station to Kaisaniemi Park and the University Botanical Gardens, and on to the tree-fringed sea inlets beyond. Walk up Mannerheimintie to see the monumental Parliament House and Finlandia Hall; then go west to Temppeliaukio Church, a copper-domed church carved out of rock.

Despite Helsinki's reputation for long, dark winters, there is much to reward the visitor throughout the year. Enjoy the restaurants, listen to the music of Jean Sibelius in Finlandia Hall or attend world-class performances at the Opera House.

You will find fewer English speakers here than in other Scandinavian countries, but Helsinkians are proud of their heritage and are eager to help visitors enjoy this cultured and self-confident Baltic city.

"Smoke" Sauna

Sauna is a way of life for Finns – apart from being healthy and relaxing, it's a social, cultural – and, some say – almost religious practice. A sauna is an insulated room that is traditionally heated by a wood-burning stove. In a "smoke" sauna, steam is generated by throwing water on the hot stones of the stove, and the correct mix of steam and heat, known as *löyly,* fills the room in which you sit naked. Plunging into icy lakes or rolling in the snow between bouts of *löyly* is also an option.

ESSENTIAL INFORMATION

TOURIST INFORMATION

• Helsinki City Tourist Office, Pohjoisesplanadi 19 ☎ 09 169 3757; fax 09 169 3839; www.hel.fi
• Finnish Tourist Board, Eteläesplanadi 4 ☎ 09 4176 9300; fax 09 4176 9301; www.mek.fi
• Hotel Booking Center, Helsinki railroad station (west wing) ☎ 09 2288 1400; fax 09 2288 1499

URBAN TRANSPORTATION

Helsinki's railroad station is located on Kaivokatu, the broad street in front of the station. It is the terminus for main train services throughout the country and to Russia. Helsinki's bus, tram and subway network is operated by Helsingin Kaupungin Liikennelaitos (HKL). The city bus terminal is next to the railroad station, on Rautatientori, the square directly in front of the station. Main tram stops are on Kaivokatu. For local bus and tram information call ☎ 010 0111 (from within Helsinki only). The long-distance bus station is located just off Mannerheimintie and Simonkatu. For information call ☎ 09 9600 4000. Helsinki has a small subway system serving mainly suburban areas. Stations have a sign marked "M." Taxis have a yellow dome light and are free when it is lit. There is a taxi stand at the railroad station. Call the Helsinki taxi center at ☎ 09 700 700.

AIRPORT INFORMATION

Helsinki Vantaa Airport is 12 miles north of the city. The airport is a modern, well-appointed complex with every facility. Finnair buses run to and from the airport to the Finnair Terminal near Helsinki railroad station. The service is every 20 minutes, daily 5:45 a.m.–1 a.m., and the journey takes about 25 minutes.
A slower, but less expensive, regular bus service also runs between the airport and the city center. For information on flight arrivals and departures call ☎ 09 9600 8100.

CLIMATE – average highs and lows for the month

JAN.	FEB.	MAR.	APR.	MAY	JUN.	JUL.	AUG.	SEP.	OCT.	NOV.	DEC.
-3°C	-3°C	1°C	7°C	14°C	18°C	21°C	19°C	13°C	7°C	2°C	-1°C
27°F	27°F	34°F	45°F	57°F	64°F	70°F	66°F	55°F	45°F	36°F	30°F
-9°C	-9°C	-5°C	0°C	5°C	9°C	12°C	10°C	6°C	2°C	-2°C	-7°C
16°F	16°F	23°F	32°F	41°F	48°F	54°F	50°F	43°F	36°F	28°F	19°F

CITY SIGHTS

Key to symbols

map coordinates refer to the Helsinki map on pages 158–159; sights below are highlighted in yellow on the map.

address or location telephone number

opening times nearest bus or tram route

ferry restaurant or café on site or nearby

admission charge: $$$ more than Fmk22, $$ Fmk8–Fmk22, $ less than Fmk8 other relevant information

ATENEUMIN TAIDMUSEO

C3 Kaivokatu 2 09 1733 6401 Tue.–Fri. 9–6 (also Wed.–Thu. 6–8 p.m.), Sat.–Sun. 11–5 Museum café All buses to Rautatientori Square bus terminus; Tram 2, 3, 4, 6 $$$

The Ateneumin taidmuseo (Ateneum Art Museum) is located in a handsome 19th-century building. Vincent van Gogh, Amedeo Modigliani and Paul Cézanne are represented, among many other international figures; but it is the significant collection of Finnish art, from the 18th century to the mid-1960s, that enhances the museum. There are some powerful works by realist painters Fanny Churberg and Albert Edelfelt, such as Edelfelt's gossiping group, *Women of Ruokalahti on the Church Hill.* Finland's master Akseli Gallen-Kallela dominates with works such as the seductive *Aino-Taru, The Aino Myth* and the earthy and very Finnish *A New House*. Gallen-Kallela pupil Hugo Simberg's mildly disturbing and surrealistic *The Wounded Angel* is another highlight. Wäinö Aaltonen's bronze of the Finnish runner Paavo Nurmi overpowers Room 24.

HELSINGIN KAUPUNGINMUSEO

D3 Sofiankatu 4 09 169 3933 Helsinki City Museum: Mon.–Fri. 9–5, Sat.–Sun. 11–5; "Street Museum": daily 24 hours Amadeus, see page 550 Tram 1, 2, 3B, 3T, 4, 7 Helsinki City Museum $$, (free Thu.) "Street Museum" free

The Helsingin kaupunginmuseo (Helsinki City Museum) is located in the "Street Museum" of Sofiankatu. The City Museum has branches throughout the city, including the nearby Sederholm House. The main museum has an informative exhibition on Helsinki's history. The "Street Museum" portrays changing styles of street architecture and accessories. Start at the harbor end and walk on cobbled surfaces past old street lamps and artifacts. You start in the early 1800s and finish in the 1930s.

KIASMA NYKYTAITEEN MUSEO

C3 Mannerheimin aukio 2 09 1733 6501 Wed.–Sun. 10–10, Tue. 9–5 Museum restaurant/café 16, 13, 21v; tram 4, 10 $$$

The Kiasma Nykytaiteen museo (Kiasma Museum of Contemporary Art) is one of the newest buildings in Helsinki. Its bold postmodern design, by American architect Steven Holl, has aroused some controversy. The exhibitions of conceptual art and often radical installations are at the forefront of European contemporary art and emphasize the sophistication of Finnish culture.

LUONNONTIETEELLINEN MUSEO

B3 Pohjoinen Rautatiekatu 13 09 1912 8804 Mon.–Fri. 9–5, Sat.–Sun. 11–4 Gallery café 16, 13, 21v; tram 3B, 3T $$$

The venerable Luonnontieteellinen museo (Natural History Museum) is guarded by a very handsome bronze elk, just one of the animals in the museum's vast and old-fashioned collection of animals, birds and insects. The museum's mammal hall is one of the best in Europe, a series of tableaux showing exotic beasts and Finnish wildlife in their native habitats.

SEDERHOLMIN TALO

D3 Aleksanterinkatu 16–18 09 169 3625 Daily 11–5, Jun.–Aug.; Wed.–Sun. 11–5, mid-Mar. to May 31, Sep.–Oct. and mid-Nov. to late Jan. Amadeus, see page 550 Tram 1, 2, 3B, 3T, 4, 7A, 7B Free

The Sederholmin talo (Sederholm House) is a rare survivor of old Helsinki and is said to be the city's oldest stone house. What distinguishes this rather unassuming

The Lutheran Cathedral in Senate Square

building is the story it tells of its one-time owner, Johan Sederholm, an 18th-century Finnish businessman who rose from poverty to great wealth and distinction. The shrewd, disciplined personality of Sederholm is so powerful that you expect him to appear, offering a few tips about wise investments.

SENAATINTORI

D3 Senaatintori Tram 1, 2, 3B, 3T, 7
Summer festivals and events

Senaatintori (Senate Square) is the focus of the Russian Imperial style. This form of architecture was encouraged by Tsar Alexander I in his bid to make Helsinki a stylistically eastern capital after it was annexed by Russia from Sweden in 1809. The square and its major buildings were designed by C. L. Engel.

Helsinki's Lutheran Cathedral dominates Senate Square and the city skyline. The cathedral is essentially classical but has Byzantine elements. Its domes are copper-sheathed and gilded, the only accents in an otherwise blinding whiteness. The buildings that flank the square and cathedral are outstanding and include the Senate House, University Building and University Library.

SEURASAAREN ULKOMUSEO

A4 Seurasaaren 09 4050 9660 Daily 11–5 (also Wed. 5–7), Jun.–Aug.; Mon.–Fri. 9–3, Sat.– Sun. 11–5, second half of May and first half of Sep.; Sat.–Sun. 11–5, second half of Sep. Museum café 24 $$ Guided tours in English at 11:30 and 3:30

The Seurasaaren ulkomuseo (Seurasaari Open-Air Museum) is a marvelous collection of Finnish regional buildings dating from as early as the 17th century. The museum, located on charming Seurasaari Island, is easily reached from central Helsinki. There are nearly 100 buildings scattered throughout the large site. Most date from the 18th and 19th centuries and include a manor house, traditional farmhouses and a church.

SUOMEN KANSALLISMUSEO

C4 Mannerheimintie 34 09 4050 9470
Tue.–Wed. 11–6, Thu.–Sun. 11–8 Museum restaurant Tram 1, 2, 4, 7 $$$

The recently refurbished Suomen kansallismuseo (National Museum of Finland) dates from 1910 and is a fine example of the National Romantic, or *Jugend* style of architecture. There are excellent exhibits on Finnish history and some compelling early artifacts, including a Stone Age sculpture of an elk's head from around 3000 BC. The throne of Alexander I is on display, from which he proclaimed Finnish "incorporation" with Russia in 1809.

SUOMENLINNA

E1 Suomenlinna Visitor Center 09 684 1880 Visitor Center: daily 10–6, May–Aug.; Mon.–Fri. 11–4, Sat.–Sun. 10–5, in Sep.; Mon.–Fri. 11–4, Sat.–Sun.11–5, in Apr.; daily 11–4, rest of year Café in Doll and Toy Museum Ferries leave at half-hourly intervals from the Market Pier $$$ Guided tours in English daily at 10:30, 1 and 2:30, Jun.–Aug.

The historic fortress of Suomenlinna is built on four interconnecting islands and was once dubbed the "Gibraltar of the North." First used by Sweden in 1748 under the name Sveaborg ("Sweden's Fortress"), the island was surrendered to Russia in 1808. It remained in Russian control until 1918, when newly independent Finland renamed it Suomenlinna ("Finland's Fortress"). There are several museums on Suomenlinna, including a main exhibition center; the Military Museum complete with a reconstructed World War II submarine; the Coast Artillery Museum; and the Doll and Toy Museum.

IMPERIAL CITY: THE BUILDINGS OF HELSINKI

Engel's Lutheran Cathedral (top), and the House of Estates – seat of government until 1906

Helsinki has some of the finest buildings in northern Europe, with the architectural heart of the city being Senate Square. Here, in the early 19th century, Berlin-born Carl Ludvig Engel was commissioned to create a new Helsinki in neoclassical Russian Imperial style. On its high podium, the gleaming white Lutheran Cathedral is the focus of the square. Leave the square at its northeastern corner and stroll up Snellmaninkatu a short distance to where the Bank of Finland (Suomen Pankki) faces the House of Estates (Säätytalo), built in the classical style with gilded Corinthian capitals.

Another great architectural theme in Helsinki is art nouveau, or *Jugend* as it is known in Finland. This style drew its motifs from Finnish culture and tradition; its materials are the timber and rough-faced granite of the country used in naturalistic ways. *Jugend* architecture is best seen in residential areas such as Eira, on the southern peninsula of the city, and on the little island to the east of the harbor, Katajanokka. The island is guarded by the magnificent Uspenski Cathedral, the most impressive expression of Orthodoxy you are likely to find in northern Europe.

Jugend architecture is characterized by turrets, castellated features and carved motifs. Yet the buildings remain elegant and restrained. Take a walk down Eira's streets of Huvilakatu and Laivurinkatu. On Laivurinkatu, look for No. 25, the Villa Johanna. Walk down Luotsikatu and Kauppiaankatu, a short distance east of the cathedral, where there are numerous examples of *Jugend* to compare with Senate Square's classicism and with the city's more modern buildings. Finlandia Hall and the Kiasma Museum maintain Helsinki's international reputation for architectural excellence.

France

"We have come five hundred miles by rail through the heart of France. What a bewitching land it is!"

From *The Innocents Abroad* (1869),
by Mark Twain

Opposite: A Gothic abbey crowns the summit of Le Mont-St.-Michel, on the Normandy coast

France

France is the largest country in western Europe, geographically one of the most diverse, and certainly among the most beautiful. Its cities contain some of the greatest treasures in Europe; its countryside is prosperous and well tended. The French combine practicality with romance; they lead a stylish life, eat delicious food and bask in a pleasant climate.

Historically, France has developed the notion of equality for all and, while retaining its sense of tradition, remains a forward-looking country. Over the past half-century, for instance, the French have forged ahead in modern technology. France is a country of contrasts, making it a delight to explore.

France Today

France was among the first European countries to permanently dispense with its monarchy. Apart from a couple of brief periods, it has been a republic almost as long as the United States. The French Revolution gave a

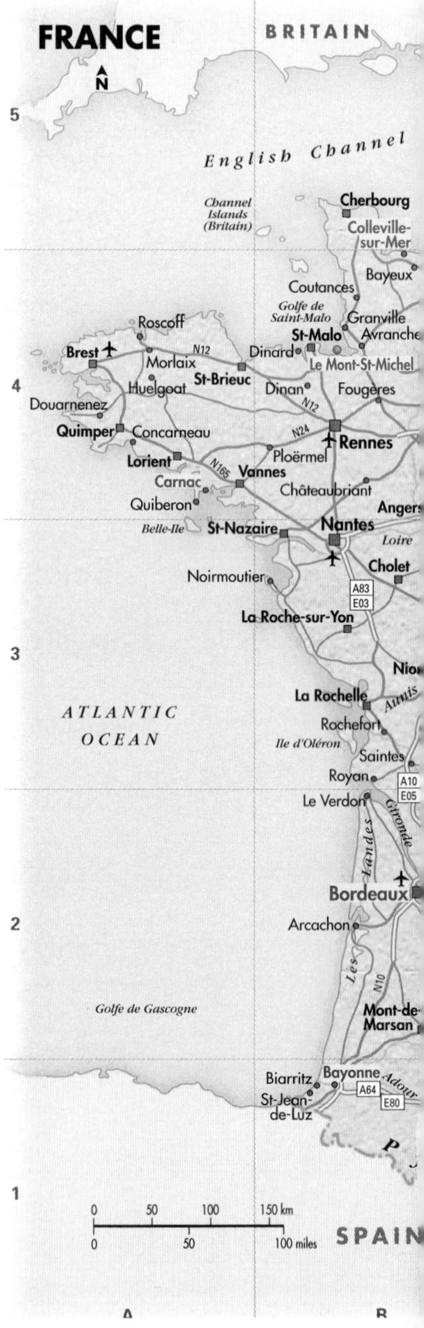

MORE TOP DESTINATIONS IN FRANCE

• Aigues-Mortes D1 • Avignon D2 • Bayonne B1 • Beaune D3 • Bordeaux B2 • Carcassonne C1 • Carnac A4 • Cirque de Gavarnie B1 • Cirque de Navacelles D2 • Colleville-sur-Mer B4 • Grasse E2 • Grotte de Lascaux C2 • Honfleur B4 • Megève E3 • Le Mont-St.-Michel B4 • Pont du Gard D2 • Rocamadour C2

tremendous sense of patriotism to all French men and women, which continues to the present day.

Despite the apparently never-ending political ups and downs, French people have a strong sense of national pride

The Renaissance château at Azay-le-Rideau – one of the grand sights of the Loire valley

and unity; they are essentially one people and one country. Every town and village in France flies the flag (*tricolore*) with pride, and displays a bust of Marianne in its town hall, the beautiful woman who epitomizes the spirit of France.

The French despair of their politicians, grumble at their government and taxation, and are quite capable of unruly demonstrations against the most surprising things, but *au fond*, at heart, they remain proud and devoted admirers of their country.

La Belle France

La belle France – beautiful France – is indeed truly beautiful. Hexagonal in shape, each of its six sides acts as a natural boundary. The English Channel and the rolling Atlantic guard the west coasts, the Pyrenees and Alps the southwest and southeast borders, the Mediterranean laps along the southern coast and the mighty Rhine river forms a barrier against Germany in the northeast. Within this area lies a huge variety of landscape, with plains, arable flatlands, forested hills, vine- and olive-growing terraces, lush river valleys, inhospitable mountain massifs and a combined coastline stretching for almost 2,000 miles.

As you travel around France you'll notice how sparsely populated the land is compared to most other European countries. Miles go past without a sign of a town or village, yet the land is mostly cultivated, forested or tended in some way. France has always been an agricultural country, and today is the largest agricultural producer and exporter in the European Union.

Cities, Towns and Villages

In a country as geographically varied as France there is bound to be a diverse range of architecture, as styles evolved to suit the environment. In southern rural areas, the population lived in easily defensible communities and worked the fields daily, leaving a legacy of picturesque hilltop villages, with narrow streets for shelter against the fierce sun. In the mountains the design was dictated by the climate, and cozy wooden chalets evolved, with steep or flat roofs depending on the region.

The whole country in general enjoyed great prosperity during the 17th and 18th centuries, and in most of the major cities there are architectural reminders of this time, in the shape of churches, fine civic buildings, spacious squares and well-planned streets. Before the French Revolution, the aristocracy spent several months a year on their estates and built fine fortified houses and châteaux in which they lived.

This wonderful mixture of style still exists, and the French have been far better than some other European nations at preserving the historic centers of their towns. The second half of the 20th century has seen some truly imaginative and innovative civic building projects in all the major cities, which you'll certainly notice.

The French Character

Other Europeans have a peculiar relationship with the French people, in which there may be more than a touch of envy. The French have much to boast about, and are rightly proud of their culture. As a result, they have gained a reputation with their neighbors for being arrogant. They are often accused of seeing themselves as decidedly superior to every other nation. For years the French have been criticized and stereotyped for their attitude. But interestingly, the minute a foreigner steps on French soil, he or she is once more seduced: by the country, the overwhelming charm of the people, the way of life.

Lifestyle

The French way of life strikes a happy balance between the work-driven culture of the northern Europeans and the wonderfully alluring, but overly relaxed, southern European approach to life. This is a prosperous country with a high standard of living, where both men and women hold down prestigious and influential jobs in every sector. It is also a highly efficient country with an excellent infrastructure, making things very easy for visitors. Public transportation is first-rate, with Europe's best and fastest train system. If you're driving, you'll find the roads fast and in good condition, although you should be aware of the sometimes erratic national driving style. Hotels are comfortable, restaurants provide good value, and tourism is a well-organized, thriving industry.

All this is augmented by the innate French sense of style, which is obvious the minute you arrive. This is evident from the way produce is artfully stacked in market stalls, to the sensible layout of an airport. You'll find a relaxed approach to most problems, and note that the wheels of daily life are oiled with a high level of politeness. Even if you don't speak the language, bear in mind that courtesy is extremely important in everyday dealings.

Yachts moored in Nice, on the French Riviera

The national game of *boules* is taken very seriously by its devotees, and is also fun to watch

People work hard in France, but indulge in relaxation as well. In the evenings they enjoy themselves over a lengthy meal or sit for hours in cafés. French citizens have always backed their country's achievements in culture and the arts, so there's a lively arts scene everywhere. You'll also find that almost everyone has strong views on a wide range of artistic, political and economic events, which they're eager to share.

Religion

France is nominally a Catholic country, with the Church separated from the State since 1905. More than 80 percent of its 58 million inhabitants have been baptized into the Catholic church, although only a small percentage regularly attend church. There are approximately one million Protestants, who for historical reasons tend to be more active churchgoers. Immigrants from France's former colonies make up a large proportion of the considerable number of Muslims, while the Jewish population in France never recovered its numbers after World War II. Every town and village has one or more churches with Sunday and daily services.

Pastimes

The French take relaxation seriously. They enjoy sports, both as spectators and participants, with soccer the national favorite. The nation was elated when France won the 1998 World Cup and again in 2000 when they won the European Championship. Tennis and golf are other popular sports, both with good facilities for tourists, and you'll find challenging golf courses all over France. Resort areas offer a huge range of pastimes, from tennis to sailing to organized hiking.

With the Alps on their doorstep, many people ski; especially during early February, when children are out of school and families head for the slopes.

You may often see *boules* being played. This is a game where players attempt to surround a small target ball on the ground by throwing larger, heavier balls from a specified distance.

The mountains around Chamonix are among the best spots for Alpine skiing

Pleasures

Food and drink are among the national pleasures of France and much time is spent shopping for and preparing food. Clearly, modern life has taken its toll but fast food, frozen meals and "grazing" items are not considered mealtime options. If the French can't be bothered to cook, they can pick up exquisite, freshly prepared dishes from a *traiteur*, a type of delicatessen. Desserts are rarely home-made, bought instead from a *pâtisserie* (cake shop), ensuring that every mouthful is of the highest quality. Every region has its own food specialties, and these are taken so seriously that some foodstuffs have an *appellation controlée* label, similar to the labeling used for wine, meaning that the product must be from the area for which it is known.

French wines need no introduction, and visitors can enjoy winery visits and tastings in all the wine-producing areas. Champagne is kept for special occasions, while everyday drinks include many varieties of beer and the *pastis* family – an aniseed-flavored spirit diluted with water so it turns milky.

Material pleasures are important in France, where shopping is an art form. This is the country that produces champagne, the world's most famous scents, and some of the world's most desirable clothes and accessories. You'll find that prices won't differ hugely from those back home, and the satisfaction is great from buying luxuries in their native land.

Expect a wealth of experience and pleasure in France: natural beauty, historic cities, and good value despite the relatively high cost of living.

Exquisite chocolate confection

TIMELINE

15,000 BC	Lascaux cave paintings; first works by tribal group in area now covered by modern France.
3000 BC	Carnac stones erected.
58 BC	Julius Caesar invades Gaul.
AD 500	Frankish King Clovis unites tribes to form France.
800	Charlemagne crowned first Holy Roman Emperor.
1431	Joan of Arc burned at the stake; resulting patriotism gives France national identity.
1763	France loses North American possessions to England at end of Seven Years War.
1789	Start of French Revolution; monarchy overthrown and republic established.
1804	Napoleon proclaimed emperor; Napoleon defeated at Waterloo in 1815.
1874	First exhibition of Impressionist art.
1889	Eiffel Tower built for Paris Exhibition; beginning of *Belle Époque* era.
1914–18	France allies with Britain, Russia and United States against Germany and Austro-Hungary to fight World War I.
1939–45	France swiftly defeated by Germans in World War II; Charles de Gaulle leads Free French Army from England.
1958	France becomes a founder member of European Community.
1985	French agents blow up Greenpeace ship, the *Rainbow Warrior*, in Auckland, New Zealand.
1998	France wins soccer World Cup; country erupts in euphoria.
1999	France is among the first countries to adopt euro currency.
2000	France wins European Soccer Championship amid national celebrations.

IMPRESSIONISM

By the 1870s a group of Parisian artists had become increasingly bored with the traditional, studio-based, graphic style of most paintings. They were obsessed with light and its effect on landscape and objects at different times of day; painting outside, they worked on several canvases at a time as the light changed throughout the day. Among these artists were Monet, Manet, Pissarro, Renoir, Dégas and Sisley. In 1874 they held their first public exhibition, where their work was ridiculed. One critic was particularly scathing about Monet's painting *Impression of a Sunrise*, and so the name of the movement was born. Literary figures such as Zola and Flaubert supported Impressionism, feeling they could do with words what artists were doing with paint, and gradually public opinion was won over.

Sunday morning entertainment at the bandstand in the Luxembourg gardens, Paris

SURVIVAL GUIDE

- You will find that many French people speak English, although they are not very willing to do so. It's polite to master the phrase "*parlez-vous anglais?*" to use before asking a question; you will notice a much better response.
- Politeness is highly regarded in France, so preface requests with "*bonjour*" and always say "*merci.*"
- French people can be among the world's best dressed, with a casual style that's difficult to emulate. Make an effort in France to be well groomed, as a smart appearance will ensure better service everywhere.
- The French government has introduced new laws governing smoking in public places, but they are frequently ignored. Smoking is often tolerated throughout restaurants and other public areas.
- It's a good idea to count your change in shops and markets, and make sure taxi meters are set at zero when starting a journey.
- It's probable you'll find a bidet in your bathroom, an appliance that looks like a toilet with faucets. This is designed for washing intimate body areas – although it's handy for washing socks, as well!
- Restrooms in museums, restaurants and many public places are generally modern, but in rural areas the toilet may consist of two floor-level porcelain plaques, on which the user squats. This often flushes automatically at high pressure, so watch out for your shoes.
- The French are notoriously inconsiderate drivers, giving little leeway to other road users. If you are considering driving long distances, use the highway system. You have to pay a toll (*péage*), but it's safer and much less crowded.
- Sodas and soft drinks are very expensive in France; a beer often costs less then a Coke.
- Iced water and ice in drinks is not served routinely in France. Ask for *des glaçons* if you want ice. Legally, restaurants must serve tap water if you ask for it, so persevere even if the waiter looks grumpy.
- French coffee is strong, so if you want a weaker cup ask for a *café américain*. Unless you ask for milk or cream, it will always be served black.

PARIS

It's hard to be indifferent to historic, hectic, elegant Paris. With all its moods, this is a city that can exhilarate you, exasperate you and leave you speechless with wonder, but it won't leave you cold. Paris is beautiful no matter when you visit: the quality of light ranges from crystalline brilliance to mellow gold; distant sounds mingle with bustling main streets; and with each season a new scent blows in to announce its arrival.

Getting Your Bearings

It would take months to explore all of Paris, so resign yourself to the idea that you're not going to be able to see everything on just one trip to this great city. Some people won't need to see the main sights, preferring to familiarize themselves with the city by wandering the different neighborhoods; others will try to see as many attractions as possible. Consider which style best suits you and then plan ahead.

You'll probably be surprised by the compressed scale; the 2 million inhabitants of inner Paris all live within an area bounded by the 21-mile Boulevard Périphérique that encircles the city. Even so, be prepared to walk considerable distances, even within the museums, some of which are on a grand scale. Your first stop should be the main tourist office on the Champs-Élysées; here you can get excellent maps, leaflets and information on excursions and events and buy a museum and monument pass (*carte musées-monuments*). It's valid for one, three or five days, and entitles you to unlimited entry at 70 monuments and museums, including the Louvre (see page 182). If you visit as few as six museums you will save money.

Tours and Excursions

Taking a city tour is an excellent way to get your bearings. Most tours cover the main sights on either side of the Seine river and take about two hours, with an audio commentary in several different languages. An alternative is to take a bus run by Paris l'Open Tour, which visits the city center but stops along the

route, allowing you to get on and off to do your own sightseeing. Tickets are valid for one or two days, and there's English commentary. You may want to take a tour outside Paris; obvious choices are the fabulous Palace of Versailles, or the old royal hunting lodge of Fontainebleau and its surrounding forest. If you'll be spending your entire stay in Paris, consider taking a day trip to the châteaux of the Loire valley, Chartres and its cathedral, or the magical island of Le Mont-St.-Michel in Normandy.

Parisian Neighborhoods

Most Parisians mentally split their city into two neat halves – Left Bank (Rive

Intriguing stores entice browsers in the atmospheric Latin Quarter – on the Left Bank

Gauche) and Right Bank (Rive Droite) – with the sinuous curve of the Seine dividing them. Traditionally, the Right Bank has stood for order and elegance, typified by the monumental architecture running from the Louvre up to the Arc de Triomphe; while the Left Bank is an altogether more raffish place. This is too simplistic, however. Paris, in fact, is a series of extremely individual *quartiers*, districts, each with its own personality, style and charm.

Riverbanks and Bridges

More than 30 bridges criss-cross the Seine, and the banks, known as *quais*, offer lovely views of the city. The best stretch of riverside for walking lies between the Pont de la Concorde (Concorde Bridge), leading to the place de la Concorde, and the Pont de Sully (Sully Bridge), at the eastern end of the Île St.-Louis. Browse in the *bouquinistes* (secondhand booksellers) stalls that line the riverbank, or simply revel in the subtly blended colors of sky, river, trees and stone. Several companies operate cruises on the Seine, an ideal way to enjoy the river.

Parisians

As inhabitants of a capital city, Parisians are surprisingly able to combine the inevitable pace of big-city life with the ability to switch off and spend hours strolling, window-shopping or endlessly chatting in a café. This is the quintessential image of the chic Parisian. To get a good taste of another side of life in the city, however, you should visit a neighborhood market: food shopping is a serious business. One characteristic you will notice is how much people seem to read: there are countless bookstores, and metro commuters seem to always have their noses in a book. Your overall impression may be that the pace of life here is hurried, and the people can seem brusque, but they can also be charming, particularly to those enthusiastic about their city.

Shopping

The selection in the stores makes shopping irresistable for some. Haute couture stores cluster mainly around the Faubourg St.-Honoré and avenue Montaigne, with boutiques selling ready-to-wear designer outfits. Paris has a number of department stores; the best known are Galeries Lafayette and Printemps, both located on the monumental boulevard Haussmann, and La Samaritaine on rue de Sèvres near the Pont Neuf. Make a point to visit some of the covered shopping arcades, built in the 18th and early 19th centuries; Galerie Colbert and Galerie Vivienne are among the most attractive. Food stores are a must. Head for the world-famous Fauchon, 26 place de la Madeleine; Androuët, 41 rue d'Amsterdam, the ultimate cheese shop; and Lionel Poilâne, 8 rue du Cherche-Midi, Paris' most famous baker.

ESSENTIAL INFORMATION

TOURIST INFORMATION
Office de Tourisme et des Congrès de Paris (Paris Convention and Visitors Bureau)

• 127 avenue des Champs-Élysées ☎ 08 36 68 31 12 (toll call); fax 01 49 52 53 00; www.paris-touristoffice.com
Branches:
• Gare de Lyon
• Tour Eiffel (May–Sep. only)

URBAN TRANSPORTATION
The easiest way to get around Paris is by the metro (subway), which runs daily 5:30 a.m.–12:30 a.m. Transportation maps are available at subway stations. Tickets are available singly or in *carnets* (books) of 10, a cheaper option; they are available at the stations and from tobacconists (*tabacs*) and must be validated before boarding. Keep your ticket until your journey is complete, as there are heavy fines for travelers without tickets. The *Paris Visite* ticket, valid for 1, 2, 3 or 5 days, is a worthwhile investment and is interchangeable with the bus and with rail (RER and some SNCF services via train) enabling you to get to Versailles and Fontainebleau. Buses run daily 6:30 a.m.–8:30 p.m. (some routes until 1:30 a.m.); tickets are interchangeable with the subway. Bus stops have route maps and show the route number of the buses stopping at each. For information on public transportation in English, phone ☎ 08 36 68 41 14 (toll call). A special tourist bus, the Balabus, operates on Sundays and holidays noon–8 from mid-April through September, circling the major tourist sights; stops are marked "Balabus (Bb)." Taxis can be hailed on the street or from one of the 470 stands around the city, and are identifiable by the light on the roof, illuminated when the taxi is free. From May through October you can take the Batobus (☎ 01 44 11 33 99) on the Seine to get around; this boat runs between the Eiffel Tower and Notre-Dame daily 10–7 (10–9, Jul.–Aug.), with stops at the main tourist attractions.

AIRPORT INFORMATION
Paris has two international airports, Roissy-Charles-de-Gaulle (CDG, ☎ 01 48 62 22 80) and Orly (☎ 01 49 75 15 15), although most U.S. visitors arrive at CDG. It is 14 miles north of Paris; taxis are available at both terminals (terminal 2 serves Air France only). Buses run at 12-minute intervals daily 5:40 a.m.–11 p.m. into central Paris, and RER trains every 15 minutes daily 4:55 a.m.–11:55 p.m.
Buses serve Orly, 8 miles south of Paris, every 12 minutes daily 6 a.m.–11 p.m.; RER trains leave every 15 minutes daily 5:45 a.m.–11:15 p.m. A bus also runs every 12 minutes daily 6 a.m.–midnight between CDG and Orly, in both directions.

CLIMATE – average highs and lows for the month

JAN.	FEB.	MAR.	APR.	MAY	JUN.	JUL.	AUG.	SEP.	OCT.	NOV.	DEC.
6°C	7°C	10°C	13°C	18°C	21°C	24°C	24°C	20°C	14°C	9°C	8°C
43°F	45°F	50°F	55°F	64°F	70°F	75°F	75°F	68°F	57°F	48°F	46°F
2°C	2°C	4°C	5°C	9°C	12°C	14°C	14°C	12°C	8°C	4°C	2°C
36°F	36°F	39°F	41°F	49°F	54°F	57°F	57°F	54°F	46°F	39°F	36°F

The neoclassic Arc de Triomphe towers over the busy thoroughfare of the Champs-Élysées

City Sights

Key to symbols

map coordinates refer to the Paris map on pages 174–175; sights below are highlighted in yellow on the map.
address or location telephone number opening times nearest subway nearest bus route restaurant or café on site or nearby admission charge: $$$ more than 75F, $$ 25F to 75F, $ less than 25F other relevant information

Arc de Triomphe

A3 place Charles-de-Gaulle 01 55 37 73 77 Daily 9:30 a.m.–11 p.m., Apr.–Sep.; 10 a.m.–10:30 p.m., rest of year RER Charles-de-Gaulle-Étoile $$ (free to all first Sun. of the month)

The Arc de Triomphe is a splendid starting point for a day's sightseeing, the view from the top giving you a chance to appreciate the grandeur of Paris' city planning. Commissioned by Napoleon for his own glorification, the 164-foot-high Arc is now dedicated to the Unknown Soldier of World War I; the eternal flame burns beneath. Twelve avenues radiate from it, giving the surrounding square its original name of place de l'Étoile (the star); today it's called place Charles-de-Gaulle, in memory of the famous general. Be warned – there are 284 steps to the top, and no elevator.

Cathédrale Notre-Dame

D2 6 place du Parvis de Notre-Dame Cathedral: 01 42 34 56 10. Towers: 01 44 32 16 72 Cathedral: Mon.–Fri. 8–6:45, Sat.–Sun. 8–7:45. Towers: daily 9:30–6:45 (also Fri.–Sun. 6:45–9:45), Apr.-Sep.; 10–4:15, rest of year Cité; RER Châtelet or St.-Michel Notre-Dame Cathedral free, Tower $$

The great Gothic Cathédrale Notre-Dame (Cathedral of Our Lady) stands on the Île de la Cité, the oldest part of Paris. It was built between 1163 and 1345. The outside elevation is as impressive as the lofty interior; walk around it to admire the twin towers, massive buttresses and the gracious symmetry of the facade. The cathedral is always packed with visitors, so arrive early if you want to climb one of the towers, and have enough room to admire the paintings, and the rose windows at each end of the transepts.

Centre National d'Art et de Culture Georges Pompidou

D3 place Beaubourg 01 44 78 12 33 Wed.–Mon. 11–10 (museum and exhibitions close at 9) Restaurant Hôtel de Ville, Rambuteau; RER Châtelet-Les-Halles Center free, musée $$ (free to all first Sun. of the month)

This controversial modern art center,

opened in the 1970s, quickly earned itself the nickname "the refinery," due to its similarity to an oil refinery. The architectural team of Richard Rogers and Renzo Piano designed it as the first post-modernist public building to show its structural elements on the outside. It's home to a movie theater, library and exhibition space, but its chief draw is the Musée National d'Art Moderne (National Modern Art Museum). Following extensive renovation, the museum reopened in 2000 and now displays 1,400 works, including Salvador Dalí's disturbing *Six Apparitions of Lénine;* Pablo Picasso's early cubist *Femme Assise*; and pop art by Andy Warhol.

Champs-Élysées

B3 avenue des Champs-Élysées Concorde, Champs-Élysées-Clémenceau, Franklin-D-Roosevelt, George V or Charles-de-Gaulle-Étoile

The stately and loved Champs-Élysées (Heavenly Fields) runs from the place de la Concorde (see page 184) to the Arc de Triomphe, and divides neatly into two sections, with the Rond-Point being the halfway mark. The lower section, nearest Concorde, is bordered with grass and chestnut trees, behind which stand the Grand and Petit Palais, both devoted to the arts. Above the bustling and lively Rond-Point are stores, offices, movie theaters and sidewalk cafés.

Cité des Sciences et de l'Industrie

Cité des Sciences E4 30 avenue Corentin-Cariou 01 40 05 80 00. Bookings: 01 40 05 12 12 Tue.–Sun. 10–6 (also Sun. 6–7) Restaurant Porte de la Villette $$ (reduced fee Sun.)
Cité de la Musique 221 avenue Jean-Jaurès 01 44 84 44 84 Tue.–Sat. noon–6 (also Fri.–Sat. 6–7:30), Sun. 10–6 Restaurant Porte de Pantin $$

On the northeast edge of Paris stands a modern park, La Villette, scattered with sculptures and fountains, and devoted to science and music. Once home to the city's slaughterhouses, the site has been remodeled and converted to house the stunning and ultra-modern Cité des Sciences (Science City). You would need a day to do it justice, but if you're pressed for time make sure you visit the main exhibition, *Explora,* focusing on life, natural resources and technological development. If you have the time, go to the Géode, a movie theater with a hemispheric screen; the Cinaxe, a multisensory movie theater; or let the kids enjoy interactive games in the Technocity. Nearby is the Cité de la Musique, an impressive complex devoted to music.

Conciergerie and Ste.-Chapelle

Conciergerie C2 1 quai de l'Horloge 01 53 73 78 50 Daily 9:30–6:30, Apr.–Sep.; 10–5, rest of year Cité; RER St.-Michel Notre-Dame $$ (free to all first Sun. of the month) Guided tours daily at 11 and 3
Ste.-Chapelle 4 boulevard du Palais 01 53 73 78 50 Daily 9:30–6:30, Apr.–Sep.; 10–5, rest of year Cité; RER St.-Michel Notre-Dame $$ (free to all first Sun. of the month) Guided tours daily at 11 and 3

The Conciergerie gained a sinister reputation during the 1790s, when Marie Antoinette, queen of France, and the infamous revolutionary Robespierre were imprisoned here. It is the only remaining part of the original royal complex on the Île de la Cité, a superb Gothic building with twin round entrance towers and a distinctive roofline. Inside, its huge

Biblical scenes in the stained glass at Ste.-Chapelle

Notre-Dame, encircled by the Seine

vaulted hall is the highlight, along with reconstructed prison cells. Nearby stands the soaring Ste.-Chapelle, commissioned by Louis IX in 1245 to house the Crown of Thorns and a fragment of the True Cross. Built as two chapels, the upper was reserved for the royal family. Here, slender pillars divide the 50-foot-high stained-glass windows, also dating from the 13th century and showing scenes from the Old and New Testaments in glowing colors.

La Défense

Off the map · La Défense · Grande Arche: 01 49 07 27 57 · Grande Arche: daily 10–7 · Restaurant · RER Grande Arche de la Défense · Grande Arche $$ · Last ascent 30 minutes before closing

It's well worth the journey out to La Défense, Paris' prestigious modern business district, with its shopping center, IMAX movie theater and the Centre of New Industry and Technology (CNIT). A pedestrian esplanade leads to the Grande Arche de la Défense, the city's triumphant architectural celebration of the French Revolution's bicentennial. Take the glass elevator 360 feet to the top of the Arche, a stark and elegant hollow white marble cube, and a great view unfolds across Paris to the Arc de Triomphe (see page 178) and the obelisk in the place de la Concorde (see page 184).

Île de la Cité

D2 · Île de la Cité · Cité

One of the loveliest parts of Paris, the Île de la Cité is the ancient heart of the city; in medieval times it was the monarch's capital and a religious and intellectual center. Here you'll find famous monuments, including Notre-Dame (see page 178) and Ste.-Chapelle (see page 179), impressive civic buildings such as the Palais de Justice, and pleasant streets and squares, all contributing to a harmonious whole.

Île St.-Louis

D2 · Île St.-Louis · Nos Ancétres les Gaulois, see page 551 · Pont Marie

Pont St.-Louis will lead you straight from the Île de la Cité on to the Île St.-Louis, ideal for a peaceful stroll, a light lunch and some expensive shopping. Once two islands, this largely residential area was developed in the 17th century, when most of its lovely streets and houses were built; since then little seems to have changed.

Jardin des Tuileries

C3 · rue de Rivoli · 01 40 20 90 43 · Daily 7 a.m.–11:45 p.m., Apr.–Sep.; 7:30–7:30, Oct.–Mar. · Concorde or Tuileries · Free

The Jardin des Tuileries (Tuileries Gardens) is a good place to recharge your batteries after the rigors of a visit to the Louvre. Designed by Le Nôtre, it's an excellent example of a 17th-century formal garden, its long central *allée* (alley) carrying the eye from the Louvre buildings and fountains to the expanse of the place de la Concorde.

Le Marais and Place des Vosges

Musée Picasso · E3 · 5 rue de Thorigny · 01 42 71 25 21 · Wed.–Mon. 9:30–6 (also Thu. 6–8), Apr.–Sep.; 9:30–5:30, rest of year · Restaurant · St.-Sébastien-Froissart; RER Châtelet-Les Halles · $$ (free to all first Sun. of the month)

Maison Victor Hugo · E2 · 6 place des Vosges · 01 42 72 10 16 · Tue.–Sun. 10–5:40 · Le Grizzli, see page 551 · Chemin Vert or Bastille · $ (free Sun. 10–1)

For many people, le Marais is the loveliest part of Paris. Its charm lies in the combination of architecture, atmosphere, the crowds that wander its streets, and its

The French Revolution

All over Paris there are reminders of France's 1789 Revolution, when the monarchy was swept away and equal rights for all citizens were established under the law. America's own Revolutionary War served as the catalyst for events in France.

By the end of Europe's Seven Years War in 1763, France had lost all its North American possessions. Louis XVI of France, thirsting for revenge, was happy to offer arms and troops to help American colonists during their struggle against the English. These soldiers came home inspired by the American ideals of liberty and equality, taking what was, in France, an intellectually led and tiny movement to a larger grass-roots level.

The palace at Versailles (top), home to the ill-fated Louis XVI, and the place de la Concorde, where he was beheaded in front of vast crowds

The Causes

France had enjoyed a Golden Age during the 17th and much of the 18th centuries; power became centralized in the hands of the monarchy, the country prospered and Paris became a center of art and sophistication. But this was at the expense of most of the population, whose standard of living dropped lower and lower. Meanwhile the nobility, deprived of any real political power, threw itself into a reckless and hedonistic lifestyle. The gap between rich and poor grew ever wider; time was ripe for republican ideas to bear fruit.

The Events

In 1789 the Third Estate, representing France's commoners, declared itself a National Assembly and demanded social and constitutional reform. On July 14 a Parisian mob stormed the Bastille prison, a hated symbol of royal power. Matters moved quickly, and within weeks France was in the grip of revolution as peasants across the country rose in revolt against the nobility and clergy.

In August, the Declaration of the Rights of Man was signed and the cry "*Liberté, égalité, fraternité*" (liberty, equality, brotherhood) was heard all over France. These high ideals soon degenerated into a bloodbath of executions; more than 40,000 people were executed. This period, aptly known as the "Terror," was halted only by Napoleon's rise to power.

Henri de Toulouse-Lautrec immortalized the dancers of the Moulin Rouge cabaret in his art

restaurants and shops. In the early 17th century Henri IV launched development by building the place des Vosges, Paris' oldest square. Its balanced brick-and-stone facades, street-level arcades and central garden make it one of the world's most harmonious and beautiful examples of city planning. Surrounding it are fine mansions built along streets such as the rue des Francs-Bourgeois – forming an unspoiled enclave of superb domestic architecture. Neglected and run-down until the 1970s, the area now boasts some excellent and informative museums, among them the Carnavalet Museum; the Picasso Museum; and Victor Hugo's House, once the writer's home, on the place des Vosges itself.

MONTMARTRE

C4 Montmartre Basilique du Sacré-Cœur: 01 53 41 89 00 Basilique du Sacré-Cœur: daily 6:45 a.m.–10:30 p.m (crypt and dome 9–6). Anvers, Abbesses or Lamarck-Caulaincourt Basilique du Sacré-Cœur free (crypt and dome $)

Over-commercialized and crammed with tourists, Montmartre still draws thousands of visitors daily. The neighborhood, once famous for its 40-odd windmills, gained a Bohemian reputation in the late 19th century when artists and writers moved in, among them Pierre-Auguste Renoir, who portrayed the area in some of his liveliest paintings. Later came a new wave of talent, when Montmartre became home to Pablo Picasso and fellow cubist painters. The place du Tertre is the hub of the quarter, nearby is the Basilique du Sacré-Cœur (Sacred Heart Basilica), an ornate 19th-century church whose domes are a familiar landmark on the skyline.

MUSÉE CARNAVALET

D2 23 rue de Sévigné 01 42 72 21 13 Tue.–Sun. 10–5:40 Le Grizzli, see page 551 St.-Paul $$ (free Sun. 10–1)

The Musée Carnavalet (Carnavalet Museum) combines a chance to see the interior of one of the finest houses in the Marais with a fascinating introduction to the history of Paris itself, from pre-Roman times to the present day. Built in 1540 and remodeled in the 17th century, this beautiful Renaissance mansion was the home of Madame de Sévigné, a famous hostess and literary figure during the reign of Louis XIV. Parts of the museum still feel like her home, where the sumptuous furnishings give some idea of the luxury of upper-class life. Allow enough time to study the models showing Paris' development, as well as the reconstructed rooms and quantities of interesting porcelain, silver and objets d'art.

MUSÉE DU LOUVRE

C3 rue de Rivoli (main entrance: Pyramide, Cour Napoléon) 01 40 20 51 51 Wed.–Mon. 9–6 (also Mon., part of museum, and Wed. 6–9:45 p.m.) Restaurants Palais-Royal Musée du Louvre $$ (reduced fee after 3 p.m. and all day Sun.; free to all first Sun. of the month) Self-guided audio tours ($$) and guided tours in English available. Sections are sometimes closed on a rotating basis, so call ahead if there is something specific you want to see

The Musée du Louvre (Louvre Museum), possibly the world's most famous art venue, started life as a palace in the 1190s. Demolished, rebuilt and extended over the centuries, this vast royal residence on the Seine assumed its present form by the 18th century, when the court of Louis XIV moved to the palace at Versailles. The Revolutionary government of 1793 transformed it into a museum to house the royal collections, and over the years donations and purchases have enabled it to be augmented.

By the 1980s the collections had outgrown their home and President François Mitterrand launched the project known as the "Grand Louvre" to renovate and extend the existing museum space. Architect I. M. Pei was commissioned to design a new entrance in the central Cour Napoléon. Below his stunning glass *Pyramide* lies a vast new foyer giving access to the main museum areas, named Richelieu, Denon and Sully. The Louvre still seems huge and confusing on arrival, but it is excellently signposted in French and English, and the bottlenecks that used to occur are largely gone. Go early, study the plan before you start and decide what you want to see, rather than galloping through everything and finishing in exhausted cultural overdose.

The museum is divided into seven departments, ranging from Egyptian, Greek, Etruscan, Roman and Oriental antiquities through a huge and outstanding painting collection, to sculpture, objets d'art, prints and drawings. Most visitors head straight for the most famous pieces, with Leonardo da Vinci's enigmatic and mysterious *Mona Lisa* topping the list. While you stand in line, admire the *Virgin of the Rocks*, also by da Vinci, a work in better shape and just as representative of his genius. The Louvre also has six wonderful paintings by Georges de la Tour, the 17th-century French painter of candlelit night scenes. Take time, too, for Jan Vermeer's light-infused *Lacemaker;* Veronese's *Marriage Feast at Cana*, the largest work in the Louvre, full of fascinating detail; and Raphael's *Beautiful Gardener*, one of the sweetest of all his Virgins.

Two superb classical sculptures draw crowds: the *Winged Victory of Samothrace*, a second-century BC marble figure, full of movement and tension and standing dramatically at the top of a grand staircase; and the *Venus de Milo*, a serene Hellenistic figure of the goddess Aphrodite from the fourth century BC. Contrast these two with Michelangelo's *Slaves*, sculpted nearly 2,000 years later but clearly inspired by classical work.

MUSÉE D'ORSAY

C2 1 rue de la Légion d'Honneur 01 40 49 48 14 Tue.–Sun. 9–6 (also Thu. 6–9:45 p.m.), Jun.–Sep.; Tue.–Sat. 10–6 (also Thu. 6–9:45 p.m.), Sun. 9–6, rest of year Restaurant and snack bar Solférino; RER Musée d'Orsay $$ (reduced fee on Sun.; free to all first Sun. of the month) Guided tours at 11:30 and 2:30. Audiotape about the collection's masterpieces available in English

The architecturally controversial Musée d'Orsay (Orsay Museum) was opened in

The glass pyramid at the Louvre was constructed to celebrate the bicentennial of the French Revolution

1986 in the old railroad station, the Gare d'Orsay. Whatever your view, the wonderful art collection inside cannot fail to impress. The whole field of visual arts – painting, sculpture, architecture and design – from 1848 to 1914 is represented.

The major draw is the superb Impressionist and post-Impressionist collection on the upper and middle levels. Here hangs Edouard Manet's *Olympia*, a glowing portrait of a naked prostitute that caused a sensation when it was painted in 1863. Also in the gallery is a series of garden scenes by Alfred Sisley and Camille Pissarro, where the light is so wonderfully expressed that you can almost tell what time of day it was that the artists were attempting to capture. You'll find world-famous paintings such as Edouard Manet's *Déjeuner sur l'Herbe*, and Claude Monet's radiant light-filled images of Rouen Cathedral and his water gardens at Giverny. Here, too, are James McNeill Whistler's portrait of his mother, glowing examples by Renoir, and Edgar Degas' pert little dancers.

Place de la Concorde

B3 place de la Concorde Concorde

Nothing better epitomizes the self-confidence, wealth and flair of 18th-century France than the vast expanse of the place de la Concorde, scene of Louis XVI's execution in 1793. No matter how many photos you've seen, nothing can prepare you for the sheer scale of this elegant square, with its sweeping views up the Champs-Élysées (see page 179) and down to the Louvre (see page 182), and from the Madeleine to the Assemblée Nationale across the river. The octagonal square is lavishly decorated with statues, while in the center rises the slender shape of a 3,000-year-old Egyptian obelisk, flanked by two graceful fountains.

What's On Where

Brochures published both weekly and monthly help you track down evening entertainment in Paris. English-language publications include *Where Paris, What's On* and *Time Out* (monthly) and the weekly *Pariscope*, which has an English section. These list an enormous selection of entertainment, including temporary events, shows and festivals. You can find them at tourist offices and English-language bookstores.

Le Quartier Latin and Vicinity

Jardin du Luxembourg C2 rue de Vaugirard Daily 7 a.m.–9 p.m. Cluny-La Sorbonne; RER Luxembourg

Panthéon D1–D2 place du Panthéon 01 44 32 18 00 Daily 9:30–6:30, Apr.–Sep.; 10–6:15, rest of year Cardinal-Lemoine or Jussieu; RER Luxembourg $$

The area around the Sorbonne, Paris' renowned ancient university, has long been known as the Quartier Latin (Latin Quarter) because until the 1789 Revolution, Latin was the language spoken by students. Centered around the place St.-Michel and its tree-lined boulevard, this maze of medieval lanes, stores and cafés is thronged with young people throughout the year. Cross the boulevard to admire the elegant Jardin du Luxembourg (Luxembourg Garden), then move on to the Panthéon, where great Frenchmen, including Voltaire and Victor Hugo, are buried.

Tour Eiffel

A3 Champ de Mars 01 44 11 23 23 Daily 9 a.m.–midnight, mid-Jun. to Aug. 31; 9:30 a.m.–11 p.m. (stairs: 9:30–6:30), rest of year Two restaurants in the Tower Bir-Hakeim; RER Champ de Mars Tour Eiffel Elevator: 1st floor $, 2nd floor $$, 3rd floor $$; Staircase: 1st and 2nd floor $

When it was built by engineer Gustave Eiffel in 1889, the Tour Eiffel (Eiffel Tower) was, at almost 1,000 feet, the tallest man-made structure in the world. Part of the World Exhibition, it was an instant success, quickly becoming a familiar symbol of Paris. Its fame has endured, and it remains on most visitors' must-see lists. You can take an elevator to each of its three levels, the views widening at each stage. Mail a letter from the first-floor post office here, and the postmark will be "Paris Tour Eiffel."

Eating and Drinking in Paris

Your hotel will probably provide you with breakfast, consisting of juice, freshly baked baguettes and a selection of croissants and *viennoiseries* (assorted pastries). Drink your coffee from a large breakfast cup, then dip your bread in the strong, steaming brew.

Main Meals

Lunch is generally served from midday until 2:30, and dinner from 7:30 until after 10. If you want either earlier, head for a *brasserie*, a French institution that serves simple, freshly cooked meals – including a daily special – and drinks and snacks throughout the day. Bistros are more modest than restaurants, although not always cheaper. You'll get the best value anywhere by choosing from the *menu* (often called *la formule*), where you'll get a choice of three or four courses for a fixed price. Some noted restaurants also serve what they term a *menu gastronomique*, which will include small portions of many of the famous house specialties. If you order water, you'll probably get bottled mineral water, for which you'll be charged. Wine can be fairly expensive, but all restaurants serve their own house wine in carafes, which is often good value. A typical meal will include a starter, frequently some type of salad; a main course with vegetables; and cheese, followed by the dessert.

Snacks, Fast Food and Picnics

If you want a light lunch you can get something to eat and drink in cafés, which usually have tables outside when the weather's nice. They serve sandwiches and other snacks, and hot, cold and alcoholic drinks. A popular lunch place in Paris is the *bar à huîtres* (oyster bar), where other seafood also is available. There also are plenty of burger joints, as well as the *boulangerie* (bakery), where you can get a variety of savory pastries. For those with a sweet tooth, head to a *pâtisserie* (cake shop) for a mouthwatering range of cakes and pastries. Summer weather may tempt you to plan a picnic: you can put together a wonderful feast at your neighborhood market.

LYON

France's second largest city has much to offer; it's a place where history and tradition, excellent civic facilities and architectural merit combine with commercial importance to give a real big-city feel on a very human level.

The City and the Presqu'Île

Lyon's sprawl may be daunting if this is your first visit, but the city's major tourist attractions are in a surprisingly compact area. Public transportation is excellent (a tram system was inaugurated in 2000), so it should take little time for you to get your bearings. Lyon's name is derived from the Latin *Lugdunum*, the capital of Roman Gaul, which was founded at the foot of Fourvière, the hill above the confluence of two great rivers known today as the Rhône and the Saône. After Rome fell, the medieval town gradually established itself, spreading out slowly to occupy the narrow spit of land immediately above the rivers' junction. This became known as the Presqu'Île (the isthmus), and here the city grew in the 17th and 18th centuries; it was only later that it expanded farther to the north and east. For visitors, the main sights are almost all either along the west bank of the Saône or on the Presqu'Île, the oldest parts of the city.

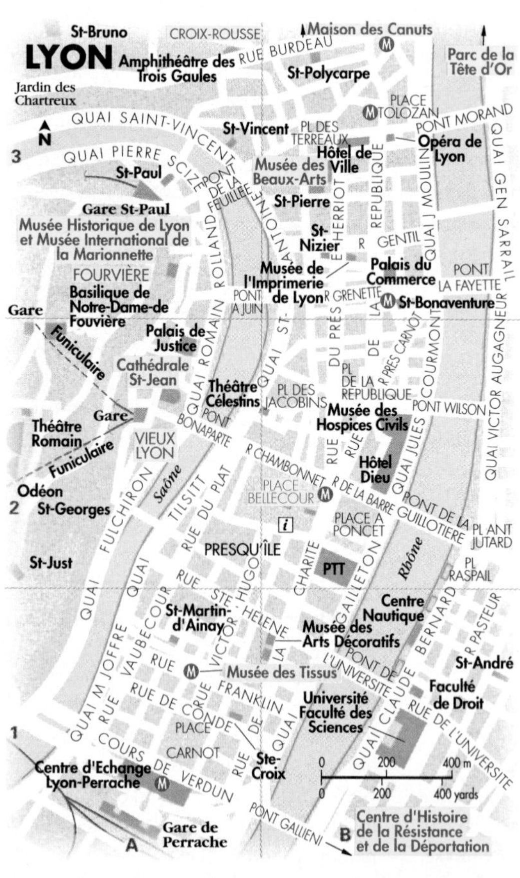

Exploring Lyon

Most visitors use the metro system, or subway, to travel around. Although it will get you from place to place effortlessly, you'll get a better sense of the city's layout if you set out on foot, and walking can actually be quicker. The hill of Fourvière (see page 190) is a useful landmark; if it's on your left you're heading north, right and you're walking south. For orientation purposes remember that the Saône is the river immediately below Fourvière, while the Rhône lies on the other side of the Presqu'Ile. Lyon is remarkably hilly, especially the climb up Fourvière and the slopes of the Croix-Rousse district (see page 189), so a trip to these places probably merits the short metro or bus ride. The two city tourist offices offer an excellent one-, two- or three-day pass called the Lyon City Card. This moderately priced ticket gives you unlimited travel on the bus and metro network, a river cruise (April through October), free admission to Lyon's best museums, a self-guided audio tour (in English) of the historic center, a guided tour on the rooftops of the Fourvière Basilica, discounts at shops and a mass of literature to help make the most of your stay. There is also a Junior Card for ages four to 18. The Lyonnais – with their reputation for common sense, wit and kindness – are helpful and friendly, and are usually happy to assist strangers.

Enjoying the Sights

Lyon, like so many historic cities, needs to be explored at leisure. Wander through picturesque neighborhoods, sit in cafés, pause in the lovely squares and linger on the bridges to admire the river scene. If pressed for time, consider taking a tour. The tourist office can provide details for both bus and walking tours, and cruises run during the summer. This prosperous city is well endowed with museums, some of which are remarkably esoteric. If you're an avid old film fan, period automobile freak or if medical history or the discovery of electricity rivets you – you'll not be disappointed. Lyon also has child-friendly attractions, including a museum of automation history, Europe's largest

Contemporary centerpiece on place Louis Pradel, on the Presqu'Île

doll collection, and a huge and well-presented natural history museum.

La Cuisine

Ask any French citizen what he or she thinks is Lyon's main attraction and the answer will probably be *"la cuisine"* (the food). This is a city where eating is taken very seriously indeed. There are hundreds of restaurants, ranging from very simple to world class, and then there is the wine. North of Lyon, miles of famous vineyards produce quality reds and whites, with names to excite a wine lover – Mâcon, Pouilly, Fleurie and Beaujolais, to name but a few. Wine enthusiasts may consider an excursion to the wine country; the tourist office can help with this.

Souvenirs of Silk

Lyon has all the shopping you would expect from a city of its size and importance. The smartest stores lie in and around rue Président Edouard Herriot, and in the streets near place Bellecour and place des Terreaux, on the Presqu'Île. All the big international names are here, from jewelers, fashion designers and interior decorators to the best of shoe, leather, china and glass stores. The modern city center, around Part-Dieu railroad station, is home to downtown malls and chain stores, and there are also branches of France's top department stores. Lyon has its own specialties, with silk topping the list, and you'll find lovely scarves, ties and fabrics to take home.

On the Town

Lyon has plenty to offer in the way of evening entertainment. Opera, ballet, classical concerts, theater, jazz, rock and movies all thrive, with constantly changing programs; listings are available from the tourist office. There are dozens of bars playing live music; cabaret restaurants; nightclubs and floor shows; discos and karaoke bars; English, Irish and Australian pubs; a casino – the list goes on and on.

ESSENTIAL INFORMATION

TOURIST INFORMATION
Office de Tourisme de Grand Lyon (Lyon Convention and Visitors Bureau)
• place Bellecour ☎ 04 72 77 69 69; fax 04 78 42 04 32; www.lyon-france.com
• 3 avenue Aristide Briand ☎ 04 78 68 13 20

URBAN TRANSPORTATION
Central Lyon is well served by an extensive bus, subway (metro) and tram system. The subway runs daily 5 a.m.–12:30 a.m., and first-time visitors may find it the easiest system to use. You can pick up subway, bus and tram maps from station service points and tourist offices. Subway stations are marked with an "M" on the city map. Tickets, available singly (valid for one or two hours' travel) or in *carnets* (books) of 10, are interchangeable between the metro, bus and tram systems. A one-day travel pass *(ticket liberté)* gives unlimited access to the transport system and is a good value. Remember to validate tickets before boarding. Taxis can be hailed or called (☎ Taxi Villeurbannais 04 78 24 44 44; Radio Taxi 04 72 10 86 86; Allo Taxi 04 78 28 23 23).

AIRPORT INFORMATION
Lyon Saint Exupéry Airport (☎ 04 72 22 72 21) is east of the city, about 30 minutes by taxi.
A shuttle bus connects the airport with the city center in 20 minutes (30 minutes on weekends). Information ☎ 04 72 68 72 17.

CLIMATE – average highs and lows for the month

JAN.	FEB.	MAR.	APR.	MAY	JUN.	JUL.	AUG.	SEP.	OCT.	NOV.	DEC.
5°C	8°C	12°C	14°C	20°C	23°C	27°C	26°C	22°C	17°C	10°C	7°C
41°F	46°F	54°F	57°F	68°F	73°F	81°F	79°F	72°F	63°F	50°F	45°F
0°C	1°C	3°C	5°C	10°C	14°C	17°C	16°C	12°C	8°C	4°C	2°C
32°F	34°F	37°F	41°F	50°F	57°F	63°F	61°F	54°F	46°F	39°F	36°F

The restored old quarter on the right bank of the Saône is the focus of Lyonnais chic

City Sights

Key to symbols

map coordinates refer to the Lyon map on page 186; sights below are highlighted in yellow on the map. address or location telephone number opening times nearest subway nearest bus route restaurant or café on site or nearby admission charge: $$$ more than 75F, $$ 25F to 75F, $ less than 25F other relevant information

Cathédrale St.-Jean

A2 place St.-Jean Cathedral: 04 78 42 28 25. Choir School: 04 78 92 82 29 Cathedral: Mon.–Fri. 8–noon and 2–7:30, Sat.–Sun. and holidays 8–noon and 2–5: Choir School: Mon.–Sat. 10–noon and 2–6 (also Sat. 6–7) Vieux Lyon Free

Post-Roman Lyon grew up around the site of the Cathédrale St.-Jean (St. John's Cathedral), a serene and lofty building with a flamboyant Gothic facade, flanked by a lovely Romanesque 11th-century choir school. Much of the interior dates from the 14th and 15th centuries. The rose windows in the transept are older; their glowing colors first illuminated the center of St. John's in the 1200s.

Centre d'Histoire de la Résistance et de la Déportation

Off the map 14 avenue Berthelot 04 72 73 33 54 Wed.–Sun. 9–5:30 Jean Macé 4, 11, 12E, 17, 18, 23, 39, 43, 47, 96 $$

World War II saw a highly organized, fearless and active resistance movement in Lyon, so it's fitting that the city should have created the fascinating Centre d'Histoire de la Résistance et de la Déportation (Resistance and Deportation Historical Center). The museum's aim is as much to educate the young as to commemorate the past, which it does admirably with permanent and temporary displays, documents, audiovisual guides and videos.

Croix-Rousse

A3 Croix-Rousse Croix-Rousse You can arrange a guided tour at either of the tourist offices

The slopes of the Croix-Rousse (Red Cross) area rise at the north end of the Presqu'Île, the neck of land between the Saône and Rhône rivers. This fascinating area, important in Roman times, was mainly occupied by religious institutions before the French Revolution, but the institutions were dissolved in 1789, leaving the area open to development. In 1804, Joseph-Marie Jacquard invented a new type of semi-mechanized silk loom, on which pattern designs could be programed. These new looms were too large to fit into the old buildings in Old Lyon, where the silk industry first began. Silk workers moved en masse to the Red Cross area, where streets of distinctive, well-lit, high-ceilinged buildings were erected to accommodate them and their machines. It was a vibrant, busy working-class district, which – later in the century – was to see huge civil unrest over low pay. Today it is a UNESCO World Heritage Site and one of the liveliest, earthiest areas of Lyon, with an atmosphere all its own and plenty to see.

Fourvière

A3 Roman theaters: 6 rue de l'Antiquaille, Fourvière 04 72 38 81 90 Daily 7 a.m.–9 p.m., mid-Aug. to mid-Sep; 7–7, rest of year Fourvière Free

One of your first impressions upon arriving in Lyon will be the hill of Fourvière, the site of Roman *Lugdunum*, with its amphitheaters (France's oldest), an odeum (a small, roofed theater) and remains of a craft district. The hill rises above the Saône river, topped by the ornate mass of the Basilica Notre-Dame de Fourvière and what appears to be a scaled-down copy of the Eiffel Tower – actually the Tour Metallique (Metal Tower), built in 1893 and now a television transmitter. Take the funicular to the top in order to avoid the steep climb, and enjoy some fabulous views across the city and its two rivers.

Maison des Canuts

B3 10–12 rue d'Ivry 04 78 28 62 04 Mon.–Fri. 8:30–noon and 2–6:30, Sat. 9–noon and 2–6 Croix-Rousse 2, 6, 13, 33, 45, 61 $

If you're interested in the history of textiles in Lyon, take time to visit La Maison des Canuts (House of Silkweavers), a splendid museum-cum-workshop devoted to the history of silk and silk weavers (*canuts*) and situated in the heart of the Red Cross area. Here you can enjoy a video, browse through old machinery displays and watch silk-weaving demonstrations on three types of traditional looms.

Musée des Beaux-Arts

B3 20 place des Terreaux 04 72 10 17 40 Wed.–Mon. 10:30–6 Hôtel de Ville 1, 3, 6, 13, 18, 19, 44 $$

The elegant mass of the Musée des Beaux-Arts (Museum of Fine Arts) dominates one side of the spacious place des Terreaux, with the impressive Hôtel de Ville (Town Hall) at right angles to it; take a moment to admire the square's fountain. The building was formerly the Benedictine convent of St. Pierre, rebuilt between 1659 and 1685, and it opened as a museum in 1803. One of France's largest art collections, the museum has exhibits from Egypt and the ancient world, and collections of pottery, porcelain, glass and sculpture. Track down the Lalique glass display and the charming animal figurines, including a cumbersome yet graceful polar bear by the 19th-century sculptor François Pompon. Above all, this is an art gallery with a vast collection of paintings. In the entrance foyer Pietro Perugino's *Ascension of Christ,* one of the artist's finest works outside Italy, is a fitting introduction to what's in store.

Musée Historique de Lyon et Musée International de la Marionnette

A3 1 place du Petit Collège 04 78 42 03 61 Wed.–Mon. 10:45–6 Comptoir du Bœuf, see page 551 Vieux Lyon 1, 3, 9, 18, 19, 31, 40, 44 $$

Two museums, the Musée Historique de Lyon (Lyon Historical Museum) and the Musée International de la Marionnette (International Puppet Museum) are housed in one of Old Lyon's stateliest Renaissance mansions, the 15th-century Hôtel de Gadagne. The first museum contains a treasure trove of objects tracing Lyon's history from the Middle Ages to the 19th century – don't miss the fascinating engravings and drawings showing how the city has evolved. Guignol, the famous French puppet, hails from Lyon and is loved all over France for his wit, sarcasm

La Cuisine Lyonnaise

Lyon is said to have more restaurants per capita than any other city in the world; no wonder that even other Frenchmen will admit, *"on mange bien à Lyon"* ("you eat well in Lyon").

Geography helps: the city stands at an agricultural crossroads, benefiting from prime beef from Charolles, wine from Burgundy and superb dairy products from the Dauphiné. The commercial fruit and vegetable gardens of France supply the freshest ingredients, and better *boulangers* (bakers) and *pâtissiers* (cake-makers) than the Lyonnais are hard to find. Here you can spend happy hours practicing the art of *lèche-vitrines*, literally "licking the windows," but in reality window-shopping for food. Have a look in the *boucheries* (butchers), *traiteurs (*delicatessens) like you've never seen before, and *épiceries* (grocer shops) piled high with olive oil, vinegar, honey and jam. Afterward, go to the morning markets on the quai St.-Antoine along the river and drool over the gleaming vegetables, glistening fish and mounds of fruit. Then you can find a restaurant and eat – *bon appetit!*

Lyon has a long tradition of professional kitchens being managed by women, a legacy from times when all restaurants were family-run and *Maman* did the cooking. Such restaurants, known as *bouchons*, still exist, and are usually small and friendly, with visible kitchens. You can count on authentic Lyonnais dishes accompanied by straightforward wines, which are served in small jugs called *pots*, holding a standard amount. Some restaurants are renowned, and it's often necessary to book ahead.

Choice galore – one of the many sidewalk cafés offering Lyon's fine cuisine

What should you eat? The cooking is classic French, with quality ingredients, subtle sauces, properly aged meat and perfectly ripe cheeses. *Boudin blanc*, a veal sausage, is a specialty, as are *quenelles*, lighter-than-air poached fish dumplings served with Lyon's classic crayfish-based *sauce Nantua*. Tripe, pigs' feet and brains may not be what you're used to, but try them. *Pommes Lyonnaises* (potatoes fried with onions) are eaten worldwide, but try *gratin dauphinois* (potatoes baked in cream and cheese) as well. Leave room for a dessert, such as a luscious fruit tart; *île flottante,* a dish with floating islands of meringue on a custard lake; sinful chocolate mousse; or the simplicity of *fromage blanc* – a fresh cream cheese eaten with sugar and cream.

and nagging wife; you can see Guignol, plus a worldwide cast of friends, in the charming puppet museum.

Musée des Tissus

A1 34 rue de la Charité 04 78 38 42 00 Tue.–Sun. 10–5:30 Chabert et Fils, see page 551 Ampère Victor Hugo $$

The Musée des Tissus (Fabric Museum) is appropriately located in Lyon – home of some of the most-beautiful silk and innovative production the industry has seen. A fine 18th-century mansion houses the collection, which has fabrics from all over the world, dating from as early as the fifth century. The Far Eastern silks and embroideries are exquisite, but the Lyon silk and costumes steal the show. These intricate pieces – including designs by Philippe de Lassalle, the greatest master of them all – are still stunningly vivid. Also exhibited are articles of clothing, featuring Mariano Fortuny's Greek-influenced gowns, as wearable today as they were in the 1920s. The Musée des Arts Décoratifs (Museum of Decorative Arts), next door at Number 30, is packed with furniture, china and glass.

Parc de la Tête d'Or

Off the map place Général-Leclerc 04 72 69 47 60 Daily 6 a.m.–11 p.m. in summer, 6–9 in winter 4 Free

Rose lovers should visit the superb 262-acre Parc de la Tête d'Or (Golden Head Park), home of Lyon's botanical gardens, which are beautifully landscaped around a lake. The *roseraie* (rose garden) has more than 60,000 bushes of 350 varieties, all thriving and filling the summer air with an overwhelming scent.

Place Bellecour

B2 place Bellecour Chabert et Fils, see page 551 Place Bellecour

The sweeping expanse of the place Bellecour – the old place Royale – is one of Europe's biggest squares. In the center is a bronze equestrian statue of Louis XIV; within the park are gravel paths and shade trees, making this a splendid oasis of calm in the heart of the busy Presqu'Île.

Vieux Lyon

A2 Vieux Lyon Comptoir du Bœuf, see page 551 Vieux Lyon Guided walking tours available with audiocassette or English-speaking guides. Apply at tourist offices

Until the 1960s, Vieux Lyon (Old Lyon) was a run-down area, many of its beautiful buildings decaying and derelict. Happily, both the French government and the city of Lyon stepped in with funds to save this historic quarter, the largest Renaissance-era urban area in France, and now a UNESCO World Heritage Site.

Here the medieval cathedral town grew and prospered as an international trade and banking center. Rich merchants and bankers built superb, ornately detailed houses along the narrow streets comprising the St.-Paul, St.-Jean and St.-Georges neighborhoods. They still stand today, rescued and restored, with their spick-and-span mullioned windows, vaulted walkways, towers and galleries. Many streets are linked by the passages known as *traboules*, which wind through courtyards and under other buildings; the name is derived from the Latin words *trans ambulare,* meaning "to walk through." Today Old Lyon hums with new life; there are studios, boutiques, and bars and restaurants, thronged in summer with both locals and visitors.

Louis XIV on horseback in the place Bellecour

Silkworms feed on mulberry leaves, which are prevalent in southern France

LYON AND THE SILK TRADITION

Nearly 5,000 years ago the Chinese discovered that the cocoon of an insignificant moth could be gently unraveled in a continuous thread and woven to produce a light and luxurious fabric. This fabric is silk, still one of the softest and most desirable of all textiles.

Silk made its way overland from China to Europe by the 12th century, and by the 1600s Lyon had become the center for European silk production. (The silkworm, *bombyx mori*, also came to Europe and is now a domesticated insect with a ravenous appetite for mulberry leaves, which grow well in southern France and elsewhere.) The industry thrived, producing sophisticated weaves to supply France's rich and demanding upper classes. Sumptuous designs in dazzling colors were achieved on hand looms; silk damask, patterned silks and brocades, and figured silk velvets poured out of the workshops of Lyon.

In 1804, Joseph-Marie Jacquard invented the mechanical loom, which enabled patterns to be programed using a punch-card system. These very large looms were moved from the Old Town into special buildings in the Red Cross area (see pages 189–190) that were designed to accommodate their size. The silkweavers (*canuts*), who also moved, were paid an abysmally low price for each pattern, with the middleman scooping the profits. Finally, in 1831 social unrest erupted, after a three-year struggle by the *canuts* to get better pay and conditions.

By 1870 the industry had recovered and Lyon silk was considered to be among the best fabrics in the world. The creation of artificial silk and other man-made fibers in the 20th century brought an end to large-scale silk production. Lyon's 30,000 weavers dwindled, and today there are only a handful of workshops where people still weave manually; hand-woven weaves are in high demand and are used to help restore the interiors of France's historic buildings.

If you're interested, follow the silk trail in Lyon, from the Old Town to the slopes of the Red Cross district, where you can visit silk workshops and working hand looms. Be sure not to miss the Fabric Museum (see page opposite), keeping in mind that the most a skilled worker could hope to weave was three to four inches a day.

NICE

Nice, France's fifth-largest city and its biggest tourist resort, is perfectly situated on the sweeping Bay of Angels (Baie des Anges). With hills as its backdrop, it is blessed with gorgeous surroundings, a superb climate, a historic past and friendly people. Until 1860 Nice belonged to Italy, and to this day both the way of life and the inhabitants seem to combine the best of both cultures: Italian charm and flair tempered with a strong dash of Gallic sophistication.

The City

The Greeks built their settlement on the hills above the bay, and 300 years later the Romans settled here. The modern city stands on the same spot and has spread down to the flat land along the sea. Sheltered to the east and west by substantial promontories, and with the Maritime Alps to the north, Nice has its own microclimate, with mild winters and perfect summers. Over the centuries city planners and gardeners have taken advantage of these conditions, resulting in one of the most graceful and flower-filled cities in Europe – the average Frenchman's retirement-home fantasy.

In recent years, Nice has marketed itself as a convention center and vacation hot spot, attested by the variety of hotels. It has more museums than any other French city outside of Paris, and plenty of festivals and events throughout the year.

Getting Around

Nice is a big city, with several districts – each of which you'll want to experience. The best way to orient yourself is to take a bus or taxi to an area, then explore on foot. Start with the atmospheric and picturesque Old Town (Vieille Ville, see page 198), which you'll probably want to visit more than once. The seafront stretches nearly 4 miles west of the Old Town, with the famous Promenade des Anglais running along much of it. Behind the promenade and situated around the place Masséna is the commercial and business center, punctuated by peaceful gardens. The upscale residential suburb of Cimiez lies on the hill behind the old port and is home to several excellent museums. As you explore,

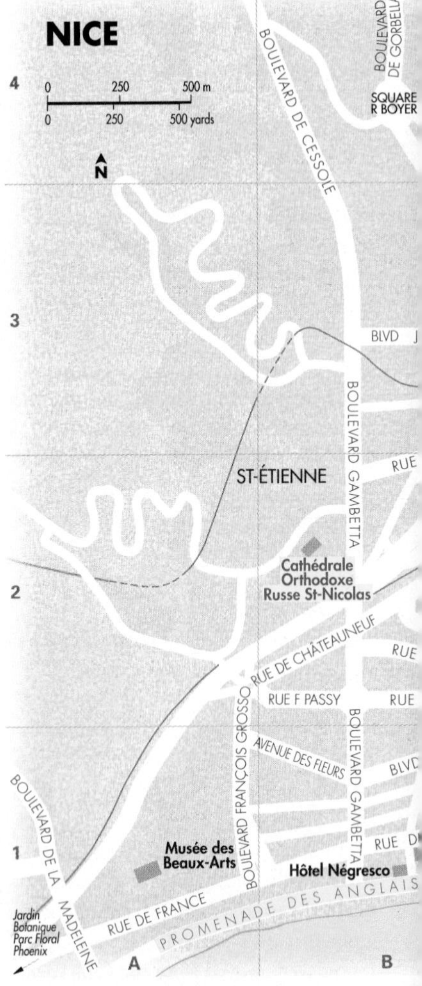

notice how the ambience varies, from the earthy gaiety in the streets of the Old Town to the haute couture you'll find along the Promenade des Anglais. You can see the different parts of Nice in style by hiring a *calèche* (horse-drawn carriage), or by taking the tourist train that trundles around the old quarter.

Flavors of the South

The French- and Italian-influenced cuisine of Nice is complemented by the sunny flavors of southern France. Look for an array of fish and seafood. Vegetable dishes include *salade Niçoise* (made of lettuce, anchovies, tomatoes, hard-boiled eggs and black olives) and *ratatouille* (Mediterranean vegetable stew), which were created here. Also try *mesclun*, a bitter selection of wild leaves. Stuffed vegetables and zucchini flowers fried in batter accompany grilled fish and meat. *Estocaficada* is a Niçois dish made from dried Norwegian cod and tomatoes. *Socca*, a type of pancake made from chickpeas, and *pissaladière*, an onion and anchovy tart, make good light lunches. The area produces several

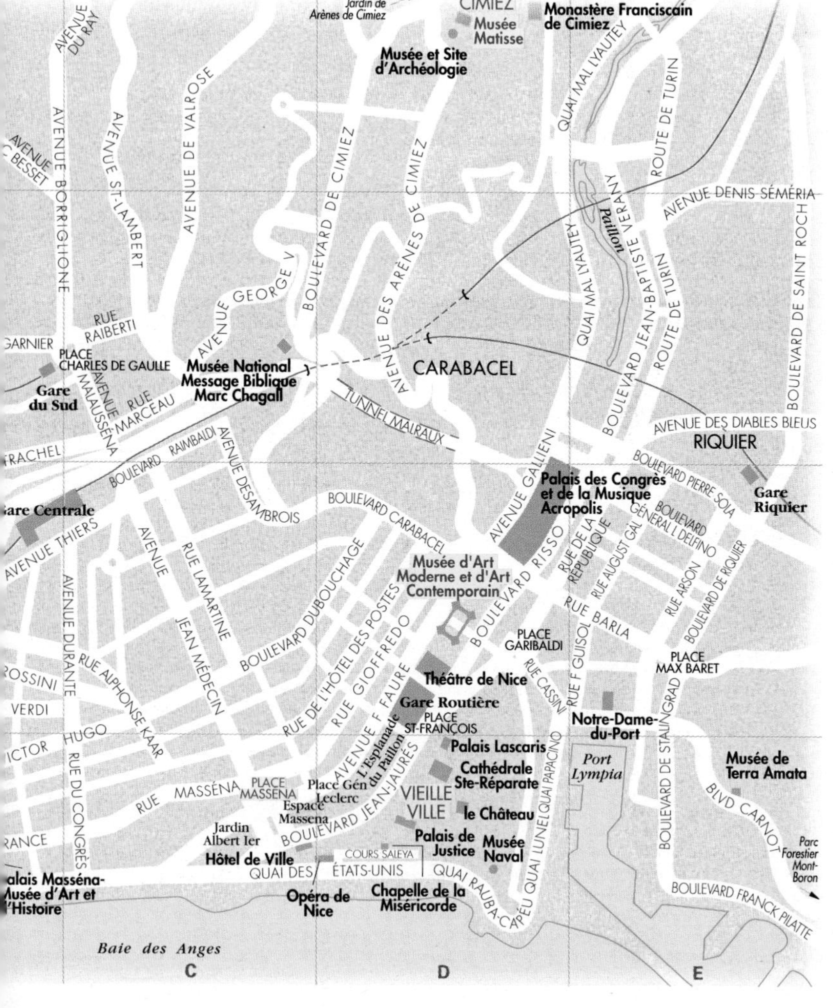

wines, Château de Bellet and Villars among them, and there's an international selection of wines and beer.

Local Wares and Souvenirs

Nice combines the temptations of big-city chain stores and designer outlets with local markets, antique shops and souvenir stores. Department stores and big-name labels are found around place Masséna, while local products are sold in the Old Town. Traditional brightly printed cottons, scents from the hills around Grasse, food, oils and wines make lovely gifts, but the best souvenirs from Nice are traditional carved figurines, known as *santons.*

Carnaval

Nice has a clutch of dynamic theaters, concert halls and an opera, as well as movie theaters, nightclubs, a casino and a host of cabaret restaurants, live-music bars and throbbing discos. The best place to learn about what's going on is through *La Semaine des Spectacles* or *L'Officiel des Loisirs* (on sale at newsstands). Enjoy the local festivals, popular no matter what time of year. The big one is the *Carnaval et Bataille de Fleurs* (Battle of Flowers) in February.

Beaches

Nice has public beaches, but to spend a day in the sun as the Niçois do, go to one of the city's 15 private beaches (open April through October). Included in the fee is an outdoor lounge chair and sun-shade umbrella, changing rooms, freshwater showers, a range of activities and access to a private bar/restaurant. Topless sunbathing is the rule rather than the exception on the French Riviera, but there's no need to partake unless you're comfortable doing so.

ESSENTIAL INFORMATION

TOURIST INFORMATION
Office du Tourisme et des Congrès (Convention and Visitors Bureau)
• SNCF railroad station, avenue Thiers ☎ 04 93 87 07 07
• 5 Promenade des Anglais ☎ 04 92 14 48 00; fax 04 92 14 48 03
• Terminal 1, Aéroport Nice-Côte d'Azur ☎ 04 93 21 44 11
• Nice Ferber, Promenade des Anglais, west end ☎ 04 93 83 32 64; www.nice-coteazur.org

URBAN TRANSPORTATION
Since Nice is so large, you'll probably want to get to each area by bus or taxi, though the latter is more expensive. Sunbus operates all over the city; maps are available from their headquarters (10 avenue Félix-Faure ☎ 04 93 16 52 10) or from any tourist office. Buy your ticket, or *carnet* (book) of tickets at a kiosk before you board; don't forget to validate it. A Sun Pass is available for unlimited travel during 1, 5 or 7 days and is a good deal. Buses run until 1 a.m. Taxis can be found at city-center cab stands (Esplanade Masséna, Promenade des Anglais and place Garibaldi are probably the most convenient locations); or call Central Taxi Riviéra (☎ 04 93 13 78 78).

AIRPORT INFORMATION
Aéroport Nice-Côte d'Azur (☎ 04 93 21 30 30 or 04 93 21 30 12) is west of the city. International flights leave from terminal 1; Paris and other French destinations are served by terminal 2. A shuttle bus (No. 23) runs every half-hour from terminal 1 to the SNCF railroad station in town daily 6 a.m.–9 p.m. Taxis can be found near the airport exits, and take about 15 to 20 minutes to reach the city.

CLIMATE – average highs and lows for the month

JAN.	FEB.	MAR.	APR.	MAY	JUN.	JUL.	AUG.	SEP.	OCT.	NOV.	DEC.
13°C	13°C	14°C	17°C	20°C	24°C	25°C	27°C	24°C	20°C	17°C	13°C
55°F	55°F	57°F	63°F	68°F	75°F	77°F	81°F	75°F	68°F	63°F	55°F
5°C	6°C	8°C	9°C	13°C	17°C	19°C	20°C	17°C	13°C	9°C	6°C
41°F	43°F	46°F	48°F	55°F	63°F	66°F	68°F	63°F	55°F	48°F	43°F

City Sights

Key to symbols

map coordinates refer to the Nice map on pages 194–195; sights below are highlighted in yellow on the map.

address or location telephone number

opening times nearest bus route

restaurant or café on site or nearby

admission charge: $$$ more than 75F, $$ 25F to 75F, $ less than 25F other relevant information

Cathédrale Orthodoxe Russe St.-Nicolas

B2 avenue Nicolas II 04 93 96 88 02

Tours: 9–noon and 2:30–6, Jun.–Aug; 9:15–noon and 2–5:30, mid-Feb. to May 31 and Sep.–Oct.; 9:30–noon and 2:30–5, Nov. 1 to mid-Feb. Daily except Sun. morning and during religious services 5, 7, 14, 15, 17 Religious services: Sat. 6 p.m. (5:30 p.m. Nov.–Feb.), Sun 10 a.m.

The Cathédrale Orthodoxe Russe St.-Nicolas (St. Nicholas' Russian Orthodox Cathedral), an exuberant pink-and-gray church with six green onion-shaped cupolas and an ornate exterior, looks out of place in southern France. Tzar Nicolas II built it from 1903 to 1912, and inside is a dazzling collection of glittering treasures, icons and memorabilia relating to the Russian presence in Nice. A commemorative chapel to Tzar Alexander II's eldest son stands in the park.

Cimiez

Franciscan Church, Monastery and Museum D4 place du Monastère 04 93 81 00 04 Mon.–Sat. 10–noon and 3–6 15, 17, 20, 22, 25 Free Concerts in monastery cloisters in Aug.

Archeological Museum and Site 160 avenue des Arènes 04 93 81 59 57 Tue.–Sun. 10–noon and 2–6, Apr.–Sep.; 10–1 and 2–5, rest of year 15, 17, 20, 22, 25 $$

Jardin des Arènes de Cimiez avenue des Arènes Gardens: dawn–dusk 15, 17, 20, 22, 25 Free

Cimiez, set above the town center, was a smart residential area in Roman times and remains so today. It's packed with interesting attractions, including the Matisse Museum (see right), a Franciscan church and monastery that have stood in their peaceful gardens since the 16th century, a small museum and harmonious cloister devoted to St. Francis, and the cemetery where artists Henri Matisse and Raoul Dufy are buried. The Roman site has been excavated, revealing the remains of an amphitheater and public baths. Housed in a nearby archeological museum are the treasures uncovered, and much more. The Jardin des Arènes de Cimiez (Cimiez's Arena Gardens), with its olive grove, is a good place for a picnic lunch.

The entrance to the remarkable Museum of Modern and Contemporary Art

Musée d'Art Moderne et d'Art Contemporain (MAMAC)

D2 Promenade des Arts 04 93 62 61 62 Wed.–Mon. 10–6 1, 2, 3, 4, 5, 6, 7, 9, 10, 14, 16, 17, 25, 30 $$

There are sweeping views from the roof of the Musée d'Art Moderne et d'Art Contemporain (Museum of Modern and Contemporary Art), or MAMAC, an architecturally stunning museum constructed of four gray marble towers linked by glass walkways. Nice artist Yves Klein founded the museum, whose collection covers European and American avant-garde art from the 1960s to the present. New realism, minimalism and pop art, including works by Roy Lichtenstein and Andy Warhol, are represented here. Look for Klein's highly original *Mur du Feu* (Wall of Fire).

Musée Matisse

D4 164 avenue des Arènes de Cimiez 04 93 81 08 08 Wed.–Mon. 10–6, Apr.–Sep.; 10–5, rest of year Café/restaurant 15, 17, 20, 22, 25 $$

The peaceful setting of the Musée Matisse

(Matisse Museum) amid olive tree groves makes a visit even more worthwhile. Inside are stunning drawings, paintings, hangings, gouache cutouts, engravings and sculptures covering the working life of this remarkable artist. The collection, given to Nice by Henri Matisse in 1954 and by his widow in 1960, is housed in an elegant, vibrantly red, Genoese-style 17th-century villa, fronted by terraced gardens. You can trace the artist's evolution; his style was influenced by late 19th- and early 20th-century art movements such as Impressionism and Fauvism.

Place Masséna and Vicinity

C1 Promenade des Anglais 3, 7, 10, 22
Gardens free

The Niçois regard the elegant, arcaded place Masséna, situated behind the Promenade des Anglais, as the heart of their city. Around the square, with its sparkling fountain representing the planets, are broad boulevards lined with designer stores. On both sides of place Masséna run more than a mile of gardens. Take time to see the palms and roses at the Jardin Albert 1er (Albert I Garden), Nice's oldest gardens, and the Jardins Suspendus du Paillon (Hanging Gardens of Paillon), a stepped garden filled with azaleas, camellias and aromatic pines.

Promenade des Anglais

A1–B1 Promenade des Anglais 3, 7, 10 22
Nice *Carnaval et Bataille de Fleurs* (Feb.), *Fête Nationale* fireworks display (Jul. 14), *Bataille de Fleurs* (Jul. and Aug.), *Nuits Estivales*, summer music evenings (Jul. and Aug.)

Early in the 19th century the English discovered that France's sheltered Mediterranean coast had mild winters, and soon they flocked here in large numbers. Afternoon strolls were fashionable, but the rocky, six-foot-wide path along the shore was hardly suitable for gentle walks. In 1820 the Reverend Lewis Way organized the construction of a sweeping promenade, planted with palm trees and decked with flowers. Not surprisingly, the locals soon called it the Promenade des Anglais (the Englishmen's Walk). Today a busy highway cuts between the sea and the ornate exteriors of the *belle époque* luxury hotels. Even amid the sprawl of ugly concrete apartment blocks, the palms, flowers, strolling crowds and views remain unchanged – a superb background for Nice's festivals.

Vieille Ville

D1 Fruit and vegetable markets: Tue.–Sun. morning. Antiques market: Mon. Flower market: Tue.–Sat. all day, Sun. morning. All on cours Saleya
6, 9, 12

Until the 1970s Nice's Vieille Ville (Old Town) was a decaying slum, with neglected buildings and narrow streets little visited by tourists. Today it's one of the liveliest, most colorful neighborhoods in the city, brimming with life, shops, bars – and noise. Interesting old houses, baroque churches, and 17th- and 18th-century civic buildings line its streets, making it an interesting place to stroll. The cours Saleya is the hub of the quarter, a spacious elongated square that is the home of Nice's famous flower, fruit and vegetable, and antiques markets. Take time to enjoy the scents, and the beautiful produce and flowers on display and for sale.

Strolling along the Promenade des Anglais

PARKS, GARDENS, TREES AND FLOWERS

Flowers at a colorful market stall in Old Nice

Many Mediterranean cities have lovely *parcs* (parks) and *jardins* (gardens), but none more so than Nice. The green swath cutting through the city's heart is only one example, and every street is decked with tubs, planters and window boxes filled with colorful flowers.

Parks

Formal parks lie within the city center, forming a green oasis for locals and visitors; the Jardin Albert 1er, L'Esplanade du Paillon and the Espace Masséna are good examples. Also in the city center, the wooded Parc du Château features winding paths and cascading water. The wilder Jardin des Arènes de Cimiez is a beautifully tended olive grove, the wind rustling the silver-gray foliage on the shapely trees.

Lovely, aromatic Aleppo pine trees, planted in 1866, abound in the Parc Forestier du Mont-Boron; they line almost 7 miles of trails that are edged with wild carnations and tiny orchids. Views from this park are spectacular: to the east is St.-Jean Cap Ferrat, and to the west is Nice's own Bay of Angels.

Gardens

Avid gardeners should head for Nice's Jardin Botanique (Botanic Garden), with a comprehensive and classic collection of Mediterranean flora. The Parc Floral Phoenix is another garden attraction, where you'll find tropical plants and fruit trees. A vast greenhouse – packed with numerous exotic and rare orchids, among other delights – dominates the 17-acre site.

Trees and Flowers

Most of Nice's trees and flowers are common to all Mediterranean countries, where this vegetation thrives in lime-rich, sandy or poor soil; can withstand months of summer heat and drought; and can endure an occasional wet or cold spell in winter. Olives, palms and pines are native; citrus trees, bougainvillea, mimosa, gerbera and many succulents have been introduced. Roses love Mediterranean conditions, which is why you'll see bigger and brighter ones here than anywhere else. If you're in the countryside – nature's own glorious garden – in April, May or June, you'll find spreads of wildflowers to rival any city park.

STRASBOURG

Strasbourg's tiny historic center, circled by arms of the Ill river, could easily lull a visitor into thinking that there was little more to the city than picturesque streets, a breathtakingly beautiful cathedral and a huge number of restaurants. But beyond its medieval core lie grandiose 19th-century civic buildings, an ancient university and the gleaming buildings housing European institutions, since Strasbourg is the seat of the European Parliament. It's a prosperous, cosmopolitan city, a beguiling blend of ancient and modern, Teutonic and French.

A Visitor's Strasbourg

For tourists, modern everyday Strasbourg need not intrude upon enjoyment of the old city. Aim to stay within the old, mostly pedestrian quarter; it's a delightful place to walk around, with an impressive choice of hotels, bars and restaurants. There's a large presence of European parliamentary officials, many of whom speak English, and the range of English-language tourist literature is excellent.

Strasbourg's appeal lies in its combination of history, architecture and culture. First impressions are of a very German city, the timbered houses and cobbled streets reminiscent of villages across the Rhine river, a little to the east. But the atmosphere is definitely French, with the style and way of life that it implies. Lying so near the German border, however, Strasbourg is a favorite destination for day and weekend visits, and you'll see and hear many Germans.

Exploring the City

Undoubtedly, it's best to explore Strasbourg on foot. Apart from visiting the wonderful cathedral, museums and fine churches, most visitors spend time simply strolling the streets. You'll find hidden corners and buildings waiting to

be photographed around every corner, so take your time. Water plays a large part in the city's layout; the center is encircled by water, divided into different channels and crossed by graceful bridges. Old mills and fortifications along the river bear witness to the city's historic importance, while the mighty Rhine, the German border, lies only a stone's throw away.

If you're interested in architecture, you could follow one of several marked routes through the heart of the old city center (see Petite France, page 204). The tram can be useful for saving your legs, and taxis are easily available. There's also the peaceful boat trip around the center (see page 205).

Sample Alsace wines in the Old Town

Eat, Drink and Enjoy

Strasbourg and Alsace is one of the few areas in Europe that produces both notable wines and beers, and it also is home to some of the finest cooking in France. There are strong German influences here, giving the cuisine a different character from typical French fare. History has played a part in this, and it's a pleasure to see the past so clearly reflected at the table – the popular dish *choucroute*, for instance, is really the same thing as sauerkraut.

But don't be fooled. There's much more to the cuisine in Strasbourg than German cooking; you'll find Italian, Chinese, Lebanese, Tex-Mex, Moroccan and others. With all these options, make sure you don't overlook the opportunity to try some real Strasbourg specialties (see page 553). Stop in a *winstub*, a small family-run restaurant often housed in an historic building, where you'll be able to sample the best of local cooking and flavors.

Alsace produces some notable wines, mainly whites, which are similar in character to the best of German wines. They are traditionally labeled with the name of the grape rather than the place of origin. Riesling, Gewurztraminer, Pinot Blanc and Muscat are all reliable varieties to look for. Beer also is big in Alsace, the home of Heineken and Kronenbourg, two of Europe's biggest sellers. Other smaller local breweries produce excellent beer.

Evening Diversions

Strasbourg has a rich cultural life, with its own orchestra participating at the renowned International Music Festival in June; in late September through early October there's the annual *Musica*, a festival of contemporary music. Opera, theater, jazz and dance performances are held year-round and are widely advertised. In summer, most tourists are drawn to the nightly folklore displays of music and dance held in some of the old city's most picturesque squares.

Malls and Markets

Shopping in Strasbourg is a real pleasure, with an excellent choice of the world's best-known designer names,

Timber-framed buildings line cobbled streets in the old part of the city

jewelers, antique shops and international bookstores clustered around the center of the old city. Across the river, Les Halles is a fair-sized shopping mall housing France's familiar chain stores. The weekly market takes place on Wednesdays in the place Kléber – stalls of fresh produce, cheese and meat jostle with inexpensive and cheerful clothes and household goods. Souvenir shops sell Alsatian handicrafts; pottery, lace and carved wood are worth looking at.

ESSENTIAL INFORMATION

TOURIST INFORMATION
Office de Tourisme de Strasbourg (Strasbourg Tourist Office)
• 17 place de la Cathédrale
☎ 03 88 52 28 28; fax 03 88 52 28 29
• place de la Gare ☎ 03 88 32 51 49
• Pont de l'Europe ☎ 03 88 61 39 23
• Aéroport ☎ 03 88 64 50 15; www.strasbourg.com

URBAN TRANSPORTATION
Walking is a delight in historic Strasbourg, although the smooth, modern trams that run across the central island are useful at the start or end of the day. Buy tickets from machines located at stops, and validate them before boarding. Outer Strasbourg is served by an efficient bus service, which you may want to use to visit the Palais de l'Europe (again, validate your ticket). Transportation maps are available at the railroad station and the tourist office. Taxis are plentiful and reasonably priced; you can pick them up at the station, place Kléber or place Gutenberg, or call for one (Taxis 13 ☎ 03 88 36 13 13).

AIRPORT INFORMATION
Strasbourg-Entzheim International Airport (☎ 03 88 64 67 67), with connections to most major European cities, is about 10 minutes south of the city by car. A shuttle bus runs every 10 minutes daily 5:30 a.m.–11:30 p.m. to Baggersee, where tram A connects directly with the city center.

CLIMATE – average highs and lows for the month

JAN.	FEB.	MAR.	APR.	MAY	JUN.	JUL.	AUG.	SEP.	OCT.	NOV.	DEC.
4°C	5°C	10°C	15°C	19°C	22°C	24°C	24°C	20°C	14°C	8°C	4°C
39°F	41°F	50°F	59°F	66°F	72°F	75°F	75°F	68°F	57°F	46°F	39°F
-2°C	-2°C	1°C	5°C	9°C	12°C	14°C	13°C	10°C	6°C	2°C	0°C
28°F	28°F	34°F	41°F	48°F	54°F	57°F	55°F	50°F	43°F	36°F	32°F

City Sights

Key to symbols

map coordinates refer to the Strasbourg map on page 200; sights below are highlighted in yellow on the map.

address or location telephone number

opening times nearest bus or tram route

restaurant or café on site or nearby

admission charge: $$$ more than 75F, $$ 25F to 75F, $ less than 25F other relevant information

Cathédrale Notre-Dame

B2 place de la Cathédrale Cathedral: daily 7–11:30 and 12:40–7. Platform: daily 8:30–7, Jul.–Aug.; 9–6:30, Apr.–Jun. and in Sep.; 9–5:30, Mar. and Oct.; 9–4:30, rest of year. Cathedral closed during Mass Au Bon Vivant, see page 553 A, D Cathedral: free; platform: $; clock: $

A superb example of Gothic architecture, the Cathédrale Notre-Dame (Cathedral of Our Lady) dominates old Strasbourg; its single steeple soars to 466 feet over the surrounding rooftops. It was built between 1176 and 1439, and it stands in a cobbled square on the site of an earlier basilica. A team of masons from Chartres worked on it in the 13th century, creating superb statuary and a harmonious interior, subtly lit by fine stained-glass windows. The main facade, a riot of sinuous, graceful biblical figures and saints, was completed half a century later. A platform constructed in the late 14th century to connect the two towers is reached by 329 stairs and offers commanding views of the city.

The astronomical clock in the south transept is a huge timepiece with a planetary dial constructed in the 1540s. Its automated figures perform daily at 12:30, when the Apostles march before Christ, a cock crows and beats its wings, and the seven ages of man can be seen. The cathedral's loveliest sculpture is the *Pilier des Anges* (*Pillar of the Angels*), a wondrously carved pillar entwined with the four evangelists and trumpeting angels, all heralding the Last Judgment.

Les Grandes Places

B1–B2 place Kléber, place Gutenberg, place de la Cathédrale A, D Christkindelsmärik, last week in Nov. through Dec.

Top: The single-steepled Cathedral of Our Lady, embellished with statuary
Above: Flying the flags – Strasbourg is the center of the European Union

Strasbourg is scattered with *grandes places* (large squares). The main three – place Kléber, place Gutenberg and the place de la Cathédrale – are all within a 5-minute walk of each other. They make an appealing and contrasting trio. The cathedral square, with its cobblestones and timber-framed houses, is distinctly medieval; 18th-century Kléber square has an elegant spaciousness; and Renaissance-style place Gutenberg nicely bridges the architectural time gap. From late November through December, all three squares are the backdrop for Strasbourg's famous *Christkindelsmärik* (Market of the Child Jesus or Christmas Market), a monthlong street market dating from 1570, when the whole town glitters with light and smells of tantalizing spice.

Musée Alsacien

B1 23–25 quai St.-Nicolas 03 88 52 50 00 Wed.–Sat. and Mon. 10–noon and 1:30–6, Sun. 10–5 Au Petit Tonnelier, see page 553 A, D $

If you only have time to visit one museum, it should be the Musée Alsacien (Museum of Alsace) – a charming regional venue housed in a disorderly canal-side building. Not only does it give a chance to see the interior courtyards and inside of a 15th-century house, but it's crammed with many attractive displays, all illustrating traditional Alsatian life. There are complete rooms and workshops, colorful pottery and glass, regional costumes and much more. Look for the votive pictures – naive religious paintings commissioned as prayer and thanks to God, and illustrating farm animals, children and loved ones far away.

Musée Archéologique

C1 · 2 place du Château · 03 88 52 50 00 · Wed.–Sat. and Mon. 10–noon and 1:30–6, Sun. 10–5 · Aux Armes de Strasbourg, see page 553 · A, D · $

Strasbourg is proud of its Musée Archéologique (Archeological Museum), one of France's most important museums of its kind. Imaginatively laid out, it's housed in the basement of the Rohan Palace, and takes the visitor through Alsace from 600,000 BC to AD 800. There are interesting prehistoric sections, but more appealing are the reminders of everyday life in Roman Gaul.

Musée d'Art Moderne et Contemporain

Off the map · 1 place Hans-Jean-Arp · 03 88 23 31 31 · Fri.–Sun. and Tue.–Wed. 11–7, Thu. noon–10 · Museum restaurant · 2, 3, 10, 20 · $$

Opened in 1998, the Musée d'Art Moderne et Contemporain (Modern and Contemporary Art Museum) is an airy building across the water from the Old Town. It covers painting and sculpture from 1870 to the present day. If you're a modern art enthusiast you will not be disappointed, as there is much to enjoy. The room devoted to Gustave Doré gives a fine introduction to his work.

Musée des Beaux-Arts

C1 · 2 place du Château · 03 88 52 50 00 · Wed.–Sat. and Mon. 10–noon and 1:30–6, Sun. 10–5 · Aux Armes de Strasbourg, see page 553 · A, D · $

The elegant first-floor rooms of the Palais Rohan (Rohan Palace) house the Musée des Beaux-Arts (Fine Art Museum), a comprehensive provincial collection covering European paintings from the Middle Ages to the late 19th century. Memling's *Polyptich of Vanity* steals the show, although the museum is justly proud of *La belle Strasbourgeoise,* by Nicolas de Largillière – a portrait of an enigmatic local lady. The ground floor of this same Renaissance building is home to Strasbourg's Musée des Arts Décoratifs (Decorative Arts Museum).

Musée de l'Œuvre Notre-Dame

B1 · 3 place du Château · 03 88 52 50 00 · Tue.–Sat. 10–noon and 1:30–6, Sun. 10–5 · A, D · $

The Musée de l'Œuvre Notre-Dame (Museum of Cathedral Works of Art) occupies a building used from the 14th to 16th centuries for cathedral maintenance. In addition to the rambling warren of fine rooms and staircases, there are courtyards, one of which is planted as a 13th-century garden with medicinal herbs and plants. Some of the cathedral's most precious sculptures are kept here, safely protected from pollution and the elements, and giving the public a chance to admire the elegance of 14th-century Gothic sculpture. The streamlined *Seven Wise Virgins* is a highlight, as is the nearby group of singularly unintimidating lions from the cathedral's main facade.

Petite France

A1 · place Benjamin-Zix · Le Baeckeoffe d'Alsace, see page 553 · The *Strolling in Strasbourg* guide – available from the tourist office – has six walking tours focusing on the architecture of six different periods

As you stroll around Strasbourg, sooner or later you'll reach the picturesque Petite France (Little France). On the banks of the Ill, at the west end of the historic center, cobbled streets are lined with some exceptionally lovely medieval and Renaissance timbered houses, dripping with colorful geraniums and shaded by ancient trees. Little France got its name in the 16th century, when sufferers of syphilis were isolated here, to keep them well away from "worthier" citizens.

Cruising down the Ill river – a perfect way to see the city

A DAY IN STRASBOURG

You awake early in the morning, and your time in this wonderful old city is limited. Here's what to do:

Spend an hour or so strolling around the historic center, visiting one of the daily produce markets and taking some photos in the morning light. Bakers and *pâtisserie* (cake) shops will be open, and you may be tempted to nibble on something as you go. Around mid-morning head for the Ill river, near the Palais Rohan, and buy your ticket for one of the 75-minute boat tours of Strasbourg. On the tour you can sit back and listen to the English commentary about the city's history and important monuments. The tour circles the central island, passing churches, fine buildings and flower-hung, timber-framed houses before heading upstream to give you a glimpse of the modernistic glass and steel palaces housing the buildings connected with the European Union.

Head next for the cathedral, timing your visit so that you'll be there at 12:30, when the marvelous astronomical clock (see page 203) swings into action. Next, it's lunchtime, with a wide choice of pretty outdoor eating places. Try a local specialty, such as *tarte flambée* (onion tart) or a beautifully presented *salade composée* (chef's salad).

If you enjoy museums, the afternoon's the time for checking out two of the best. At the top of the list is the Museum of Alsace (Musée Alsacien), closely followed by the Gothic treasures in the Museum of Cathedral Works of Art (Musée de l'Œuvre Notre-Dame). After this, you may be ready for a drink at a sidewalk café.

Evenings in Strasbourg feature a special dinner in one of the dozens of superb restaurants; be sure to eat a local dish, or follow the set menu, which is bound to be good. Afterward you can go to the movies (in English), a concert or enjoy a folklore display. For many people, a late-night stroll through the atmospheric old streets, followed by a nightcap at a music bar, will nicely round off the day. For others, there are discos and clubs into the early hours.

ℹ Boat tours leave from the landing stage near the Palais Rohan daily on the half-hour 9:30–9, Apr.–Oct.; less frequently 10:30–1 and 2:30–4, rest of year. Call Strasbourg-Fluvial (☎ 03 88 84 13 13) for details. $$. Consult the tourist office about a Strasbourg Pass and for evening events.

GERMANY

"IN Germany one breathes in love of order with the air..."

From the 1900 novel *Three Men on the Bummel* by English writer Jerome K. Jerome

Opposite: Tree-clad gorges and dramatic river views of Bad Schandau, in the Bastesti region

GERMANY
N
NORTH SEA
DENMARK
Westerland
Nord-friesische Inseln
Sylt
Flensburg
Schleswig
Kieler Bucht
Puttgarden
Fehmarn
Mecklenburger Bucht
Nord-Ostsee-Kanal
Kiel
Neumünster
Heide
Bad Doberan
Rostock
Deutsche Bucht
Ostfriesische Inseln
A23
Itzehoe
Lübeck
Wismar
A19
E55
Cuxhaven
Brunsbüttel
A7
A1
Güstrow
E22
Wilhelmshaven
Bremerhaven
Stade
E45
Schwerin
Mecklenburg
Hamburg
A24
E26
Emden
Parchim
A1
E22
Ludwigslust
Oldenburg
Lüneburg
Elbe
Bremen
A7
Wittenberge
Ems
Soltau
Havel
Uelzen
Aller
Cloppenburg
E45
Salzwedel
A1
Nienburg
Celle
Lingen
E37
Weser
Wolfsburg
Stendal
Osnabrück
Minden
A2
NETHERLANDS
Rheine
Hannover
Braunschweig
Gronau
E30
A30
Hildesheim
Wolfenbüttel
Magdeburg
Herford
A31
Lemgo
Hameln
Saltzgitter-Bad
Bocholt
Münster
Bielefeld
Brocken 1142m
Halberstadt
Detmold
Goslar
A43
A2
Gütersloh
Wesel
Northeim
Quedlinburg
Dessau
A57
E34
Paderborn
Harz
Oberhausen
Gelsenkirchen
Saale
Moers
Bochum
Lippstadt
Scherfede
Göttingen
Halle
Duisburg
Essen
Dortmund
A44
Nordhausen
Düsseldorf
Wuppertal
Ruhr
Kassel
Mühlhausen
Naumburg
Mönchengladbach
Solingen
Werra
Buchenwald
Eder
Fulda
Leverkusen
A4
Weimar
COLOGNE
A7
Gotha
Jena
E45
Eisenach
Erfurt
A45
Marburg
Gera
Aachen
Siegburg
Siegen
Alsfeld
Bad Hersfield
Arnstadt
A1
Lahn
E41
Bonn
Thüringer Wald
BELGIUM
Euskirchen
Giessen
Saale
Plauen
Remagen
A3
Westerwald
Rhein
Limburg
Wetzlar
Fulda
Rhön
Koblenz
Bad Ems
Bad Nauheim
Bad Neustadt
A72
Cochem
Taunus
Bad Homburg
E35
Bad Kissengen
Hof
Eifel
A61
Rheintal
Coburg
A9
Mosel
Wiesbaden
Frankfurt am Main
Bitburg
Offenbach
Schweinfurt
E51
A1
Rüdesheim
Main
A48
Main
A70
Aschaffenburg
Bad Kreuznach
Mainz
LUXEMBOURG
E31
Darmstadt
Trier
Bamberg
Bayreuth
Worms
Michelstadt
Würzburg
A1
A3
E45
Idar-Oberstein
A5
Odenwald
Erlangen
Weiden
Fränkische Alb
Kaiserslautern
A6
Mannheim
Wertheim
Fürth
Saarlouis
Homburg
Ludwigshafen
Heidelberg
Bad Mergentheim
Rothenburg ob der Tauber
Nürnberg
Amberg
Neckar
Saarbrücken
Neustadt-an-der-Weinstrasse
Ansbach
A3
Pirmarsens
Bad Wimpfen
Landau
A6
A9
E56
A93
Heilbronn
Öhringen
Dinkelsbühl
Karlsruhe
Maulbronn
Regensburg
Rastatt
Schwäbisch Hall
Pforzheim
Eichstätt
Baden-Baden
Stuttgart
A7
Nördlingen
E43
Ingolstadt
Tübingen
Donau
Amper
Offenburg
Reutlingen
A81
Schwäbische Alb
Freudenstadt
Ulm
A8
Dachau
Freising
FRANCE
Rhein
Schwarzwald
A5
Hechingen
Augsburg
E35
Triberg
Lech
MUNICH
Villingen
Sigmaringen
Freiburg
Donaueschingen
A96
Rosenheim
Titisee
Ravensburg
Ottobeuren
Überlingen
Meersburg
Kempten
Oberammergau
Lorrach
Friedrichshafen
Füssen
Garmisch-Partenkirchen
Konstanz
Allgäuer Alpen
Bodensee
Lindau
2962m Zugspitze
Mittenwald
SWITZERLAND
Oberstdorf
5
4
3
2
1
A
B
C

GERMANY

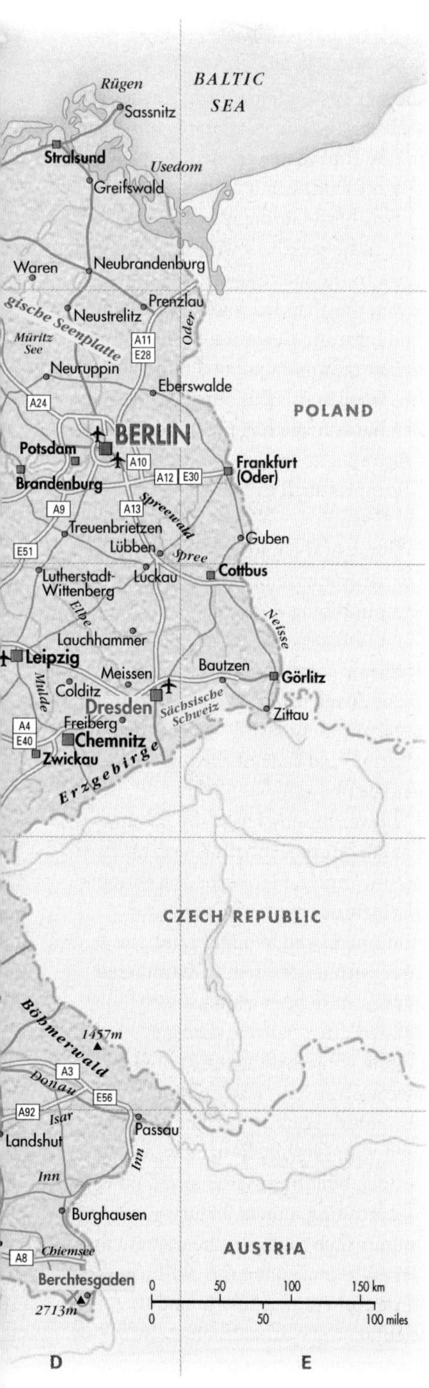

Germany is not easily summed up. Before 1871 there was no single, unified German state: the area was made up of several territories, loosely knit together in alliance. Their local languages and loyalties still have first claim on many Germans' hearts.

After World War II, the country was split between two opposed powers: the West, whose territory was known as the Federal Republic of Germany, and the Soviets, who created the German Democratic Republic (G.D.R.). In 1989, faced with popular protests and a retreating Soviet authority, the G.D.R.'s government opened the Berlin Wall, which had divided the city's eastern and western zones since 1961. A year later the country was reunited, and a new Germany was born. But within its unified political boundaries, this is still a nation of diversity, where the people and cultures vary as dramatically as the landscapes.

MORE TOP DESTINATIONS IN GERMANY

• Bamberg C2 • Berchtesgaden D1 • Bodensee (Lake Constance) B1 • Dresden D3 • Freiburg B1 • Goslar C4 • Hamburg C5 • Heidelberg B2 • Lübeck C5 • Mecklenburgische Seenplatte D4 • Regensburg D2 • Rheintal B2 • Sächsische Schweiz E3 • Trier A2 • Tübingen B1 • Ulm C1

Traveling in Germany

Germany's 16 administrative states (*Bundesländer)* extend from the tail of Denmark south to the Swiss and Austrian Alps; the Netherlands, Belgium, Luxembourg and France border on the west, Poland and the Czech Republic on the east. Each state has enough of interest for the visitor to occupy a whole vacation in its own right, and Germans are themselves often tourists in their own country, especially as westerners and easterners explore each other's previously unknown territories.

Traveling – by automobile or by public transportation – is not a problem, despite the country's size. The road network in western Germany is excellent, from the highways (*Autobahnen*) to minor roads. In the east, roads were in poorer condition for many years, but there have been recent improvements.

The biggest culture shock to drivers is likely to be the speed of traffic. There is no official upper limit on highways, and many drivers ignore the recommended 130 k.p.h., the equivalent of which is 80 m.p.h. Driving etiquette is taken seriously, though: you can be stopped and fined for swearing or making rude gestures.

Taking the train is a convenient way to cover large areas. The quickest and most comfortable trains are the InterCity (ICE) and Eurocity trains, linking major centers – but the InterRegios, connecting smaller towns, are also fast.

The North and the Baltic

Northern Germany has a maritime character. Schleswig-Holstein, a province Germans and Danes have often fought over, is made up of two former dukedoms and shares the coastline with Lower Saxony. Together they take in a shore ranging from the fjords and hills of the Baltic coast to the wind-lashed North Sea beaches. Inland, the countryside is wide, rolling farmland and peat bogs; offshore, the North Friesian islands are favorite summer destinations, with beaches and brisk sea air. The inhabitants of coastal Friesland have maintained their own separate culture and dialect.

Northern Germany's cities were a force to be reckoned with in the Middle Ages. In the interests of trade and power, they banded together to form the Hanseatic League, a protected market that monopolized trade between the North and Baltic seas. The league's merchants made huge fortunes and had impressive houses and churches built in seaports such as Hamburg, Lübeck and Bremen.

Some of their legacies have survived – or at least have been rebuilt after the heavy bombing raids of World War II. The Gothic/Renaissance architecture of Bremen's Town Hall and Lübeck's Music Academy, both converted from merchant homes, still suggests the affluence and style of the region's medieval heyday.

Lower Saxony has many features that are quintessentially German. Its historic center, Hannover, is a thriving commercial city; towns such as Hildesheim and Wolfenbüttel, the latter with its painted, half-timbered facades, have been immaculately restored after wartime damage.

The winter sports resort of Goslar, once a silver- and lead-mining town, has picture-book streets and squares lined with Gothic, Renaissance and baroque buildings, some inscribed with gold lettering, others featuring curving, sinuous slate roofs. To the east are the Harz Mountains, on the old East/West border, where witches are said to celebrate their Sabbath on *Walpurgisnacht*, the eve of May Day.

Sumptuous Renaissance and baroque style draws the crowds to Linderhof Castle

The Rhine

The great 820-mile Rhine flows from the Swiss Alps across the western regions of Germany, through the ancient city of Koblenz and the recently deposed seat of West German government, Bonn, and through the industrial country of Ruhr toward Rotterdam. Its valleys and those of its tributaries, the Mosel, Main, Nahe and Neckar, have been producing wines (mainly white) since Roman times. Castles with fairy-tale Gothic towers loom over the river, built for their powerful princes' protection and profit, which was gleaned from tolls on passing river traffic.

On the Lorelei rock, above the twisting Rhine gorge, the beautiful siren Lorelei is said to lure sailors to their death with her enchanting song. This is a romantic, myth-laden part of the country, and a river cruise is one of the most popular ways of seeing it.

The East

After years of restricted travel, border guards and obsessive document checking, eastern Germany is now completely open to visitors. When the Berlin Wall came down, East Germans poured into the West, eager to boost incomes, and some West Germans raised their voices against the sudden influx and resulting unemployment and uneasiness. After the initial euphoria of reunification came the backlash of mutual resentment and offshoots of xenophobia. Integration has pressed on, nevertheless, and financial investment in the east (another grievance to some western taxpayers) has brought new business and better facilities, although there is still a marked difference compared to the affluent west. English is less likely to be spoken here.

One of eastern Germany's highlights is Dresden, which re-created itself after devastation by more than 2,000 Allied

Bavarian craftsmanship – the astrological clock on the Old Town Hall in Munich

bombers in 1945. Fine 18th-century buildings surround its Brühlsche Terrace, an elevated section on the bank of the Elbe river, and the nearby baroque Zwinger pavilions house a marvelous collection of museums. Leipzig, the famous medieval university town, is also worth visiting, with its pedestrian-only center and attractive gardens and squares.

Weimar, once the home of poet and dramatist Johann Wolfgang von Goethe, composers Franz Liszt and Richard Strauss, and philosopher Friedrich Nietzsche, has a core of lovely historic buildings, parks and boulevards. The gentle hills and red-roofed villages of the Thüringian Forest form a stretch of popular walking country, despite some parts suffering the effects of industrial pollution; the region has a growing industry of family-run lodgings and restaurants.

The Black Forest and Bavaria

Two states make up southern Germany: Baden-Württemberg in the southwest and Bavaria in the southeast. As the name suggests, Baden-Württemberg is itself made up of two distinct areas: mainly Catholic Baden, where the inhabitants are reputed to be amiable and easy-going, and traditionally Protestant Württemberg (Swabia), where the work ethic is strongly established and the Swabian dialect is spoken.

Lovers of the outdoors flock to the Black Forest (Schwarzwald), a swath of highlands reaching over 3,900 feet and encompassing attractive villages, lush valleys, orchards and meadows as well as woods. Clock-making has been a successful industry here since the 1660s, and cuckoo clocks are on sale at every gift shop. The other notable local product is Black Forest cake – the authentic and superior original is called *Schwarzwälder Kirschtorte.*

East of the Black Forest is a range of limestone cliffs and hills known as the Swabian Jura, where castles peer down at the Danube (Donau) river as it begins its long journey to the sea. Pleasant resorts surround the "Swabian Ocean," Lake Constance (Bodensee), which straddles the German-Austrian border. The Neckar river flows through Swabia's vineyards and past romantic Heidelberg, where students and tourists really do raise huge beer tankards over tavern tables, as they did in Sigmund Romberg's operetta *The Student Prince.*

Clichés also come true in southern Bavaria. Here the people are characterized by their detractors as loud and brash, and by their admirers as humorous, warm and fun-loving. They are often seen in traditional leather trousers (*Lederhosen*) or embroidered dresses, and are primarily Catholic and conservative: the standard daily greeting here is *"Grüss Gott,"* or "God's greeting."

Between the Bavarian capital, Munich (München), and the magnificent Alpine peaks lie the wooded hills, pretty villages, lakes and castles that attract so many visitors to this part of the country. The spectacular Alpine Road takes in the mountain scenery and passes the theatrical 19th-century castles of Linderhof, Herrenchiemsee and Neuschwanstein – all three are almost always packed to the brim with sightseers.

Northern Bavaria has its own character. In fact, not everyone here appreciates being labeled "Bavarian": this is the region known as Franconia (Franken), and its main city is Nuremberg (Nürnberg). Architecture and art come into their own here. During the late Middle Ages and early Renaissance, artists such as Lucas Cranach and Albrecht Dürer were prominent in Germany, and Nuremberg's wonderful German National Museum displays some of their best work. A more sinister aspect of the city's past is recalled in the giant stadium and Hall of Congress, built for Hitler's mass rallies, and preserved as chilling memorials to that era.

The hugely popular Romantic Road, running from ancient Würzburg and the Franconian wine country all the way to the Alps, 217 miles south, links several unspoiled medieval towns. On the way, it passes Rothenburg ob der Tauber, one of the loveliest old towns in Germany – and as a result one of the most crowded. Also on the route are the old walled, half-timbered town of Dinkelsbühl and the splendid Renaissance city of Augsburg.

Spa Towns

Health and fitness are national preoccupations, apparent in the German love of soccer, skiing and tennis, and in the spa towns that thrive all over the country. In addition to their statutory annual vacation, German employees are given six weeks a year to reap the benefits of medicinal waters and enjoy the spas' other facilities, which can include mud baths, saunas and steam treatments.

Germany's oldest casino is one of the features of Baden-Baden, a celebrated spa town with graceful 19th-century hotels. Other spas are also worth investigating. Bad Ems, in the Rhineland's picturesque Lahn valley, was 19th-century ruler Kaiser Wilhelm's personal favorite. A steam train travels from Bad Doberan, near Rostock in eastern Germany, to the country's oldest seaside resort, Ostseebad Heiligendamm, founded in 1793. Bad Kissingen, Bavaria's most popular spa, is on the banks of the Saale river.

TIMELINE

800–700 BC	Celtic tribes settle around the Rhineland.
AD 800	Franks overrun the territory; Charlemagne, the Frankish king, is crowned Holy Roman Emperor.
1273	Rudolf of Habsburg is elected emperor, founding the 600-year Habsburg dynasty.
1517	Martin Luther precipitates the Reformation.
1740	Frederick the Great is crowned king of Prussia.
1871	Franco-Prussian War ends with states united under the Prussian Kaiser Wilhelm and chancellor, Otto von Bismarck.
1914–19	Habsburg claims to the Balkans lead to World War I; the Treaty of Versailles demands huge war reparations and surrender of territories from defeated Germany.
1930	The Nazis gain power in elections.
1933	Adolf Hitler is made chancellor; under Hitler's dictatorship, millions of Jews and minorities are persecuted and killed.
1939	Hitler invades Poland; Britain and France declare war.
1945	Allied forces enter Berlin; Hitler kills himself.
1949	Western occupying powers create the Federal Republic of Germany; Russia forms the German Democratic Republic.
1961	The Berlin Wall is built.
1990	A year after the demolition of the wall, East and West Germany reunite; Germany leads support for a politically and economically integrated European Union.
1999	Newly refurbished, glass-domed Reichstag unveiled in preparation for the return of seat of government to Berlin.

MAD KING LUDWIG

Ludwig II of Bavaria lost all interest in running his kingdom after it was drawn first into war and then into the German Empire by the Prussian Chancellor, Otto von Bismarck. The late 19th-century ruler was left with nothing to do but amuse himself, which he did by having three flamboyant castles built – Herrenchiemsee, Linderhof and Neuschwanstein – and watching them take shape through his telescope. Ludwig found other ways to spend his money, too, supporting Richard Wagner while he wrote his operas, but eventually he ran out of cash altogether. This and his eccentric manner made him an increasing liability to the Bavarian government. Its ministers plotted with Ludwig's uncle Luitpold to depose him and certify him insane. Only days later, Ludwig and his doctor drowned in the Starnberger See, a boating lake near Munich – whether by accident or design, no one knows.

SURVIVAL GUIDE

- Formality plays an important part in everyday German life. Don't address people by their first names unless invited to; always use *Herr* (Sir) or *Frau* (Madam) at first.
- Job titles are used frequently in social exchange; doctors, for instance, are addressed as *Frau Doktor* or *Herr Doktor.*
- People tend to shake hands upon meeting, but women are often kissed on both cheeks, Continental-style.
- Local dishes, particularly in southern Bavaria, use the classic German ingredients of *Sauerkraut* (pickled cabbage), *Wurst* (sausage), dumplings, pork and potatoes. German cooking (*Gutbürgerliche Küche*) can be sampled at a *Gasthaus*, a restaurant serving simple meals.
- German wine is mainly white. *Tafelwein* is table wine, less expensive and harsher than the quality stuff; *Deutscher Tafelwein* is guaranteed to be wholly German, rather than a mix of different countries' grapes. *Qualitätswein* is the better product, from a specified range of vineyards. Some of the best grapes are *Riesling*, the fruity *Müller-Thurgau* and the spicy *Gewürztraminer.*
- Brewing is big business in Germany. *Bock* is a strong beer, light or dark, popular in Bavaria; *Weisse* is pale wheat beer, and *Malz*, an unfermented black malt beer.
- *Imbiss* (snack) stands are found everywhere and sell hamburgers, meatballs, sausages and other fast food.
- Stores in the main cities are usually open from 9 a.m. until 6:30 p.m. Many close on Saturday afternoons, but some stay open until 4 p.m.
- Germany has a long tradition of toy-making, particularly china dolls and the famous Steiff teddy bears. Antiques sell for enormous sums.
- Beer and wine festivals take place all over the country. Munich's September/October *Oktoberfest* is the best known; *Weinfeste*, celebrations held in the Rhine-Mosel area during the harvesting of the grapes, also are worth attending.
- Dinkelsbühl's 10-day *Kinderzeche* festival, held in July, recalls the Thirty Years' War, when local children persuaded Swedish soldiers not to ransack their town. It features plays, a pageant and the boys' band, the *Knabenkapelle*, dressed in 18th-century military garb.
- The music of Richard Wagner is performed in the summer *Bayreuth Festival*, northeast of Nuremberg near the composer's former home. Tickets are often snapped up a year in advance; for information contact Bayreuther Festspiele, Kartenbüro, Postfach 100262, D-95402 Bayreuth, Germany.

Traditionally decorated beer mugs

BERLIN

No other city better illustrates the upheaval in late 20th-century Europe than Berlin. For nearly 30 years it was, for all intents and purposes, two cities. Tourists posed on the Western side of the Berlin Wall, and those who crossed the East-West boundary at Checkpoint Charlie did so with the trepidation of travelers to another planet.

Then, in 1989, Berlin changed virtually overnight. The wall has all but vanished; Checkpoint Charlie is a museum; the No Man's Land that lay between the two zones is now the site of a new complex of ministries, offices, stores and hotels, ready for the return of the German parliament and government. Reunified Berlin is an exciting, restless place, reinventing itself at a fast pace.

Berlin Flavors

There are many restaurants and cafés in Berlin, serving every imaginable kind of food. The most popular restaurant areas are around Savignyplatz and Hardenbergstrasse and on the Ku'damm, and all buzz late into the night. Berlin has a larger Turkish community than any other city outside Turkey, and many live in the old quarter of Kreuzberg, where inexpensive Turkish meals are served in dozens of restaurants, especially in the neighborhood of Kottbusser Tor.

Kaffee und Kuchen (coffee and cakes) is an institution, usually indulged at about 4 p.m., but it doesn't come cheap. The café that started it all – Café Kranzler, which opened in 1835 – still operates on the Ku'damm.

Heavy, hearty German food can be sampled all over the city, in restaurants or in a tavern (*Kneipe*). There are more than 4,000 taverns, many offering *Hackepeter* (meatloaf), *Aal grün* (eel in parsley sauce) and *Solei* (pickled eggs).

If you find the traditional fare daunting, try the lighter new German cuisine (*neue Deutsche Küche*) at restaurants such as Trio, on Klausenerplatz.

Beer is, of course, a favorite beverage. One custom is to have a *Korn* – a light beer with a *Schnapps* chaser; another, a summer choice, is *Berliner Weisse mit Schuss*, light beer turned pink with raspberry liqueur or green with extract of woodruff.

Music and Cabaret

In the 1920s Berlin had a reputation for "divine decadence," as portrayed in the 1972 film *Cabaret*. The cabaret tradition has been revived, albeit in a milder form, and there are clubs all over the city; there also are folk, jazz and other music venues. For the latest details consult *Berlin TutGut* (from tourist offices), which has English-language listings, or the *Berlin Das Magazin* (*Berlin – The Magazine*, published three times a year). The busiest district for entertainment is in Scheunenviertel.

The Berlin Philharmonic, perhaps the world's best-known orchestra, has its home at the Philharmonie, in the Kulturforum, a complex of concert halls and museums on Potsdamer Strasse. The Berlin Symphony Orchestra performs in the 19th-century Konzerthaus Berlin (Berlin Concert House), at

Gendarmenmarkt. Berlin's oldest opera house is the Staatsoper (State Opera), a lovely baroque concert hall on Unter den Linden – its glittering list of past directors includes Franz Liszt.

Store of the West

One of Europe's biggest department stores – second only to Harrods of London – is found in Berlin: the KaDeWe (Kaufhaus des Westens, or Store of the West), which stocks more than 250,000 items in its building on Tauentzienstrasse and stays open late on Thursdays.

A branch of the Paris flagship, Galeries Lafayette, is on Friedrichstrasse, near the designer shops on the same street. In the leisure and shopping complex Europa-Center, not far from KaDeWe, there are more than 100 stores, cafés and bars.

Berlin porcelain makes a perfect souvenir. It's been produced here since 1763, when the Royal Porcelain Factory (K.P.M.) opened, and the factory's main store is on the Ku'damm.

Street markets flourish in this city; try Nollendorf flea market, which operates from Wednesday to Monday in the old Nollendorf S-Bahn station. The popular morning Winterfeldtmarkt, a lively affair on Winterfeldtplatz, has anything and everything for sale.

Berlin Classicism

Sculptor, painter, set-designer and architect Karl Friedrich Schinkel left his mark all over Berlin. After designing the Prussians' military medal, the Iron Cross, he was commissioned to create a series of civic buildings, including the National Theater, the museums on Museum Island and St. Nicholas' Church in Potsdam. He mixed his own Romantic tastes with the royally approved Classical style to form "Berlin Classicism," and gave his undivided attention to every detail, right down to the doorknobs.

ESSENTIAL INFORMATION

TOURIST INFORMATION

Berlin Tourismus Marketing GmbH

• Am Karlsbad 11 ☎ 030 264 748-0 or 0190 754 040 (information); fax 030 264 748-99; www.berlin-tourism.de
• Europa-Center, Budapester Strasse 45
• Brandenburger Tor (Brandenburg Gate), Pariser Platz
• Kaufhaus des Westens, Tauentzienstrasse 21–24
• Flughafen Tegel (Tegel Airport)

URBAN TRANSPORTATION

There are two city rail networks: the subway (U-Bahn) and the city railroad (S-Bahn), and tickets are interchangeable. The S-Bahn is marked on the Berlin city map as an "S" in a red circle. Buy tickets (valid for all forms of transport) in the station foyer and validate them in the machine on the platform. Trains run daily 5 a.m.–12:30 a.m.; U-Bahn lines 9 and 12 and S-Bahn line 7 run all night Friday and Saturday. Bus route 100 runs through the center from Bahnhof Zoo (Zoo station) in the west to Unter den Linden in the east. The main bus terminal is Funkturm (☎ 030 301 8028). Trams are mainly confined to eastern parts of the city. Taxi stands are all over the city. Use only metered cabs (☎ 030 261 026 or 030 210 101).

AIRPORT INFORMATION

Berlin has three international airports: Tegel (northwest), Schönefeld (southeast) and Tempelhof (south). Bus 109 runs from Tegel to Zoologischer Garten and bus X9 to Ku'damm. From Schönefeld S-Bahn lines 9 and 45 and from Tempelhof U-Bahn line 6 all run to the city center. For airport information ☎ 0180 500 0186.

CLIMATE – average highs and lows for the month

JAN.	FEB.	MAR.	APR.	MAY	JUN.	JUL.	AUG.	SEP.	OCT.	NOV.	DEC.
2°C	3°C	8°C	12°C	18°C	21°C	23°C	23°C	18°C	13°C	7°C	3°C
36°F	37°F	46°F	54°F	64°F	70°F	73°F	73°F	64°F	55°F	45°F	37°F
-3°C	-3°C	0°C	2°C	7°C	11°C	13°C	13°C	10°C	5°C	2°C	-1°C
27°F	27°F	32°F	36°F	45°F	52°F	55°F	55°F	50°F	41°F	36°F	30°F

CITY SIGHTS

Key to symbols
map coordinates refer to the Berlin map on pages 216–217; sights below are highlighted in yellow on the map. address or location telephone number opening times nearest subway nearest bus route restaurant or café on site or nearby admission charge: $$$ more than DM8, $$ DM3–DM8, $ less than DM3 other relevant information

ALEXANDERPLATZ

E3 Alexanderplatz Fernsehturm: 030 242 3333 Fernsehturm: daily 9 a.m.–1 a.m., Mar.–Oct.; 10 a.m.–midnight, rest of year. St. Marienkirche: Mon.–Thu. 10–noon and 1–5, Sat. noon–4:30 Zum Nussbaum, see page 554 or restaurant in Fernsehturm U-Bahn/S-Bahn to Alexanderplatz 100, 157, 348; tram 2, 3, 4, 5, 6, N54, N92 Fernsehturm $$$

Alexanderplatz, the marketplace known to Berliners as "Alex," was the heart of the old city. After World War II it was rebuilt in a bleak style but is now scheduled for renovations. Two old buildings have survived: the Rotes Rathaus (Red City Hall), built from 1860 to 1868 to emulate the Italian Renaissance style; and the 15th-century Marienkirche (St. Mary's Church), Berlin's second-oldest parish church. At the center of the square, Fernsehturm, a 1,207-foot television tower, soars above the city; there's a revolving restaurant and a viewing platform at the top.

BAUHAUS-ARCHIV

C2 Klingelhöferstrasse 14 030 254 0020 Wed.–Mon. 10–5 Café on site U-Bahn to Nollendorfplatz 100, 129, 187, 341, X9 $$

Following World War I Walter Gropius founded a new architectural movement in Weimar, stressing function above beauty and encouraging collaboration between art and industry. The Bauhaus (Building House) school had an immense influence on 20th-century design, but was condemned by the Nazis and moved first to Dessau and then to Berlin before being closed in 1933. The Gropius-designed Bauhaus-Archiv (Bauhaus Museum), built in 1979, shows examples of the style – from chairs to models of buildings – and explains the aims of the Bauhaus artists.

Symbol of reconciliation – East meets West at the Brandenburg Gate

BERLINER DOM

D2 Am Lustgarten 030 2026 9119 Mon.–Sat. 9–8, Sun. noon–8, Apr.–Sep.; Mon.–Sat. 9–7, Sun. noon–7, rest of year. Last admission to dome at 5, Apr.–Sep.; at 4, rest of year Lutter & Wegner, see page 554 U-Bahn/S- Bahn to Alexanderplatz; S-Bahn to Hackescher Markt 100, 157, 348; tram 2, 3, 4, 5, 6, 15, 53 $$ (including dome $$$) Guided tours of dome

Berliner Dom, Berlin's Protestant Cathedral, is a monument to imperial wealth and power, containing 100 sarcophagi and tombs of the royal Hohenzollern dynasty in its vault. Completed in 1905, its dome is intricately decorated with mosaics.

BRANDENBURGER TOR

D2 Pariser Platz Borchardt, see page 554 S-Bahn to Unter den Linden 100, 147, 248, 257, 348

Built from 1788 to 1791 as an "arch of peace," the Brandenburger Tor (Brandenburg Gate) was modeled after the entrance to the Acropolis temple in Athens. A sculpture of the goddess Viktoria and her chariot, added to the top in 1794, was stolen by Napoleon 12 years later. On its return, Karl Friedrich Schinkel added a triumphal wreath and iron cross to the goddess' staff. During the East-West split, it stood in No Man's Land. Now a symbol of reconciliation, it forms a backdrop for pop concerts.

Modern sculpture at the Kulturforum

Haus am Checkpoint Charlie

D2 Friedrichstrasse 43–45 030 253 7250 Daily 9 a.m.–10 p.m. Café on site U-Bahn to Kochstrasse 129 $$–$$$

The crossing point of the Berlin Wall, known as Haus am Checkpoint Charlie (House at Checkpoint Charlie), is now a tourist attraction. The Eastern border guards' hut was taken down in 1990 and moved to the Deutsches Historisches Museum on Unter den Linden. The site has a display of paraphernalia and photographs illustrating the effects of the wall and various escape attempts. A video on the history of the wall includes a look at the graffiti artists who decorated the Western side.

Kaiser-Wilhelm-Gedächtnis-Kirche

B2 Breitscheidplatz 030 218 5023 Memorial Hall: Mon.–Sat. 10–4; New Chapel: daily 9–7 Berliner Stube, see page 554 U-Bahn/S-Bahn to Zoologischer Garten; U-Bahn to Kurfürstendamm 100, 109, 119, 129, 146 Free

Although it stands in poverty-ridden Breitscheidplatz, the landmark Kaiser-Wilhelm-Gedächtnis-Kirche (Kaiser William Memorial Church) is worth visiting as a memorial to the devastation of World War II. The 19th-century Romanesque hall was all that remained of Kaiser Wilhelm II's church after the 1943 air raids; it has been left as it was, and a modern octagonal chapel and hexagonal blue stained-glass tower were added to it from 1959 to 1961. Inside, the church displays a cross of nails donated by Coventry, in Britain – another city devastated by bombs.

Kulturforum

C2 Gemäldegalerie and Kunstgewerbemuseum: Matthäikirchplatz. Musikinstrumenten–Museum: Tiergartenstrasse 1. Neue Nationalgalerie: Potsdamer Strasse 50 Kulturforum complex: 030 2090 5555; Musikinstrumenten-Museum: 030 254 810 Gemäldegalerie: Tue.–Wed. and Fri.–Sun. 10–6, Thu. 11–10; Kunstgewerbemuseum: Tue.–Fri. 10–6, Sat.–Sun. 11–6; Musikinstrumenten-Museum: Tue.–Fri. 9–5, Sat.–Sun. 10–5; Neue Nationalgalerie: Tue.–Fri. 10–6 (also Thu. 6–10 p.m.), Sat.–Sun. 11–6 Cafés on site U-Bahn/S-Bahn to Potsdamer Platz; U-Bahn to Mendelssohn–Bartholdy–Park 129, 142, 148, 248, 341, 348 Gemäldegalerie and Neue Nationalgalerie $$–$$$ (day ticket for all state museums); Musikinstrumenten-Museum and Kunstgewerbe-museum $. All museums free first Sun. of the month

This complex of galleries, halls and museums, all angles and curves, was designed in the 1960s and houses some outstanding collections of art. The Gemäldegalerie (Picture Gallery) displays European art from the 13th to the 18th centuries; look for works by the 16th-century Dutch master Pieter Brueghel and the collection of Italian Renaissance art. In the glass-and-steel Neue Nationalgalerie (New National Gallery) 20th-century paintings, drawings and sculpture include works by Salvador Dalí, Paul Klee and others.

A highlight of the Kulturforum complex is the Kunstgewerbemuseum (Arts and Crafts Museum), where gold, silver, glass, porcelain and jeweled arts and crafts are displayed. The star item is the eighth-century Burse Reliquary, a casket glittering with silver, pearls, gems and gold inlay. Next door to the Philharmonic Hall, the Musikinstrumenten-Museum (Museum of Musical Instruments) has everything from ancient bagpipes to synthesizers.

Museumsinsel

D3 Museumsinsel 030 2090 5555 Tue.–Sun. 10–6 (also Thu. 6–10 p.m.) Borchardt, see page 554 U-Bahn/S-Bahn to Friedrichstrasse; S-Bahn to Hackescher Markt 100, 157, 348; tram 1, 2, 3, 4, 5, 13, 15, 53 $$–$$$ (day ticket for all state museums); free first Sun. of the month

THE BERLIN WALL

Ray of hope – a segment of the Berlin Wall (top) and colorful fragments after its demolition in 1989

On August 13, 1961, the German Democratic Republic began work on an "Anti-Fascist Protection Wall." Relations between the Eastern and Western sectors of Berlin had never been easy. The Soviets closed off their access routes in 1948, so supplies had to be flown in from the West in a year-long airlift. There had been popular protests against the Soviet authorities, and a steady exodus of East Berliners to the West. Finally the Eastern government decided to mark its boundary with bricks and barbed wire.

The border was based on a 1920 map of Berlin, and this was the course taken by the wall, without regard for any houses, or streets that might be in the way. The houses on Bernauer Strasse (Bernauer Street), which happened to be on the route, became part of the barrier, and their exits were bricked up. Residents tried to jump to freedom from the upper windows; 20 people were shot down. One border guard took the opportunity to leap over the partially built wall before it grew too high. Those who didn't make it across were cut off from the West and from their friends and families as the 13-foot barricade took shape.

After the escape of 30 people through a tunnel from a bakery cellar in 1964, a large part of Bernauer Street was demolished, and a No Man's Land was created, guarded by dogs and 295 watchtowers. Booby traps were sunk into the Teltow canal, at the point where the border crossed the Spree river, after Gunter Litfin was shot trying to swim his way to the West. As the restrictions increased, the escapes grew more daring. One steamship's crew got the captain drunk and shut him in his cabin before sailing to the western bank. A homemade hot-air balloon was used to float over the wall. But the risks were very high: 80 people were killed in these attempts, including 25 guards.

At 9:15 p.m. on November 9, 1989, under pressure from an increasingly impatient crowd, border guards lifted the barriers and let Easterners cross the border freely for the first time since 1961. Fittingly, the first to cross were residents of Bernauer Street.

The first of a group of imposing museum buildings was begun on an island in the Spree river in 1830. In 1841, Frederick William IV designated the area a "space for art and science," and now many of Berlin's antiquities, dispersed during World War II, are being brought together for display in the complex. Altes Museum (Old Museum) has been restored after its destruction in 1943. It is being stocked with ancient sculpture and art, as is the Pergamon-museum, whose main exhibit is the 52-foot Pergamon Altar, from a 164 BC royal temple in Bergama, Turkey. The Bodemuseum displays medieval sculpture, art and coins (closed until 2005). The Egyptian collection is in the Neues Museum (New Museum); 18th- and 19th-century German art is in the Alte Nationalgalerie (Old National Gallery).

SCHLOSS CHARLOTTENBURG

A3 Luisenplatz 030 320 911 Old Palace: Tue.–Fri. 9–5, Sat.–Sun. 10–5; New Wing: Tue.–Fri. 10–6, Sat.–Sun. 11–6 Altes Luxemburg, see page 553 U-Bahn to Richard-Wagner-Platz or Sophie-Charlotte-Platz, or S-Bahn to Westend 109, 110, 121, 126, 145 Old Palace $$–$$$; New Wing $$

When building started on the huge Schloss Charlottenburg (Charlottenburg Palace) in 1695, it was designed as an understated rural home for Sophie-Charlotte, wife of the future King Frederick I of Prussia. Over the next 100 years it grew into a sprawling palace with a suite of royal apartments, dazzling rooms such as the White Hall and Golden Gallery, and gardens in formal French and landscaped English style, sloping down toward the Spree river.

Statue of Frederick the Great on Unter den Linden

TIERGARTEN

C2 surrounds Strasse des 17 Juni S-Bahn to Tiergarten 123

Once a hunting ground well stocked with boar and deer, now the Tiergarten (Animal Garden) is a 524-acre breath of fresh air in the center of the city, with woodlands, lakes and waterways, gardens and open-air concerts. Originally landscaped in the 1830s, the park is divided by the wide avenue Strasse des 17 Juni, where an 1873 Siegessäule (victory column) crowned with a golden goddess commemorates Prussian successes against Denmark, Austria and France.

TOPOGRAPHIE DES TERRORS

D2 Niederkirchnerstrasse 8 030 2548 7603 Daily 10–8, May–Sep.; 10–6, rest of year U- Bahn to Kochstrasse; S-Bahn to Anhalter Bahnhof 129, 248, 341 Free

The grim Topographie des Terrors (Topography of Terror) occupies the site of the former Nazi secret police headquarters, where prisoners were interrogated and tortured. Photographs trace the emergence of Nazism, and a nearby viewing platform overlooks the enormous Regierungsviertel (Government Quarter), where the Third Reich had its administrative offices.

UNTER DEN LINDEN

D2 Museum: Unter den Linden 3 Museum 030 203 040 Museum: Thu.–Tue. 10–6 Borchardt, see page 554 U-Bahn to Französische Strasse 100, 157, 348; tram 1, 2, 3, 4, 5, 13, 15, 53 Museum free

Unter den Linden (Under the Lime Trees) was laid out in 1648 as a route to the Tiergarten. It runs from the Brandenburg Gate to Museum Island and the river, and is lined with baroque and neoclassic buildings. Included in the line up is the 1695 Zeughaus (Arsenal), which houses the Deutsches Historisches Museum (German History Museum). An equestrian statue of Frederick the Great stands at the eastern end – turned by the Communist regime to ride toward the East rather than the West.

Popular day trip – the extravagant Sanssouci Palace, where Frederick the Great spent his summers

AN EXCURSION TO POTSDAM

Visits to several palaces can be combined on a trip to Potsdam, southwest of Berlin. The setting for the 1945 Potsdam Conference, at which Allied leaders redrew the European map, is Cecilienhof Palace (Schloss Cecilienhof), a mock-Tudor 1916 building now partly used as a hotel. It was built for Kaiser Wilhelm II; although his nation was two years into a war with Britain, the Kaiser chose to have it built in the style of an English country house. The royal Hohenzollern family lived here until 1945. The conference hall, delegates' studies and the reception rooms used by Churchill, Truman and Stalin are unchanged and can all be seen.

The palace that really draws crowds to Potsdam is the Sanssouci Palace (Schloss Sanssouci), on the town's western outskirts. This summer retreat was where Frederick the Great could enjoy life "without care" (*sans souci*). A green dome tops the single-story, yellow rococo facade; inside the richly furnished rooms are artworks and ornaments. Sanssouci Park has fountains, temples, gardens, an 18th-century Chinese teahouse and the third Potsdam palace: Frederick's New Palace (Neues Palais), with its vast marble hall and indoor grotto decorated with shells.

The town of Potsdam also is worth seeing. St. Nicholas' Church (Nikolaikirche) is one of Karl Friedrich Schinkel's classical monuments. In the Old Town, sculptures of rearing horses mark the site of the former royal stables, the 17th-century Marstall building, now a movie museum. The New Town was actually built in 1732, and became the focus of Potsdam's exiled French Huguenot (Protestant) community. In the Dutch Quarter, several streets of redbrick, gabled houses survive; they were built for Dutch construction workers who came to build the New Town.

Cecilienhof: Tue.–Sun. 9–5, Apr.–Oct.; 9–4, rest of year. Sanssouci: daily 9–5 (each building has its own schedule; some may only open mid-May to mid-Oct.). Park: daily dawn–dusk. New Palace: Wed.–Mon. 9–5, Apr.–Oct.; 9–3, rest of year All can be reached by bus 695 or the S-Bahn (Potsdam Stadt). Private tour operators in Berlin offer day trips by bus (inquire at the tourist office).

Surrounded by soaring spires and shaded by trees, Cologne's cafés serve a variety of delicious fare

COLOGNE

The two spires of Cologne (Köln) Cathedral soar above the Rhine, reminders of its past glory as a center of pilgrimage and the biggest city in medieval Germany. Despite the destruction of most of its central core in World War II, the city has retained and restored considerable evidence of its long and distinguished past. Today Cologne is thriving again, in business, trade, the arts and education, and its renowned sense of fun adds to the character that makes this one of Germany's most attractive cities.

Old Town

Cologne's Old Town (Altstadt) forms a vast semicircle on the west bank of the Rhine (Rhein) river, hemmed in by the Ring, a long boulevard that changes names along its route. It extends along the line of the former city fortifications and passes the old city gates of Eigelseintor, Hahnentor and St. Severinstor. Within this area, the Cathedral (Dom, see page 227) is the main attraction and, in fact, the most visited monument in Germany. The railroad station and a group of major museums are within easy reach of it.

The Gothic-Renaissance Town Hall (Rathaus, see page 228) stands at the heart of the Old Town, just south of the Old Market Square; to the east, toward the river, is the 12th-century church of Gross St. Martin (see page 227), one of 12 wonderful pre-Gothic churches still standing in the city. These sights form the old core. Head across the river via the Deutzer Brücke or Hohenzollern Brücke bridges for a look back at an unrivaled view of historic Cologne.

Cafés and Taverns

There are 24 breweries here, more than in any other German city. All produce the local beer, *Kölsch*, which is light and clear and served in tall, slim glasses. Beerhalls, known in the local dialect as *Weetschaften*, also serve food at very reasonable prices. Specialties at these establishments include rolls with cheese (*Halve Hahn*) or rye bread with black sausage (*Kölsche Kaviar*).

You will find plenty of restaurants in the historic center, ranging from the traditional *Gasthaus* (tavern) to trendy bistros, and the range of cuisines includes Japanese, French, Burmese, Chinese, Turkish and East European. Wine bars and cellars are another source of refreshment, serving wines from the Rhine valley. There are many excellent cafés serving the ubiquitous *Kaffee und Kuchen* (coffee and cakes).

Karneval and Concerts

To see Cologne at its most boisterous, come before Easter for Carnival (*Karneval*) week. Precise dates change every year, but the fun always reaches its peak before Ash Wednesday, in time for the abstinence of Lent. On the Thursday before the seventh Sunday prior to Easter, the festival begins in a morning ceremony at Old Market Square, and everyone gears up for the three "crazy days" (*Tolle Tage*) – Thursday, Sunday and Monday. There are costume balls at night, and more informal revelry on the streets and in the taverns. On Sunday there's a procession of floats, and on Monday a spectacular parade provides the lively and colorful climax.

For the rest of the year, there's calmer entertainment at the city's main cultural centers. Concerts are performed at the Philharmonie, in the Wallraf-Richartz/Ludwig museums building on Bischofsgartenstrasse. Other concerts take place regularly in the city's churches, and are usually free.

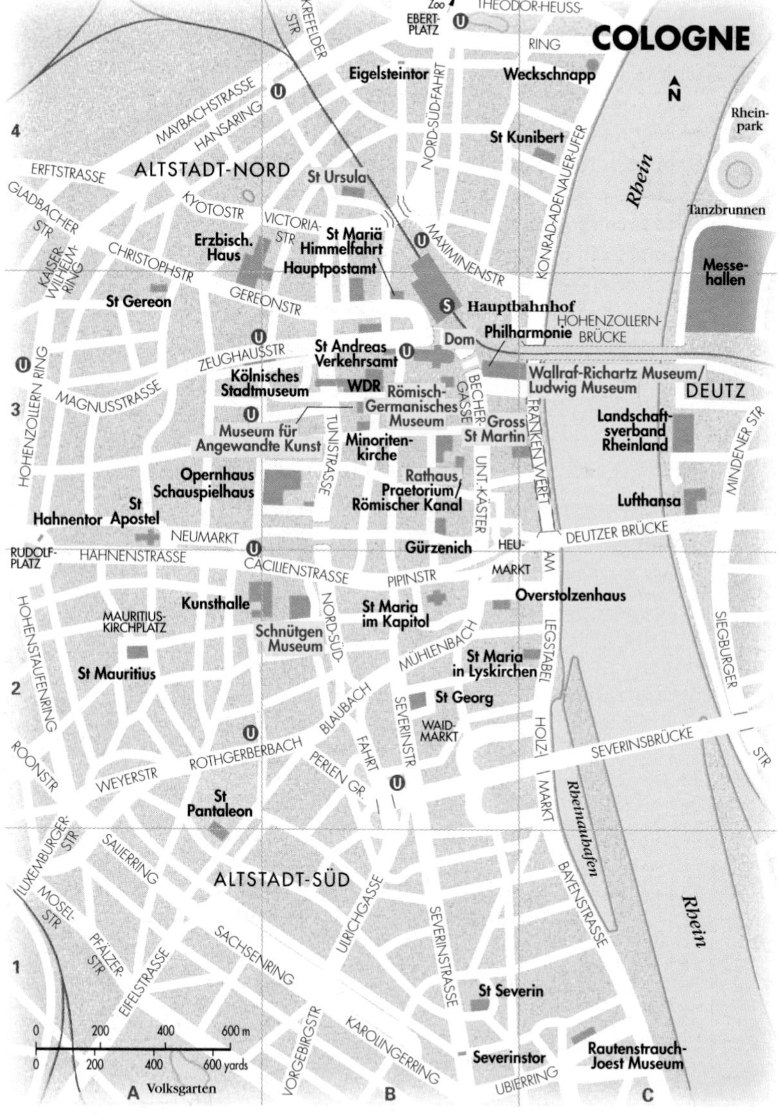

Opera is staged at the Opernhaus. Cologne has a famous puppet theater – the Puppenspiele – but dialogue is in the local *Kölsch* dialect.

Listings for movies, theater and concerts are published in the magazines *Kölner Illustrierte* and *Stadt Revue*, and in the tourist office's own monthly *Köln-Monatsvorschau*. Nightclubs and discos are concentrated on the streets around Gross St. Martin; in the St. Severin quarter, Südstadt; and in the university quarter – the Quartier Lateng, in the southwest part of the city.

Eau de Cologne

Probably the most appropriate Cologne souvenir is a bottle of *eau de Cologne*, first distilled from flower blossoms in the 18th century and intended as an aphrodisiac. Known here as *Kölnisch Wasser*, it's made by about 20 businesses, including one of the originals, Farina, which has been in operation since 1709. Stores all over the city sell it, but the Old Town is the best place to browse for gifts. An all-day market takes place Friday in Old Market Square. On spring weekends (April and May) the same square is taken over by flower stalls. A wine market sets up in New Market in late May and early June. All shops close during Carnival's crazy days.

Crazy Days

On the first of the crazy days of Carnival, a procession takes place based on the local legend of Jan and Griet. Jan von Werth was a cavalry officer in the 17th century, and Griet was his sweetheart, who nobly urged him to follow his career as a soldier rather than stay with her. Jan went on to become a hero, saving Cologne from destruction during the Thirty Years War, but he and his love never crossed paths again – until he was a distinguished general, entering the city at the head of his troops, and watched by the old spinster Griet.

ESSENTIAL INFORMATION

TOURIST INFORMATION
Köln Tourismus
• Unter Fettenhennen 19, in front of the cathedral ☎ 0221 2212 3345; fax 0221 2212 3320; www.koeln.org/koelntourismus

URBAN TRANSPORTATION
Cologne has a peculiarly integrated transportation system. Trams travel through the Old Town, some above ground (east-west lines), some underground (north-south lines); they also share some lines with freight trains. Subway stations are marked on the Cologne city map as the letter "U" in a red circle. Tickets are sold individually or for groups of up to 5 persons; you can also buy a 24-hour, 3- or 7-day travel card. The bus and railroad stations are next to the cathedral. For information call Cologne transportation information ☎ 0221 547-0.

AIRPORT INFORMATION
The Cologne/Bonn airport is less than 30 minutes from the city center. Bus 170 travels to and from the airport and the main railroad station (near the cathedral) every 15 or 30 minutes daily 5:30 a.m.–11:20 p.m. Beginning in 2002, suburban (S-Bahn) trains will operate from the airport to the city center and InterCity (ICE) trains to other destinations in Germany. Taxis operate from the airport to the city center. For flight information, call ☎ 02203 40 40–1 (24 hours).

CLIMATE – average highs and lows for the month

JAN.	FEB.	MAR.	APR.	MAY	JUN.	JUL.	AUG.	SEP.	OCT.	NOV.	DEC.
3°C	4°C	10°C	14°C	19°C	22°C	24°C	24°C	20°C	14°C	8°C	3°C
37°F	39°F	50°F	57°F	66°F	72°F	75°F	75°F	68°F	57°F	46°F	37°F
-2°C	-2°C	0°C	4°C	8°C	12°C	14°C	13°C	10°C	6°C	3°C	0°C
28°F	28°F	32°F	39°F	46°F	54°F	57°F	55°F	50°F	43°F	37°F	32°F

City Sights

Key to symbols
map coordinates refer to the Cologne map on page 225; sights below are highlighted in yellow on the map.
address or location telephone number opening times nearest subway nearest bus or tram route restaurant or café on site or nearby admission charge: $$$ more than DM8, $$ DM3–DM8, $ less than DM3 other relevant information

Dom

B3 Am Hof Cathedral: 0221 9258 4740; Treasury: 0221 2728 0120 Cathedral: daily 6 a.m.–7:30 p.m. Treasury: daily 10–5. Tower: daily 9–6, May–Sep.; 9–5, Mar.–Apr. and Oct.; 9–4, rest of year Brauhaus Sion, see page 554 Lines 5, 12, 16, 18 to Dom/Hbf Cathedral Free; Treasury $$; Tower $$ Free guided tours of cathedral daily

It took more than 600 years to complete the Dom (Cathedral), a Gothic masterpiece that incorporated the original architects' plans right to the end. The purpose of the project (begun in 1248) was to provide an appropriately grand setting for the relics of the Three Magi, which were snatched from Milan and kept here in a golden shrine. The final result is majestic, with intricately worked masonry serving to lighten the great mass of the facade and the two 515-foot spires – at the time they were built, the tallest structures in the world.

The golden shrine is, of course, the main focus of the interior, but there are many other treasures. In the south ambulatory chapel, the altarpiece of the *Adoration of the Magi* is a superb work by Stefan Lochner, one of the 15th-century artists of the Cologne School. In the north chapel is the ninth-century Gero Crucifix. One of the church's most inspiring features is the stained glass, ranging from the 13th-century Bible Window in the ambulatory to the Bavarian windows in the nave, donated by King Ludwig I in the 19th century.

Gross St. Martin

C3 An Gross St. Martin 0221 1642 5650 Mon.–Fri. 10:15–6, Sat. 10–12:30 and 1:30–6, Sun. 2–6 Päffgen in der Altstadt, see page 555

The glorious Gero Crucifix in Cologne Cathedral

Lines 5, 12, 16, 18 to Dom/Hbf Tram 7, 9 to Heumarkt

From its consecration in 1172 until the 19th century, the church of Gross St. Martin was the most distinctive feature of Cologne's skyline. Its tower, with four turrets at the corners, makes an interesting contrast to the lacy stonework of the cathedral's spires. Originally this was a monastery church, built for Benedictine monks from Ireland and Scotland.

Museum für Angewandte Kunst

B3 An der Rechtschule 0221 2212 3860 Tue.–Sun. 11–5 (also Wed. 5–8) Lines 5, 12, 16, 18 to Dom/Hbf $$

The Museum für Angewandte Kunst (Museum of Applied Art), has an exquisite collection of applied arts ranging from medieval to contemporary times. One of the most interesting pieces is a panel of *The Nativity* by Hans Memling, a Flemish painter whose calm, precise style was very popular in his time. There is also a fine collection of art nouveau works.

Rathaus

B3 Rathausplatz 0221 2210 Mon.–Sat. 8 a.m.–10:30 p.m., Sun. 9 a.m.–10:30 p.m., May–Oct.; Mon.–Sat. 8 a.m.–9 p.m., Sun. 9:30–7, rest of year Päffgen in der Altstadt, see page 555 Lines 5, 12, 16, 18 to Dom/Hbf Tram 1, 7, 9 to Heumarkt

The Rathaus (Town Hall) is a Cologne landmark at the heart of the Old Town. A flamboyant, octagonal 15th-century tower tops off the 14th-century body of the building. The Renaissance *loggia* (porch) was added in the 1570s. Under a glass pyramid in front of the hall is a 12th-century Jewish bathhouse, the *Mikwe*. There was once a ghetto here, where the city's Jewish community lived until they were expelled in 1424.

Römisch-Germanisches Museum

B3 Roncalliplatz 4 0221 2212 4438 Tue.–Fri. 10–5 (also Thu. 5–8), Sat.–Sun. 11–5 Lines 5, 12, 16, 18 to Dom/Hbf $$ During special exhibitions, hours and admission may vary

For hundreds of years Cologne was under Roman rule; city status was granted in AD 50 by Emperor Claudius. The Römisch-Germanisches Museum (Roman-Germanic Museum) gives some idea of day-to-day life in the Roman Empire through items that were excavated locally. The main exhibit is the astonishing 230-foot Dionysus Mosaic, once part of a third-century Roman villa: it shows Dionysus, god of wine – also known as Bacchus – indulging in drunken revelry. An older exhibit is the 49-foot-high tomb of a legionnaire called Poblicius, who died about AD 40. Cologne's glass workshops were busy producing their own designs in the third and fourth centuries, and there's a display of their work, as well as a collection of jewelry found at Frankish burial sites.

St. Ursula

B4 Ursulaplatz 24 0221 133 400 Mon.–Fri. 9:45–1 and 2–5:15, Sat. 9–1 and 2–4, Sun. by appointment Bosporus, see page 554 Lines 5, 12, 16, 18 to Dom/Hbf

North of the city center is the church of St. Ursula; it was named after the daughter of a fourth-century king of Britain, who was said to have been killed in the city by Huns, along with her 11,000 virgin companions. The popularity of the cult of St. Ursula contributed to the city's development as a center of pilgrimage, and she appears in the Cologne coat of arms. The church sacristan can provide visitor access to the baroque Goldene Kammer (Golden Chamber).

Schnütgen Museum

B2 Cäcilienstrasse 29 0221 2212 3620 Tue.–Fri. 10–5 (also first Wed. of the month 5–8), Sat.–Sun. 11–5 Brauhaus Sion, see page 554 Lines 3, 4, 12, 16, 18 to Neumarkt Tram 1, 2, 7, 9 to Neumarkt $$

Some of the best religious art and furnishings in the city can be seen at the Schnütgen Museum, which occupies the deconsecrated church of St. Cäcilien. Among other treasures are original carvings from the cathedral altar and some beautiful ivory pieces. The carved *memento mori* (reminders of mortality) are chilling depictions of human bodies in a state of decay.

Wallraf-Richartz Museum/Ludwig Museum

B3 Bischofsgartenstrasse 1 0221 2212 2379 Tue.–Fri. 10–6 (also Tue. 6–8), Sat.–Sun. 11–6 Lines 5, 12, 16, 18 to Dom/Hbf $$ During special exhibitions, hours and admission may vary

Cologne's major collection of German and international art is here, with works through the 19th century shown in the first-floor Wallraf-Richartz Museum, and 20th-century art shown in the Ludwig Museum, which occupies the rest of the building. At the Wallraf-Richartz you can study the work produced in Cologne in the 15th century, when the city was at the forefront of artistic development. In particular, look for the triptychs by the artist known as the Master of St. Bartholomew, one of the last of the Cologne School, whose brightly colored paintings resemble carvings.

Many 20th-century greats are represented in the Ludwig Museum, including Otto Dix and Max Ernst; the section on pop art has works by Andy Warhol and Roy Lichtenstein.

An Excursion to Kloster Altenberg

Kloster Altenberg, about 11 miles northeast of Cologne, is set on the Dhün river in the woods of the hilly country called Bergisches Land. This former Cistercian monastery is better known as the Bergischer Cathedral (Bergischer Dom). The original monastery church was built using stone from the manor of the Count of Berg, who left it to the monks after moving his headquarters elsewhere in 1133. It took a little more than 100 years to finish building the present monastery, which was begun in 1255 – only seven years after work had started on the cathedral in Cologne (which took more than six centuries to complete).

The end result is one of Germany's best examples of 13th-century Gothic style: no elaborate embellishments and no tower, but a marvelous sense of space and light, enhanced by the simple, silvery stained-glass windows in the chancel. The window representing *Holy Jerusalem* is the biggest stained-glass window in the country. There are tombs of the past counts of Berg in the north transept.

During the Napoleonic Wars in the late 18th and early 19th centuries, the church fell into disuse and was in danger of crumbling. Luckily, King Frederick William IV took an interest in its restoration, and it was opened again to worshipers on the condition – laid down by the king – that both Catholics and Protestants could attend. This holds true today, and on Sundays both Catholic and Protestant congregations from the city come here for services. The outbuildings now house restaurants; at any of these *Küchenhof*, you can ask for the key to the oldest standing part of the monastery, the 13th-century chapel Markuskapelle. One of the most exquisite features of the whole complex is the choir surrounded by chapels, viewed most rewardingly from the slope east of the monastery.

It takes an hour to reach Kloster Altenberg from Cologne's center: the underground trams (U-Bahn lines 4, 15 and 16) take you to Wiener Platz for a connection with bus 434.
Guided excursions from Cologne can be arranged by the Cologne tourist information office (Koln Tourismus – see Essential Information box, page 226).

Nestled in the woods – Bergischer Cathedral

Munich

The capital of Bavaria is one of Germany's most appealing and popular cities. Even though Munich (München) is the country's third-largest city, with a cosmopolitan society and culture, it has also retained a village-like atmosphere with parks and a pedestrian-only center. It's only an hour from the Alps, and also has the easygoing feel of a Mediterranean town. Even on the briefest German tour, Munich is a city not to be missed.

Munich on Foot

Central Munich is compact and attractive, and easy to explore on foot. Long pedestrian streets (Neuhauser Strasse and Kaufingerstrasse) run from the main railroad station and from Karlstor, one of the city gates, to Marienplatz, the square at the heart of the Old Town. Here you can watch the mechanical characters of the carillon (*Glockenspiel*) at the front of the New Town Hall (Neues Rathaus, see page 234) and visit the twin-towered cathedral. To the north of the square is the tree-lined Maximilianstrasse, which leads to the Bavarian Parliament building and the Residenz (palace). Great art collections – the Old and New Picture Galleries (and opening in summer 2002, the Modern Art Picture Gallery) – are a short distance northwest of the city center; to the south are the history museum and, on an island in the Isar river, one of the world's foremost museums of science and technology, the German Museum.

Bavarian Eateries

There are innumerable restaurants and cafés in Munich, and its large foreign population ensures a wide range of cuisines. At specifically Bavarian cafés, the Munich *Weisswürste* (white veal sausage with parsley) is a staple, served in hot water to be peeled and covered in mustard before eating. This delicacy is usually eaten at about 11 a.m. Meals are generally early in Munich, as people start work at 7 or 8 a.m. Lunch can begin at 11:30 but is often substantial, and the "lunch hour" can last until 2 p.m. Dinner is served between 6:30 and 11 p.m., but locals tend to stick to a light supper, or *Abendbrot*. The Schwabing district, north of the city

center, is a busy area of sidewalk cafés and taverns. Snack bars (*Lokal* or *Schnellimbiss*) and even butcher shops (*Metzgereien*) sell tasty meatloaf and sausages all day. And don't leave the city without visiting one of the beer gardens.

Music and Film

Munich is a major European cultural center, with thriving movie and publishing industries and a proud musical tradition. There are no fewer than three symphony orchestras based here, and the Residenz provides an impressive venue – either in the concert hall or, in summer, in the courtyard. Opera and ballet are staged at the National Theater, where the July Opera Festival is the highlight of the city's calendar. The main cultural center is the modern Gasteig, home of the Munich Philharmonic Orchestra; students from

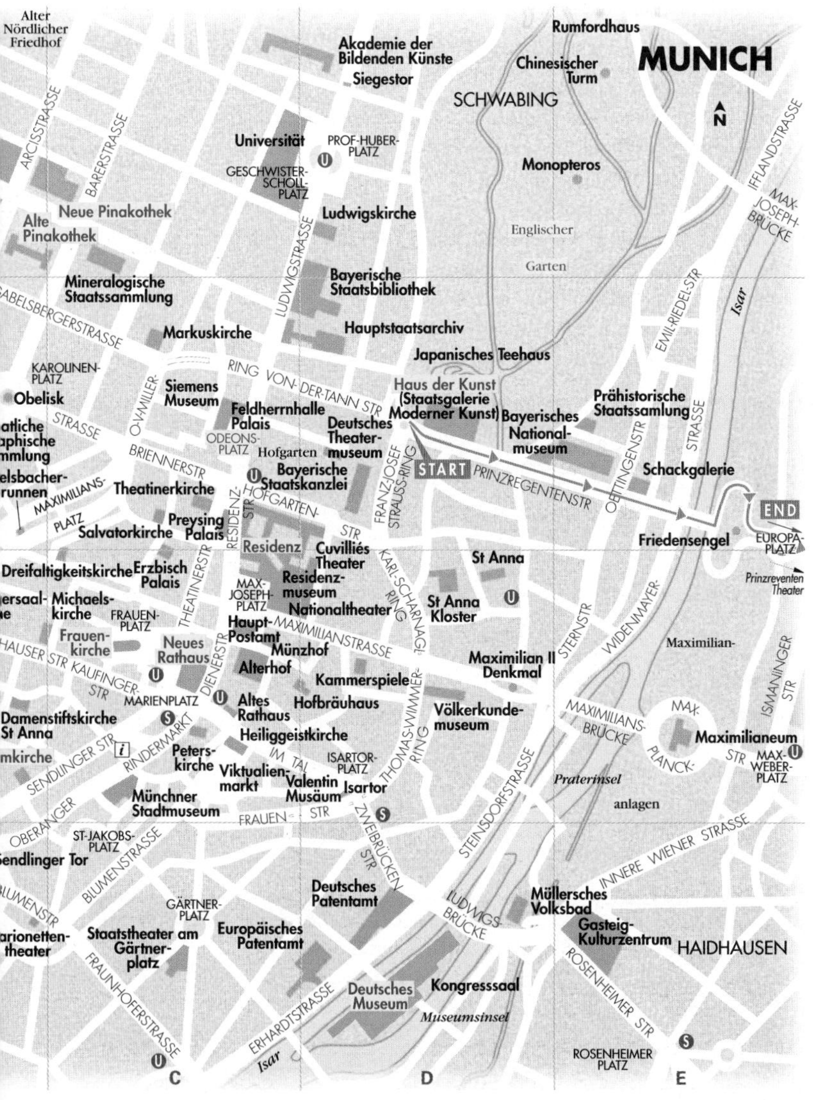

the Richard Strauss Conservatory give free lunchtime recitals in the Little Concert Hall during the week. The annual International Film Festival takes place at the Gasteig in late June and early July – the high point of a series of festivals devoted to the movies.

Munich tends to shut down early, but Schwabing has many cabarets, theaters and live music venues ranging from rock to folk to jazz – including the well-known Jazzclub Unterfahrt on Kirchenstrasse 96.

City of Monks

Munich's city emblem is the *Münchener Kindl*, or "little monk," recalling its origins as a monastic settlement. The first recorded mention of *Munichen*, "the home of monks," was in AD 777. The city itself was founded nearly 400 years later by Henry the Lion, Duke of Saxony.

Boutiques and Markets

There's good window-shopping all over the old center of Munich, especially along the pedestrian-only Neuhauser Strasse and Kaufingerstrasse. Maximilianstrasse is a browser's paradise, lined with designer fashion boutiques, art galleries and jewelers. More stores can be found in the arcades and lanes leading off Residenzstrasse. Antiques, less expensive fashion and second-hand stores are concentrated in the student area of Schwabing, and Bavarian crafts can be found in the streets that run off Max-Joseph-Platz. Munich's famous open-air food market, Viktualienmarkt, with its formidable women vendors and fresh goods ranging from local cheese to Alpine flowers, sets up south of the Marienplatz every day except late Saturday afternoon and Sunday.

ESSENTIAL INFORMATION

TOURIST INFORMATION
Fremdenverkehrsamt München (Munich Tourist Office)
• Sendlinger Strasse 1 ☎ 089 233 03 00; fax 089 23 33 02 33; www.muenchen-tourist.de
• Hauptbahnhof, Bahnhofplatz 2 ☎ 089 23 33 02 57 or 089 23 33 02 58
• Neues Rathaus (New City Hall), Marienplatz ☎ 089 23 33 02 72 or 089 23 33 02 73

URBAN TRANSPORTATION
A U-Bahn (subway) and S-Bahn (suburban) train network covers the city center and beyond. The U-Bahn is marked on the Munich city map by the letter "U" in a red circle; the S-Bahn is marked by the letter "S" in a red circle. Trains run daily 5 a.m.–1 a.m. Buy tickets from machines at MVV stations. You can purchase tickets individually, in strips or for 1 or 3 days: multiple tickets are valid for buses and trams, too. Validate your ticket in the automatic stamping machine as you board, except for tickets bought from machines on trams (these will stamp automatically). One ticket is good for up to four bus/tram or two train stops; two tickets for additional stops. For MVV information call ☎ 089 41 42 43 44. Taxi stands can be found all over the city. Call Taxi-München ☎ 089 21610, or IsarFunk Taxizentrale ☎ 089 45 05 40.

AIRPORT INFORMATION
The international airport, Flughafen München Franz-Josef-Strauss, is 19 miles north of the city center. S-Bahn trains run 24 hours a day to the main railroad station (Hauptbahnhof), a 36-minute journey; airport buses run to the station from the North Terminal daily 7:05 a.m.–8:05 p.m., a 45-minute journey. For flight information call ☎ 089 97 52 13 13.

CLIMATE – average highs and lows for the month

JAN.	FEB.	MAR.	APR.	MAY	JUN.	JUL.	AUG.	SEP.	OCT.	NOV.	DEC.
2°C	3°C	8°C	11°C	17°C	20°C	22°C	23°C	19°C	13°C	7°C	3°C
36°F	37°F	46°F	52°F	63°F	68°F	72°F	73°F	66°F	55°F	45°F	37°F
-4°C	-4°C	0°C	2°C	7°C	10°C	12°C	12°C	8°C	4°C	0°C	-3°C
25°F	25°F	32°F	36°F	45°F	50°F	54°F	54°F	46°F	39°F	32°F	27°F

City Sights

Key to symbols

map coordinates refer to the Munich map on pages 230–231; sights below are highlighted in yellow on the map. address or location telephone number opening times nearest subway nearest bus or tram route restaurant or café on site or nearby admission charge: $$$ more than DM8, $$ DM3–DM8, $ less than DM3 other relevant information

Alte Pinakothek

B4 Barerstrasse 27 089 23 80 52 16 Tue.–Sun. 10–5 (also Thu. 5–10) U-Bahn to Königsplatz Tram 27 $$$

Over 850 pre-18th-century paintings are being rehoused in the huge Alte Pinakothek (Old Picture Gallery), built in 1836 to store the expanding royal art collection. After suffering extensive war damage, the gallery was restored in the 1950s and underwent a further renovation in the 1990s, during which time its paintings were shown in the Neue Pinakothek (New Picture Gallery, see page 234). Among the treasures are works by Albrecht Dürer and the world's best collection of work by Peter Paul Rubens.

Asamkirche

B2 Sendlinger Strasse 62 Daily 8–5:30 U-Bahn to Sendlinger Tor 31, 56; tram 17, 18, 20, 21, 27

The Asamkirche (Asam Church) is a stunning example of rococo architecture. It was built as a private chapel in 1729 by architect and sculptor Ägid Quirin Asam and his brother Cosmas Damian Asam, and was opened to the public in 1746. Every inch is decorated with gold leaf, sculptures and frescoes. One of Asam's works is at the altar, showing the crucified Christ in God's embrace – *The Throne of Mercy*.

BMW Museum

Off the map Petuelring 130 089 38 22 33 07 Daily 9–5 U-Bahn to Olympiazentrum or Petuelring 36, 41, 43, 80, 81, 136, 184; tram 27 $$ Last admission at 4

The BMW Museum occupies a half-spherical silver structure next to the Bavarian Motor Works headquarters – itself a striking building with four silver cylinders. Cars, motorcycles, videos and slides illustrate the history of the automobile and its place in our lives, and visitors can even design their own cars with the aid of computer graphics.

Deutsches Museum

D1 Museumsinsel 1, Ludwigsbrücke 089 21 79-1 Daily 9–5 Café on site S-Bahn to Isartor Tram 18 $$$

One of the biggest science and technology museums in the world has more than 17,000 items on display, and deals with everything from lightning demonstrations to space travel to hydraulics to the first German submarine. Audiovisual displays and hands-on exhibits add to the fun.

Englischer Garten

D4–E4 Kutscherei Hans Holzmann Daily dawn–dusk Beer gardens, cafés and restaurants in park U-Bahn to Odeonsplatz, Universität, Giselastrasse or Münchener Freiheit 44, 54, 154; tram 17

Stretching along the bank of the Isar river, the landscaped park Englischer Garten (English Garden) was created in 1789 on a former hunting ground. Today it is busy with street entertainers and people lunching, boating and taking in the fresh air. Boats can be rented at the Kleinhesseloher See, and there is a beer garden, the Seehaus, near the lake. Enjoy good city views from the circular "temple," the *monopteros*; other popular attractions are the Chinese Tower

Early touring car at the BMW Museum

The onion domes of Munich's cathedral

and beer garden, the Japanese Tea House, and the carousel.

FRAUENKIRCHE

C2 Frauenplatz 1 089 290 08 20 Towers: Mon.–Sat. 10–5, Apr.–Oct. U-Bahn/S-Bahn to Marienplatz 52; tram 19

Munich's twin-towered cathedral, a famous city landmark, was built between 1468 and 1488, but was left without a roof. In 1524 its green onion domes were "temporarily" added – and have been there ever since. Near the entrance is a footprint in the floor, said to be that of the devil, who stamped with glee thinking that the architect had forgotten to put in the windows. In fact, the windows can't be seen from where the devil was standing – but they are there.

HAUS DER KUNST

D3 Prinzregentenstrasse 1 089 211 27-0 Daily 10–10 for exhibitions only Café in gallery U-Bahn to Odeonsplatz or Lehel 53; tram 17 Exhibition admission varies

The Haus der Kunst (House of Art) was opened by the Nazis in 1937 as a white-columned building known to its detractors as the *Weisswurst* (white sausage) gallery. It was part of Hitler's campaign against modern artists such as Paul Klee and Max Beckmann: While their work was ridiculed in an exhibition of "degenerates" in the Hofgarten, this gallery showed state-approved art. It now gives pride of place to the work denounced by the Third Reich in a series of alternating temporary exhibitions.

LENBACHHAUS

B3 Luisenstrasse 33 089 23 33 20 00 Tue.–Sun. 10–6 Café in gallery U-Bahn to Königsplatz $$$

A 19th-century Italianate villa, home of aristocratic painter Franz von Lenbach, the Lenbachhaus is now the city's art gallery. It shows the progression of art in Munich from the Gothic art of the 15th and 16th centuries to the 18th- and 19th-century Romantics. Highlighting the collection are works by the Munich Expressionists, the so-called *Blaue Reiter* (Blue Rider) group of the 20th century, including more than 90 abstract paintings and 900 other works by Wassily Kandinsky. In all, there are around 1,000 works by Kandinsky.

NEUE PINAKOTHEK

C4 Barerstrasse 29 089 238 05-195 Wed.–Mon. 10–5 (also Thu. 5–10) Café in gallery U-Bahn to Königsplatz Tram 27 $$

Across the street from the Renaissance-style Old Picture Gallery (see page 233) is Neue Pinakothek (New Picture Gallery), a modern concrete, granite and glass building featuring art from the late 18th to the 20th centuries. It covers French and German Impressionists, Romantic paintings, and the art nouveau style known in Germany as *Jugendstil*.

NEUES RATHAUS

C2 Marienplatz 089 233 03 00 Tower: Mon.–Fri. 9–4, Sat.–Sun. 10–7, May–Oct.; Mon.–Thu. 9–4, Fri. 9–1, rest of year Ratskeller, see page 555 U-Bahn/S-Bahn to Marienplatz 52 Tower $$

A forest of neo-Gothic turrets, towers, spurs and gargoyles, the 19th-century Neues Rathaus (New Town Hall) sprawls around six courtyards on the north side of Marienplatz. On its central tower (Rathausturm) is a 43-bell clock (Glockenspiel), which comes to life every day at 11 a.m. and noon (also at 5 p.m. in summer) as life-size figures from Munich's history come dancing out to its four melodies. The *Schäfflertanz*, a dance which celebrates the end of the plague in 1517, is performed by dancers in the city streets every seven years (the next performance is due in 2005).

HOFBRÄUHAUS

Wilhelm V of Bavaria founded Munich's Hofbräu brewery in 1589 to brew a dark ale more to his liking than the local beer. At this time, beer was a drink restricted to the Bavarian upper classes: they had made it their own preserve after losing their vineyards in a series of bad winters. In 1828, the brewery became an inn, and the delights of its beer were made accessible to all.

The huge beer hall and its tree-shaded courtyard has been the scene of political upheaval and violence in recent history. The Nazi party held its early mass meetings here, and a fight broke out during one of Adolf Hitler's speeches that became known as the Battle of the Hofbräuhaus.

Nowadays, there is nothing sinister about the hall's fame: tourists flock to the long benches, listen to the Bavarian brass bands and drink beer served by traditionally dressed waitresses. They no longer practice the customary quality test for *Bock* beer, though, which is probably just as well. The test apparently consisted of drinkers sitting at one of the Hofbräuhaus' beer-soaked benches and consuming *Bock* beer for hours at a time, staying put even while nature took its course. If, at the end of the session, they stuck to the benches when they tried to get up, the beer was reckoned to be thick enough and ready to sell.

The Hofbräuhaus is the city's most popular beer hall and fills up very quickly, especially during the world-famous, 16-day *Oktoberfest*, a beer festival that ends on the first Sunday in October. Barbecues, processions and music all play their part in this annual jamboree, but beer is the main ingredient.

If the Hofbräuhaus is too crowded, there are other options all over town, plus numerous beer gardens where you can even bring your own food. The *Oktoberfest* action takes place on the fairground at Theresienwiese, west of the city.

Whether you drink at the Hofbräuhaus or elsewhere, make sure you don't sit at the regulars' table (*Stammtisch*). You'll know you're there if the waitress refuses to take your order!

Service with a smile at Munich's most famous beer hall

ODEONSPLATZ

C3 Halali, see page 555 U-Bahn to Odeonsplatz 53

This regal square was laid out for Ludwig I early in the 19th century and marks the beginning of two great Munich boulevards – Ludwigstrasse and Prinzregentenstrasse. The Bavarian Ministry of Finance now has its offices in the Leuchtenberg-Palais, built in Italian Renaissance style along one side of the square. The Feldherrnhalle (Military Commanders' Hall) was added as a tribute to the Bavarian army, and is guarded by two bronze lions – one roaring, the other mute. Overlooking Odeonsplatz is the lovely baroque, golden-stone Theatinerkirche, the church where Wittelsbach family members were laid to rest. The immaculate gardens of Hofgarten are next to the square.

OLYMPIAPARK

Off the map Spiridon-Louis-Ring 21 089 30 67 24 14 Olympiaturm: daily 9 a.m.–midnight (last admission at 11:30 p.m.). Stadium: daily 8:30–6, Apr.–Oct.; 9–4:30, rest of year Revolving restaurant, Olympiaturm U-Bahn to Olympiazentrum 36, 41, 43, 81, 136, 184; tram 20, 21, 27 Olympiapark $$; Olympiaturm $$

North of the city center, beyond Schwabing, the park built for the 1972 Olympics has become a focus for strollers, joggers and swimmers. Its television tower, the Olympiaturm, is the highest reinforced concrete tower in Europe, and has a platform and revolving restaurant with fantastic Alpine views. A tour train takes visitors around the Olympiasee Lake, the Olympiaberg Hill, made of wartime debris, and the Olympic Village – scene of the terrible shooting of Israeli athletes during a terrorist siege on September 5, 1972.

Ceiling detail at the fabulous Residenz

RESIDENZ

C3 Residenzstrasse 1/Max-Joseph-Platz 3 089 29 06 71 Daily 9–6 (also Thu. 6–8 p.m.), Apr. to mid-Oct.; 10–4 rest of year Spatenhaus, see page 555 U-Bahn to Odeonsplatz; U-Bahn/S-Bahn to Marienplatz 53; tram 19 $$

The Wittelsbach dynasty's dazzling palace took 40 years to restore after wartime damage. Its 112 rooms are once again a treasure-trove of artworks, ornaments, furnishings and statues – too much to take in during just one visit. Some of the highlights are the vaulted Antiquarium hall, built in 1568; the rococo Cuvilliés Theater; the crown jewels in the Treasury; and the Ahnengalerie (Ancestral Portrait Gallery) featuring 121 Wittelsbachs.

SCHLOSS NYMPHENBURG

Off the map 089 17 90 80 Palace: Tue.–Sun. 9–12:30 and 1:30–5, Apr.–Sep.; 10–12:30 and 1:30–4, rest of year. Gardens: daily 7–dusk Schlosscafé Palmenhaus, see page 555 U-Bahn to Rotkreuzplatz 41; tram 17 All attractions $$$; Castle and Gallery $$; Marstallmuseum $$

For centuries the mighty Wittelsbach family ruled Bavaria, with Munich as their base. Schloss Nymphenburg (Nymphenburg Palace), on the city's western outskirts, was built as their summer villa by Agostino Barelli between 1664 and 1674. Every generation of Wittelsbachs subsequently added to his creation, and the palace now measures 1,640 feet from end to end. In the central section is the Schönheitsgalerie, or Gallery of Beauties – 36 paintings of beautiful women produced between 1827 and 1850 for Ludwig I. Some are believed to have been his mistresses. The former palace stables house the Marstallmuseum, a museum of porcelain and a collection of state carriages and sleighs, and on the grounds a Hall of Mirrors (in the 1734 Amalienburg hunting lodge) lets you see yourself many times over.

A WALK ALONG PRINZREGENTENSTRASSE

Fountain in the Hofgarten

This grand old boulevard runs east from the 17th-century Court Garden (Hofgarten), with its beautiful fountains and Renaissance arcades. A startling modern addition, the steel-and-glass Staatskanzlei, houses the Bavarian State Chancellery. Prinzregentenstrasse was laid out at the end of the 19th century and named for Prince Luitpold, who ruled as regent after his nephew, Ludwig II, had been declared mad and deposed.

Today it takes visitors through one of the city's main museum and gallery quarters. Running past the southern end of the English Garden, the boulevard first reaches the Haus der Kunst (House of Art, see page 234), formerly a gallery of Nazi-approved art. It exhibits the kind of work the Nazis had condemned. Next door is the Bavarian National Museum (Bayerisches Nationalmuseum), in a turn-of-the-20th-century building incorporating many different architectural styles.

The next notable monument is the former Prussian embassy, now the Schack-Galerie, named for one of the 19th century's great patrons of the arts, Count Schack. His own collection of paintings is represented by such artists as Franz von Lenbach and Arnold Böcklin, who relied on the count for their livelihoods. The gallery is open Wed.–Mon. 10–5.

Prinzregentenstrasse continues across the Isar river and past the *Angel of Peace* (*Friedensengel*), a golden monument to peace, erected to commemorate the end of the Franco-Prussian War. Nowadays citizens gather on New Year's Day to enjoy fireworks displays and the view of Munich. Farther along, past the Europaplatz, is the Villa Stuck, a 19th-century house built in a mix of styles by artist Franz von Stuck. Von Stuck was part of the 1890s *avant-garde* school known as the Munich Secession, and his own work is displayed inside; open Tue.–Sun. 10–6 (also Thu. 6–9 p.m.).

The boulevard continues east to the Prinzregententheater (☎ 089 21 85–28 99), which stages drama, concerts and musicals. It was designed in 1900 to emulate the neoclassical Wagner Festival Theater in Bayreuth and sits on Prinz-regentenplatz, where there is a U-Bahn station; trains travel back to Odeonsplatz and the Hofgarten. For the walking route, see the city map on pages 230–231.

GREECE

"*MIGHTY indeed are the marks and monuments of our empire we have left. Future ages will wonder at us, as the present age wonders at us now...*"

From *The Peloponnesian War*, circa 400 BC, by Athenian historian Thucydides

Opposite: Verdant olive groves on the fertile Lasithi plateau in eastern Crete

GREECE

Somewhere, subconsciously, we all feel we have a stake in Greece. Our language, our political systems, our values and ethics are inextricably connected to this beautiful country's ancient civilization. Visitors arrive with high expectations and romantic notions, muddled snippets of myths and folklore, history and hearsay mingled in their minds. Those experiencing the country for the first time are likely to be dazzled. Greece evokes strong feelings, and months of travel would scarcely be enough to do this stunning country justice.

The Land

Islands are by definition beautiful, and there are 166 inhabited islands in Greece, scattered on three sides of the mainland. Some are studded with pine and eucalyptus, and some are arid or mountainous. Most have idyllic beaches and picturesque villages, and many have superb ancient sites, Frankish castles or Venetian fortifications.

You could spend years discovering them all, so spare at least a few days to visit one or two. Greek islands are a vital part of the country and have bedazzled travelers for centuries. Ferry

services are excellent and even in the height of summer you can find somewhere to stay, so an island-hopping trip can be a spur-of-the-moment decision.

Much of mainland Greece is very mountainous. The slopes of Olympus and Parnassus are carpeted with huge spreads of wildflowers in spring, offering superb vistas and alluring hiking. But there's more: the eerie and stony landscape of the Mani and the gentle coastal hills of the Péloponnese. Traveling is easy by public transportation, and renting a car is simple to arrange. If you do decide to drive, beware of aggressive Greek motorists and be prepared for roads in poor condition.

Traditional Culture

Greece has one of Europe's most vigorous cultures, perpetuated through architecture, crafts, music and dance. Traditional ways permeate everyday life, despite the growing impact of Western consumer values. If you can, see traditional dancing and listen to the music – the real thing is often easier to find in rural areas.

As in many other Mediterranean countries, much of life is lived in the full gaze of the public eye, hence the strolling crowds and packed cafés. Tempers can quickly flare, and you'll see the ubiquitous worry beads carried by Greek men, which serve mainly as an outlet for their stress.

The Greeks and You

Tourism is not a slick operation in Greece; everything works, things eventually happen, but not necessarily with streamlined efficiency. So relax, slow down and you'll get much more out of your trip.

The Greeks have been dealing with foreign invaders for centuries, so the late 20th-century tourist influx hardly threw them at all. The classical Greek tradition of hospitality to strangers is still strong, which makes for a matter-of-fact and laid-back attitude toward visitors, particularly when you go off the beaten track.

Hospitality often takes the form of innumerable personal questions, among which "How much do you earn?" is usually near the top of the list. Don't be offended, as this is considered an acceptable and friendly exchange. If someone offers you something – a drink, some fruit, a flower – accept it graciously, as the donor is acting out a tradition that goes back thousands of years in time.

Greeks have a strong code of honor, which helps to make Greece one of the safest countries to visit. It's highly unlikely you'll be cheated in any way, and you can safely walk most streets at night without worrying. Society has changed beyond recognition in the last 40 years and young Greeks – especially boys – are far more emancipated than their parents. However, especially in the country, girls are still sheltered and virginity still counts, so foreign girls are an attractive target for local youths.

There's still a large peasant class in Greece, and outside cities and tourist areas you'll see black-garbed figures laboring in tiny fields as they have for centuries, their lifestyle a million miles from that of city dwellers.

MORE TOP DESTINATIONS IN GREECE

• Ágios Efstrátios B3 • Alónnisos B2 • Delfoí B2 • Ioánnina A3 • Kefalloniá A2 • Léros C2 • Máni B1 • Metéora A3 • Mykonos C2 • Náfpaktos A2 • Ólympos A3 • Óros Píndos A3 • Samothráki B3 • Skópelos B2 • Thíra/Santorini C1

TIMELINE

776–700 BC	City-states established; first Olympic Games.
499–400 BC	Persian Wars; Golden Age of classical Greek culture; Peloponnesian Wars against Sparta.
336–323 BC	Alexander the Great conquers the known world.
146 BC	Greece becomes a Roman province.
AD 394	Christianity established throughout the Roman Empire; the Olympic Games finish and the Delphic Oracle is closed.
476–1453	Greece ruled from Constantinople; fall of Constantinople in 1453; Greece ruled by Turks for next 400 years.
1821–29	Greek War of Independence; Greece becomes an independent modern state.
1917–18	Greece sides with Allies in World War I.
1940–44	Axis occupation during World War II.
1945–60	Many Greeks emigrate to the United States and Australia; others flood into Athens from the countryside.
1974	Conflict with Turkey over Cyprus; situation remains tense into the 1990s.
1975	Tourist boom begins with foreigners visiting classical sites, islands and coastal resorts.
1981	Greece joins European Community; community funding catapults much of the country into mainstream Europe.
1996	Macedonian claims by former Yugoslavs seen as implicit threat to northern Greek region of Macedonia.
2001	Greece adopts the euro as its new national currency (euro bills and coins appear in 2002).

THE GOLDEN AGE OF CLASSICAL GREECE

The peace following the defeat of the Persians in the fifth century BC marked the start of a cultural, artistic and intellectual blossoming for Athens and the other city-states. Much of what truly epitomizes "the glory that was Greece" dates from this era. The great architectural triumphs, the start of drama and comedy, and the first steps in philosophical thought can all be traced to Athens at this time. The Acropolis took the form whose remains are seen today, decorated by Pheidas' sublime marbles, and subtly harmonious temples were built everywhere. The names Sophocles, Euripides, Aristophanes, Socrates and Plato are familiar worldwide; it's worth remembering that they lived and worked in this tiny state in the eastern Mediterranean more than 2,500 years ago.

Survival Guide

- Athens is best avoided during the sweltering summer months, when temperatures can soar, noise levels are high around the clock, and the ever-present pollution is at its worst.
- Head for restaurants and *tavernas* where locals eat; the food will be good and it's a delight to watch Greek families dining together. If you don't understand the menu in a *taverna* you'll probably be invited into the kitchen for a look – choose what you want and point! Remember, too, that Greeks firmly believe that hot food harms the stomach, so food is generally served lukewarm.
- Remember to *never* flush toilet tissue down the toilet – it goes in the basket provided. Greek plumbing is antediluvian, and you'll flood the bathroom if you put paper down the drains. This applies to *all* toilets throughout Greece, even restaurant and museum facilities. Greek public restrooms are few and far between and leave much to be desired, so seize every opportunity to use them in cafés, museums and restaurants.
- Athens is a capital city, and you should dress appropriately. Greeks are generally cool and comfortable rather than stylish, but usually don't wear shorts in the city. It's respectful to cover bare shoulders and upper arms in churches. Unlike some European countries, topless and nude sunbathing are unacceptable in this deeply religious country, except at some island resorts.
- Taxis are inexpensive, but check the meter before starting out; it's not unknown for the price to mysteriously triple for foreign visitors.
- Don't rent a scooter; more tourists have accidents on them than by any other means.
- At important sites you'll be inundated by guides wanting to be paid for their services; some are good, others barely speak English. If you want guide service, use an official one or take a tour.
- There's a plethora of attractive, handmade items to buy in Greek stores and markets. Leather goods, hand-woven rugs, sponges, olive-wood bowls, sweaters and antique reproductions are all worth looking for; just make sure the piece you choose is of good quality. Most prices are fixed, but you can try a little gentle haggling in markets, where you'll also find some of the world's best honey and olive oil.

Parliamentary guard in traditional uniform

ATHENS

Athens is one of the Mediterranean's great cities, boasting some of the world's most treasured relics; it's also noisy, crowded and polluted, with sprawling, unattractive suburbs. Summertime heat and the lack of green, shady spots can be oppressive, but the city is exhilarating, fascinating and stimulating, as much for its past as its present. Accept it and enjoy it for the colorful place it is.

Tackling Athens

You'll probably spend most of your visit in Athens' tiny historical center. Base yourself near Syntagmatos Square or Pláka, which are only a 10- to 15-minute walk from most of the main tourist sights. Try to plan your day carefully, getting an early start, so you can lay low during the heat of the afternoon. If you need information or advice, you will find that most people connected with tourism speak English, ranging from a few words to polished and idiomatic speech.

Moving around the city is easiest by taxi, although a ride on a trolley bus or the subway is a real, if not particularly enjoyable, Athenian experience. The existing subway system is being extended as Greece prepares for the 2004 Olympic Games, resulting in mounds of building debris and greater chaos than usual around the city. There's heavy traffic, and drivers often have a light-hearted disregard for other drivers and pedestrians, so take care when crossing busy roads.

Athenian Flavors

Sitting at a shady café table, lingering over a gargantuan lunch, munching sunflower seeds, melon, pistachio and pine nuts, or eating ice cream as you stroll on balmy evenings are true Athenian pleasures.

In a country where hospitality to strangers is one of the bedrock rules of society, it's not surprising that eating and drinking socially play an important role. Eating establishments are known as *estiatorio* (restaurants) or *tavernas* (less expensive, simpler and often family-run).

Greek food is delicious and healthy – fresh salads with feta cheese and olives, fantastic hors d'oeuvres (*mezédhes*), grilled meats, moussakas, and tasty stews and vegetables, washed down with *retsina,* the barrel-stored, pine-resonated white wine.

Dessert is normally fresh local fruit; if you want something sweeter, head for a *zaharoplastío*, a café serving the honey-soaked pastries much loved by the Greeks. The cuisine seems at times to have more in common with the Middle East than with the rest of mainstream Europe.

Festivals and Theater

Athens has theater, movies, dance, galleries and nightlife; everything changes rapidly, so pick up a free copy of such English-language magazines as *Athens Today* or *Now in Athens* to find out schedules.

In summer, the main tourist attractions are the sound-and-light show at the Acropolis from April through October and the Athens Festival, which runs from June through September. The festival offers a wonderful program of excellent cultural events, although it's most famous for classical Greek theater, stunningly staged in the second-century Herodes Atticus Theater.

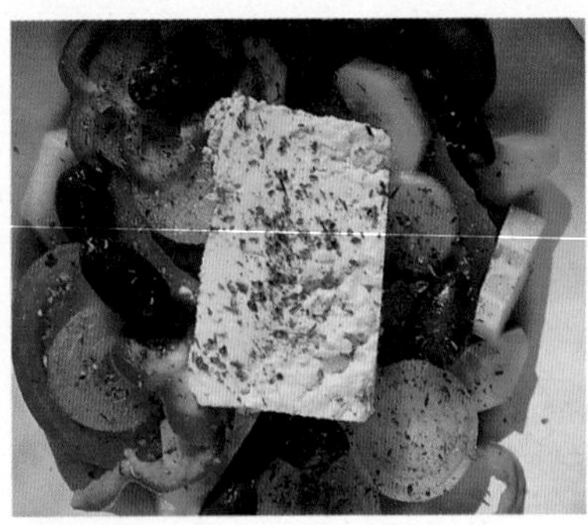

The delicious Greek salad, topped with feta cheese and oregano

The Greek Alphabet

At first it may be daunting to see Greek script everywhere, but it won't be a major inconvenience. All street signs are in both Greek and Roman letters, as are signs to museums and most restaurants and shops. Public transportation is usually signed in Greek. But you'll get the hang of it and will feel a real sense of achievement when you do.

Ceramics and Honey

There's a wide range of shopping in Athens, from international labels to traditional Greek products. In Kolonáki and on and around Ermoú Street, the smartest retail areas, you'll find familiar merchandise.

Ethnic buys are another matter, with much to hunt down around Pláka and vicinity. Leather and woolen goods, traditional ceramics and tapestries, felt slippers, natural sponges, fruity olive oil, honey and pistachios are all excellent buys. For something special, check out jewelry or religious stores; Greece has a long tradition of fine gold craftsmanship, and traditional icons are still made. Watch for Athens' kiosks – much more than newsstands, they sell everything from snacks and drinks to bus tickets, simple medicines and cassette tapes. In central Athens many are open 24 hours a day.

ESSENTIAL INFORMATION

TOURIST INFORMATION

• Odós Amerikis 2 ☎ 01 331 0565 or 01 331 0692; fax 01 325 2895
• East Airport ☎ 01 961 2722
• Zea Marina, Piraeus ☎ 01 411 5716 or 01 413 5730; www.gnto.gr

URBAN TRANSPORTATION

The easiest way to get around Athens is to walk or take one of the numerous inexpensive yellow taxis, as public transportation can be jam-packed and unbearably hot. Taxis are hailed on the street and often shared; you pay for your segment of the journey, so check the meter when you get in. Alternatively, your hotel can arrange a taxi for you. Buses, trolley buses and the subway operate daily 5 a.m.–midnight; tickets are available at kiosks and are interchangeable with subway tickets, which can be bought at stations or kiosks. Remember to validate bus and trolley bus tickets on board and subway tickets at entrances to platforms.

AIRPORT INFORMATION

Athens' Ellenikou Airport has two terminals, connected by trolley bus 19; the west (☎ 01 997 2816) is used by Olympic Airways, the east (☎ 01 969 4529) by all other airlines. Ellenikou is about 10 miles south of the city and is easily accessible by taxi or by the bus to Stadiou Avenue, which runs every 20 minutes (5 a.m.–11:55 p.m.) and hourly (11:55 p.m.–5 a.m.). Buy your ticket in the terminal before boarding.

CLIMATE – average highs and lows for the month

JAN.	FEB.	MAR.	APR.	MAY	JUN.	JUL.	AUG.	SEP.	OCT.	NOV.	DEC.
13°C	13°C	15°C	19°C	24°C	30°C	31°C	32°C	28°C	23°C	17°C	14°C
55°F	55°F	59°F	66°F	75°F	86°F	88°F	90°F	82°F	73°F	63°F	57°F
6°C	6°C	7°C	11°C	15°C	20°C	22°C	22°C	19°C	15°C	11°C	8°C
43°F	43°F	45°F	52°F	59°F	68°F	72°F	72°F	66°F	59°F	52°F	46°F

Room with a view – a quiet place to stop for a picnic

Stunning under floodlights, the Acropolis rises serenely above the city

City Sights

Key to symbols

map coordinates refer to the Athens map on pages 244–245; sights below are highlighted in yellow on the map.
address or location telephone number
opening times nearest subway nearest bus or tram route restaurant or café on site or nearby admission charge: $$$ more than Dr2000, $$ Dr1000 to Dr2000, $ less than Dr1000 other relevant information

Agorá

B2 Adrianou or Theorias 01 321 0185
Daily 8:30–3 Theseion or Monastiráki
$ (free to all Sun.)

The stately civic center and marketplace of ancient Athens is at the foot of the Acropolis, to which it was linked by the Panathenaic Way. Today the site is a jumble of atmospheric, tree-shaded ruins, and you'll need to use your imagination to visualize its glorious heyday. Dominating one end is the virtually reconstructed, fifth-century BC Doric temple known as the Thieío. Opposite, the two-story Stoá Attálou, a second-century BC arcade, has been restored by the American School of Archeology to give an idea of the glory of these ancient public buildings. It contains a museum with finds from the site.

Akrópoli

B2 Akrópoli 01 323 6665 or 01 321 0219
Mon.–Fri. 8–7, Sat.–Sun. 8:30–3, Apr. 1 to mid-Oct.; Mon.–Fri. 8–5, Sat.–Sun. 8:30–3, rest of year. Closed holidays Psaras, see page 556 Thission
1, 5, 9, 230, 231 $$ Acropolis Sound and Light, in English nightly, Apr.–Oct.; tickets from Athens Festival Box Office 4 Stadiou 01 322 1459

The Akrópoli (Acropolis) should top your sightseeing list. This naturally defensible rock was the sacred focal point of ancient Athens, and what you see today dates mainly from the fifth century BC, an era of peace and prosperity.

You reach the summit through the Propylaia, a magnificent stepped gateway, with the graceful little temple of Athena Nike to your right. Ahead rises the great Doric temple of the Parthenón; built using no perpendicular lines, its columns actually taper, giving the whole structure a feeling of lightness. It was decorated by leading Athenian sculptors and dedicated to the goddess Athena Parthenos, whose statue by the sculptor Pheidias stood inside. To the left of the Parthenón stands the Erechtheion, shrine to Athena and Poseidon, and said to be the place where the goddess created the first olive tree. The roof of the south portico is supported by six caryatids, stately maidens dressed in pleated tunics.

At the Acropolis' foot you can see two Roman theaters, the Théatro Iródou Attikoú and the Théatro Dionysou.

Ethnikó Archaiologikó Mouseío

C4 44 Patission 01 821 7717 or 01 821 7724
Tue.–Fri. 8–7, Sat.–Sun. 8:30–3, Mon. 12:30–7, Apr. 1 to mid-Oct.; Tue.–Fri. 8–5, Sat.–Sun. 8:30–3, Mon. 11–5, rest of year Café in museum Omonia 2, 3,

11, 13, 15, 18 $$ (free to all Sun. and public holidays)
For lovers of classical art the Ethnikó Archaiologikó Mouseío (National Archeological Museum) is one of the world's top sights. This vast and varied collection covers all the finest from ancient Greece, with the bonus of an exceptional Egyptian collection. The museum needs a full day to do it justice, and some perseverance to track down the main highlights in a very poorly organized venue.

The best approach is to concentrate on only the finest examples. Head first for the treasures from the royal tombs at Mycenae, opposite the entrance, dating from 1500 BC; they include exquisite gold funerary masks, necklaces and filigree flowers. Next, take in the sixth-century BC *kouros*, vibrant statues of nude male athletes; Aristodikos' superbly tactile athlete is one of the finest ever carved. Move on to admire the huge statue of Poseidon and the little jockey urging on his horse, both found in the sea in 1927. There's also a stunning bronze by the famous sculptor Praxiteles in room 28. Upstairs you'll find frescoes from Thera, buried 3,500 years ago during a volcanic eruption, showing charming riverside scenes. Next door are the fascinating pottery collections; look for the rare *lekythoi* (white-ground clay ware), and the exquisite red and black Attic vases.

ETHNIKÓS KÍPOS

C2 Amalias Museum: 01 721 1178
Daily dawn–dusk (museum: Tue.–Fri. 7:30–3, Sat.–Sun. 8:30–3) 2,4,11,12
The green and somber Ethnikós Kípos (National Gardens) provide a wonderful oasis of cool. Laid out in the 19th century by Queen Amalia, this is a true southern Mediterranean garden – no colorful flowerbeds, but deep shade and sylvan green. With plenty of benches and cafés, the gardens are a good place for a picnic. On the grounds is a botanical museum with samples of all the gardens' plants, many rare.

Greek head at the National Archeological Museum

LYKAVITTÓS AND KOLONÁKI

D3 Kolonáki Funicular: Fri.–Wed. 8:45 a.m.–midnight, Thu. 10:30 a.m.–midnight Terrace café at top 3, 13 $$
From Kolonáki Square, the hub of one of Athens' smartest shopping areas, the slopes of Lykavittós (Lykabettus) rise steeply to the 912-foot-high summit, one of the city's great vantage points. You can walk up or take the funicular to enjoy panoramic views over the city, from the Acropolis down to the sea at Piréas. Aim to get there for sunset, and leave time to visit the whitewashed chapel of Agios Giorgios (St. George) at the top.

MONASTIRÁKI

B2 Monastiráki Museum of Greek Ceramics: 01 324 2066 Market open daily, but largest on Sun. Museum: Wed.–Mon. 9–2:30
Monastiráki Museum $ (free to all Sun.)
This cacophonous area centers round Monastiráki square, named after a former monastery on this site. Today the square's focal point is the 18th-century Tzistarakis Mosque, a relic of Turkish rule, which houses the Keramiki Silogi (Museum of Greek Ceramics). However, most people head straight for Monastiráki's famous flea market, where you can find anything from clothes and kebabs to icons and compact discs. Sunday is the big day.

MOUSEÍO AKRÓPOLEOS

B2 Akrópoli 01 323 6665 or 01 321 0219
Mon.–Fri. 8–7, Sat.–Sun. 8:30–3, Apr. 1 to mid-Oct.; Mon.–Fri. 8–5, Sat.–Sun. 8:30–3, rest of year
Psaras, see page 556 Thission
1, 5, 9, 230, 231 $$ (included in Acropolis entrance)
Tucked behind the Parthenon is the Mouseío Akrópoleos (Acropolis Museum), housing a fine collection of sculptures found on the Acropolis. The original caryatids from the Erectheion are best known, but spend time admiring the superb fragment of a horse and rider and the splendid marble hound, straining forward, in room IV.

The great Doric temple of the Parthenon, the crowning glory of the Acropolis

MOUSEÍO KYKLADIKIS KAI ARCHAÍAS ELLINIKÍS TÉCHNIS

D2 4 Neofytou Douka 01 722 8321 Wed.–Fri. and Mon. 10–4, Sat. 10–3 3, 7, 13 $$

The beautifully presented Mouseío Kykladikis kai Archaías Ellinikís Téchnis (Goulandris Museum of Cycladic Art), once a shipowner's private collection, took its present form in 1986. Packed with fine antiquities, it's primarily famous for its collection of artifacts and statuettes from the Cycladic civilization, which flourished on the Greek islands from 3000 until 2000 BC. The figures, carved from local marble, could be taken for 20th-century work; elegant and minimalist, yet full of powerful feeling.

OLYMPÍEION ZEUS AND PYLI ADRIANOÚ

C1 2 Vasilissis Olgas 01 922 6330 Mon.–Sat. 8:30–3 Achillion, see page 556 2, 4, 11 $ (free to all Sun.)

Along with the Tower of the Winds in the Roman Agora, Olympíeion Zeus and Pyli Adrianoú (Temple of Olympian Zeus and Hadrian's Arch) are Athens' most impressive Roman legacy. Both were completed around AD 130 by the Emperor Hadrian; the temple as a shrine to this paramount Roman god, and the arch to mark the boundary between the old Greek city and Hadrian's new one. Fifteen massive columns remain of what was once Greece's largest temple.

PIRÉAS

Off the map Piréas Vassilenas, see page 556

Piréas is a town in its own right, although it's only five stops on the subway from Athens' center. It's a noisy, bustling port, one of the biggest in the Mediterranean, and many of the inter-island boats leave from its harbor. It boasts a magnificent cathedral, rebuilt after World War II; a fine archeological museum; and Greece's naval museum. Sunday is a good day to browse in the flea market, then enjoy a delicious fish dinner at one of the restaurants around Mikrolimano Harbor.

PLÁKA

B2 Pláka Thission 9, 11, 15, 18

Visitors return time and again to the picturesque Pláka neighborhood, at the foot of the Acropolis. The maze of colorful narrow streets, flower-bedecked squares and huge range of stores and *tavernas* may be touristy, but also radiate charm. Bustling Kidhathineon and Adrianoú, the main streets, teem with street life and are lined with mainly 19th-century, colorfully painted houses. Don't miss the dazzling white alleys that comprise Anafiotika, on the northern slopes of the Acropolis; built in the 1840s by masons from the Cycladic islands, they still retain a village atmosphere.

PLATÉIA SYNTAGMATOS

C2 Syntagmatos 1, 2, 4, 5, 12, 15, 18 Changing of the guard at varied times Mon.–Fri., at 11:25 a.m. on Sun.

Noisy, crowded and commercial, Platéia Syntagmatos (Constitution Square) is the heart of modern Athens, where you'll find hotels, offices, banks, restaurants, cafés and myriad jostling Athenians. The vast neoclassical edifice at the top is the Voulí (Parliament Building), once the royal palace. In front of it is the Tomb of the Unknown Soldier, patrolled around the clock by the Evzones, a guard of honor whose dress uniform features a short pleated kilt and pom-poms on their shoes.

The Athenian Treasury and Sacred Way at Delphi

An Excursion To Delphi

The sacred site of Delphi (Delfoí), 93 miles northwest of Athens, is the obvious choice for a day trip. The greatest shrine of the ancient Greek world, the center of their earth, lies in an unrivaled position below the great peaks of Mount Parnassós. Dedicated to the god Apollo, in ancient times Delphi was independent – belonging to no state – so enemies could worship there together. It was famed for its oracle, which gave enigmatic and prophetic advice through the medium of a priestess.

In return for this, petitioners brought gifts and erected treasure houses to hold them; ancient writers referred to the marble and precious stones of the sanctuary. For centuries, pilgrims trudged through the mountains to bathe in the sacred Castalian spring and worship here, but in the fourth century Christianity triumphed and the last oracle slipped away. Below the site, olive groves spread down to the sea, the ground is carpeted with flowers and the sky is full of birds.

The French excavated Delphi in the 1890s, and today it lies on a series of terraces below Parnassós. The paved Sacred Way leads past treasure houses – one sensitively reconstructed – to the Temple of Apollo. Six columns still stand, giving an idea of its former size and grandeur. Up the hill you'll find the 5,000-seat theater, and higher still, the marvelously evocative athletic stadium, set amid pine trees. To visit the ruins of the Sanctuary of Athena, leave the main site and cross the modern road. Use the columns of the fourth-century BC Tholos, undoubtedly the most photographed of all Delphi's wonders, as your guide.

Delphi Museum

The adjacent museum contains the finds from Delphi, some of the finest in Greece. Sculptures from the Temple of Apollo, two superb examples of archaic *koroi* (statues), ivory, jewelry and pottery are all here. The highlight is the bronze *Charioteer*, dating from 478 BC, an artistic and technical masterpiece.

See page 240, grid reference B2 Delphi 02 658 2313 Mon.–Fri. 7:30–6:15, Sat.–Sun. 8:30–2:45, Apr.–Oct.; Mon.–Fri. 7:30–5, Sat.–Sun. 8:30–2:45, rest of year A guided excursion is the easiest way to visit Delphi

Excursion Operators

Chat Tours (Intermed Travel, 46 Eleftheriou Venizelou 01 957 8441) is the best-known and most experienced tour operator in Athens.

HUNGARY

"BEYOND the river the hills...behold they lead to Heaven."

By early 20th-century Hungarian poet Árpád Tóth

Opposite: View across the rooftops from the Firewatch Tower in Sopron, western Hungary

HUNGARY

Hungary is situated at the heart of Europe. Surrounded by Austria, Slovakia, the Ukraine, Romania, Serbia/Yugoslavia, Croatia and Slovenia, it has absorbed the cultures of such peoples and conquerors as the Romans, Magyars, Turks and Habsburgs. Its majestic capital, Budapest, sits on the Danube river, which has brought trade and settlers through the country on its course from Austria to Serbia. For centuries Hungary has been a nation in flux, its territories expanding or diminishing through a series of invasions, occupations and liberations. It is today undergoing yet more change after emerging from 40 years of life behind the Iron Curtain.

Landscape of History

Northern, western and southern Hungary are different worlds. In the north, beyond the urban centers of Budapest and Miskolc, are the uplands and their wide, rolling, forested hills. The vineyards here produce famous Tokay and Bull's Blood wine.

In the west there are strong links with Western European culture. The rich farmlands are punctuated with historic towns that are packed with Renaissance and baroque buildings. In the south the landscape changes completely. Vast, flat grasslands form the Great Plain (*puszta*), dotted with tiny farmsteads and presided over by the capital, Debrecen. In the far south, the medieval city of Pécs preserves many relics of its 143 years under Turkish rule.

Making Contact

The Hungarian language, related to Finnish and Estonian, can be daunting for visitors. Some English may be spoken in the tourist areas, but German is more frequently used. When you find a common language, however, you will discover that Hungarians are courteous, generous and formal. Hungary is a proud, multiracial nation, and despite its proximity to the Balkan region, considers itself to be European.

Hungarian Heritage

Hungarians have strong folk traditions and customs, especially music and dance. You can enjoy them at a dance

house (*táncház*); there are several in Budapest. Bands usually include bagpipes and a hurdy-gurdy, and the dancing is fast and furious.

In Kiskunság National Park, between the Danube and the Tisza river, a horse-drawn buggy takes visitors to see farmsteads, long-horned cattle and curly-horned Podokan sheep. There also are displays at Hortobágy National Park – Hungary's first national park.

In the Cserhát hills of the north, the village of Hollókő sits at the foot of a 13th-century castle. The village is home to the Palóc people, who speak a distinct regional dialect and wear colorful embroidered costumes and elaborate headdresses. For another insight into Hungary's heritage, visit the famous Király thermal baths in Budapest and enjoy the luxury of a Turkish-style bath or massage.

MORE TOP DESTINATIONS IN HUNGARY

• Balatonfüred B2
• Bugac-Puszta C1 • Eger D3
• Fertöd A2 • Gödöllö C3
• Hollókö C3 • Hortobágyi Nemzeti Park D3 • Kecskemét C2
• Mátra C3 • Pécs B1 • Sopron A2
• Szabadtéri Néprajzi Múzeum C3
• Szentendre C3 • Tihany B2
• Tokaj D3 • Visegrád C3

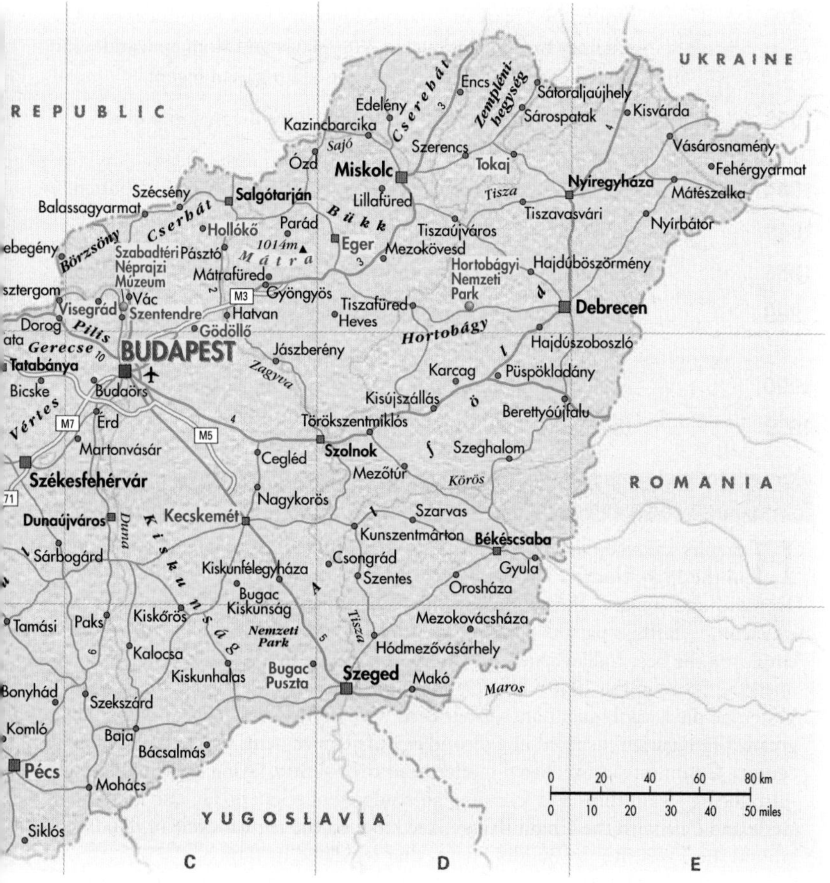

Timeline

13 BC	The Roman province of Pannonia is established on the west bank of the Danube; nomadic tribes occupy the east.
AD 896	Seven Magyar tribes cross the Carpathian Mountains and invade the Hungarian plains.
1000	King Stephen is crowned and makes Hungary a centralized, Christian state.
1526	Sultan Suleiman I and his Turkish army defeat the Hungarians at Mohács; most of the country is brought under his rule.
1686	Habsburg troops recapture Buda, on the west bank of the Danube (later united with Pest, on the east).
1896	The Great Exposition celebrates the 1,000th anniversary of the Magyar Conquest.
1919	Hungary briefly becomes a Bolshevik republic.
1920	Under the Treaty of Trianon, Hungary loses two-thirds of its territory to Czechoslovakia, Yugoslavia and Romania, and comes under the rule of an Austro-Hungarian regent.
1943	After regaining its lands, Hungary loses the majority of its army at Stalingrad.
1944	German occupation; most of the Jewish population is deported.
1948	Communists take power.
1956	Rebellion against Communist rule is crushed by Soviet troops.
1989	Hungary opens its borders to Austria and the Iron Curtain begins to lift.
1990	Free elections are won by a center-right coalition.
1999	Hungary officially joins NATO.

The Good Old Days

Hungary enjoyed two "golden ages" – one in the 15th century and another in the 19th. Under 15th-century ruler King Matthias, the son of a Transylvanian general, the nation expanded its borders and established its court in Vienna. Matthias patronized some of Europe's most brilliant scholars, and employed the best Italian artists to work on his palace in Visegrád. Ruins were unearthed here in the 1930s. His reign became a byword for good government. When he died, say Hungarians, justice died with him. The man known as "the greatest Hungarian" ushered in a second age of achievement. In the 19th century Count István Széchenyi modernized the country, laying surfaced roads, introducing steam ships and founding an academy of sciences. He also linked Buda and Pest with the Chain Bridge, and stopped the regular cycle of floods around the Tisza river by building dams that regulated its flow.

SURVIVAL GUIDE

- Hungarian cuisine's best-known export, *gulyás* (goulash), is made with beef, onions, potatoes, paprika, tomatoes and garlic. Salami is a regular item, as is *lecso*, a mix of peppers, tomatoes, onions and bacon fried in pork fat. Pastries also are specialties, sold in the *cukrászda* (pastry shop). Try *palacsinta,* thin pancakes filled with chocolate or curd cheese.
- Rural Hungarians produce and sell beautifully crafted items such as embroidered blouses and carved wood furniture. You can buy these in city stores, at national parks and from street sellers like the brightly costumed Transylvanian (Romanian) Hungarians.
- Wine is another good Hungarian buy, sold by dealers in the main vineyards, such as Eger. Many give tastings in their barrel-lined cellars.
- Go to street markets in the main towns and cities, such as the popular morning flea market on the southwest outskirts of Pécs. This is one of the biggest open-air markets in the country, selling antiques, crafts and food. On Sundays it also sells livestock, and the place is packed with country people.
- Some of the most fascinating ethnic communities have inevitably become big tourist magnets. Hollókő is filled with visitors for the August Palóc Festival and for Easter – an important celebration everywhere, marked with processions, egg-painting and a ceremony involving splashing girls with water or perfume.
- Summer festivals attract the crowds to Pécs and Sopron in June, and on St. Stephen's Day on August 20. There are fireworks, fairs and processions all over Hungary.

A miscellany of merchandise on display at one of the many antique shops in Budapest

- The state railroad, Hungarian Railways (MÁV), travels to most of the country. There are special tickets offering unlimited use of the network for seven or 10 days: contact the MÁV (✉ Andrássy út 35, Budapest ☎ 1 353 2722, fax 1 353 2187).
- Accommodations are not limited to city hotels. The Danube bend, a spectacular deep gorge north of Budapest, is lined with attractive towns where many private homes offer rooms, often for negotiable rates. The resorts around Lake Balaton are another option.
- For overnight stays on the Great Plain, try the Epona Hotel in Hortobágy National Park (✉ H-4071 Hortobágy-Máta, Czinege utca 1 ☎ 52 369 020 or 52 369 092) or Pongrácz-Major Hotel near Kesckemét (✉ H-6041 Kerekegyháza, Kunpuszta 76 ☎ 76 371 240).

BUDAPEST

Until the 19th century, two communities faced each other across the Danube. Royal, medieval Buda, with its majestic architecture, stood on the hilly western bank; and modern Pest, a flat area of busy boulevards, was on the east bank. Then the Chain Bridge (Széchenyi lánchíd) was built and Budapest, "Queen of the Danube," was created, linking the western and eastern landscapes of Hungary: the green uplands behind Buda, and the flat fields of the Great Plain beyond Pest.

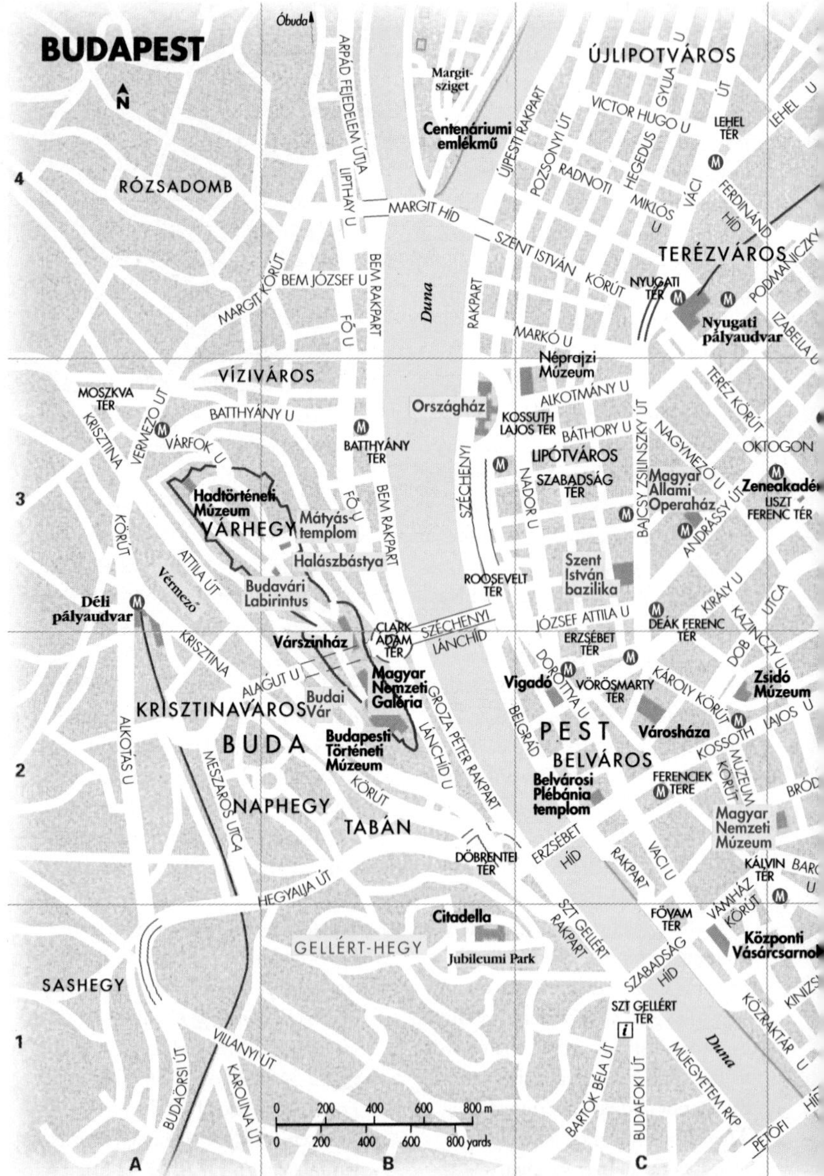

Crossing the Divide

The best place to get a feel for the capital's character and history is at Buda. Here you will find the oldest and grandest architecture, a cluster of museums and galleries, and countless cafés and bars. You can survey the whole city from Gellért Hill (Gellérthegy), and visit Castle Hill (Várhegy), a renovated medieval quarter reached by funicular railroad (from the Buda end of Chain Bridge). This is where you'll find the Buda Castle (Budai Vár) and the Fishermen's Fortress (Halászbástya).

Pest has a much more contemporary feel; its main landmark is the Gothic parliament building (Országház) dominating the riverbank. Also worth visiting are the Hungarian State Opera House (Magyar Állami Operaház) and the Museum of Fine Arts (Szépművészeti Múzeum). Between the riverbanks is tranquil Margaret Island (Margit-sziget), providing a haven of gardens in the middle of the Danube.

Local Flavors

In the late 19th and early 20th centuries, Budapest ranked with Vienna and Paris as part of the European café society drawing artists and intellectuals to argue, work and read newspapers. After World War II, few of these hubs of creative life remained. For a terrific art nouveau interior and a hint of the former literary and theatrical clientele, try the Café Restaurant New York, at Erzsébet körút 9–11.

Traditionally, Hungarian meals rely on the staples of spices, meat and cream and include intriguing specialties such as *túrós csúsza* (pasta with curd and sour cream). Since 1989 the range of international restaurant options has increased immeasurably.

Budapest at Night

The main home of opera and ballet is the Hungarian State Opera House (Magyar Állami Operaház, Andrássy út 22), a massive neo-Renaissance confection. Classical concerts take place in the art nouveau Franz Liszt Academy of Music (Zeneakadémia), at Liszt Ferenc tér 8.

Panoramic view of Budapest from the top of Gellért Hill

There are many bars, clubs, rock venues and discos, and rock bands have emerged from their underground status of the Communist years. The weekly English-language magazine *Budapest Week* has entertainment listings.

Shopping

Pedestrian-only Váci utca, on the Pest side of the river, is the perfect place to start shopping trips, and to look for antiques and art bargains. The other main boulevards in central Pest also are lined with stores. In Buda, there's a good browsing area around Móricz Zsigmond körtér.

A well-known flea market (Ecseri) sets up at Nagykrősi út from Monday to Saturday. It's also a pleasure to wander among the heaped food stalls of the renovated Vásárcsarnok (Central Market Hall) on Fövám Körút. The market is open all day Monday to Friday and on Saturday until 2 p.m.

ESSENTIAL INFORMATION

TOURIST INFORMATION
Tourism Office of Budapest
Written inquiries only:
• 1364 Budapest, P.O.B. 215
Fax: 1 266 7477; www.budapestinfo.hu
In person:
• Király utca 93 ☎/fax 1 352 1433
• Liszt Ferenc tér 11 ☎/fax 1 322 4098
• Tárnok utca 9–11 ☎ 1 488 0453; fax 1 488 0474
• Nyugati palyaudvar (Western Railroad Station) ☎/fax 1 302 8580.

URBAN TRANSPORTATION
Subway lines are color coded: yellow (M1), red (M2) and blue (M3). Buy tickets from the counter (*pénztár*) until 8 p.m., then from the section called *forgalmi ugyelét.* Trains run daily 4:30 a.m.–11 p.m. Buses with red or black numbers and no letter stop all over the city; avoid the express buses, which have a letter "E." Trams and trolley buses also have an extensive network. Tickets for all three are available from transport terminals, subway stations, vending machines or post offices. Subway stations are marked with an "M" on the city map. Do not take taxis that don't display a sign, and check that the meter is on and running. The biggest city company is Fötaxi (☎ 1 222 2222).

AIRPORT INFORMATION
Ferihegy Airport 2 is 12 miles south-east of the city. An airport shuttle (☎ 1 296 8555) travels to any downtown area, and farther for a small surcharge. Purchase tickets from the LRI counter at the airport. Centrum–Airport–Centrum minibuses run every 30 minutes to and from Erszébet tér bus station (daily 5:30 a.m.–10 p.m.), and bus 93 runs to Kőbánya-Kispest subway station. For airport flight information ☎ 1 296 7155.

CLIMATE – average highs and lows for the month

JAN.	FEB.	MAR.	APR.	MAY	JUN.	JUL.	AUG.	SEP.	OCT.	NOV.	DEC.
2°C	4°C	10°C	15°C	22°C	24°C	26°C	26°C	22°C	15°C	7°C	3°C
36°F	39°F	50°F	59°F	72°F	75°F	79°F	79°F	72°F	59°F	45°F	37°F
-4°C	-3°C	1°C	5°C	10°C	14°C	15°C	15°C	11°C	6°C	1°C	-3°C
25°F	27°F	34°F	41°F	50°F	57°F	59°F	59°F	52°F	43°F	34°F	27°F

City Sights

Key to symbols
map coordinates refer to the Budapest map on pages 258–259; sights below are highlighted in yellow on the map.
address or location telephone number
opening times nearest subway nearest bus, trolley bus, or tram route restaurant or café on site or nearby admission charge: $$$ more than 1,000Ft, $$ 600Ft–1,000Ft, $ less than 600Ft
other relevant information

Budai Vár

Budapesti Történeti Múzeum B2 Szent György tér 6 1 355 8849 Daily 10–6, mid-May to mid-Sep.; Wed.–Mon. 10–6, Mar. 1 to mid-May and mid-Sep. to Oct. 31; Wed.–Mon. 10–4, rest of year For all attractions: 5, 16, 78, Várbusz (Castle Bus) from Moszkva tér; tram 18; funicular from west end of Chain Bridge $; free to all Wed.
Kortárs Müvészeti Múzeum 1 375 9175 Tue.–Sun. 10–6 $; free to all Tue.
Magyar Nemzeti Galéria 1 375 7533 Tue.–Sun. 10–6, mid-Mar. to Oct. 31; 10–4, rest of year Café in Nemzeti Galéria $; free to all Wed.
Országos Széchényi Könyvtár 1 224 3700 Tue.–Sat. 9–9, Mon. 1–9, May–Jun. and Nov.–Jan.; Tue.–Sat. 9–5 (also Wed. and Fri. 5–9), Mon. 1–9, rest of year $; free to all Wed.

Budai Vár (Buda Castle) looks down over the Danube from its clifftop setting at the southern end of Várhegy (Castle Hill). Hardly anything is left of the earliest castle, which was built in the 13th century. What remains is in the cellars and underground passages, now part of the Budapesti Történeti Múzeum (Budapest History Museum), in Wing E. Before the building was flattened during World War II, it was an amalgam of 18th- and 19th-century Habsburg architecture. This is the version that has been carefully restored.

The Magyar Nemzeti Galéria (Hungarian National Gallery) collection of Hungarian art is housed in the Central Wings B, C and D, under a landmark dome.

A walk from here through a garden square and past the lovely Matthias Well fountain takes you to the West Wing (F) and the Országos Széchényi Könyvtár (National Széchényi Library), which stores about 2 million books.

Take a back seat for a view of Buda Castle

Contemporary art is displayed in the Kortárs Müvészeti Múzeum (Museum of Contemporary Art – Ludwig Museum), in Wing A.

Statues outside the palace include Prince Eugene of Savoy, who routed the Turkish armies; King Matthias, in the west courtyard; and a mythical bird called the Turul.

Budavári Labirintus

B3 Uri utca 9 1 375 6858 Daily 9:30–7:30 16, Várbusz (Castle Bus) $$

A maze of catacombs extends for 16 miles under Várhegy (Castle Hill), made up of caverns linked by passageways originally built for use by the Turkish military. Only a tenth of the Budavári Labirintus (Buda Castle Labyrinth) complex can be visited, but even this gives a vivid impression of a strange, enclosed, underground world. Waxworks illustrate the history of Hungary from the misty past to the golden Renaissance age of King Matthias. During the siege of Budapest in World War II, thousands of people took shelter down here while their city was destroyed.

Magyar chiefs stand guard in Heroes' Square

GELLÉRT-HEGY

B1 Between Erzsébet híd (Elizabeth Bridge) and Szabadság híd (Freedom Bridge) Duna, see page 557 27; tram 18, 19, 47, 49

Bishop Gellért failed to convert the pagan Magyars to Christianity; legend has it they stuck him in a barrel and threw him into the river from this 771-foot-high limestone cliff. His statue stands at the bottom of Gellért-hegy (Gellért Hill). At the top is the Citadella, a stronghold built after the 1848–49 War of Independence to keep an eye on the restive citizens. The Freedom Monument, also at the top, was erected by the Russians in 1947. Before the fall of Communism, the monument featured a Soviet soldier as well as the now lone woman brandishing a palm leaf.

HALÁSZBÁSTYA

B3 Szentháromság tér, Várhegy Tue.–Sun. 8:30 a.m.–11 p.m. Alabárdos, see page 557 16, Várbusz (Castle Bus) from Moszkva tér $ One ticket for fortress and crypt; free to all Mon.

Halászbástya (Fishermen's Fortress) is one of the city's greatest tourist draws: a fairy-tale seven-towered rampart in pale stone wedged into the eastern rim of Castle Hill. The architect, Frigyes Schulek, designed the fortress as part of the city's millennial celebrations of Magyar nationhood in 1896. There are great river views, and plenty of souvenir stalls and shops.

HŐSÖK TERE

D4 Városliget Hősök tere red 4, black 20, 30; trolley bus 79

At the end of the grand Andrássy út boulevard and on the edge of Városliget (City Park) is magnificent Hősök tere (Heroes' Square), part of the city's 1896 millennial celebrations. On either side are the Műcsarnok (Art Gallery) and the Szépművészeti Múzeum (Museum of Fine Arts, see page 264); between them is a monument to Hungarian successes. Perched on a 118-foot-high column is the Archangel Gabriel; guarding the foot of the column are statues of the seven fierce and triumphant Magyar chiefs, with Árpád, their leader, in the center. They are flanked by colonnades bearing the figures of Fame, Knowledge, Peace and War; between the columns are more Hungarian icons, including King Stephen (who would later be sainted).

MAGYAR ÁLLAMI OPERAHÁZ

C3 Andrássy út 22 1 331 2550 Tours daily at 3 and 4 Müvész, see page 557 Opera red 4 Tour $

Take one of the daily 40-minute guided tours of the Magyar Állami Operaház (Hungarian State Opera House) building to marvel at its marble, gold leaf and frescoes. Opened in 1884, it celebrates the musical world with statues of composers Wolfgang Mozart, Guiseppe Verdi, Richard Wagner and Ludwig van Beethoven, which stand on the stone cornice of the front terrace. Pride of place goes to Hungarians Franz Liszt and opera composer Ferenc Erkel, whose statues flank the entrance. Inside the building an enormous bronze chandelier hangs over the auditorium, which is decorated with Greek gods.

MAGYAR NEMZETI MÚZEUM

D2 Múzeum körút 14–16 1 338 2122 Tue.–Sun. 10–6, mid-Mar. to mid-Oct.; 10–5, rest of year Empire, see page 557 Astoria, Kálvin tér 9; tram 47, 49 $

Five collections form the Magyar Nemzeti Múzeum (Hungarian National Museum), Hungary's largest museum, covering an

The Chain Bridge crosses the Danube, linking Buda and Pest

area of 861,111 square feet. They include archeology, medieval and modern displays, a numismatic collection and historical portraits. The great prize among the exhibits is St. Stephen's 11th-century crown, which was stolen by Hungarian fascists after World War II and kept in the United States until President Jimmy Carter ordered its return. The upper part of the crown, a gold cap set above the jeweled headband, may date even earlier. Other curiosities are the inscribed brick from a 13th-century monk's tomb and the tent of a Turkish commander taken at the siege of Vienna in 1683.

MÁTYÁS-TEMPLOM

B3 Szentháromság tér 2 1 355 5657 Daily 9:30–7:30, mid-Feb. to mid-Jan. 16, Várbusz (Castle Bus) from Moszkva tér

Fifteenth-century King Matthias was married twice in the Mátyás-templom (Matthias Church), which had already been in existence for two centuries. It later served the Turks as a mosque, and was subsequently remodeled in the 19th century in striking neo-Gothic style. Medieval touches have been reproduced in the interior, along with dramatic features such as the soaring 262-foot spire. The tombs of 12th-century monarch Béla III and his wife, Anne of Châtillon, are in the Trinity Chapel near the main door.

ORSZÁGHÁZ

B3 Kossuth Lajos tér 1-3 1 441 4904, 1 441 4415 or 1 441 4138 English guided tours daily at 10 and 2. Tours subject to parliamentary sessions Empire, see page 557 Kossuth tér 15; tram 2; trolley bus 70, 78 $$$

Bristling with neo-Gothic spires and turrets, the Országház (Parliament) building sits on the eastern bank of the Danube, covering an area of nearly 200,000 square feet. Its magnificent red dome is 315 feet high and rises above a 16-sided hall between the upper and lower houses of parliament.

SZENT ISTVÁN-BAZILIKA

C3 Svent István tér 1 317 2859 Daily 9–5, Apr.–Sep.; 10–4, rest of year Arany János utca

Budapest's biggest church, Szent István-bazilika (St. Stephen's Basilica), took 55 years to finish. It can house a congregation of 8,500, and its dazzling interior includes 90 pounds of 24-carat gold, as well as frescoes, paintings and tapestries by Hungarian artists. Transylvanian and Hungarian heroes are represented by 88 statues, and the most cherished item – the mummified right hand of St. Stephen – is displayed in a glass case. Its 315-foot-high dome provides good views of the city.

The golden dome of St. Stephen's Basilica

SZÉPMŰVÉSZETI MÚZEUM

D4 Hősök tere 1 343 9759 Tue.–Sun. 10–5:30 Hősök tere red 4, black 20, 30; trolley bus 79 $

The Szépművészeti Múzeum (Museum of Fine Arts) is a neoclassic temple built to celebrate the millennial anniversary of the Magyar nation and to house the nation's art. Its exhibits are now restricted to foreign work and include ancient Egyptian mummy cases and a world-renowned collection of old masters. Of particular note are works by Spanish artists El Greco and Pablo Picasso.

VÁROSLIGET

Magyar Mezőgazdasági Múzeum E4 Vajdahunyad vára 1 343 0573 Tue.–Sat. 10–5, Sun. 10–6, Apr. 1 to mid-Nov.; Tue.–Sat. 10–4, Sun. 10–5, rest of year Gundel, see page 557 Széchenyi fürdő red 4, black 20, 30; trolley bus 70, 72, 79 $

Fővárosi Nagycirkusz E4 Állatkerti út 12 1 343 8300 Mon. and Thu.–Fri. at 3, Sat. at 10, 3 and 7, Sun. at 10 and 3 Gundel, see page 557 Széchenyi fürdő red 4; trolley bus 70, 72, 79 $

Közlekedési Múzeum E4 Városligeti körút 11 1 343 0565 Tue.–Fri. 10–5, Sat.–Sun. 10–6, May–Sep.; Tue.–Fri. 10–4, Sat.–Sun.10–5, rest of year Gundel, see page 557 Széchenyi fürdő tram 1; trolley bus 70, 72, 74 $

Állatkert D4 Állatkerti út 6–12 1 268 1970 Daily 9–7, May–Aug.; 9–5, rest of year Gundel, see page 557 Széchenyi fürdő red 4; trolley bus 72 $

Vidámpark Állatkerti út 14–16 Daily 10–8, Apr.–Sep.; Sat.–Sun. 10–7, rest of year Gundel, see page 557 Széchenyi fürdő red 4; trolley bus 72 Free entrance (rides $)

Petőfi Csarnok/Repüléstörténeti Múzeum E4 Zichy Mihály út 14–16 1 251 7266; Museum 1 343 0009 Tue.–Fri. 10–5, Sat.–Sun. 10–6, May–Sep.; Tue.–Fri. 10–4, Sat.–Sun. 10–5, rest of year Gundel, see page 557 Széchenyi fürdő tram 1; trolley bus 70, 72, 74 $

Beyond the bustling boulevards of Pest is Városliget (City Park). It was laid out in the 18th century and has acquired several extras over the years. The oddest is Vajdahunyad vára (Vajdahunyad Castle), built for the 1896 exhibition. Based on a Transylvanian fortress, its popularity ensured permanent survival. Inside the walls is the Magyar Mezőgazdasági Múzeum (Hungarian Agricultural Museum). The Állatkert (zoo), with art nouveau animal houses, is another favorite. There's also the Fővárosi Nagycirkusz (circus) and a slightly faded Vidámpark (amusement park).

In the park's southeast corner are the Közlekedési Múzeum (Transportation Museum) and the Petőfi Csarnok youth center, where local youth come to hear pop music and watch open-air movies in the summer. The hall is home to the Repüléstörténeti Múzeum (Aviation Museum), which exhibits the space capsule of the first Hungarian cosmonaut.

The Danube Esplanade

Running alongside the river on the Pest bank, between Chain Bridge (Széchenyi lánchíd) and Elizabeth Bridge (Erzsébet híd), is the tree-lined Danube Esplanade (Duna korzó). In the 19th century, this was the most fashionable place to be seen. Café tables were set out in the evening, and gypsy bands played by lamplight under the stars. The elaborate Vigadó is a legacy of that era, and still a venue for classical music concerts.

Esztergom's cathedral entrance, dominated by eight Corinthian pillars

Excursion to Esztergom

Hungary's largest cathedral towers over the stunning scenery of the Danube Bend at Esztergom, former royal city and the birthplace of King Stephen I (975–1038). There has been a settlement here, guarding the western approach to the gorge, since Roman times. Medieval Esztergom was destroyed by the Turks in 1543, but the city rose again, and it now boasts a center full of baroque buildings.

The cathedral is by far the most imposing: it is 328 feet from the floor to the top of its huge, glittering dome. It includes one of the world's biggest paintings – an altarpiece based on the work of 16th-century Italian artist Titian. The white marble altar itself was designed in 1519 and made by expert craftsmen from Florence, Italy.

Among other treasures are the impressive Renaissance interior of the Bakócz Chapel and a gold and enamel Gothic cross known as the Calvary of Matthias Corvinus. The dome offers a spectacular view over Esztergom and its surroundings.

The present version of the cathedral was begun in the 1820s: Hungarian composer Franz Liszt celebrated its reconsecration in 1856 with a mass. Long before this second lease of life, Esztergom was the seat of the Hungarian Primate – head of the nation's Catholic Church – and an important royal base. King Stephen was crowned in a church on the site in AD 1000, and the remains of a royal palace are housed in the Castle Museum (Vár Múzeum) next door.

Two other museums are worth a visit. The Museum of Christian Art (Keresztény Múzeum) has a superb collection of medieval religious paintings and works by Italian artists such as Duccio di Buoninsegna, Lorenzo di Credi and Giovanni di Paolo. The Danube Museum (Duna Múzeum) features displays that clearly illustrate (despite Hungarian-only captions) the role of the river and its effects on the life of the town.

Esztergom is 41 miles north of Budapest. Buses travel from Budapest's Árpád híd bus station and there is a regular service from Nyugati (Western) railroad station.

For tour information contact Gran Tours (✉ H-2500 Esztergom, Széchenyi tér 25 ☎ 33 417 052; fax 33 413 756).

IRELAND

"THERE lay the green shore of Ireland, like some coast of plenty."

On arriving in Ireland, from *English Traits*, 1856, by essayist and philosopher Ralph Waldo Emerson

Opposite: This view of the mountains and lakes of Killarney is known as "Ladies View"

IRELAND

People long for Ireland in a way that they pine for few other countries. Call it romantic, call it sentimental, but there is something about this remarkable country that tugs at the heartstrings of even those who have no Irish blood. The beauty of the country, its powerful Gaelic traditions and the irrepressibly romantic and creative nature of the Irish people underscore this potent appeal. This is a country that is not without problems, however, and its political and religious divide has had far-reaching, universal impact.

Mists of Time

Ireland claims with pride that it was a "land of saints and scholars" when the rest of Europe was deep in the Dark Ages. It is often described as a Celtic country, with all the myth-making that goes along with that term. The Celts are seen as being a distinctive lost race of Iron Age people who, in the face of first Roman and then Anglo Saxon aggression, retreated into Scotland, Ireland, Wales and Cornwall, from where they passed down the cultural values of their time. They did not call themselves Celts, and the term may be only a convenient label, but what is certain is that the influence of the earliest Bronze Age and Iron Age cultures survives on the peripheries of the British Isles. This is especially true in Ireland, where the evocative Gaelic language, still heard today, is its greatest expression.

There are thousands of prehistoric sites in Ireland: on the remote western seaboard, on the Beara peninsula, in County Kerry, and at exceptional places such as the Newgrange burial complex, in County Meath north of Dublin. Even where they are ruinous and vestigial, these ancient sites are hauntingly evocative.

You will find within the same landscape the music, song, wit and drama of Ireland that have been enshrined in hundreds of films, songs, dances and stories. A sense of the past is intense here; it has shaped Ireland in a seminal way, for better or for worse.

MORE TOP DESTINATIONS IN IRELAND

- Aran Islands
- Beara Peninsula
- Blarney Castle
- The Burren
- Clifden
- Dingle
- Galway
- Giant's Causeway
- Glendalough
- Kilkenny
- Killarney
- Newgrange

From Dublin to Kerry

Dublin is the boisterous heart of Ireland, the "family home." It should not be missed, of course, but Dublin will only whet your appetite for the rest of the country. Save time to explore other areas for the essential Irish experience. South of the capital lie the Wicklow Mountains, with the popular Glendalough at their heart – half religious site, wholly spectacular from a scenic point of view.

Farther south lies the fascinating Viking town of Wexford, from where the long, rambling southern coast of Ireland runs through endless great bays toward the distant west (and the most spectacular scenery). The western coast stretches for nearly 180 miles north to south, but measures much more if all the sinuous indentations, bays, river

Irish music played on traditional instruments beneath the craggy outline of the Rock of Cashel in County Tipperary - one of the most spectacular historical sites in Ireland

mouths, peninsulas and islands are taken into account.

Try to visit the far southwest. Take in the charming historic city of Kilkenny on the way; and visit Cork, the Irish Republic's second largest city, where you can kiss the nearby Blarney Stone if you feel that you should. Beyond Cork lies the glorious Beara peninsula. The bigger Iveragh peninsula is part of exquisite County Kerry to the north, land of the great mountains of Macgillycuddy's Reeks and the delightful lakes, and town, of Killarney.

Islands and Lakes

North of County Kerry lies the lovely Dingle peninsula and County Clare. Clare's southern half is mundane, but becomes increasingly spectacular the farther north you go, past the huge, echoing Cliffs of Moher and into the limestone country of the Burren, with its natural pavements of moonscape rock, dramatic stone burial chambers and hill forts.

In the pubs of Clare you will encounter the heart-stopping, foot-tapping essence of Irish music and

The great open spaces of the peat country as seen from Sligo Bay

song, in an environment that preserves the best of the past with energy, vitality and lyricism.

Off Clare's northwestern coast are the stunning Aran Islands, the magic names of Inishmor, Inishmaan and Inisheer resonating with all things Irish. Beyond Clare is Galway Bay and Galway city, the latter a vibrant, unfailingly charming place on the threshold of the Gaeltacht, the major area of Gaelic-speaking Ireland. Here, the mountains of Connemara and the broad lakes Loughs Corrib and Mask match an astonishing coastline of raw, rocky wilderness that lies to either side of the romantic town of Clifden.

Inland, Ireland also has much to offer. The heart of the country is a green bowl of rich farmland, of lakes, rivers and isolated ranges of rounded hills. Landlocked Ireland is outshone by the stupendous coastline of the far west, but it is a charming country full of character and tradition, where you will hear talk of horses and history and where lakes and rivers throng with fish.

Traveling North

Farther north is the remote county of Mayo, where you can follow the pilgrims' route up the Holy Mountain of Croagh Patrick, if you feel fit enough for the grueling four-hour clamber over rough rocks. Beyond Mayo are Sligo and Donegal, and golden beaches and tumbling Atlantic surf. Lakes and remote peninsulas enhance north Donegal, where the coast turns east toward the beautiful yet troubled city of Londonderry, gateway to Northern Ireland and the six counties of Ulster.

This British-ruled area has been riven for decades by sectarian violence and a divisiveness that is still struggling to resolve itself. Ulster's image has suffered much from "the Troubles" (the resumption of political violence since 1969), yet the beauty of its coast and countryside is of classic Irish quality.

"Organ-pipe" cliffs of the Giant's Causeway – County Antrim

The Giant's Causeway area, on County Antrim's north coast, is an astonishing landscape of perfectly formed hexagonal rock sections. Farther east lies the seaside town of Ballycastle, beyond which are the towering cliffs of Fair Head and then the green and peaceful Antrim Glens. South of Antrim lies Belfast, Ulster's capital, a city that has shown a grim face for far too long, and one that might yet be recognized, along with all of Ulster, for its majority of law-abiding, determined and hardworking citizens and for its deeply rooted Ulster-Irish traditions.

The Gaelic Lifestyle

In Dublin you will find museums, stores, theaters and restaurants to match those anywhere else in Europe, all suffused by the richness of Irish culture and by a modern sophistication.

In parts of rural Ireland things are different. You may come across an easygoing attitude, a relaxed approach reflecting the fact that the Irish have been around for a long time and often see no reason to rush things. At the same time, you may find yourself swept off your feet in places like beautiful, bustling Galway city, where a vigorous student population adds a contemporary note to the Gaelic culture most young people continue to embrace.

If you travel through Ireland, you will find the Irish hospitable and friendly. Often, if you ask a local for directions to a nearby site or place in town, you will be taken there rather than given complicated directions.

The Irish are fired by an all-consuming curiosity and have an almost total lack of pretension. They are a people whose history has often been terrible, bleak and unforgiving. Yet they have survived as the inheritors of a bewitching country that lies off the western edge of the Continent but is also an integral part of modern Europe.

Timeline

circa 3000 BC	Neolithic, Stone Age farmers construct sacred burial chambers at Newgrange and Knowth in the valley of the River Boyne.
AD 430	"Saint" Patrick begins the conversion of Ireland to Christianity.
circa 795	Vikings settle on the River Liffey, thereby founding Dublin.
1170	Powerful Anglo-Irish hegemony established in Ireland.
circa 1610	The six counties of Northern Ireland are confiscated by the English Crown.
1845–51	The Great Famine; a million Irish people die and a million emigrate, chiefly to America.
1921	Anglo-Irish Treaty partitions Ireland into the Irish Free State and mainly Protestant Ulster, which remains under British rule.
1948	Ireland is declared a republic.
1969	Beginning of "the Troubles" in Northern Ireland.
1972	Republic of Ireland becomes a member of the European Community, or, as it is now known, the European Union.
1985	The Anglo-Irish Agreement is signed by British Prime Minister Margaret Thatcher and the Irish Prime Minister Garrett Fitzgerald.
1998	"Good Friday" agreement paves the way for a Northern Ireland Assembly.

Divided Ireland

Ireland has been a divided country for long, bitter centuries. The reasons for this are immensely complex and lie in historical developments over hundreds of years. The larger, southern part of modern Ireland is the Republic of Ireland, *Poblacht na h' Eireann* – mainly Roman Catholic, with a small minority of Protestants. There is a strong Irish Gaelic culture and identity in this part of the country. After years of stagnation, the nation is now enjoying economic success and modernization, partly through its early embracing of the European Community.

The smaller, northern part of Ireland is Ulster, or Northern Ireland, part of the United Kingdom of Great Britain. It is mainly Protestant, with a substantial Roman Catholic minority, and has a culture and identity that is essentially Irish, but with strong British elements. Ulster Protestants consider themselves Irish but wish to maintain a union with Britain. In Ulster, Roman Catholics, many of whom wish to be thought of as Northern Irish, are seen by many Protestants as representing a rival religion as well as representing southern Irish Republicanism. The tensions of this duality in Ulster have given rise to violent conflict that in the past 30-odd years has caused immeasurable suffering. The "Good Friday" agreement in 1998 began a process to create a multiparty governing assembly that is still under way.

Survival Guide

- If you visit Dublin in the early spring, try to be there on March 17, St. Patrick's Day, when the city is bursting with activity. For the literary-minded (and the lively) there is Bloomsday, held on June 16. It celebrates the great Irish novelist James Joyce, and especially his most famous work, *Ulysses* (see page 278).
- If you're interested in shopping for Celtic crafts, don't miss the Kilkenny Design Centre in Dublin. This is the city's finest showcase for stylish Irish housewares, glass, books, fashion and jewelry. The upstairs restaurant serves generous portions of delicious homestyle food.
- Ireland is rapidly modernizing its road system, but there are still some very poor public roads, especially in the rural parts of the country. Look for unexpected potholes on otherwise smooth surfaces.
- Politics in Ireland is a very serious subject. It is best not to get involved in too much political discussion, especially in Northern Ireland. The subject is hugely complex and emotive. In the Republic of Ireland you should avoid referring to the "United Kingdom" or the "British Isles." The republic is emphatically a separate country. Speak of Ulster as Ulster or as Northern Ireland.
- Visit the local pubs in rural Ireland, especially in Clare, where in towns like Ennis you will find some of the greatest Irish music of all.
- Visit popular places such as Glendalough in County Wicklow, Killarney in Kerry and the Cliffs of Moher in Clare outside the peak season of July and August. Glendalough, especially, can become jammed with traffic.
- Enjoy the beautiful and often remote beaches of Ireland's west coast, but always be careful if you go swimming. Tides are very strong and there can be unexpected currents.
- Street signs in Ireland are often confusing because just about anyone who has something to sell attaches his own sign to an already groaning signpost. You'll find this is true for location markers, hotels, guest houses and local attractions as well.
- Ireland's Roman Catholic churches are extremely important places to the communities they serve, and you'll usually find someone praying if you visit. Be as discreet as possible when walking around the interiors of churches, and especially when in front of the altar. People may not take kindly to photographs being taken inside churches.

Shoppers frozen in time

DUBLIN

All roads seem to lead to Dublin in the end; it is a homecoming city where the visitor will feel as welcome as the Irish do. Dublin is celebrated today as one of Europe's most vibrant, colorful cities, something that Dubliners have always known. It is a rich distillation of all things Irish – music, conversation and laughter amid the city's lively streets, buzzing pubs and magnificent Georgian buildings.

Finding Your Way

The Dublin tourist office is located in the handsome old church of St. Andrew's, just southwest of Trinity College in the city center. Here you can obtain information about guided summer walking tours. Central Dublin is a reasonably easy and rewarding place to explore on foot. The main museums and notable buildings are concentrated in more fashionable south Dublin, but there are not-to-be-missed attractions across the River Liffey in north Dublin. A good starting point is the famous

Historic O'Connell Street - the principal thoroughfare linking the city's northern and southern districts

O'Connell Bridge, where Dublin begins with a rush.

Take time to adjust to the breezy pace of it all. To the north is O'Connell Street – the "broadest street in Europe." Lively shopping streets such as Abbey Street Lower and Earl Street North lead off to either side. On Earl Street you will find a genial, roguish statue of James Joyce, Ireland's most famous writer and the masterful chronicler of Dublin life. Go down Earl Street and turn left onto Marlborough Street to visit St. Mary's Pro-Cathedral, a magnificent neoclassical building that's always thronged with worshipers.

Opposite Earl Street is very busy Henry Street, with the huge ILAC Shopping Centre and the adjoining fruit and vegetable market on Moore Street. The women who work the stalls are famous for their lively Joycean banter. On O'Connell Street, just before Henry Street, is the site of the Easter Rising of 1916, when Irish nationalists staged an uprising against British rule and took over the General Post Office.

At the north end of O'Connell Street, by the Parnell Monument, is Parnell Square; on the square's north side is the Hugh Lane Municipal Gallery of Modern Art (see page 279) and the Dublin Writers Museum (see pages 277 and 279).

The Heart of Dublin

South of O'Connell Bridge is the brimming heart of Dublin. From the south side of the bridge, walk down Westmoreland Street to College Green, a frantic concentration of traffic that initially detracts from the stupendous buildings that surround it. Admire the neoclassical splendor of the Bank of Ireland and the elegant entrance to Trinity College, through which you can escape to the crowded but relaxing college campus. Otherwise, carefully cross College Green to the south and then continue past the buxom statue of Molly Malone, heroine of the famous "Cockles and Mussels" refrain, wheeling her cart in the midst of Dublin shoppers. The statue has become cheerfully known, through irrepressible Dublin wit, as "The Tart with the Cart."

Ahead lies pedestrian-only Grafton Street, crammed with interesting stores and delightful side streets on both sides. Expect street performers of all kinds, from guitarists and mimes to harpists or half an orchestra of music students. Stop at Bewley's Coffee House, a famous Dublin institution. Head east to Leinster House, seat of Irish government, and to the National Museum and National Gallery.

Beyond these lie the 19th-century Georgian splendors of Merrion Square and Fitzwilliam Street. Alternatively, go west from Grafton Street along store-lined Wicklow Street, then on to Dublin Castle and Christ Church Cathedral; or head back north across Dame Street and into Temple Bar, the rejuvenated old riverside district that is the exciting focus of Dublin by night.

The Ha'penny Bridge

Dublin's Ha'penny Bridge, over the River Liffey, is best reached from Temple Bar by going down the narrow Merchant's Arch – look closely for the symbols of nearby stores carved into the pavement. The bridge dates from 1816 and is made of cast iron; its elegant arches are lit up at night. It was officially named the Wellington Bridge after England's Duke of Wellington, but gained its popular name from the half-penny toll once charged for crossing it.

Elegant 19th-century Georgian architecture frames Ha'penny Bridge on the Liffey

Vary your Dublin experiences. Enjoy Temple Bar's restaurants and lively streets like Crow Street and Crown Alley, or visit St. Patrick's Cathedral on Patrick Street, where Jonathan Swift, writer of *Gulliver's Travels,* was dean. Enjoy outstanding drama at Dublin's Abbey Theatre on Abbey Street, or classic Irish entertainment at the Olympia on Dame Street. Above all, visit Dublin's famous pubs (see page 281) for great music and talk. There is a quicker, sharper edge to the Irish here, as befits a busy, cosmopolitan city.

ESSENTIAL INFORMATION

TOURIST INFORMATION

Dublin Tourism Centre

• Suffolk Street ☎ 01 605 7755; fax 01 605 7757; www.visitdublin.com

Also at: • 14 Upper O'Connell Street
• Baggot Street Bridge
• The Square, Tallaght

URBAN TRANSPORTATION

Dublin has two main railroad stations: Heuston Station, Kingsbridge, is where services from southern and western Ireland terminate. Connolly Station, on Amiens Street, is where ferry connections arrive and the termination point for trains arriving from the south-east, north and northwest, including the Belfast train. The Dublin Area Rapid Transit (DART) railroad line runs north to Howth and south to Greystones. There are 28 stations en route, but Connolly Station and Pearse Station, on Westland Row south of the River Liffey, are convenient city center stops. For train information call ☎ 01 836 6222.

There is a good citywide bus service run by Dublin Bus (✉ 59 Upper O'Connell Street, ☎ 01 873 4222). The main bus station, Busáras, is on Amiens Street.

Dublin taxis are expensive and are often difficult to hail on the street. Stands are at O'Connell Street, St. Stephen's Green (near the Shelbourne Hotel) and College Green. Call ☎ 1800 727 272 (toll-free).

AIRPORT INFORMATION

Dublin Airport is located 7 miles north of the city. It contains a tourist office, open daily 8 a.m.–10 p.m. (to 10:30 p.m. Jul.–Aug.) An Aircoach runs between the airport and the city center. The service runs every 15 minutes, 5:30 a.m.–11:30 p.m. The journey takes 30 minutes; for information call ☎ 01 844 7118. There is also the slower, regular bus service (No. 41) from Eden Quay. Taxis run from the airport and are less expensive than single bus fares if the ride is shared by a group. Only accept taxis with meters turned on.

CLIMATE – average highs and lows for the month

JAN.	FEB.	MAR.	APR.	MAY	JUN.	JUL.	AUG.	SEP.	OCT.	NOV.	DEC.
8°C	8°C	9°C	11°C	14°C	17°C	19°C	18°C	16°C	13°C	10°C	8°C
46°F	46°F	48°F	52°F	57°F	63°F	66°F	65°F	61°F	55°F	50°F	46°F
3°C	3°C	4°C	5°C	7°C	10°C	12°C	12°C	10°C	8°C	5°C	4°C
37°F	37°F	39°F	41°F	45°F	50°F	54°F	54°F	50°F	46°F	41°F	39°F

City Sights

Note: Due to copyright permission issues the Ireland country and Dublin city maps do not appear in this edition.

Key to symbols

address or location telephone number opening times nearest DART station nearest bus route restaurant or café on site or nearby admission charge: $$$ more than £4, $$ £2 to £4, $ less than £2 other relevant information

Christ Church Cathedral

Christ Church Cathedral Christchurch Place 01 677 8099 Daily 9:45–5:30 50, 78A Suggested donation $

Dvblinia St. Michael's Hill 01 679 4611 Daily 10–5, Apr.–Sep.; Mon.–Sat. 11–4, Sun. 10–4:30, rest of year 50, 78A $$

Dublin's great cathedral dates from the 12th century, but much of the surviving building is a 19th-century refurbishment in Gothic revival style. The interior has numerous fine memorials and features, but the most authentic parts of Christ Church are the late 12th-century transepts and the ancient crypt, one of the largest medieval crypts in Europe. It is 175 feet long. Thickets of rough stone pillars support the entire weight of the massive building above; the air is dense with age. Weird monuments and artifacts lurk menacingly in niches and dark corners. They include battered statues of English kings, medieval carved stones and oddities such as a mummified cat and rat, thought to have become trapped during a chase through organ pipes. Linked to the cathedral by a covered stone bridge is Synod Hall, where the colorful exhibition "Dvblinia" details Dublin's history from the medieval period.

Dublin Castle

Dame Street 01 677 7129 Mon.–Fri.10–5, Sat.–Sun. 2–5 Castle restaurant 50, 50A, 54, 56A, 77, 77A, 77B $$ Guided tours only; advance reservations are required. State apartments may be closed at times for official functions

Ornate interior decoration at Dublin Castle

Dublin Castle dates from the early 13th century but has been largely rebuilt and expanded. It is a powerful and at times brooding reminder of the past. Look for deep scars in the stonework of the Guardroom, at the main (north) entrance leading to the cobbled upper yard. They are the result of repeated bayonet sharpening, an eerie symbol of 950 years of British rule. The state apartments that are open to the public include St. Patrick's Hall, the Throne Room, the State Drawing Room and the Picture Gallery, all of which have sumptuous decorations and furnishings. A reconstruction during the 1980s uncovered original ninth- and 10th-century Viking defenses, a fascinating other world. The castle's Chapel Royal is a glorious neo-Gothic indulgence dating from 1814. Its exterior bristles with pointed Gothic motifs and 90 or so carved heads of historical figures. The interior has lavish plaster vaulting and superb carved oak galleries.

Dublin Writers Museum

18 Parnell Square North 01 872 2077 Mon.–Fri. 10–6, Sat. 10–5, Sun. 11–5, Jun.–Aug.; Mon.–Sat. 10–5, Sun. 11–5, rest of year Museum restaurant 10, 11, 11A, 11B, 13, 13A, 16, 16A, 19, 19A $$–$$$

Literary Dublin in all its glory is represented by this engrossing museum's large collection of documents, artifacts, portraits and general memorabilia of famous Irish writers, including Oscar Wilde and Samuel Beckett. The combined buildings that contain the museum date from the late 18th century

JAMES JOYCE

Ireland's most controversial novelist, James Joyce, was one of world literature's most important figures. Joyce was an innovator of the highest order, a writer of dazzling intellect. He was born in 1882 into a Dublin Catholic family of some gentility, although poverty overtook the family while Joyce was in his teens. He was educated at Ireland's leading Jesuit school and then at Catholic University College in Dublin.

Joyce rebelled early against the tenets of his class and religion and against Ireland's prevailing politics and culture, both of which he felt were too "nationalistic." He left Ireland in 1904 with Nora Barnacle, who became his lifelong partner. After a visit in 1912, Joyce never returned to Ireland and remained in Europe until his death in Zurich in 1941.

Joyce wrote several books of poetry and novels; his most famous novels were *Ulysses* and *Finnegan's Wake*. *Ulysses* was a monumental work, an allegorical saga describing the daylong wandering of its central character, Leopold Bloom, through the streets of Dublin. The novel developed new literary forms in its exploration and use of language and in its epic structure. It was published in Paris in 1922 but was banned for obscenity in Britain and in the United States until 1936. *Finnegans Wake* was published in 1939 and carried the "stream of consciousness" style of writing to revolutionary limits.

Joyce is a national hero in Ireland, something that would have amused this complex and essentially solitary man. The James Joyce Cultural Centre is at No. 35 North Great George's Street in north Dublin. And each year on June 16 Dublin celebrates Bloomsday, during which there are guided walks, readings and numerous events based on Leopold Bloom's progress through the Dublin of *Ulysses*. Visits to famous Dublin pubs play a lively part in the festivities; participants dress in Edwardian clothes from the period featured in the novel and readings, and other celebrations of *Ulysses* are staged.

A portrait of the artist by Jeffrey Morgan (top) and the James Joyce Martello Tower at Sandycove in south Dublin, which houses a small museum of Joycean memorabilia

and are themselves an experience. There is magnificent stucco, especially in the first-floor rooms. The colonnaded main salon, now the Gallery of Writers, has busts and paintings of famous names, a decorative ceiling and boisterous friezes.

Guinness Storehouse

St. James Gate 01 408 4800 Daily 9:30–7, Apr.–Sep.; 9:30–5, rest of year 51B, 78A, 123 Museum café/bar $$$

Dublin without Guinness is like the earth without air. You can sample Guinness in its creamy, lip-smacking originality in the city's multitude of pubs (see page 281), but to reach the heart of things visit the enlightening and entertaining Guinness Storehouse, located in an original hop store at the brewery. Admission includes a pint of the famous stout; visitors have been known to burst into song.

Hugh Lane Municipal Gallery of Modern Art

Parnell Square North 01 874 1903 Tue.–Thu. 9:30–6, Fri.–Sat. 9:30–5, Sun. 11–5 Gallery café DART Connolly Station (10 mins) 10, 11, 11A, 11B, 13, 16, 16A, 19, 19A, 22, 22A, 36 Free

The Hugh Lane Gallery is located in the delightful Charlemont House. The collection, bequeathed by Sir Hugh Lane to Dublin Corporation in 1905, comprises 19th- and 20th-century Irish and international painters, including Claude Monet, Sir John Everett Millais and Edgar Degas. There are several outstanding works, not the least of which is Renoir's *Les Parapluies*. Notable Irish artists include Jack B. Yeats, and there are contemporary Irish works and temporary exhibitions, often of daring conceptual art. The gallery also has a fine collection of stained glass and is a venue for music recitals, poetry readings and lectures. Francis Bacon's studio was gifted to the gallery in 1998. Painstakingly removed from its London home, the studio was reconstructed here and opened to the public in 2001. An audiovisual display documents the process.

Compelling atmosphere at Kilmainham Gaol

Kilmainham Gaol

Inchicore Road 01 453 5984 Daily 9:30–6 (last admission at 4:45), Apr.–Sep.; Mon.–Fri. 9:30–5 (last admission at 4), Sun. 10–6 (last admission at 4:45), rest of year Tearoom on site 51, 78A, 79 $$

The notorious Kilmainham Gaol (prison) has been the scene of great misery. A visit to this awesome place is a sobering experience. Kilmainham opened in 1796 and until 1924 when it closed, just about every famous name in the struggle for Irish independence and statehood was a "guest" at one time. They included Robert Emmet, Charles Stewart Parnell and Eamon de Valera. Fourteen leaders of the 1916 Easter Rising were executed in the prison yard. Explore the warren of gloomy cells and chilly corridors. Guided tours give a graphic picture of Irish history.

National Gallery

Merrion Square West 01 661 5133 Mon.–Sat. 10–5:30 (also Thu. 5:30–8:30), Sun. 2–5 Gallery restaurant DART Pearse Station (5 mins) 5, 7, 7A, 10, 44, 48A, 62 Entrance free Guided tours: Sat. at 3, Sun. at 2:15, 3 and 4

Ireland's national art collection eschews quantity for quality, and this fine building holds a collection that represents all major schools of European art. The gallery's interiors are splendid. The Shaw Room, dedicated to early benefactor George Bernard Shaw, is an elegant statement in its own right. Painters represented include

The National Gallery under the shadow of its founder, William Dargan

Titian, Francisco de Goya and Nicolas Poussin. Thomas Gainsborough and J. M. W. Turner are here as well, and there are strong collections of leading Irish artists such as Nathanial Hone, Jack B. Yeats and Roderic O'Conor. The gallery has computer facilities to find information about its paintings.

National Museum

Kildare Street 01 677 7444 Tue.–Sat. 10–5, Sun. 2–5 Museum café DART Pearse Station 7, 7A, 8, 10, 11, 13 Entrance free; guided tours $

This museum is part of a splendid complex of buildings that date from 1890. Together with the National Library, opposite the museum, the complex forms the approach to Leinster House, the seat of Irish government. This is an excellent museum with a relaxing atmosphere that inspires curiosity instead of exhausting it. The Bronze and Iron Age gold artifacts are dazzling. Included are the Tara Brooch, Broighter Hoard and the Ardagh Chalice. Displays also depict prehistoric and Viking Ireland and the Irish independence struggle.

St. Stephen's Green

St. Stephen's Green Mon.–Sat. 8–dusk, Sun.10–dusk 11, 13, 44, 46, 48

The delightful St. Stephen's Green has been a public park since 1664, when Dublin Corporation set aside 27 acres of open ground, albeit for use by its more well-to-do citizens. Access was by payment only until 1880, when the park was made free to all. There are numerous statues and busts of famous Irish men and women, including James Joyce, Robert Emmet, Wolfe Tone and Sir Arthur Guinness. The park is surrounded by some of the finest buildings in Dublin. They include the Shelbourne Hotel, and the neo-Byzantine interior of the Roman Catholic University Church, Cardinal Newman's great indulgence of 1856.

Trinity College

Campus College Green 01 608 2320 Daily All city buses Free Walking tours leave regularly from main gate Mon.–Fri. 11–3, Sat–Sun. at 11, noon and 3, May–Sep.; Fri–Sun. at noon, rest of year $$$ **Old Library** College Green Mon.–Sat. 9:30–5, Sun. 9:30–4:30, Jun.–Sep.; Mon.–Sat. 9:30–5, Sun. noon–4:30, rest of year. Closed 10 days from late Dec. to early Jan. All city buses $$$ **"Dublin Experience"** College Green Daily 10–5, late May–early Oct. Closed 10 days from late Dec. to early Jan. All city buses $$

Dublin's Trinity College is one of the world's great campuses, an outstanding architectural and cultural oasis at the heart of a busy city. It was founded in 1592, but all of the present buildings date from after 1700. The complex is best entered from College Green, between statues of poet Oliver Goldsmith and orator Edmund Burke, and then through the Corinthian facade of the Palladian Regent House. This leads into cobbled Parliament Square, with its tall campanile, and lined with grand buildings. Trinity's Old Library and its Long Room contain a number of outstanding artifacts, including the ninth-century *Book of Kells*, an illuminated manuscript of the four gospels of the New Testament. Another attraction is the "Dublin Experience," an audiovisual overview of the city, housed in the modern Arts and Social Science Building.

Dublin's Pubs

Irish pubs are fueled by good drink, but are rooted in the gregarious nature of the Irish, and in lively gossip. Many pubs also are outstanding folk music venues, inevitable in a country so well suited to such spontaneous music.

A local favorite is the Brazen Head, at 20 Lower Bridge Street, hailed as the oldest pub in Dublin. Davy Byrne's, on Duke Street just off busy Grafton Street, has an art deco lounge with lively murals that were painted by Irish playwright Brendan Behan's father-in-law. For Victorian authenticity try the Stag's Head, on Dame Court.

You can hear great Irish music with your Guinness in busy Temple Bar pubs like Oliver St. John Gogarty's, on the corner of Fleet and Anglesea streets. One of the best Dublin music pubs is O'Donoghues, on Merrion Row down from St. Stephen's Green. This was the favored haunt of the Dubliners folk group in its 1960s heyday, and the city's best folk musicians regularly raise the roof here.

Other good traditional pubs are Doheny and Nesbitt's on Lower Baggott Street; The Palace on Fleet Street; O'Neill's, at the corner of Pearse and Shaw streets; and old-fashioned Mulligan's on Poolbeg Street, a last outpost of Joycean Dublin amid the chilly lifelessness of modern office blocks. South of St. Stephen's Green at the corner of Camden Street Upper and Harcourt Road is The Bleeding Horse, formerly a blacksmith's shop and a church; its warren of little rooms are called "snugs."

If you want Dublin sophistication try the Horse Shoe Bar in the Shelbourne Hotel or the Kildare Bar next to the Kildare Hotel; the latter is favored by Irish politicians from nearby Leinster House and the Irish Parliament. For a down-to-earth atmosphere visit Joxer Daly's on Dorset Street Upper in north Dublin, where Old Dublin reigns unchanged. These are just a small selection from the multitude of Dublin's pubs.

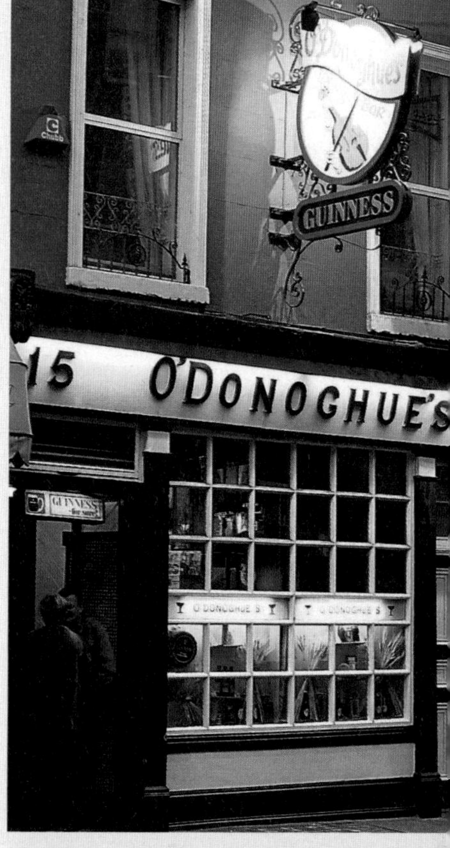

Guinness in lights (top), and behind the bar at one of Dublin's 800 pubs

ITALY

"LUMP the whole thing! Say that the Creator made Italy from designs by Michael Angelo."

From Mark Twain's 1869 novel *The Innocents Abroad*

Opposite: The village of Altangnana nestles on a hillside beneath Italy's magnificent Alpi Apuane

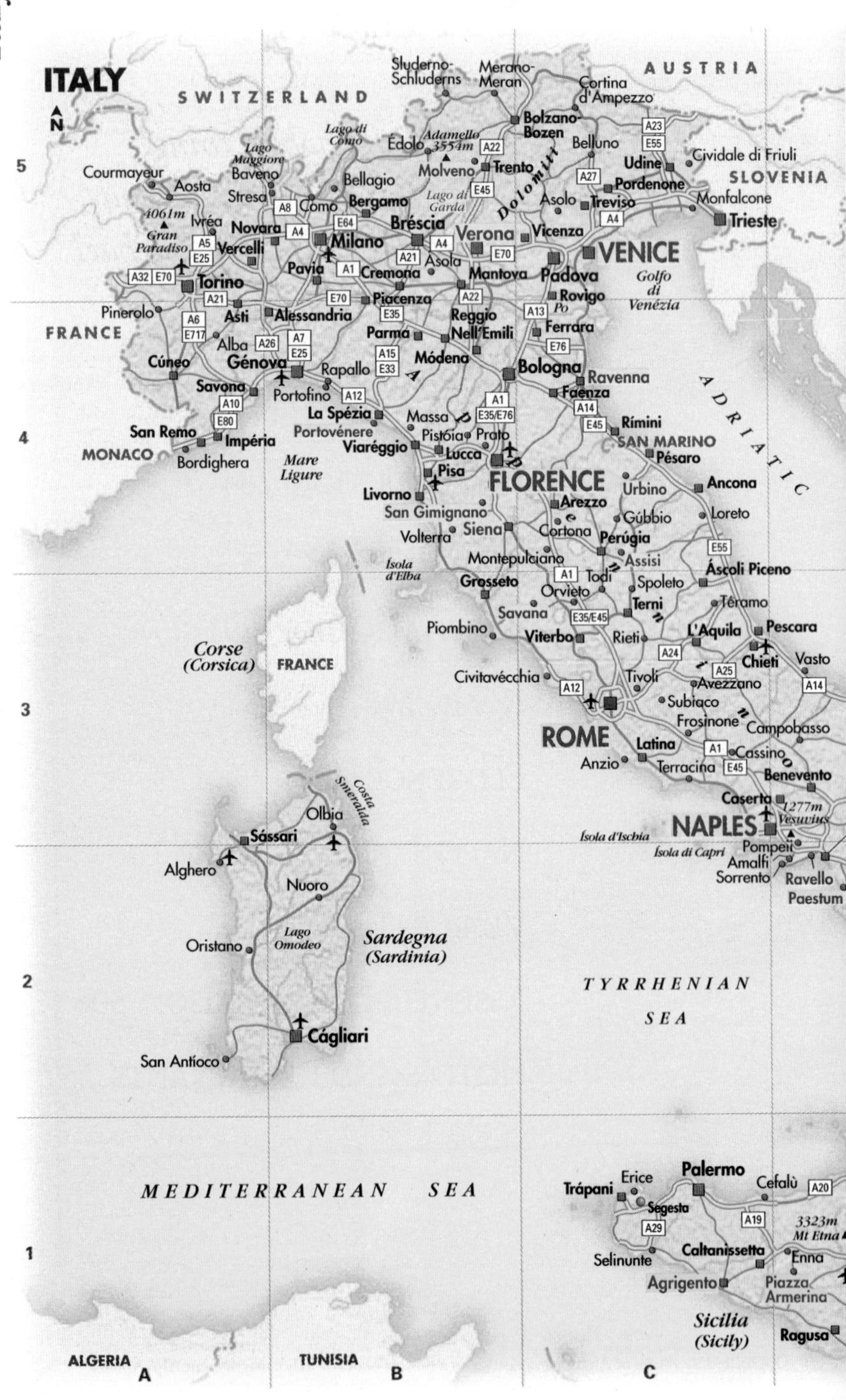
ITALY
N
SWITZERLAND
AUSTRIA
SLOVENIA
FRANCE
MONACO
SAN MARINO
ADRIATIC
Golfo di Venézia
Mare Ligure
TYRRHENIAN SEA
MEDITERRANEAN SEA
Corse (Corsica)
FRANCE
Sardegna (Sardinia)
Sicilia (Sicily)
ALGERIA
TUNISIA
Apennino
Dolomiti
Sluderno-Schluderns
Merano-Meran
Cortina d'Ampezzo
Bolzano-Bozen
Lago di Como
Lago Maggiore
Adamello 3554m
Édolo
Belluno
Cividale di Friuli
Udine
Courmayeur
Aosta
Baveno
Bellagio
Molveno
Trento
Pordenone
Stresa
Como
Bergamo
Lago di Garda
Asolo
Treviso
Monfalcone
4061m Gran Paradiso
Ivréa
Novara
Brescia
Verona
Vicenza
Trieste
Vercelli
Milano
Asola
VENICE
Torino
Pavia
Cremona
Mantova
Padova
Piacenza
Rovigo
Po
Pinerolo
Asti
Alessandria
Reggio Nell'Emili
Ferrara
Alba
Parma
Cúneo
Génova
Módena
Rapallo
Bologna
Ravenna
Savona
Portofino
Faenza
La Spézia
Massa
Rímini
San Remo
Impéria
Portovénere
Pistóia
Prato
Bordighera
Viaréggio
Lucca
Pésaro
Pisa
FLORENCE
Urbino
Ancona
Livorno
Arezzo
San Gimignano
Gúbbio
Loreto
Volterra
Siena
Cortona
Perúgia
Ísola d'Elba
Montepulciano
Assisi
Áscoli Piceno
Grosseto
Todi
Spoleto
Orvieto
Terni
Téramo
Savana
Piombino
Viterbo
Rieti
L'Aquila
Pescara
Chieti
Vasto
Civitavécchia
Tivoli
Avezzano
Subiaco
Frosinone
Campobasso
ROME
Latina
Cassino
Anzio
Terracina
Benevento
Caserta
1277m Vesuvius
Ísola d'Ischia
NAPLES
Ísola di Capri
Pompeii
Amalfi
Sorrento
Ravello
Paestum
Costa Smeralda
Olbia
Sássari
Alghero
Nuoro
Lago Omodeo
Oristano
Cágliari
San Antíoco
Trápani
Erice
Palermo
Cefalù
Segesta
3323m Mt Etna
Selinunte
Caltanissetta
Enna
Agrigento
Piazza Armerina
Ragusa
A1
A4
A5
A6
A7
A8
A10
A12
A13
A14
A15
A19
A20
A21
A22
A23
A24
A25
A26
A27
A29
A32
E25
E33
E35
E35/E45
E35/E76
E45
E55
E64
E70
E76
E80
E717
5
4
3
2
1
A
B
C

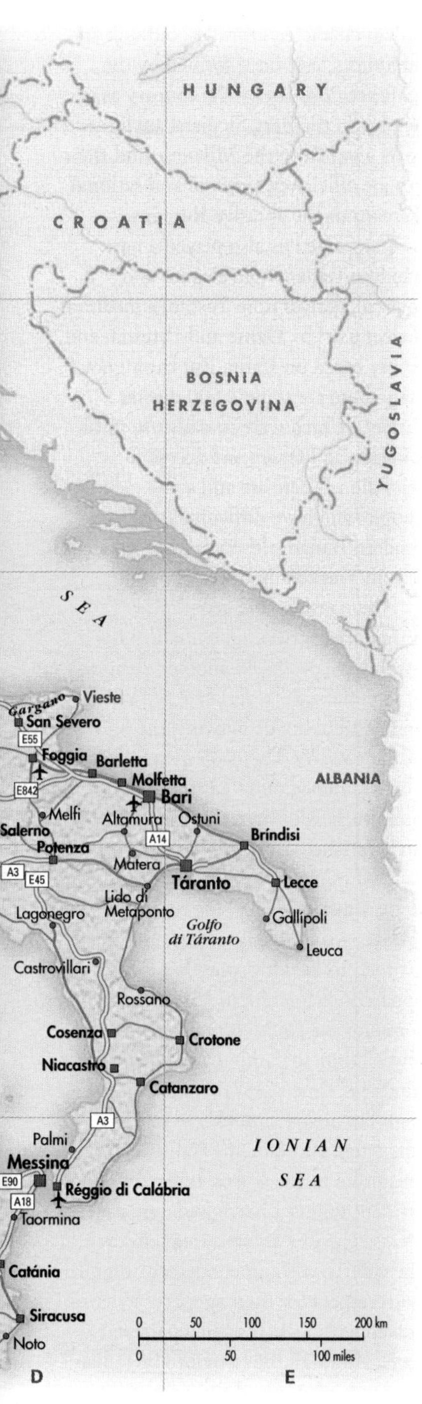

ITALY

Few countries have as much to offer as Italy (Italia), with its warm and passionate people; varied and beautiful landscape; a rich artistic, historic and cultural heritage; some of the world's best food and wine; and a stylish and relaxed philosophy on life. Italy truly has something for everyone, whether the visitor is seeking great cities, tiny villages, idyllic countryside or beautiful beaches.

Bella Italia

Of all European countries, Italy is the one to which travelers return time and again, their love affair blossoming with each trip. Whether your visit is a chance opportunity or the dream of a lifetime, Italy will fulfill and exceed your expectations, capture your heart and senses, and send you away longing to return.

From the Alps in the north, through the prosperous and fertile heartland to the stark beauty of the deep south, Italy is blessed with some of the world's most beguiling landscapes. The northern half features Tuscany's classic olive, vine and cypress-studded rolling countryside; the dramatic peaks of the Dolomites

MORE TOP DESTINATIONS IN ITALY

• Agrigento C1 • Assisi C4 • Lago di Garda B5 • Molveno B5 • Paestum D2 • Piazza Armerina D1 • Portovénere B4 • Ravello D2 • Ravenna C4 • San Gimignano B4 • Savana C3 • Siena B4 • Urbino C4 • Verona B5 • Vieste D3

(Dolomiti); pine-clad white cliffs and turquoise seas; and the eerie loveliness of mist-laden mornings in the great river valleys. The south is equally lovely, with an arid and fierce beauty during the long hot summers, when the intense color of the sea offsets the bleached ocher mountains.

Most of Italy is mountainous, the long spine of the Apennines (Appennini) running almost from top to bottom and stretching virtually from coast to coast. Some hilly areas are immensely fertile, as in Tuscany and Umbria in central Italy, while in other places, such as Basilicata and Calabria in the south, the combination of altitude and extreme climate make the land unproductive.

The largest area of flatland is the great plain of the Po river valley in the north, which extends down the eastern seaboard, an agriculturally rich and productive swath. Much of upland Italy is wooded, and there is a wide variety of indigenous plants.

Diverse Regions

Until 1870 Italy was a collection of separate and disparate states with a complex history, which does much to explain the diversity of people and attitudes. Camillo Cavour (statesman and first prime minister of a united Italy) remarked after unification in 1860, "We have made Italy, now we must make Italians." This aim still seems to await fruition, such is the gulf between the different regions. Italy has been a republic since 1946, the 21 regions (*regione*) enjoying a large degree of self-government; some, such as Sicily and Sardinia, are semi-autonomous.

Italians would be the first to agree that there is no such thing as "an Italian." Ask an Italian where he's from and the answer will be "from Tuscany, from Rome, from Naples, from Sicily," but never "from Italy." Primary loyalties are firmly local and regional. The Italian character, attitudes, outlook and prejudices have been formed by the native region, not by the country as a whole. So the fiery Sicilians are light years away from the Milanese and their urbane efficiency, the cool and rational Tuscans or the abrasive Romans.

Language has also played a part. Modern Italian, rich, elegant and musical, derives from Tuscan, a medieval dialect used by Dante and Petrarch and firmly based on Latin. But throughout Italy there are some 1,500 diverse dialects, which were in daily use until widespread literacy and access to television. There are still some elderly people who have difficulty speaking modern Italian, although mass media is rapidly weakening dialects.

The considerable geographic differences between the north and south have produced another element of regionalism – a very real economic and cultural divide between the halves of the country. The cooler, more fertile north is richer, more advanced and more successful than the arid and impoverished south.

The People

All Italians do seem to share the same attitude toward life, one that is instantly apparent to foreigners. Life is for living, for enjoying, for savoring. There's always time to pause to chat, time for kindness, time to laugh; passions run high but anger is quickly over and forgotten. Pause in any Italian piazza and listen to the voices; there are no strident tones or harsh and ugly notes. Watch the way Italians treat children or the elderly, without condescension but with respect for their age. Problems are solved with little fuss on a personal level, although the labyrinth of Italian bureaucracy might drive visitors crazy.

Opposite: The medieval Campo, in the heart of Siena

CALZATURE
PELLICCERIA AL CAMPO
CREMERIA
ENOTECA BAR

Despite having the world's lowest national birthrate, family ties are exceptionally close, with children often living with their parents into their 30s, and elderly people are still mainly cared for at home. The mother's role is pivotal; Italian men, it is said, spend their whole lives searching for a woman to live up to their mother – hence the constant philandering.

If you want to attract the opposite sex, you have to look good. This helps explain the importance of the *bella figura*, literally "beautiful form," but meaning infinitely more. Italians have an innate sense of style, and it matters greatly that clothes, cars and personal possessions are stylish and contemporary.

Bella figura dictates that these must all be admired, and what better way to display them than during that great Italian tradition, the *passeggiata*? This nightly outdoor perambulation occurs in every village, town and city in the land, when citizens exit en masse from their homes, strolling through the streets, exchanging news and gossip, but above all admiring and hoping to be admired in return.

Country of Contrasts

A rich historical and cultural past has shaped the townscape in Italy. Cities, towns and villages are crammed with fine buildings, churches and works of art, a legacy of pre-Unification days. But over the past century, and notably since World War II, there has been huge development and growth in urban areas, with unattractive spreads of industrial buildings and blocks of soul-less apartments on the outskirts of countless towns. Every town still retains its central piazza, with civic buildings and a church grouped around or near it.

In many rural areas, people have traditionally lived in villages rather than on the land they work, traveling daily to the fields, so in some areas isolated country farmhouses are rare. There has always been a huge gulf between the urban and rural populations, possibly due to the very early development of Italian towns.

The middle class was a late arrival in Italy and only really emerged during the great economic boom of the '50s and '60s. Even now there are still large numbers of *contadini*, peasant farmers and small shareholders, working the land as it has been worked for centuries, while their cousins may be employed in hi-tech industries.

Exploring Italy

Prosperous Italy has one of Europe's highest standards of living, making traveling easy and pleasurable. Tourism is a major industry, so you'll find English widely spoken in city hotels and restaurants, although not away from the main tourist areas.

Italian engineering prowess has produced an excellent road network, with both toll roads and good highways. Minor roads are often unsurfaced. Italians drive fast and aggressively but mostly safely, and once you're accustomed to the style of driving you should have no problems. All major cities have an airport, with frequent internal flights. Trains are cheap and punctual, although cross-country routes can be slow and complicated; it's safer to stick to the inter-city services. Buses connect even the smallest villages.

Italian hotels are all rated and inspected by regional authorities; regardless of the price range, they are spotlessly clean. Bathtubs are rare except in deluxe establishments, and showers frequently dribble when turned on; water is precious in many parts of the country. Air-conditioning is becoming more widespread but is by no

A wedding party make their way through Venice in a specially decorated gondola

means universal, and buildings can be stifling in summer. By law, heating in public places is not turned on until November 1.

Culinary Traditions

Italian cooking is regional and simple, relying on the superb quality of the ingredients, and you'll find wonderful dishes wherever you go. In a country where frozen food is practically nonexistent, menus are dictated by the seasons, with a rich variety of dishes punctuating the different months.

The different types of restaurant can be confusing. The terms *ristorante, osteria* and *trattoria* are fairly interchangeable; *tavola calda* and *pizzeria* imply something a bit more humble. Lunch has traditionally been the main meal, but there is a trend toward making dinner the extravaganza. The evening menu often consists of *antipasto* (hors d'oeuvre), the first course (*primo*) of pasta, soup or rice, the meat or fish second course (*secondo*) with its accompanying *contorni* (vegetables) or *insalata* (salad), followed by *formaggio, dolce* or *frutta* (cheese, dessert or fruit). If a meal this size seems a bit daunting, choose just a couple of courses.

Italians automatically drink wine with their meals. *Denominazione d'Origine Controllata* (DOC) is a method of classification that guarantees the origin of the wine, and that it has been made following the guidelines for a particular area. However, it is no indication of quality.

Pastimes

The favorite Italian pastimes are probably eating, drinking and talking; preferably all together. Immensely sociable people, Italians tend to relax en masse, making group activities of every type very popular. Soccer is the national sport, and almost every Italian male either attends or follows Sunday matches. Deeply traditional, Italians prefer their pleasures to be family-oriented; a Sunday drive, a day at the beach or a gentle stroll, accompanied by a non-stop stream of chatter, constitutes most people's idea of leisure.

TIMELINE

3000–1800 BC	First traces of migratory peoples in peninsula.
700–300 BC	Etruscan federation exists alongside Roman republic.
264–146 BC	Punic Wars against Carthage.
AD 200–400	Decline of Roman Empire.
550–770	Peninsula fragmented with different areas under Byzantine, Papal, Lombard and Frankish influence.
1300–1400	Emergence of the city-states in north; Renaissance era.
1500–1848	Fragmentation of peninsula under foreign domination.
1848–61	Struggle for unification, with brief republic established in 1848; kingdom of Italy proclaimed in 1861.
1870	Rome and the Papal States become part of a unified Italy.
1915–18	Italy sides with Allies during World War I.
1940	Italy enters World War II on Axis side.
1943	Fall of Mussolini and armistice with Allies; Mussolini reinstated by Germany as head of puppet republic; Rome liberated in 1944.
1946	Italian Republic established.
1957	Treaty of Rome; Italy becomes a founding member of European Community.
1960–85	Period of political confusion, inflation and terrorism.
1985–2000	Corruption is rife, but Italy flourishes as desire for political and institutional reform grows.
2000	Bologna designated a European City of Culture for 2000.

THE ETRUSCANS

Travelers in central Italy will frequently come across signs of the Etruscans in monuments, tombs and museums. For centuries historians have questioned exactly who they were. This enigmatic race preceded the Romans and were at the height of their power from 800 to 400 BC. They formed a confederacy of 12 cities, built towns, passed laws, traded overseas and believed firmly in an afterlife. A lively and imaginative people, they also had highly developed cultural, political and social systems. The Romans, admirers of Etruscan culture, absorbed much of it as they rose to power. By the third century BC the Romans had virtually assimilated the entire nation, along with much of its language, customs and religious beliefs. Today only the monuments remain, particularly those to the Etruscan dead. Wonderful finds have been made in these tombs – jewelry, vases, sculpture and frescoes. They are preserved in museums all over ancient Etruria, the name given to the area they inhabited. You can visit Etruscan sites at Tarquinia and Cerveteri, both a short distance north of Rome, and see the finest Etruscan collection in the world at the Villa Giulia museum in Rome.

SURVIVAL GUIDE

- The fashion-conscious Italians spend much time and thought on looking good, and appreciate it if tourists do as well. Dressing appropriately means no shorts in cities. If you do show too much leg or arm, you won't be allowed to enter churches.
- Inevitably, Italy's star attractions in Rome, Venice, Florence and other major cities become packed during the hot summer. Get out early to avoid the main rush or, better still, visit in the late fall or winter when it's quieter and cooler.
- Italy closes down from around 12:30 until 4:30 or 5 while most of the population eats a large lunch and has a siesta. Plan your day around this, remembering that museums, churches, galleries and stores will all be closed for several hours. You'll enjoy your sightseeing more if you do as the locals do and take a midday rest.
- Italians enjoy wine, which they drink at all meals, but they disapprove of people who drink to excess.
- It is unusual to eat dinner before 7:30 or 8, and lunch is served from around 12:30 to about 2:30. Some restaurants offer fixed-price set menus, but you'll get a better meal if you choose some of the local specialties. Vegetarians will find plenty of choices in most restaurants. As for children, Italians genuinely love them, and most restaurants – even upscale ones – welcome them. Italian coffee is extremely strong, so if you want it weaker just ask for a *caffe americano.*
- Bars are much more than the name suggests. They are open from dawn until midnight or later, and offer coffee, tea, soda, snacks and pastries, as well as alcohol. All bars have restrooms and a public telephone.
- Smoking is common in public places throughout the country.
- One of the joys of Italy is shopping in little local stores and at the colorful street markets; there are very few department stores and virtually no shopping malls. Shop and market prices are fixed.
- Facilities for visitors with disabilities are improving, but are not yet as good as those back home. If you need help it's best to check ahead with local tourist offices.

Italians make serious choices at a colorful city market

ROME

There's almost too much to Rome (Roma); too much history, too much art, too much noise, confusion, traffic. This is an overwhelming city in every way, with splendors and frustrations in equal measure. Nowhere else will your senses be assaulted by such a glorious mélange of ancient, medieval, Renaissance, baroque and modern sights. Expectations run high, and every visitor comes with preconceptions of sun-filled days of *dolce vita* and romantic strolls through ancient streets. Put them aside, take it slow, accept Rome not as you think it should be, but

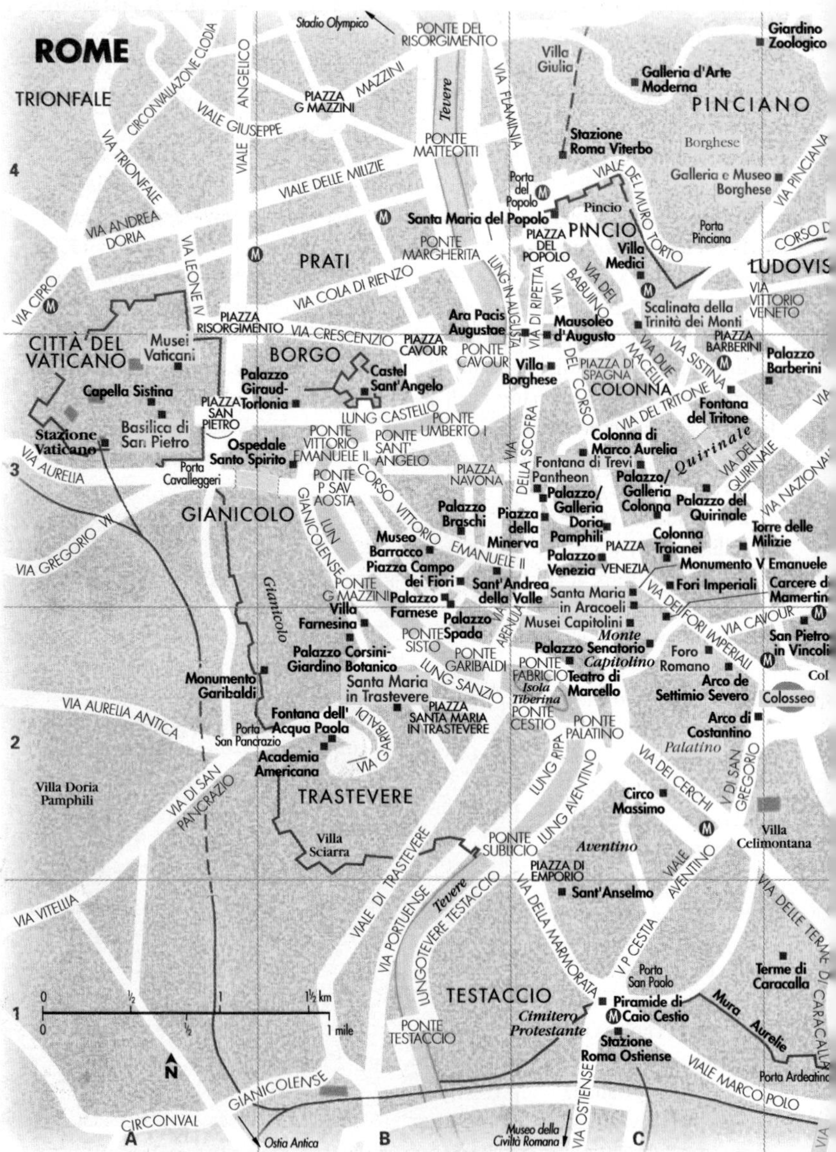

as it is, and you'll discover a city that is virtually impossible to describe.

Mapping the City

It's a good idea to stay as centrally located as you can, but avoid the unwholesome area around the central railroad station, Stazione Termini, and keep in mind that few areas of the city offer peace and quiet. You'll quickly realize that Rome has no discernible center, although Piazza Venezia, dominated by the vast, wedding cake-like monument of Victor Emmanuel, is a good place to orient yourself. From here, the Via del Corso stretches north, and to the south lies the Forum (Foro Romano), the heart of classical Rome.

Between the Corso and the Tiber (Tevere) river lies the *centro storico*, or historic center, a maze of narrow medieval streets and Renaissance squares and one of the city's most beguiling areas. On the other side of the Corso are Rome's most elegant shopping streets, more sun-dappled piazzas, some lovely green spaces and the charms of the Via Veneto, with its luxury hotels and galaxy of smart cafés. Across the river lies Trastevere, filled with charming streets and squares and noted for its excellent restaurants. To the north is Vatican City (Citta del Vaticano), home of the Pope and St. Peter's Basilica (Basilica di San Pietro).

Seeing the Sights

It would take months to see all of Rome, so before you arrive, decide where your priorities lie. It's a mistake to rush out, exhausted from travel, and see the Vatican on your first day; instead wander around the back streets or linger over a cup of coffee before you plunge into serious sightseeing. If you're not a sightseer, enjoy the street life and the stylish stores and restaurants.

It's best to tackle the highlights early in the day, before the crowds and heat intensify and while you're still fresh. Make a point of resting during the early afternoon; most stores and attractions are closed then anyway, and you can venture out again refreshed and relaxed in the late afternoon. If time is short and you want to see a lot, think about taking a tour; your hotel will be able to

Running repairs at the fountain in Piazza Navona

advise you. Other options include walking tours with local experts to explore off-the-beaten-track areas or a boat trip on the Tiber river.

Peace and Quiet

Tranquility is in short supply in Rome, but there are moments when it seems within reach. In addition to the Villa Borghese (see page 296), other green spaces exist around the city, where the roar of the traffic is at least muted. One of the best is Palatine Hill (Palatino) above the Forum, a good place to picnic after a morning's sightseeing, with scattered ruins, cypresses and wildflowers. The Botanical Gardens (Giardino Botanico) in Trastevere provide cool shade amid the 7,000 botanical species, while Colle Oppio garden, with its strolling mothers and babies, is a good bet after a morning at the Colosseum.

Roman Cuisine

Romans enjoy dining out, and there are plenty of restaurant choices. Trastevere and the streets around Piazza Navona are packed with eateries; as always in Italy, look for places patronized by locals. Roman specialties center heavily around the less attractive parts of animals, such as offal, brains and tripe, but staples like grilled meat and the delicious *saltimbocca alla Romana* (veal scaloppine cooked with prosciutto and sage) are easy to find. Pasta dishes include spicy *rigatoni all'amatriciana* (pasta with bacon, chili and tomato), and the delicious and familiar *spaghetti alla carbonara*, with bacon, egg and fettuccine.

Artichokes are a great Roman specialty, eaten either deep fried or raw; look for asparagus in early summer. Desserts are simple, but Roman ice cream is mouthwatering, and it's worth forgoing restaurant desserts and opting instead for a *gelateria*. Pizzas are excellent. Local wines come from the hills outside Rome, in an area known as the Castelli Romani; Frascati is the best known. You'll also find wines from all over Italy, as well as herbal aperitifs and liqueurs.

Boutiques and Markets

Shopping can be a pleasure in self-indulgent Rome, where there is a superb range of luxurious silk, linens,

Roman Fountains

Lovely fountains are scattered around Rome, and their beauty will stick in your mind when much else has faded. They provide cool places for a few minutes of rest, and the soothing sound of splashing water somehow manages to make itself heard over the noise of Rome's frenetic traffic. Be sure to pause at the Fontana delle Naiadi in Piazza della Repubblica, with its bronze nymphs; the dolphin-decorated Fontana del Tritone in Piazza Barberini; and the charming tortoise fountain, the Fontana delle Tartarughe, in Piazza Mattei.

leather and accessories. Shoes, bags, handmade evening wear, and exquisite china and porcelain are found in the smartest stores clustered around the Via Condotti and the Via Frattina, just off the Piazza di Spagna. You'll find moderately priced shops along the Via del Corso and the Via Nazionale; knitwear and sweaters are good buys. Rome also has several department stores, including the upscale La Rinascente in Piazza Colonna; Upim and Standa are inexpensive and cheerful chain stores with plenty of surprisingly stylish buys. If you enjoy markets, head for the daily food and vegetable market in the lovely Campo dei Fiori, or the main city market in Piazza Vittorio Emanuele II.

Nightlife

Romans consider a restaurant meal the pinnacle of evening entertainment, but there are other events going on as well. Pick up a copy of *Roma c'è* or *Trovaroma* for up-to-date information. There are plenty of music bars and discos. Opera is a good option, either at the Teatro dell'Opera or outdoors in summer at the Villa Borghese gardens. Rome has a clutch of movie theaters showing films in their original language. Concerts and recitals are frequently held in the city's churches.

ESSENTIAL INFORMATION

TOURIST INFORMATION

- Via Parigi 5 ☏ 06 4889 9253
- Largo Goldoni ☏ 06 6813 6061
- Piazza San Giovanni in Laterano ☏ 06 7720 3535
- Via Nazionale ☏ 06 4782 4525
- Piazza delle Cinque Lune ☏ 06 6880 9240
- Piazza Pia ☏ 06 6880 9707
- Piazza del Tempio della Pace ☏ 06 6992 4307
- Via dell' Olmata ☏ 06 4788 0294
- Via Marco Minghetti ☏ 06 678 2988
- Piazza Sonnino (Trastevere) ☏ 06 5833 3457

www.romaturismo.com

URBAN TRANSPORTATION

Public transportation in Rome can be slow, consisting of orange buses and trams and a two-line subway system. Subway stations are marked on the Rome city map by the letter "M" in a red circle. Bus tickets must be purchased from automatic machines before boarding, or from shops and newsstands displaying an ATAC or COTRAL sticker. They are valid for any number of bus trips plus one subway trip within a 75-minute period, and must be validated at the rear of the vehicle when boarding. The *biglietto integrato* is valid for a day's unlimited travel on buses, trams, the subway and the suburban train service. A weekly pass, the *carta integrata Settimanale*, also is available. Taxis are yellow or white and can be picked up from one of the stands indicated by a blue-and-white sign; they do not stop on the street. You can call a taxi from Radio Taxi (☏ 06 3570, 06 8433 or 06 4994) or Radio Taxi Eurocosmo (☏ 06 88177 or 06 8822); the meter will start running immediately after your call. Do not trust anyone offering private taxi service, and be sure the meter is set at zero if you begin your ride at the taxi stand.

AIRPORT INFORMATION

Rome has two airports: Leonardo da Vinci, at Fiumicino (west of the city); and Ciampino, south of Rome, which handles charter flights. The easiest way to get to and from Leonardo da Vinci is by train from Stazione Termini (the central railroad station); trains leave every 30 minutes 6:51 a.m.–10:37 p.m. Trains also run from the airport to Fara Sabina and Tiburtina train stations; if you use these you will have to make a connection. There is a nightly bus service between the airport and Tiburtina Station. To reach Rome from Ciampino, take the subway line A to Anagnina and connect with the COTRAL bus service; both are scheduled to run daily 6:50 a.m.–11:40 p.m.

CLIMATE – average highs and lows for the month

JAN.	FEB.	MAR.	APR.	MAY	JUN.	JUL.	AUG.	SEP.	OCT.	NOV.	DEC.
13°C	13°C	15°C	17°C	21°C	25°C	28°C	28°C	26°C	21°C	17°C	14°C
55°F	55°F	59°F	63°F	70°F	77°F	82°F	82°F	79°F	70°F	63°F	57°F
4°C	4°C	5°C	8°C	12°C	16°C	19°C	19°C	17°C	13°C	8°C	5°C
39°F	39°F	41°F	46°F	54°F	61°F	66°F	66°F	63°F	55°F	46°F	41°F

The Colosseum – the world's largest surviving structure from Roman antiquity

CITY SIGHTS

Key to symbols

map coordinates refer to the Rome map on pages 292–293; sights below are highlighted in yellow on the map.

address or location telephone number

opening times nearest subway station

nearest railroad station nearest bus or tram route restaurant or café on site or nearby

admission charge: $$$ more than L5,000, $$ L3,000 to L5,000, $ less than L3,000 other relevant information

BASILICA DI SAN PIETRO

A3 Piazza San Pietro, Citta del Vaticano 06 6988 4466 Daily 7–7, mid-Mar. to Oct. 31; 7–6, rest of year Ottaviano 23, 64, 98, 492 Admission free ($ for elevator to terrace/steps to dome)

The spiritual heart of Catholicism, the Basilica di San Pietro (St. Peter's Basilica) stands on the site of the saint's burial place. This is architectural grandeur on a triumphant scale, from the sweeping colonnades branching from the magnificent facade to the soaring dome above the twisted columns of Giovanni Bernini's High Altar *baldacchino*. There's a lot that dates from 1506 to 1626, when Donato di Angelo Bramante and Bernini were the principal architects. Near the end of his life, Michelangelo designed the dome, from which there are superb views; inside you can see the sublime *Pietà*, one of his earliest works. The right nave contains a bronze statue of St. Peter, his right foot worn away by pilgrims' caresses.

BORGHESE, VILLA

C4 Porta Pinciana Daily dawn–dusk Flaminio 52, 53, 116, 910

The time will come when you're sated with art and architectural splendors and long for some cool green grass. This is the moment to head for the Villa Borghese gardens, central Rome's largest park, an oasis of verdant lawns, umbrella pines, lakes and fountains. The adjoining Pincio Gardens offer wonderful views across the rooftops to St. Peter's.

COLOSSEO

D2 Piazza del Colosseo 06 700 4261 Daily 9–1 hour before sunset Colosseo 27, 81, 85, 87 $$$; free admission to lower levels

The massive Colosseo (Colosseum) dates from AD 72, and the design has never been bettered. This is a functional stadium seating 55,000, but can be cleared in less than 20 minutes; its sophisticated "backstage" facilities even allow the arena to be flooded. Most ancient entertainment featured animals, slaves and gladiators, sometimes fighting to the death, but few Christians were martyred here. During the Middle Ages the Colosseum was an excellent source of building stone, which explains the missing sections.

FONTANA DI TREVI

C3 Piazza di Trevi Spagna or Barbarini 492

Among Rome's delightful fountains, none is more famous than the Fontana di Trevi (Trevi Fountain), tucked into a tiny piazza set in a maze of lanes that makes its impact all the more dramatic. There's been a fountain here since Roman times; the present example dates from 1732 and takes its name from the three roads – *tre vie* – that converged here. Throw two coins in the fountain before you leave Rome; legend claims that the first coin grants a wish and the second guarantees your return.

FORO ROMANO E PALATINO

C2 Via dei Fori Imperiali 06 699 0110 Daily 9–1 hour before sunset Colosseo 11, 27, 81, 85, 186 $$$ (includes Palatino)

Heart of the Roman Empire, the Foro Romano (Roman Forum) contained all of the ancient city's most important political, religious and municipal buildings. Today, it's a romantic jumble of tumbled columns and walls set amid cypresses and wildflowers. It's worth spending time here, tracking down the fine second-century Arch of Septimius Severus, the Temple of Antoninus and Faustina (AD 141), the stately columns of the fourth-century Portico of the Dei Consentes, and the House of the Vestal Virgins, home of the guardians of the sacred fire. On the Palatino (Palatine), overlooking the Roman Forum, the ruins of the homes of wealthy Romans, emperors and aristocrats also may be explored.

GALLERIA E MUSEO BORGHESE

D4 Villa Borghese, Piazzale Scipione Borghese 5 06 841 7645 Tue.–Sun. 9–7 (also Sun. 7–8) Spagna 52, 53, 116, 910 $$$

The Galleria e Museo Borghese

Rome's magical Trevi Fountain

(Borghese Museum and Gallery), housed in the 17th-century summer palace of Cardinal Scipione Borghese, is a treasure-trove of sculpture, mainly collected by the cardinal. He admired Giovanni Bernini, whose works dominate – the *David* is said to be a self-portrait. Look for Antonio Canova's *Paolina Borghese*; this little minx, with her come-hither look, was Napoleon's sister, married off to a later Borghese. Stunning paintings include Caravaggio's famous *Boy with a Fruit Basket.*

MUSEI CAPITOLINI

C2 Piazza del Campidoglio 06 6710 2071 Tue.–Sat. 9–7, Sun. 9–1 44, 46, 64, 70, 81, 110 $$$

The two palazzi housing the great classical collection of the Musei Capitolini (Capitoline Museums) are set on either side of a Michelangelo-designed square. Look for the *Dying Gaul* and the tautly muscled *Discobolus* (Discus Thrower). Bronzes include the famous fifth-century BC *Capitoline Wolf Suckling Romulus and Remus* and, finest of all, the superb equestrian statue of *Marcus Aurelius*. Paintings include some major works by Titian and Paolo Veronese.

Musei Vaticani

A3 Viale Vaticano, Citta del Vaticano 06 6988 3333 Mon.–Fri. 8:45–4:45, Sat. and last Sun. of month 8:45–1:45 Ottaviano 32, 49, 64, 110, 492 $$$; free to all last Sun. of month

The Musei Vaticani (Vatican Museums) make up the world's largest museum complex, with around a dozen self-contained museums in 1,400 rooms. It would take days to see everything, so it makes sense to follow either one of the color-coded routes or pick out the highlights that personally appeal to you. However, do not miss the Cappella Sistina (Sistine Chapel), with its frescoes by Michelangelo covering the ceiling and the altar wall, showing scenes from the Old Testament and the powerful *Last Judgment*. The Stanze di Raffaello (Raphael Rooms), one of the artist's masterpieces, were executed in 1508.

Classical sculpture, an Egyptian collection and modern religious art are among the other features at this rich venue.

Pantheon

C3 Piazza della Rotunda 06 6830 0230 Daily 9–6:30, holidays 9–1 (also Sat. 9–11:45 p.m., Jun.–Sep.) Spagna 64, 70, 75, 116 Free

The superbly engineered Pantheon, erected between AD 118 and AD 128 and still in use today, fires the imagination and gives a better idea of the splendor of ancient Rome than any other monument. Built as a temple, it became a Christian church in AD 609 and now houses Raphael's tomb and also those of two Italian kings.

Piazza di Spagna e Scalinata della Trinità dei Monti

C3–C4 Piazza di Spagna Museum: 06 678 4235 Museum: Mon.–Fri. 9–1 and 3–6, Sat. 11–2 and 3–6 Spagna 117 Museum $$

The Scalinata della Trinità dei Monti (Spanish Steps), curving gracefully up from Piazza di Spagna to the church of Trinità dei Monti, attracts myriad visitors; this is a favorite meeting place, situated at the heart of Rome's smartest shopping area. The steps, built in 1723, get their name from the piazza, which once housed the Spanish embassy. The eccentric-looking "sunken boat" fountain dates from 1627, while on the right of the steps (at No. 26) you'll find the Keats–Shelley Memorial House, in the lodgings where John Keats died in 1821.

Detail from Bernini's *Il Moro* in Piazza Navona

Piazza Navona

B3 Piazza Navona Spagna 56, 60, 62, 64

Piazza Navona owes its unmistakable shape to the Roman racetrack, used well into the Middle Ages, that once stood here. Pope Innocent X, who commissioned Giovanni Bernini to design the focal point, the *Fountain of the Four Rivers*, rebuilt the piazza in 1644. The 17th-century church of Sant' Agnese is Francesco Borromini's work.

San Clemente

D2 Via di Giovanni in Laterano 06 7045 1018 Daily 9–12:30 and 3:30–6 15, 85, 13 $

No church in Rome gives a better idea of history than San Clemente, a multilayered structure whose newest part dates from the 12th century. In its dim interior, the apse mosaics glitter above the marble panels of the choir screen and pulpits. From here, descend to the fourth-century lower church, with its ghostly traces of eighth- to 11th-century frescoes, before plunging deeper to examine the fine altar of the Roman Mithraic temple.

THE VATICAN

Vatican City (Citta del Vaticano), an area covering about 109 acres around the Basilica of St. Peter (Basilica di San Pietro), is the world's smallest independent state. Until Italian unification in 1870, the Papacy had held territory covering a large part of central Italy, known as the Papal States. These became part of the new united Italy, and the Pope, Pius IX, retreated to the Vatican, a virtual prisoner. The supreme head of a worldwide religion clearly needed some type of sovereign territory to retain his independent spiritual authority, and in 1929 the Treaty of the Lateran was thrashed out with Benito Mussolini, bringing the Vatican State into existence.

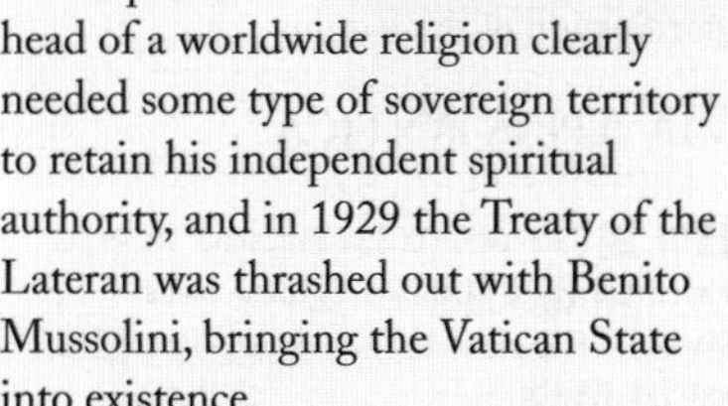

St. Peter's Basilica (top) and the spiral staircase in the Vatican (left)

The Vatican Today

The Pope, as well as being head of the Catholic church, is also Europe's only absolute monarch, ruling over the 200-odd inhabitants of the Vatican. The Vatican retains worldwide diplomatic relations; foreign ambassadors to the Holy See live around Rome, as do more than 800 other workers who commute across the "border" daily. The Vatican has its own judiciary, currency, bank, stores and postal system – you can send cards home from the post office outside the Basilica. It issues a daily newspaper, the *Osservatore Romano,* and broadcasts 24 hours a day from its radio station. A branch railroad line runs from the Italian State system into the Vatican. Despite the vernacular spoken at Mass, Latin is still the official language.

Defending the Pope

The Pope has been defended by the Swiss Guard since 1506. Their colorful striped red, yellow and blue dress uniform, said to have been designed by Michelangelo, is instantly recognizable. The 90 members are indeed Swiss, young men recruited between the ages of 19 and 25, from Switzerland's four Catholic cantons. They then serve tours of duty ranging from two to 20 years.

Papal Audiences

The Pope gives a weekly general audience on Wednesdays at 11 a.m. in the Papal Audience Chamber, and occasionally in the Basilica of St. Peter or in the Piazza. These occasions, for up to 7,000 people, are open to everyone and tickets are free. The Pope also gives a blessing from the windows of his rooms overlooking the piazza on Sundays at midday.

Audience tickets are available by writing to Prefettura della Casa Pontificia, 00120 Citta del Vaticano, or by visiting the office through the bronze doors in the right-hand colonnade of Piazza San Pietro, open daily from 9–1.

A calm retreat from the crowds – St. Mary Major houses the Pintoricchio frescoes

Santa Maria in Aracoeli

C2–C3 Piazza d'Aracoeli 06 679 8155 Daily 7–noon and 4–6:30, Jun.–Sep.; 7–noon, rest of year 44, 56, 90

Santa Maria in Aracoeli (Our Lady of the Altar of Heaven) was built around 1260 to replace an older church. Approached by 124 steep steps, built in 1348 to celebrate the end of a plague epidemic, the church's plain facade hides a superb interior. The nave columns were taken from Roman buildings, while the gilded ceiling, lit by chandeliers, dates from the 1570s.

Santa Maria Maggiore

D3 Piazza di Santa Maria Maggiore 06 483 195 Daily 7–6:45 Cavour 16, 27, 70, 71

As you enter Santa Maria Maggiore (St. Mary Major), remember that Mass has been said daily here since the fifth century, when it was built on a site marked by an alleged miraculous summer snowfall. The mosaics in the nave date from the fifth century, those in the apse from the 13th century. The gilding on the coffered ceiling reputedly comes from the first gold to arrive from the New World, a gift from Spain.

Santa Maria in Trastevere

B2 Piazza Santa Maria in Trastevere 06 581 4802 Daily 7:30–1 and 3–7 44, 56, 60, 170

The facade of Santa Maria in Trastevere, with its lustrous 12th-century mosaics, overlooks an atmospheric fountained piazza. The charming portico, added in 1702, leads to an interior with nave columns that once supported Roman buildings. The 12th-century, Byzantine-style mosaics of the apse represent the glorification of the Virgin.

Via Appia Antica

D1 Catacombe di San Sebastino: Via Appia Antica 136 06 5130 1580 Catacombs: Mon.–Sat. 8:30–noon and 2:30–5, Dec.–Oct. 78, 118, 127 $$$

A short bus ride from central Rome takes you to the Via Appia Antica (Old Appian Way), built in the fourth century BC to link Rome with Brindisi. Here, Spartacus and his men were executed, and St. Paul marched to prison. This cobbled way, shaded by pine trees, is lined with monuments and tombs; you can visit the catacombs, with their mementos of early Christian life.

Villa Giulia

C4 Piazzale di Villa Giulia 9 06 320 1951 Tue.–Sat. 9–7 (also Sat. 9–11:45 p.m., Jun.–Sep.), Sun. 9–8 Flaminio 19, 52, 95 $$$

Visit the Villa Giulia to learn more about the Etruscans (see page 290). The collection is housed in a late Renaissance villa; its architects included Michelangelo. Highlights are the Castellani exhibits, fine Greek vases, and gold, silver and ivory artifacts. Be sure to see the *Sarcofago degli Sposi*, sixth-century BC figures of a reclining married couple, and the terracotta *Hercules* and *Apollo*.

Water is the dominant feature in the gardens of the Villa d'Este

EXCURSION TO TIVOLI

Most visitors to Rome seize the chance to escape the city's noise and heat by taking an excursion to Tivoli, a small town in a lovely wooded location some 19 miles northeast of Rome. Its main attractions are the gardens of the Villa d'Este, among the world's most beautiful, and the vast classical site of Villa Adriana (Hadrian's Villa), about 4 miles southwest of Tivoli.

It's easy to make an independent trip to Tivoli, either by train from the central railroad station, Stazione Termini, then local bus, or by bus from central Rome. There also are guided excursions from the city that take you there, while an English-speaking guide tells you all you need to know.

Villa d'Este

The Villa d'Este is famous not so much for the villa itself, built by Cardinal d'Este in 1550, but for the gardens, terraces and fountains. The main attractions are two Giovanni Bernini fountains, the elegant Fontana di Biccierone and the Fontana dei Draghi, and the breathtaking Avenue of a Hundred Fountains (Viale delle Cento Fontane). Nearby lies the Villa Gregoriana, where a pair of waterfalls cascade into a gorge.

Villa Adriana

Many prosperous Romans built retirement villas at Tivoli, and in AD 125 the Emperor Hadrian embarked on the construction of his own. The villa and its gardens grew and grew, eventually covering as much ground as Imperial Rome itself. The site is vast and romantic, and you'll need a map to make sense of it all. Don't miss the Maritime Theater (Teatro Marittimo), a palace on an island in the lake.

Villa d'Este See page 284, C3 Piazza Trento 0774 22070 Tue.–Sun. 9 a.m.–1 hour before dusk COTRAL bus from via Gaeta to Tivoli Train to Tivoli Refreshments available in gardens $$$

Villa Adriana Via Tiburtina 0774 530203 Tue.–Sun. 9 a.m.–90 minutes before dusk COTRAL bus from via Gaeta to Tivoli Train to Tivoli Refreshments available at villa site $$$

Tour Companies

Appian Line Piazza dell'Esquilino 6/7 06 4878 6604

Vastour Via Piemonte 34 06 481 4309

American Express Piazza di Spagna 38 06 676 42413

FLORENCE

More than 3 million tourists annually visit Florence (Firenze), the capital of Tuscany, whose resident population is under 393,000. Visitors come with high expectations of beauty, stunning art, history and stylish people. Sadly, they are often so overwhelmed by heat, crowds, noise and cultural overload that the city fails to live up to expectations. When touring Florence, more so than most cities, planning pays off.

Choose the time you visit carefully. If art and architecture are the main purpose of your trip, try to come off-season when Florence is quieter and the

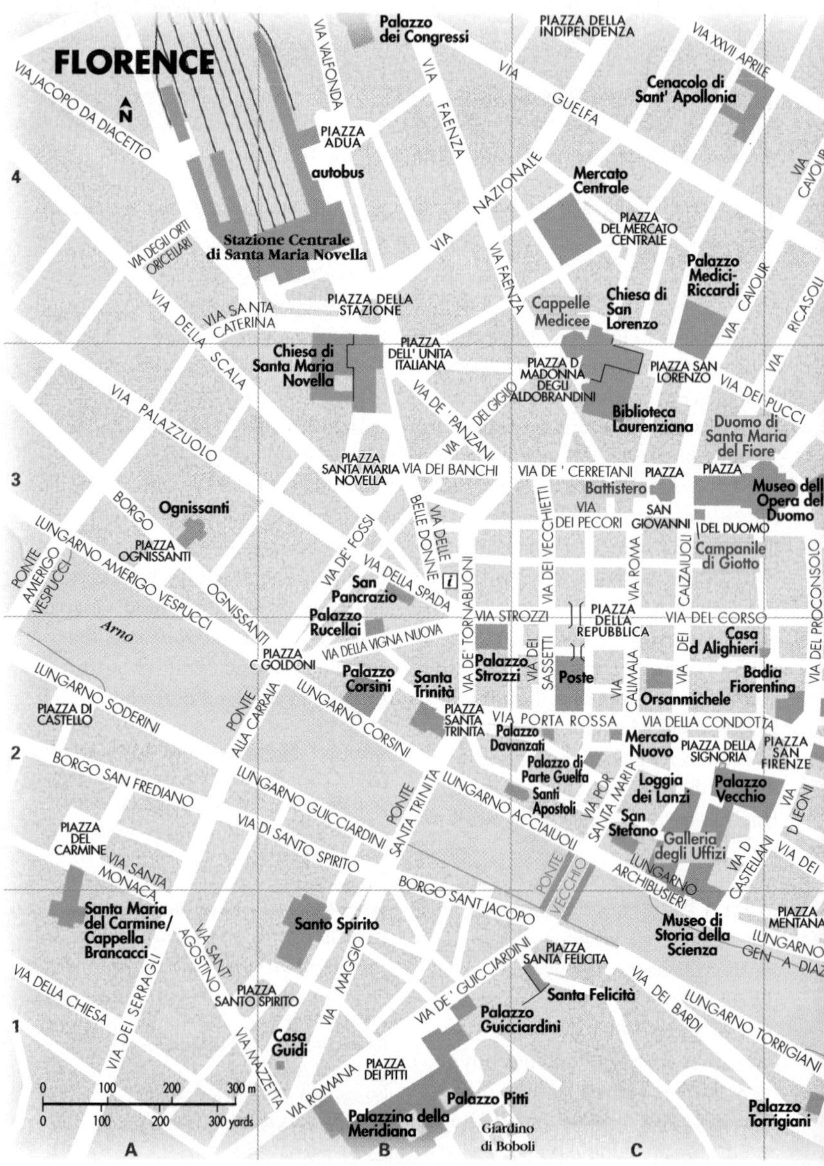

heat in this largely non-air-conditioned city won't wipe you out. If the city is one stop on a summer tour, be prepared for crowds, time museum visits for early and late in the day, and don't try to do too much. Book accommodations before you come, and don't plan to use Florence as a base for touring the rest of Tuscany.

Florence and Florentines

Florentines are Tuscans – restrained and rational, and less given to fiery displays than other Italians. They are also more reserved, without the superficial and easy charm of people from other regions. Accustomed to huge numbers of visitors, they do not go out of their way to befriend tourists, but are courteous and professional in their everyday dealings.

Florence is not as instantly appealing as Rome or Venice – let it grow on you and experience it as a living city, not merely as a vast treasure house of art. Get away from the major sights and explore the quieter areas, with atmospheric streets and a wealth of traditional activities. Vary the artistic glories with a bit of hedonism, and give yourself time to relax. The best way to see Florence is on foot. Most of the main attractions are clustered together in the largely pedestrian central core, making walking easier (but watch out for ebullient scooter riders).

Eating in Tuscany

Florence is well endowed with restaurants of every type, from fast-food joints to world-class establishments. Many are specifically aimed at tourists and have prominently displayed fixed-price (but mediocre) menus. To ensure a memorable meal, eat where the Italians eat and be prepared to pay somewhat high prices. For a simple lunch, try a slice of fresh-baked pizza to go or a quick snack in a *vinaio* or *fiaschetteria*, traditional wine bars. Food markets are particularly tempting, with the makings to put together a picnic. Tuscan food is simple and excellent, with plenty of soups, superb pork dishes, grilled meats and vegetables. Bean dishes are especially popular (Tuscans are fondly nicknamed *mangiafagioli*, or "bean-eaters"). The most famous wine is

Chianti, but look for Brunello di Montalcino, a superb red from Tuscany.

Pucci, Gucci and More

Intriguing stores, markets and boutiques are scattered throughout the center of Florence. Shoes and leather goods are famous, as are fine china, exquisite bed and table linen, and gold jewelry. Designer-label fans can visit Pucci and Gucci on their home ground; other tempting gifts include brilliantly glazed majolica pottery, marbled paper, prints and antiques.

Via Tornabuoni and the surrounding streets house the most elegant stores; less expensive fashion is found around Piazza della Repubblica and Via Calzaiuoli, while jewelers line the Ponte Vecchio. There are many factory leather outlets near Santa Croce. Be sure to spend time browsing in a market; the huge Mercato San Lorenzo is probably the most enjoyable. Most stores will ship direct to the United States.

Festivals Galore

A summer visit is likely to coincide with one of the cultural festivals, the *Estate Fiesolana* or the *Maggio Musicale Fiorentino*. Together they run from May through August, with concerts, opera and ballet – often performed outdoors in an historic setting – creating an unforgettable experience.

Excursions

Even if your time in Tuscany is limited, try to fit in an excursion outside Florence, viewing the timeless landscape en route to another of the region's superb historic towns. Possibilities include Pisa, Siena, San Gimignano and the wine country of Chianti, all easily reached by tour bus or public transportation. Nearer still lies Fiesole, a picturesque hill town just above Florence, the perfect escape from noise and heat.

ESSENTIAL INFORMATION

TOURIST INFORMATION

- Via Manzoni 16 ☎ 055 23320
- Piazza Stazione 4 ☎ 055 212 245
- Borgo Santa Croce 29r

☎ 055 234 0444
www.firenze.turismo.toscana.it

URBAN TRANSPORTATION

Buses, both regular and electric, run from Sta Maria Novella station all over town. Tickets must be purchased before boarding. They are available from machines and tobacconists and are valid for an unlimited number of trips over a period of 70 or 120 minutes; 24-hour passes also are available. You can pick up a map and timetable from the ATAF office (✉ Piazza del Duomo 57r). Stamp tickets as you get on, in the orange box on the bus. Taxis can be hailed at various central locations, or by calling Radio Taxi Cotafi (☎ 055 4390 or 055 4499) or Radio Taxi Socata (☎ 055 4242 or 055 4798).

AIRPORT INFORMATION

Most visitors arrive and leave from Pisa's Galileo Galilei Airport (☎ 050 500 707), connected to Florence's Sta Maria Novella railroad station (where luggage can be checked) by hourly trains. Florence's own airport is at Perètola (☎ 055 537 3498), about 4 miles outside the city and easily reached by bus or taxi; if you're flying to another Italian destination, it's likely you'll leave from here.

CLIMATE – average highs and lows for the month

JAN.	FEB.	MAR.	APR.	MAY	JUN.	JUL.	AUG.	SEP.	OCT.	NOV.	DEC.
4°C	8°C	13°C	18°C	23°C	26°C	28°C	27°C	23°C	17°C	10°C	6°C
39°F	46°F	55°F	64°F	73°F	79°F	82°F	81°F	73°F	63°F	50°F	43°F
0°C	2°C	5°C	9°C	13°C	17°C	20°C	19°C	16°C	11°C	5°C	2°C
32°F	36°F	41°F	48°F	55°F	63°F	68°F	66°F	61°F	52°F	41°F	36°F

City Sights

Key to symbols

map coordinates refer to the Florence map on pages 302–303; sights below are highlighted in yellow on the map.
address or location telephone number
opening times nearest bus or tram route
restaurant or café on site or nearby admission charge: $$$ more than L5,000, $$ L3,000 to L5,000, $ less than L3,000 other relevant information

Cappelle Medicee

C4 Piazza Madonna degli Aldobrandini 6 055 238 8602 Tue.–Sat. 8:30–5, Sun. 8:30–1:50 1, 6, 10, 17 $$$

Set behind San Lorenzo, the Cappelle Medicee (Medici Chapels) were built as the mausoleum for Florence's most powerful family. The *Sagrestia Nuova,* built by Michelangelo between 1520 and 1534, contains some of his most powerful sculpture. Reclining figures representing *Night* and *Day* and *Dawn* and *Dusk* decorate the tombs of Lorenzo the Magnificent and his son, Giuliano. The figures' fluid lines are a perfect foil for the austerity of the architecture, and are offset by the artist's lovely *Madonna.*

Duomo, Battistero e Campanile di Giotto

C3–D3 Piazza del Duomo Duomo and Campanile: 055 230 2885. Battistero: 055 294 514 Duomo: Mon.–Sat. 10–5 (also Thu. and first Sat. of the month 5–5:30), Sun. 1:30–5. Cupola: Mon.–Fri. 8:30–7, Sat. 8:30–5 (8:30–3:20 on the first Sat. of the month). Battistero: Mon.–Sat. 8:30–6:30, Sun. 8:30–1:30. Campanile: daily 9–6:50, Apr.–Sep.; 9–4:20, rest of year 1, 14, 17, 23 Duomo free. Cupola, battistero and campanile: $$$ each

The Gothic Duomo (Cathedral) of Santa Maria del Fiore, the first domed structure erected in Europe since Roman times, was built between 1296 and 1436. Its austere interior, with a fine Paolo Uccello fresco, leads to the 463 steps to the top of Brunelleschi's Cupola (Dome). The chief draw of the 11th-century marble Battistero (Baptistery) is the three sets of bronze doors, with their Old Testament scenes. Andrea Pisano cast the south pair in 1326, and they inspired Lorenzo Ghiberti to design those at the north and east in the 1400s.

The Campanile (Bell Tower), designed by Giotto, was built between 1334 and 1359. Its marble walls are decorated with superb relief sculptures. The 280-foot, 414-step climb offers lovely, if vertiginous, views over Florence.

Sculptures by Michelangelo adorn the tombs of his patrons at the Medici Chapels

Galleria dell'Accademia

D4 Via Riccasoli 60 055 238 8609
Tue.–Sun. 8:30–6:50 (also Sat. 6:50–10 p.m.)
Gauguin, see page 559 6, 14, 17, 23 $$$

Founded as an art school in 1784, the Galleria dell'Accademia (Academy Gallery) today houses the world's most important collection of Michelangelo sculptures, as well as works by other artists. The main attraction is his *David*, a huge, anatomically precise and technically perfect nude male figure, possibly the most famous in the history of sculpture. More moving by far are the other sculptures by the artist, particularly the four *Prisoners,* the figures struggling to escape the stone.

Galleria degli Uffizi

C2 Loggiato degli Uffizi 6 055 238 8651
Tue.–Sun. 8:30–6:50 (also Sat. 6:50–10 p.m.)
Ponte Vecchio, see page 559 14, 23
$$$

Arguably the world's greatest collection of Renaissance paintings, the Galleria degli Uffizi (Office Gallery) is housed in an elegant arcaded building designed by Vasari as administrative offices – hence the name. Here, in chronological order, are paintings representing the greatest names in art, among them Giotto, Paolo Uccello, Botticelli, Piero della Francesca, Leonardo da Vinci, Michelangelo, Raphael and Caravaggio. Come early or late to try to avoid the lines.

Museo Nazionale del Bargello

D2 Via del Proconsolo 4 055 238 8606
Daily 8:30–1:50 (except alternating Sun. and Mon., when it's closed) Dino, see page 559 14, 19
$$$

Surrounding a courtyard, in a building dating from 1255, the Museo Nazionale del Bargello (National Bargello Museum) houses Italy's finest collection of Renaissance sculpture. The first floor has works by Michelangelo, Benvenuto Cellini and the flamboyant Giambologna, but the vaulted second-floor hall contains the museum's masterpieces. Here are Donatello's jaunty bronze of *David*, his exquisite *St. George,* and the superb Baptistery door reliefs by Lorenzo Ghiberti and Brunelleschi, made for a competition in 1401. Upstairs are bright enameled terracottas by the della Robbia family.

Ponte Vecchio

C1–C2 Ponte Vecchio 14, 23

Not the most beautiful Florentine bridge, but certainly the most photographed, the Ponte Vecchio (Old Bridge) was built in 1345 to replace an earlier one. It has been picturesquely lined with exclusive goldsmiths and jewelers' shops since 1593. Above it runs a corridor used by members of the Medici family to travel from the Pitti to the Uffizi. It was not only the sole bridge not destroyed by the Germans in World War II, but also survived the floods in 1966.

San Marco

D4 Piazza San Marco 055 238 8608
Mon.–Fri. 8:30–1:50, Sat. 8:30–6:50, Sun. 8:30–7
6, 14, 17, 23 $$$

Rebuilt in 1437, the convent of San Marco, decorated by Fra Angelico, is one of Florence's loveliest treasures. It's a peaceful religious house, where each monk's cell is adorned with a tiny fresco to aid prayer. The pilgrim's hall contains many paintings by Angelico and his school, and additional works are on view in the cloisters and on the stairs, notably the radiant *Annunciation.*

Santa Croce

E1 Piazza Santa Croce 16 055 244 619
Mon.–Sat. 8–6:30, Sun. 3–5:30 14, 23

This huge, plain Franciscan church was built in 1294, but was badly damaged by the 1966 floods. Today it contains superb early frescoes telling the story of the Santa Croce (Holy Cross). Michelangelo is buried here, along with Machiavelli and Galileo Galilei. In the serene cloisters stands the Cappella dei Pazzi (Pazzi Chapel), among the most beautiful of Renaissance buildings.

A DAY IN FLORENCE

A detail from the bronze east door at the Baptistery, by Lorenzo Ghiberti (1378-1455)

Many Florentines start working by 8 a.m., when food stores also open. Italian cities don't have American-style suburbs – most people live in centrally located apartments – so visitors have the chance to see the neighborhoods waking up. Housewives go to market early, children walk to school and people pause for a quick bar breakfast on their way to work.

For the tourist in Florence an early start makes sense. Head straight for major sights such as the Uffizi, Accademia, Duomo or Pitti Palace while you're still fresh and before the big tour groups arrive. Most of the museums open at 8:30 a.m. and the churches earlier, so it's feasible to pop into a specially noted church first thing. Pause mid-morning for a drink and a rest, but bear in mind that some attractions shut for several hours in the middle of the day, as do stores. It's a good idea to follow the siesta habit – a leisurely lunch and a quiet hour or so digesting all you've seen will leave you fresh for more touring in the late afternoon. Early evening is a popular time for Florentines to shop, and a good opportunity for you to track down that must-have leather bag, beautiful fabric, silk tie or marbled paper souvenir.

Florentines are back at work and out on the streets again some time after 4:30, looking rested, relaxed and ready for the rest of the day and evening. By 6:30 the town is thronged with well-dressed crowds, strolling, meeting friends and wholeheartedly enjoying the evening *passeggiata* through the streets of their beautiful city. Crowds thin out and shops close around 8:30, when people head home or to a restaurant for dinner, and there's a break before the evening's activities. Florence has plenty of nightlife to choose from, with a wealth of cultural offerings such as theater, opera and classical music, movies, and numerous discos and bars with live music. The streets are busy well into the early hours – especially in summer – with locals and foreigners alike enjoying the balmy night air.

Shopping is important to the fashionable Florentines

NAPLES

Vibrant, noisy, crumbling Naples (Napoli), the capital of southern Italy and one of Europe's most beautifully located cities, is light years removed in atmosphere from the prosperous north. The city epitomizes southern Italy: confusing, passionate, dirty and charming, redolent with a rich and complicated history that has physically shaped it and emotionally shaped its residents. Naples can feel alien and intimidating, but also inspires fierce loyalty as visitors are quickly won over by its exuberance, way of life, attractions and, above all, its people.

The people of southern Italy are charming, warm and enthusiastic, and Neapolitans are no exception. They live at what appears to be a fever pitch of excitement and noise, which you'll be very aware of on the street. You'll find people genuinely eager to help, and anxious for you to enjoy Naples. In recent years authorities have encouraged citizens to welcome tourists, and have succeeded admirably. The friendliness of locals to visitors here far exceeds that of any other big Italian city.

Old and new – a view of Naples

Getting Around

Once you get your bearings, central Naples is best tackled on foot, as the traffic is so horrendous that any form of transportation can be excruciatingly slow. Much of what you'll want to see is walkable, and sights are grouped together in different areas, so take a bus or cable car to your general destination and then walk. Wandering around is an essential part of the Naples experience, as the street life is lively and beguiling – but stick to well-frequented areas.

You'll want to travel down the coast to Pompeii and the Sorrento peninsula; both can be reached by train. The best way to appreciate the beauty of Naples' spectacular setting on the bay is from the sea; you could combine this with a boat trip to Sorrento or to the ravishing islands of Capri and Ischia.

Mediterranean Flavors

Neapolitan cooking ranks among the best in Italy, with a strong emphasis on the freshest fish and seafood, and local fruit and vegetables from the fertile volcanic soil of the hinterland. Flavors are intense, and the combination of ingredients unusual and interesting. There are pasta dishes with shellfish, grilled fish of all varieties, mozzarella cheese dripping with freshness, and numerous salamis, as well as some excellent local prosciutto.

Naples is the home of thin, tasty and crisp pizzas; they are always baked in wood-fired ovens, and can be eaten as a snack or light meal. Neapolitan cakes and pastries are famous and best enjoyed from a *pasticceria* (a specialist pastry and cake shop). Don't miss out on the ice cream – the flavors encompass every imaginable type of fruit. Local wines to try are Lacryma Christi and Greco di Tufo. Be sure to sample Limoncello, a lemon-flavored liqueur made all along the coast.

Shopping and Nightlife

Naples' upscale stores are clustered along the Via Toledo and the Via Chiaia, where you'll find outlets for Italy's top designers, as well as local

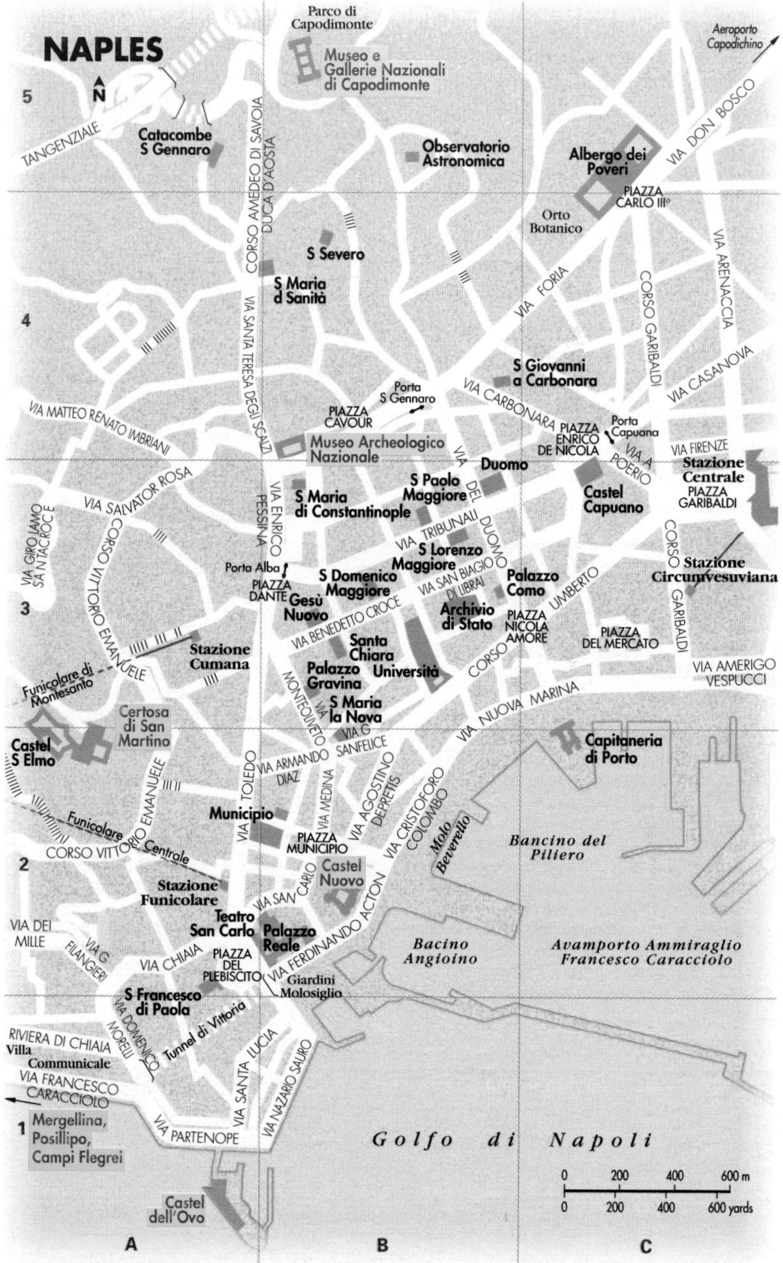

stores selling fine leather goods, fashion and knitwear. Jewelers abound near Via San Biagio; the traditional best buys in Naples are coral necklaces, bracelets, earrings, and cameo brooches. If you like antiques, head for Via Domenico Morelli, where stores specialize in 18th-century furniture and paintings.

Wonderful traditional nativity figurines are still made in the historic area around San Biagio, along with dolls and masks. There are shopping centers at Galleria Vanvitelli and Galleria Scartelli in the Vomero district, and you'll find a branch of the department store la Rinascente in downtown Naples.

If you like opera and classical music, a performance in the wonderful San Carlo opera house should be high on your list. Traditional Neapolitan music is easy to find, and even the least tourist-oriented restaurants have musicians serenading diners.

Safety in Naples

The city authorities have done much in recent years to clean up Naples in every way, making it a safer and more attractive city. However, it is still wise to avoid the labyrinthine back streets, the docks and, at night, the railroad station. Avoid carrying a lot of cash, and be aware of pickpockets, particularly in crowded tourist areas.

Be careful when crossing the street: Neapolitan drivers often ignore pedestrian crossings, and unless you step off the pavement you could be stranded for what seems like hours. Scooters appear to come out of nowhere, and they frequently use the sidewalks or go against the direction of traffic.

ESSENTIAL INFORMATION

TOURIST INFORMATION

- Piazza dei Martiri ☎ 081 405 311
- Stazione Centrale ☎ 081 268 779
- Stazione Mergellina ☎ 081 761 2102
- Capodichino Airport ☎ 081 780 5761

www.ept.napoli.it

URBAN TRANSPORTATION

Neapolitan traffic makes any form of transportation slow, so it's best to walk if it's feasible. Longer distances can be covered by subway, bus and cable car *(funiculari)*, all of which are slow. There are two types of *Giranapoli* transport tickets, valid for either 90 minutes or all day; they are interchangeable between buses, cable cars and the subway, and obtainable from tobacconists or newsstands. They must be validated in the special machines on board buses; before boarding cable cars; and at the entrance to subway platforms. To travel around the bay, use the Circumvesuviana railway, which leaves from the railroad station on Corso Garibaldi every half-hour and takes an hour to reach Sorrento, its farthest point. You can also travel to Sorrento by ferry or hydrofoil from the Mergellina or Molo Beverello docks; the same companies also serve Capri, Ischia and the other islands. There are taxi stands throughout the city, or you can call Taxi Napoli (☎ 081 556 4444), Taxi Free (☎ 081 551 5151) or Taxi Partenope (☎ 081 556 0202). Taxis also will take you sightseeing outside Naples for fixed rates.

AIRPORT INFORMATION

Naples' Capodichino Airport (☎ 081 789 6259), with internal and European flights, is northwest of the city center. Airport buses (☎ 081 531 1646) run at 50-minute intervals to Piazza Municipio via Piazza Garibaldi, daily 6 a.m.–midnight. Bus 14 runs every 15 minutes as far as Piazza Garibaldi.

CLIMATE – average highs and lows for the month

JAN.	FEB.	MAR.	APR.	MAY	JUN.	JUL.	AUG.	SEP.	OCT.	NOV.	DEC.
12°C	13°C	15°C	18°C	22°C	26°C	29°C	29°C	26°C	22°C	17°C	13°C
54°F	55°F	59°F	64°F	72°F	79°F	84°F	84°F	79°F	72°F	63°F	55°F
4°C	5°C	7°C	9°C	13°C	17°C	19°C	19°C	17°C	13°C	8°C	5°C
39°F	41°F	45°F	48°F	55°F	63°F	66°F	66°F	63°F	55°F	46°F	41°F

City Sights

Key to symbols

map coordinates refer to the Naples map on page 309; sights below are highlighted in yellow on the map. address or location telephone number opening times nearest subway nearest bus or tram route restaurant or café on site or nearby admission charge: $$$ more than L5,000, $$ L3,000 to L5,000, $ less than L3,000 other relevant information

Castel Nuovo

B2 Piazza Municipio 081 795 2003 Mon.–Sat. 9–7 Trattoria Medina, see page 559 R2, R3 $$$

The five massive towers of the 15th-century Castel Nuovo (New Castle) dominate the Naples waterfront. A magnificent Renaissance gateway accesses the central courtyard, which is surrounded by buildings housing the Museo Civico (Civic Museum), the splendid Gothic Sala dei Baroni (Baron's Hall) and the Cappella Palatina (Palatine Chapel), the only surviving part of a 13th-century building. Nearby is the imposing 17th-century Palazzo Reale (Royal Palace) and the famous San Carlo opera house.

Castel dell'Ovo

A1 Borgo Marinaro La Cantinella, see page 559 R3; tram 1

Encircled by the sea, Castel dell'Ovo (Egg Castle), Naples' oldest castle, was built between the ninth and 16th centuries. Run-down and dilapidated by the 1970s, it has been restored and is now used for cultural events.

Certosa di San Martino

A2 Al Vomero 081 578 1769 Mon.–Fri. 8:30–7:30, Sat.–Sun. 9–7:30 Montesanto V1 $$$

Visible from all over Naples is the hilltop complex of the Certosa di San Martino (St.

Pompeii

The 20,000 inhabitants of first-century Roman Pompeii enjoyed a civilized lifestyle in their prosperous city, which boasted fine civic amenities, temples, public baths, and housing suitable for every taste and pocket. The one drawback was Pompeii's location on the slopes of Vesuvius, an active volcano. In AD 79 its worst eruption occurred, engulfing the city and many of its inhabitants in a thick layer of pumice and volcanic ash.

For nearly 1,700 years Pompeii remained buried, perfectly preserved beneath a hard layer of volcanic debris. About 1750 it was rediscovered, excavations started, and gradually the city emerged. It's a complete small city that can be explored like any other, wandering the streets and visiting the sites that appeal. It has the main features of every Roman city – the forum that was the center of public life; two theaters; an amphitheater; a sports stadium; and symmetrical rows of streets laid out in a grid pattern.

Start at the forum and make your way through the paved streets, looking into houses and shops as you go. Track down the covered market, the bakery, the laundry and the numerous taverns, some advertising bargain prices on the outside walls. The House of the Vetii, with its lovely garden and frescoed dining room, is a highlight, as is the House of the Tragic Poet, whose owners had a portrait mosaic of their dog laid by the front door with "*cave canem*," "beware of the dog," carefully inscribed.

Pompeii 081 5365 154 Daily 9–1 hour before dusk Self-service restaurant and bar outside forum, many in modern Pompeii Pompeii (Circumvesuviana) $$$

The hilltop complex of St. Martin's Charterhouse looks down on the city of Naples

Martin's Charterhouse), constructed mainly between the 16th and 18th centuries. Highlights include the sumptuous baroque church, the arcaded Chiostro Grande (Main Cloister) and the lavishly decorated Quarto del Priore (Prior's Quarters). Don't miss the exhibition of *presepe* (crib figures), a charming collection of figures, animals and everyday objects fashioned for Christmas cribs in the 19th century, in the Museo Nazionale de San Martino (San Martino National Museum).

MERGELLINA

Off the map · Mergellina · Mergellina · R3, C21

This waterfront area, traditionally the fishermen's quarter, is a delightful place to stroll and enjoy ice cream. Fishing boats and island ferries still leave from the harbor here.

MUSEO ARCHEOLOGICO NAZIONALE

B4 · Piazza Museo · 081 440 166 · Wed.–Mon. 9–7:30 · Al 53, see page 559 · 1, 24, 42 · $$$

The Museo Archeologico Nazionale (National Archeological Museum) houses one of the world's most important collections of classical sculpture, mosaics, gems, glass, silver and Egyptian antiquities. Finds from Pompeii are here; don't miss the graceful fresco portrayal of Flora. The *Farnese Hercules* and *Farnese Bull* are equally impressive; the *Bull* is the largest classical sculptural group to have survived, dating from 200 BC. Allow two or three hours for your visit to do the museum justice.

MUSEO E GALLERIE NAZIONALI DI CAPODIMONTE

B5 · Parco di Capodimonte · 081 749 9111 · Tue.–Sun. 8:30–7:30 · R4, 24 · $$$

Built in the 18th century as a palace and museum, and surrounded by a wooded park, Capodimonte has been recently restored and rearranged. Be sure to see Masaccio's *Crucifixion*, which is the star of the Renaissance painting collection, and the majolica and porcelain collection, much of it made by the Capodimonte factory.

POSILLIPO AND THE CAMPI FLEGREI

Off the map · Posillipo · Mergellina or Campi Flegrei

Posillipo and the Campi Flegrei (literally "Burning Fields," named because of the area's volcanic activity) lie east of Naples on a lovely stretch of coast. Classical ruins, fishing villages, beaches, inlets and grottos, dot the area, which is well worth exploring.

EXCURSION TO CAPRI

A favorite with the Roman emperors, Capri has been a tourist hot spot for more than 150 years. This tiny island, with its spectacular scenery and crystal-clear waters, now welcomes more than 2 million visitors annually.

Capri's Marina Grande is the starting point for visiting this enchanting island

Getting There

You can travel from Naples' Mergellina or Molo Beverello docks by ferry or hydrofoil, a lovely trip across the Bay of Naples that takes between 50 and 90 minutes. Spectacular views open up back to the city and across to Mount Vesuvius as you approach the steep hills of the Sorrento peninsula, with Capri lying off its tip. Boats dock at Marina Grande, the island's main harbor.

What to See

The charm of Capri lies in the combination of lovely scenery, picturesque villages and a laid-back holiday atmosphere. The two main settlements are Anacapri and Capri; their whitewashed houses and narrow, winding streets are crammed with boutiques, outdoor cafés and lively fish restaurants, and many visitors do no more than enjoy these. Most, however, take a boat trip to the Grotta Azzurra (Blue Grotto), a spectacular sea cave filled with refracted turquoise light. Another highlight is the beautiful Villa San Michele in Anacapri. Built in the late 19th century by Swedish physician Axel Munthe, this dreamlike villa is filled with classical statues. There also is a peaceful green garden, and from its shady pergola you can enjoy some of the island's loveliest views.

Walk to the ruins of Villa Jovis, Emperor Tiberius' clifftop villa, from where he allegedly threw his enemies into the sea. Or stroll to a lookout above the Faraglioni, a cluster of offshore rocks rising more than 360 feet above the water.

Capri See page 284, C2 Tourist offices: Banchina del Porto, Marina Grande 081 837 0634; Piazza Umberto I, Capri 081 837 0686; Via G. Orlandi 59, Anacapri 081 837 1524 From Marina Grande to Marina Piccola, Capri and Anacapri Ferry operator: Caremar, from Molo Beverello, Naples (081 551 5384). Hydrofoil operators: Caremar, from Molo Beverello (081 551 3882); NLG, from Molo Beverello (081 552 7209); SNAV, from Mergellina (081 761 2348)

Blue Grotto 081 837 0634 Daily 9–1 hour before dusk (weather permitting) From Marina Grande $$$

Villa San Michele, Anacapri 081 837 1401 Daily 9:30–6, May–Sep.; 9:30–5:30, in Apr.; 9:30–5, in Oct.; 9:30–4:30, in Mar., 10:30–3:30, rest of year From Capri $$$

Villa Jovis Daily 9–1 hour before sunset From Capri $

VENICE

No matter how many pictures or films you've seen, nothing can prepare you for the real Venice (Venezia), one of the world's most captivating cities. Whether it's sparkling in late spring sunshine or shrouded in winter mist, it will enchant you in every way.

Tackling Venice

When you first arrive in Venice, don't head straight for the main sights (which will invariably be packed); take time to get a feel for the city, either from the

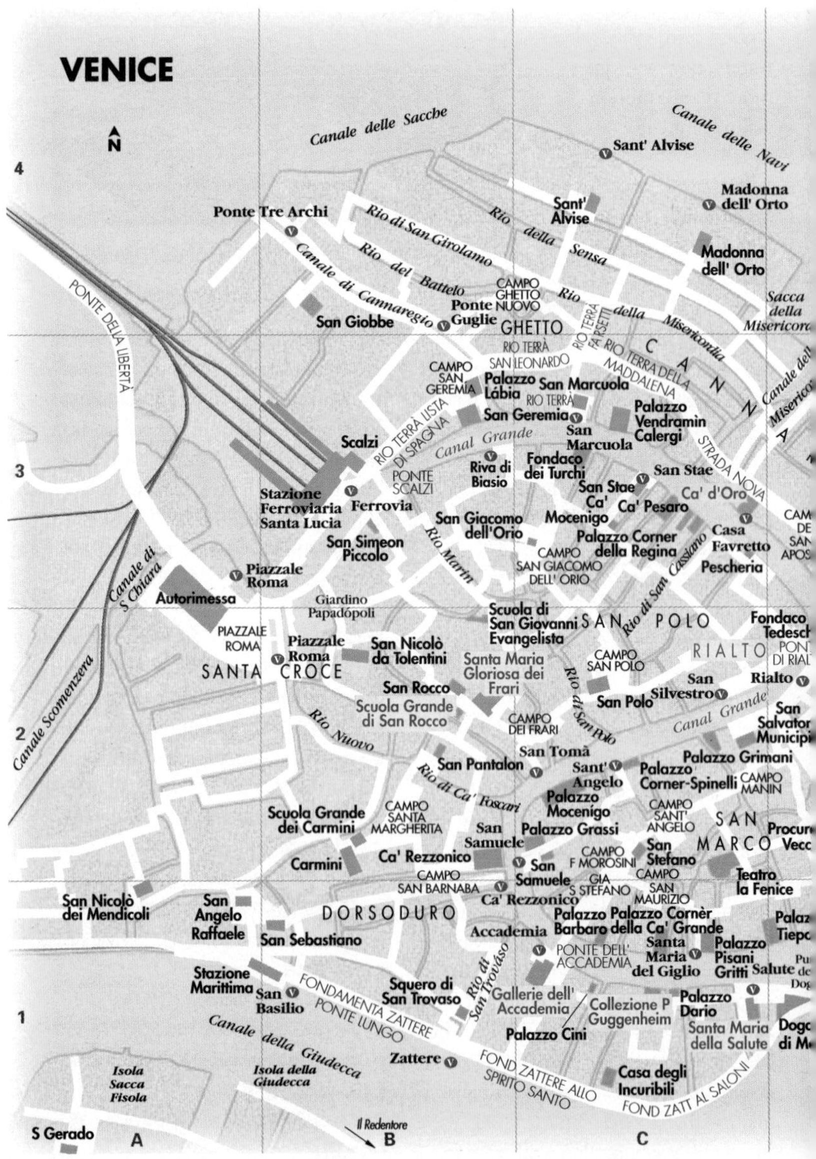

vantage point of a ferry or by strolling the streets and squares. As for accommodations, luxury hotels lining the Grand Canal (Canale Grande) are clearly the optimum choice, but there are many with great charm elsewhere. The *sestiere* (city areas) of Dorsoduro, San Marco, Castello and San Polo are among the nicest parts of the city to stay. Avoid the area around the train station, which is noisy and less attractive. Under no circumstances should you stay in Mestre, an industrial sprawl across the causeway on the mainland.

Accept that you will do a great deal of tiring walking around the city, and come prepared with comfortable shoes. Take time working out your daily itinerary; shortcuts across the city save valuable time. Main routes are clearly marked along the streets by yellow signs. There are numerous tour options; if time is short these can be helpful, and you'll have the benefit of English-speaking guides.

Venetian Glass, Velvet Slippers

The city's main fashion and leather stores cluster along the Calle dei Fabbri, the Frezzeria and the so-called Mercerie, made up of the streets connecting Piazza San Marco with the Rialto district. Glass is a true Venetian specialty, made for centuries on the island of Murano. Marbled paper is another good buy, and Venetian masks make wonderful souvenirs. Other typical products are velvet slippers in jewel-bright colors or a real gondolier's hat; you'll find one at Emilio Ceccato, near the Rialto.

Gondolas

The shiny black gondola – symbol of Venice – is a shallow-draft vessel propelled by a single oarsman, the gondolier, who stands at the back of the boat. A ride in a gondola is a great Venetian experience for many visitors, but they are expensive and normally follow a set route. Be sure to ascertain what you're getting before you set out.

Festivals

Carnival lasts for 10 days before the start of Lent, when thousands of people wearing costumes parade the city streets. The summer sees several ancient festivals, notably the feast of *La Sensa*, when the mayor and his entourage sail out in the state barge and enact a symbolic marriage to the waters. This is followed in July by the *Festa del Redentore*, a thanksgiving festival for deliverence from a plague. During the *Regata Storica* in September, there are races of decorated craft manned by crews in period dress.

Getting Around

No cars, taxis, motorcycles or trucks are permitted within the city of Venice. If you arrive in a wheeled vehicle you must leave it in a parking lot on the city outskirts and enter Venice by boat or on foot. Every single item, from paper and pens to vegetables and vinegar, arrives at its destination by water, and so must every visitor. Take a water bus, water taxi or gondola to the landing point nearest your destination and then walk.

ESSENTIAL INFORMATION

TOURIST INFORMATION

• Palazzina dei Santi, Giardini ex Reale ☎ 041 522 6356
• San Marco 71f, Ascenzione ☎ 041 520 8964
• Aeroporto Marco Polo ☎ 041 541 5887
• Stazione Santa Lucia ☎ 041 529 8727
• Viale Santa Maria Elisabetta, Lido di Venezia ☎ 041 526 5721; www.provincia.venezia.it/aptve

URBAN TRANSPORTATION

If you arrive by car, you must leave the vehicle in one of the parking lots on the outskirts of the city. The parking at Piazzale Roma is the nearest to the city center. Venice's public transportation system is operated by ACTV (office at Piazzale Roma, ☎ 041 528 7886) and uses two types of boats, *vaporetti* (big and slow) and *motoscafi* (small and fast). All are numbered on the front of the boat and follow set routes. Check to make sure the routes given here are still valid. *Vaporetti* boats leave from *pontile* (floating docks), which are clearly marked with service numbers and a route map. As the same numbers head in two directions, check that you are going the right way before you board; there are normally separate boarding points for each direction. Tickets can be bought at the *pontile* or at shops showing the ACTV sticker. You can save money by buying a 1-, 2- or 3-day pass. All tickets must be validated at the machine on the dock before boarding. There is a limited night service on most routes. *Vaporetti* stops are marked on the Venice city map with a "V." *Taxi motoscafi* (water taxis) are fast and expensive; they can be hailed on various canals, but it is easier to call (☎ 041 523 5775, 041 522 2303 or 041 522 1265). Gondolas can penetrate even the narrowest canals, but are very expensive. As there are only three bridges over the Grand Canal, the seven *traghetti* (ferries) crossing at various points are useful. These ferries are old gondolas and are marked by yellow signs. Pay as you board and watch your balance, as it is customary to stand.

AIRPORT INFORMATION

Venice's Marco Polo airport (☎ 041 260 9260) is 5 miles from the city center on the northern edge of the lagoon, and handles both domestic and international flights. For city connections you can take a bus (shuttle bus ATVO or ACTV bus no. 5) from outside the terminal to the Piazzale Roma at the edge of the city, where the road ends, and then connect with your hotel by *vaporetto* (water bus). The transfer takes 15 minutes by ATVO bus and 25 minutes by ACTV bus; tickets must be purchased from the office inside the airport arrivals terminal before boarding. A *vaporetto* leaves from the dock outside the terminal for San Marco and the Lido; the transfer takes around 50 minutes. The fastest way to reach the city is by water taxi; they leave from the dock outside the terminal and take only 20 minutes to reach the center, but are expensive.

CLIMATE – average highs and lows for the month

JAN.	FEB.	MAR.	APR.	MAY	JUN.	JUL.	AUG.	SEP.	OCT.	NOV.	DEC.
5°C	8°C	12°C	17°C	21°C	24°C	27°C	26°C	23°C	18°C	12°C	8°C
41°F	46°F	54°F	63°F	70°F	75°F	81°F	79°F	73°F	64°F	54°F	46°F
0°C	2°C	5°C	9°C	13°C	17°C	19°C	18°C	16°C	12°C	7°C	3°C
32°F	36°F	41°F	48°F	55°F	63°F	66°F	64°F	61°F	54°F	45°F	37°F

Crowds converge on St. Mark's Basilica – one of the world's greatest medieval buildings

CITY SIGHTS

Key to symbols

map coordinates refer to the Venice map on pages 314–315; sights below are highlighted in yellow on the map.

address or location telephone number

opening times nearest boat or ferry stop

restaurant or café on site or nearby

admission charge: $$$ more than L5,000, $$ L3,000 to L5,000, $ less than L3,000 other relevant information

BASILICA DI SAN MARCO

D2 Piazza San Marco 041 522 5205 or 041 522 5697 Mon.–Fri. 10–5, Sat.–Sun. 1–5 1, 82 Basilica free; Tesoro $, Pala d'Oro $

The Basilica di San Marco (St. Mark's Basilica), glittering with mosaics and flickering candles, is an architectural hybrid, a fusion of western and Byzantine styles. Dating from 1094, it stands on the site of the ninth-century basilica built to house the body of St. Mark. Pause before entering to admire the Romanesque carvings, then proceed inside to take in the ornate marble pavements; the gem-encrusted altar screen, the Pala d'Oro, a masterpiece of Gothic-Byzantine goldsmith art; and the third-century bronze horses, which once adorned the facade.

CA' D'ORO

C3 Calle di Ca' d'Oro, off Strada Nova 041 523 8790 Daily 9–2 1 $$

The picture-book facade of the Ca' d'Oro (House of Gold), so called because it was once gilded, is a perfect example of the finest Venetian-Byzantine architecture. Behind the facade is a beguiling small museum with an impressive *St. Sebastian* by Andrea Mantegna and a lovely *Madonna* by Giovanni Bellini, as well as sculptural fragments, bronzes and tapestries. All pieces are arranged in rooms around the palazzo's central *portego*, or inner courtyard.

CAMPANILE

D2 Piazza San Marco 041 522 4064 Daily 9:30–5:30 (opening hours vary; check before visiting) 1, 82 $$$

The graceful Campanile, Venice's tallest building, is less than 100 years old. The original bell tower, reputedly built in AD 912, collapsed in 1902, killing no one and leaving St. Mark's unscathed. A cry of *"Dov'era e com'era"* ("where it was and how it was") went up, and 10 years later a perfect replica was completed. Take the elevator up for superb views – on a clear day you can see as far as the Alps.

Canal Grande

B2, C1, C2, C3, D2, D3 1, 82

The allure of the Canal Grande (Grand Canal), Venice's magical highway, never fades. It divides Venice in two and is crossed by three bridges. The canal is lined with a wondrous procession of palaces, built over the course of 500 years and each lovelier than its neighbor. By day numerous boats chug up and down; at night it epitomizes romance, with reflected lights twinkling on the water. Take a number 1 or 82 water bus from any of the stops on the Grand Canal.

Collezione Peggy Guggenheim

C1 Palazzo Venier dei Leoni, Calle San Cristoforo 041 520 6288 Wed.–Mon. 11–6 1, 82 $$$

American Peggy Guggenheim's modern art collection is installed in her 18th-century palazzo on the Grand Canal. Here you'll find works by Pablo Picasso and Salvadore Dalí and fine examples of Jackson Pollock and Mark Rothko, all beautifully displayed. The garden makes a wonderful background for some Henry Moore sculptures and Marino Marini's *Angel of the Citadel.*

Gallerie dell'Accademia

C1 Campo della Carità 041 522 2247 Tue.–Sat. 9–9, Sun. 9–8, Mon. 9–2 Taverna San Trovaso, see page 560 1, 82 $$$

Allow plenty of time for the Gallerie dell'Accademia (Academy Gallery), the finest collection of Venetian painting in the world. Arranged chronologically, the gallery's 24 rooms contain masterpieces such as Giorgio Giorgione's enigmatic *Tempest*, Giovanni Bellini's luminous *Virgins*, and superb Mantegnas. Don't miss the dramatic *Translation of the Body of St. Mark* by Jacopo Tintoretto and Paolo Veronese's sumptuous *Feast in the House of Levi.* Among other highlights are the cycles of paintings in rooms 20 and 21; *The Miracle of the True Cross* had several contributors, while the *Life of St. Ursula* is wholly by Vittore Carpaccio.

Museo Storico Navale

E1 Campo San Biagio 041 520 0276 Mon.–Sat. 8:45–1:30, Sun. 8:45–1 1 $

Venice's Museo Storico Navale (Maritime Museum) is fittingly housed near the Arsenale, the great shipyards that once manufactured the city's fleets. It tells the story of the city's sea power through displays of every type of maritime artifact; the highlight is the collection of gondolas and other historic boats, which are housed in one of the Arsenale's old sheds.

Palazzo Ducale

D2 Piazzetta San Marco 041 522 4951 Daily 9–7 (last admission at 5:30), Apr.–Oct.; 9–5 (last admission at 3:30), rest of year. Guided tours a.m. only 1, 82 $$$

The huge Gothic complex of the Palazzo Ducale (Ducal Palace) was the seat of Venice's government, where the Council of Ten met, ambassadors were received and the Doge held councils of state. The present building dates from the 15th century, with later alterations following two fires in the 1500s. The marked route leads through a succession of sumptuous rooms to the vast Sala del Maggior Consiglio (Great Council Chamber), dominated by Jacopo Tintoretto's *Paradiso*, the world's largest oil painting. Be sure to have a look at the famous Ponte dei Sospiri (Bridge of Sighs), spanning a canal to the right of the Palazzo's waterfront facade.

Piazza San Marco

D2 Piazza San Marco 1, 82

The only piazza in Venice (all the others are officially *campi*) is thronged around the clock with strolling and chattering crowds. Go early or late to avoid the worst crush, and marvel at the harmony of this wonderful open space. Highlights here are the 15th-century Torre dell'Orologio (Clock Tower) and its zodiac clock, the graceful architecture of the Libreria Sansoviniana (Sansoviniana Library), and the two columns near the waterfront, topped by the lion of St. Mark and St. Theodore with his crocodile emblem.

Time to reflect on the beauty of Venice – sample the local fare with a view of the Rialto Bridge

RIALTO

D2 Rialto 1, 82

Throughout the Middle Ages the Rialto was Europe's financial and banking center; the name had the same connotations as does Wall Street now. Today, you can admire the bridge and browse in Venice's food markets, one of the city's great sights. Wander through the fruit and vegetable stalls, but leave time to enjoy the scents and sights of the fish market, full of delicious delights.

SAN GIORGIO MAGGIORE

E1 Campo San Giorgio, Isole San Giorgio 041 522 7827 Mon.–Sat. 9:30–12:30 and 2:30–5, Sun. 9:30–10:30 and 2:30–5. Hours can vary in winter 82 $

To visit the superb Palladian church of San Giorgio Maggiore (St. George the Great), whose serene bulk dominates the view of St. Mark's Basin, you must take a waterbus across the canal of St. Mark's to St. George's island. Built by Andrea Palladio in 1559, the church embodies order, grace and harmony. Take the elevator up the Campanile (bell tower) to enjoy fine views across to the Doge's Palace and the Campanile tower.

SANTA MARIA DEI MIRACOLI

D3 Campo dei Miracoli 041 528 3903 Mon.–Sat. 10–noon and 3–5 1, 82

The tiny jewel-like church of Santa Maria dei Miracoli (Our Lady of the Miracles) was built around 1480 to house a miraculous image of the Virgin. Pietro Lombardo, who faced his church with colored marble and porphyry rock, created the harmonious interior as a frame for some fine sculpture and intricate carvings.

SANTA MARIA DELLA SALUTE

C1 Campo della Salute 041 522 5558 Daily 9–noon and 3–6:30 Taverna San Trovaso, see page 560 1

During the 1630 plague, the Senate promised to build a church in honor of the Virgin if she would save the city. The pestilence passed, an architect was commissioned, and the great dome of Santa Maria della Salute (Our Lady of Health and Salvation) rose at the entrance to the Grand Canal. One of the city's outstanding skyline features, the interior has fine sculptures and paintings.

The Annunciation by Jacopo Tintoretto in the Scuola Grande di San Rocco

Santa Maria Gloriosa dei Frari

B2 Campo dei Frari 041 522 2637 Mon.–Sat. 9:30–6, Sun. 1–6 1, 82 $; free to all Sat.–Sun.

Santa Maria Gloriosa dei Frari (Glorious Virgin Mary of the Brothers), a lofty Franciscan church, is the resting place of Titian and the composer Claudio Monteverdi. Built as a preaching church about 1250, it contains Titian's great *Assumption*, prominently hung over the high altar, and his *Madonna of Ca' Pesaro*. Best of all, though, is Giovanni Bellini's *Madonna and Child with Saints,* considered among the world's finest paintings. You'll find it tucked away in the right transept.

Santi Giovanni e Paolo

D3 Campo SS Giovanni e Paolo 041 523 5913 Mon.–Sat. 9–noon and 3–6 52

More than 20 of Venice's Doges are buried in the Gothic church of Santi Giovanni e Paolo (St. John and St. Paul), rising majestically on one side of its *campo* (square). The focal point is the great equestrian statue of Bartolomeo Colleoni, a 15th-century Venetian army officer. The 13th-century church contains many tombs, their monuments representing the best of Venetian medieval sculpture, and some lovely paintings, including Giovanni Bellini's *St. Vincent Ferrer.*

Scuola di San Giorgio degli Schiavoni

E2 Calle dei Furlani 041 522 8828 Tue.–Sun. 9–noon and 3–5 Da Franz, see page 560 1, 52, 82 $$

Carpaccio painted one of the city's most delightful picture cycles between 1502 and 1508 for the headquarters of Venice's Dalmatian, or Slavic, community – the Scuola di San Giorgio degli Schiavoni (School of St. George of the Slavs). He used Dalmatia's patron saints, St. George, St. Tryphon and St. Jerome, as his inspiration, painting scenes from the lives of all three. Highlights are *St. George Slaying the Dragon* and *St. Augustine in his Study*, accompanied by his dog.

Scuola Grande di San Rocco

B2 Campo San Rocco 041 523 4864 Mon.–Fri. 10–1, Sat.–Sun. 10–4 1, 82 $$$

In 1564, the brotherhood of St. Roche ran a competition to choose an artist to decorate the walls of their Scuola Grande di San Rocco (Grand Meeting Halls of the Confraternity of St. Roche). Tintoretto won, and spent the next 23 years working on a stupendous cycle of paintings. There are 54 paintings in all; highlights include the wonderful *Crucifixion*, in a room off the gallery upstairs. New Testament scenes line the walls of the main hall on the ground floor.

The Lagoon Islands

You can spend a delightful day exploring some of the islands in the lagoon. Most visitors opt for Murano, famous for its glass; Burano, with its lace-making; or Torcello, a virtually deserted island with an ancient cathedral and church. Guided excursions run to all three, but a more flexible option is to take boat number 12, which leaves from the Fondamenta Nuove and takes around 40 to 50 minutes to reach Burano and Torcello, the two farthest islands.

Colorful waterfront at Burano

Murano

Venetian glass has been made on Murano since 1291, when the furnaces were moved away from the city as a fire precaution. A visit to the fascinating Glass Museum (Museo Vetrario) will give you an idea of glass-blowers' skills through the ages. Murano also has two exquisite churches: San Pietro Martire, which contains a glowing altarpiece by Giovanni Bellini, and Santi Maria e Donato, a 12th-century structure with mosaics on its walls and floor.

Burano

Burano's colorful canal-side houses, narrow streets and sun-splashed squares are as picturesque as anything in Venice itself. This is still a fishing community, with a robust workaday atmosphere, and you'll see moored fishing boats and nets drying in the sun. Local ladies have always been skilled lace-makers, and you can admire the fragility of their exquisite work in the Lace-Making School (Scuola dei Merletti).

Elaborate glass candlestick produced on the Venetian island of Murano

Torcello

Timeless Torcello is one of the most evocative and magical places in Venice. This sleepy island, with its overgrown canals and green fields, was the lagoon's first settled area, and once had fine buildings and palaces. Silt and malaria caused its 12th-century decline. Today the only remaining signs of its past importance are the Cathedral of Santa Maria Assunta and the adjacent church, Santa Fosca. The cathedral's main glories are two 12th-century mosaics, which completely cover the apse and the opposite rear wall. High above the seventh-century altar stands a lovely Byzantine *Madonna and Child*, their poignant beauty highlighted by the simple gold background, while the graphic *Judgment* scenes make a telling contrast. The nearby church of Santa Fosca, with its arcaded porch full of nesting swifts, is as lovely in its own way.

LUXEMBOURG

"ALL that we see is superb, the Ardennes are enchanting..."

From a letter written by French author Victor Hugo

Opposite: Castle Vianden overlooks the valley of the Our, on the border with Germany

LUXEMBOURG

Luxembourg lies at the heart of the European landmass. It is a minuscule country, measuring 50 miles from north to south and a mere 35 miles from east to west. Belgium lies to the north and west, France to the south and Germany to the east. Because of its attractive financial laws and constitutional stability, it has become a center of European politics and finance. And despite a turbulent history, Luxembourg retains its independence and sovereignty; it is a true survivor of the Continent's stormy past.

Luxembourg Landscapes

Luxembourg is a Grand Duchy, with the city of Luxembourg as its main focus, although its rural areas are remarkably varied for such a small country. They include part of the delightful Ardennes region, the hilly area that lies across the northern third of Luxembourg and extends into Belgium. The Ardennes have a distinctive landscape of forested plateaus sliced through by deep valleys that are drained by beautiful rivers. Fairy-tale castles crown wooded bluffs. At Vianden a medieval castle, one of the Grand Duchy's finest historic sites, dominates the landscape. The equally magnificent Bourscheid Castle stands above the Sûre and Wark rivers. At Clervaux, the castle is matched by the red-roofed Clervaux Abbey, which stands amid the wooded heights above the beautiful town.

View over the Old Town, city of Luxembourg

At the southern edge of the Ardennes, where the hills meet the flatter, more fertile land known as the Bon Pays, or "Good Land," lies the picturesque town of Diekirch. Only a short distance southwest is Ettelbrück, where there is a monument to General George Patton and a Patton Museum commemorating World War II's bitter Battle of the Bulge.

Southern Luxembourg is the country's economic powerhouse. Here in the "Good Land" are farms and orchards, forests and even more castles. In fact, the lovely valley of the Eisch river is known as the Valley of the Seven Castles.

MORE TOP DESTINATIONS IN LUXEMBOURG

- Abbaye Benédictine C3
- Abbaye St.-Maurice B4
- Château Bourscheid B3
- Diekirch B3
- Esch-sur-Sûre A3
- Grevenmacher C2
- Mondorf-les-Bains B1
- Vallée du Mullerthal C3
- Vallée des Sept Châteaux B2
- Vianden B3

Farther south and west from the city of Luxembourg is the "red earth" country around Dudelange and Pétange, where much of the country's industry is located. West of here is the delightful Mondorf-les-Bains, a fashionable spa town on the edge of the Moselle region. This area, running north to south along the border with Germany, is Luxembourg's wine-growing district.

Exploring the Country

You will find Luxembourgers are very cosmopolitan and friendly, and a large percentage of them speak English. The duchy has an excellent road system and distances are short between the many towns and villages, making independent travel a good option. There also are numerous day trips organized from the city of Luxembourg.

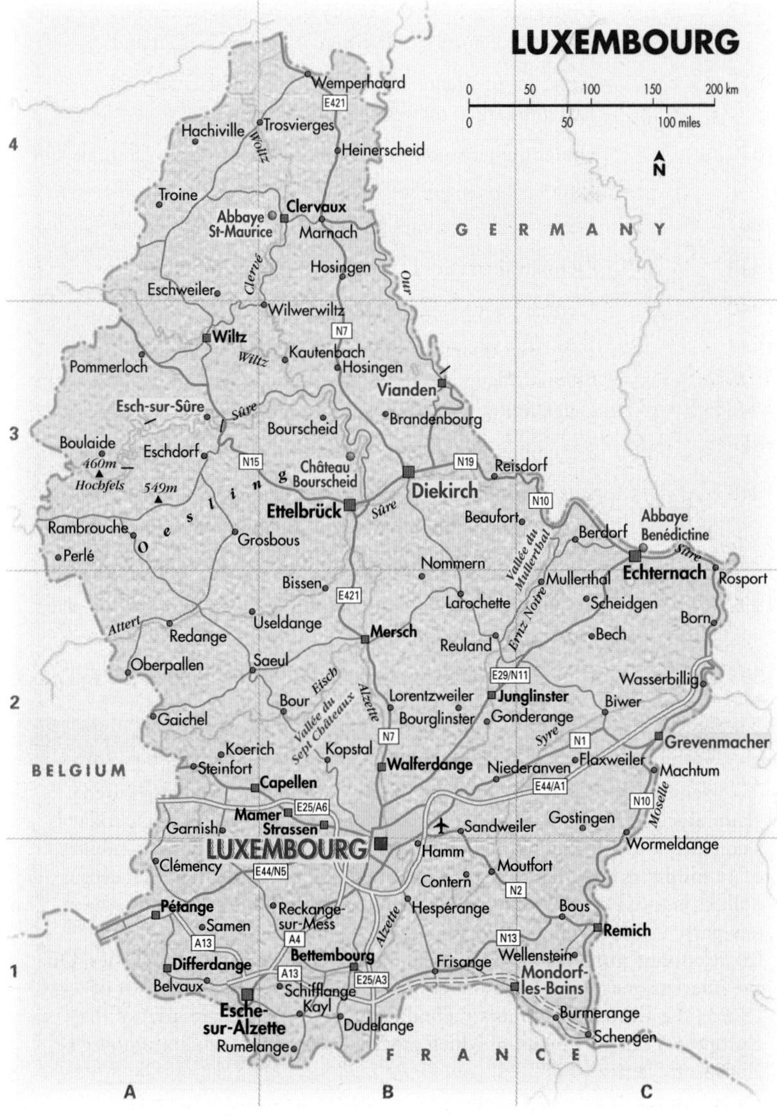

Timeline

AD 963	Count Siegfried of the Ardennes builds a castle on the Bock promontory called the Lützelburg ("Little Castle").
1354	Luxembourg becomes a duchy.
1447	The Duchy of Luxembourg comes under the rule of the Habsburgs through marriage.
1542	The city of Luxembourg is captured by the French.
1554	The Spanish capture the city of Luxembourg.
1713	Under the terms of the Treaty of Utrecht, Luxembourg comes under the control of the Kingdom of the Netherlands.
1815	Congress of Vienna establishes the Grand Duchy of Luxembourg as a sovereign, neutral state.
1839	Under the terms of the Treaty of London, the western part of the Grand Duchy is ceded to Belgium.
1867	Luxembourg becomes an independent state.
1914	Germany occupies Luxembourg in World War I.
1940	Germany invades Luxembourg again in World War II.
1944	American troops liberate Luxembourg; in December, Germany launches its "Ardennes Offensive"; the Battle of the Bulge follows as chiefly American forces repel the attack.
1945	Luxembourg becomes a member of the United Nations.
1948	Luxembourg joins Belgium and the Netherlands in forming BENELUX, a trading and economic union.
1949	Luxembourg abandons neutrality and joins NATO.
1992	Luxembourg ratifies the Maastricht Treaty, securing its place in the European Union.
1994	City of Luxembourg declared a World Heritage Site by UNESCO.

Luxembourg: The Great Survivor

Luxembourg, with its long history at the heart of Europe, has secured a major part in the working of the European Union. The country today is a constitutional monarchy ruled by Grand Duke Jean, who heads a cabinet of 12 ministers appointed from an elected chamber of deputies. Consensus politics is used in Luxembourg's government, and coalitions of more than one party usually hold power. So open is Luxembourg's government that the telephone numbers of ministers are often listed in public directories. On the international front, Luxembourg is home to the European Court of Justice, the European Monetary Fund and the General Secretariat of the European Parliament – all of which are based in the city of Luxembourg's European Center.

Sidewalk cafés amid the downtown bustle of the city of Luxembourg

SURVIVAL GUIDE

- If you are in Luxembourg during September, visit the city of Luxembourg during the *Schueberfouer* Fair.
- For lunchtime treats try Oesling ham from the Ardennes, or a selection of cold meats and sausages with salad. In rural areas look for *friture*, delicious fried river fish.
- Most shops in the city of Luxembourg are closed on Monday mornings but often stay open until 8 p.m. on Thursdays.
- There are numerous stores in the Gare district of the city of Luxembourg, especially on avenue de la Liberté. Enjoy an evening in the Grund district. There are lovely areas, good bars and restaurants, and a different ambience to the city center, known as the Ville area.
- Both Belgian and Luxembourg francs are used in Luxembourg, but only Belgian francs are good in Belgium. Use the new euros wherever possible—valid tender in both countries.
- The city of Luxembourg has many designer shops, such as Hermès, Dolce & Gabbana, Armani, Louis Vuitton and Claudia Sträter, along Grande Rue and Neuve rue Philippe II. There also are tempting treats in Leonidas, the renowned Belgian chocolatiers. Try rue de la Boucherie for antique and specialty shops.
- Typical Luxembourg souvenirs include cast iron from the Mersch foundry, in the heart of the duchy. Designs incorporate castles and coats of arms. Authentic Luxembourg porcelain and earthenware are produced by Villeroy & Boch.
- If you travel in the Moselle wine-producing region, enjoy some of Luxembourg's dry white and sparkling vintages, such as the subtle Rivaner; Pinot Blanc to go with fish dishes; or the satisfyingly strong Pinot Gris to complement a meal of *judd mat gaardebounen* (roast, smoked pork).
- Children will especially love the Butterfly Garden in Grevenmacher. They also will enjoy Parc Merveilleux in Bettembourg, at the southern tip of Luxembourg, where there are attractions from fairy-tale tableaux and exotic birds to children's animal enclosures and games of all types.

City of Luxembourg

The city of Luxembourg is known as the landlocked "Gibraltar of the North" because of its once-fortified location. It is set above the cliffs that flank the canyon-like valleys of the Alzette and Pétrusse rivers. Today, the city of Luxembourg is more fairy tale than fortress. The old city, especially, is a pleasing mix of the past and present. Its elegant towers, spires and turrets and its attractive walls of golden sandstone helped win Luxembourg the United Nations' designation of World Heritage Site in 1994.

The steep-sided plateau on which Luxembourg stands explains its origins. The Romans first set up camp here. They had one eye on military control and the other on the advantages of a strategic trading position at the crossroads of northern Europe. In AD 963, Count Siegfried of the Ardennes built a castle on the narrow Bock promontory above the Alzette river.

Over the next 900 years Luxembourg evolved into one of the mightiest fortifications in Europe. In 1867 the terms of the 1831 Treaty of London were applied, and Luxembourg became a neutral state. The military fortress was dismantled and the encircling walls were replaced by the present city's outer boulevards.

A Lift in Luxembourg

You can reach the riverside Grund district in the Alzette valley by public elevator from place du St.-Esprit, near the intersection with boulevard Franklin-Roosevelt. Look for the glass-fronted elevator shelter in the corner of the place du St.-Esprit. The elevator takes you to a tunnel that emerges at montée du Grund.

Ville and *Gare*

The main parts of Luxembourg are the city center, known as *Ville*, perched on the high plateau above the Pétrusse and Alzette river gorges; and the more modern district, known as *Gare*, south of the river. The two are connected by bridges across the Pétrusse gorge; the main ones are the pont Adolphe and the pont Viaduc, the latter known locally as *Passerelle*. Below the cliffs lies Grund, the main part of the city's valley settlements.

The area around the railroad station is emphatically modern and downtown. Buses leave regularly from outside the station and take you – within minutes via the pont Adolphe – to place E.-Hamilius, on the western side of Ville. This is a different world from down-to-earth Gare. From here a short walk east along rue de la Poste leads to the large central square of place d'Armes.

At the east end of place d'Armes is the handsome City Palace (Cercle Municipal), where the tourist information office is located. Ask for details about guided tours and the Luxembourg Card, which is good for one, two or three days for free entry or discounts on admission fees to numerous museums and attractions and free use of public transportation. The largely pedestrian-only city center makes Luxembourg a very walkable place. The maze-like streets of the Old Town (Vieille Ville, see page 332) and the marvelous complex of steps and terraces that connect plateau and valley floor can be easily enjoyed on foot.

Conversation and Music

The place d'Armes is a public space shaded by lime trees. In summer it is filled with the chairs and tables of the surrounding restaurants and cafés, where you can enjoy the hum of relaxed conversation and the music of regular concerts on the nearby bandstand.

All around the place d'Armes are the city's pedestrian-only shopping streets. To the north is Grande Rue, known locally as *Groussgaass*, the city's main shopping street. Here, and in the adjoining streets of rue Phillipe II and rue des Capucins, are fashion boutiques, as well as good restaurants and cafés. Stop for coffee at Namur, on the corner

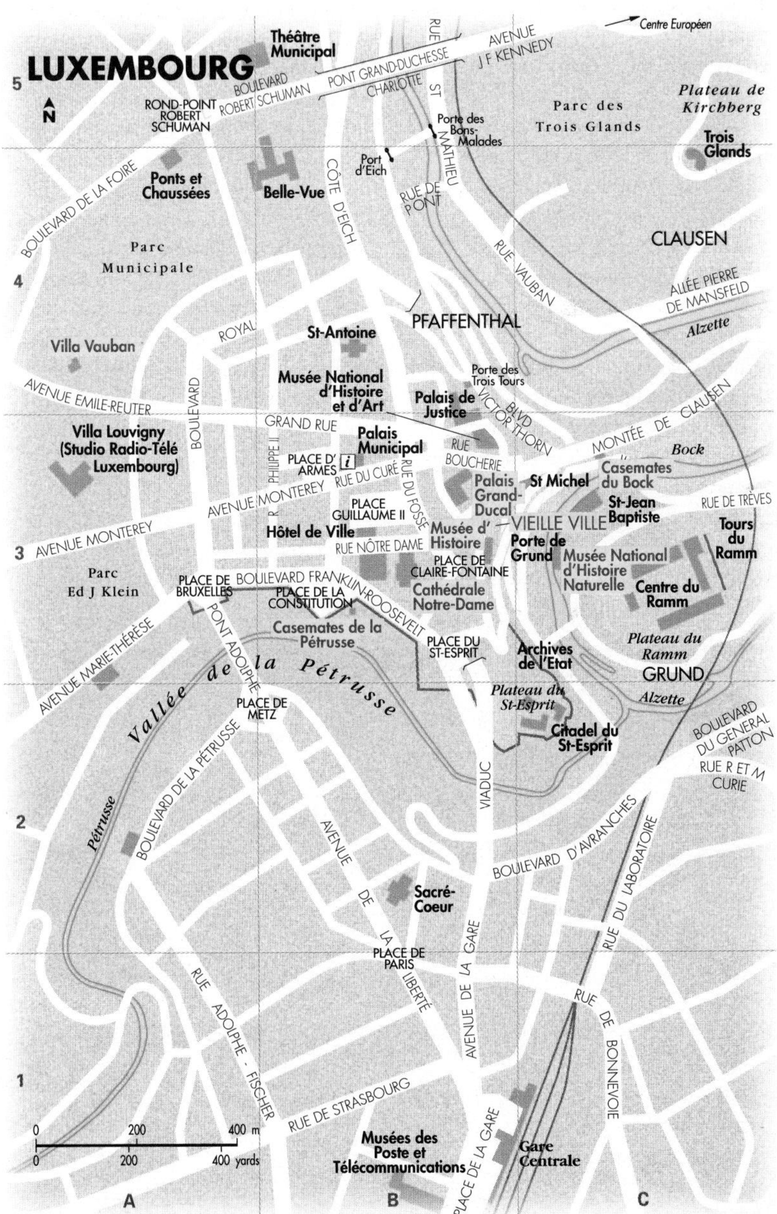

of Grande Rue and rue des Capucins. At the east end of Grande Rue look for the fountain known as Hämmelsmarsch, “The March of the Sheep.”

Exploring Historic Luxembourg

To reach historic Luxembourg, leave the southeast corner of place d’Armes, where a covered passage leads between bookshops and into the large place Guillaume II. A colorful flower market is held here on Wednesdays and Saturdays. From here you can quickly reach the Grand Ducal Palace on rue du Marché aux Herbes.

Behind the palace lies the Old Town. Look for rue de l’Eau, with its cluster of restaurants known collectively as Ilot Gastronomique. Then head down rue Sigefroi to the stunning viewpoint of the Bock, above the Alzette gorge.

From here you can see the famous Grand Duchess Charlotte Bridge, known as the Red Bridge because of its color. It connects the city center plateau with the Kirchberg plateau and the ultramodern European Center (Centre Européen), home of numerous European Community institutions. Visit the famous Bock Casemates, the maze of underground tunnels in the cliffs, and then walk the Corniche, the terrace that leads south above the Alzette gorge.

Visit the valley district of Grund, a riverside haven of well-preserved old houses and attractive restaurants and taverns. From here you can turn left and wander along the paths and terraced lanes of the Alzette to reach the riverside church of St. John on the Stone, with its rich baroque altar and famous Black Madonna statue.

Luxembourg’s Ville is more relaxed than the centers of other, more cosmopolitan European cities, although city life is sophisticated in its restrained way. Fine music can be enjoyed at the city’s Municipal Theater, Capuchin Theater and Music Conservatory. The top fashion stores of Grande Rue speak for themselves, and Ville restaurants are second to none for international cuisine; there are some superb fish restaurants as well.

ESSENTIAL INFORMATION

TOURIST INFORMATION

- place d’Armes ☎ 22 28 09 and 22 75 65; fax 46 70 70 www.luxembourg-city.lu/turistinfo
- Findel Airport ☎ 42 82 82-21
- Luxembourg railroad station ☎ 42 82 82-20

URBAN TRANSPORTATION

Buses are the only form of public transportation in the city of Luxembourg. There is a reliable and regular bus network, mainly serving the outlying districts. Visitors will probably require service only between the railroad station and the city terminus at place E.-Hamilius. Taxis are expensive, but can be hired by calling ☎ 43 43 43.

AIRPORT INFORMATION

Luxembourg’s Findel Airport is located 4 miles east of the city of Luxembourg. Luxair runs a bus service between the airport and the railroad station in Gare and to the city. Public bus No. 9 runs between the airport and the city center and railroad station, and is much cheaper. Taxis between airport and city are expensive. For airport information call ☎ 47 981.

CLIMATE – Average highs and lows for the month

JAN.	FEB.	MAR.	APR.	MAY	JUN.	JUL.	AUG.	SEP.	OCT.	NOV.	DEC.
3°C	4°C	9°C	14°C	18°C	21°C	23°C	22°C	19°C	13°C	7°C	4°C
37°F	39°F	48°F	57°F	64°F	70°F	73°F	71°F	66°F	55°F	45°F	39°F
-2°C	0°C	2°C	4°C	8°C	11°C	13°C	12°C	10°C	6°C	3°C	0°C
28°F	32°F	36°F	39°F	46°F	52°F	55°F	54°F	50°F	43°F	37°F	32°F

City Sights

Key to symbols

map coordinates refer to the Luxembourg map on page 329; sights below are highlighted in yellow on the map.
address or location telephone number
opening times nearest bus route
restaurant or café on site or nearby
admission charge: $$$ more than 150F, $$ 100F–150F, $ less than 100F other relevant information

Casemates

Casemates du Bock C3 montée de Clausen 22 28 09; 47 96-27 09 for guided tours Daily 10–5, Mar.–Oct. $
Casemates de la Pétrusse B3 boulevard Franklin-Roosevelt 22 28 09; 47 96-27 09 for guided tours Daily 11–4, Jul.–Sep. (also 11–4, Easter and Whitsunday) $

The great cliffs of the Pétrusse and Alzette gorges are honeycombed with tunnels, stairways and chambers, called the Casemates, hollowed out of rock during the 17th and 18th centuries. Originally the network of Casemates measured over 14 miles and accommodated thousands of soldiers. There was room for the stabling of their horses, and for all necessary garrison services from bakeries to workshops. Today about 10 miles of the Casemates survive. Two sections, the Casemates du Bock (Bock Casemates) and the Casemates de la Pétrusse (Pétrusse Casemates), are open to the public in summer. There are spectacular views from openings in the cliffs.

Cathédrale Notre-Dame

B3 boulevard Franklin-Roosevelt Daily 10-noon and 2-5:30, except during services Free

The steeples of the Cathédrale Notre-Dame (Cathedral of Our Lady) are a striking image on the city's skyline. Inside, the lavish high altar is a shrine to Our Lady, "Comforter of the Afflicted." To reach the crypt you must go down stone steps; at the rear, two menacing bronze lions guard the barred entrance to the burial chamber of the Grand Ducal family. A solitary sarcophagus lies in a dark blue marble setting.

The steeples of the Cathedral of Our Lady

Musée d'Histoire de la Ville de Luxembourg

B3 14 rue du St.-Esprit 47 96-30 61 or 22 90 50-1 Tue.–Sun. 10–6 (also Thu. 6–8 p.m.) Museum café $$$

A late 1990s restoration of the Musée d'Histoire de la Ville de Luxembourg (Museum of the History of the City of Luxembourg) has created a superb must-see venue. Take care in some rooms where sunken channels containing hidden lighting run around the edges of the room. The museum is located in several old 17th-, 18th- and 19th-century town houses. This is a sophisticated, interactive museum; visitors are given a card to operate audiovisual displays and touch screens that explain the city's history. Follow the room numbers counter-clockwise and do not miss a trip in the big glass elevator that rises through layers of history and architecture.

Musée National d'Histoire Naturelle

C3 25 rue Munster 46 22 33-1 Tue.–Sun. 10–6, mid-May to mid-Sep.; Tue.–Fri. 2–6, Sat.–Sun. 10–6, rest of year Museum café $$

The Musée National d'Histoire Naturelle (National Museum of Natural History) is tucked away in the Grund area, below the cliffs. It is housed in the old Hospice of St. John, later a women's prison. The

The statue of William II, Grand Duke of Luxembourg, dominates the place de Guillaume II

building's splendid entrance survives. It was refurbished in the late 1990s and features modern interactive activities. There are no English-language programs, but there is enough visual excitement to entertain everyone who visits.

Palais Grand-Ducal

B3 rue du Marché aux Herbes Guided tours run Mon.–Fri. afternoon and Sat. morning, mid-Jul. through Aug. Contact the city tourist office for details (22 28 09) $$$

The Palais Grand-Ducal (Grand Ducal Palace), the home of Grand Duke Jean of Luxembourg and his family, is in the narrow rue du Marché aux Herbes. The building is a much-renovated and extended replacement of a medieval town hall, which was destroyed in a fire in 1554. The 16th-century Spanish rulers of Luxembourg rebuilt it after the fire, and you can see the architectural influences of southern Spain in its Renaissance facade. The interiors are exquisite, especially the Main Hall, the King's Room and the Banqueting Hall.

Vieille Ville

C3

Luxembourg's Vieille Ville (Old Town) lies between the rear of the Grand Ducal Palace and the Bock promontory. The area of the Old Town is small, lying within narrow streets and squares such as rue de l'Eau, rue de la Loge, rue du Rost and the Marché aux Poissons (Fish Market). The feeling of medieval Luxembourg is palpable here, although today's immaculate streets and elegantly preserved buildings hardly reflect the din and dirt of those days. The market was once the bustling heart of the community outside the castle walls. Down rue Sigefroi from the Marché aux Poissons is St. Michael's Church. It is the oldest church in the city and is located on the site of the 10th-century castle church, but its oldest surviving parts date from the 17th century. The church's baroque altar is superb, and there is a wonderfully vivid carved oak *pietà*.

Villa Vauban

A4 avenue Emile-Reuter 47 96-30 61 Tue.–Sun. 10–6 (also Thu. 6–8 p.m.) $$

The elegant Villa Vauban (Municipal Art Gallery) stands among flowerbeds and neat lawns in City Park. The late 19th-century building is on the foundation of the former Vauban Fortress. Today's gallery has a fine collection of the works of Dutch and Flemish masters and of later European painters. There also are temporary exhibitions.

FORTRESS LUXEMBOURG

The history of the city of Luxembourg as a medieval fortress is fascinating. Ringed by impregnable cliffs on every side but the west, it was easy to secure the western approach by building a defensive wall. The narrow and rocky Bock promontory offered the first natural fortification.

It was here on this narrow shelf, 300 feet above the Alzette valley, that prehistoric settlers may have established a camp. The Romans established their own fortifications on the Bock and called it *Castellum Lucilinburhuc*. Then, in AD 963, Count Siegfried of the Ardennes built his castle and linked it to the main plateau by a drawbridge. This *Lützelburg,* the "Little Castle," gave the city and the country its present name.

By 1050 a defensive western wall nearly 30 feet high, with numerous towers and gateways, protected the castle and the community that was growing around it to the west. In 1554 a massive explosion of stored gunpowder destroyed much of the settlement. New fortifications were built during a period of Spanish rule. They included excavation of the Pétrusse Casemates (Casemates de la Pétrusse, see page 331); the Beck Bastion; and the ramparts known today as the Corniche and dubbed the "Balcony of Europe" because of the spectacular views.

In the late 17th century the French military engineer, de Vauban, reshaped and extended the ramparts. In the 18th century the Austrians extended them once more and excavated the Bock Casemates (Casemates du Bock, see page 331). Such was the strategic importance of Luxembourg as a fortification that all buildings on the Bourbon Plateau, where Gare (the modern town) now stands, were built of wood so that they could be quickly destroyed before an attack on the fortress, thus robbing the enemy of cover.

Medieval tranquility on the Alzette river below the Pétrusse Casemates

On May 11, 1867, Luxembourg became an independent state. As part of the agreement, the city's fortifications were dismantled or destroyed. At that time, the fortress walls enclosed an area to the west that was larger than the city.

What remains today are the Casemates, the retaining walls of the cliffs and numerous ruins concentrated on the cliff edges, all adding drama to the city's already spectacular position. City boulevards and parkland lie where great walls and towers once protected the western approach.

NETHERLANDS

"*IN what other country can one find such absolute freedom...*"

17th-century French philosopher René Descartes

Opposite: View from the West Church tower across the rooftops and canals of Amsterdam

NETHERLANDS

The Netherlands is a country where freedom has come with responsibility and hard work. It is a country where the word "land" means something special – a valuable resource won from the sea. For in literal terms, when you walk on dry land in the Netherlands, your head is barely above sea level in some places, and well below it in others. Amsterdam itself is 10 feet below sea level.

Dutch Icons

To the outside world, the enduring image of the Netherlands is of a land unremittingly flat, criss-crossed by canals and dotted with windmills. Popular imagination conjures up pictures of clogs, cheese and swaths of brightly colored tulips. Then there is Amsterdam, its lively, lovely and evocative capital, seen by many as a slightly wicked city.

The Kingdom of the Netherlands is, of course, a far more complex and fascinating entity than such assumptions imply. Although the country is often known as Holland, this name actually only relates to the country's heavily populated western provinces of Noord (North) and Zuid (South) Holland. These provinces contain the main cities, such as Amsterdam, Rotterdam and The Hague, known collectively as the Randstad, the "Ring Town." Compared with this heavily urbanized area, the Netherlands' other provinces offer the visitor a remarkably diverse landscape and regional cultures that will correct any misconception that the country is homogeneous.

MORE TOP DESTINATIONS IN THE NETHERLANDS

• Arnhem C2 • De Hoge Veluwe B2 • Delta Expo A2 • Edam B3 • Enkhuizen B3 • Haarlem B3 • Het Loo B2 • Heusden B2 • Keukenhof B2 • Maastricht B1 • Orvelte C3 • Scheveningen A2 • Utrecht B2 • Zwolle C3

Land from the Sea

The Netherlands is a small country, just under 15,500 square miles in area. Its eastern neighbor, Germany, is nine times larger. To the south lies Belgium, once part of the United Provinces of the Netherlands (see page 50) but an independent nation since 1830. To the north and west of the Netherlands lies the North Sea, and it is with this near neighbor that the Dutch have their most pressing relationship. You will not be too aware of the sea in Amsterdam or The Hague. You need to go north to Noord Holland and Friesland, or south to Zeeland, to fully appreciate the astonishing control over their watery environment that the Dutch have engineered.

For the definitive story of land reclamation, visit the Zuiderzee Museum in Enkhuizen or travel across the Afsluitdijk, a 20-mile dam that seals the great inland lake of IJsselmeer and connects Noord Holland to Friesland. You could go south to Zeeland, a glittering mosaic of water within a vast web of land. There you'll want to visit the Delta Expo Museum to learn about the Delta Plan. This system of huge dams and movable barriers was built after the storm-driven North Sea breached the existing dykes in 1953, killed more than 1,800 people and devastated the countryside.

Exploring Inland

Beyond these water lands – beyond the great dunes and beaches of the North Sea coast, and the red, white and neon-bright lights of Amsterdam – lie the delights of the landlocked Netherlands. In the south, Limburg is known as the Dutch "hill country." In the province of Noord Brabant, the De Kempen region's landscape of sandy heath and woodland is a very different image than that of the "flat" Holland most people envisage. You can explore Gelderland meadows and orchards; the serene villages and waterways of Overijssel; and the moorlands and flower-filled bogs of Drenthe, so beloved by van Gogh. They all add to the variety of the rural Netherlands. In the north country, in Groningen, the quintessential Dutch images of windmills, clogs and flat green landscapes reassert themselves. In neighboring Friesland you will find

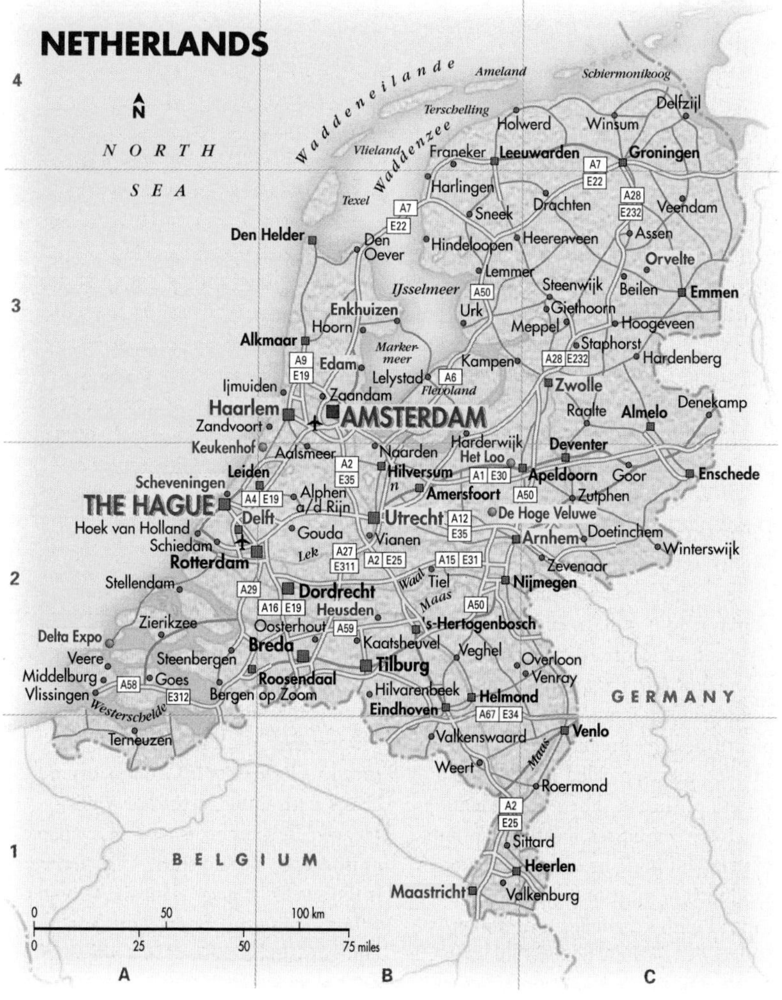

another country altogether, a province with its own language and distinctive cultural heritage.

Reaching these fascinating districts is not difficult. Public transportation in Holland is efficient and generally inexpensive. Virtually every place is within a three-hour train ride from Amsterdam. Excellent bus services run between cities, and there is an extensive bus network linking towns and villages in the provinces. Driving in rural areas is convenient and reasonably straightforward, but in urban areas it can be stressful.

The Dutch

The Dutch people are self-confident, accomplished and tolerant, qualities that have been shaped by their history and surroundings. Although they could easily boast of the way in which their environment has been mastered, they are refreshingly modest and restrained. Once the ice is broken, however, people are enthusiastic and friendly. Above all, the Dutch blend tolerance with a powerful sense of mutuality. Mutual respect is the secret of Dutch maturity and of the success that they have made of their country.

Pancakes and Beer

Modern Dutch cuisine, especially fish dishes, is fast reversing the view that Dutch food is dull. In larger cities – especially in Amsterdam – Holland's colonial past has left a fine tradition of Indonesian cooking. Most hotels have plentiful buffet breakfasts, including smoked meats, pickled herring and a variety of cheeses. For a traditional lunch try *erwtensoep*, a satisfying soup of peas and pork; or *uitsmijter*, an open sandwich of meat or ham with cheese, topped with a fried egg. For dinner have a *hutspot* stew of vegetables, smoked bacon and meat; or *stampott*, mashed potatoes and vegetables with smoked sausage or bacon. For more exotic experiences, eat Indonesian specialties, especially *rijsttafel* ("rice table"), or any of several dozen other spiced, sauced, tangy, exquisite dishes. For sweets try *pannekoek*, pancakes with *stroop* (molasses) or *poedersuiker* (powdered sugar). If you're on the move, street stalls also serve a smaller type of pancake, *poffertjes*.

As in Belgium, beer is the most popular drink. Dutch beers tend to be lighter, although you will know that you are drinking something substantial when you sample lager in a Dutch "brown café" – a traditional bar. An excellent light beer is Grölsch, often drunk with meals instead of wine. Heavier Belgian beers also are available, as is *jenever*, a grain spirit. *Oude jenever* is the sweetest; *jonge* is for the stronger palate. These and vintage gins and liqueurs can be enjoyed in a *proeflokaal*, or "tasting house."

Canal homes – Amsterdammers have traditionally lived on houseboats and barges

Porcelain and Jewelry

Some stores in Holland are closed on Sunday and Monday mornings, but many are open every day, and stores in the larger cities usually stay open late one night a week. Cities such as Amsterdam and The Hague have a variety of international clothing stores, but the real shopping experience is in antique and craft districts, looking for such specialties as jewelry and porcelain. In the provinces, search around and you will find some excellent regional buys.

Take a break in Amsterdam's largest and oldest municipal park, the Vondelpark

TIMELINE

AD 50	Iron Age Frisian and Batavi tribes settle in present-day Netherlands; they build settlements above the tide line on artificial mounds called *terpen*.
751	Charlemagne, the Holy Roman Emperor, rules the Low Countries, the lands alongside the North Sea.
12th century	Herring fishermen settle at the mouth of the Amstel river, later site of Amsterdam.
1519	Charles V of Spain is crowned Holy Roman Emperor; the Low Countries come under Spanish rule.
1566–67	Repression by Spain leads to lengthy struggle against Spanish control.
1579	Formation of Republic of the United Provinces of the Netherlands.
1602	Formation of Dutch East India Company; "Golden Age" of Amsterdam as a world trading center lasts for most of the 17th century.
1814	Northern and southern Netherlands become a united kingdom after fall of Napoleon.
1831	Southern Netherlands becomes independent Belgium.
1914–18	The Netherlands remains neutral during World War I.
1940	Germany invades the Netherlands; Amsterdam finally liberated in 1945.
1947	Formation of Benelux Trade Treaty between Belgium, the Netherlands and Luxembourg.
1957	The Netherlands signs up as a founding member of the European Community.
1992	The Netherlands signs the Maastricht Treaty, the key to the European Union.
2002	"Floriade," the world horticultural exhibition (every 10 years) takes place in Haalemmermeer, south of Haarlem (mid–April to mid-October).

TULIPS

Tulips are a universal symbol of the country. They also are part of the Dutch flower trade, which accounts for 70 percent of the world market in exported flowers. In the 17th century the importation of tulip bulbs from Turkey led to "tulip mania"; during the 1630s, single bulbs sold for thousands of dollars. The tulip has been a major focus of Dutch flower growing since, although carnations, roses and chrysanthemums outsell tulips today. The great floral experience is in late April, when the fields just inland from the east coast are vibrant with color. Visit the Keukenhof Gardens at Lisse, north of Leiden, for floral extravaganzas from late March to late May and from early August to mid-September.

SURVIVAL GUIDE

Great way to get around; there are over half a million bicycles in Amsterdam

- Large cities have regulated routes for pedestrians, cyclists, trams and automobiles. Next to the sidewalk there may be a bicycle lane. Always remember that bicycles approach silently, and always check to your left. Beyond the cycle lane you may find a second sidewalk, then a tram track, then the main thoroughfare for buses and automobiles. This sequence is the same on each side of the road. Remember that trams also approach quietly from the left.
- There are few public restrooms, and those that exist are not known for their cleanliness. Railroad and bus stations, restaurants and the bigger cafés have public bathrooms with attendants. You are expected to pay the equivalent of about 10 cents to use them.
- Eating out in the Netherlands is considered a fashion event as much as an eating experience. The Dutch tend to dress their best when going out for a meal, although attitudes are relaxing.
- You may tip for good restaurant service. Always tell the waiter or waitress that you're tipping them, and the amount; don't leave a cash tip on the table when you leave.
- You may be tempted to sample raw herring. Follow local custom: dip the herring in a bowl of diced onions, hold it by its tail, tip your head back, and savor.
- For tasty snacks, try the always-available *patat* (french fries) with mayonnaise or spicy sauce dips; *kroketten*, small rolls of meat filling covered in bread crumbs and fried; and do not forget pickled herring or smoked eel. *Broodjes*, like their Belgian counterparts, are baguettes filled with smoked sausage, spicy meat and cheeses.
- If you buy a present in a shop, especially chocolates, tell the assistant and it will be carefully wrapped in gift paper.
- If you buy Delftware porcelain, make sure the trade name has a D, and buy from reputable outlets.

Not always the traditional blue and white, Delft pottery comes in a variety of styles and colors

Amsterdam

AMSTERDAM

Amsterdam is a city whose dramatic past, generous people, remarkable canals, cobbled streets and decorative buildings have made it into one of the most exciting and seductive capitals in western Europe.

The city, like much of Holland, has triumphed over water. It began life in the 13th century, when fishermen built a dam across the mouth of the Amstel river and settled nearby in rough wooden houses. By the end of the 17th century the city was the leading commercial port of the post-medieval world, its success based on canals and land reclamation.

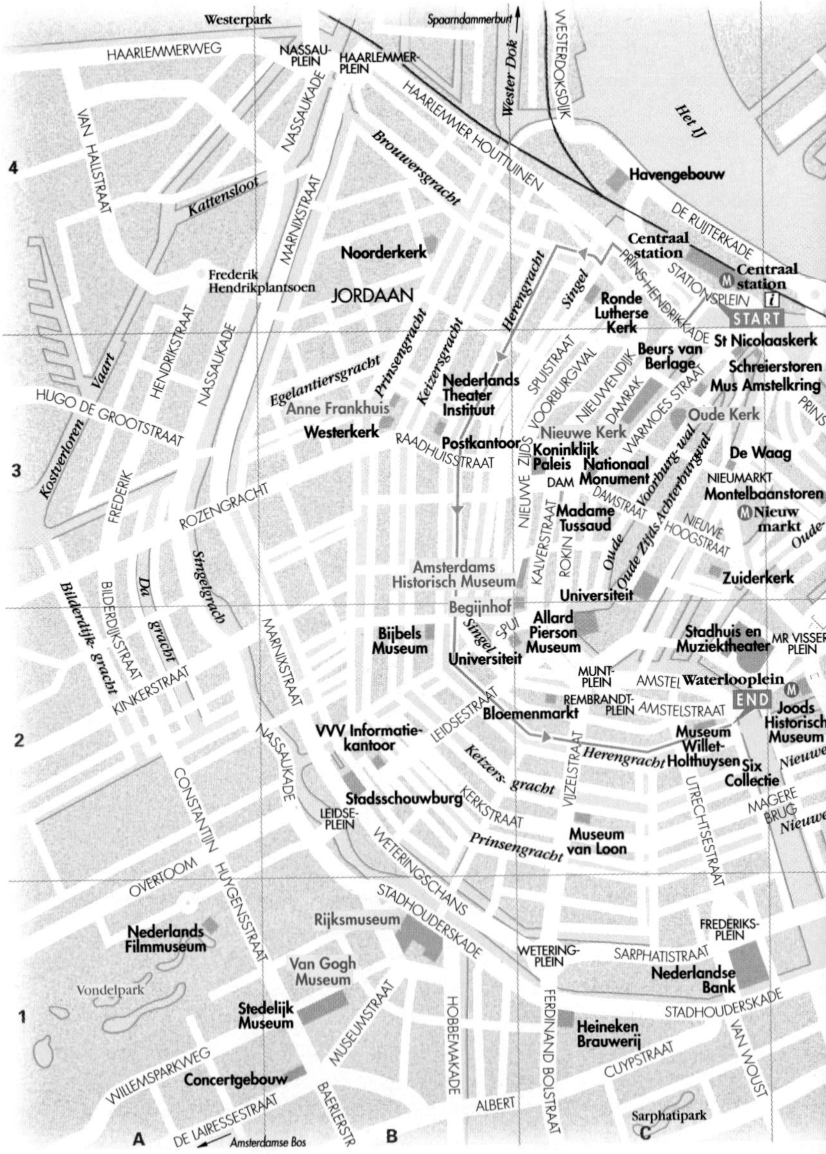

For most of the 18th century Amsterdam prospered – until its ships lost command of the seas to England. The city became the capital of the Netherlands in 1813. During World War II, Amsterdam was occupied by the Germans. Its position over the past 50-odd years has been one of consolidation, urban maturity and social liberalism – influences that have produced the vigorous and tolerant city of today.

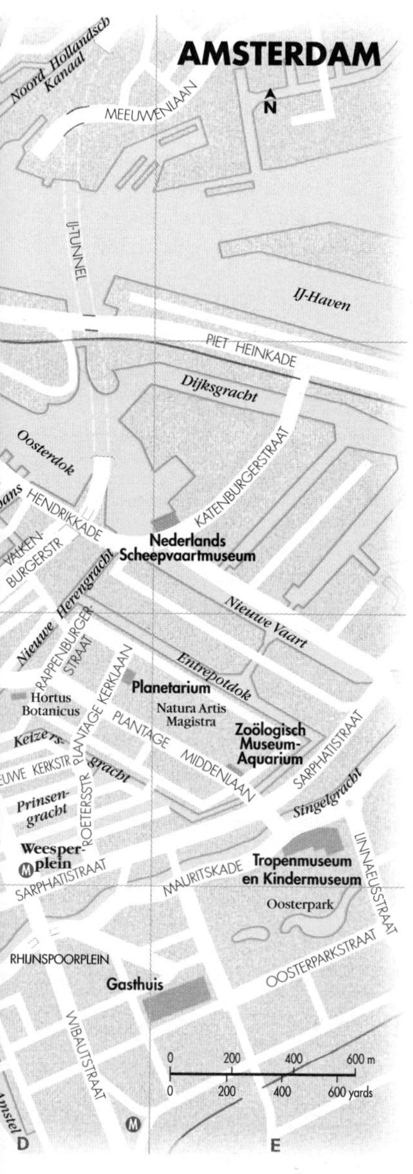

First Impressions

Most visitors arrive by train at Amsterdam's Centraal Station, a smoothly run modern complex within a handsome 1880s neoclassical building. A helpful tourist information office is on platform (*spoor*) 2; the main tourist office (see page 344) is just outside the railroad station. Immediately in front of the station is the busy Stationsplein, a mix of tram line, bus track, bicycle lane and pedestrian concourse with street entertainers and crowds of people. Straight ahead lies the Damrak thoroughfare; watch out for traffic here, and always wait patiently for the green light at pedestrian crossings.

A Cultural and Liberal City

Amsterdam's liberal traditions are apparent in the notorious Red Light District (Walletjes), located mainly between Warmoesstraat and Oudezijds Achterburgwal. Be advised – do not take photographs of prostitutes' booths. As in any crowded location, be on the lookout for pickpockets.

Amsterdam also is notorious for its "coffee shops," where hashish and marijuana sold for personal use is tolerated by the authorities. *Eetcafes* and cafés, on the other hand, are conventional places where coffee is served. "Brown cafés" are traditional bars where liquor is sold.

All this alternative culture is a minor aspect of the larger Amsterdam, a sophisticated city and a working community. There are peaceful canals and tree-shaded, cobbled streets lined with narrow gabled houses. It's a flower-filled city of exhilarating art museums, glorious civic buildings, medieval churches, quality stores, superb restaurants and an entertaining street life.

Getting to Know Amsterdam

Try a 50-minute round-trip ride on the famous Circle Tram 20, which leaves every 12 minutes in both directions (daily 9–7) from in front of Centraal Station. For a taste of the city's canal culture, take a cruise on one of the sleek, efficient tour boats; you can even enjoy a candlelit wine and cheese cruise. Walking tours show you the city's architecture, history, art and special neighborhoods.

Amsterdam also is a rewarding city to explore by foot on your own. Step away from the city center and discover the serenity of canal-side walks. Enjoy street theater in Leidseplein, or visit the Stoeltie Diamond works in Wagenstraat, near the neon-lit square of Rembrandtplein. The major shopping street of Kalverstraat leads to the busy open space of Spui, or try wandering down to the Bloemenmarkt (Flower Market) along the Singel canal.

Supporting the City

Amsterdam is built on hundreds of thousands of pilings that have been driven through the surface layers of soft peat to rest soundly on hard sand. The 17th-century Royal Palace (Koninklijk Paleis, see page 346) on the Dam rests on 13,659 wooden pilings. Concrete pilings sunk to 65 feet have replaced the original ones.

ESSENTIAL INFORMATION

TOURIST INFORMATION

Tourist information centers are known as **VVV (Vereniging Voor Vreemdelingenverkeer)**

- Amsterdam Tourist Board, Box 3901, 1001 AS Amsterdam, The Netherlands ☎ 0900 400 4040 (toll call); fax 020 625 2869; www.visitamsterdam.nl
- VVV Centraal Station, spoor (platform) 2
- VVV Stationsplein 10 (opposite Centraal Station entrance)
- VVV Leidseplein 1, corner of Leidsestraat
- VVV Argonautenstraat 98, corner of Stadionplein
- Holland Tourist Information (HTI), Amsterdam Airport Schiphol (arrival hall 2)

URBAN TRANSPORTATION

Trains run from Centraal Station (central railroad station), Stationsplein. The city transportation authority is Gemeentevervoerbedrijf Amsterdam (GVB). For information and tickets there is a GVB office opposite Centraal Station; open Mon.–Fri. 7 a.m.–9 p.m., Sat.–Sun. 8 a.m.–9 p.m. Amsterdam's subway (metro) mainly serves suburban areas and is not of great use to visitors. Subway stations are marked with an "M" on the city map. There is a station and information desk at Centraal Station. For information on all public transportation call ☎ 0900 9292 (toll call). Taxis are expensive, but can be picked up at the stands at Amsterdam Airport Schiphol, Centraal Station, Dam and Leidseplein. You also can call Taxicentrale (☎ 020 677 7777, 24-hour service).

AIRPORT INFORMATION

Amsterdam Airport Schiphol, 11 miles southwest of the city, is one of the most modern facilities in Europe. Fast, efficient trains run from a station just south of the airport complex to Amsterdam's Centraal Station; the journey takes 20 minutes. They depart every 15 minutes daily 6 a.m.–midnight, on the hour midnight–6 a.m. Buses run regularly to Amsterdam and leave from Schiphol Plaza in front of the airport. There are post offices, banks, numerous shops and a Holland Tourist Information office in arrival hall 2, and there is a restaurant and hotel in the airport complex. For airport information call ☎ 020 601 2182.

CLIMATE – average highs and lows for the month

JAN.	FEB.	MAR.	APR.	MAY	JUN.	JUL.	AUG.	SEP.	OCT.	NOV.	DEC.
5°C	5°C	9°C	11°C	15°C	18°C	20°C	21°C	18°C	13°C	9°C	7°C
41°F	41°F	48°F	52°F	59°F	64°F	68°F	70°F	64°F	55°F	48°F	45°F
1°C	0°C	3°C	5°C	8°C	11°C	13°C	13°C	10°C	8°C	4°C	2°C
34°F	32°F	37°F	41°F	46°F	52°F	55°F	55°F	50°F	46°F	39°F	36°F

City Sights

Key to symbols

map coordinates refer to the Amsterdam map on pages 342–343; sights below are highlighted in yellow on the map.
address or location telephone number
opening times nearest tram route
Museum Boat stop restaurant or café on site or nearby admission charge: $$$ more than 10f, $$ 5f–10f, $ less than 5f other relevant information

Amsterdams Historisch Museum

C3 Kalverstraat 92/Nieuwezijds Voorburgwal 359 020 523 1822 Mon.–Fri. 10–5, Sat.–Sun. 11–5 Museum café Tram 1, 2, 5 $$

Amsterdam's story is well told in the enjoyable Amsterdams Historisch Museum (Amsterdam Museum of History), in the heart of the city. Once a monastery, and then a city orphanage for four centuries, the museum is now an elegant complex of bright and airy rooms. (Watch for awkward steps in some of them.) Highlights include a superb model of a Dutch East India sailing ship and the silver drinking horn of the medieval Guild of St. George. To the right of the entrance is the glass doorway into Schuttersgalerij. This was once an open street and is now the Civic Guard Gallery, with splendid group portraits of 17th-century city militiamen.

Anne Frankhuis

B3 Prinsengracht 263 020 556 7100 Daily 9–9, Apr.–Aug.; 9–7, rest of year. Closed Yom Kippur Tram 13, 14, 17, 20 Museum Boat stop $$$

No matter how often you have heard the Anne Frank story, a visit to Het Achterhuis, "The Secret Annexe," is unforgettable. Here, in the Anne Frankhuis (Anne Frank House), the Frank family and their friends lived secretly in Nazi-occupied Amsterdam until their arrest only months before the Liberation. The only one to survive the concentration camps was Anne's father, Otto. The lively, passionate diary kept by Anne during her years in hiding was later published to worldwide acclaim. The museum has absorbing displays and multimedia installations, but the secret annex is the haunting heart of it all. The stark emptiness intensifies the experience, and the atmospheric rooms throng with ghosts. From every corner Anne Frank bears witness on behalf of millions of Nazi victims. After your visit, a quiet walk through the peaceful, reflective Jordaan district, just across the canal, is recommended.

Visitors pay homage at Anne Frank House, preserved exactly as it was in 1944

Begijnhof

C2–C3 Gedempte Begijnsloot Daily dawn–dusk Tram 1, 2, 5 Free

Amsterdam's secluded Begijnhof (Courtyard of the Beguines) is an outstanding example of a medieval almshouse community. It was built in the 14th century to accommodate Beguines, pious single women of the Catholic faith, who lived a religious and charitable life without the stricture of holy vows. The Beguines were later ostracized because of their faith, and today the discreet facade of the Begijnhof's once clandestine Catholic church masks a

Tomb of Admiral du Ruyter, Holland's most valiant naval hero, honored in the Gothic New Church

haunting little Italianate chapel. Opposite stands the original church that was transferred to the city's Protestant community in the late 16th century. In the south corner of the Begijnhof is the 15th-century Houten Huys, one of Amsterdam's oldest houses, wooden-fronted and steeply gabled. Today's Begijnhof still accommodates single women of modest means.

NIEUWE KERK

C3 Dam Kerk: 020 638 6909. Paleis: 020 620 4060 (020 624 8698 for guided tours) Kerk: daily 10–6 (also Thu. 6–10 p.m.); hours may vary depending on the event. Paleis: daily 11–5, Jun.–Aug.; usually Tue.–Thu. and Sat.–Sun. 12:30–5, rest of year (subject to official functions) Tram 4, 9, 14, 16, 24, 25 Kerk $$$, Paleis $$

The 17th-century Nieuwe Kerk (New Church) was new only in its original form, as compared with the more venerable Oude Kerk (Old Church). The New Church is a fine counterpoint to Dam square's Koninklijk Paleis (Royal Palace), with its beautifully decorated rooms. Today the church is used for major art exhibitions. There are a dozen or so side chapels and a magnificent vaulted roof. The church's baroque pulpit and its splendid organ are permanent highlights. Dutch monarchs have been crowned here, including the present Queen Beatrix.

OUDE KERK

C3 Oudekerksplein 23 020 625 8284 Mon.–Sat. 11–5, Sun. 1–5, late Mar.–Nov. 30; daily 1–5, rest of year Tram 4, 9, 16, 20, 24, 25 $$ Art exhibitions and music recitals at various times

The Oude Kerk (Old Church) is the oldest building in Amsterdam. It has been much restored, but retains an authentic medieval atmosphere. The church stands on the banks of the Oudezijds Voorburgwal canal in the heart of the Red Light District. Its glorious stained-glass windows, featuring Lambert van Noorts' *Annunciation* and *The Visit of Mary to Elizabeth*, look down on prostitutes' booths in the narrow Enge Kerk Straat, much as they might have done in medieval times. A triple nave and high-vaulted roof give added spaciousness to the dramatically bare interior of the Old Church. A poignant feature is the gravestone of Rembrandt's wife Saskia van Uylenburg, set among slabs below the choir organ.

RIJKSMUSEUM

B1 Stadhouderskade 42 020 674 7047 Daily 10–5 Museum café/restaurant Tram 2, 5, 6, 7, 10, 20 Museum Boat stop $$$ Audio tour available

The Rijksmuseum (National Museum) contains some of the world's greatest works of Dutch art. The building dates from 1885 and was designed by Pierre Cuypers.

Its elegant neo-Gothic facade is something of a mirror image to Cuypers' Centraal Station.

Start on the second floor with rooms 201–206, which display Dutch works from the 15th and 16th centuries. There are dozens of superb paintings and numerous highlights, such as Frans Hals' supremely cheerful marriage portrait of *Isaac Abrahamsz Massa and Beatrix Van der Laen* and Johannes Vermeer's *The Kitchen Maid*, a masterpiece of complementary colors. The sequence ends with the Gallery of Honour, displaying Rembrandt's *The Night Watch* or, under its original title, *The Company of Captain Franz Baning Cocq and Lieutenant Willem van Ruytenburch.* Other sections of the Rijksmuseum have dazzling displays of sculpture, Delftware, Meissen porcelain and historic artifacts.

Entrance to the Rijksmuseum, Amsterdam's national collection

Van Gogh Museum

B1 · Paulus Potterstraat 7 · 020 570 5200 · Daily 10–6 · Museum café/restaurant · Tram 2, 5, 20 · Museum Boat stop · $$$

To view the finest and largest collection of Vincent van Gogh's paintings, visit the Van Gogh Museum, where the artist's works (200 paintings and nearly 500 drawings) chart his intense and ultimately tragic life. The collection takes you through his early period, when he was a missionary in the Dutch coal fields; pieces include such dark social commentary as *The Potato Eaters*. His later Parisian work reflects the influence of the Impressionists, but it is the paintings inspired by his life at Arles, in sunny Provence (France), that exhilarate with their fiery yellows and oranges. The most famous works are the iconic *Sunflowers* series. Conversely, *The Garden of St. Paul's Hospital,* painted at St.-Rémy mental asylum the year before van Gogh's death, is a heartrending evocation of a dejected figure. The trees are as rigid as the bars of a cell. But the sum of the Van Gogh Museum, the painter's legacy of outstanding work, is wholly positive and uplifting. There are other works by such contemporaries of Van Gogh as Tolouse-Lautrec, Gauguin and Redon. The adjacent Stedelijk Museum is one of the finest and most exuberant collections of modern art in the world.

Vondelpark

A1 · Stadhouderskade · Daily dawn–dusk · Ronde Blauwe Theehuis ("The Round Blue Teahouse," by the lake) · Tram 1, 2, 3, 5, 6, 12 · Museum Boat stop · Excellent open-air theater and concerts during summer

The Vondelpark, Amsterdam's principal park, is named after 17th-century playwright Joost van den Vondel. The park starts modestly enough as a green avenue that leads southwest from a busy corner on Stadhouderskade, a short distance south of Leidseplein. Soon it opens invitingly into a broad green space peppered with trees and interspersed with ornamental lakes and linked waterways. There are children's playgrounds, a sweetly scented rose garden, teahouses, a bandstand and the Nederlands Filmmuseum (Netherlands Film Museum). During the summer, music, theater and entertainment in the sun enliven the park even more.

Amsterdam's Canals

Flower stalls are an essential part of the Amsterdam scene

So many northern European capitals claim the title "Venice of the North" that the epithet has become devalued. Some say there is no substitute for the real thing, but perhaps Amsterdam has the strongest claim to the title. The city lacks the romantic splendor of Venice, but there is a cool, restrained beauty about Amsterdam's canals (*grachten*) and their attendant buildings.

The finest canals are west of the city center, beyond the bustling main streets of Damrak and Nieuwezijds Voorburgwal, both of which were canals at one time. A stroll along narrow side streets from Nieuwezijds Voorburgwal and across the busy Spuistraat brings you suddenly to the great waterways of Singel, Herengracht, Keizersgracht and Prinsengracht.

Herengracht

Herengracht is the finest canal of the *grachtengordel*, the ring or girdle of canals that were built in the early 17th century to defend the city. The name Herengracht translates into English as the "Gentlemen's Canal," a sign of contemporary male ascendancy. This was the district where the wealthiest Amsterdam merchant families built themselves handsome canal-side mansions notable for their superb ornate gables. The houses were designed to be tall and narrow because of limited space.

Take a stroll down Herengracht to appreciate it all. You can start from the canal's northern end at its junction with Brouwersgracht. The Brouwersgracht is the short stretch of canal that links Herengracht to the Singel canal at the Haarlemmer Sluis, one of the 40 or so sluices that are opened each night to flush clean water through the canal system. Haarlemmer Sluis can be reached from Centraal Station by walking northwest along Prins Hendrikkade for about 300 yards and then turning left. Cross the wide sluice bridge. (There is a superb cheese shop on the opposite corner.) Go left, then turn right along Brouwersgracht to reach the tree-shaded bridges at the junction with Herengracht.

Walk south for a mile of scenic history to where the Herengracht meets the Amstel river. You can stroll down either side of the great canal and cross over bridges to get the best views of canal-side houses. Visit the Theater Museum and garden at Herengracht 168, and the exquisite Bartolotti House next door. The latter is a 17th-century Renaissance mansion built by the head of the Bartolotti Bank. Enjoy the *Golden Bocht*, which translates as

Houseboats and barges line the picturesque Prinsengracht, in Amsterdam's Jordaan district

"Golden Bay" or "Bend," between Leidsestraat and Vijzelstraat – note the decorative double-fronted houses along the elegant curve of the canal.

The curve is an engaging motif amid Amsterdam's general flatness – in the decorativeness of house gables, the elegant bridges, the sweep of railings, even in the curved handlebars of the wonderful old upright bicycles still favored by Amsterdammers. There are said to be 600,000 bicycles in the city, and it seems that everybody cycles in Amsterdam. Elderly *dames* and *heren* (ladies and gentlemen) cruise past to the tinkling of bells like songbirds. Stylishly dressed young people skim along with their backs straight and a wary eye on the tourist's uncertain bid to run across the street in front of them.

Connections

Explore the Prinsengracht and the Keizersgracht, as well as the main canals, and don't neglect the connecting waterways. There's the Leidsegracht on the Golden Bend, or the peaceful, leafy Egelantiersgracht near the Anne Frank House (Anne Frankhuis, see page 345) that takes you into the quiet heart of the Jordaan district. Sidestep into enchanting streets between Herengracht and Singel canals, such as Gasthuismolen Steeg or Oude Spiegelstraat, where craft and antique shops and boutiques rub shoulders with delightful little cafés and restaurants. And try a nighttime walk along the great canals, when many of the finest houses are floodlit and the numerous bridges twinkle with lights.

In summer the canals become venues for concerts by the water, rowing regattas, Chinese dragon boat races and various other events. Amsterdam is many things to many people, but the city's fascinating network of canals will always be the enduring motif of this very special city. For the walking route, see the city map on pages 342–343.

The Hague

The Hague (Den Haag), third-largest city in the Netherlands, is justly proud of its status as the political and royal capital of the country and as a focus of international affairs. It lacks the fast pace and excitement of Amsterdam, yet a sense of well-being and security underpins the rich cultural and political heritage.

The city's name derives from *Gravenhage,* which means "the Count's hedge." In the 13th century the Count of Holland built a hunting lodge among sand dunes – this is where The Hague's historic center, the Binnenhof ("inner court") now stands. The settlement that developed around the lodge was the Count's "hedge" sheltering him against the outside world.

In the 16th century the States General of the United Netherlands met at The Hague, and since then the city has been the seat of Dutch government. The Hague Convention of 1907, which formulated laws governing warfare worldwide, gave this city international status. The 1913 opening of the Peace

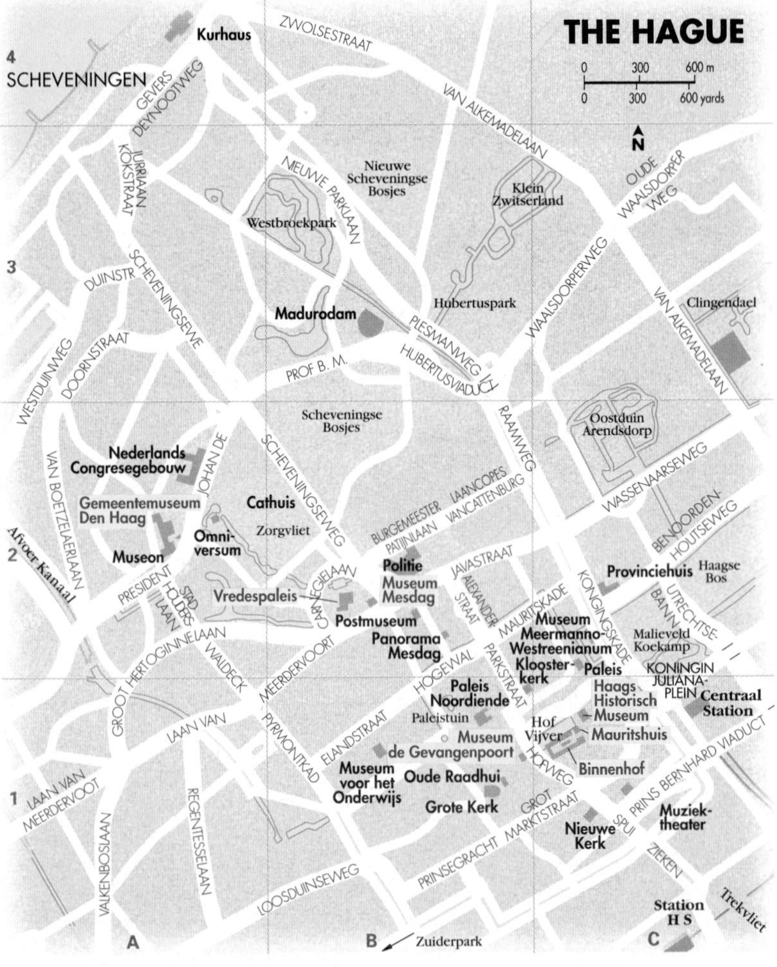

Palace (Vredespaleis, see page 354) further enhanced The Hague's standing, and it is today considered a center of international diplomacy and business. The Permanent Court of Arbitration and the International Court of Justice are located at the Peace Palace; numerous embassies, ministries and headquarters of international organizations also are based here. In 1980, after the Dutch queen, Juliana, abdicated in favor of her daughter Beatrix, the royal residency was relocated from Utrecht to The Hague, adding even more luster to this small but fascinating city.

Arrival

The Hague's main railroad station, Den Haag Centraal Station, is plain but functional. Local tram and bus stations stand next to it, and the helpful tourist information center is located at the front of the Babylon shopping center, by the railroad station's main entrance. From here you can see the skyline of modern buildings that lies between the station and the city itself. A short walk southwest leads to the sedate, elegant heart of The Hague, where the Binnenhof and several fine museums cluster around a graceful little lake, Hofvijver.

Guided city tours are offered during the summer. A Royal Tour by bus (May to August only) takes in the main sights, including the seaside resort of Scheveningen and outside views of three royal palaces (none are open to the public). Tours can be booked through the tourist information center.

On Your Own

Exploring The Hague on your own can be a very rewarding experience. The oldest section centers on the Hofvijver, the "Court Pond." On its south side the Hofvijver laps against the walls of the Binnenhof and the Mauritshuis (see page 354), which houses The Hague's outstanding art collection. Its northern side is lined with trees and is backed by the elegant 18th-century street Lange Vijverberg.

From the Hofvijver you can stroll north beneath the lime trees on the wide avenue Lange Voorhout. A colorful antiques market is held here on Thursdays and Sundays from May through September. Continue past the grand facade of the Des Indes Inter Continental Hotel to reach Denneweg, a charming street with a Parisian flavor and a host of interesting antique and craft galleries, delicatessens, restaurants, cafés and distinctive fashion boutiques.

Quickening Pace

West of the Hofvijver and the Binnenhof lies the bustling open area of the Buitenhof, where the pace

Gate at the Binnenhof – the complex where The Hague had its beginnings

quickens to that of a busy city. Beyond the Buitenhof is The Hague's commercial and shopping district and the pedestrian-only streets that lead to the Kerk Plein (Church Square) and the imposing, hexagonal-towered church, the Grote Kerk.

North of the church is the Hofkwartier, one of the oldest areas of The Hague. There are many specialty shops, small restaurants and cafés here. Be sure to stroll along the Palace Promenade (Hoogstraat) and on into Noordeinde, one of The Hague's most attractive streets. Here you will find a marvelous selection of art galleries, antiques, craft shops and fashion boutiques, restaurants and the Royal Palace (Paleis Noordeinde).

A good way to enjoy this fine city is to keep a relaxed pace. Fill your day with activities involving the arts and history; eat well in any of the excellent restaurants and cafés; and seek out the numerous musical and cultural events that take place in the summer.

A short journey on tram 1, 8 or 9 will take you to the coast and the popular resort of Scheveningen. You can break the journey halfway at the miniature "town" of Madurodam, a favorite with children. In addition to Scheveningen's superb beach and promenade, the numerous attractions include the Holland Casino, the Sea Museum and a pier. (Proper pronunciation of the name Scheveningen is the sign of a true local; try "Shravin-eeng-e" and you might get by.)

Hooigracht canal

Several ring canals were built around The Hague during the 17th century. Although many of them have been filled in, you can walk east from Denneweg to reach the serene little stretch of surviving canal, the Hooigracht, its leafy banks lined with elegant and attractive old buildings.

ESSENTIAL INFORMATION

TOURIST INFORMATION

Tourist information centers are known as **VVV (Vereniging Voor Vreemdelingenverkeer)**

- VVV, Koningin Julianaplein 30, Babylon shopping center ☎ 0900 340 3505 (toll call); fax 070 361 7915
- VVV, Gevers Deynootweg 1134, Palace Promenade shopping center, Scheveningen ☎ 0900 340 3505 (toll call); www.denhaag.com

URBAN TRANSPORTATION

Den Haag Centraal Station (The Hague's central railroad station) is on Koningin Julianaplein. Service to and from Amsterdam is at 15-minute intervals; travel time between Amsterdam and The Hague is about 45 minutes. For information and tickets for buses and trams inquire at the tourist information office or call ☎ 0900 9292 (toll call). Taxi stands are at the central railroad station and at the Buitenhof. To call a taxi, try ATC Taxi ☎ 070 317 8877, HCT City Taxi ☎ 070 383 0830 or HTMC ☎ 070 390 7722.

AIRPORT INFORMATION

Amsterdam Airport Schiphol (see page 344) serves The Hague. Trains for The Hague leave the airport at regular intervals, and travel to Den Haag Centraal Station in about 40 minutes. Trains from Schiphol and Amsterdam stop first at Den Haag Station Hollands Spoor, south of the city center. If you are going to the city center, stay on the train until Centraal Station.

CLIMATE – average highs and lows for the month

JAN.	FEB.	MAR.	APR.	MAY	JUN.	JUL.	AUG.	SEP.	OCT.	NOV.	DEC.
5°C	5°C	9°C	11°C	15°C	18°C	20°C	21°C	18°C	14°C	9°C	7°C
41°F	41°F	48°F	52°F	59°F	64°F	68°F	70°F	64°F	57°F	48°F	45°F
1°C	0°C	3°C	5°C	8°C	12°C	14°C	13°C	11°C	9°C	4°C	3°C
34°F	32°F	37°F	41°F	46°F	54°F	57°F	55°F	52°F	48°F	39°F	37°F

The picturesque Hofvijver, lined with an impressive ensemble of public buildings

CITY SIGHTS

Key to symbols

map coordinates refer to The Hague map on page 350; sights below are highlighted in yellow on the map. address or location telephone number opening times nearest bus or tram route restaurant or café on site or nearby admission charge: $$$ more than 10f, $$ 5f–10f, $ less than 5f other relevant information

BINNENHOF

C1 8a Binnenhof 070 364 6144 Mon.–Sat. 10–4; closed holidays and 2 days in mid- to late Sep. for the opening of parliament 4, 5, 22; tram 1, 2, 3, 6, 7, 8, 9, 16, 17 $$ (Parliament Exhibition free) Last tour at 3:45. Advance reservations recommended. May be closed to the public on other occasions

The Binnenhof (Inner Court) of the original lodge of the Counts of Holland is the oldest part of The Hague. The turreted Knight's Hall, where medieval guests were received and entertained, stands at the heart of a central square; behind it is the parliament building. The complex retains a timeless atmosphere; the main room of the Knight's Hall is the Ridderzaal, an impressive grand hall, restored in 1900 to its medieval glory, and full of coats of arms, Dutch provincial flags, stained glass and artifacts. Ceremonies, including *Prinsjesdag*, the day of the Queen's speech to the Dutch parliament, are held here. There are guided tours of the Ridderzaal and the two chambers of parliament when they are not in use. The entrance to the ticket office is on the right side of the Knight's Hall.

GEMEENTEMUSEUM DEN HAAG

A2 41 Stadhouderslaan 070 338 1111 Tue.–Sun. 11–5 Museum café 4, 14; tram 7, 10, 11 $$$

Renovations completed in 1998 have added to the attractions of the Gemeentemuseum Den Haag (The Hague Municipal Museum), which is located just northwest of the city center. The museum has outstanding collections of musical instruments and ceramics, including delftware and The Hague silverware. The modern art collection includes works by Vincent van Gogh and Claude Monet, and there is a large collection of paintings by Piet Mondrian. A recent addition is a fashion gallery featuring temporary exhibitions of Dutch and international fashion.

HAAGS HISTORISCH MUSEUM

C1 7 Korte Vijverberg 070 364 6940 Tue.–Fri. 11–5, Sat.–Sun. noon–5 4, 5, 18, 22; tram 1, 7, 8, 9, 12 $$

Haags Historisch Museum (Historical Museum of The Hague) is very much a Dutch institution; there are no English translations to supplement the almost exclusively Dutch labeling of the paintings. A visit is nonetheless rewarding, especially to see such big paintings as Jan van Goyen's *View of The Hague*. In the attic there is a permanent exhibition illustrating the history of The Hague; look for the explanatory panels that are translated in English.

The Peace Palace – seat of the International Court of Justice

MAURITSHUIS

C1 8 Korte Vijverberg 070 302 3456 Tue.–Sat. 10–5, Sun. and holidays 11–5 4, 5, 18, 22; tram 1, 7, 8, 9, 12 $$$

The original Mauritshuis (Maurit's House) was built as a private home in the 17th century by Johan Maurits van Nassau-Siegen and was reconstructed after a disastrous fire in 1704. Today it contains an outstanding collection of Dutch art. Highlights include Johannes Vermeer's *Girl with a Pearl Earring* and the crowning glory, Rembrandt's famous *The Anatomy Lesson of Doctor Nicolaes Tulp*. Don't miss Andy Warhol's charming portrait of Queen Beatrix in the cloakroom area.

MUSEUM DE GEVANGENPOORT

B1 33 Buitenhof 070 346 0861 Tue.–Fri. 11–5, Sat.–Sun. noon–5 4, 5, 22; tram 1, 2, 3, 6, 7, 8, 9, 16, 17 $$ Tours on the hour (last tour at 4), extra tours Jul.–Aug.

A guided tour of the Museum de Gevangenpoort (Prison Gate Museum) is great fun, but is not for the fainthearted. The Prison Gate Museum was The Hague's notorious prison for hundreds of years. Wood-paneled cells, interrogation rooms and a debtors' chamber give a vivid and gruesome picture of medieval justice. The tour commentary is mostly in Dutch, but information sheets in other languages are available and the guide will answer questions in English. The final visit to the torture room in the basement should finish you off nicely. The Dutch treat the whole thing with a commendable black humor. Be sure to bring yours along with you.

MUSEUM MESDAG

B2 7f Laan van Meerdervoort 070 362 1434 Tue.–Sun. noon–5 4, 5, 13, 22; tram 7, 8 $$

Hendrik Willem Mesdag was a leading figure in the art world of The Hague during the 19th century. Famous for his *Panorama Mesdag* (a cylinder-shaped painting of nearby coastal resort Scheveningen in 1881), Mesdag was himself a painter and an avid collector of works, especially of the Barbizon School of French painters, including Jean François Millet, Gustave Courbet and Jozef Israëls, whose works – along with Mesdag's – grace the salons of the museum. Mesdag built the museum as an annex to his house, and the carpets and artifacts are all original.

VREDESPALEIS

B2 2 Carnegieplein 070 302 4137 Mon.–Fri. 10–4, Apr.–Sep.; 10–3, rest of year 4, 13; tram 7, 8 $$ Tours at 10, 11, 2, 3 and 4. Tour times are subject to change. Inquiries and reservations can be made at the tourist information office

The Vredespaleis (Peace Palace) is an awe-inspiring building symbolizing the power of statehood. Scottish philanthropist Andrew Carnegie, who made his fortune in America, paid for its Gothic splendor in the early years of the 20th century. Its exquisite furnishings and artifacts were donated by the nations of the world. A guided tour of the building includes a visit to the International Court of Justice and is conducted in several languages, including English. Due to security control, you must wait in the open at the palace gates for the hourly tour to begin. Peace and justice are worth the wait, but choose a dry day.

DELFT

Fine ceramics and architecture are the main features of Delft. The ceramics have been exported worldwide, but Delft's buildings remain much as they were when immortalized on canvas by Johannes Vermeer, a native of the town.

There are organized coach trips to Delft from The Hague, and seats can be reserved through the tourist information office at the Babylon shopping center. The town is only 20 minutes from The Hague via tram 1, and takes even less time by train. Tram and train both land you on a two-lane highway, but a few steps along cobbled lanes transport you into a delightful medieval world enclosed by Delft's tranquil canals. It's centered on an imposing main square, the Markt, where there is a tourist information office as well as numerous stores, cafés and restaurants.

Delft is a popular tourist destination, and in summer the Markt can be especially crowded. Explore farther afield; follow the canal-side street of Oosteinde from behind the New Church (Nieuwe Kerk) to reach the medieval city gate of Oostport. Visit the Old Church (Oude Kerk) west of the Markt, at the head of the lovely street of Oude Delft. The Old Church is a splendid Gothic building full of interest and charm. View it from the Peperstraat Bridge, three bridges to the south on Oude Delft, to fully appreciate its remarkable leaning tower. Close to the Old Church is the Prinsenhof Museum, with a fine collection of paintings. Stop for coffee and crêpes at Stads Pannekoeckhuys, Oude Delft 113–115.

Many stores on the Markt sell Delft china. The Huis Lambert van Meerten Museum at Oude Delft 199 has a superb collection of Delft earthenware and tiles from around the world. The Koninklijke Porceleyne Fles, a factory involved in producing delftware since the 17th century, is located a short distance out of town on Rotterdamsweg 196 and offers guided tours.

Take a break from a spring shopping expedition and relax with coffee by one of Delft's canals

NORWAY

"NOVEMBER always seemed to me the Norway of the year."

American poet Emily Dickenson, from a letter to friends, 1864

Opposite: Clean air, clear water and majestic mountains at Sognefjord, in Norway's dramatic fjord region

NORWAY

Norway is the edge of Europe's most northerly land mass, where sea and mountains have merged to produce one of the world's most breathtaking landscapes. This is a country whose ancient peoples, the Vikings, helped shape the history of northern Europe. The Vikings once controlled half of Britain, and sent mariners as far west as Newfoundland and as far south as the Straits of Gibraltar.

It is this vigorous and resourceful national character, reflected in Viking tradition, that still exemplifies modern Norway. This is a nation that has mastered an inhospitable landscape without despoiling it, even becoming a leading oil producer in the hostile environment of the North Sea.

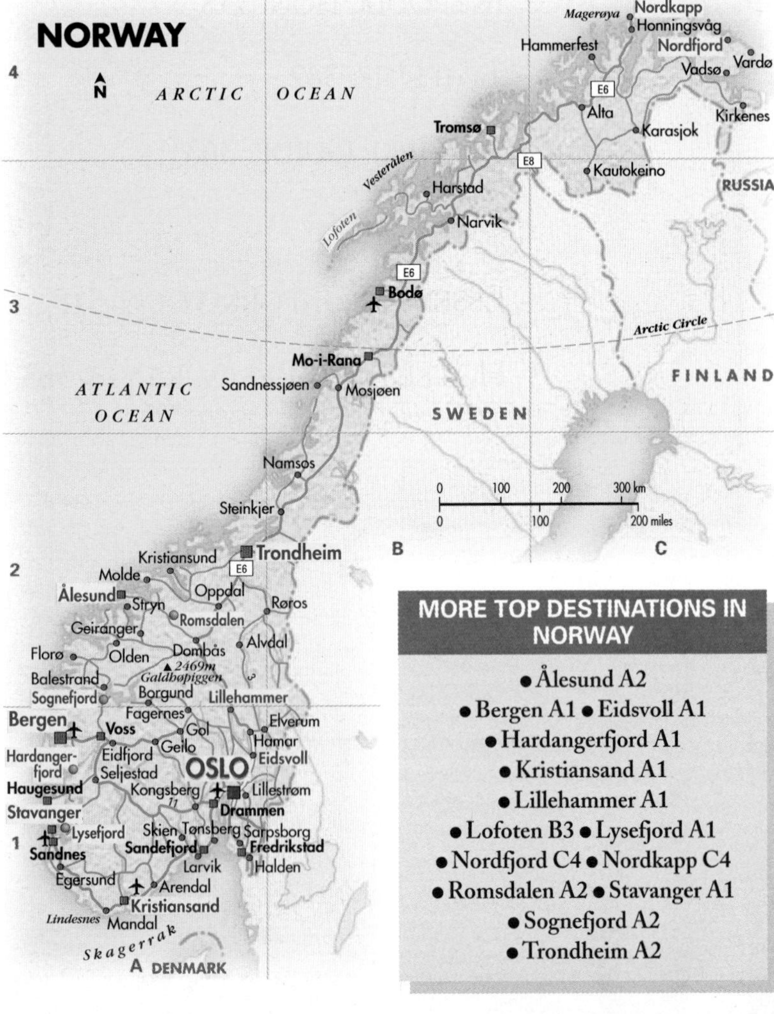

MORE TOP DESTINATIONS IN NORWAY

- Ålesund A2
- Bergen A1 • Eidsvoll A1
- Hardangerfjord A1
- Kristiansand A1
- Lillehammer A1
- Lofoten B3 • Lysefjord A1
- Nordfjord C4 • Nordkapp C4
- Romsdalen A2 • Stavanger A1
- Sognefjord A2
- Trondheim A2

Landscape

Norway's landscape is dominated by intervening seas – the Barents Sea to the north, the Norwegian Sea to the west and the North Sea to the southwest. All three are vast and often stormy. The corrugated coastline measures nearly 13,600 miles, including fjords and the country's 150,000 offshore islands. This scattered mosaic of islands – the "Skerry Guard" – is Norway's natural sea defense. The islands break the onslaught of the ocean, creating the country's sheltered seaways to north and south and protecting the gateways to the fjords.

Norway is shaped like a Viking club, narrowing in the north and with a broad base in the south. The country's mountain system runs from northeast to southwest and reaches its greatest height at Galdhøppigen, at 8,100 feet. The mountains separate the rugged western seaboard, the Vestlandet, from the gentler eastern region, the Øslandet.

The broad southwestern half of the country is known as Sørlandet, the South Country. Here, on the coastal fringe and around Oslo, is lowland Norway, where the sheltered coast is a favorite vacation destination for Norwegian families – a landscape of mellow woods and fields and tranquil blue waters. On the southern tip of Sørlandet is the sunny town of Kristiansand, with its flock of offshore islands. Southwest along the coast is Mandal, where attractive beaches catch the best of the summer sun; nearby is the promontory of Lindesnes, whose lighthouse marks Norway's southernmost point.

Then the coast turns to the northwest, twisting through a rugged landscape of rocky headlands and deeply indented fjords, past the pleasant town of Egersund and finally through rich farming country to Stavanger and the open west.

Fjordland

Norway's famous Fjordland begins at Stavanger. Stretching for more than 375 miles is one of the most spectacular landscapes and seascapes in the world. In the Ryfylke area, northeast of Stavanger, lies the stunning Lysefjord, with its flat-topped and sheer-sided Pulpit Rock. Farther north is the mighty Hardangerfjord, with its massive cliffs, and the silver-white waterfalls of Skykkjedalsfoss and Vøringfoss, set off by snowcapped mountains.

Farther north into Hordaland lies fascinating Bergen, against a setting of islands and mountains. Bergen is the starting point for boat journeys to the north along the coastal islands and into the 120-mile-long Sognefjord, the deepest and longest fjord in the world. Its side fjords twist between towering cliffs and penetrate as far as Flåm and Gudvangen, at the head of Nærøyfjord (the narrowest fjord in Europe), and to Fjærland, below the southernmost edge of the great Jostedal glacier.

Along Sognefjord are lovely villages such as Balestrand. Throughout the area, ancient pagoda-like stave churches survive at settlements such as Vik, Kaupanger and Urnes. Inland to the east lies the mighty mountain range of Jotunheimen, known as the "Land of the Giants."

The Northern Fjords

Beyond the Sognefjord lies Nordfjord and then the county, or *fylke*, of Møre og Romsdal. The coastal town of Ålesund is renowned for its art nouveau architecture of turrets, towers and medieval motifs. Inland is the Geirangerfjord and its magnificent waterfalls. From Ålesund, spectacular roads lead over the mountains to the

Traditional embroidered costume, worn at festivals

town of Åndalsnes and the Romsdalsfjord. Along the coast farther north lies the Atlantic Road, a highway linking a chain of islands. Northeast from here lies Trollheimen, the mountainous "Home of the Trolls," and then comes the great expanse of Trondheimsfjorden and Trondheim itself – once called Nidaros – the ancient capital of Norway.

Beyond Trondheim is the narrowing edge of Norway's northwestern seaboard, fertile coastal lands backed by barren mountains that reach into Nordland and to the Arctic Circle. At Narvik, you look out across the waters of Vestfjorden to the spectacular Lofoten Islands before continuing north to Tromsø. You then go on through Finnmark, the land of the Sami people and of the midnight sun, to the Arctic island of Honningsvåg and Nordkapp (North Cape), the symbolic northern end of Europe.

Traveling in Norway

Norway is a pleasant country in which to travel, but to enjoy this magnificent land you should be selective about how and where to explore. Roads are well maintained throughout. Good driving skills are required, however, where roads are narrow and twisting and where they pass through long tunnels. Norway's public transportation system is excellent.

This is a country that copes impressively with some of the most difficult winter conditions in Europe. Only in severe conditions are train services to the northwest likely to be curtailed. Buses serve more remote villages throughout the north and west. Travel by boat is a way of life in Norway, especially on the western seaboard. There is no finer way of touring Fjordland than by boat.

Most of Norway has a comparatively mild, wet maritime climate. The west coast and mountains have high rainfall even in midsummer. But there can be long spells of fair weather, when Fjordland is glorious. In eastern and southeastern Norway, summers can be warm and dry. Winter in the higher elevations is cold and extremely snowy, creating excellent skiing conditions at Norway's winter resorts. The Norwegians are philosophical about their weather, preferring to think of it as invigorating.

The Norwegians

Norway, as a constitutional monarchy, is extremely well run. The moderate Labor Party has dominated government since the 1930s. The Norwegians are a level-headed, open and generous people. They are unfailingly courteous, and only in busy Oslo does an occasional impatience with visitors emerge.

The people share the Scandinavian tendency toward self-effacement, but they are understandably proud of their success at shaping a modern nation out of such a wild landscape.

Stunning mountain pass at Stalheim

TIMELINE

2000–1000 BC	Early Neolithic and Bronze Age people leave numerous rock carvings throughout Scandinavia.
AD 787	Viking expansion begins with increased expeditions to Britain and northern Europe.
870	Vikings settle in Iceland.
1000	Christianity is introduced to Norway; Lief Eriksson reaches the coast of Labrador.
circa 1300	Oslo becomes capital of Norway.
1350	The Black Death kills over half of Norway's population.
1397	Union of the Three Crowns of Denmark, Sweden and Norway signed at Kalmar.
1536	Norway is reduced to a "province" of Denmark and remains so for nearly 300 years.
1814	The country is forced into union with Sweden.
1905	Prince Carl of Denmark is invited to become king of an independent Norway.
1914–18	Norway remains neutral during World War I.
1925	City of Christiana reverts to its original name of Oslo.
1940	Invasion of Norway by Germany, in spite of Norway's declaration of neutrality.
1945	German troops surrender; Norway becomes one of the founders of the United Nations.
1949	Norway becomes a founding member of NATO.
1970s	Oil and gas extraction from Norwegian sector of North Sea boosts Norway's economy.
1994	In a referendum, Norwegians reject membership in the European Union.
2000	Oslo celebrated its 1,000th anniversary.

THE VIKING SETTLERS

History has painted the Vikings as aggressive, anarchic sea raiders, but this view has changed somewhat in recent times. The restless voyaging that took the Vikings around the coasts of Britain and into the deep estuaries of northern France led to bloody conflict. There seems no question that the Vikings plundered and destroyed. But modern theory argues that a desire for new territory made them settlers in foreign lands more often than just violent raiders. In later, more stable times, the Vikings' commercial success was just as powerful as their military ferocity had been.

SURVIVAL GUIDE

- Mid-June through July is the national vacation period, and many Norwegians depart cities and towns for the fjords, mountains and countryside. Oslo is quieter than normal during this period and it can be a good time to visit the city.
- During the peak summer vacation season, North Cape (Nordkapp) and its approaches are very busy with traffic and visitors.
- When driving in Norway, dimmed headlights must be kept on even during daylight hours.
- Because of Norway's strict control on the sale of alcohol, you will have difficulty buying your own wines and spirits outside larger towns. Some rural areas are virtually "dry." You cannot buy alcohol (except beer) from supermarkets. Special state-controlled *Vinmonopolet* are the only liquor stores, and they are very expensive. Most restaurants are licensed, and you may be able to buy beer in some grocery stores.
- Norwegians are catching up on international fashion, but there is more interest in good outdoor clothing than fancy styles. For something truly Norwegian, such as vividly designed knitwear, try the Oslo sweater stores AS, at the SAS Scandinavia Hotel (✉ Tullins gate 5, ☎ 22 11 29 22), or Thv. L. Holm AS (✉ H. Heyerdahls gate 1, ☎ 22 41 15 74). Other souvenirs include ceramics, pewter, wooden troll figures, enamel jewelry and woven wall hangings.
- You can eat very well in Norway, especially in Oslo and the larger towns. Norwegians are experts at buffet preparation, the ideal lunch experience, often with elaborate fish specialties. Smoked salmon and trout, and lamb dishes such as *fenalår* (smoked leg of lamb) are delicious. You can always try reindeer or elk for a real taste of mountain Norway.
- You will find that, as in Sweden and Finland, some things are about 30 percent more expensive in Norway than in the rest of Europe. Hotel accommodations and restaurants are more expensive. Overall, prices are higher than elsewhere in Europe. If you're on a budget, watch for *Lavpris* (low-price) food stores.

A troll statue greets visitors to Lillehammer

OSLO

Oslo is a small, modern city of great character, but without the grandeur of many larger European capitals. Its spacious suburbs, forests and parks, all within sight and sound of the sea, give the city great vistas. It has outstanding art galleries and maritime museums, music venues, cafés, restaurants and fashionable boutiques. Yet there is always that inescapable feeling that wide-open spaces are not too far away.

Oslo Through History

Oslo was founded in 1000 (it celebrated its 1,000th anniversary in 2000) but Oslo's progress to capital city was checkered. It was significant only as a fjord settlement during the Viking age. In the 11th century, the Norwegian King Harald Hardråde chose to make Oslo a rival to the northern capital of Trondheim. Oslo's fortunes rose and fell thereafter, and in the 17th century, following a devastating fire and while under Danish rule, the settlement was rebuilt to the west of its original site and renamed Christiana, after the Danish King Christian IV.

Christiana became the capital of Norway in 1814. Throughout the 19th century the profitable timber trade and the economic advantages of union with Sweden increased its prosperity. By 1905, when Norway broke with the union, Christiana was a mature city economically and politically, and by 1925 the country was confident enough to reinstate the traditional name of Oslo.

The story of Oslo in the final decades of the 20th century was one of rapid modernization, as much on cultural as on social, political and economic terms. Wealth from the oil industry, the internationalization of Norwegian culture and a growing Norwegian self-confidence transformed the city into the cosmopolitan, vibrant capital of today.

The hub of the city; try Karl Johans gate for shopping, relaxing and eating out

The City's Stage

The most impressive way to arrive in Oslo is by sea. Viewed from the narrow neck of the Oslofjorden, the city's buildings are set against a backdrop of serene peninsulas and wooded hills. The hills are dotted with houses and accented by the great white pylon of the famous Holmenkollen ski jump.

Arrival by train, however, lands you at Jernbanetorget, the big open space in front of Oslo's central railroad station. This is not the most attractive part of the city, but a short walk along Karl Johans gate takes you quickly to Oslo Cathedral (Oslo Domkirke) and the busy open space of Stortorget, with its colorful flower market.

A few steps farther on is the Parliament (Stortinget). Before it lies the open space of Eidsvollsplass, the busy city center, alive with action and entertainment in summer, its pond a skating rink in winter.

To the northwest of Eidsvollsplass is the neoclassic Nationaltheatret (National Theater), guarded by statues of Norwegian dramatists Bjørnstjerne Bjørnson and Henrik Ibsen. Farther northwest is tree-lined Slottsparken, which encompasses the unfenced and accessible Royal Park and the Royal Palace within its bounds.

To the south of the National Theater, down busy Olav V's gate and Roald Amundsen gate, lies Rådhuset (City Hall) and the open space of Rådhusplassen. Adjoining this square is Rådhusbrygge (City Hall Pier) and the local ferryboat dock on Pipervika inlet. A short distance northwest on Brynjulf Bullsplass, located in the old railroad station building, are the Norwegian tourist information center and the main tourist information office in Oslo.

Exploring Oslo

Central Oslo is easily explored on foot, but you should become familiar with the transportation system so you can take one of the many day trips within easy reach. Public transportation is very efficient and easily understood; travel on city trams is a relaxing experience in itself. Visit the outlying Bygdøy peninsula, with its clutch of outstanding museums, or Frogner Park and Vigelandsparken (Vigeland Park), Norway's most visited attraction (see page 368).

Oslo's main street, Karl Johans gate, is full of stores of all kinds, including David-Andersen AS at No. 20 (☎ 22 41 69 55), Scandinavia's largest jewelry store. The Paléet shopping mall has a mix of fashion boutiques and restaurants. Stop for coffee and fruit-speckled pastries at the Grand Café at No. 31, one of Henrik Ibsen's former haunts.

A short distance north of the Royal Palace is the busy shopping street of Hegdehaugsveien and its continuation,

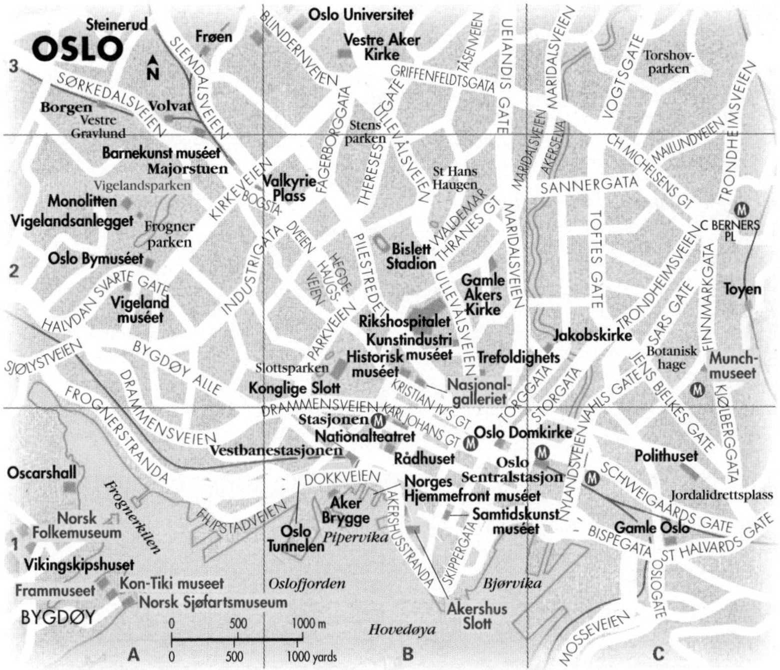

Bogstadveien. Down at the harbor, on the western side of Pipervika inlet and beyond the tourist information center, is Aker Brygge, a modern complex with numerous stores, restaurants, cafés and entertainment venues. The area's attractive waterside setting adds to the character.

Eating out in Oslo offers a remarkable choice of local and international cuisine. Try traditional restaurants such as Blom-Kunsterernes Restaurant (see page 563) on Karl Johans gate, where you can enjoy seasoned or smoked Norwegian specialties. Feast on excellent music too, in the Konserthus on Munkedamsveien, to the west of Aker Brygge.

The Oslo experience is a relaxed one, because of the compactness of the city center and because of the ease with which you can reach the outlying attractions and surrounding countryside. The openness of the city is reflected in the people, who are brisk but friendly in their attitude. English is a second language, especially to younger Norwegians, and you are never far away from advice and guidance to help you make the most of your stay.

Nobel Peace Prize

The Nobel Peace Prize awards for physics, chemistry, physiology and medicine, peace and literature have been awarded in Oslo City Hall since 1990. The awards were founded at the end of the 19th century by Swedish inventor and industrialist Alfred Bernhard Nobel. The Peace Prize winner is based on criteria in Nobel's will citing "the person(s) who shall have done the most or the best work for brotherhood between nations." The ceremony takes place each year on December 10, the anniversary of Nobel's death.

ESSENTIAL INFORMATION

TOURIST INFORMATION
Oslo Promotion (Oslo Visitors and Convention Bureau)
• Brynjulf Bullsplass 1 ☎ 23 11 78 80 (Mon.–Fri. 9–4); fax 22 83 81 50; www.visitoslo.com
• Oslo Sentralstasjon, Jernbanetorget 2 (walk-in only)

URBAN TRANSPORTATION
Oslo's main railroad station is Sentralstasjon (Central Station), known as Oslo S; it has modern facilities and is only minutes from the city center. For local trains contact Trafikanten (☎ 177 or 22 17 70 30). For other services call ☎ 81 50 08 88. Oslo has an efficient bus and tram network. The bus terminal is next to Oslo Sentralstasjon. Eight tram lines run east to west. The city also has a subway system, called the T-Bane, with five lines identified by a "T" sign. Its main junction is at Stortinget Station. Taxis are available from Oslo Taxi (☎ 02323). For general information on transportation in the city contact Trafikanten, near Oslo Sentralstasjon (☎ 177 or 22 17 70 30).

AIRPORT INFORMATION
Oslo Airport is located at Gardermoen, 31 miles north of the city. An airport express train, Gardermobanen, runs between the airport and Oslo S (Central Station) every 10 minutes; the trip takes 19 minutes. Regular train services also stop at the airport. Airport buses run between the airport and Oslo Busterminal, located alongside Central Station. Agents for Oslo Airport are Braathens (☎ 81 52 00 00), SAS (☎ 81 00 33 00) and Widerøe (☎ 67 11 60 00).

CLIMATE – average highs and lows for the month

JAN.	FEB.	MAR.	APR.	MAY	JUN.	JUL.	AUG.	SEP.	OCT.	NOV.	DEC.
0°C	0°C	4°C	9°C	16°C	19°C	22°C	20°C	16°C	9°C	4°C	0°C
32°F	32°F	39°F	48°F	61°F	66°F	72°F	68°F	61°F	48°F	39°F	32°F
-7°C	-7°C	-3°C	1°C	7°C	10°C	12°C	12°C	7°C	3°C	-2°C	-5°C
19°F	19°F	27°F	34°F	45°F	50°F	54°F	54°F	45°F	37°F	28°F	23°F

CITY SIGHTS

Key to symbols
map coordinates refer to the Oslo map on page 365; sights below are highlighted in yellow on the map.
address or location telephone number
opening times nearest subway nearest bus or tram route Bygdøynes Boat restaurant or café on site or nearby admission charge: $$$ more than KR50, $$ KR15-50, $ less than KR15
other relevant information

AKERSHUS SLOTT

Slott B1 Oslo Mil./Akershus 22 41 25 21 Mon.–Sat. 10–4, Sun. 12:30–4, early May–Oct. 31 Engebret Café, see page 563 Stortinget 60; tram 10, 12, 13, 15, 19 $$
Festning Oslo Mil./Akershus 23 09 39 17 Outdoor area: daily 6 a.m.–9 p.m. Engebret Café, see page 563 Stortinget 60; tram 10, 12, 13, 15, 19 Free
Norges Hjemmefgrontmuseet Oslo Mil./Akershus 23 09 31 38 Mon.–Sat. 10–5 (also Tue. and Thu. 5–6), Sun. 11–5, mid-Jun. to Aug. 31; Mon.–Sat. 10–4, Sun. 11–4, mid-Apr. to mid-Jun. and in Sep.; Mon.–Fri. 10–3, Sat.–Sun. 11–4, rest of year Engebret Café, see page 563 Stortinget 60; tram 10, 12, 13, 15, 19 $$

Akershus Slott (Akershus Castle) stands on a rocky height on the eastern side of the harbor inlet of Pipervika. It was founded in 1299 as a royal residence, but by the end of the 17th century it had been transformed into the powerful Festning (Fortress) by the addition of ramparts. There are guided tours of the fortress and of the castle's halls and subterranean passages. The Norges Hjemmefrontmuseum (Norway's Resistance Museum) at the fortress is a compelling record of Norway's experiences in World War II, when the Nazi occupation headquarters were located at Akershus.

FRAMMUSEET

A1 Bygdøynes 22 43 83 70 Daily 9–6:45, mid-June to Aug. 31; daily 9–5:45, mid-May to mid-Jun.; daily 10–4:45, May 1 to mid-May and in Sep.; daily 10–3:45, in Oct.; daily 11–3:45, Mar.–Apr.; Mon.–Fri. 11–2:45, Sat.–Sun. 11–3:45, rest of year 30 Bygdøynes Boat 91, from Rådhusbrygge 3 (May–Sep.) $$

The centerpiece of the Frammuseet (Polar Ship *Fram* Museum) is the preserved Arctic exploration vessel *Fram,* with a bow like a battering ram and a hull as solid as a castle wall. The *Fram* was built in 1892 and was used by Norwegian explorers Fridtjof Nansen, Otto Sverdrup and Roald Amundsen in polar expeditions. Go aboard the *Fram* to see its sturdiness and get a sense of the tough, determined life that its crew led.

KON-TIKI MUSEET

A1 Bygdøynesveien 36 23 08 67 67 Daily 9:30–5:45, Jun.–Aug.;10:30–5, Apr.–May and in Sep.; 10:30–4, rest of year 30 Bygdøynes Boat 91, from Rådhusbrygge 3 (May–Sep.) $$

The Kon-Tiki museet (Kon-Tiki Museum) is a colorful celebration of Thor Heyerdahl's voyages. It complements the general maritime themes of the adjacent *Fram* Museum and the Norwegian Maritime Museum. Heyerdahl's ethos of adventure, linked to environmentalism and international cooperation, is vividly expressed. The original *Kon-Tiki* balsa wood raft of his 1947 Pacific crossing and the papyrus vessel *Ra II* of his 1970 Atlantic crossing both reflect the Norwegian genius for maritime exploration.

MUNCH-MUSEET

C2 Tøyengata 53 23 24 14 00 Daily 10–6, Jun. 1 to mid-Sep.; Tue.–Sun. 10–4 (also Thu. and Sun. 4–6), rest of year Museum café Tøyen 20 $$$

The Munch-museet (Munch Museum) is a fitting celebration of Norway's most famous artist. Edvard Munch's *The Scream,* on display at the National Gallery, is a world-famous cultural icon, but the artist's huge body of work merits even greater attention. The Munch Museum provides an insight into the complex personality of this intense and compelling artist.

NASJONALGALLERIET

B2 Universitetsgaten 13 22 20 04 04 Mon.–Fri. 10–6 (also Thu. 6–8 p.m.), Sat. 10–4, Sun. 11–4 Grand Café, see page 563 Nationaltheatret Buses to Nationaltheatret;

Gustav Vigeland's Monolith at Frogner Park

tram 11, 13, 15, 17, 18, 19 Free
Oslo's Nasjonalgalleriet (National Gallery) is primarily a Norwegian art experience. The gallery has works by painters such as Georges Braque and Pablo Picasso, but its main collection is of work up to 1945 by Norwegian masters such as Christian Krohg, Johan Christian Dahl, Thomas Fearnley and Edvard Munch. Highlights include Krohg's lively portrait *Oda Krohg, the Painter*, a charming rendition of artist Oda Krohg in vivid red and blue clothes. The romantic Fjordland paintings of Johan Christian Dahl and Thomas Fearnley will encourage you to visit the fjords. Look on the top floor for Ernst Josephson's *The Spanish Blacksmiths*. The room devoted to Munch shows some classic masterpieces, including the iconic *The Scream*, the powerful *Dance of Life*, the sensual *Day After* and the ravishing *Madonna*.

NORSK FOLKEMUSEUM

A1 Museumsveien 10 22 12 37 00 Daily 10–6, mid-May to mid-Sep.; 11–3 (also Sun. 3–4), rest of year. Park: Mon.–Fri. 9–8, Sat.–Sun. 9:30–8, mid-May to mid-Sep.; Mon.–Fri. 9–6, Sat.–Sun. 9:30–6, rest of year Museum café 30 Bygdøynes Boat 91, from Rådhusbrygge 3 (May–Sep.) $$$ (reduced admission mid-Sep. to mid-May)
The Norsk Folkemuseum (Norwegian Folk Museum) gives an excellent view of Norway's folk culture and traditional life. It is located at the heart of the Bygdøy peninsula and includes a large parklike area with more than 150 traditional buildings and reconstructed 19th-century village streets. The main buildings have displays of traditional crafts, folk costumes and haunting reconstructions of rural interiors. There is a significant exhibition on the culture of the Sami, the indigenous people of northern Scandinavia. Children will be delighted by the toy exhibition.

NORSK SJØFARTSMUSEUM

A1 Bygdøynesveien 37 22 43 82 40 Daily 10–7, mid-May to Sep. 30; 10:30–4 (also Tue. and Thu. 4–7), rest of year Museum café 30 Bygdøynes Boat 91, from Rådhusbrygge 3 (May–Sep.) $$
The Norsk Sjøfartsmuseum (Norwegian Maritime Museum) stands on the tip of the Bygdøy peninsula, overlooking the waters of the Oslofjorden. In the main hall, Christian Krogh's great marine painting, *Leiv Eriksson's Discovery of America,* sets the scene for numerous exhibits on shipping and the sea. The basement theater shows a video on Norway's maritime history. Look on the main floor for the escape boat, secretly made from rough planking by Norwegian sailors while they were imprisoned aboard their ships in West Africa by the Germans during World War II.

VIGELANDSPARKEN

A2 Kirkeveien 22 54 25 30 Daily 24 hours (visitor center: daily 9:30–8, mid-May to mid-Sep.; Mon.–Fri. 9:30–4, Sat. 11–4, Sun. 11–5:30, rest of year 20, 45, 81; tram 12, 15 Free
Vigelandsparken (Vigeland Park) is a memorial to Norwegian sculptor Gustav Vigeland. It also is a celebration of the human body. This is celebratory nudity without a hint of prurience. The centerpiece is the famous Monoliten (Monolith), a tall granite column composed of writhing human figures struggling upward. The park lies within the larger Frogner Park, a green area within easy reach of central Oslo.

FJORD AND MOUNTAIN LINE

Most visitors to Norway go to the western fjords at some time during their stay. Even if your time is limited you can still make the famous "Norway in a nutshell" journey by train, bus and boat. The trip takes you from Oslo to the Sognefjord via the well-known Flåm mountain railroad. Some people make the round trip from Oslo in a day, but it is a very long day. An alternative is to take an early train from Oslo to Bergen, from where you can catch the fast coastal ferry into the Sognefjord.

Try to stay in Bergen, a delightful city amid spectacular surroundings. The ferry from Bergen to the Sognefjord is an experience in itself. The boat races under high bridges, skims past scores of islands and rugged peninsulas, and slows only at narrow channels with feet to spare. You travel deep into the mighty Sognefjord to Balestrand, a village at a beautiful part of the fjord. Here fruit trees flourish in the fjordland summer, yet glaciers are only a few miles away in the mountains. It is possible to stay overnight here.

From Balestrand, a final boat trip takes you to the very end of Sognefjord, the high cliffs crowding ever closer. Flåm (pronounced Flum) is not a traditional fjord village; its purpose is to cater to bus and car parking, and the crowds who arrive by ferry and cruise ship. The famous Flåm to Myrdal railroad is the reason for it all. The stylish train, with its comfortable quarters, takes 50 minutes to travel along the valley floor behind Flåm. It climbs steadily through spectacular scenery to the head of the valley, where the track rises through a series of S-bends, protected in places by snow shelters. Finally, the train reaches the plateau and the Myrdal railroad station, where you connect with the Oslo train for the last leg (5 hours) of one of the world's great round trips.

You can arrange this tour yourself through Norwegian State Railways (NSB), (☎ 81 50 08 88; www.nsb.no), or ask at the Oslo Promotion tourist information center (see page 366) for details about organized tours.

Within easy reach of Bergen is the spectacular Hardangerfjord, looking towards the Folgefonn glacier

PA SB 461 L

PORTUGAL

"THERE is something very extraordinary in the nature of the people of the Peninsula, the most loyal and best-disposed..."

The Duke of Wellington, in an early 19th-century dispatch

Opposite: Spectacular display of color at the fishing village of Sesimbra, south of Lisbon

PORTUGAL

Portugal, lying on the western edge of the Continent and overshadowed by Spain, its powerful neighbor to the east, is sometimes considered the poor relation of southwestern Europe. Political turmoil and poverty have long hindered development, but after joining the European Union in 1986, billions of dollars have poured into the country, helping to modernize its economy.

The Land

For travelers who knew Portugal 20 years ago, some things have changed beyond recognition; others remain stubbornly the same. In many ways Portugal is still old-fashioned and underdeveloped, a real bonus for visitors seeking something a little different from mainstream European travel. The country is small, diverse and beautiful. Stretching 350 miles from north to south, it is packed with mountains, plateaus, river valleys, flat dry plains, rolling forested hills and a truly beautiful coastline. Portugal borders the Atlantic, and weather conditions can range from hot and sunny to stormy and wet. In the northern Douro region, winter temperatures drop well below freezing; in summer, it is not uncommon for the thermometer to top 100 degrees.

The Algarve, a popular vacation area on the southern coast that's often visited by northern Europeans, enjoys a Mediterranean climate, and the vegetation is subtropical. On the whole, summers are warm and dry, winters mild and wet, although it can be cold in the mountains. Portugal's highest mountain is Torre, in the Serra da Estrela, which rises above 6,500 feet. The Tagus (Tejo) river roughly divides the country in half. The Tagus and two other important rivers, the Douro and the Guadiana, rise in Spain, and Portugal must share their waters with its bigger neighbor, a factor leading increasingly to difficulties in supply and environmental problems.

MORE TOP DESTINATIONS IN PORTUGAL

• Alcobaça B3 • Batalha B3 • Braga B4 • Bragança C4 • Castelo de Vide C3 • Chaves C4 • Coimbra B3 • Douro B4 • Évora B2 • Fátima B3 • Guimarães B4 • Monsanto C3 • Óbidos B3 • Parque Nacional da Peneda-Gerês B4 • Sagres B1 • Serra de Monchique B1 • Silves B1 • Tomar B3 • Torres Vedras A2

Portuguese Empire

It's easy to forget that Portugal was once at the head of a powerful empire. From the early 15th century, Portuguese explorers pushed far into the unknown, challenging the traditional view that the world ended somewhere west of Gibraltar. Madeira and the Azores were the first to be discovered, and these islands remain part of Portugal. Portuguese ships rounded the Cape of Good Hope in 1488, and in 1497 Vasco da Gama reached Calicut, India. By 1560, Portugal had claimed Brazil and had an empire stretching east as far as Japan, with missionary and trading posts in Africa, India, Malaysia, Macao and Timor.

Despite strong rivalry between Portugal and Spain over discoveries in the Americas, the 16th century was a Golden Age, with spices, slaves and gold making Portugal hugely rich. But the voyages and maintenance of an overseas empire were extremely costly, and the home economy was worsening. By 1580, Philip II of Spain had claimed the throne, becoming Philip I of Portugal the following year. Within 100 years, many of the overseas possessions had fallen to the English and Dutch.

The legacy of the empire still exists, however. Portugal extricated itself from Africa in the 1970s, when Angola, Mozambique and Guinea became independent; East Timor in Indonesia

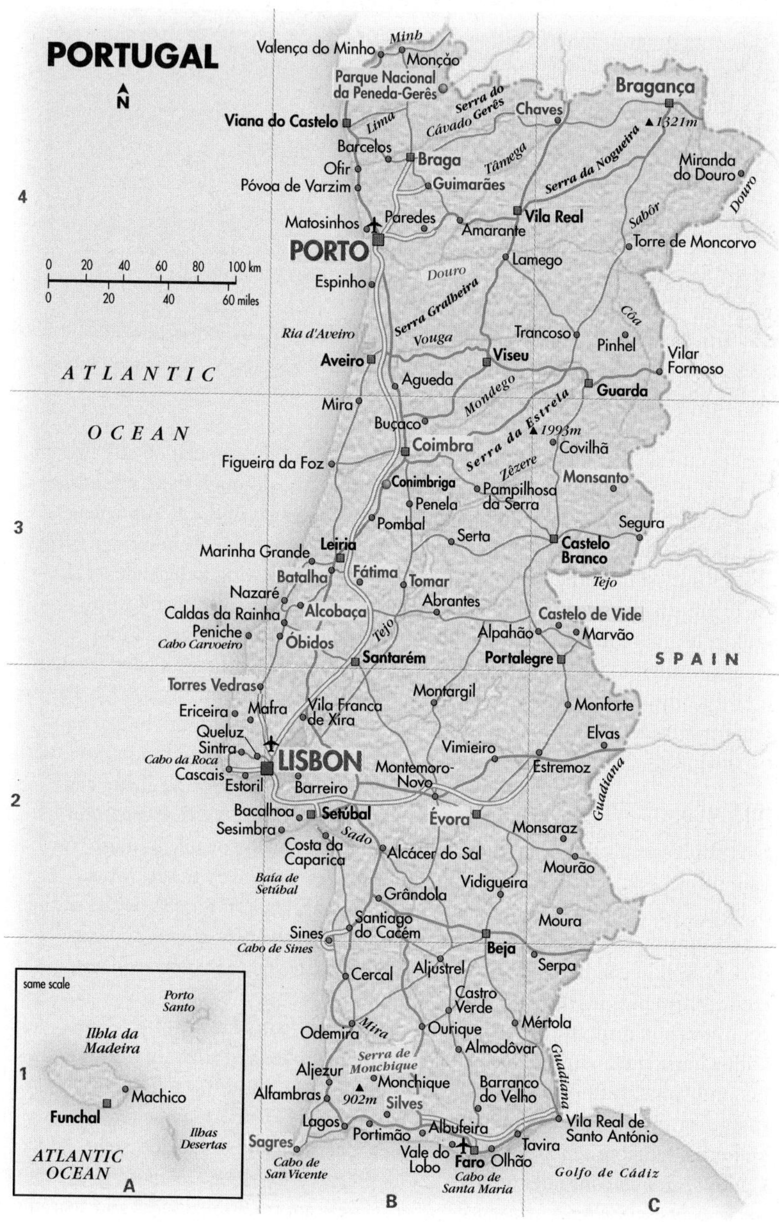

Perched on a ridge overlooking the Alentejo valley and the Spanish border, the 13th-century castle of Marvao dominates the surrounding landscape

was relinquished at the same time. Today there are buildings, churches and monuments wherever the Portuguese held power, but language became the country's most important legacy. Portuguese is the seventh most widely spoken language in the world. Brazil retains strong ties with Portugal and, unlike many other former colonies, there is genuine respect between the two countries.

The People

Geographical isolation from most of Europe has kept Portuguese bloodlines pure, and you'll notice a definite racial type – most people are short, with dark eyes, skin and hair. They are conservative people who are generally courteous and respectful. Northerners, with a harsher climate and historically poorer living conditions, tend to be less easygoing than people in the south, and more religious. Even so, the Catholic church continues to hold great sway everywhere.

Most of the population still lives in rural areas, although there was a large urban increase in the 1970s, when people came home from former African colonies following independence. In Lisbon in particular, many Afro-Portuguese have integrated into Portuguese life; there's a good level of interracial harmony.

The country still has one of Europe's highest emigration rates, with around 3 million people living and working abroad. With few natural resources, many people in northern Portugal are forced to seek work overseas; you can see the results of their labors in the new houses and cars found in even the poorest villages.

Society and Language

Being polite and friendly will smooth your path as you travel through Portugal. The Portuguese tend to be welcoming and unhurried, so be prepared for things to take a long time. There are traditional ideas and attitudes

The narrow, picturesque streets of Porto cluster together on the hillsides of the city

toward women, and the farther away from major towns you travel the more obvious this becomes. It's considered disrespectful to wear skimpy clothing, and it is customary to speak formally and politely until you get to know the people you are talking to.

One of the major hurdles in getting to know the Portuguese is the language barrier. Don't try your Spanish in Portugal. Despite – or because of – proximity to Spain, the Portuguese don't appreciate being addressed in Spanish. However, if you can read Spanish you'll have no problem reading Portuguese. It's a romance language with Latin roots, similar to Spanish and Italian. Pronunciation is a different matter altogether, however, and spoken Portuguese, with its sibilants, nasal vowels and guttural consonants, reminds some people of Russian and Slavic languages.

The Portuguese are very aware that they speak a difficult language and are excellent linguists; you'll find English spoken in major tourist areas, although rarely in the deep countryside. Do try and tackle one or two words; your efforts will be appreciated and faces will light up when you try to communicate.

Changing Portugal

Since the watershed year of 1986, huge changes have occurred in Portugal. From being one of the poorest nations in Europe, the country now has one of the highest economic growth rates, while unemployment has plummeted. Despite a recession in the early 1990s, things still look good for the country as the economy continues to expand. But this has been achieved at the cost of a widening gap between the rich and poor, noticeable wherever you travel. Education levels are low, with an embarrassing percentage of the population having few if any literacy skills. Agriculture still lags far behind the rest of Europe, and a high proportion of national earnings comes from money earned overseas or spent by tourists within Portugal.

For visitors, the blend of old and new is alluring and adds an extra dimension to the travel experience. Recent investment has improved the infrastructure to the visitor's benefit, while the uneven wealth distribution means that a rustic way of life is still evident throughout the country.

TIMELINE

1000 BC to AD 400	Occupation by Phoenicians, Carthaginians, Iberians, Celts, Romans and Visigoths.
AD 713	Moors control most of the country and remain in power for 400 years.
1179	Pope recognizes Kingdom of Portugal.
1255	Afonso III makes Lisbon the capital of Portugal.
1480–1500s	Age of Discovery.
1488	Bartolomeu Dias rounds Cape of Good Hope.
1580	End of Golden Age with invasion by Philip II of Spain, who declares himself Philip I of Portugal.
1668	Treaty of Lisbon recognizes Portuguese independence.
1755	Lisbon earthquake.
1910	Portuguese monarchy overthrown and replaced by republic.
1916–18	Portugal joins Allies in World War I.
1933	*Estado Novo* (New State) established.
1939–45	Portugal neutral throughout World War II.
1950–70	Rapid industrial growth.
1960s	Portuguese colony of Goa occupied by India; local nationalist uprisings in Angola, Guinea and Mozambique.
1976	New constitution drawn up after the fall of the *Estado Novo* in 1974.
1986	Portugal admitted to European Union; start of period of huge economic growth and social reform.
1999	Portugal joins European Monetary System.
2001	Porto named European Capital of Culture for 2001.

PRINCE HENRY THE NAVIGATOR

The impetus for the great Portuguese "Age of Discovery" of the late 15th century came from the son of João I, Prince Henry, who was born in 1394. He can be credited with transforming Portugal into a great maritime power whose success was based on a scientific approach to exploration, navigation and cartography. At his base in the Algarve, Henry collected accomplished shipbuilders, sailors, instrument makers and astronomers, encouraging them to prepare for long voyages into the unknown. The highly successful caravel was designed, a speedy ship that made the great voyages possible. Motivated by religion as well as commerce, Henry's ships sailed ever farther south, rounding Cape Bojador in West Africa, then thought to be the end of the world, in 1434. By Henry's death in 1460 the Portuguese had reached Sierra Leone, and the known world had become a bigger place.

SURVIVAL GUIDE

- The Portuguese are committed wine drinkers. Generally, when you order house wine in restaurants you'll get something highly acceptable, even if it appears in an earthenware jug.
- Water everywhere is safe to drink, although sometimes less than delicious. Avoid tap water in the Algarve during the summer and drink bottled water instead, to be on the safe side.
- The modest Portuguese are shocked by scanty clothes worn anywhere except at the beach. If you are wearing a sleeveless top, take along a scarf to wrap around your shoulders as needed.
- Portuguese drivers are among Europe's worst, and the country also has the Continent's highest accident rate.
- Portugal's telephone system is improving, but is still not up to the standards of other European countries. If you call from your hotel room, you'll pay a high surcharge. Use an on-street "Credifone," which accepts plastic phone cards available from street kiosks.
- Be prepared for Portugal to be different in many ways from its neighbor, particularly if you've already visited Spain. Despite their proximity, the two countries are very different.
- Public restrooms are few and far between, but it's acceptable – even if you're not a customer – to ask to use hotel or restaurant facilities. Men's toilets are marked "H" and women's are marked "S."
- Try not to let grime and shabbiness in Portuguese cities affect you; look for the positive qualities, such as daily clean sheets in many hotels.
- Don't be surprised by the sometimes startling amount of garbage in public places. In Portuguese bars and cafés, it's acceptable to throw paper wrappings on the floor.
- You probably won't find luxury accommodations or excellent service if you're away from the major tourist centers; Portugal is still considered a poor country.
- Portuguese food can be monotonous, and some dishes are unappealing to foreigners. If you are not feeling adventurous, stick to grilled fish and chicken.
- Leave small change in a bar; otherwise about 10 percent is an adequate tip.
- *Pousadas* are by far the nicest places to stay when traveling in Portugal. These are government-run, deluxe hotels located in historic or beautiful places such as former monasteries, palaces and castles. Advance reservations are recommended.

Strong ties with Brazil – a restaurant entrance in Rua Garret, Lisbon

LISBON

Lisbon (Lisboa) is a beguiling city. It has a great past and a promising future. It may easily strike the visitor as old-fashioned and crumbling – but these elements also are an essential part of its charm. Look for the positive: the port city's vigor and life; its great colonial past; the atmospheric old trams; and the evocative sights and scents – laundry flapping in the wind, shoeshine men hawking their trade, the smell of roasting coffee and chestnuts. Most sights of interest are within walking distance of downtown, with the exception of the glorious attractions of suburban Belém, an easy bus or tram ride away.

Lisbon Flavors and *Bacalhau*

Lisbon has a wide range of restaurants at every price level, with the emphasis on traditional Portuguese cooking, although fast-food outlets are easy to find as well. Breakfast consists of small cakes and pastries, but hotels can usually prepare meals tailored to foreign tastes. Lunch is more substantial than in other European cities.

Heavy soups are popular, salads are surprisingly hard to find, and fresh fruit juice virtually non-existent. Lisbon inhabitants eat a lot of fish and seafood, including *bacalhau* (a dried, salted codfish), and the warming winter stews can be good.

You may be surprised at the number of pastry and cake shops; the Portuguese are notoriously sweet-toothed, and Lisbon has many old-fashioned shops selling traditional specialties like the delicious *pastéis de Belém* (pastries filled with custard). Portugal makes good red and white wine, national and foreign beers are everywhere, and all the usual spirits and aperitifs are available.

Souvenirs from Lisbon

Shopping is great fun in Lisbon, and there are many stores selling lovely Portuguese crafts. The area known as the Chiado, in downtown Lisbon, is the

smartest shopping district, with streets lined with numerous classy clothing and jewelry boutiques.

Carpets from the village of Arraiolos are a superb buy, as is the exquisite porcelain manufactured by Vista Alegre. Linen and cotton sheets and tablecloths are another Portuguese specialty. You can even have the lovely glazed tiles, *azulejos,* made to order, or

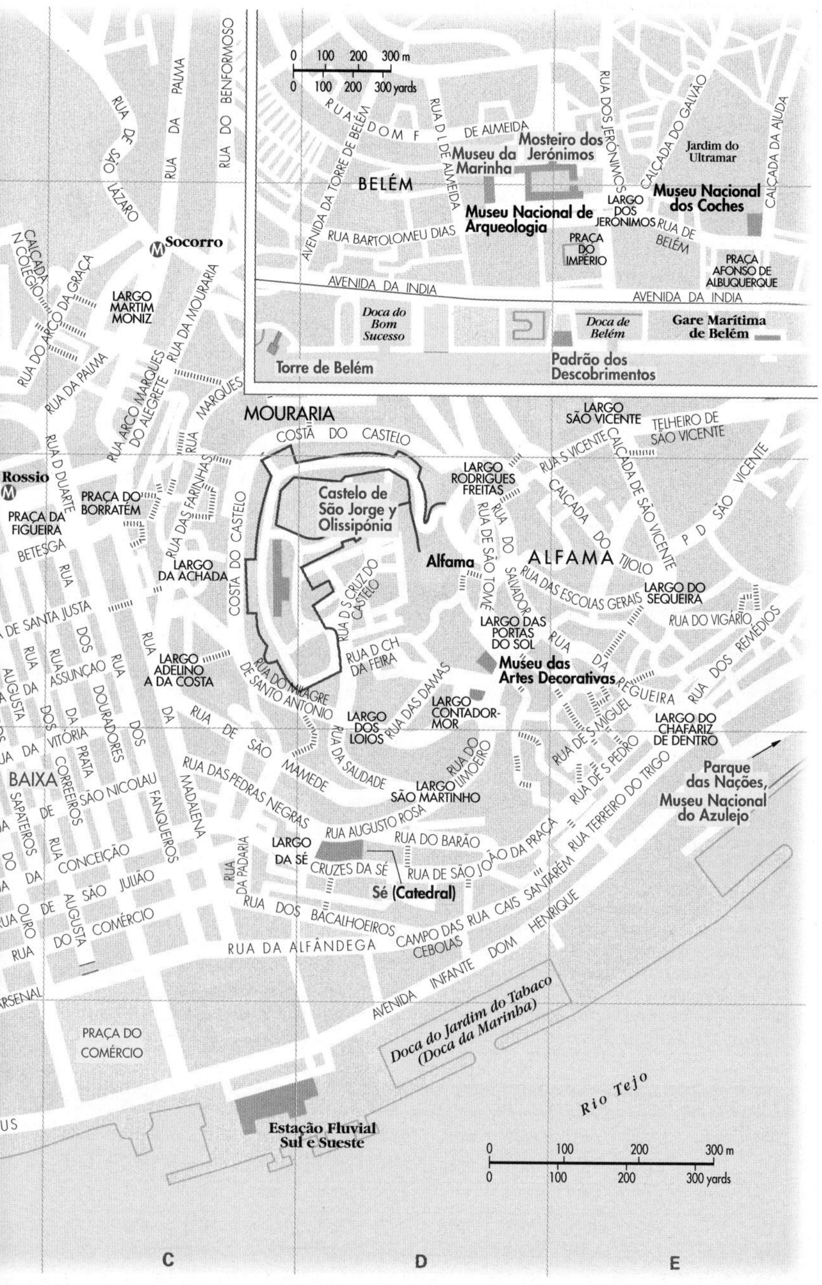

track down something made from cork, one of Portugal's biggest exports.

Film, Music and *Fado*

As befits its capital status, Lisbon offers a variety of music, theater and ballet. Moviegoing is a particular pleasure, as films are all shown in their original language with subtitles, rather than dubbed, so you can catch the latest releases from home.

Fado, a unique style of Portuguese music, is heard at its best in Lisbon and should at least be experienced. This melancholy and passionate music is traditionally sung by a woman, accompanied by guitar. Its origins lie deep in history, a mix of Moorish and African elements, and can be described as a kind of light operetta. The best place to hear it is at one of the *fado* houses in the Upper Town (Bairro Alto, see page 381), or in the Alfama district.

The Lisbon Earthquake

On All Saints Day (November 1) 1755, the Lisbon earthquake struck. Churches were packed for this major feast day, and thousands of lighted candles toppled during the tremors, starting fires that were as destructive as the quake itself. A massive tidal wave followed, swallowing Lisbon's fleet and flooding the already-destroyed lower city.

During the aftermath, corpses were sent to sea on barges and sunk in order to avert the plague. Hospitals opened, prices were fixed and a tax was levied to cover re-building costs, including the renovation of the lower city, today known as the Baixa district. Although Lisbon largely recovered, 1755 marked the end of its role as Europe's leading port city.

ESSENTIAL INFORMATION

TOURIST INFORMATION
Turismo de Lisboa (Lisbon Tourist Office)
• Palácio Foz, Praca dos Restauradores ☎ 21 346 3314
• Santa Apolónia (railway station) ☎ 21 882 1604
• Aeroporto-Chegadas (airport) ☎ 21 844 6473/4/5
• Tourist information helpline ☎ 0800 296 296 (toll-free); www.atl-turismolisboa.pt

URBAN TRANSPORTATION
There's a wide choice of transportation in Lisbon; a fairly limited, although useful, subway system, buses, trams, funiculars and even ferries. Subway stations are marked with an "M" on the city map. For visitors, the Lisboa Card, valid for 24, 48 or 72 hours, gives free unlimited travel and free entry into 27 museums, monuments and other tourist attractions. Cards are available from tourist offices (see above). Otherwise you can buy bus and tram tickets when boarding, and subway tickets from a machine or office at the subway station. The trams and funiculars are one of Lisbon's glories, so make a point of traveling on them; the modern tram 15 is a particularly useful line. Ferry tickets are available from offices at the ferry stations; again, a ferry trip is recommended as part of your sightseeing. Taxis are beige, or occasionally green and black. There are taxi stands on the open squares of the Rossio and the Praça da Figueira,or you can call a cab (☎ 21 811 1100 or 21 793 2756).

AIRPORT INFORMATION
Portela Airport (☎ 21 841 3500, or 21 841 3700 for flight information) is about 4 miles (a 20-minute drive) north of the downtown area. The Aero-Bus shuttle service leaves every 20 minutes daily 7 a.m.–9 p.m. from outside the terminal.

CLIMATE – average highs and lows for the month

JAN.	FEB.	MAR.	APR.	MAY	JUN.	JUL.	AUG.	SEP.	OCT.	NOV.	DEC.
13°C	15°C	17°C	19°C	21°C	25°C	28°C	29°C	27°C	21°C	18°C	14°C
55°F	59°F	63°F	66°F	70°F	77°F	82°F	84°F	81°F	70°F	64°F	57°F
8°C	9°C	10°C	12°C	12°C	15°C	18°C	18°C	17°C	14°C	10°C	9°C
46°F	48°F	50°F	54°F	54°F	59°F	64°F	64°F	63°F	57°F	50°F	48°F

CITY SIGHTS

Key to symbols

map coordinates refer to the Lisbon map on pages 378–379; sights below are highlighted in yellow on the map.
address or location telephone number opening times nearest subway nearest bus or tram route nearest ferry restaurant or café on site or nearby admission charge: $$$ more than 500Esc, $$ 250Esc to 500Esc, $ less than 250Esc other relevant information

BAIRRO ALTO

A3 Area on slopes to west of Baixa Restauradores Tram 28

The Bairro Alto (Upper Town) is one of the five areas that constitute Lisbon's historic center. It was virtually untouched by the 1755 earthquake, and the atmospheric jumble of streets and squares tumble down steep slopes to the Baixa (the Lower Town) below. At night it's one of the city's liveliest quarters, where in *fado* houses you can hear melancholy, evocative Portuguese songs. The Elevador de Santa Justa, a wonderfully clanky funicular built in 1902, runs up the hill.

BAIXA AND ROSSIO

B2–B3 Praça Dom Pedro IV and streets between it and Praça do Comércio Rossio All services to Rossio and Praça do Comércio

Rossio Square, properly known as Praça Dom Pedro IV, and the grid of streets forming the Baixa district will repeatedly draw you back. The Teatro Nacional (National Theater) and a soaring column topped by a statue of Dom Pedro IV dominate the spacious Rossio, which is lined with stores and cafés. The square has an ancient history and was the scene of Inquisition burnings in the 16th century. Between Rossio and the waterfront lies Baixa, a perfect example of rational 18th-century planning, erected at the Marquês de Pombal's instigation after the 1755 earthquake. The orderly streets are lined with lovely old stores, gracious buildings and tiled facades.

CASTELO DE SÃO JORGE Y OLISSIPÓNIA

D3–E3 Rua do Chão da Feira 21 887 7244 Castle: daily 9–9. Olissipónia: daily 10–7 37; tram 12, 28 $$$

Visible from many parts of Lisbon, the Castelo de São Jorge (St. George's Castle) stands on the site of the earliest settlement. Fortified by the Romans, Visigoths and Moors, it was besieged in 1147 by Afonso Enriques and his Christian army and finally fell after 17 weeks – a turning point in the struggle to evict the Moors from Portugal. The Moorish battlements still stand, giving superb views over the rooftops to the river. Today, extensive restoration within the main structure has made a verdant, cool

Shady cloisters of the 16th-century Jerónimos Monastery enclose formal gardens

oasis, with terraces, pools and fountains. A multimedia exhibition (Centro de Interpretação da Cidade de Lisboa – Olissipónia) gives insight into the history of Lisbon. The Alfama district around the palace is worth exploring.

Mosteiro dos Jerónimos

See map inset Praça do Império 21 362 0034 Tue.–Sun. 10–6:30, May–Sep.; 10–5, rest of year São Jerónimo, see page 564 Train: Belém 27, 28, 29, 43, 49, 51; tram 15, 17 Belém $$$

The stunning architectural ensemble of the Mosteiro dos Jerónimos (Jeronimos Monastery), a UNESCO World Heritage Site, stands on the site of an earlier chapel, visited by Portuguese explorers before their great voyages. Building began on the present church in 1501 to celebrate Vasco da Gama's successful voyage to the Indies. It took almost 100 years to complete, by which time various architectural fashions had come and gone. The church and adjoining cloisters are a glorious mix of Gothic, Renaissance and Manueline styles. Pause first at the great south door. Its intricate carving includes the figure of Henry the Navigator; the west door, equally splendid, features Manuel I, who originally started the construction. The soaring interior contains the simple tomb of Vasco da Gama, a contrast to the surrounding riot of stone-work. The two-story cloisters are equally elaborately carved, a wonderful combination of delicacy and weighty strength.

Museu Nacional do Azulejo

Off the map Rua da Madre de Deus 4 21 814 7747 Wed.–Sun. 10–6, Tue. 2–6 Café in museum 18, 42, 104, 105 $$

Throughout Lisbon and Portugal, you'll notice the exquisite tiles, or *azulejos*, which adorn the walls of countless buildings. The Museu Nacional do Azulejo (National Tile Museum) traces the history of the painted glazed tile, which has been used in Portugal since the 15th century. You can see how the art developed from simple early tiles to complex, multicolored modern examples. Blue and white has predominated since Chinese porcelain arrived in Europe; the wonderful tiled view of Lisbon, made in 1738, is a fine example.

Museu Calouste Gulbenkian

Off the map Avenida de Berna 45A 21 782 3000 Wed.–Sun. 10–6, Tue. 2–6 Restaurant and café in museum S. Sebastião or Praça de Espanha 16, 18, 26, 31, 56 $$–$$$; free to all Sun.

Portugal's greatest museum, the Museu Calouste Gulbenkian (Calouste Gulbenkian Museum) was financed by a bequest from the Armenian magnate, whose private collection makes up the bulk of the exhibits. It comprises two sections: European art and artifacts, and Oriental and ancient pieces. The museum is not vast, but everything it contains is of the highest quality. Most visitors are particularly enthralled by the Lalique jewelry and glass, distinctive art deco pieces displayed in a darkened room.

Museu da Marinha

See map inset Praça do Império 21 362 0019 Tue.–Sun. 10–6, mid-Jun. to Sep. 30; 10–5, rest of year Train: Belém 27, 28, 29, 43, 49, 51; tram 15 $$; free to all Sun.

The Museu da Marinha (Maritime Museum), located at Belém, is one of the best of its kind in Europe, as befits this seafaring nation. It's a huge collection, with full-size boats and royal barges, paintings, uniforms and archaic navigational instruments. Most evocative, perhaps, is the polychrome wooden statue of the Archangel Raphael, said to have accompanied Vasco da Gama on his epic voyage to the Indies in 1497.

Padrão dos Descobrimentos

See map inset Avenida de Brasília 21 3031 1950 Tue.–Sun. 9:30–6:30 São Jerónimo, see page 564 Train: Belém 27, 28, 43, 49, 51; tram 15 $$ (temporary exhibitions free)

The eye-catching white mass of the Padrão dos Descobrimentos (Monument to the Discoveries) soars up from the water's edge at Belém, serving as a reminder of Portugal's great maritime past. It was erected in 1960 to mark the 500th anniversary of the death of Henry the Navigator, and has an angular

Topiary gardens on the Italianate grounds of the Fronteira Palace, in north Lisbon

LISBON LIFE

Everyday life in Lisbon, a relatively small city, is far more relaxed than in other capitals. The day starts around 7:30, when commuters are on the move and children make their way to school. Trams, the subway and buses all are crowded. Some people travel to town on the ferries that crisscross the Tagus. Many grab breakfast in a bar before work. Breakfast is usually tea or coffee, with one of the cloyingly sweet pastries so loved by the Portuguese.

Lunch in Lisbon is taken seriously, and many people eat a full meal rather than a snack, although they eat it fast, often standing at a bar counter. Workers also use the lunch hour to shop for food or browse in stores. At the end of the afternoon, commuters head home but will often re-emerge later to meet friends for a drink or more tea and cakes. Midweek evenings are often spent at home, although in summer the streets will be thronged for a few hours as people stroll and chat outside.

Weekends are a different matter; people head for the Upper Town to eat and drink before going to concerts, movies or the theater, while young Portuguese enjoy the old district's waterfront clubs.

Saturday and Sunday are popular shopping days when crowds flock to huge malls on the outskirts of the city, which stay open until late. Sundays, too, are high points for soccer fans, with the big matches attracting large crowds. Lisbon is blessed by its proximity to a beautiful coastline, and it's easy in summer to drive or catch a train to the coast for a day at the beach and dinner in an excellent fish restaurant. In midsummer, an outing to the cool green countryside around Sintra (see page 385), some 15 miles away, is another weekend option.

Statue in the Praça Sao Roque

front and curving form that represents a ship's prow and sails. Figures crowd the prow, led by Henry, who holds a ship. An elevator rises more than 435 feet to the top, offering panoramic views. Below, a mosaic map traces the Portuguese voyages of exploration.

Parque das Nações

Off the map · Parque das Nações · 21 891 9333 · Park: Sun.–Thu. 9:30 a.m.–1 a.m., Fri.–Sat. 9:30 a.m.–3 a.m. Oceanarium: daily 10–7 · Oriente · 28, 81 · Park: free; Oceanarium: $$$

The Parque das Nações (Park of the Nations), the name given to the site occupied by Expo '98, is now used for trade fairs and exhibitions. Impressive buildings, moorings, landscaped gardens, street cafés and restaurants front the Tagus. From the water rises Oceanário (Oceanarium), a state-of-the-art aquarium that was the focal point of the 1998 fair. Europe's largest aquarium features a vast central tank, surrounded by four others representing the main oceans. Marine mammals and seabirds thrive, as well as fish, underwater creatures and vegetation, making this one of Lisbon's most impressive new attractions.

Belém Tower, rising beside the Tagus, an enduring symbol of Portugal's maritime past

Praça do Comércio

C1 · Praça do Comércio · Rossio · All buses to Praça do Comércio; tram 15 · Terreiro do Paço for ferries to Cacilhas

One side of the spacious Praça do Comércio (Comercial Square) opens on the water, emphasizing its original purpose as an imposing gateway to the city from the sea. To experience its original perspective, take the five-minute ferry trip from nearby Terreiro do Paço (Palace Square) across the Tagus to the suburb of Cacilhas. The vista of the square and the triumphal arch leading to the streets of the Baixa opens up to buildings, churches and monuments, an excellent chance to feel the city's past.

Sé

D2 · Largo da Sé · 21 886 6752 · Tues.–Sat. 9–7, Sun.–Mon. 9–5 · Rossio · 37; tram 12, 28 · $

Construction of the Sé (Cathedral) started in 1150, soon after the expulsion of the Moors. It was the city's first church, a solid and harmonious Romanesque edifice. Its two massive towers are a city landmark. It largely escaped damage in the 1755 earthquake, making it a superb symbol of Lisbon's history. Inside, be sure to see the font where Lisbon-born St. Anthony of Padua was baptized.

Torre de Belém

See map inset · Avenida de Brasília · 21 362 0034 · Tue.–Sun. 10–5 · São Jerónimo, see page 564 · Train: Belém · 27, 28, 29, 43, 49, 51; tram 51 · $$

In the nearby suburb of Belém, the Torre de Belém (Belém Tower) rises beside the Tagus. This exquisite honey-colored stone tower, a triumph of Renaissance and Manueline design, is a symbol of Portugal's maritime past. Built between 1515 and 1520, it was designed by Francisco de Arruda, a Portuguese architect whose earlier Moroccan travels influenced his style. His work shows delightful Moorish elements – little domes topping the battlements, corner towers, and arcaded windows and loggias. Built as a bastion against pirate attack, it later served as a prison and is considered by UNESCO to be a World Heritage Site.

SINTRA

By far the most popular day trip from Lisbon is to beautiful Sintra, a small town packed with delights, set in lush and mountainous country some 15 miles northwest of Lisbon. Once there, the attractions are scattered over a wide area, so unless you have plenty of time, it makes sense to take a tour or rent a car and drive from the city. As a bonus, most tour operators include a detour to Cabo da Roca, the Continent's westernmost point.

Palaces

For more than 500 years Sintra was the summer resort of Portuguese kings – a legacy that is apparent in the town's two astounding palaces. The National Palace (Palácio Nacional) was first built by João I in the 15th century and remained in use until the end of the late 1800s.

Architecturally imposing, it's nevertheless a stylistic muddle. The interior is worth exploring. Note the superb ceramic tiles, as well as the elaborately decorated ceilings: one is painted with gold-collared swans and another with magpies.

The other main palace is the Pena Palace (Palácio da Pena), built in the 1840s by Ferdinand of Saxe-Coburg-Gotha, husband of Queen Maria II. It's a creation rivaling the best of Disney, complete with towers, turrets and battlements. Inside is a riot of flamboyant furniture, wall hangings and paintings, including a whole room of nudes.

Nearby is the eighth-century Castelo dos Mouros, a ruined Moorish stronghold with superb views.

Gardens

The other outstanding attractions in Sintra are its gardens and parks. The warm, damp climate is ideal for a profusion of exotic trees, shrubs and roses, and you'll see everything from rhododendrons and camellias to tree ferns and palms. The Pena Gardens, below the Pena Palace, are lovely, with lakes and mock temples. But the highlight is the Monserrate Gardens, west of Sintra. Two Englishmen laid out the gardens between 1790 and 1860, and they ramble over 74 acres.

Around Sintra lies the Sintra-Cascais National Park (Parque Nacional de Sintra-Cascais), a wonderful area stretching from the tree-clad mountains of Sintra down to the dramatic Atlantic coastline at Guincho.

Ornate stonework at Sintra's National Palace

Tour Operators

Cityrama ✉ Avenida Praia da Vitória 12-B ☎ 21 319 1090, 21 319 1091 or 21 319 1092; fax 21 356 0668

Gray Line ✉ Avenida Praia da Vitória ☎ 21 319 1090; fax 21 356 0668

Portugal Tours ✉ Avenida Defensores de Chaves ☎ 21 351 1220; fax 21 351 1229

PORTO

Porto, Portugal's second-largest city with about 300,000 residents, stands on the steep and rocky north bank of the Douro river, just a couple of miles from its outlet on the Atlantic. The suburbs sprawl to the coast. Many visitors encounter Porto on their way up the beautiful Douro valley. The city also is known for its long association with port wine, which has been shipped from Vila Nova de Gaia, a suburb of Porto, since the 17th century. It has long been referred to as "Oporto," a name never used by the Portuguese and now declining in use elsewhere.

Development of Porto

Founded in pre-Roman times, the city gave its name to the country, and was the birthplace of Prince Henry the Navigator in 1394. Traditionally liberal, its residents have always had a strong rebellious streak, which goes well with the city's industrious and down-to-earth image.

Porto is a refreshing antidote to the faded elegance of Lisbon – a bustling city lying at the center of Portugal's most important economic area, whose layout is inextricably entwined with the history of the port trade. Grandiose buildings testify to 18th- and 19th-century wealth, but the true spirit of the city lies in the maze of narrow streets below the cathedral, the old docks and the waterfront houses.

Suggested Itineraries

Two or three days is sufficient to see Porto. Nearly everything of interest is within a short walk or bus ride of the city center. The streets are steep and hilly, so wear comfortable shoes. If you're just passing through on your way up the Douro valley, visit the port lodges in Vila Nova de Gaia, Porto's main tourist attraction. If you've got more time, the city can be neatly divided into cultural itineraries, focusing on medieval, baroque and neoclassic monuments and churches. Pockets throughout the city are endowed with *azulejo* decoration (glazed ceramic tiles). There are good views of the city and tantalizing glimpses of the Douro river from many street corners.

The heart of modern Porto centers around Avenida dos Aliados, a broad avenue with the monumental town hall at one end and the Praça da Liberdade, a transportation hub, at the other. Seething with people, this stretch is a good place to observe locals going about their daily business. The main shopping areas are east and north of this avenue. You can use the river to help orient yourself to the city.

Porto Flavors

The people of Porto have traditionally been known as *tripeiros*, or "tripe-eaters," allegedly because they sacrificed all their meat except the tripe to their army during a legendary battle – an historic indicator that refined cooking doesn't top the priority list here. Expect hearty, tasty meals, plenty of fish, the much-beloved *bacalhau* (dried, salted cod) and super-sweet desserts on every menu.

On the other hand, a glass of smooth, unctuous and subtle port – drunk on its native soil – may convert even the most inveterate port-hater. An especially atmospheric place to dine is beside the river at Ribeira, in the heart of the oldest part of Porto. Until recently it was run-down and decayed, but most of the area has now been given a face-lift, and it is filled with good, lively restaurants with tremendous tourist appeal.

Crafts and Shopping

Porto is the place to track down northern handicraft specialties, fine port, locally made shoes and the village of Minho's traditional gold filigree jewelry. The city's wonderfully old-fashioned stores, many of which still retain their turn-of-the-20th-century facades and details, are worth a visit even if you're not buying. Highlights include the Lello and Irmão bookstore on Rua do Carmelitas, with its superb double staircase and somber wooden paneling, and Cardoso Cabeleiro on Rua do Bonjardim, a shop specializing in wigs and toupees. Similar stores cluster together in Porto, so you'll find streets packed with hardware stores, seed merchants, jewelers and linen stores. Marques Soares, a chic department store on Rua do Carmelitas, carries exquisite leather goods.

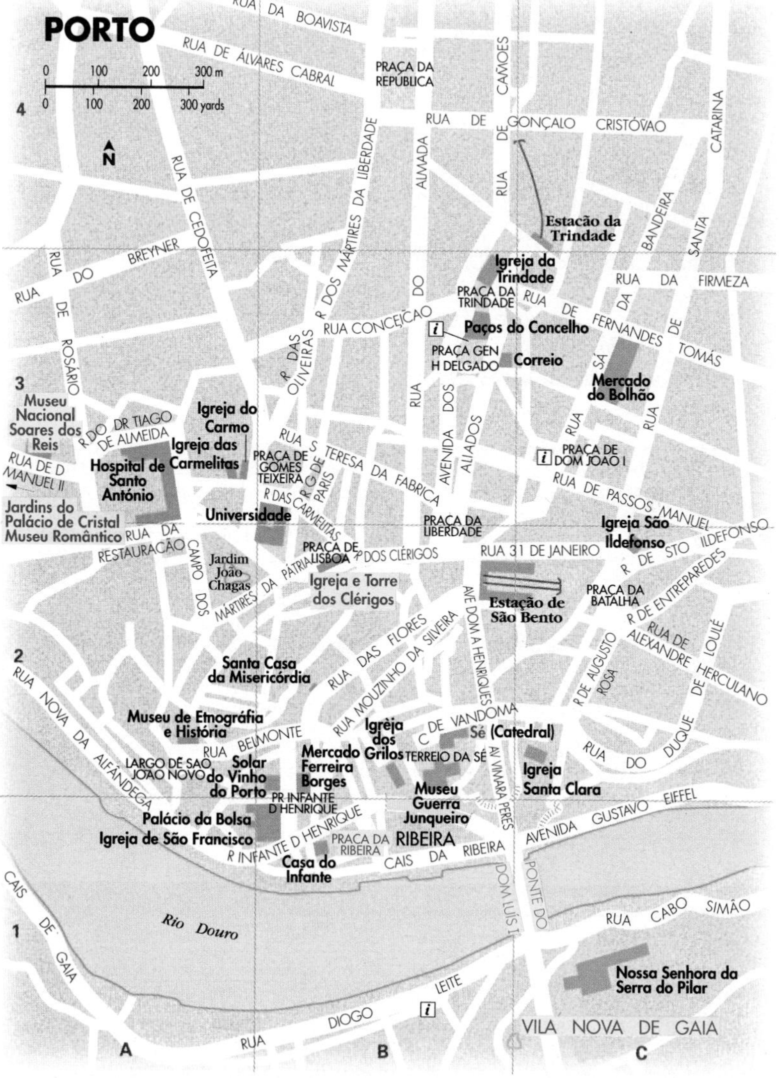

The Douro river runs through the Ribeira docks

Excursions and Entertainment

Various operators run cruises on the Douro river, ranging from a weeklong trip up the river in a luxury cruiser to a couple of hours puttering around the lower reaches in a reproduction of a *rabelo*, the glorious old boats once used to carry barrels of port downstream from the vineyards. Sections of the 19th-century narrow-gauge railway still operate in the Douro valley – a fun way to do a little exploring. Tour operators also run bus trips in, around and out of Porto; Diana Tours (☎ 22 377 1230, or toll-free 800 203 983) is a reliable operator with English-speaking guides. Alternatively, tickets may be bought at the tourist office. Be sure to visit the port lodges in Vila Nova de Gaia (see page 390), an essential stop on any Porto visit.

For evening entertainment, locals attend theaters, concerts and the movies, although many people prefer to while away the hours at one of the terrace cafés or simply strolling along the riverbank.

ESSENTIAL INFORMATION

TOURIST INFORMATION
Turismo do Porto (Porto Tourism)
• Rua Clube dos Fenianos 25
☎ 22 339 3470; fax 22 332 3303
www.portoturismo.pt
• Rua do Infante D Henrique 63 ☎ 22 200 9770

URBAN TRANSPORTATION
Getting around Porto is difficult because there isn't a reliable transportation guide to the city, so it's hard to know where bus stops are located and what routes run where. If you take the bus or the tram, pay as you get on; all buses serving the city center pass through the Praça da Liberdade. You can buy a one-, four- or seven-day travel pass from kiosks in the city center, a considerable saving on single tickets. Taxis are inexpensive and can be flagged down; there is an additional charge to cross the river to Gaia.

AIRPORT INFORMATION
Francisco Sá Carneiro International Airport (☎ 22 941 3260) is about 12 miles northwest of central Porto. Bus 56 runs daily every 20 minutes from 6 a.m. until midnight, with a journey time of 30–60 minutes, depending on traffic. It terminates at Praça Lisboa, next to Torre dos Clérigos. The faster Aero-Bus service to downtown Porto is an alternative; for information ☎ 808 200 166 (toll-free).

CLIMATE – average highs and lows for the month

JAN.	FEB.	MAR.	APR.	MAY	JUN.	JUL.	AUG.	SEP.	OCT.	NOV.	DEC.
13°C	13°C	15°C	17°C	18°C	22°C	23°C	23°C	23°C	19°C	17°C	14°C
55°F	55°F	59°F	63°F	64°F	72°F	73°F	73°F	73°F	66°F	63°F	57°F
6°C	7°C	7°C	9°C	10°C	13°C	14°C	14°C	14°C	12°C	8°C	7°C
43°F	45°F	45°F	48°F	50°F	55°F	57°F	57°F	57°F	54°F	46°F	45°F

City Sights

Key to symbols

map coordinates refer to the Porto map on page 387; sights below are highlighted in yellow on the map. address or location telephone number opening times nearest bus or tram route restaurant or café on site or nearby admission charge: $$$ more than 500Esc, $$ 250Esc to 500Esc, $ less than 250Esc other relevant information

Igreja e Torre dos Clérigos

B2 Rua dos Clérigos 22 200 1729 Church: Mon.–Tue. 10–noon and 2–5, Sat. 10–noon and 2–8, Sun. 10–1. Tower: daily 10–10, in Aug.; 10–noon and 2–7, Jun.–Jul.; 10–noon and 2–5, rest of year 6, 20, 35 $

The soaring Torre dos Clérigos (Tower of Clérigos), attached to an 18th-century granite church (Igreja dos Clérigos), is a Porto landmark, and most visitors climb it to admire the views. Nicolau Nasoni designed the oval church, with its elaborately festooned facade of swags and garlands, in the 1730s in Italian baroque style.

Jardins do Palácio de Cristal

Off the map Rua de Dom Manuel II 22 609 3192 Daily 9–6 Cafeteria in gardens 3, 20, 52, 78

The green oasis of the Jardins do Palácio de Cristal (Crystal Palace Gardens), a few minutes' walk from Porto's center, offers one of the best vantage points in the city. A lime tree-lined avenue leads from pools and fountains past rhododendrons, magnolias and camellias to rose gardens and terraces high above the river. Summer concerts are held in the park's pavilion.

Museu Nacional Soares dos Reis

A3 Rua Dom Manuel II 22 339 3770 Wed.–Sun. 10–1 and 2–6, Tue. 2–6. Frequently closed for restoration or rearrangement 3, 20, 35, 37, 52, 78 $$

The Museu Nacional Soares dos Reis (Soares dos Reis National Museum), named after the 19th-century sculptor Soares dos Reis, is Porto's most important museum. It's housed in an impressive 1795 neoclassic edifice, occupied in the early 1800s during the Peninsular War by both the French and English. The museum emphasizes pieces by dos Reis, and the exhibits of glass and porcelain are eye-catching; look for some early pieces from the famous Vista Alegre factory.

Museu Romântico

Off the map Rua de Entre-Quintas 220 22 609 1131 Tue.–Sat. 10–noon and 2–5, Sun. 2–5 3, 20, 52,78 $

For insight into how the prosperous bourgeois of Porto lived in the 19th century, visit the Museu Romântico (Romantic Museum), housed in a pretty villa overlooking the river. Wander through the house at will, viewing the furniture and paintings; many of the furnishings have connections with the last king of Piedmont, who lived here in exile. The basement houses the Solar do Vinho do Porto (Port Wine Rooms), where you can sample a wide selection of ports.

Ponte do Dom Luís I

C1 Ponte do Dom Luís I 32, 57, 91

Five bridges span the Douro river, all built dramatically high above the water to span the gorge cut by the lower reaches of the river. Perhaps the most impressive is the Ponte do Dom Luís I (Luis I Bridge), a striking bi-level iron construction designed by Téofilo Seyring (one of Gustave Eiffel's collaborators) and dating from 1886. The bridge effectively links four city areas, so if you can tolerate heights, walk across the upper level for spectacular city views. The lower level will take you directly to the port warehouse area of Gaia.

Praça da Ribeira

Casa do Infante B1 Rua da Alfandega, Ribeira Mon.–Fri. 9–5 49, 88
Centro Regional de Artes Tradicinais Rua de Reboleira 37, Ribeira 22 332 0076 Tue.–Fri. 10–noon and 1–6, Sat.–Sun. 1–7 88

The waterfront Praça da Ribeira (Ribeira Square) is the focal point of the Ribeira district, by far the most atmospheric area of Porto and designated a World Heritage Site. Many of the buildings – arcaded neo-classic constructions – were erected between 1776 and 1782. Although you can approach the area by descending the steep rua de Alfândega past Casa do Infante (Prince Henry the Navigator's reputed birthplace), the easiest way is to walk through the warren of canyon-like streets tumbling down to the river from the cathedral.

There's no better place to experience historic Porto than in this spruced-up district, which has plenty of bars and restaurants. While you're here, visit the Centro Regional de Artes Tradicinais (Regional Center for Arts and Crafts), selling a wonderful range of traditional northern handicrafts.

SÉ

B2 Terreiro da Sé 22 205 4837 Mon.–Sat. 9–12:30 and 2:30–5:30, Sun. and holidays 2:30–5 3, 6, 71, 78 $$

Porto's Sé (Cathedral) stands imposingly high above the steep slopes leading to the river, with the clean classical lines of the adjacent Episcopal Palace providing an elegant contrast to its venerable bulk. Built in the 12th century as a fortress church, it was extensively altered in the 1700s in the baroque style, although the vast silver altarpiece in the north transept dates from the mid-16th century. The two-storey cloisters are more appealing than the cathedral itself; the solid granite lines are enlivened with beautiful tiles, and there are good views over the town. A museum in the treasury houses archeological finds from pre-Roman to Gothic times plus liturgical objects from the 15th to 19th centuries.

VILA NOVA DE GAIA

C1 Vila Nova de Gaia Most lodges open Mon.–Fri. 10–noon and 2–6 (also Sat. in summer) Porto Ibérico, see page 565 57, 91

Officially a separate municipality, Vila Nova de Gaia lies across the Douro river from Porto itself. Its name is synonymous with port, for until 1987 all port had to be matured here to be so named. The riverside slopes are dominated by the solid granite buildings of the port warehouses, or lodges. There are many oportunities for free tours and tastings. This is *the* place to buy port; the white aperitif variety – subtly sweet yet dry – is hard to find overseas. The huge complex high above the river is the old monastery of Serra do Pilar, now a military installation and closed to the public.

The cathedral cloisters are beautifully lined with 18th-century *azulejos* (glazed ceramic tiles). This form of tile is Arabic in origin, but the large designs of blue-on-white tiles are characteristically Portuguese

Port Wine

Port is drunk all over the world, as an aperitif and a digestif. In the 18th century, its production area was the world's first demarcated wine zone, helping to make port one of the few wines with a flavor that has remained untouched for centuries. Be sure to try it in Porto, a city more associated with port than any other.

No longer used commercially to transport barrels of port along the Douro valley, *barcos rabelos* (flat-bottomed boats) now decorate the waterfront

The Wine

Port is a fortified wine, which means that brandy is added to the grapes during the production process. This both "fortifies" the wine, making it stronger, and halts the fermentation process, leaving half the natural grape sugar in the wine. These two factors give port its strength, sweetness and smoothness; its complex flavors come from the soil and climate where the grapes are grown.

To people accustomed to the lush vineyards of other countries, those in the upper Douro valley, which produce port, are a revelation. It's a stony, barren area, a micro-climatic zone where temperatures reach extremes of heat and cold. The soil is a thin layer on top of schist, and the vine roots must force their way through the rock as much as 20 feet to find water. The Portuguese insist, probably rightly, that these conditions are what gives port its unique character.

The vineyards grow on steep terraces, so much of the harvest is done by hand, and until recently the grapes were still trodden by foot. Today more than 90 percent are crushed and fermented at a controlled temperature, sometime between mid-September and mid-October. The new wine is stored up-river to clear until the following spring. In March it's ready for transportation. Following strict tradition, until 1987 it could not be called port unless the maturation had taken place in Vila Nova de Gaia, across the Douro from Porto. Now it can mature on site, although much is still stored and bottled down-river.

Drinking Port

Port comes in several varieties: white, a semi-sweet light wine; ruby, a clear, intense red; tawny, which is older and more complex; and late bottled vintage and vintage port. Vintage port is aged in the bottle and comes from grapes from a single year; late bottled is matured for up to four years before further maturing after bottling. White port is delicious chilled before a meal; ruby goes down well with a cup of coffee after lunch or in the early evening. Tawny and vintage port are best after dinner, savored slowly to appreciate the depth of flavor.

SPAIN

"MEN have no idea of time in any country that is or has been connected with Spain."

From *The West Indies and the Spanish Main* by English novelist Anthony Trollope

Opposite: Exploring the enchanting streets of the Barrio de Santa Cruz, Seville

SPAIN

Spain is a country of diverse landscapes, climates, peoples and cultures, forged over the centuries into a political unity. Physically separated from the rest of Europe by the Pyrenees mountain chain, Spain also found itself isolated internationally, during General Francisco Franco's dictatorship (1939–75). Since Franco's death, however, and with the restoration of its monarchy, Spain has

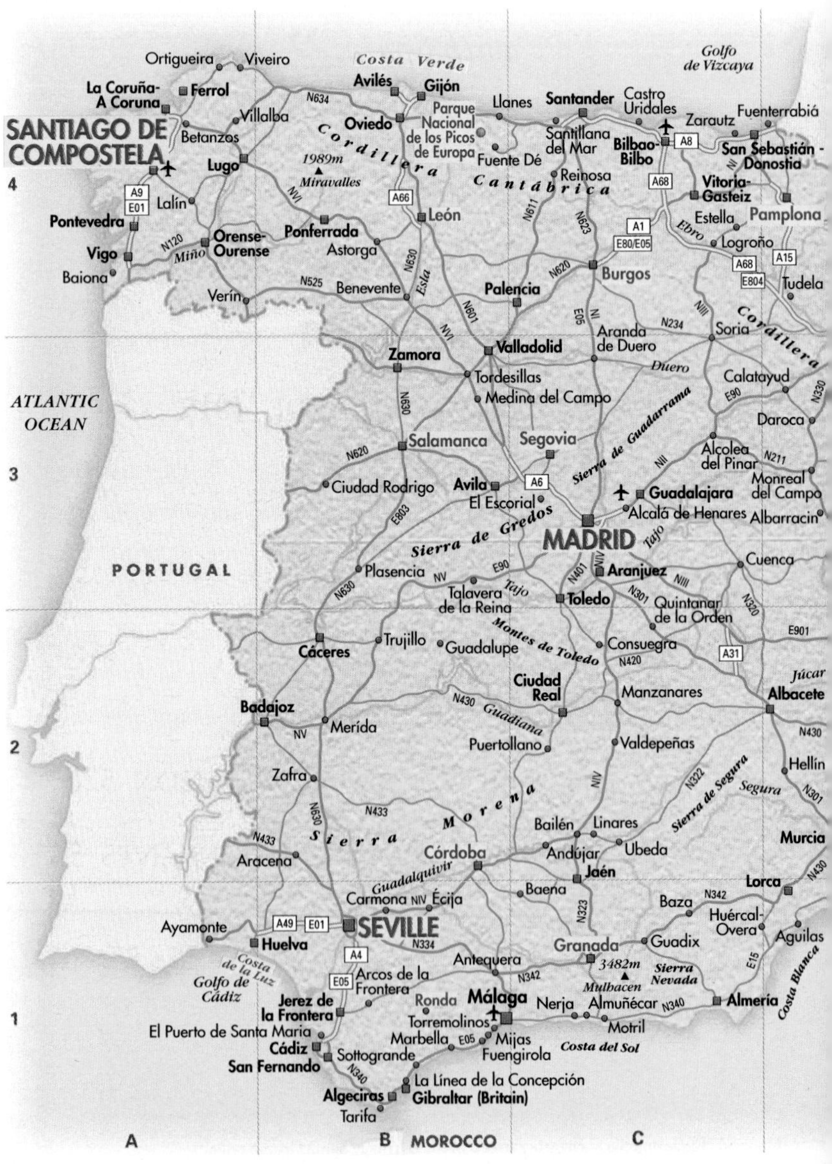

regained its place politically, economically and culturally within mainstream Europe. But despite the rate of progress, many aspects of life remain untouched, and Spain still retains much of its traditional character.

Spain Today

Spain's long and checkered history peaked in the Golden Age of the 16th century, when it was one of the most influential nations of the world. It had immense power across Europe and possessed many overseas colonies. The following centuries saw a gradual decline and increasing isolation from the rest of Europe, culminating in the bitter Civil War (1936–39) and Franco's long dictatorship.

In Spain today, political, cultural and artistic life flourishes, along with national confidence. In 1992 Madrid was chosen as the Cultural Capital of Europe, the same year that dynamic Barcelona hosted the Olympic Games and Seville the World Fair.

From Pyrenees to Portugal

One of Europe's most mountainous countries, Spain occupies most of the Iberian peninsula, stretching southwest from the Pyrenees. Much of the land area is covered by the Meseta, a huge plateau surrounded by long mountain ranges. These stretch from the Sierra Nevada in the south to the Cordillera Cantábrica in the north, and give Spain an average altitude of 2,100 feet. The highest mainland peak is 11,424-foot Mulhacen in the Sierra Nevada, although Mount Teide on the island of Tenerife is nearly 1,000 feet higher.

MORE TOP DESTINATIONS IN SPAIN

• Burgos C4 • Córdoba B2 • Costa Brava E4 • Costa de la Luz A1 • Costa Verde B4 • Granada C1 • León B4 • Monestir de Poblet E3 • Pamplona D4 • Parque Nacional de los Picos de Europa B4 • Peñíscola D3 • Ronda B1 • Salamanca B3 • Segovia C3 • Sierra de Montserrat E3 • Zaragoza D3

Originally from southern Spain, flamenco music is now heard all over the country

The mild, moist Atlantic coast of the Costa Verde in the north contrasts with the sun-baked Mediterranean beaches of the southern Costa del Sol. The grandeur of the Pyrenees is more than rivaled by the dramatic peaks of the Asturian mountains on Spain's northern coast, probably the most beautiful region in Spain. East of Asturia the Ebro valley slashes southeast toward the Mediterranean, where it bisects the coastal plain southwest of Barcelona.

The fertile gardens of Murcia and the agricultural flatlands of the Quadalquivir yield harvests rivaled only by the tourist crop drawn from the golden sands of the Mediterranean beaches. The Mediterranean coast ends on the northern shore of the Straits of Gibraltar, only 9 miles from Africa. Such diversity is echoed in Spain's climate, which varies from the mild, wet weather of the northern Atlantic coast to the typical Mediterranean hot, dry summers and mild, wet winters in the south. Winter inland can be very cold. The island groups of the Balearics and the Canaries have their own geographical and climatic characteristics.

Diversities of Spain

Regional differences are reflected in the Spanish people, their looks, their character, their attitudes and above all, their cuisine. The 800 years of Moorish occupation, the eventual unification of a number of small kingdoms, and the power and wealth of 16th-century colonial Spain have all played their part in the evolution of diverse provincial characteristics.

The concept of centralized power is alien to many Spaniards, and regionalism is still strong in Spain. It has its base in the peninsula's linguistic groups: Galician, spoken in the northwest; Basque, another northern language; Castilian, or pure, central Spanish; and Catalan, based in the southeast, with Valencian a variation of this. These different languages are still spoken every day.

In 1977, when the present constitution was established, ethnic groups were provided for in regions such as Catalonia and Galicia, which are both autonomous. Others fared less well, notably the Basques, whose struggle for a separate identity has been marked by decades of conflict.

Spanish Characters

There are physical differences between Spaniards from different parts of the peninsula. With a population of 40 million, there's room for diversity; contrary to popular belief, not all

Exuberant, spontaneous and passionate – dancing the flamenco outside the Plaza de España, Seville

Spaniards are dark-eyed and olive-skinned. The Moorish genetic legacy is strongest in Andalucia, where many are delicate-featured and dark, personifying the Spanish stereotype.

Spaniards are sometimes thought of as an exuberant, passionate and light-hearted people, much like the Italians, but nothing could be further from the truth. They are certainly passionate, but there's a strong streak of self-control and melancholy in the national character. History has given them loyalty and tolerance. Kindness to children and respect for the elderly are the norm. You will find a tendency to delay until tomorrow (*mañana*) anything that can wait.

Young Spaniards enjoy a freedom and lifestyle their grandparents could never have imagined, yet society is still in a state of flux, and there are huge contrasts between different regions, towns and rural areas. But wherever you go you'll find the same level of hospitality and friendliness, particularly if you speak a little Spanish. English is widely spoken along the Mediterranean coast and by hotel staff in big cities, but very rarely elsewhere.

Cities, Towns and Villages

For visitors the three great cities are Madrid, Barcelona and Seville, but in Spanish eyes the industrial centers of Zaragoza and Bilbao are of equal importance, and the inhabitants of each region claim their capital as the most beautiful in Spain. Andalucia, with the architectural treasures of Granada and Córdoba, is rich in Moorish history. The region of Castille has Christian castles built during the struggle to oust the Moors.

The Mediterranean coast has many remains from centuries of Roman occupation, while the Atlantic port of Cádiz boasts 2,000 years of maritime history. Rural Spain continues largely unchanged; agriculture is more mechanized, but the way and pace of life are still deeply rooted in the past.

Spanish Lifestyle

Daily life in Spain differs in one major way from other southern European countries; mealtimes are very late. Breakfast in hotels is served from around 7:30 until 9:30 or 10. Most Spaniards rise early and eat very little first thing, so they are ready for a snack around 11. This delays lunch until 2 at the earliest, and therefore dinner is often around 10:30 or later.

An early start means you can take advantage of the cool mornings, vital in a country where air-conditioning is not universal. Virtually everything – stores, offices, churches and museums – closes from 1 until 5, and most people sleep after lunch for a couple of hours, during the fabled siesta.

This bypasses the worst heat and leaves people ready to stay up late and enjoy the comparatively fresh evening air. It's a pleasure to sit at a café or restaurant table until 1 or 2 in the morning, as long as you've had a midday rest.

You'll find that most entertainment begins very late, around 10 p.m., and clubs don't get going until the early hours of the morning. Along the Mediterranean coast things are more geared toward foreigners, and you should be able to have dinner soon after 8:30 p.m.

Spain is a deeply Catholic country. When you visit churches, cover the tops of your arms and shoulders and avoid wearing shorts. The many local fiestas held in every town and village are always in honor of the Virgin or some favorite local saint, and if you get the chance to watch one, you will see how religion plays an integral part in everyday life.

Traveling in Spain

The economic boom of the last two decades has resulted in a sound infrastructure. Spain has an excellent network of well-signed toll roads and highways. Spaniards drive fast but safely, and you should have no problems if you rent a car. Public transportation is good, with a choice of internal flights, inexpensive and punctual trains, and long-distance buses going to even the most remote corners.

Hotels are graded and inspected by the government, so you are guaranteed a clean and adequate room no matter how little you pay. Try to spend at least a few nights at one of the *paradores.* These are state-owned hotels housed in historic buildings such as castles and monasteries, often furnished with antiques and offering a high standard of comfort and service.

Spanish Passions

Spaniards throw themselves wholeheartedly into eating out, shopping, going to a soccer match or spending a day on the beach. Their most famous, and often misunderstood, passion is bullfighting (see page 429), but soccer has more supporters. Huge crowds follow the fortunes of teams such as Real Madrid and Barcelona.

Spain has some of Europe's finest golf courses, chiefly along the Mediterranean coast, where you'll also find excellent marinas and water-sports facilities, as well as untouched wilderness areas. Young people travel from all over Europe to experience Spain's club scene, at its most frenetic on the Balearic island of Ibiza.

The Moorish legacy of color and decoration is boldly kept alive in Alicante

22
CASA
DEL
RINGUI

Timeline

15,000–12,000 BC	Caves at Altamira painted; earliest sign of habitation.
218–210 BC	Rome begins conquest of Iberian peninsula.
AD 411	Visigoths invade and establish powerful kingdom at Toledo.
711	Moors defeat Visigoths and begin period of occupation.
1478–79	Spanish Inquisition against Jews, Moors and Protestants.
1492	Christopher Columbus discovers New World.
1519	Spanish conquistadores move across America.
1588	Spanish Armada is sent against Protestant England; fleet destroyed and maritime pre-eminence lost.
1808–14	Peninsular War (War of Independence) sees expulsion of French and defeat of Napoleon.
1898	Phillippines and Cuba rebel against Spanish rule; the United States occupies Puerto Rico; end of Spanish Empire.
1914–18	Spain remains neutral in World War I.
1936–39	Spanish Civil War; General Francisco Franco leads Nationalist troops from Morocco against Republicans.
1939	Franco becomes head of state; Spain enters period of isolation and remains neutral throughout World War II.
1955	Spain joins United Nations.
1975	Death of Franco; Juan Carlos becomes king.
1986	Spain joins the European Union.
1992	Barcelona hosts Olympic Games; Madrid declared Cultural Capital of Europe; Seville is the venue for Expo 92.

The Moorish Occupation

In AD 711 a faction of the ruling Visigoth tribe in Spain went to Islamic Africa to seek help with some domestic political problems. They returned with an army of 7,000; after victory at Cádiz, the Moors encountered little resistance in taking over all but a small strip of northern Spain over the next 30 years. Their tactics were a blend of intelligent strategy and diplomacy; they never demanded religious subordination, as long as Christians paid taxes. Beginning in AD 744, however, resistance against the invaders spread south from the small, unoccupied northern territory, fueled by the legend of St. James the Moorslayer. El Cid succeeded in capturing Toledo from the Moors in 1085, and despite some setbacks a coalition of Christian armies were finally victorious at the Battle of Navas de Tolosa in 1212, the last great battle between Moors and Christians. The Moorish occupation left important legacies, however – they brought mathematics, papermaking, oranges, spices and rice to Spain, which were then introduced to the rest of Europe.

SURVIVAL GUIDE

- English is not widely spoken, even in large cities. Keep in mind that the Spanish you may have learned in high school differs in accent, pronounciation and some vocabulary from that spoken in Spain.
- It's best not to discuss politics, since Spaniards are very proud and the subject could be sensitive.
- Beachwear, shorts and revealing necklines are not acceptable away from coastal resorts.
- Public restrooms are few except in museums, but it's acceptable to use the facilities in a bar; leave a small tip on the counter or stop and have a cup of coffee while you're there.
- Inebriation is frowned on in Spain; the Spanish drink alcohol every day, but in moderation.
- The Spanish are formal and polite; it is best to ask, in Spanish, if the person you're addressing speaks English before you start to speak, and shake hands at the end of casual conversations.
- Water is precious in many parts of Spain; you may find that hotel bathrooms have a shower rather than a tub. Shower pressure is generally low.
- You can safely drink the water throughout Spain, although you may prefer to drink bottled mineral water, which is inexpensive and served chilled. Ice is not generally served in drinks unless you ask.
- Throughout Spain, especially along the Mediterranean, bars specialize in *tapas*, delicious selections of hot or cold savory mouthfuls served with drinks. Be sure to try some of the dozens available: fish, smoked ham, stewed peppers, salads, local almonds, olives. Two or three little dishes will make a delicious lunch.
- All large cities have malls, usually away from the town center; downtown department stores; and a range of antique stores, designer boutiques, local craft and souvenir shops, gourmet food stores, and clothing and bric-a-brac markets.
- Prices in Spain are comparable to the rest of Europe; meals are a little cheaper.
- Try to arrange your trip so that it coincides with a major local festival. Spain has some of the most colorful and exotic celebrations in Europe.

Colorful flower market in La Rambla, Barcelona

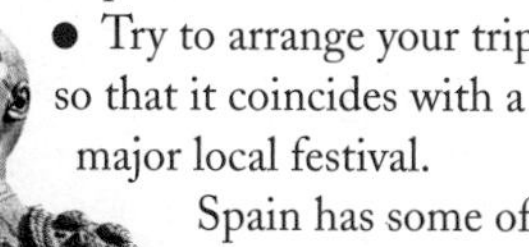

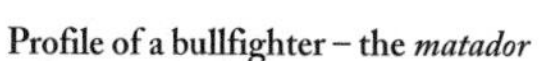
Profile of a bullfighter – the *matador*

MADRID

Unlike most European capital cities, Madrid did not evolve as the nation's capital. It was chosen. In 1561, Philip II settled the court permanently in Madrid, as much for its position in the center of Spain as for political reasons.

Today Madrid is noisy, vibrant and chaotic – a city of great wealth and grueling poverty, with both a booming economy and high unemployment.

Like so much of Spain, Madrid's spirit is elusive and diffused, and will surprise you repeatedly. Plan to stay in the city center, so you can easily reach your hotel in the middle of the day,

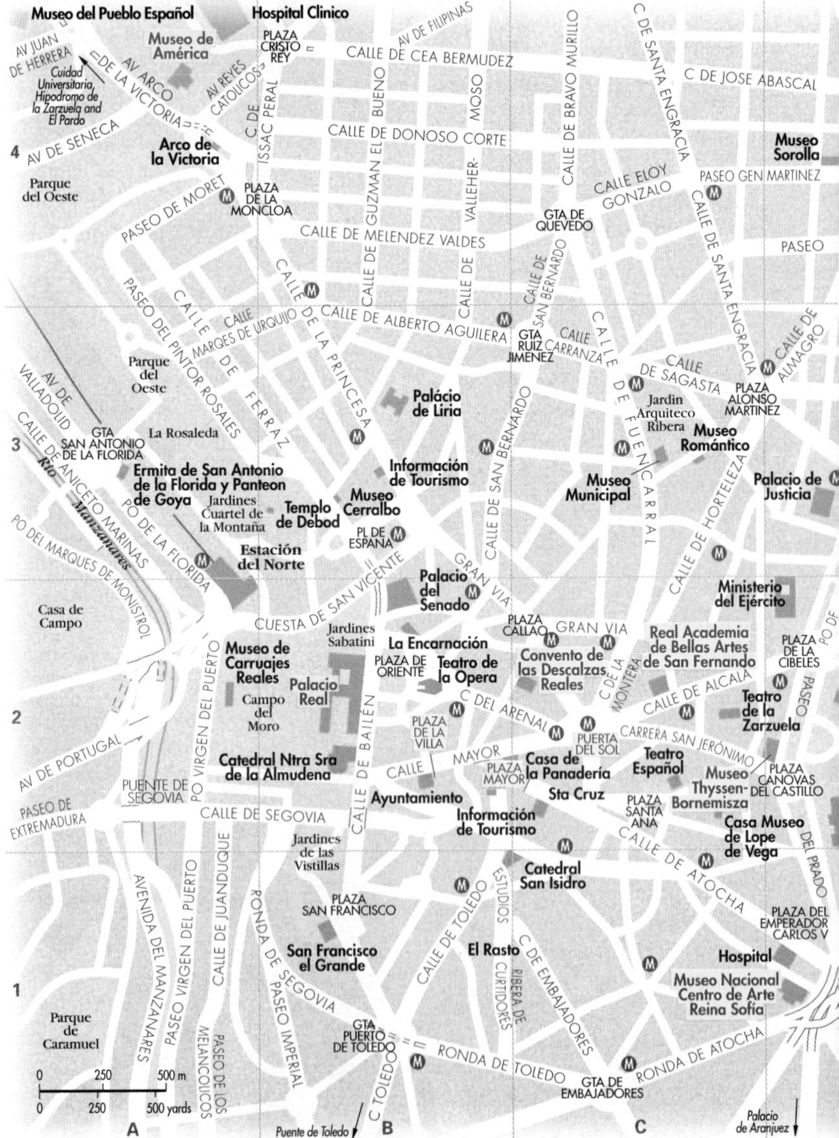

when many museums and monuments are closed for the siesta. The best way to tackle sightseeing is to concentrate on one section at a time. There are three historical areas of interest in the vicinity of the city's main plaza, Sun's Gate (Puerta del Sol): Old Madrid (Viejo Madrid), centering on the Plaza Mayor; the Eastern Quarter (Barrio de Oriente), by the Palacio Real; and Bourbon Madrid, the heart of which is the sweeping avenues and sparkling fountains around the Prado museum.

A convenient tourist bus, Madrid Vision (☎ 91 767 1743), links all three, allowing passengers to get on and off when they want to. Tickets are valid for one or two days, and there's English commentary. The city also has an efficient subway system. Plan your day in advance and also take along a good English-Spanish dictionary, because English is not widely spoken here.

Dining Out

Eating is a real pleasure in Madrid, and there is much to choose from. Local specialties such as offal, blood sausage and pig's ear are usually unpopular with visitors. But there are many regional restaurants featuring traditional dishes from all over Spain. The cuisine of the Basque country and Catalonia is particularly good, or you could try a Latin American restaurant, where even the meat is imported from Argentina. Fast-food outlets are everywhere; take your pick of hamburgers, tortillas or even paella-to-go.

By law, all restaurants have to offer a fixed-price menu, which is usually a good value and includes a choice of first and second courses, a dessert and drink. Madrid has innumerable bars, where you'll find everything from tea and coffee to beer, champagne and exotic cocktails. In summer, bar life moves onto the sidewalks, with hundreds of outdoor venues (*terrazas)* crowded until 4 or 5 in the morning.

Malls and Markets

The central department stores, such as the nationwide chain Corte Ingles, are clustered in the commercial area around the Puerta del Sol. If you're looking for malls, the large Vaguada is in northern

Madrid; the ABC Serrano, between Serrano and Castellana in the center of Madrid is smaller and more upscale. The smartest shopping area is the Salamanca district around the streets of Calle de Serrano and Goya, where you'll find a range of expensive and elegant stores. Madrid is a good place to find Spanish souvenirs from all over the country, and there are many antique stores; the Salamanca district alone has more than 50. Visit the Rastro flea market on a Saturday or Sunday morning and browse in some of the tiny boutiques.

Evening Entertainment

Classical music, opera and theater thrive in Madrid, and the tourist office publishes a monthly guide, *Qué hacer en Madrid*, with excellent listings. You might enjoy a *zarzuela* performance, a traditional form of musical combining elements of opera, vaudeville and melodrama. Jazz is very popular, with nightly performances at some of Europe's best venues. If you're looking for flamenco, there are several clubs (*tablaos*) where it is staged. Madrid has an exceptional nightclub scene. A number of movie theaters show movies in their original language.

Late, Late Nights

People eat late and go to bed late all over Spain, especially in the capital. Locals do not eat dinner much before 10 or 11 at night, even in winter; in summer the "night" is still young at 3:30 in the morning. In recent years the siesta has become threatened, as Spanish business practices come in line with the rest of Europe. One result of this is that *Madrileños* are functioning on less and less sleep – a fact beginning to worry Spanish health watchdogs.

ESSENTIAL INFORMATION

TOURIST INFORMATION

Oficinas de Información Turística de la Comunidad de Madrid (Madrid Community Tourist Information Offices)

- Calle Duque de Medinaceli 2 ☎ 91 429 4951; fax 91 429 3705
- Plaza Mayor 3 ☎ 91 366 5477
- Mercado Puerta de Toledo (market), Glorieta Puerta de Toledo ☎ 91 364 1876
- Aeropuerto de Madrid-Barajas (airport), international arrivals terminal ☎/fax 91 305 8656
- Estación de Chamartín (railroad station), central hall (gate 16) ☎/fax 91 315 9976; www.turmadrid.com

URBAN TRANSPORTATION

Getting around Madrid is simple on the subway (metro) and bus systems. Subway stations are marked on the Madrid city map as the letter "M" on a blue background inside a red diamond. The subway has 11 lines and runs daily 6 a.m.–1:30 a.m. Purchase tickets from machines or ticket offices in the stations, where you also can pick up a map of the system. The Metrobus ticket, valid for 10 trips on the subway and bus systems, is available from metro stations, tobacconists (*estancos*) and Municipal Transport Company (EMT) booths at some bus stops. Buses run daily 6 a.m.– midnight, with a limited all-night service. Pay the driver or stamp your pass in the machine when you board. Taxis are cheap and can be hailed on the street; a green light on top means they are free. To call a taxi dial Tele-Taxi (☎ 91 445 9008), Radio-Teléfono Taxi (☎ 91 547 8200) or Radio-Taxi Independiente (☎ 91 371 2131).

AIRPORT INFORMATION

Madrid's Barajas Airport (☎ 91 305 8343) is 8 miles northeast of the city center, about a 30-minute drive. Buses run every 12 minutes into Madrid, where they terminate beneath the Plaza de Colón, across the square and downstairs from the subway station of the same name.

CLIMATE – average highs and lows for the month

JAN.	FEB.	MAR.	APR.	MAY	JUN.	JUL.	AUG.	SEP.	OCT.	NOV.	DEC.
9°C	12°C	15°C	18°C	21°C	27°C	32°C	31°C	26°C	19°C	13°C	10°C
48°F	54°F	59°F	64°F	70°F	81°F	90°F	88°F	79°F	66°F	55°F	50°F
1°C	2°C	4°C	6°C	9°C	14°C	17°C	17°C	13°C	9°C	4°C	2°C
34°F	36°F	39°F	43°F	48°F	57°F	63°F	63°F	55°F	48°F	39°F	36°F

City Sights

Key to symbols

map coordinates refer to the Madrid map on pages 402–403; sights below are highlighted in yellow on the map.
address or location telephone number opening times nearest subway restaurant or café on site or nearby admission charge: $$$ more than 900PTA, $$ 600PTA–900PTA, $ less than 600PTA other relevant information

Convento de las Descalzas Reales

C2 Plaza de las Descalzas Reales 3 91 542 0059 Tue.–Thu. and Sat. 10:30–12:45 and 4–5:45, Fri. 10:30– 12:30, Sun. 11–1:30 Sol, Calloa or Opera $$

The oddly named Convento de las Descalzas Reales (Convent of the Royal Shoeless Nuns) was founded in 1560 as a convent for aristocratic ladies seeking the religious life. Pious and wealthy, they and their families endowed and decorated 33 chapels, each more opulent than the last, with treasures by mainly Spanish artists.

Iglesia de los Jerónimos

D2 Calle Moreto 4 91 420 3078 Daily 8–1:30 and 5–8:30 Atocha

Iglesia de los Jerónimos (St. Jerome's Church) is the traditional royal church where princes were consecrated and monarchs married until King Alfonso XIII married Queen Victoria in 1878. Rebuilt in 1505 by King Ferdinand for his queen, Isabella, this simple Gothic church, with its single nave and side chapels, is in marked contrast to the flamboyance of many other churches in the country.

Museo de América

A4 Avenida Reyes Católicos 6 91 549 2641 Tue.–Sat. 10–3, Sun. 10–2:30 Moncloa $

The Museo de América (America Museum), an archeological and ethnological museum, is devoted to pre-Columbian and Hispanic artifacts telling the story of European ties with America. The information is in Spanish, but anyone can appreciate the powerful Quimbayas Treasure and the collection's high point, the Cortesiano

An allegorical statue outside the America Museum

Codex, which records in Mayan runes the arrival of the Spaniards in the New World.

Museo Nacional Centro de Arte Reina Sofía

D1 Calle Santa Isabel 52 91 467 5062 Mon. and Wed.–Sat. 10–9, Sun. 10–2:30 Café and snack bar in museum Atocha $ (free Sat. after 2:30 p.m. and Sun. to senior citizens and under 18)

The Museo Nacional Centro de Arte Reina Sofía (Queen Sofía National Art Center),

Golden altar inside the Descalzas Convent

The Royal Palace viewed from the Campo del Moro

Olivareo by Velázquez, in the Prado

the city's modern art museum, is housed in the former Hospital de San Carlos. Exterior glass elevators whisk you up to the permanent exhibitions. Most visitors flock to Pablo Picasso's great *Guernica*. When it was commissioned for the 1937 World's Fair, his only instruction was to paint a big picture; this searing black-and-white composition has become the icon of 20th-century antiwar symbolism. Other highlights include paintings by Salvador Dalí, spanning his stylistic development and surreal sexual imagery, and Joan Miró.

MUSEO DEL PRADO

D2 Paseo del Prado 91 330 2800 Tue.–Sat. 9–7, Sun. 9–2 Café and snack bar in museum Banco de España or Atocha $ (free Sat. after 2:30 p.m. and Sun. to senior citizens and under 18)

Since its opening in 1819 the Museo del Prado (Prado Museum), with its unrivaled collection of Spanish paintings, has been among the world's finest. Once the royal collection, the Prado represents the personal taste of the Spanish monarchs, with a noticeable emphasis on religious and courtly paintings. Because of space limitations only about 1,500 of the 7,000 works are on display. Paintings are frequently moved around or loaned to other museums, but the most famous are normally on view; pick up an up-to-date floor plan as you arrive. Some works, particularly those by Diego Velázquez and Francisco Goya, attract huge crowds and you may have to wait to see them.

Highlights include Velázquez' *Las Meninas*, often described as "the finest painting in the world." Goya's work occupies many rooms; look for his *Majas*, two paintings thought to be of the Duchess of Alba, one demure and clothed, the other sensuously naked. His *pinturas negras*, the dark pictures, stand in stark contrast; disturbing and pessimistic, they represent the apocalyptic vision of a man on the edge of madness. The Spanish monarchs were fascinated by the surreal work of Hiëronymous Bosch; his *Garden of Earthly Delights*, with its wealth of weird detail, is one of his finest works.

MUSEO THYSSEN-BORNEMISZA

D2 Paseo del Prado 8 91 369 0151 Tue.–Sun. 10–7 Café and restaurant in

Madrid's Plaza Mayor, begun in medieval times and still a focus for the social activities of its citizens

museum Banco de España $$ ($ for temporary exhibitions)

Acquired in 1993 for about $350 million, the Museo Thyssen-Bornemisza (Thyssen-Bornemisza Museum) provides Spain with another world-class museum. It contains more than 700 works. Western paintings from the 13th to 20th centuries are arranged chronologically, so start on the top floor and work down. Early portraits and Renaissance works are grouped together, followed by Dutch interiors. Nineteenth-century American paintings include a portrait of George Washington's cook by Gilbert Stuart and a fine sea scene by Winslow Homer. The 20th century is well represented by Joan Miró, Salvador Dalí and Mark Rothko.

Palacio Real

B2 Calle Bailén 91 542 0059 Palacio/Museo: Mon.–Sat. 9–6, Sun. 9–3, Apr.–Sep.; Mon.–Sat. 9–5, Sun. 9–2, rest of year. Closed when official events are held Opera $$$

The vast white bulk of the Palacio Real (Royal Palace) looks particularly striking from the Campo del Moro, a peaceful garden behind the palace where you'll also find the Museo de Carruajes Reales (Royal Carriage Museum). After a fire destroyed the Moorish original, the palace was planned to be three times its existing size. Funds ran out, leaving the structure built between 1737 and 1764. In use until 1931, it is now occasionally used for state receptions. Everything is opulent and awesomely large. Madrid's 1993 Cathedral of the Almudena stands nearby; the Plaza de Oriente is a pleasant square across the road .

Parque del Retiro

D2 Main entrance: Plaza de la Independencia Retiro, Ibiza, Atocha or Menéndez Pelayo

The Parque del Retiro (Retreat Park) was laid out in the 1630s as part of the immense French-style pleasure gardens surrounding the Buen Retiro Palace. The building itself was destroyed during the Napoleonic Wars. Today it is Madrid's favorite park, bright with flowers and scattered with statues and fountains. Many people head straight for the lake, with its ornate statue of Alfonso XII, but other attractions include the Palacio de Cristal (Crystal Palace), a wonderful 19th-century glass palace.

Plaza Mayor

B2 Plaza Mayor Sol

One of Europe's most dazzling squares, the present Plaza Mayor (Main Square) stands on the site of the medieval market, the Plaza del Arrabal. When Madrid became Spain's capital, Philip III ordered it to be rebuilt as the focal point, and it was completed in 1620. Harmonious brick facades are punctuated with elegant stonework and arcades. The plaza was used for fiestas, bullfights and royal proclamations, and was the scene of many executions during the dark days of the Inquisition.

The Alcalá Gate – Madrid's finest example of neoclassic architecture

PLAZA MONUMENTAL DE TOROS DE LAS VENTAS

Off the map · Avenida de los Toreros · 91 356 2200 (Museo Taurino: 91 725 1857) · Museo Taurino: Tue.–Fri. 9:30–2:30, Sat.–Sun. 10–1 · Ventas · Museum $; tickets for fights $–$$$

Madrid's Plaza Monumental de Toros de las Ventas (Las Ventas Bullring) was opened in 1934, and for aficionados is the most important in the world. The Museo Taurino (Bullfight Museum), devoted to some of bullfighting's famous names, features the "suit of lights" worn by Manolete during his fateful fight in 1947.

PLAZA DE LA VILLA

B2 · Plaza de la Villa · 91 588 2908 · Buildings: Mon. 5–6 · Sol or Opera

Despite their different dates, the three main stone buildings around this little plaza (Town Square) coexist harmoniously. The Gothic Torre de los Lujanes (Lujanes Tower), one of Madrid's few surviving 15th-century structures, is balanced by the Casa de Cisneros, a restored 1537 Plateresque-style palace. The Casa del Ayuntamiento was designed as the meeting place for the town council in 1640, a function it still serves today.

PUERTA DE ALCALÁ

D2 · Plaza de la Independencia · Retiro

Surrounded by roaring traffic, the Puerta de Alcalá (Alcalá Gate) is a symbol of Madrid, along with the equally splendid Plaza de la Cibeles, a street away. Designed in 1778 as the main entrance to the Spanish court, it's a gateway on a monumental scale, with five grandiose arches topped by lion heads, cherubim and coats of arms.

PUERTA DEL SOL

C2 · Puerta del Sol · Sol

Puerta del Sol (Sun's Gate) has been a plaza since 1570, when the original gate was demolished. This is the heart of Madrid. The headquarters of the regional government are housed on the south side, where a stone in the sidewalk marks Kilometer Zero, from which all distances in Spain are measured.

REAL ACADEMIA DE BELLAS ARTES DE SAN FERNANDO

C2 · Calle Alcalá 13 · 91 522 1491 · Tue.–Fri. 9–7, Sat.–Mon. 9–2:30 · Sol · $ (free to all Sat.–Sun.)

Art lovers will enjoy the peaceful Real Academia de Bellas Artes de San Fernando (Royal Academy of Fine Arts), founded in the 18th century to emulate art venues in Paris and London. The academy has some fine paintings by Francisco Goya and a good Diego Velázquez portrait of Philip IV. The highlight is *Spring* by Italian artist Giuseppe Arcimboldo, a portrait in which the sitter's features are entirely composed of fruit and vegetables.

MONASTERIO DE EL ESCORIAL

Harmonious facade of the Monastery of El Escorial

Twenty-five miles northwest of Madrid, on the southern slopes of the Sierra da Guadarrama mountain range, stands the massive religious complex known as El Escorial. One of the most impressive monuments in Spain, it's easily accessible from Madrid and gives a true insight into the extraordinary wealth and power of the 16th-century Spanish monarchy.

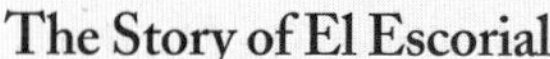

The Story of El Escorial

In 1557 the Spanish forces of Philip II defeated the French at St. Quentin. To give thanks to God, Philip conceived the idea of building a monastery dedicated to St. Lawrence (San Lorenzo), which would also serve as a royal palace and burial place.

The vast complex was principally designed in 1584 by Juan de Herrera, and it required 1,500 laborers to complete the work. It has more than 1,200 doors, 2,600 windows and 16 courtyards, and measures nearly 670 feet long. The granite stone accentuates the severe lines of the building, which is built on a grid plan, and the clear air has kept the stone and tiles pristine. Later Bourbon monarchs also left their stamp on the palace by means of decoration, furnishings and pictures.

El Escorial Today

Philip II's modest private apartments are in marked contrast to his grand throne room. He lived in a suite of relatively small rooms with direct access to the chapel.

Later Bourbon monarchs extended these royal Habsburg apartments near the church to the third floor. You will find sumptuously painted ceilings, frescoes and a wonderful tapestry collection. A frescoed courtyard gives access to the marbled staircase leading down to the Royal Pantheon (Pantéon de los Reyes), where many Spanish kings from the time of Charles V onward are buried.

The church itself, in the heart of the monastery, is on a monumental scale. Its 100-foot-high altarpiece with onyx, marble and jasper columns is punctuated by bronze sculptures. Move on to the equally opulent library, with its rare wood shelves, marble tables and ornate ceiling.

One of the highlights is the art museum. Among numerous paintings by Peter Paul Rubens, Titian and Jacopo Tintoretto are Roger van der Weyden's thought-provoking *Calvary* and the acidic angularity of El Greco's *Martyrdom of St. Maurice*.

C3 El Escorial 91 890 1554 Tue.–Sun. 10–6, Apr.–Sep.; 10–5, rest of year Trains from Atocha and Chamartín (91 328 9020) Autobuses Herranz (91 890 4100); buses leave from outside Moncloa subway station in Madrid $$$

BARCELONA

Barcelona, the capital of the autonomous Spanish region of Catalonia (Catalunya), is one of the Mediterranean's most vibrant cities. Catalonia is Spain's leading economic region, the most innovative and prosperous area of the country, with a proud history, an independent spirit and a strong sense of identity.

In 1975 King Juan Carlos restored Catalonia's status as an autonomous region, which marked the beginning of Barcelona's renaissance. The pride and self-confidence engendered by a thriving economy and urban renewal culminated in the Barcelona Olympic Games of 1992. Since then, the city has continued to forge ahead. With its 2,000-year-old history, exhilarating atmosphere and superb architecture from nearly every age, it can't fail to please.

The City and Its People

Wherever you stay, the excellent public transportation system gives easy access to the entire city. For atmosphere, you might want to be somewhere near the street La Rambla or in the old town, and thus within easy walking distance of many of the main sights and the waterfront. The architecturally interesting Eixample area is more spacious, with excellent shopping and restaurants; other hotels are relatively far out of the city center. Barcelonans are exceptionally helpful and polite, with an ability to combine efficiency with a relaxed Mediterranean attitude.

English is not widely spoken, although most hotel staff speak it adequately. All signs are in both Catalan and Spanish. Both are official languages in Barcelona; like Spanish, Catalan is a romance language with Latin roots.

Barcelonan Themes

Since there's so much to see in Barcelona, concentrate on specific areas and themes. Spend a day on the waterfront taking in the Old Port district, Little Barcelona and the ultra-modern Olympic Port. There's a choice of boat tours around the harbor and up the coast, which is the best way to admire the port.

Head for l'Eixample, the Passeig de Gràcia and the Sagrada Família to enjoy the Modernista architecture for which the city is so well known. Barcelona is blessed with two hills, the Montjuïc and Tibidabo; each offers a refuge from the summer noise and heat and has magnificent views over the city and sea.

Barcelona has more than 50 museums and galleries. The Maritime Museum, the Pedralbes Monastery, the Football Museum, the City History Museum and the Comic Book and Illustrations Museum cater to a wide range of interests and are all fascinating. Modern-art lovers shouldn't miss the

Gaudí

Antoni Gaudí was born in Barcelona in 1852, and lived and worked in the city throughout his life. His architectural vision was flamboyant and unique, and he designed some of Barcelona's most outstanding Modernist buildings. Curved lines, pinnacles, organically inspired stone and towers are his trademarks, seen at their best in the remarkable Holy Family Temple (Temple Expiatori de la Sagrada Família). He was run over by a tram in 1926 and died, unrecognized, in a hospital. When his body was identified, the people of Barcelona lined the streets for his funeral.

Contemporary Art Museum and the Modern Art Museum. If time is short, there are plenty of English-language guided tours and excursions that take in the main city sights by day and night, and also offer a chance to explore other parts of Catalonia.

Parks and Pools

Barcelona is rich in parks offering a welcome contrast to the bustle and noise of city streets. The Parc de la Ciutadella, near the Old Town and waterfront, is particularly nice. It has shady trees, a lake and Spain's best zoo, with more than 7,000 animals. Other parks in the city include the Parc Joan Miró, with its flamboyant ceramic sculpture, and the Parc Espanya Industrial, laid out in the early 1980s. Good beaches are within easy reach, and Barcelona also has excellent swimming pools.

Where to Shop

Prosperous Barcelona is a great shopping center. You'll find serious shopping along the Passeig de Gràcia and on its surrounding streets, which have all the big fashion names, expensive antique stores and some enticing interior design outlets. The wide avenue of Diagonal is lined with good stores, while the Plaça de

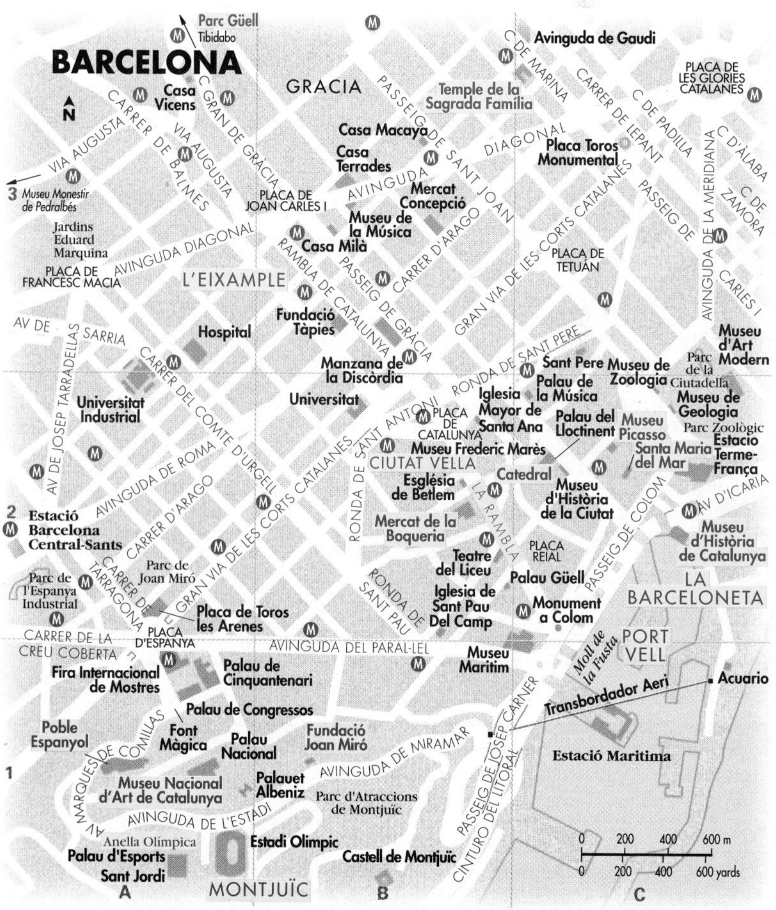

Quirky decoration on a corner of La Rambla

Catalunya has a large branch of the department store Corte Ingles.

For Spanish souvenirs, porcelain, fans and items made of wood, try the stores on Portal de l'Angel and around La Rambla. Mercat de les Encants is a second-hand market held on the Plaça de les Glòries on Monday, Wednesday, Friday and Saturday (8 a.m. to 7 p.m.).

Nightlife

Classical music, jazz, rock, dance, theater and movies are popular forms of entertainment; there are comprehensive listings in the *Guía del Ocio,* available from newsstands. Dancing is very popular, and the club scene is one of the best in Spain, ranging from the elegant to the avant-garde. As everywhere in the country, nightlife reaches its peak around 3 a.m. and continues until dawn.

Barcelona has some superb festivals throughout the year, often featuring decorated floats, fireworks and processions of the huge dragon and demon figures known as *capgrossos,* or "big heads."

ESSENTIAL INFORMATION

TOURIST INFORMATION

Barcelona Turisme (Barcelona Tourism)

- Plaça de Catalunya 17-S ☎ 93 304 3135; fax 93 304 3155; www.bcn.es
- Palau de Congressos, Avenida Reina María Cristina ☎ 93 233 2439
- Estació Barcelona-Sants (railroad station) – walk-in only
- Barcelona Airport (arrivals hall) ☎ 93 478 4704

URBAN TRANSPORTATION

Getting around is easy on the subway and bus systems. Subway stations are marked on the Barcelona city map by the letter "M" in a red circle. There are five color-coded lines on the subway; trains run Sun.–Thu. 5 a.m.–11 p.m., Fri.–Sat. 5 a.m.– 2 a.m. Combination tickets valid for one, three or five days give unlimited use of the bus, subway and urban trains; tickets and maps are available from subway stations. Don't forget to validate tickets by stamping them at the turnstile before boarding trains, or when you get on the bus. Bus Turístic operates daily 9–7:45 from March through December and has two routes which cover Barcelona's main attractions, taking you closer to the sights than the regular city service. A cable car links La Barceloneta and Montjuïc, and there are two funiculars, serving Montjuïc and Tibidabo; the latter also is served by Barcelona's one surviving tram route. You can pick up a black-and-yellow taxi at a stand, hail one on the street, or call Taxi-Radio-Móvil (☎ 93 358 1111), Servi-Taxi (☎ 93 330 0300) or Radio-Taxi (☎ 93 225 0000).

AIRPORT INFORMATION

Barcelona International Airport (☎ 93 289 3838) connects to most major European cities and is 7 miles southwest of the city center, about a 30-minute drive. A train connects to Estació Barcelona-Sants every 30 minutes daily 6:15 a.m.–10:10 p.m. (journey time 30 minutes). The Aerobus runs to and from Plaça de Catalunya every 15 minutes, 5:30 a.m.–10:05 p.m. (journey time 30 minutes).

CLIMATE – average highs and lows for the month

JAN.	FEB.	MAR.	APR.	MAY	JUN.	JUL.	AUG.	SEP.	OCT.	NOV.	DEC.
13°C	14°C	15°C	17°C	21°C	24°C	28°C	28°C	25°C	21°C	17°C	14°C
55°F	57°F	59°F	63°F	70°F	75°F	82°F	82°F	77°F	70°F	63°F	57°F
5°C	6°C	8°C	10°C	12°C	17°C	20°C	20°C	19°C	13°C	9°C	8°C
41°F	43°F	46°F	50°F	54°F	63°F	68°F	68°F	66°F	55°F	48°F	46°F

City Sights

Key to symbols

map coordinates refer to the Barcelona map on page 411; sights below are highlighted in yellow on the map.
address or location telephone number opening times nearest subway nearest bus or tram route restaurant or café on site or nearby admission charge: $$$ more than 900PTA, $$ 600PTA–900PTA, $ less than 600PTA other relevant information

Anella Olímpica

A1 Montjuïc 93 426 0660 Olympic Stadium: Mon.–Fri. 10–2 and 4–8, Sat.–Sun. 10–2, Jul.–Sep.; Mon.–Fri. 10–2 and 4–7, Sat.–Sun. 10–2, Apr.–Jun.; Mon.–Fri. 10–1 and 4–6, Sat–Sun. 10–2, rest of year Espanya 61 $

The 1992 Olympic complex, the Anella Olímpica (Olympic Ring), centers around the 1936 Olympic Stadium, which was enlarged to seat 70,000 people. Its basement now houses the Olympic Gallery, recalling the 1992 games with videos and souvenirs. Nearby are Barcelona's sports university; the steel-and-glass Sant Jordi Stadium; and the pools, all dominated by the silhouette of the communications tower, one of the city's modern landmarks.

La Barceloneta

C2 La Barceloneta Barceloneta 14, 17, 51, 64

The district of La Barceloneta (Little Barcelona) occupies a triangle of reclaimed land between the harbor and the sea. Developed in the 18th century to house seamen, fishermen and dock workers, the neighborhood retains its maritime atmosphere. It's a great place to eat; many seafood restaurants (*chiringuitos*) line the seafront, where you'll find local fresh fish specialties.

Catedral

C2 Plaça de la Seu 93 315 1554 (museum: 93 310 2580) Mon.–Fri. 8–1:30 and 4–7:30, Sat.–Sun. 5–7:30 p.m. Museum: daily 11–1 Nou Celler, see page 566 Jaume I 17, 19, 40, 45 Cathedral free (clock tower $; museum $)

Nothing more strongly represents

Barcelona's fortress-like Cathedral

Barcelona's historic past than the great Catedral (Cathedral). It was built between the 13th and 15th centuries (with a 19th-century neo-Gothic facade), and the soaring space beneath the Catalan Gothic arches and numerous side chapels houses a wealth of treasures. The tranquil 14th-century cloister, with its fountains, magnolias and palms, is particularly beautiful.

Ciutat Vella

B2 Bounded by Rambla, Universitat, Laietana and Ferran Nou Celler, see page 566 Jaume I 14, 17, 19

A maze of narrow streets and squares comprises the Ciutat Vella (Old City). It was built within the old Roman walls when Barcelona was one of the richest and most important Mediterranean trading cities. At its heart lies the Barri Gòtic (Gothic Quarter), centered around the Catedral and Plaça Sant Jaume. This plaza, once the power center of Catalonia's kings, is still the site of city hall and the administrative buildings of the government of Catalonia.

The Plaça del Rei, formerly the medieval marketplace, is said to be where King Ferdinand and Queen Isabella welcomed Christopher Columbus home from America in 1493. Nearby is the Plaça Reial, a fine arcaded square built in 1848. Gothic mansions line the streets, and you'll find museums, historic churches, bars and restaurants.

Gaudí's exuberant Casa Batlló

L'Eixample

A3 Diagonal, Catalunya or Girona
Between 1860 and 1920 Barcelona expanded into a grid of uniform streets parallel to the sea, an area known as l'Eixample (the Extension). Today this is a residential, commercial and business district, divided in half by the Diagonal, a grand avenue cutting through the grid at a 45-degree angle. An interesting example of innovative town planning, it contains Barcelona's finest Modernist buildings. Some of the best are in the Passeig de Gràcia; look for No. 43, Casa Batlló, with a mosaic facade and wavy roofline that represent St. George's dragon. The block at No. 92 is known as La Pedrera, Gaudí's last secular work, built with no single straight line or sharp corner.

Fundació Joan Miró

B1 Plaça Neptú, Parc de Montjuïc 93 443 9470 Tue.–Sat. 10–7 (also Thu. 7–9:30 p.m.), Sun. 10:30–2:30 Café in museum Espanya 61; Montjuïc funicular to Miramar $$
More than 200 instantly recognizable and vibrantly colored paintings, along with sculptures, tapestries and drawings, are displayed in the white, bright space of the Fundació Joan Miró (Joan Miró Foundation). Born in Barcelona in 1893, Miró spent most of his life in the city before retiring to Mallorca in 1956. In 1971 he established the foundation to house the world's largest collection of his works and to promote contemporary art.

Mercat de la Boquería

B2 Plaça de la Boquería Mon.–Sat. 8–8 Liceu 14, 38, 59
Make time to visit the glorious Mercat de la Boquería (Boquería Market), housed since the 1830s in a covered hall just off the Rambla. If you arrive at lunchtime, take advantage of the snack bars here. The scents and colors of the fish, hams and sausages, succulent fruit and freshly picked vegetables, and the babble of noise from the shoppers and stall vendors will be one of the most enduring memories of your visit to Barcelona.

Montjuïc

A1 Montjuïc Font Màgica displays: Thu.–Sun. evenings, late Jun. to late Sep. Take the subway to Parallel station, then the funicular to Parc de Montjuïc and the *telefèric* cable car to Mirador and Castell 61
The green hill of Montjuïc, 698 feet high, dominates Barcelona's southern suburbs. Once known as the "Mountain of the Jews," Montjuïc today is a pleasant recreational area, dotted with gardens, museums, galleries and sports facilities. The most impressive approach is through the monumental Plaça de Espanya to the Font Màgica (Magic Fountain). The fountain stands below the pavilions built for the 1929 International Exhibition, many of which now house galleries.

Museu d'Història de Catalunya

C2 Plaça Pau de Vila 3 93 225 4700 Tue.–Sat. 10 –7 (also Fri.–Sat. 7–8 p.m.), Sun. 10–2:30 Café in museum Barceloneta or Drassanes 14, 17, 36, 39, 40, 45, 57, 59, 64 $
The Museu d'Història de Catalunya (Catalonian History Museum), Barcelona's newest museum, helps explain Catalonia, a "nation within a nation." It is located in a

converted 19th-century warehouse, and exhibits depict the political, historical, cultural and everyday life of this vibrant region. The museum uses state-of-the-art and hands-on displays, interactive screens and special effects to convey its story.

Museu Nacional d'Art de Catalunya (MNAC)

A1 Palau Nacional, Parc de Montjuïc 93 622 0376 Tue.–Sat. 10–7 (also Thu. 7–9 p.m.), Sun. 10–2:30 Café-bar in museum Espanya 9, 13, 38, 50, 55, 56, 57, 61, 65, 109, 157 $$ (free first Thu. of the month)

Still in the middle of ongoing renovations, the Museu Nacional d'Art de Catalunya (National Museum of Catalonian Art) is among the world's finest medieval art museums. Catalan Romanesque art, with its solid rounded forms and stunning simplicity, is represented by sculpture and carving, gold, enamel and textiles. The outstanding treasures are the 11th- and 12th-century murals, removed from isolated country churches and reassembled in the museum in order to preserve them. The ornate forms of the Gothic sculptures and altarpieces, which form the other major part of the museum, make a perfect contrast.

Museu Picasso

C2 Calle Montcada 15–19 93 319 6310 Tue.–Sat. 10–8, Sun. 10–3 Café-restaurant in museum Jaume I, Liceu or Arc de Triomf 14, 17, 19, 39, 40, 45, 51, 59 $$ (free to all first Sun. of the month)

Pablo Picasso, born in Andalucia in 1881, lived in Barcelona from 1895 until 1904, and he held his first exhibition in the city in 1900. The Museu Picasso (Picasso Museum), Barcelona's top attraction, is the most important collection of his works in Spain. It contains examples from each of his stylistic periods, from early street scenes to the major cubist works and ceramics he produced in later years.

Parc Güell

Off the map Calle Olot 93 424 3809 Daily 10–9, May–Aug.; 10–8, Apr. and Sep.; 10–7, Mar. and Oct.; 10–6, rest of year Vallcarca 24, 25, 31, 32, 74

With its views and green spaces, Parc Güell (Güell Park) would be worth visiting even without the architectural elements by Antoni Gaudí scattered throughout its 50 acres. Originally planned as a residential landscaped area by Gaudí's main patrons, the Güell family, only the grand entrance, the plaza, paths and steps were completed. These are interspersed with colorful and weirdly shaped sculptures, fountains and columns, many intricately decorated with thousands of pieces of broken ceramics.

Mosaic fountain by Gaudí on Güell Park steps

Poble Espanyol

A1 Avenida de Marqués de Comillas 93 508 6330 Tue.–Sat. 9 a.m.–2 a.m. (also Fri.–Sat. 2–4 a.m.), Sun. 9 a.m.–midnight, Mon. 9–8 Espanya 9, 13, 27, 38, 50, 52, 53, 55, 56, 57, 61, 65, 91, 127, 141, 209, L52, L90, L93, EA, EB $$$

The streets and squares of the Poble Espanyol (Spanish Village), built for the 1929 World Exhibition, give a glimpse of the country's many architectural styles. Reproductions range from the gleaming white houses of Andalucia to the flat granite facades of Galicia, all blended to form one "village." The buildings house restaurants, cafés and workshops where you'll find crafts and artifacts from all over Spain, while evening brings dinner, live music and flamenco.

The soaring interior of the Gothic church of Santa Maria del Mar

Port Vell

C1 Port Vell Drassanes or Barceloneta 17, 36, 64

The Port Vell (Old Port) district, once decayed and run-down, was transformed for the 1992 Olympics. An integral part of the city again, it is a busy recreation area, with a new marina and elegant new bridges and walkways connecting its various attractions. The centerpiece is Maremagnum, a shopping, eating and leisure center, complete with IMAX movie theater and Europe's largest aquarium.

La Rambla

B2 La Rambla Catalunya, Drassanes or Liceu 13, 48, 59

La Rambla, Barcelona's most famous street, runs from Plaça de Catalunya to the waterfront. It's an exuberant tree-lined promenade effectively joining the old and new parts of the city, divided into seven distinctive sections. Here is Liceu, Barcelona's opera house, restored after a fire in 1994. The name Rambla is Arabic, from *ramla,* "a torrent," a reminder that the street follows an old watercourse. From here head to the statue of Christopher Columbus on a 164-foot iron plinth near the waterfront; take the elevator to an observation deck near the top for views of the city and port.

Temple de la Sagrada Família

C3 Plaça de la Sagrada Família 93 207 3031 Daily 9–8, Apr.–Aug.; 9–7, Mar. and Sep.–Oct.; 9–6, rest of year Sagrada Família 18, 19, 33, 34, 43, 44, 50, 51, 54 $$

The famous Catalan Modernist architect, Antoni Gaudí, worked on the Temple de la Sagrada Família (Church of the Holy Family) for over 40 years. He envisioned a vast cathedral, with facades to show the birth, death and resurrection of Christ, and 18 towers to represent the Twelve Apostles, the Four Evangelists, the Virgin and Christ. At his death in 1926 only the nativity facade, the crypt and one of the towers was complete, and it seems unlikely the project will ever be completed.

Santa Maria del Mar

C2 Plaça de Santa Maria 93 310 2390 Daily 9–12:30 and 4:30–8 Jaume I 14, 17, 51

Built between 1329 and 1384 at the height of Barcelona's medieval prestige, the beautiful Gothic church of Santa Maria del Mar (Our Lady of the Sea) is tucked away in the Gothic streets of the Ribera district. Its stark, serene interior allows the elegant architecture to speak for itself.

CATALAN FARE

You can eat as well in Barcelona as anywhere in Spain, sampling local Catalan dishes, fresh fish and seafood, and specialties from other parts of Spain and abroad. Since restaurants here cater to foreigners, dinner is served much earlier than elsewhere in Spain.

Fish and Seafood

Be sure to eat fish during your visit, preferably in one of Little Barcelona's restaurants where it is a specialty. Appetizers often include a selection of shellfish, tiny grilled sardines or giant prawns. Local main fish dishes are often a type of *sarsuela,* fish stew, or *suquet de peix,* a soupy fish and potato casserole. Although not the home of paella (that's Valencia), there are wonderful *arròs* dishes, where rice, subtly flavored with vegetables and spices, is combined with fish and its stock. Try *fideuà,* cooked like paella but using fine pasta in place of rice.

Mar i Muntanya

Mar i muntanya (sea and mountain), or surf 'n' turf, has inspired some of Catalonia's best recipes. Using local ingredients, cooks have created combination dishes featuring rabbit, shrimp, prawns, chicken and meat. Look for *mar i cel* (sea and sky) on local menus, or try some of the excellent pork products. Main dishes are usually accompanied by intensely flavored vegetables, a saffron sauce, a garlic mayonnaise or a crisp salad. The local bread, baked several times a day, is crisp and light, a reminder of Barcelona's proximity to the French border. Cured ham, spicy sausages and garlic snails are often part of a *tapas* lunch, a good time to try a variety of tastes.

Above: Spain's national dish – paella

Below: Catalan mussels served in a marine sauce

Thirst-quenchers

Bars serve tea, coffee, soda and fruit juice as well as every conceivable form of alcohol. You'll find many familiar drinks, and a range of Spanish beers and wines.

Beer comes in bottles or on tap, and you can buy wine by the glass. Local red, white and rosé wines come from the Penedès area; Torres and Masia Bach are reliable labels. Cava makes a great aperitif; a light sparkling dry wine, it's made the same way as champagne.

SANTIAGO

Tucked away in the green fringes of Galicia, in northwest Spain, is Santiago de Compostela – one of the great shrines of medieval Christendom. Millions of pilgrims braved hazardous travel to worship at the shrine of St. James, the patron saint of Spain. People still come here on pilgrimages today, especially during holy years, which occur when St. James' Day falls on a Sunday.

Santiago is one of Europe's most perfect medieval cities – a mix of religious and secular buildings, with an ancient and thriving university and a unique spiritual atmosphere. It is also home to the parliament of Galicia, which is an autonomous region, and there is a lively and prosperous modern town surrounding the central core.

Old Santiago

The historic heart is pedestrian-only and can be traversed on foot in less than a half-hour; everything you'll want to see lies within this small area. Santiago offers quality, not quantity, so most visitors find a stay of a few days ample.

The two main streets, Rúa do Franco and Rúa do Vilar, lead south from the cathedral square and are lined with stores, bars and restaurants. Pick up a map at the tourist office; it's easy to lose your bearings in the maze of streets and squares behind the cathedral.

Santiago Flavors

Galician cooking is delicious, robust and tasty, and relies on the excellent quality of local ingredients. Seafood and shellfish are extensively farmed in the *rias*, deeply indented coastal inlets, and are of superb quality. Regional specialties include *pulpo* (octopus) cooked in various ways; blood puddings and sausages; and *empanadas*, a flat pie with a meat or fish filling.

This is one of the few Spanish regions where lamb is eaten, and local beef also is particularly good. Santiago

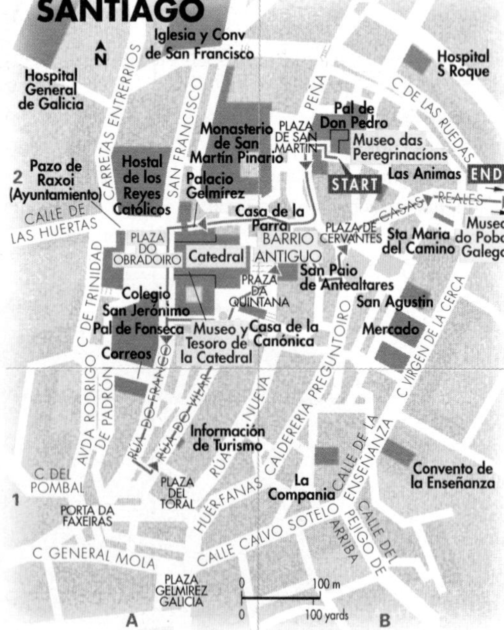

Stone carvings adorn the medieval buildings in the old quarter of the city

has many pastry shops, where you'll find wonderful cakes and cookies. Local wine varieties include Ribeiro and Valdeorra, straightforward whites, and the excellent red Amandi and Condado. If the weather's cold try a cup of hot chocolate; thick enough to eat, it's some of the best in Spain.

Souvenirs and Entertainment

Santiago's streets are lined with stores selling pilgrim souvenirs – medals, rosaries, key rings, holy pictures and statues, all decorated with the image of St. James and his scallop shell emblem. The traditional material for pilgrimage souvenirs is jet, polished and cut, or fashioned into the *figa,* a clenched-fist amulet. The guild of silversmiths, hugely important in the past, is still active and makes some fine pieces.

This is a university town with a thriving cultural life, and there are year-round classical concerts, as well as clubs frequented by students. You'll hear bagpipes, Galicia's national instrument, played on the streets; this is a favorite way for students to make extra cash.

Santiago Festivals

Santiago's biggest festival is July 25th, the feast of St. James, when the city is packed with pilgrims, tourists and local people. The night before sees the Apostle's Fire (Fuego del Apóstol), a spectacular fireworks display in front of the cathedral. The feast itself represents a solemn Mass, with music, choirs and Galician bagpipes, and the huge incense burner, the *botafumeiro*, is swung in the cathedral. The feast falls in the middle of Santiago's folklore festival, a two-week celebration of Galician culture, with street music, parades, concerts and markets. An international music festival is held in August and September.

ESSENTIAL INFORMATION

TOURIST INFORMATION

• Plaza de Galicia ☎ 981 584 400 or 981 573 990
www.turgalicia.es

URBAN TRANSPORTATION

Santiago's historic center is pedestrian-only; the only vehicular access is for taxis and delivery vehicles. It takes around 15 to 20 minutes to walk from one end of the center to the other, and everything you'll want to see is within this area, even the farthest hotels. If you are staying outside the historic center, take a taxi to the edge of the old town and then walk. Taxis can be found at stands outside the old city, or you can call them (☎ 981 561 082, 981 561 028 or 981 595 964 for night service).

AIRPORT INFORMATION

Santiago-Lavacolla International Airport (☎ 981 547 500), with services to many European cities, is 7 miles east of the city, about a 15- to 30-minute drive. Buses into Santiago run hourly from outside the terminal, Mon.–Sat. 7:15 a.m.–10:15 p.m., Sun. 10:30–10:15 (journey time 20 minutes). Taxis also leave from outside the airport terminal.

CLIMATE – average highs and lows for the month

JAN.	FEB.	MAR.	APR.	MAY	JUN.	JUL.	AUG.	SEP.	OCT.	NOV.	DEC.
13°C	14°C	15°C	17°C	19°C	22°C	25°C	25°C	24°C	20°C	17°C	14°C
55°F	57°F	59°F	63°F	66°F	72°F	77°F	77°F	75°F	68°F	63°F	57°F
5°C	6°C	7°C	8°C	10°C	14°C	16°C	16°C	14°C	12°C	9°C	7°C
41°F	43°F	45°F	46°F	50°F	57°F	61°F	61°F	57°F	54°F	48°F	45°F

The baroque facade of the Cathedral

City Sights

Key to symbols

map coordinates refer to the Santiago map on page 418; sights below are highlighted in yellow on the map.
address or location telephone number
opening times restaurant or café on site or nearby admission charge: $$$ more than 900PTA, $$ 600PTA–900PTA, $ less than 600PTA other relevant information

Barrio Antiguo

B2 Barrio Antiguo

The Barrio Antiguo (Old Quarter) of Santiago is packed with beautiful, historic buildings. The main streets are lined with arcaded old granite houses in the traditional Galician style. East of the cathedral, the spacious Plaza da Quintana is surrounded by notable buildings, including the arcaded Casa de la Canónica (Canon's Residence). This faces a gracious flight of steps leading up to the 17th-century Casa de la Parra (House of the Bunch of Grapes). On the third side is the austere facade of San Paio de Antealtares Monastery, founded in the ninth century. Opposite, the Puerta del Perdón (Door of Pardon) opens onto the east end of the cathedral – this is only used during holy years. On the cathedral's north side stands the huge complex of the Monasterio de San Martín Pinario, with its church and three cloisters. Behind the monastery lies the 17th-century Convento de San Francisco, commemorating a pilgrimage by St. Francis of Assisi in 1213. It is now a museum devoted to the Holy Land and incorporates a hotel.

Catedral

A2 Plaza do Obradoiro 981 561 527
Daily 9–9; hours sometimes vary Botafumeiro, see page 567

The present Catedral (Cathedral) dates from the 11th to 13th centuries. The simple Romanesque lines of the interior provide a superb contrast to the ornate facade, added in 1750, at the cathedral's main entrance. Here stands the 12th-century triple doorway known as the Pórtico de la Glória (Doorway of Glory), one of the sculptural glories of Spain. Prophets and Apostles surround Christ the Savior and the Four Evangelists, all carved with exceptional imagination and fluidity. Behind the worn entrance pillar and the figure of St. James is a figure said to be Maestro Mateo, the cathedral's designer. It's customary to bump your head against his in the hope some of his artistic genius may rub off.

You'll notice a pulley system high above the transept; this operates the *botafumeiro*, a monster incense burner used during major feasts, which requires eight men to swing it through a huge arc above the transept. The silverwork and gilded figures of the High Altar glitter under the lights of the candelabra.

Museo das Peregrinacíons

B2 Rúa San Miguel 4 981 581 558
Tue.–Fri. 10–8 , Sat. 10:30–1:30 and 5–8, Sun. 10:30–1:30 $

The Museo das Peregrinacíons (Pilgrimage Museum) tells the story of pilgrimage in general, and the Santiago pilgrimage in particular. Exhibits show how the cathedral and town grew around the apostle's tomb,

ST. JAMES AND SANTIAGO

The pilgrims' well-trodden route into Santiago

To medieval Europeans, a pilgrimage (*peregrinacíon*) was a means of earning extra grace and thus attaining heaven faster. Pilgrimages were made to many holy places, but the great goals were Jerusalem, Rome and Santiago de Compostela. The apostle St. James is known as "Sant Iago" in Spanish. The city which bears his name also is the site of his shrine and burial place. According to legend, he had preached in Spain before returning to martyrdom in Judea in AD 44. His disciples brought his body back to Spain, where it lay hidden until AD 844.

Legend tells that he appeared in a vision to Christian leaders and led them to victory against the Muslim invaders, earning him the title of *Matamoros*, the Moorslayer. His body and relics were rediscovered at Compostela, which soon became the center of devotion for Spain's new patron saint. By the 11th century, pilgrims were traveling from all over Europe to pray at Santiago.

The *Camino de Santiago*

Pilgrims traveled from France, Britain, Germany, Italy and Scandinavia, as well as Spain and Portugal, many of them taking years to complete their journey. By the mid-12th century, between 500,000 and 2 million people were on the move annually, a vast number in relation to the total population.

Roads to Spain threaded their way across the Continent, but once across the Pyrenees converged into a well-organized route across northern Spain. This became known as the *Camino de Santiago*, the Way of St. James. Administered by a religious military order, the *camino* was policed and marked along its length, with hostels, inns and churches offering practical and spiritual sustenance to travelers. Towns grew up around the stopping points, with their own churches, hospitals and hospices.

Dressed in sandals and heavy capes and armed with stout staffs, pilgrims also wore the scallop shell emblem of the saint in their broad-brimmed hats. On arrival in Santiago, the custom was to enter the cathedral and embrace the golden effigy of the saint placed high above his tomb, while giving alms and thanks in gratitude for the safe completion of the pilgrimage.

The *Camino* Today

The custom of walking the *camino* died out during the 16th century, but was revived around 1880. Today thousands of people make the journey to Santiago, by car, train, plane and on foot.

Relax amid the grandeur of Obradoiro Square

how the routes west across Europe developed, what the pilgrims wore and how they traveled. There's a copy of the fascinating *Codex Calixtinus,* a 13th-century guide to the route, full of tips about travel and information about Santiago. Look for the collection of souvenirs 14th-century pilgrims took home.

Museo do Pobo Galego

Off the map Moistero de San Domingos de Bonaval 981 583 620 Mon.–Sat. 10–1 and 4–7 $

Santiago is more than a noted shrine, it's also one of the main towns in Galicia. The Museo do Pobo Galego (Museum of the Galician People), located in the old convent of San Domingo, explains Galicia and the many aspects of traditional life in this remote corner of Spain. There are displays of tools, pottery, costumes and exhibits on Galicia's dolmens, stone circles and hill forts. The museum's galleries encircle the 17th-century cloister; in one corner a superb staircase, with three intertwining flights of steps, rises to different floors of the building.

Museo y Tesoro de la Catedral

A2 Plaza do Obradoiro 981 560 527 Mon.–Sat. 11–1:30 and 4:30–6:30, Sun. 10–1:30 and 4–7 Botafumeiro, see page 567 $$

The Museo y Tesoro de la Catedral (Cathedral Museum and Treasury) is housed around the magnificent 16th-century cloisters adjoining the cathedral. It also includes the Romanesque Old Cathedral (a crypt beneath the Pórtico de la Glória) and the Chapel of San Fernando, which opens off the interior of the cathedral. In the latter you can see gem-encrusted gold crucifixes and statues still used for important feasts. The museum includes a fine collection of tapestries from the most prestigious workshops.

The cloisters, a lovely blend of Castilian-Gothic and Renaissance architecture, are some of the largest in Spain. Stairs lead up to the gallery, completed in 1590, which offers a good vantage point over the cathedral square. The building adjoining the left of the cathedral is the old Bishop's Palace.

Plaza do Obradoiro

A2 Plaza do Obradoiro Botafumeiro, see page 567

The sweeping expanse of Plaza do Obradoiro (Obradoiro Square), in front of the cathedral, is surrounded on its other sides by three harmonious buildings. These are the Hostal de los Reyes Católicos (Hostel of the Catholic Monarchs), the Colegio de San Jerónimo (College of St. Jerome) and the Pazo de Raxoi, or Ayuntamiento (City Hall). The oldest building is the hostel (now a hotel), originally founded by Ferdinand and Isabella as a pilgrims' lodging house. It has an elegantly plain facade centered by a superb Plateresque doorway. Inside, the building is laid out around four lovely patios.

Across from the hostel is the college and its charming balcony, which dates mainly from the 17th century – although its doorway is 200 years younger. Facing the cathedral, the classical lines of the City Hall, built in the 18th century, seem to unite the whole ensemble.

The Cathedral of St. James dominates the city skyline

A Day in Santiago

A Spiritual Morning

Your first stop should be a visit to the excellent Pilgrimage Museum (Museo das Peregrinacíons, see pages 420–422), where you can learn about the history of pilgrimage. This will give you a sense of perspective and will pave the way for a visit to the cathedral, next on the list. As you go in, place your hand on the worn stones of the entrance pillar, the first gesture of arriving pilgrims.

Spend time admiring the architecture and artistic treasures, then join the line and mount the steps behind the altar to embrace the effigy of St. James, as pilgrims have done for more than 1,000 years. You could time your visit to coincide with the daily noontime Pilgrims' Mass.

A Secular Afternoon

Head up Rúa do Franco or Rúa do Vilar, the main streets, and choose one of the many restaurants for lunch – shellfish or octopus are both traditional Galician specialties. After lunch, you could head back toward the cathedral and visit the Cathedral Museum and Treasury (Museo y Tesoro de la Catedral) before walking back across town to the Museum of the Galician People (Museo do Pobo Galego). At about 6 p.m. the streets begin to fill with shoppers and university students, and the bars become busy.

A Peaceful Evening

There's no problem finding an excellent restaurant for dinner; try some fish or one of the flavorful Galician meat dishes, often pork-based, with potatoes and turnip tops. Be sure to order some of the local dome-shaped cheese, and finish with a slice of *tarta de Santiago*, a special almond pastry made only here. As you wander through the ancient streets after dinner, you'll probably hear the strains of bagpipes echoing through some hidden courtyard. For the walking route, see the city map on page 418.

SEVILLE

Some of Spain's quintessential images are of whitewashed streets, Moorish architecture, flamenco dresses, orange trees and proud horsemen. This mental picture actually reflects Andalucia and its capital, Seville (Sevilla). It is the fourth-largest city in Spain, the seat of a university, an important industrial city and the center of a rich agricultural region. Renowned for architectural treasures, great festivals and a relaxed lifestyle, Seville has attracted visitors for many years, and cares for them far better than many other Spanish cities.

Seville on Foot

In Seville, every building, garden and street is designed as an escape from the sun. If you're visiting in summer, take lengthy siestas during the hottest hours. The central old core is relatively small, and you'll be able to walk to many of the main sights. The narrow, twisting streets can be confusing, so always take a city map with you; maps are free and available at the tourist office and many hotels. Blue-and-white signs direct visitors to the main sights. There's plenty of information in English, and helpful multilingual guides – often university students – offer assistance at the main attractions.

There's plenty to see in Seville besides the main attractions. The range of museums, fine churches and civic buildings attracts many visitors: the Casa de Pilatos, an elegant private palace, is a favorite. Also look for the Tobacco Factory (Fabrica de Tabacos), now part of the university but also where Carmen (of opera fame) worked.

Walking is only one option. Visitors can take an open-carriage drive from outside the cathedral that takes in many of the sights. Alternatively, half-hourly cruises run from the Torre del Oro on the Guadalquivir River, one of Spain's greatest waterways, and this is a relaxing way to admire Seville.

Festivals in Seville

Seville has two major festivals: the *Semana Santa* (Holy Week), the last week of Lent, and the *Feria de Abril*

Bathed in light – the Moorish "Tower of Gold"

(April Festival), held the last week in April. If you plan to visit the city during either of these, reserve a room far in advance. Holy Week is a deeply religious time, celebrated by *pasos* processions held by rival brotherhoods in Seville's different districts. *Pasos* are huge carriers supporting religious statues, sumptuously decorated and carried by up to 60 men. The April Festival is completely secular, a weeklong celebration of Andalucia's love affair with horses, music and beautiful women. Carriages filled with laughing girls in flounced dresses, accompanied by horseback riders in traditional dress, parade the streets, and the graceful *sevillana* is danced all night.

Eating Southern Style

Eating is a pleasure in Seville, with a wide range of restaurants and *tapas*

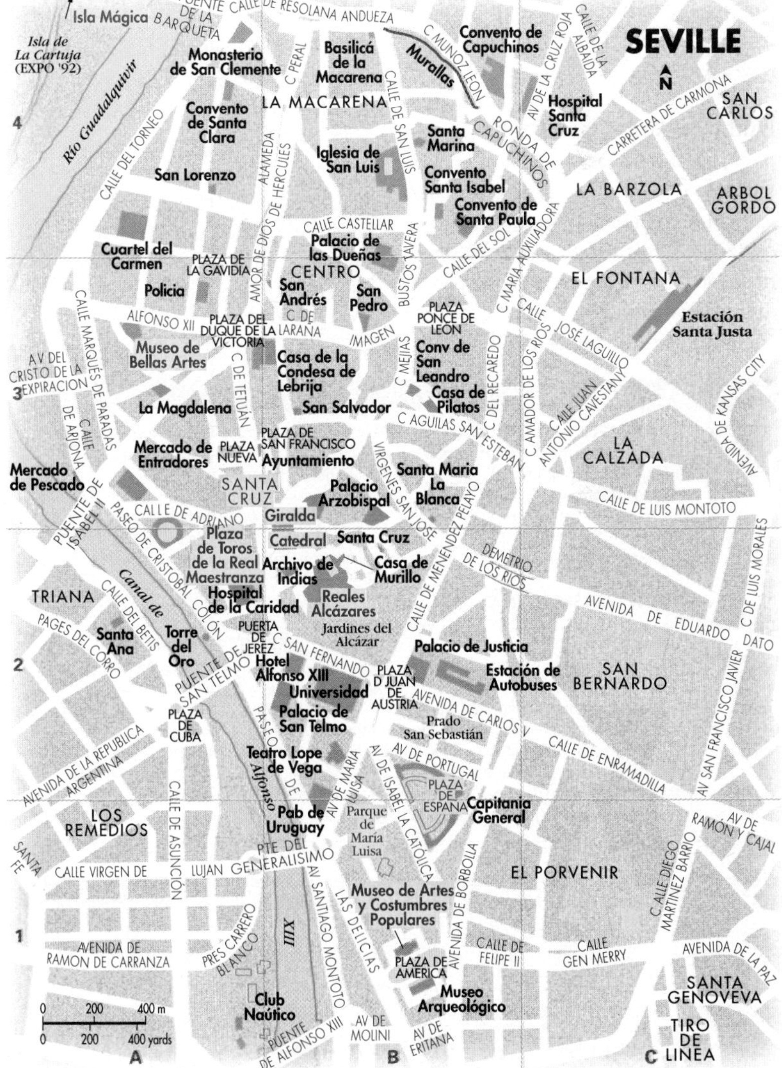

bars. More than almost anywhere else in Spain, *tapas* has a special place here. There's a fabulous choice of dishes, traditionally eaten with a glass of *copa,* or sherry, the fortified wine from Jerez – a lovely city south of Seville.

Mealtimes are late, particularly in summer, with lunch often finishing around 4 or 5 and dinner starting at midnight. The more cosmopolitan restaurants are geared to foreigners' dining habits. Andalucian coffee is very strong, so it's best to ask for a *café con agua* (coffee with water) if you like it weaker.

Mantillas and Castanets

Shoppers throng Sierpes – "the Serpent" – the winding pedestrian-only street running north from near the cathedral. Stroll around and enjoy the traditional storefronts; it's a good place to find Sevillian fans, mantillas, shawls, flamenco dresses, castanets and gourmet candies. You'll find attractive pottery at tiny stores in Santa Cruz or across the river in the Triana district, where they also make fine wrought-iron goods, saddles and guitars.

Flamenco

Flamenco is a synthesis of dance and music, ideally performed spontaneously to express joy and sorrow about everyday life, religion and work. Its heartland lies in Andalucia, but its origins stretch as far afield as Egypt and India. It reaches its zenith in the songs known as *cante jondo* (deep song), expressions of deep feelings. The profound meaning of flamenco is hard for foreigners to grasp, but the music and dance, the distinctive costume and the click of castanets can be enjoyed by all.

ESSENTIAL INFORMATION

TOURIST INFORMATION
Oficinas Municipales de Turismo (Municipal Tourist Offices)
• Paseo de la Delicias 9
☎ 95 423 4465
• Naves del Barranco, Calle Arjona 28
☎ 95 450 5600; www.sevilla.org

URBAN TRANSPORTATION
Seville has an efficient bus system that mainly services the sprawling residential suburbs, with only a few buses going into the heart of the old city. Some city-center routes run past the cathedral to the Plaza Nueva, and other lines terminate at Plaza de la Incarnación. Maria Luisa Park and the surrounding area also is well served from the center. Buy single tickets when you board, or show your three- or seven-day tourist pass, available at newsstands or from the Tussam bus office. There's also a special tourist bus, run by Sevirama (☎ 95 456 0693). This hop-on-and-off service covers the main sights, with an English commentary, and runs from March through November; tickets are valid all day. Beige-colored taxis can be hailed on the street or at a stand, or you can call Radio Taxi (☎ 95 458 0000 or 95 458 1111), Tele Taxi (☎ 95 462 2222) or Radio Teléfono Giralda (☎ 95 467 5555).

AIRPORT INFORMATION
Seville International Airport (☎ 95 444 9000), with connections to major European cities, is about 5 miles northeast of the city, a 15- to 30-minute drive. An airport bus runs hourly from the terminal to Puerta Jerez, Mon.–Fri. 6:15 a.m.–9:15 p.m., with less frequent service on weekends. Taxis are available outside the airport terminal.

CLIMATE – average highs and lows for the month

JAN.	FEB.	MAR.	APR.	MAY	JUN.	JUL.	AUG.	SEP.	OCT.	NOV.	DEC.
15°C	16°C	18°C	22°C	27°C	32°C	35°C	35°C	32°C	25°C	20°C	16°C
59°F	61°F	64°F	72°F	81°F	90°F	95°F	95°F	90°F	77°F	68°F	61°F
5°C	7°C	8°C	10°C	13°C	17°C	18°C	19°C	18°C	14°C	10°C	4°C
41°F	45°F	46°F	50°F	55°F	63°F	64°F	66°F	64°F	57°F	50°F	40°F

CITY SIGHTS

Key to symbols

map coordinates refer to the Seville map on page 425; sights below are highlighted in yellow on the map. address or location telephone number opening times nearest bus route restaurant or café on site or nearby admission charge: $$$ more than 900PTA, $$ 600PTA–900PTA, $ less than 600PTA other relevant information

BARRIO DE SANTA CRUZ

A3 Santa Cruz 21, 22, 23, 24, 25, 26, 30, 31, 33, 34, 40, 41, 42, C3, C4

The Barrio de Santa Cruz (Santa Cruz Quarter), with its narrow white streets, ironwork grilles and sun-splashed squares shaded by orange trees, typifies Seville and draws visitors night and day. Originally the Jewish quarter, it was popular with 17th-century nobility, who added mansions along its alleyways.

CATEDRAL

B2 Plaza Virgen de los Reyes 95 421 4971 Mon.–Sat. 10:30–5, Sun. 2–6 El Giraldillo, see page 567 21, 22, 23, 24, 25, 26, 30, 31, 33, 34, 40, 41, 42, C3, C4 $$

Seville's magnificent Catedral (Cathedral), built on the site of the Moorish mosque, is the third largest in Europe; only St. Peter's in Rome and St. Paul's in London are larger. Vast, rich and harmoniously balanced, it was built between 1401 and 1507, a blend of Gothic austerity and Spanish flamboyance. Almost as wide as it is long, the interior is dominated by the chancel, the *Capilla Mayor*, its splendid, richly carved Flemish altarpiece glistening with gold leaf behind immense grilles. Opposite lie the choir stalls. Stand between the two and look up at the transept roof, 184 feet above your head; this riot of stone filigree is supported by massive arches and columns, but even their huge size is dwarfed by the scale of the cathedral. Other highlights include Christopher Columbus' tomb in the south transept; the treasury and sacristy, packed with paintings and precious altar vessels; and the domed Royal Chapel, the burial place of Alfonso X of Castille.

Dine beneath the beautiful 12th-century Giralda

GIRALDA

B3 Plaza Virgen de los Reyes 95 421 4971 Mon.–Sat. 10:30–5, Sun. 2–6 El Giraldillo, see page 567 21, 22, 23, 24, 25, 26, 30, 31, 33, 34, 40, 41, 42, C3, C4 $$

When Christians destroyed the mosque to build the cathedral, they kept the minaret and transformed it into the new cathedral's bell tower. Nicknamed the *Giralda,* the "weather-vane," the 322-foot-tall tower was built in the 12th century. Instead of stairs, you climb the series of interior ramps; 17 levels lead to the top, from where there are views over Seville. Below the tower lies the lovely Patio de los Naranjos (Courtyard of the Orange Trees), once part of the mosque.

ISLA MÁGICA

Off the map Pabellón de España, Isla de la Cartuja 902 16 17 16 or 902 16 00 00 Daily 11 a.m.–2 a.m. late Jul.–early Sep.; days and times vary mid-Mar. to late Jul. and early Sep.–late Oct.

C1, C2 $$$ (reduction for evening)
Seville hosted Expo '92 on the Isla de la Cartuja, an island between two branches of the Quadalquivir river. This is now the site of Isla Mágica, a theme park devoted to the Spanish discovery of the New World in the 15th and 16th centuries. It has a range of state-of-the-art attractions.

Museo de Artes y Costumbres Populares

B1 Plaza de América, Parque de María Luisa 95 423 2576 Tue. 3–8, Wed.–Sat. 9–8, Sun. 9–2 6, 34, 35 $
The Museo de Artes y Costumbres Populares (Museum of Arts and Popular Traditions), located in one of the 1929 International Exhibition pavilions, the Mudéjar Pabellón (Mudéjar Pavilion), is devoted to traditional everyday life in Andalucia. There are reconstructions of workshops where you can see how guitars and castanets are made, old agricultural implements, pottery, furniture and much more. Upstairs are intricately embroidered costumes, painted fans and delicate lace. You also can learn about the history of Seville's great Spring Festival, the *Fiesta Primaverales.*

Museo de Bellas Artes

A3 Plaza del Museo 9 95 422 0790 Tue. 3–8, Wed.–Sat. 9–8, Sun. 9–2 43, C1, C2, C3, C4 $
Seville's Museo de Bellas Artes (Fine Arts Museum), housed in an 18th-century convent built around three courtyards, concentrates on the Golden Age of Spanish painting. The former church is devoted to the Spanish religious painter Bartolome Murillo, and pride of place is given to his *Immaculate Conception*. Francisco de Zurbarán, another great master, is also well represented, his masterpiece being the stark, sculptural *Christ on the Cross.*

Plaza de España and Parque de María Luisa

B1–B2 Plaza de España 6, 34, C1, C2
Built as the centerpiece for the 1929 International Exhibition, the Plaza de España overlooks Parque de María Luisa (María Luisa Park). Traditionally styled and lavishly decorated with thousands of colored tiles, the 650-foot-wide plaza is framed by a semicircular range of buildings and encircled by a canal. The park, laid out in the 19th century, is a tranquil stretch of shady paths, punctuated by pools and fountains. It plays a central part in Seville's Spring Festival, when hundreds of horsemen accompany carriages of smiling girls, dressed in silk, around the park.

Plaza de Toros de la Real Maestranza

A2 Paseo Colón 12 95 422 4577 Daily 9:30–2 and 3–6. Museum: daily 10:30–2 and 4–6 (on bullfight days 10–3) 5, 41, C3, C4 $$
Seville's Plaza de Toros (Bullring) is one of the oldest and most prestigious in Spain. Once built of wood, the present 14,000-seat ring was designed around the Prince's Balcony and is oval rather than round. Tours, in Spanish only, include the Museo Taurino (Bullfighting Museum), stables, chapel and modern operating theater.

Reales Alcázares

B2 Plaza del Triunfo 95 450 2323 Tue.–Sat. 9:30–5, Sun. 9:30–1:30 El Giraldillo, see page 567 21, 22, 23, 24, 25, 26, 30, 31, 33, 34, 40, 41, 42, C3, C4 $$
Less swamped with tourists than its cousin in Granada, the unforgettable Reales Alcázares (Royal Palace) epitomizes the elegance and charm of Mudéjar secular architecture. Little remains of the original Moorish Alcazar, and most of the palace you see today was built by Pedro the Cruel in the 1360s, long after the Moors left Spain. But the builders were Christianized Moors, the inventors of Mudéjar style, and this "Arabian Nights" complex is one of the purest examples of their art remaining today. It's a labyrinth of courtyards, delicate stucco and tile rooms, terraces and coffered chambers, fountains and arched patios. From here you pass into the 16th-century Palace of Charles V, with its tapestries and lavish rooms. Outside are gardens with terraces, pools, and shady magnolia and orange trees. Labeling and information are poor, so your best option is to rent the English-language audio guide.

Bullfighter at work: the first stage, assessing the ability of the animal

Bullfighting

Bullfighting is the least understood of all Spanish traditions. Performed on horseback until the 18th century, bullfighting had attained its present form by the 19th century, with established rules and a strict pattern to the *corrida,* or fight. Not all Spaniards enjoy bullfighting, but they are tolerant of it. True aficionados spend years studying the careers of the fighters and the bloodlines of the fighting bulls.

The *Corrida*

Six four-year-old bulls are killed during a *corrida,* which starts at 5 p.m. Bred on huge estates on the rolling grasslands of Andalucia and Castille, the 1,000-pound bulls have never seen an unmounted man until the moment they enter the ring. The afternoon starts with a parade, the *paseo,* by three *matadors*, glittering figures in their "suits of light" who will each kill two bulls. The *matadors* are accompanied by their teams, known as *cuadrillas.*

Each fight falls into three parts, marked by a trumpet call. First the *matador* must appraise the bull, using a cape to make the animal turn so he can judge its speed and dexterity. Bred for aggression, it will charge at the two mounted team members, the *picadores,* who attack its flanks with pikes.

The next act allows the bull to regain its wind while it is further enraged by the *banderillas,* who pierce the neck muscles with ribboned darts. The pikes and darts gradually weaken the bull's immensely strong neck and cause its head to drop, allowing the matador access to the heart.

The final stage of the drama belongs to the matador alone. Working with the *muleta,* a small red cloth, he draws the bull in a series of passes across his body, which can be as elegant as they are fearless. Finally, the bull will stand still, tired but still mesmerized by the *muleta.* This is the moment for the matador to take his sword and, reaching over the horns and shoulder blades, strike the bull cleanly through the heart.

Bullfighting can be seen throughout Spain at all the major summer festivals, although those bothered by a bullfight's inherent cruelty should avoid attending.

SWEDEN

"THE further I came north, the more like New England everything grew to look..."

American historian Henry Adams

Opposite: Houses on stilts at the waterfront town of Orust

SWEDEN

Sweden is the largest of the Scandinavian countries, famed for the perceived efficiency of its people and the pragmatism of its government. This is a land of wide-open spaces, where even a large city like Stockholm seems to merge urban and rural elements in a way that benefits the people.

Swedish Landscapes

Southern Sweden is an area of forests and farmland punctuated by a vast number of lakes, of which two – Vänern and Vättern – dominate the landscape. The south also is the center of Sweden's industrial powerhouse. The main cities are Gothenburg (Göteborg) and Malmö on the southwest coast.

The southernmost province, Skåne, is a rich farming area where you will find a hint of Danish features, both in the people and in the landscape. This is Sweden's vacation land. Off the east coast, the islands of Gotland and Öland have superb beaches that benefit from calm waters and warm summer sunshine.

Stockholm lies on the east coast of Sweden, within a beautiful mosaic of inland lakes and offshore islands. In the surrounding provinces there is a richly varied countryside centered on mighty Lake Mälaren. North of Stockholm is Sweden's ancient capital, the lively university town of Uppsala. This entire area is accessible by ferries and cruise boats that ply a network of waterways and lakes.

MORE TOP DESTINATIONS IN SWEDEN

• Göteborg A2 • Gotland B2
• Kalmar A1 • Lund A1 • Malmö A1
• Siljan A3 • Skokloster B2
• Uppsala B2

Northern Sweden is known as Norrland, with similarities to northern Finland, and it enjoys the same "Land of the Midnight Sun" tag. It is a country of vast forests and tumbling rivers that are fed by icy, crystal waters from the mountains. Lapland, or Sápme (see page 434), is a vast and magnificent wilderness of mountains, moor land, birch forest and tundra.

Travel and Climate

Sweden has an extensive road network, but public transportation throughout the country also is a very efficient and convenient way to get around. Trains are modern and comfortable, and buses serve even the most remote northern parts of the country.

Sweden's climate is similar to that of its neighbors, but the country is generally much drier than Norway's western regions. Summers can be as warm and sunny as anywhere else in northern Europe, and along the southern coast you may even find yourself enjoying a Scandinavian heat wave. Conversely, visitors need to be prepared for wet weather in Sweden's maritime climate.

A remarkable number of Swedes are fluent in English, and most people in the cities have at least some command of English. The people are generally very helpful, and have a great awareness of the world in general; they are politely curious about visitors and are lively conversationalists, once their initial reserve is overcome.

Swedes are conservative by nature, and on first impression may seem overly serious about life. They are very aware that their society operates on the basis of co-operation and willingness to accept the norm. You may mistake Swedish directness for impatience, especially in Stockholm, but this simply reflects a national confidence about how things work.

Sweden's Geography

Like its neighbors Norway and Finland, Sweden is a long, narrow country, but uniform in breadth. It shares its longest border with Norway, with the Scandinavian mountain chain running along this frontier for more than 1,000 miles. Northern Sweden borders Finland, with the Arctic Circle sweeping across the farthest reaches of the land, part of an area known as the "Nordic Cap."

East of Sweden lies the Gulf of Bothnia, which eventually gives way to the Baltic Sea in the southeast. To the southwest, a shorter coastline borders the North Sea within the protective shadow of neighboring Norway and northern Denmark.

TIMELINE

8000 BC	Hunter-gatherers move throughout Scandinavia in the wake of retreating ice sheets; the Sami (Lapp) people are thought to descend from these early settlers.
1500 BC	Germanic tribes in southern Sweden develop trading links with the European lands to the south, from which they came.
AD 750	Battle of Bråvalla; the Svear emerge as the dominant tribe and give their name to the country (Sverige).
800–1000	Swedish "Vikings" travel east via the great rivers of eastern Europe, as far as Constantinople.
1397	Union of Kalmar unites Denmark, Sweden and Norway under Queen Margaret of Denmark.
1523	Gustav Vasa establishes Sweden's independence, he becomes King Gustav I; Lutheran Protestantism becomes the country's main religion.
1658	Treaty of Roskilde secures all of southern Swedish mainland from Danish control.
1814	Sweden wins control of Norway from Denmark.
1905	Norway achieves independence from Sweden.
1914–18	Sweden remains neutral during World War I.
1939–45	Sweden again remains neutral during World War II.
1946	Sweden maintains neutrality but joins the United Nations.
1989	The Sami people are granted their own parliament, known as the Sametinget.
1995	Sweden joins the European Union.
1998	Stockholm is named Cultural Capital of Europe.
2000	The 10-mile Øresund Bridge and Tunnel linking Malmö and Copenhagen opens.

THE SAMI

The Sami are the indigenous people of Sápme, the area popularly called Lapland. They are known historically as Lapps, but this is not a native name and is one that the Sami themselves feel is derogatory. The ancient name Sápme, a form of Sami which is said to mean "the people of the interior," is now considered accepted usage. Sápme covers the Scandinavian Arctic region from the Russian Kola peninsula to the northwest coast of Norway, and extends down either side of the Norwegian-Swedish border to the central area of both countries. There are about 60,000 Sami people today, of which about 17,000 live in Sweden. A minority of Sami are reindeer herders, but the Sami also are developing alternative lifestyles while strengthening their self-awareness and political position within Scandinavia. Tourism is increasing in Scandinavian Lapland, but some Sami people are concerned about what they believe is too much intrusion on their fragile environment and culture.

SURVIVAL GUIDE

- For lunch you must experience smörgåsbord, a Scandinavian institution. The name translates as *smörgås* for "bread," *bord* for "table." The reality of a true smörgåsbord means much more than this simple image implies. There may be more than 100 different dishes in a true smörgåsbord, with items ranging from *gravad lax* (salmon slices in herbs) to *köttbullar* (tasty meatballs), *sillbullar* (herring rissoles) or *kåldolmar* (stuffed cabbage rolls).
- Sweden has the same tight control over alcohol sales as does Norway and Finland, and alcohol is expensive. The government-controlled liquor monopoly, *Systembolaget,* has branches throughout the country, which are open Mon.–Fri. 9:30–6 (some also open evenings, Saturdays and holidays). Emphasis is on the sale of good wines. Try some *aquavit* with your food if you want a taste of Sweden. The beverage is distilled from grain or potatoes and is then given added taste with spices or herbs. Drink it in small quantities, consumed in one gulp.
- July is a popular month for vacations in Sweden. You will find the countryside and coast very busy, and especially populated with Swedes.
- Swedish design is world famous, especially in silver, ceramics, glassware and stainless steel. The Småland area in southeast Sweden is particularly noted for its fine glassware. Stores such as NK in Stockholm's Hamngatan have good selections of glassware, as does Nordiska Kristall, a store in Österlånggatan.
- Home furnishings are a Swedish specialty. Visit the big IKEA store at Kungens Kurva, outside Stockholm. A free bus leaves every hour between 11 and 5 (except weekends) from Regeringsgatan, the street leading north from Hamngatan, a short distance east of the NK department store. Or try the very stylish Nordiska Galleriet, in Nybrogatan.
- In mid-June, don't miss the lively Stockolm Jazz Festival, a 6-day event that draws an ever-increasing number of enthusiasts. They flock to Stockholm to listen to world-famous Swedish and international artists and groups playing jazz, blues, soul and Latin American music.
- In big cities you'll find public restrooms along some main streets, as well as in main subway stations and some department stores. Signs are *Damer* for ladies and *Herrar* for men. If there is an attendant the charge is normally 5SKr.

Replica of the Hand of God by Swedish-American sculptor Carl Milles

STOCKHOLM

Stockholm is probably the only city in the world where you can catch a salmon at a busy road intersection under the walls of a royal palace, and where the city's subway stations double as eye-catching art galleries. The salmon thrive in Stockholm's clean waters at the very heart of the city, and local anglers fish from the Strömbron bridge. And the artwork that enlivens the subway stations is just one expression of the vigorous cultural life that makes Stockholm one of the world's most civilized cities.

Subway Art

Subway art in Stockholm is not freelance graffiti but spectacular and eclectic art. When the Stockolm *Tunnelbana* was built in the late 1940s an inspired decision was made to decorate each station with individual artworks. T-Centralen, the hub of the system, has the most, with examples ranging from terazzo sofas to wrought-iron gates and ceramic figures on a white-stone background. Visit the Blue Line's amazing Kungsträdgården station; not only is it enormously deep, but it has outstanding sculptures. Stockholm's subway art evolves year by year, a stunning reflection of this sophisticated city.

City of Islands

Modern Stockholm is a large, exhilarating city. The scale of its public buildings is monumental, the bustle of its streets all-embracing; yet the city is given a uniquely open character by the thousands of islands in its archipelago and by the mirror images of lakes that pepper its hinterland. Stockholm stands on 14 interlocking islands; the city is a mosaic of land, lake and waterway stitched together by more than 40 bridges, an exhilarating urban environment that also seems to ensure that people are not overwhelmed.

Gamla Stan is the heart of old Stockholm, a dramatic and fascinating expression of heritage and tradition. It stands on an island in the middle of the narrow bottleneck channel between the salty Baltic Sea and the inland freshwater lake of Mälaren. To the south is the hilly island of Södermalm, a suburban area with generous expanses of grass and trees. North of Gamla Stan and the buildings of state (the Royal Palace and the Parliament House) is Norrmalm, the business and commercial district. This is the heart of the modern city – glass, steel, concrete and good Swedish design – a cityscape of towering buildings, stylish shopping malls, busy streets and traffic-free concourses that satisfy the demands of both vehicles and pedestrians. East of Norrmalm is the residential district of Östermalm and the city's great island park, Djurgården. To the west, the island mosaic spreads across the waters of Lake Mälaren, Stockholm's magnificent "inland" sea.

Compass Bearings

Most visitors arrive at the city's big, bustling central railroad station in Norrmalm, and the experience can be disorientating at first. Just east of the railroad station along Klarabergsgatan is the big sunken square of Sergels Torg, with its landmark *Kristall* tower of glass and steel and a huge glass facade on the south side. This is Stockholm's contemporary hub. You can orient yourself here and, within the pedestrian concourse, even relax in spite of the surrounding traffic and the bustle.

Running north and south of Sergels Torg are busy shopping streets, such as the pedestrian-only Drottninggatan. Here you will find Åhléns, a huge department store. The northern section of Drottninggatan runs past many additional stores.

Continuing east from Sergels Torg into the street of Hamngatan takes you past elegant NK, the best name in Swedish shopping. This massive department store has floor after floor of fine shops and such fashionable restaurants as Bobergs Matsal, where Greta Garbo is said to have whiled away the time. Also in Hamngatan is Gallerian, a big shopping mall. Farther along are the offices of the Stockholm tourist center and the great open swath of the Old Royal Gardens (Kungsträdgården). They sweep south to the waters of Strömmen, to the magnificent Royal Palace, and to enchanting Gamla Stan.

Seeing Stockholm

For all its size Stockholm is a city that can be enjoyed on a human scale. You can see it by tour bus, or you can book a knowledgeable personal guide or a taxi tour, although the latter is expensive. Try a boat trip for the wider view of

View over Stockholm's Old Town, with Riddarholm in the foreground

Stockholm's islands, and visit some attractions, such as Djurgården and Drottningholm Palace, by ferry boat.

Ask at the tourist center about the Stockholm Card, with special discounts on museum and attraction admissions, among other benefits.

One of the most appealing aspects of Stockholm is that the city is neatly packaged into separate entities because of its island nature; you can plan your visit one day at a time. At night the city becomes even more majestic when it is lit up and vibrant with music and lively entertainment.

Stockholmers

Stockholm's confidence is infectious. Listen closely to advice and don't be afraid to ask for clarification or guidance. Then let the magic of the city take over; relax. Stockholmers have created one of the most endearing and enchanting cities in the world, and know how to enjoy it.

ESSENTIAL INFORMATION

TOURIST INFORMATION

Stockholm Information Service

- Sweden House, Hamngatan 27, Kungsträdgården ☎ 08 789 24 90; fax 08 789 24 91; www.stockholmtown.com
- Hotellcentrallen, Central Station
- Kaknäs Tower, Ladugårdsgärdet
- Gamla Stan, Västerlånggaten 66/Kornhamnstorg 49.

URBAN TRANSPORTATION

Stockholm Central Station (✉ Klarabergsviadukten ☎ 08 762 25 80) is the main train station. A very large and comprehensive bus system serves Stockholm and its environs. The subway (*Tunnelbana*) is known as T-Bana and radiates out from Central Station. Subway stations are indicated by a blue "T" sign on the street. On the Stockholm city map subway stations are marked with the letter "T" in a red circle. Public transportation in Stockholm has a unified ticket system, allowing you to transfer between systems. There is a Transit Authority information center in the T-Centralen subway station, accessible from the railroad station. For information on schedules and routes, call ☎ 08 600 10 00. Several taxi companies also operate in and around the city. For information on rates, call ☎ 08 30 00 00 or 08 15 00 00.

AIRPORT INFORMATION

Stockholm-Arlanda Airport is 28 miles north of the city center and is Stockholm's main air terminal (information: ☎ 08 797 60 00). The new Arlanda Express train links the airport and Central Station at 15-minute intervals (information: ☎ 08 595 114 40). The journey takes about 20 minutes. Airport buses (Flygbussar) run at 10-minute intervals and take 35 minutes to reach the City Terminal at Klarabergsviadukten (information: ☎ 08 600 10 00). Taxis also depart from the airport. Bromma Airport is 5 miles west of Stockholm and handles domestic flights only. For information call ☎ 08 797 68 74.

CLIMATE – average highs and lows for the month

JAN.	FEB.	MAR.	APR.	MAY	JUN.	JUL.	AUG.	SEP.	OCT.	NOV.	DEC.
-1°C	-1°C	3°C	8°C	15°C	19°C	21°C	20°C	15°C	9°C	4°C	0°C
30°F	30°F	37°F	46°F	59°F	66°F	70°F	68°F	59°F	48°F	39°F	32°F
-5°C	-6°C	-3°C	0°C	5°C	11°C	13°C	13°C	9°C	4°C	1°C	-2°C
23°F	21°F	27°F	32°F	41°F	52°F	55°F	55°F	48°F	39°F	34°F	28°F

City Sights

Key to symbols

map coordinates refer to the Stockholm map on page 437; sights below are highlighted in yellow on the map.
address or location telephone number
opening times nearest subway nearest bus or tram route nearest ferry stop
restaurant or café on site or nearby admission charge: $$$ more than 35SKr, $$ 15SKr–35SKr, $ less than 15SKr other relevant information

Drottningholms Slott

Drottningholms Slott Off the map
Drottningholm 08 402 62 80 Daily 10–4:30, May–Aug.; daily noon–3:30 in Sep.; Sat.–Sun. noon–3:30, rest of year Café in palace T-Brommaplan 301, 323 Stadshusbron $$$
Kina Slott Drottningholm 08 402 62 70
Daily 11–4:30, May–Aug.; noon–3:30, in Sep.; 1–3:30, Apr. and Oct. Café in palace T-Brommaplan
301, 323 Stadshusbron $$$
Palace Theater Drottningholm 08 759 04 06
Guided tours daily, May–Sep. Café in palace
T-Brommaplan 301, 323 Stadshusbron
$$$

Drottningholms Slott (Drottningholm Palace) is located on Lovön island, west of the city center. The palace, home of Sweden's royal family, is a superb 17th-century baroque building in the style of Versailles. It overlooks Lake Mälaren amid wooded countryside and its own gardens, a mix of French and English styles. French details enhance the palace's interiors. On the grounds is the 18th-century Kina Slott (Chinese Pavilion), where Asian meets rococo in a delightful piece of extravagance. Nearby is the 18th-century Palace Theater, which has its original stage. It is a venue for classical concerts and ballet in summer, and there is a small museum.

Kungliga Slottet

HM Konungens representationsvåningar and Skattkammaren B2
Kungliga Slottet 08 402 61 30
Daily 10–4, mid-May to Aug. 31; Tue.–Sun. noon–3, rest of year
T-Gamla Stan 46, 55, 59, 76 $$$
Livrustkammaren Slottsbaken 3 08 519 555 44
Daily 10–5, Jun.–Aug.; Tue.–Sun. 11–5 (also Thu. 5–8), rest of year T-Gamla Stan 43, 46, 55, 59, 76 $$$

The northern corner of Old Town is dominated by the monumental Kungliga Slottet (Royal Palace), a stunning mix of classical styles developed throughout the 17th and 18th centuries on the site of the original Castle of the Three Crowns. There are several museums within the palace. Among them is the Livrustkammaren (Royal Armory), where Sweden's military history is depicted in a colorful way. Visit the basement *Vagnhall* (Wagon Hall), where there is a collection of royal coaches, including a Viennese rococo sleigh that is impossibly romantic. Also visit the Skattkammaren (Royal Treasury), where the state regalia are on display. The palace's Konungens representationsvåningar (State Apartments) are a dazzling expression of French baroque, rococo and imperial styles. In summer, time your visit to observe the changing of the guard in the palace's courtyard (12:15 p.m. Mon.–Sat., 1:15 Sun.).

Medeltidsmuseet

B2 Strömparterren 08 508 317 90
Daily 11–4 (also Tue.–Thu. 4–6), Jul.–Aug.; Tue.–Sun. 11–4 (also Wed. 4–6), rest of year
T-Gamla Stan 43, 62 Museum café in summer $$$

The Medeltidsmuseet (Medieval Museum) is one of Stockholm's most fascinating attractions, not least because of its underground location below the Riksdagshuset (Parliament House) on the tiny island of Helgeandsholmen, between Gamla Stan and the main city. Here, in the late 1970s, layers of medieval remains, including sections of old city wall, were

Thespian pose – statue outside Drottningholm Palace Theater

Colorful sculptures in the snow outside the Modern Museum

uncovered during excavations for an underground parking lot below the terrace of Parliament House. Admirably, the parking plan was abandoned in favor of preservation. The museum is entered via steps leading down from Norrbro, the bridge between Gustav Adolfs Torg and Gamla Stan.

MODERNA MUSEET

C2 Skeppsholmen 08 519 552 00 Tue.–Thu. 11–8, Fri.–Sun. 11–6 Museum restaurant and café T-Kungsträdgården 65 from Slussen $$$
Arkitekturmuseet Skeppsholmen 08 587 270 00 Tue.–Thu. 11–8, Fri.–Sun. 11–6 T-Kungsträdgården 65 from Slussen $$$
Visit Stockholm's Moderna Museet (Modern Museum), on the little island of Skeppsholmen, as much for its excellent restaurant as for the art. The collection of contemporary art includes works by Roy Lichtenstein, Willem de Kooning, Rene Magritte and Pablo Picasso. Don't miss Salvador Dalí's startling *The Enigma of William Tell* and Marcel Duchamp's *Fountain*. There are compelling works by such Swedish luminaries as Viking Eggeling and Isaac Grünewald.

NATIONALMUSEUM

C3 Södra Blasieholmshamnen 08 519 543 00 Wed.–Sun. 11–5 (also Thu. 5–8, Feb.–May and Sep.–Dec.), Tue. 11–8 Museum restaurant and café T-Kungsträdgården 46, 55, 59, 62, 65, 76 $$$ (cheaper Wed.)
The Nationalmuseum (National Museum of Fine Arts) is a dignified Italianate building on little Blasieholmen peninsula, across the water east of Gamla Stan and facing the Royal Palace. The museum has a superb collection of Swedish and international art and applied art exhibited in a series of elegant rooms. Among the paintings are works by Rembrandt, Paul Cézanne and Paul Gauguin. Swedish art is well represented and includes superb watercolors by Carl Larsson and fine works by Anders Zorn. The applied art section is a feast of furnishings and artifacts, and there are additional displays of sculpture and Russian icons. The museum restaurant is located in a lovely, glass-roofed atrium.

NORDISKA MUSEET

C3 Djurgårdsvägen 6–16, Djurgårdsbron 08 519 560 00 Tue.–Sun. 10–5 (also Tue. and Thu. 5–8) Museum restaurant 44, 47, 69 $$$
The building housing the Nordiska Museet (Northern Museum) is a splendid work in its own right. Standing at the entrance to Djurgården, its gabled facade of brick and stone has elegant turrets and a handsome central steeple. The exhibits are a comprehensive and absorbing collection illustrating Swedish and general Nordic cultural life from the medieval period onward. There is an excellent section depicting the life of the Sami (Lapp) people and delightful exhibits of Swedish traditional dress. Pay your respects as you enter to the powerful oak statue of

Gustav Vasa, the 16th-century warrior who established the Swedish state.

SKANSEN

Off the map · Djurgården · 08 442 80 00 · Park and zoo: daily 10–10, Jun.–Aug.; 10–8, in May; 10–5 in Sep.; 10–4, rest of year. Traditional buildings: daily 11–5, May–Sep.; 11–3, rest of year · Museum restaurant and café · 44, 47 · Djurgårdsfäjan from Slussen/Nybrohamnen · $$–$$$

The Skansen open-air museum is located on Djurgården, Stockholm's island park. This area was the old hunting domain of Swedish royalty and is now preserved as an urban escape zone for Stockholmers and visitors. Individual attractions on Djurgården include the Vasamuseet (Vasa Museum, see below) and the Nordiska Museet (Northern Museum, see opposite), but the island offers numerous other diversions. Make a day of it, enjoying delightful woodland walks or a stroll alongside the quiet waters of the Djurgärdsbrunnsviken. At the heart of Djurgården, Skansen features more than 150 traditional buildings and a lively working environment in summer for artisans. You can sample traditional Swedish delicacies here, such as herring sandwiches and waffles with cream and cloudberries. Skansen's other attraction is its zoo and animal park, which boasts elk, bear and lynx. There are several smaller museums and art galleries scattered around Djurgården, and fun for everyone at Gröna Lunds Tivoli amusement park.

STADSHUSET

B2 · Hantverkargatan 1 · 08 508 290 58 · Guided tours daily at 10, 11, noon, 2 and 3, Jun.–Aug.; at 10, noon and 2, in Sep.; at 10 and noon, rest of year. Tower: daily 10–4:30, May–Sep.; Sat.–Sun. 10–4:30, in Apr. · Restaurant in City Hall · T-Centralen, T-Rådhuset · 3, 62 · City Hall $$$, Tower $$

Stockholm's Stadshuset (City Hall) is perhaps the city's finest example of early 19th-century Scandinavian Romantic Nationalist style. This was the same style that produced the *Jugend* buildings of Helsinki. Built of red brick and with a magnificent Italianate tower, it stands on the shore of Lake Mälaren, a striking focus

The steeple and facade of the Northern Museum

for inland Stockholm. The tower tapers gently to an upper platform and lantern that supports the gleaming *Tre Kroner*, the three crowns symbol of the city. Interiors are no less striking, the highlight being the Golden Hall with its mosaic walls and gleaming marble floor.

Admission to City Hall is by guided tour only. Daily from May to September and weekends in April you can climb the 450-foot tower – or take the elevator.

VASAMUSEET

C2 · Galärvarvet, Djurgården · 08 519 548 00 · Daily 9:30–7, Jun. 10–Aug. 25; 10–5 (also Wed. 5–8), rest of year · Museum restaurant and café · 44, 47, 69 · $$$ · Guided tours in English daily at 12:30 and 2:30 (also Sat.–Sun. at 10:30 and 4:30)

The unmistakable Vasamuseet (Vasa Museum) is truly exceptional, a great celebration of a unique historical event. The focus of the museum is the sailing ship *Vasa*, which sank spectacularly in Stockholm harbor within minutes of starting its maiden voyage in 1628. The sheer drama of the event is enough to grip you, but the reality of the *Vasa*, 230 feet long and fully restored and rigged, is just as breathtaking. No ordinary ship, the *Vasa* was ornamental as well as functional, and the vessel's finest features were preserved in the muddy waters of the Baltic for more than 330 years. The museum also tells the story of the people who salvaged the *Vasa*, and exhibits show some of the 12,000 artifacts recovered, bringing the ship and its story to vivid life.

A Stroll Around Gamla Stan

Stockholm's Gamla Stan (Old Town) – or *staden mellan broarna,* "the city among the bridges," as it is more lyrically known to Swedes – is not a perfectly preserved medieval townscape by any means. Disastrous fires in 1407 and 1640 destroyed the original wooden buildings of medieval Gamla Stan. But the island nature of the settlement, its small area and its crowded layout have spared Gamla Stan from too much modernization. What remains today is a superb enclave of old stone buildings dating from the 15th–18th centuries.

You can wander at will through the Old Town without getting lost. On this tiny island you are never far from the waterside or a bridge to re-orient yourself. Pick up an enlarged Gamla Stan map, widely available in stores, restaurants and tourist venues, to help you find specific places.

There are many easily missed treasures hidden away from the busy main streets of Västerlånggatan and Österlånggatan. Pay a visit to the Great Church (Storkyrkan), Stockholm's 13th-century cathedral, which lies just south of the courtyard of the Royal Palace. The church's finest artifact is the oak- and elkhorn-gilded sculpture of *St. George and the Dragon*, a 15th-century Gothic masterpiece of thorny carving. You may be lucky and catch a lunchtime organ recital or other musical performance in the church.

From the church, go into the narrow street of Trångsund and then turn left past a charming old phone booth to reach Great Square (Stortorget). This was the scene in 1520 of the notorious Stockholm "Blood Bath," when Christian II of Denmark slaughtered 82 Swedish nobles and citizens in a bid to seal with blood his overlordship of Sweden. This brutal act inspired Gustav Vasa, son of a murdered nobleman, to rebel successfully against Denmark and to secure Sweden's independence. On Stortorget's west side are a row of splendid gabled houses with little cafés and restaurants on their ground floors. The 18th-century Bourse, or Stock Exchange, commands the north side of the square. The Swedish Academy, the body that selects Nobel prize winners, meets at the Bourse.

Leave the square via the east side and walk down Köpmangatan, "Street of the Merchants," the oldest street in the Old Town and home to several fine antique shops with attractively painted ceilings. At the end of Köpmangatan, in the little square of Köpmantorget, is a dramatic reprise of the Great Church's statue of *St. George and the Dragon*, this time in bronze but just as powerful. Farther east is Österlånggatan, a long, winding street that was once the Old Town's shoreline.

Bear right, down the short slope of Köpmanbrinken street, and then keep right along Österlånggatan, past stylish restaurants, antique and craft stores, and fashion salons. There are lots of gift possibilities here, especially for children, in shops such as Textilarna, Kalikå and Tomtar & Troll. The narrow streets running east to the sea, such as Drakens Gränd, Ferkens Gränd and Packhusgränd, mark the old piers of the early medieval era. Near the end of Österlånggatan is the well-known restaurant Den Gyldene Freden (see page 568).

Soon you reach Iron Square (Järntorget), a name probably derived from the days when the Old Town's fortunes were built on its status as the

A rest from sightseeing – sample the delights of Swedish food in the Old Town

main outlet for the Swedish iron and copper trade. Here, against the wall of the old Central Bank, is the remarkably lifelike statue of Stockholm poet Evart Taube, a popular performer who died in 1976. Check out the nearby Sundbergs Konditori, a long-established institution selling coffee and delicious pastries.

From Järntorget, turn right onto Västerlånggatan, the busiest street in the Old Town, crammed with stores and tempting restaurants and cafés. On the right, just past the Mårten Trotzig restaurant, you'll pass the narrow entrance to Mårten Trotzigs Gränd, reputed to be the narrowest alleyway in Stockholm and named after a German medieval copper trader who had a business here.

All the way along Västerlånggatan you will be tempted by souvenir stores such as Thorndahl, at No. 17; the exotic Indiska at No. 50, with Indian clothes and artifacts; the Swedish craft stores Imagolit and Gallery S; and a host of specialty shops. Note the glass-paneled ceilings of many of the stores. Wandering along the delightful side streets is equally rewarding.

To end your Old Town excursion, stroll to where the bridge over the canal Stallkanalen leads through the arched passage to the gate at Riksgatan. Follow this back into Stockholm via the shopping street of Drottninggatan.

SWITZERLAND

"SWITZERLAND is simply a large, humpy, solid rock, with a thin skin of grass stretched over it."

From *A Tramp Abroad* by Mark Twain

Opposite: Mountains, green pastures and picture-postcard villages – all ingredients for a Swiss landscape

SWITZERLAND

With stunning Alpine scenery, lush meadows, a medley of beautiful lakes and attractive cities and towns, Switzerland has a wonderful variety of natural and man-made attractions.

Neutral Territory

The Swiss Constitution, modeled on that of the United States, was drawn up in 1848 and revised in 1874; it is still in force today. Modern Switzerland is thus a federation of democracies and neutrality is the cornerstone of state policy: Switzerland interferes in no foreign conflicts and makes no alliances.

Remaining neutral through both world wars, Switzerland emerged in 1945 as a powerful commercial player. Banking has long thrived here due to the political stability of the country and because of Swiss financial acumen. The superb infrastructure of railroads, tunnels and roads has overcome the mountainous terrain and allows the country to exploit a trading position at the center of Europe.

The Swiss Landscape

Europe's continental watershed runs through Switzerland, a landlocked, oval-shaped nation, with a central lowland sandwiched between the Jura mountains to the north and the mighty Alps. The high mountain glaciers and dramatic peaks of the Swiss Alps occupy 60 percent of the country (mostly in the south). Forests cover another quarter of the land. The rest is a delightful mix of lakes and meadow pasture, beautiful throughout the year. Much of Switzerland's weather is typical of central Europe; Ticino canton, south of the Alps, has a Mediterranean climate. You may encounter days when the *föhn* – a warm, dry wind – blows from the northern slopes of the Alps.

MORE TOP DESTINATIONS IN SWITZERLAND

• Ascona D1 • Baden C3 • Basel B3 • Bern B2 • Brienz C2 • Château de Chillon B2 • Engelberg C2 • Fribourg B2 • Grindelwald C2 • Gstaad B2 • Interlaken C2 • Lausanne A2 • Montreux B2 • St.-Moritz E2 • Schaffhausen C3 • Wilderswil C2 • Villars B1 • Zermatt C1

Language and Manners

Reflecting Switzerland's location in central Europe, the Swiss speak four different languages: Schwyzerdütsch, a Swiss-German dialect (although German is used for reading and writing); French; Italian; and Romansch, an ancient Latin tongue. This linguistic diversity results in very different types of people, and you'll notice this as you travel.

On the whole, the Swiss are extremely law-abiding, and consider punctuality very important. Manners are extremely formal, with hand-shaking and serious toasts in all social circumstances. Efficient, civic-minded and polite, they make Switzerland one of Europe's best-run countries.

Vacationing in Switzerland

The fabled Swiss efficiency has positive benefits for visitors: trains run punctually, hotels are clean and comfortable, opening times for attractions are reliable, and everyone connected with tourism speaks English. You'll also discover that Switzerland is expensive, so if you're watching your budget, don't plan on staying too long. There's something to enjoy throughout the year – skiing in the mountains during the winter; walking, sailing and other outdoor pursuits all summer. Late spring sees the countryside at its best, with carpets of mountain and meadow wildflowers; autumn, when the leaves turn and the first snow whitens the lower peaks, also is magnificent.

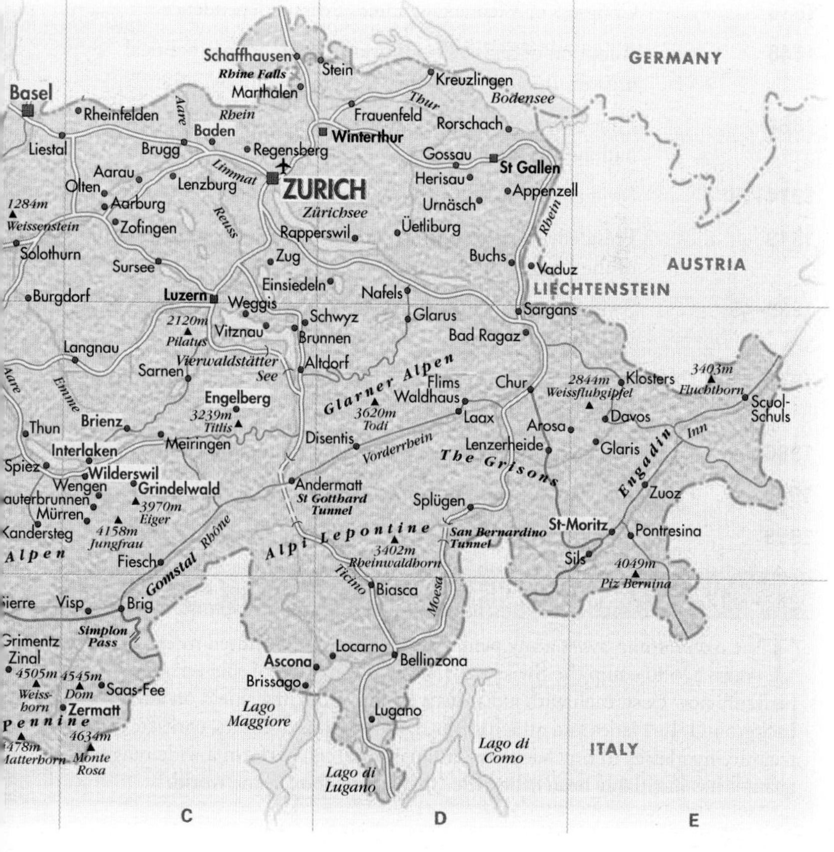

TIMELINE

3,000 BC	Evidence of earliest neolithic settlers by Lake Neuchâtel.
circa 100 BC	Romans invade from the south, incorporating Helvetic tribes.
circa AD 400	Romans expelled southward; Burgundians occupy western areas (modern French-speaking Switzerland) and Alemans the north and east (German-speaking Switzerland).
1032	Existing country incorporated into Holy Roman Empire, followed by gradual emergence of powerful independent nobles.
1515	Defeat at Battle of Marignano inaugurates neutrality.
1526	Zwingli's Reformation takes hold in Zurich, continued by John Calvin in Geneva beginning in 1532.
1648	Treaty of Westphalia recognizes Swiss neutrality and independence of 13 cantons.
1798	French invasion and rule under Napoleon, who establishes Helvetic Republic.
1815	Congress of Vienna guarantees Swiss independence.
1848	Adoption of Swiss Constitution, which defines political organization of the country.
1864	First Convention of Geneva is accepted and signed by 16 nations; the Red Cross is founded.
1914–18	Switzerland remains neutral during World War I.
1919	President Woodrow Wilson chooses Geneva as headquarters of the League of Nations.
1939–45	Switzerland remains neutral during World War II, but image is tarnished by pro-Nazi activities.
1946	United Nations takes over role of League of Nations; Geneva retained as European headquarters.
1986	Swiss vote in a referendum against joining the United Nations.
1990	Population votes to freeze nuclear power development.
1999	Ruth Dreifuss becomes Switzerland's first woman president.

THE SWISS ARMY PENKNIFE

The oxymoronic Swiss army penknife was first manufactured more than 100 years ago to equip the Swiss army. Over 200 models of this versatile penknife now exist, each with a distinctive white cross in a shield on a red background. Its blades and attachments, ranging from tweezers, corkscrews and magnifying glasses to tiny hacksaws and nail files, can perform a wide range of tasks; it has justifiably been called the "smallest toolbox in the world."

SURVIVAL GUIDE

- Keep more money available than you think you will need; cash seems to be spent alarmingly fast throughout Switzerland. Credit cards are widely accepted.
- Although most Swiss are excellent linguists, it's polite to ask if they speak English before starting a conversation or asking a question.
- Be polite to everyone – *bitte, prego* or *je vous en prie* is the equivalent of "you're welcome," and it's important to use one of these expressions when you're thanked. When you use public transportation, it's customary to give up your seat for elderly people, pregnant women and people with disabilities.
- Be punctual; if you're likely to be arriving later than planned at your hotel, let them know you've been held up.
- It is considered rude to eat or drink on the street. If you purchase food to go, find somewhere to sit down and eat it.
- Don't drop litter; it is a finable offense. When getting rid of trash, make sure you put it in the compartment designated for that particular type of waste.
- In Protestant Switzerland, decorous behavior is expected on Sunday.
- Dress conservatively in cities: avoid shorts, halter tops and beachwear.
- There is no state medical health service in Switzerland; treatment must be paid for on the spot. Therefore, it is very important to carry medical travel insurance valid in Switzerland. Many drugs can be bought over the counter. If you need a prescription drug, the prescription must be written by a Swiss doctor.
- In large towns and cities, stores are often closed on Monday mornings. Museums are usually closed on Mondays.
- Always cross the street at designated crossings, and wait for the green man symbol.
- Each canton and community is responsible for its own laws and law enforcement. The police uniform differs widely from place to place, as do local bylaws. Respect authority at all times, even if you see no point in what you are being requested to do.
- Use the superbly efficient public transportation system rather than the inordinately expensive taxis.
- You'll save money by eating and drinking in smaller establishments away from the more upscale areas.
- There is no need to tip in Switzerland; a service charge is automatically added to all bills.

St. Bernard – icon of Swiss mountain rescue

GENEVA

Sparkling Geneva (Genève), beautifully situated by the shores of Lake Geneva (Lac Léman) and backed by the Jura mountains and Alps, is indeed an elegant city. With its key role as an important international meeting place, many visitors are here on business, but others come to enjoy the scenic location, excellent museums, stores, restaurants and lively cultural life.

The Modern City

Strategically positioned at the head of the Rhône river, Geneva joined the Swiss Confederation in 1815, after Napoleon's downfall. Since then the city has grown, prospered and become increasingly cosmopolitan.

Today Geneva hosts meetings, exhibitions, conventions and many organizations involved with humanitarian and social causes. It plays a major part in Swiss industry, finance and commerce, but has succeeded in retaining much of its French style and attitude, resulting in a pleasing blend of charm and efficiency.

An important university and scientific center, Geneva also is home to CERN, the European Center of Nuclear Research. The city is ringed with attractive countryside – the ski slopes of the French Alps are less than an hour away, and Lake Geneva offers superb water sports facilities.

The steeple of St. Peter's Cathedral

Old Town and Beyond

Geneva is used to foreign visitors, and it's an easy city with which to become familiar. Getting around by public transportation is simple, and the center of the city is small enough to cover on foot, with much of the Old Town pedestrian-only. It's worth spending a couple of hours getting your bearings by walking around the town center, which lies on either side of the Rhône river.

Much of what you'll want to see is in or around the Old Town and is well signed, although with more than 30 museums to choose from, you are likely to take a bus at some point. Tourist trams run through the Old Town, leaving from the place Neuve every half-hour; they're a relaxing way to enjoy the city, although guided walking tours are available.

Tour buses travel to Lausanne and Château de Chillon, and into the Alps to Mont Blanc, Zermatt and Gstaad. Many lake cruises are offered, most lasting from one to three hours and many with an English commentary.

Gourmet Geneva

Like all Swiss cities, Geneva has a large range of restaurants offering cuisine from around the world. It also has its own specialties, many of which have more in common with France than the rest of Switzerland. Eating out can be expensive, although away from the city center you'll find friendly and atmospheric neighborhood restaurants where prices are considerably lower.

Many places serve Swiss specialties such as fondue and *rösti*, but you can choose from French, Italian, Thai, Japanese, Korean, Chinese, Russian, Spanish, Australian, Moroccan and many more. You'll find all the usual fast-food outlets in the center, and it's fun to shop for a picnic to eat in one of the lakeside parks. There's a plethora of bars throughout the city; the nicest are in the Old Town and along the lakeside.

Festivals and Fun

Geneva's biggest traditional festival is the *Escalade*, a December commemoration of a 1602 battle. A wonderful costumed parade marches through the Old Town, and the whole city is out in the streets. Summer is festival time, with many celebrations centering around the lake and featuring some of Europe's most spectacular fireworks displays. On July 4th, Geneva stages the largest Independence Day celebration outside the United States.

The globe of unity outside the Palace of Nations

Designer Style and Souvenirs

Geneva stores do not close at lunchtime and are open until 8 p.m. on Thursdays. There are vast malls on the city outskirts, but it's likely you'll be shopping in the downtown area, where the most attractive and elegant stores are located. Many of them are along the rue du Rhône, the rue du Mont Blanc and neighboring streets.

Don't miss Globus in the Grand Passage, a large department store that's a Geneva institution. You'll find watches, jewelry, high fashion and superb leather goods from outlets such as Boucheron and Piaget, Christian Dior, Giorgio Armani, Gucci, Hermes and Chanel.

If you're looking for souvenirs to take home, try the tourist boutique in Globus in the Grand Passage, Swiss Corner on the rue des Alpes, or l'Ours de Berne on the place du Port.

ESSENTIAL INFORMATION

TOURIST INFORMATION
Genève Tourisme (Geneva Tourism)
- rue du Mont Blanc 18
☎ 022 909 7000; fax 022 909 7011
www.geneve-tourisme.ch
- Pont de la Machine ☎ 022 311 9827
- Aéroport (airport) arrivals ☎ 022 717 8083

URBAN TRANSPORTATION
Geneva is efficiently served by swift and punctual trolley buses and buses that cover the city's various areas; it's likely you'll be traveling mainly inside Zone 10, which covers the city center. You buy and validate your ticket from the machines at each bus stop, which also have route maps and clear instructions about using the system. The best ticket for visitors to buy is the daily or multifare ticket, which provides either unlimited travel for 3 hours or 1 day, or 6 or 12 trips spread over several days. To board or leave the bus, press the red button near the door; the doors will open and close automatically. You can get more information from the Transports Publics Genevois (TPG) head office, route de la Chapelle 1, or at the information and ticket sales offices at Bachet-de-Pesay, Rive or Cornavin; for information ☎ 022 308 3311. Taxis can be found at stands in the city center and also can be hailed on the street or called from your hotel. Try AA New Cab SA (☎ 022 320 2020) or Taxi Phone Genève (☎ 022 331 4133).

AIRPORT INFORMATION
The Aéroport Internationale de Genève-Cointrin (Geneva International Airport, ☎ 022 717 7111) is 3 miles north of the city center. It is linked to the central railroad station by trains departing every 10 minutes, daily 6:30 a.m.– 12:30 a.m., with a 6-minute journey time. Bus No. 10 runs approximately every 10 minutes between the airport and the city center; the trip takes around 20–25 minutes. Taxis are available outside the airport terminal.

CLIMATE – average highs and lows for the month

JAN.	FEB.	MAR.	APR.	MAY	JUN.	JUL.	AUG.	SEP.	OCT.	NOV.	DEC.
4°C	5°C	10°C	13°C	18°C	22°C	25°C	25°C	20°C	13°C	8°C	4°C
39°F	41°F	50°F	55°F	64°F	72°F	77°F	77°F	68°F	55°F	46°F	39°F
-2°C	0°C	2°C	3°C	7°C	12°C	14°C	14°C	11°C	6°C	2°C	0°C
28°F	32°F	36°F	37°F	45°F	54°F	57°F	57°F	52°F	43°F	36°F	32°F

City Sights

Key to symbols

map coordinates refer to the Geneva map on page 451; sights below are highlighted in yellow on the map.

address or location telephone number

opening times nearest bus or tram route

restaurant or café on site or nearby admission charge: $$$ more than SF10, $$ SF7–SF10, $ less than SF7 other relevant information

Cathédrale St-Pierre

B2 cour St.-Pierre 022 311 7575; tours 022 310 2929 Cathédrale: Mon.–Sat. 9–7, Sun. noon–7, Jun.–Sep.; Mon.–Sat. 10–noon and 2–5, Sun. 11–12:30 and 1:30–5, rest of year. Site archéologique: Tue.–Sat. 11–5, Sun. 10–5, Jun.–Sep.; Tue.–Sat. 2–5, Sun. 10–noon and 2–5, rest of year 2, 7, 12, 16, 17 Cathedral free; site archéologique $

Begin your visit to the Cathédrale St-Pierre (St. Peter's Cathedral) at the site archéologique (archeological site), a huge complex beneath the cathedral that has been undergoing excavations since 1976. Here you'll see the remains of the earliest church, built in the fourth century, and learn the history of the site via an audio-visual show. Move on to the vast and austere cathedral, a Protestant church since 1536. It was built in the 12th and 13th centuries; its facade added in the 18th century. This is where John Calvin preached; his seat is still in the north aisle. Visitors can climb the 158 steps up the tower for fine views over Geneva and the lake.

Collections Baur

C1 rue Munier-Romilly 8 022 346 1729 Tue.–Sun. 2–6 1, 8 $

A solidly elegant 19th-century mansion houses the Collections Baur, connoisseur Alfred Baur's collection of Asian art. Here you'll find exquisite Chinese ceramics and jade, snuff bottles, prints and *netsuke* (Japanese carved toggles), and some stunning Japanese and Chinese lacquerwork covering the 1,000 years between the 8th and 18th centuries. It's worth lingering over the porcelain and marveling at the depth and translucency of the yellow and celadon-green glazes.

Jardin Anglais

B2–C2 promenade du Lac Daily dawn–dusk Cafés and restaurants 6, 8, 10

Statues, trees and colorful flowers help make the lakeside Jardin Anglais (English Garden) and its mountain views the perfect place to escape the city's bustle. Admire the 1862 fountain, complete with numerous reclining nymphs, before spending a few minutes at the Floral Clock. This huge timepiece, made entirely of 6,500 flowers and plants, was installed in 1955 as a symbol of the Geneva watch industry. A short walk along the lake will bring you to Parc de la Grange, a lovely rose garden seen at its best in mid-June.

Musée d'Art et d'Histoire

B1 rue Charles-Galland 2 022 418 2600 Tue.–Sun. 10–5 Restaurant 2, 3, 5, 7, 12, 16, 17 Free; temporary exhibitions $

Behind the grandiose facade of Geneva's Musée d'Art et d'Histoire (Museum of Art and History) lies a dauntingly large collection of paintings, archeological finds and objets d'art. Ancient history fans will enjoy the Egyptian, Greek, Roman and Etruscan rooms. The galleries cover the full range of European painting but concentrate on Swiss specialties, such as Ferdinand Hodler's powerful work *The Drinkers* or Konrad Witz's 1444 altarpiece; its background is one of Europe's first accurate landscape representations. Other rooms contain applied arts collections, fine furniture, silver and porcelain.

Musée d'Histoire Naturelle

C1 route de Malagnou 1 022 418 6300 Tue.–Sun. 9:30–5 Café and snack bar 1, 6, 8; tram 12, 16 Free, except some exhibitions

The splendid Musée d'Histoire Naturelle (Natural History Museum) is immensely popular, so get there early. The exhibits cover everything from the history of the Earth through the dinosaur age to comprehensive displays of animals, birds, reptiles and fish from all over the world. It's all excellently displayed, with some very realistic sound effects to help your

Place de Bourg-de-Four – the heart of old Geneva

imagination. Don't miss the relief map of Switzerland on the fifth floor.

Musée International de l'Automobile

Off the map · Voie-des-Traz 40, Grand Saconnex · 022 788 8484 · Tue.–Sun. 10–6 · Cafeteria · 5, 10, 18 · $$$

It's worth the trip out of town to Palexpo, Geneva's impressive exhibition complex, which houses the Musée International de l'Automobile (International Automobile Museum), a must for automobile fans. Four hundred vehicles are grouped in chronological order, from early speedsters to General George Patton's jeep and Elvis Presley's Cadillac. Space is devoted to cars of the future, rally and Formula 1 models, and there are numerous movie clips, posters, models and hands-on games.

Musée International de la Croix-Rouge et du Croissant-Rouge

Off the map · avenue de la Paix 17 · 022 748 9525 · Wed.–Mon. 10–5 · Restaurant · 8, F, V, Z · $$ · Guided tours

It's well worth visiting the state-of-the-art Musée International de la Croix-Rouge et du Croissant-Rouge (International Red Cross and Red Crescent Museum), which explains the principles and history of the Red Cross and the Red Crescent during some of the most serious crises of the 20th century.

Palais des Nations

Off the map · avenue de la Paix (Porte 39) · 022 907 4896 or 022 907 4539 · Guided tour: daily 9–5, Jul.–Aug.; daily 10–noon and 2–4, Apr.–Jun. and Sep.–Oct.; Mon.–Fri. 10–noon and 2–4, rest of year · Cafeteria and café · 5, 8, 11, 14, 18, F, V, Z · $$

Built between 1929 and 1936 to house the League of Nations, the Palais des Nations (Palace of Nations) is now the European seat of the United Nations. The vast marble and travertine-stone complex is beautifully situated on the slopes above the lake, with views of Mont Blanc. You can tour some of the interior and see the Salle des Pas-Perdus, a room decorated with marble donated by United Nations member countries, and the 2,000-seat Salle des Assemblées, one of the world's most active conference centers. After the tour, learn more through the multilingual interactive games.

Petit Palais

C1 · terrasse St.-Victor 2 · 022 346 1433 · Mon.–Fri. 10–6, Sat.–Sun.10–5 · 1, 3, 5, 8, 17 · $$ · Currently closed

This imposing 19th-century mansion contains the Petit Palais (Little Palace) museum, Geneva's Impressionist gallery, featuring many paintings from the private collection of the museum's founder, industrialist Oscar Ghez de Castelnuovo. Here you'll see Degas' *Nude Woman Washing*, some fine pointillist paintings by Paul Signac, and early works by Pablo Picasso and Marc Chagall.

Place du Bourg-de-Four

B1 · place du Bourg-de-Four · Cafés and restaurants nearby · 8, 17

Bourg-de-Four square is the heart of Old Geneva, historically the site of the Roman market, medieval trade fairs, and political and religious meetings. Today the square and its surrounding streets are a lovely place to stroll or enjoy a drink at one of the bars and cafés. Many of the fine buildings date from the 16th century; note their extra floors, added later to accommodate the flood of Protestant religious exiles.

Headquarters of the International Red Cross, in Geneva

The Red Cross

In 1859 Henri Dunant, son of a prominent Genevan family, set off to appeal to Napoleon III of France on a personal matter. Dunant caught up with Napoleon the day after the Battle of Solferino, where he saw more than 40,000 wounded men desperately in need of care and attention.

Dunant returned to Geneva and wrote a moving book, *Souvenir of Solferino*, in which he proposed the establishment of a body of volunteer male nurses to impartially care for the wounded in wartime. He further suggested that these men be recognized through an international agreement. Three friends added their support, the book was published and the International Committee of Help for the Wounded in Case of War (Comité Internationale de Secours aux Blessées en Cas de Guerre) was set up.

In 1864, the First Convention of Geneva was accepted and signed by 16 nations; a revised version of its standards of treatment for prisoners of war is still in effect today. An easily recognizable logo for the new movement was needed, and a reverse version of the Swiss flag was used; a red cross on a white background, rather than a white cross on a red background, and a symbol known the world over.

The Red Cross, present in more than 50 countries throughout the world, works hand in hand with the Red Crescent, an identical body functioning in Muslim and other non-Christian countries. Henri Dunant was awarded the Nobel Peace Prize in 1901.

The Red Cross functions at both international and national levels. The international headquarters are in Geneva, and it is from here that major humanitarian relief work is coordinated. Each participating country has its own national committee that deals with day-to-day work in that particular country. The Red Cross is still manned largely by volunteers, who cover everything from terrorist attacks and natural disasters to organizing collections for war victims and refugees, as well as training the public in emergency aid procedures.

ZURICH

Primarily a business center, with an emphasis on international finance and banking, this prosperous and clean city has plenty for visitors to enjoy. It is dotted with fine buildings, museums, historic churches and green spaces, the perfect background for affluent stores, elegant cafés and well-dressed citizens.

Lakeside City

Zurich surrounds the northern end of Zürichsee (Lake Zurich), from which the Limmat river flows to bisect the city. The oldest part lies on either side of the river, with the 19th-century

Swiss precision watch

Peaceful St. Peter's

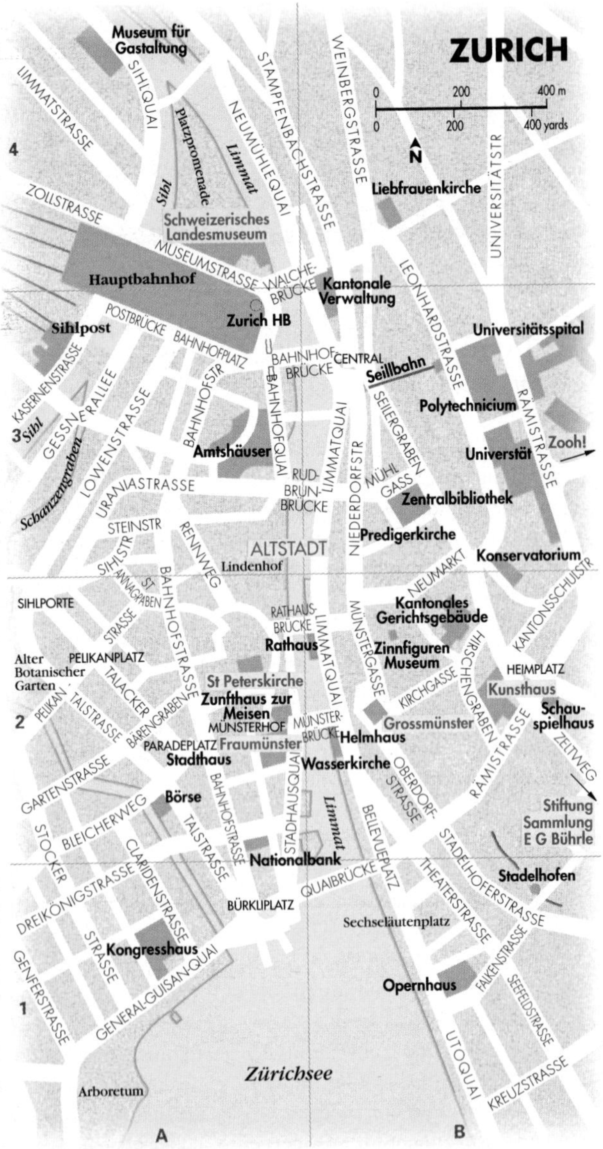

ZURICH
0 200 400 m
0 200 400 yards
N
Museum für Gastaltung
LIMMATSTRASSE
SIHLQUAI
Platzpromenade
Limmat
NEUMÜHLEQUAI
STAMPFENBACHSTRASSE
WEINBERGSTRASSE
UNIVERSITÄTSTR
Liebfrauenkirche
Sihl
ZOLLSTRASSE
Schweizerisches Landesmuseum
MUSEUMSTRASSE
Hauptbahnhof
WALCHEBRÜCKE
Kantonale Verwaltung
LEONHARDSTRASSE
Zurich HB
Universitätsspital
POSTBRÜCKE
Sihlpost
BAHNHOFPLATZ
BAHNHOFBRÜCKE
CENTRAL
Seilbahn
KASERNENSTRASSE
GESSNERALLEE
LOWENSTRASSE
BAHNHOFSTR
BAHNHOFQUAI
LIMMATQUAI
SEILERGRABEN
Polytechnicium
RÄMISTRASSE
Sihl
Schanzengraben
Amtshäuser
Universtät
Zooh!
URANIASTRASSE
RUDBRUNBRÜCKE
NIEDERDORFSTR
MÜHLGASS
Zentralbibliothek
STEINSTR
RENNWEG
ALTSTADT
Predigerkirche
SIHLSTR
ST ANNAGRABEN
Lindenhof
Konservatorium
NEUMARKT
KANTONSSCHULSTR
SIHLPORTE
BAHNHOFSTRASSE
RATHAUSBRÜCKE
Kantonales Gerichtsgebäude
STRASSE
Rathaus
LIMMATQUAI
MÜNSTERGASSE
Zinnfiguren Museum
HIRSCHENGRABEN
Alter Botanischer Garten
PELIKANPLATZ
HEIMPLATZ
St Peterskirche
KIRCHGASSE
Kunsthaus
PELIKAN
TALSTRASSE
TALACKER
Zunfthaus zur Meisen
BÄRENGRABEN
MÜNSTERHOF
MÜNSTERBRÜCKE
Grossmünster
Schauspielhaus
RÄMISTRASSE
PARADEPLATZ
Fraumünster
Helmhaus
ZELTWEG
Stadthaus
Wasserkirche
OBERDORFSTRASSE
GARTENSTRASSE
Börse
Stiftung Sammlung E G Bührle
BLEICHERWEG
TALSTRASSE
BAHNHOFSTRASSE
STADHAUSQUAI
Limmat
BELLEVUEPLATZ
STADELHOFERSTRASSE
STOCKER
CLARIDENSTRASSE
Nationalbank
THEATERSTRASSE
Stadelhofen
DREIKÖNIGSTRASSE
QUAIBRÜCKE
BÜRKLIPLATZ
Sechseläutenplatz
STRASSE
Kongresshaus
GENFERSTRASSE
GENERAL-GUISAN-QUAI
FALKENSTRASSE
SEEFELDSTRASSE
Opernhaus
UTOQUAI
Zürichsee
Arboretum
KREUZSTRASSE
4
3
2
1
A
B

grandeur of the Bahnhofstrasse area on the west. East of the river, gentle hills rise to the impressive university complex, while wide boulevards, parks and gardens run along the lake.

A tram ride is an essential experience; these efficient vehicles ensure that city streets are virtually traffic-free. If you feel in need of exercise, the tourist office will loan you a bike to get around like the locals do (May through late September; ID and deposit required).

Evenings Out

There's a wide range of excellent restaurants in Zurich, most of them expensive. It is possible to eat well and relatively cheaply on the east side of the river. You'll find the usual fast-food outlets, excellent cafés and tearooms, and cozy taverns and wine cellars.

Notice boards all over the city list movie theaters (often showing American films in English), concerts, theater and opera. For a relaxed evening with the locals, you'll find plenty of packed bars, open late, in and around the Limmatquai; on summer nights there is an array of street performers. Zurich also has a number of cabarets and discos.

Chocolates and Watches

Bahnhofstrasse, running from the main railroad station to the lake, is one of Europe's great shopping streets. Lined with expensive stores, it is where you'll find luxury items, including fashion, jewelry, watches, porcelain, furs and accessories. It's also home to Schweizer Heimatwerk, a lovely store specializing in every type of Swiss handicraft.

Don't miss Sprüngli, one of the most mouthwatering chocolate shops you'll ever visit. And the narrow old streets on each side of the river are packed with antiques stores, clock and watch outlets, and fun places for picking up souvenirs.

ESSENTIAL INFORMATION

TOURIST INFORMATION

Zürich Tourismus (Zurich Tourism)
• Bahnhofbrücke 1 ☎ 01 215 4000; fax 01 215 4099
www.zurichtourism.ch

URBAN TRANSPORTATION

Zurich's superbly efficient tram and bus system runs daily 4:30 a.m.–12:30 a.m. It is easy to use, fast and never, ever late. Tickets must be purchased and validated before boarding; all bus stops have ticket machines with detailed transportation maps and instructions for buying and validating your ticket. If you are going to be in Zurich for a couple of days or more, you can buy 24-hour, 48-hour or multiride tickets; like normal tickets, these also are valid for trams, buses, local trains and some boats. Numbers and stops (which are all named) are displayed on the front of the vehicles as well as inside. You must press the red button on the door to open the door before getting off; it will close automatically. For further English-language information call ☎ 0848 80 18 80 (only from within Switzerland). Taxis are an expensive option; call Züri Taxi (☎ 01 222 2222), Taxi Jung (☎ 01 271 1188) or Taxi Zürich (☎ 01 444 4444). Boats run on the lake April through October; their timetables are listed at departure points.

AIRPORT INFORMATION

Zurich-Kloten Airport (☎ 01 157 1060) is just under 6 miles north of the city center. Trains run every 10–15 minutes from the Hauptbahnhof, daily 5:30 a.m.–12:30 a.m., with a ride time of around 10 minutes. There are two terminals, A and B, which are interconnected. Taxis are available from outside the terminals.

CLIMATE – average highs and lows for the month

JAN.	FEB.	MAR.	APR.	MAY	JUN.	JUL.	AUG.	SEP.	OCT.	NOV.	DEC.
2°C	3°C	8°C	12°C	16°C	19°C	22°C	22°C	18°C	12°C	6°C	3°C
36°F	37°F	46°F	54°F	61°F	66°F	72°F	72°F	64°F	54°F	43°F	37°F
-2°C	-2°C	2°C	4°C	8°C	11°C	14°C	14°C	11°C	7°C	2°C	0°C
28°F	28°F	36°F	39°F	46°F	52°F	57°F	57°F	52°F	45°F	36°F	32°F

The twin towers of Grossmünster overlook the Limmat river and the Old Town

CITY SIGHTS

Key to symbols

map coordinates refer to the Zurich map on page 456; sights below are highlighted in yellow on the map. address or location telephone number opening times nearest bus or tram route restaurant or café on site or nearby admission charge: $$$ more than SF10, $$ SF7–SF10, $ less than SF7 other relevant information

ALTSTADT

A3–B3 Altstadt 4, 6, 7, 15 Guided tours: Mon.–Fri. at 2:30, Sat.–Sun. at 10 and 2:30, May–Oct.; Wed. and Sat. at 10, rest of year (information: tourist office, see page 457) $$$

The narrow streets and peaceful squares on either side of the Limmat river make up the Altstadt (Old Town). Beautifully preserved old buildings house antique and specialty stores, and there's a lovely riverside walkway and plenty of relaxing cafés and bars. Take in the Lindenhof, a square planted with lime trees on the site of the original Roman settlement, before crossing the river to amble down the east side's lively Niederdorfstrasse and Hirschengasse.

FRAUMÜNSTER

A2 Münsterhof 01 211 4100 Daily 9–12:30 and 2–6, May–Sep.; daily 10–noon and 2–5, Mar.–Apr.; daily 10–12:30 and 2–5, in Oct.; Mon.–Sat. 10–noon and 2–4, rest of year 2, 4, 6, 7, 8, 9, 11, 13 Free

The graceful spire of the Fraumünster (Our Lady's Minster Church), founded in the ninth century by two German princesses, rises near the west riverbank in the Old Town. The interior dates from 1250 and earlier; against its gray stone serenity, Marc Chagall's stained-glass choir windows vibrate with green, blue and yellow. Alberto Giacometti designed the transept glass.

GROSSMÜNSTER

B2 Grossmünsterplatz 01 252 5949 Mon.–Sat. 9–6 (tower 1:30–5), mid-Mar. through Oct. 31; 10–4 (tower 1:30–4:30), rest of year. Open Sun. for services 4, 15 $

Grossmünster church played a major part in Zurich's Reformation (a 16th-century movement which aimed at reforming the Roman Catholic Church and resulted in the establishment of Protestant churches). It was here that Ulrich Zwingli, the father of Swiss Protestantism, preached and taught. He transformed this Catholic foundation into a theological college that became the focal point of the University of Zurich. The church, galleries and three naves were built between 1100 and 1260, a superb Romanesque basilica with some outstanding sculpture on the capitals of its columns. Be sure to visit the tranquil cloister, which has exhibits telling the story of the Reformation, and save energy to climb up the tower, which has lovely views over Zurich and the lake.

KUNSTHAUS

B2 Heimplatz 1 01 251 6765 Tue.–Thu. 10–9, Fri.–Sun. 10–5 Café and restaurant 3, 31 Free

Zurich's Kunsthaus (Art Gallery), a lively museum that often mounts important temporary exhibitions, is mainly devoted to 19th- and 20th-century paintings and artworks. Earlier times are represented by a clutch of Venetian paintings, as well as some splendid Dutch works. The exhibits of modern art are housed in the newer wing. Here you'll find the largest collection of Edvard Munch outside Scandinavia, paintings by Marc Chagall, and a good cross-section of modern work by Mark Rothko, Francis Bacon and Roy Lichtenstein, whose contribution is a baked potato oozing with butter.

SCHWEIZERISCHES LANDESMUSEUM

A4 Museumstrasse 2 01 218 6511 Tue.–Sun. 10:30–5 Café and restaurant 3, 6, 7, 10, 15 $

Housed in a bizarre looking castle complete with towers and turrets, the Schweizerisches Landesmuseum (Swiss National Museum) should top your sightseeing list. This is the place to learn about Switzerland's history and development, and it is one of Europe's best organized museums. From prehistoric times, you can follow the flowering of Swiss civilization through frescoes, religious woodcarvings and exquisite jewelry, wood-paneled interiors, and furniture and costumes from every corner of the land. The 16th-century globes, showing all that had so far been discovered, are fascinating, and most visitors will enjoy the reconstruction of rooms from different eras.

ST. PETERSKIRCHE

A2 St. Peterhofstatt 01 211 2588 Mon.–Fri. 8–6, Sat. 9–4 6, 7 Free

The oldest church foundation in Zurich stands in a tranquil square at the heart of the Old Town, its delightfully restrained baroque interior perfectly typifying Zurich's God-fearing prosperity. Four churches predated the existing one, which preserves the late Romanesque choir and 13th-century tower. All is harmony and balance, from the richly carved choir stalls to the superb plasterwork. The clock in the tower is Europe's largest clock-face, measuring an impressive 28½ feet across.

STIFTUNG SAMMLUNG E. G. BÜHRLE

Off the map Zollikerstrasse 172 01 422 0086 Tue. and Fri. 2–5, Wed. 5–8 77 $$

A lovely suburban villa houses the Stiftung Sammlung E. G. Bührle (E. G. Bührle Collection), a wonderful range of Impressionist and post-Impressionist works of art collected by a German industrialist between 1934 and 1956. The exhibits are outstanding and the building a delight, so allow plenty of time.

There are delicate Jean Honoré Fragonards and François Bouchers – all flowery pinks and blues – sun-filled Camille Pissarros, the dazzling *Poppies near Vétheuil* by Claude Monet and the stunning *Chestnut Tree* by Vincent Van Gogh. Upstairs you'll find Pablo Picasso, Henri Matisse and Georges Braque, among others. Linger in the room devoted to Pierre Renoir, where there's also a lovely painting by Monet of his garden at Giverney. The 22 Degas bronzes of *The Dancer* are another highlight.

ZOOH!

Off the map Zürichberg 01 252 7100 Daily 8–6 Cafés and restaurant on zoo grounds 6 $$$

Zurich's zoo enjoys a parkland setting on a hill overlooking Zurich. More than 2,000 animals are exhibited, with emphasis on species from South America, Africa and Asia. If you're traveling with kids, arrange to be here at 10 a.m. when the elephants and monkeys enjoy their daily bath. The zoo has a successful breeding program; a board near the entrance gives information about any new arrivals.

A tasty shared experience – fondue, the Swiss national dish

Swiss Flavors

Switzerland has a range of regional dishes – German, French and Italian – rather than a national cuisine. With many foreigners working in the country, there's plenty of choice, and in the cities you'll find everything from Japanese to Tex-Mex. The Swiss call a restaurant menu the *Karte* or *carte*; *menu* means the "dish of the day."

Swiss Cheese Specials

The country's best-known specialty, fondue, is made by melting a selection of Swiss hard cheeses, such as Gruyère, Emmental and Vacherin, in white wine spiked with garlic and then adding spices and kirsch. The bubbling pot sits in the middle of the table on a little brazier, and you help yourself by dipping forkfuls of bread into the unctuous mixture. Be careful not to drop the bread in the pot – traditionally the culprit has to buy the next bottle of wine. Fondues also are made by cooking cubed beef in either hot oil (*fondue bourguignonne*) or beef stock (*fondue chinoise*); these are served with a variety of tasty dips. In French Switzerland you'll find raclette; a whole block of cheese is toasted and melted with slices scraped off and draped over boiled potatoes to be eaten with gherkins, smoked ham and sausage. It's delicious!

Main Dishes

Bündnerfleisch – raw, dried smoked beef – is well worth sampling, as are the many kinds of *wurst*, sausages eaten raw, grilled or boiled. The traditional accompaniment is *rösti,* a mouthwatering, crisp potato cake studded with onions and bacon. Hungry diners might enjoy the *Berner Platte*, a groaning plate of sausage, beef and ham served with potatoes and sauerkraut. The Swiss also are fond of liver, pork and veal. Traditional fish recipes in this landlocked country feature lake trout, carp and perch.

A Little Something Sweet

Chocolate and cream feature heavily in Swiss desserts, and you should certainly try some of the smooth Swiss chocolate during your trip; in addition to the ubiquitous Nestlé and Cailler, Lindt, Sprüngli, Teuscher and Tobler are varieties worth sampling. There are some splendid local cakes; try *leckerli* (spiced bread with honey), meringues, and delicious kirsch-flavored cakes and fruit breads. Start the day with a breakfast bowl of muesli, a tasty mixture of grains, fruit and nuts.

ESSENTIAL INFORMATION

"LET your boat of life be light, packed only with what you need..."

From *Three Men in a Boat*
by English author Jerome K. Jerome

PRE-TRIP ESSENTIALS...

WHAT YOU NEED

ESSENTIAL FOR TRAVELERS

● Required ● Recommended ● Not required

- Passport
- Visa
- Travel, medical insurance
- Round-trip or onward airline ticket
- Local currency
- Traveler's checks
- Credit cards
- First-aid kit and medicines
- Inoculations*

*see also HEALTH section

ESSENTIAL FOR DRIVERS*

- Driver's license
- International Driving Permit
- Car insurance (for nonrental cars)
- Car registration (for nonrental cars)

*see also DRIVING section

IMPORTANT ADDRESSES

Austrian National Tourist Office
PO Box 1142
New York, NY 10108-1142
☎ (212) 944-6880
Fax (212) 730-4568
www.experienceaustria.com

Österreich Werbung/Urlaubsinformation Österreich (Austrian National Tourist Office)
Margaretenstrasse 1
A-1040 Vienna, Austria
☎ 01 587 20 00
Fax 01 588 66 48
www.austria-tourism.at

American Embassy
Boltzmanngasse 16
A-1090 Vienna, Austria
☎ 01 31 339-0
Fax 01 310 06 82
Personal callers should phone for an appointment, Mon.–Sat. 8:30–5.

COUNTRY ESSENTIALS...

CUSTOMS

YES

Duty-free limits on goods brought in from non-European Union countries:
200 cigarettes or 50 cigarillos/cigars or 250 g. tobacco; 1 L. alcohol over 22% volume; 2 L. alcohol under 22% volume; 60 ml. perfume; 250 ml. toilet water; plus any other duty-free goods (including gifts) to the value of S2,500. Personal allowance from Hungary, Slovenia, Czech or Slovak republics: S1,000 (unless you arrive by air, when it is S2,500, as above). This information applies to visitors aged 17 and over. There are no currency regulations. There is no limit on the importation of tax-paid goods purchased within the European Union, provided they are for your own personal use.

NO

No unlicensed drugs, weapons, ammunition, obscene material, pets or other animals, counterfeit money or copied goods, meat or poultry.

For customs limits for returning U.S. citizens see page 16.

MONEY

Austria's currency is the schilling (S or Sch), which is divided into 100 groschen (g). The denominations of bills are 20, 50, 100, 500, 1,000 and 5,000S. There are coins of 10 and 50g and 1, 5, 10 and 20S. You can exchange dollars or traveler's checks *(Reiseschecks)* at a bank *(Bank)*, exchange office *(Wechselbüro)*, post office *(Postamt)* and at hotels. Credit cards are widely accepted. On Jan. 1, 1999, the euro became the official currency of Austria, and Austrian schillings became a denomination of the euro. Euro bills and coins were introduced on Jan. 1, 2002. Both euro bills and coins and the old national currency will be in use during a transitional period, after which time the euro will be the only currency accepted.
Exchange rate at press time: $1 = S15

TIPS AND GRATUITIES

Tips *(Trinkgeld)* are welcomed and expected in restaurants and cafés.

Restaurants (even when service is included)	10%
Cafés/bars	10%
Taxis	10%
Porters	at your discretion
Chambermaids	at your discretion
Hairdressers	5% (and change to shampooer)

COMMUNICATIONS

POST OFFICES

Buy stamps *(Briefmarken)* singly at a post office *(Postamt)* or newsstand/ tobacconist *(Tabak Trafik)* or from a hotel.

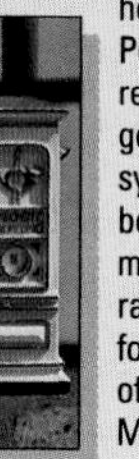

Post offices can be recognized by a golden trumpet symbol and can often be found close to the main square or railroad station.Hours for out-of-town post offices may vary. Mailboxes are yellow or orange.

TELEPHONES

You can use cash or a prepaid phone card *(Wertkarte)* to make a call in Austria. Telephones have direct dialing for national and international calls. Use S1, S5 and S10 coins. Phone cards can be bought from newsstands, gas stations, post offices and hotels. Some city phone booths take credit cards.

Phoning inside Austria
All Austrian telephone numbers in this book include an area code: dial the number that is listed.

To call the operator dial 1611.

Phoning Austria from abroad
The country code for Austria is 43. Note that Austrian numbers in this book do not include the country code; you will need to prefix this number if you are phoning from another country. To phone Austria from the United States or Canada, omit the first zero from the Austrian number, and add the prefix 011 43. (Note that the number of digits in Austrian area codes varies.)
Example: 01 12 23 34-4 becomes 011 43 1 12 23 34-4.

Phoning from Austria
To phone the United States or Canada from Austria, prefix the area code and number with 001.
Example: (111) 222-3333 becomes 001 111 222-3333.

To call European information dial 1613
To call international information dial 1614.

EMERGENCY TELEPHONE NUMBERS

Police *(Polizei)*	133
Fire *(Feuerwehr)*	122
Ambulance *(Krankenwagen)*	144

Emergency calls are free from phone booths.

HOURS OF OPERATION

- Stores Mon.–Sat.
- Museums/monuments
- Offices Mon.–Fri.
- Pharmacies
- Banks Mon.–Fri.
- Post offices Mon.–Fri.

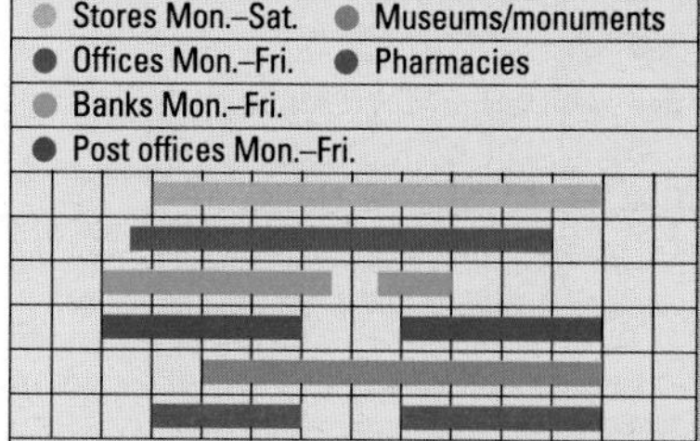

Saturday is early closing day; shops close between noon and 5 p.m. Thursday or Friday is late night shopping (until 7 or 8). Some shops close for 1 or 2 hours for lunch.

Grocery stores and other food stores may have longer hours of operation.

Banks stay open until 5 p.m. on Thursday. Post offices may also open 8–10 on Saturday. In cities, main post offices are open 24 hours a day.

Pharmacies usually follow store opening hours with a 2-hour lunch break. There is always one pharmacy open late in each city: details are displayed in pharmacy windows.

Facilities at tourist resorts may have special hours of operation.

NATIONAL HOLIDAYS

Banks, businesses and most stores close on these days. Also, some museums may be closed or have restricted hours.

Jan. 1	**New Year's Day**
Jan. 6	**Epiphany**
Mar./Apr.	**Easter Monday**
May 1	**Labor Day**
May	**Ascension Day**
May/Jun.	**Pentecost Monday**
May/Jun.	**Corpus Christi**
Aug. 15	**Assumption of the Virgin**
Oct. 26	**National Day**
Nov. 1	**All Saints' Day**
Dec. 8	**Immaculate Conception**
Dec. 25	**Christmas Day**
Dec. 26	**St. Stephen's Day**

PHOTOGRAPHY

Magnificent and varied subject matter awaits the photographer in Austria. Make sure you choose a perspective that will do justice to the architectural masterpieces and narrow city lanes. Away from the city, the Alpine peaks give enormous scope for landscape photography, and the light is generally very good.

HEALTH

MEDICAL INSURANCE

The cost of medical treatment in Austria is high, and private medical insurance is recommended. The American Medical Society can suggest a doctor *(Arzt)* or hospital *(Krankenhaus)*: Lazarettgasse 13, Vienna, ☎ 01 4054 5680. The south and east are home to *Zecken* – a kind of tick that can transmit encephalitis. This disease is potentially lethal, and it is essential you seek medical advice if you are bitten. An inoculation is available.

DENTAL SERVICES

Dentists *(Zahnarzt)* will charge for any treatment given. Dental work is expensive, so check that it is covered by your medical insurance. Dentists are listed in the telephone directory, or ask for English-speaking dentists at your embassy, a tourist office or hotel.

SUN ADVICE

Austria has strong sun during the summer months so sun protection is needed. Wear a hat, cover shoulders, drink plenty of fluids and use sunblock.

DRUGS

Pharmacies *(Apotheken)* can dispense prescriptions. Many assistants speak English, and a schedule displayed on the door enables you to find a late-opening or 24-hour pharmacy in every town.

SAFE WATER

Tap water is safe to drink throughout Austria. Mineral water *(Mineralwasser)* is widely available.

RESTROOMS

Public restrooms *(Toiletten/WC)* are generally easy to find and immaculately clean. A small charge is levied.

ELECTRICITY

Austria has a 220-volt power supply. Electrical sockets take plugs with two round pins; American appliances will need a plug adapter and will require a transformer if they do not have a dual-voltage facility.

NATIONAL TRANSPORTATION

TRAIN *(Zug)*

The Austrian Federal Railways (Österreichische Bundesbahnen or ÖBB) runs a comfortable and efficient service, with connections to all European countries. If you like a slower pace try a steam train journey through valleys and along lakesides, or a cable car trip; local tourist offices can give details. For rail information ☎ 01 93 00 00.

BUS *(Bus)*

Austria has a good network of local, federal and private bus companies. Bus travel is slower but less expensive than the train; for information ☎ 01 711 01. The Eurolines international bus service also operates in Austria: ☎ 01 71 20 453.

FERRY *(Fähre)*

From Easter to the end of October you can enjoy steamer services on the Danube; some continue into neighboring countries. Steamers ply the larger Austrian lakes from May to September. Wiener Tourismusverband can supply details on steamer companies: ☎ 01 211 14-222.

DRIVING

DRIVE ON THE RIGHT

SPEED LIMITS

Police impose on-the-spot fines (for which receipts are issued), although a foreign motorist may refuse and instead be asked to make a surety payment.

Limited-access highways *(Autobahnen)*
130 k.p.h. (80 m.p.h.)

Main roads
100 k.p.h. (62 m.p.h.)

Urban areas
50 k.p.h. (31 m.p.h.)

SEAT BELTS

Must be worn in front and back seats at all times. Children under 12 are not allowed to use a front seat.

BLOOD ALCOHOL

The legal blood alcohol limit is 0.05%. Random breath tests on drivers are carried out frequently, especially late at night, and the penalties for offenders are severe.

DRIVING continued

TOLLS

To use toll highways, purchase a windshield sticker *(Vignette)* at automobile clubs in Austria or abroad, or at a border crossing, gas station, post office or tobacconist. Nonpayment of tolls results in a fine.

CAR RENTAL

The leading rental firms have offices at airports and train stations. Hertz offers discounted rates for AAA members (see page 15). For reservations:

	UNITED STATES	AUSTRIA
Alamo	(800) 327-9633	01 799 6176 (Europcar)
Avis	(800) 331-2112	01 587 6241
Budget	(800) 527-0700	01 714 6565
Hertz	(800) 654-3080	01 512 8677

FUEL

Many gas stations *(Tankstelle)* are self-service, and 24-hour facilities are common. Unleaded gas *(Bleifrei)* is available at 91, 95 and 98 octane. Diesel is available and credit cards are accepted in most garages.

AAA AFFILIATED MOTORING CLUB
Österreichischer Automobil-, Motorrad-und Touring Club (ÖAMTC)
Schubertring 1-3, 1010 Vienna
☎ 01 711 99-0, fax 01 713 18 07

If you break down while driving, phone ☎ 120 (ÖAMTC breakdown service). Not all automobile clubs offer full services to AAA members.

BREAKDOWNS AND ACCIDENTS

There are 24-hour emergency phones at regular intervals on highways.

All accidents involving personal injury must be reported to the police (☎ 133).

Most car rental firms provide their own free rescue service; if your car is rented, follow the instructions given in the documentation. Use of a car repair service other than those authorized by your rental company may violate your agreement.

OTHER INFORMATION

The minimum age for driving a car is 17 (may be higher for some car rental firms).

An International Driving Permit (IDP) is recommended; some rental firms require them, and they can speed up formalities if you are involved in an accident. A Green Card (international motor insurance certificate) is recommended if you are driving a private car; see page 16 for more information.

Cars must carry a first-aid kit and warning triangle.

In winter, snow tires or chains are essential, and are legal from Nov. 15 to the first Monday after Easter. Rent chains at automobile clubs and border crossings.

USEFUL WORDS AND PHRASES

The official language in Austria is German, although Austrians are very proud of their brand of the language *(Österreichische)*, and are offended if it is treated as a mere dialect of "standard" German *(Hochdeutsch)*. On paper, the differences between the two varieties are not obvious, but the Austrian accent is distinctive, and especially strong in rural regions.

There are numerous words that are peculiar to Austria and the south of Germany. The Austrian diminutive is *-el* or *-lein* compared with the German *-chen*, so *Mädchen* (girl) in German becomes *Mädel* in Austrian. A small number of Austrian words, such as *Fauteuil* (armchair) and *Plafond* (ceiling), are in fact of French origin.

See page 493 for a pronunciation and basic vocabulary guide to the German language; the following list is an eclectic sample of words peculiar to Austrian German.

Everyday life

a maiden, or a girl's dress	*Dirndl*
masked ball	*Fetzenball*
hello	*Grüss Gott*
policeman	*Gendarm*
friend, guy	*Haberer*
legs	*Haxen*
funny	*Hetzig*
work	*Hockn*
guitar	*Klampfe*
goodbye	*Pfiat di*
slippers	*Schlapfen*

Food and drink

blood sausage	*Blunzn*
potato	*Erdäpfel*
green beans	*Fisole*
green salad	*Häuplsalat*
carrot	*Karotte*
croissant	*Kipferl*
lemonade	*Kracherl*
doughnut	*Krapfen*
corn	*Kukuruz*
milky coffee	*Melange*
mushroom	*Schwammerl*

Common words and phrases

how much?	*wieviel kostet es?*
excuse me	*entschuldigen*
I don't understand	*Ich verstehe nicht*
I'd like	*Ich möchte*
where is...?	*wo ist...?*
no smoking	*nicht rauchen*
closed	*geschlossen*
open	*geöffnet*
please	*bitte*
thank you	*danke*
key	*schlussel*
room	*zimmer*
shower	*dusche*
breakfast	*frühstück*

Belgium - Essential Information

PRE-TRIP ESSENTIALS...

WHAT YOU NEED

ESSENTIAL FOR TRAVELERS

● Required ● Recommended ● Not required

Passport	● Required
Visa	● Not required
Travel, medical insurance	● Required
Round-trip or onward airline ticket	● Not required
Local currency	● Required
Traveler's checks	● Required
Credit cards	● Required
First-aid kit and medicines	● Required
Inoculations	● Not required

ESSENTIAL FOR DRIVERS*

Driver's license	●
International Driving Permit	●
Car insurance (for nonrental cars)	●
Car registration (for nonrental cars)	●

*see also DRIVING section

IMPORTANT ADDRESSES

Belgian Tourist Office
780 Third Avenue, Suite 1501
New York, NY 10017
☎ (212) 758-8130
Fax (212) 355-7675
www.visitbelgium.com

Belgian Tourist Information Center
rue du Marché-aux-Herbes 63/Grasmarkt 63
1000 Bruxelles, Belgium
☎ 02 504 0390
Fax 02 504 0270
www.belgium.tourism.net

American Embassy
boulevard du Régent 27/Regentlaan 27
1000 Bruxelles/1000 Brussel,
Belgium
☎ 02 508 2111
Fax 02 511 2725
Personal visa inquiries: Mon.–Fri. 9–noon and 2:30–4

COUNTRY ESSENTIALS...

CUSTOMS

YES

Duty-free limits on goods brought in from non-European Union countries: 200 cigarettes or 100 cigarillos or 50 cigars or 250 g. tobacco; 1 L. alcohol over 22% volume or 2 L. alcohol under 22% volume; 2 L. wine; 50 ml. perfume; 250 ml. toilet water; plus any other duty-free goods (including gifts) to the value of 3,800BF. There is no limit on the importation of tax-paid goods purchased within the European Union, provided the goods are for your own personal use. There are no currency regulations.

NO

No unlicensed drugs, weapons, ammunition, obscene material, pets or other animals, counterfeit money or copied goods, meat or poultry.

For customs limits for returning U.S. citizens see page 16.

MONEY

Belgium's currency is the Belgian franc (BF), which is divided into 100 centimes. The denominations of franc bills are 100, 200, 500, 1,000, 2,000 and 10,000. There are coins of 50 centimes and 1, 5, 20 and 50BF. Be sure to differentiate between 5BF and 20BF coins, as they are very similar in shape and color. Credit cards are widely accepted but can be unwelcome for small amounts. On Jan. 1, 1999, the euro became the official currency of Belgium, and the Belgian franc became a denomination of the euro. Euro bills and coins were introduced on Jan. 1, 2002. Both euro bills and coins and the old national currency will be in use during a transitional period, after which time the euro will be the only currency accepted. Exchange rate at press time: $1 = 45BF

TIPS AND GRATUITIES

Tips are not obligatory; a service charge is usually included for restaurants, cafés and taxis.

Restaurants (where service is not included)	10%
Cafés/bars	change
Taxis	change
Porters	50BF per item
Chambermaids	change
Cloakroom attendants	20BF

COMMUNICATIONS

POST OFFICES

Buy stamps *(timbres/postzegels)* at a post office *(bureau de poste/ postkantoor)*, a tobacconist or newsstand *(tabac/ tabaksverkoper)*, or from a vending machine.

Allow a week for mail to reach the United States.

Mailboxes are painted red.

Hours for out-of-town post offices may vary.

TELEPHONES

Coin-operated public phones take 5BF and 20BF coins, but phone card booths are more common. Phone cards *(télécartes/kaarttelephoon)* are available from post offices, train stations, bookstores and some newsstands for 100BF, 500BF or 1,000BF (phone card booths do not take credit cards). Dialing instructions in English are often displayed in public booths.

Phoning in Belgium
All Belgian telephone numbers in this book include an area code: dial the number listed.
To call the operator dial 1307 (French-speaking areas) or 1207 (Flemish-speaking areas).

Phoning Belgium from abroad
The country code for Belgium is 32.
Note that Belgian numbers in this book do not include the country code; you will need to prefix this number if you are phoning from another country. To phone Belgium from the United States or Canada, omit the first zero from the Belgian number and add the prefix 011 32. (Note that Belgian area codes are two or three digits.)
Example: 01 122 3344 becomes 011 32 1 122 3344.

Phoning from Belgium
To phone the United States or Canada from Belgium, prefix the area code and number with 001.
Example: (111) 222-3333 becomes 001 111 222-3333.

To call international information dial 1204 (French-speaking areas) or 1304 (Flemish-speaking areas).

EMERGENCY TELEPHONE NUMBERS

Police *(police)*	101
Fire service *(pompiers)*	100
Ambulance *(ambulance)*	100

Emergency calls are free from phone booths.

HOURS OF OPERATION

- Stores Mon.–Sat.
- Museums/monuments
- Offices Mon.–Fri.
- Pharmacies Mon.–Sat.
- Banks Mon.–Fri.
- Post offices Mon.–Fri.

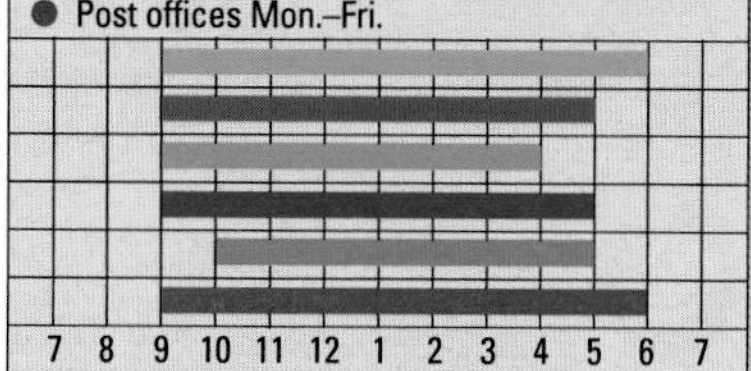

While Sunday is the official closing day, souvenir shops in many towns stay open.

Many bakeries and *patisseries* open at 7:30 or 8 a.m. and also open on Sunday morning.

Department and other major stores often stay open until 7 p.m. on weekdays and 9 p.m. on Friday.

Smaller stores and out-of-town post offices and banks may close for lunch.

Some city post offices and banks open on Saturday morning. Post offices and banks outside cities and large towns may close for 2 hours at lunch.

It is common for museums to close on Monday (except in Bruges, where they close on Tuesday or Wednesday, or in Tournai, where they close on Tuesday) and open later one evening a week. Many close for 2 hours at lunch.

NATIONAL HOLIDAYS

Banks, businesses and most stores close on these days. Most cities, towns and villages celebrate their patron saint's day, but most places stay open.

Jan. 1	**New Year's Day**
Mar./Apr.	**Easter Monday**
May 1	**Labor Day**
May	**Ascension Day**
May/Jun.	**Pentecost Monday**
Jul. 21	**National Day**
Aug. 15	**Assumption of the Virgin**
Nov. 1	**All Saints' Day**
Nov. 11	**Armistice Day**
Dec. 25	**Christmas Day**

PHOTOGRAPHY

Belgium is not renowned for bright sunshine, so pack plenty of 200 ASA-speed film. Check that flash photography is permitted before taking pictures in museums. Film and camera batteries are readily available from tourist stores. Rapid-developing services are also widely available.

POLICE 101 *(Police)*

HEALTH

MEDICAL INSURANCE
Private medical insurance is recommended. Visitors from non-European Union countries can receive treatment in a hospital emergency room but are charged if admitted to a hospital *(hôpital/ziekenhuis)*.

DENTAL SERVICES
Dental treatment is not available free of charge; all dentists practice privately. A list of dentists *(dentiste/tandarts)* can be found in the yellow pages *(pages jaunes/beroepenlijst)*. Check that dental treatment is covered by your private medical insurance.

SUN ADVICE
The warmest months are July and August, with average daytime temperatures of 60°F. Belgian weather can be unpredictable and although the sun is not often very fierce, protection is still required.

DRUGS
Prescription and nonprescription medicines are available from a pharmacy *(pharmacie/apotheek)*. If you need a medicine outside regular hours, the addresses of 24-hour facilities are posted on the door of all pharmacies.

SAFE WATER
Tap water is safe to drink and mineral water *(eau minérale/mineraalwater)* is widely available. The origin of the English word "spa" is in fact the Belgian town of Spa, especially popular during the 19th century for its mineral springs.

RESTROOMS

Public restrooms *(toilettes/toilets)* are not always easy to find, but are usually clean. If you need to use the facilities at a restaurant or café purchase a drink first. Restrooms in the larger restaurants and cafés sometimes have attendants; you should tip them 20BF, which goes toward their wages.

ELECTRICITY

Belgium has a 220-volt power supply. Electrical sockets take plugs with two round pins; American appliances will need a plug adapter and will require a transformer if they do not have a dual-voltage facility.

NATIONAL TRANSPORTATION

TRAIN ***(train/trein)***
The national rail network is the SNCB/NMBS (Societé Nationale des Chemins de fer Belges in French, and Nationale Maatschappij der Belgische Spoorwegan in Flemish). It runs an efficient system with many special deals on fares. Reservations can only be made for international journeys; ☎ 0900 10177 for information.

BUS ***(bus/bus)***
Details on the good local services are available at tourist offices, but there are few national long-distance buses. Open the door yourself on buses and trams; where there is no handle, press the black strip or button. International Eurolines buses operate in Belgium; ☎ 02 274 1350 (daily 9 a.m.–11 p.m.).

FERRY ***(ferry/veerboot)***
A fast ferry (hydrofoil) across the English Channel from Oostende (Ostend) to Dover takes 2 hours ; Hoverspeed ☎ 059 55 99 11. A conventional ferry from Zeebrugge to Hull (northern England) takes around 14 hours; P&O North Sea Ferries ☎ 050 543 430.

DRIVING

DRIVE ON THE RIGHT

SPEED LIMITS
Police impose on-the-spot fines (for which receipts are issued), although a foreign motorist may refuse and instead be asked to make a surety payment.

Limited-access highways *(autoroutes/autoweg)* **120 k.p.h. (74 m.p.h.)**
Minimum speed on straight, level stretches **70 k.p.h. (43 m.p.h.)**

Main roads
90 k.p.h. (55 m.p.h.)

Urban areas
50 k.p.h. (31 m.p.h.)

SEAT BELTS
Must be worn in front and back seats at all times; children under 12 must travel in the rear. If a child is sitting in the front, a seat belt/child restraint appropriate to his or her size/weight must be used.

BLOOD ALCOHOL
The legal blood alcohol limit is 0.5 g/L. Random breath tests on drivers are carried out frequently, especially late at night, and the penalties for offenders are severe.

DRIVING continued

TOLLS

Limited-access highways are free.

CAR RENTAL

The leading rental firms have offices at airports, train stations and ferry terminals. Hertz offers discounted rates for AAA members (see page 15). For reservations:

	UNITED STATES	BELGIUM
Alamo	(800) 327-9633	02 753 2060
Avis	(800) 331-2112	02 720 0944
Budget	(800) 527- 0700	02 721 5097
Hertz	(800) 654-3080	02 726 4950

FUEL

Gasoline *(essence/benine/benzine)* and diesel are priced in liters and are expensive. There are two grades of unleaded gas *(sans plomb/loodvrij)*: normal (92 octane) and super (97 octane). Most gas stations are self-service, and 24-hour facilities are common.

AAA AFFILIATED MOTORING CLUB

Touring Club de Belgique (TCB)
44 rue de la Loi, 1040 Brussels
☎ 02 233 2211, fax 02 233 2205

If you break down while driving, phone ☎ 070 344 777 (TCB breakdown service) or, on a limited-access highway, use one of the emergency telephones located every 1.2 miles. Ask for *"Touring-Secours."* Not all automobile clubs offer full services to AAA members.

BREAKDOWNS AND ACCIDENTS

Most car rental firms have their own free rescue service; if your car is rented, follow the instructions given in the documentation. Use of a car repair service other than those authorized by your rental company may violate your rental agreement.

If you are involved in an accident phone 101 for police assistance.

OTHER INFORMATION

The minimum age for driving a car is 18 (may be higher for some car rental firms).

An International Driving Permit (IDP) is recommended; some rental firms require them, and they can speed up formalities if you are involved in an accident.

A Green Card (international motor insurance certificate) is recommended if you are driving a private car; see page 16 for more information.

Beware of cobbled roads, in both cities and rural areas, which can be slippery in wet weather.

USEFUL WORDS AND PHRASES

A linguistic battle has existed in Belgium for many centuries; settlers have long entered from neighboring countries, and there are three marked language communities in Belgium: French, Dutch and German.

The two dominant languages are Walloon (a form of French, spoken in the south) and Flemish (a dialect of Dutch, spoken in the north). Passions run deep between the two groups; prosperity has moved back and forth between them over the centuries, and their relationship is still difficult to this day. The Flemish fear their language is being diminished, aware of the strength that French has as a world language.

Both Walloon and Flemish hold equal status as official languages, and although the bilingual signs can be confusing to the visitor, English is widely spoken.

In Brussels, where Flemish and French are both spoken, the street signs also are in both languages. Place names are not usually a problem, since the Flemish and French proper names have similarities, but there can be differences. Following is a selection of locations:

English	Flemish	French
Aalst	*Aalst*	Alost
Antwerp	*Antwerpen*	Anvers
Bruges	*Brugge*	Bruges
Brussels	*Brussel*	Bruxelles
Ghent	*Gent*	Gand
Jodoigne	*Geldenaken*	Jodoigne
Kortrijk	*Kortrijk*	Courtrai
Liège	*Luik*	Liège
Leuven	*Leuven*	Louvain
Mechelen	*Mechelen*	Malines
Mons	*Bergen*	Mons
Mouscron	*Moeskroen*	Mouscron
Nivelles	*Nijvel*	Nivelles
Ostend	*Oostende*	Ostende
Roeselare	*Roeselare*	Roulers
Ronse	*Ronse*	Renaix
Scheldt	*Schede*	Escaut
Tongeren	*Tongeren*	Tongres
Tournai	*Doornik*	Tournai
Veurne	*Veurne*	Furnes
Ypres	*Ieper*	Ypres

For useful phrases in French, see page 489; for phrases in German, see page 493; for phrases in Dutch, see page 517.

PRE-TRIP ESSENTIALS…

WHAT YOU NEED

ESSENTIAL FOR TRAVELERS

● Required ● Recommended ● Not required

Item	Status
Passport	Required
Visa	Not required
Travel, medical insurance	Required
Round-trip or onward airline ticket	Not required
Local currency	Required
Traveler's checks	Required
Credit cards	Required
First-aid kit and medicines	Required
Inoculations	Not required

ESSENTIAL FOR DRIVERS*

Item	Status
Driver's license	Required
International Driving Permit	Required
Car insurance (for nonrental cars)	Required
Car registration (for nonrental cars)	Required

*see also DRIVING section

IMPORTANT ADDRESSES

British Tourist Authority
551 Fifth Avenue, 7th Floor
Suite 701
New York, NY 10176-0799
☎ (212) 986-2200 or (800) 462-2748
Fax (212) 986-1188
www.travelbritain.org

British Tourist Authority
Thames Tower
Black's Road
Hammersmith
London W6 9EL, U.K.
☎ 020 8846 9000
Fax 020 8563 0302
www.visitbritain.com

British Visitor Centre (walk-in only)
1 Regent Street, Piccadilly Circus,
London SW1 4XT, U.K.

American Embassy
24 Grosvenor Square
London W1A 1AE, U.K.
☎ 020 7499 9000
Fax 020 7495 5012 (consular service)
Personal and telephone inquiries:
Mon.–Fri. 8:30–5:30

COUNTRY ESSENTIALS…

CUSTOMS

YES

Duty-free limits on goods brought in from non-European Union countries: 200 cigarettes or 100 cigarillos or 50 cigars or 250 g. tobacco; 2 L. wine; 1 L. alcohol over 22% volume or 2L. alcohol under 22% volume; 60 ml. perfume; 250 ml. toilet water; plus any other duty-free goods (including gifts) to the value of £145. There is no limit on the importation of tax-paid goods purchased within the European Union, provided the goods are for your own personal use. If you are bringing in more than £10,000 worth of U.S. dollars, customs must be notified and proof of ownership will be required.

NO

No unlicensed drugs, weapons, ammunition, obscene material, pets or other animals, counterfeit money and copied goods, meat or poultry.

For customs limits for returning U.S. citizens see page 16.

MONEY

Britain's currency is the pound sterling (£), which is divided into 100 pence (p). The denominations of pound bills are 5, 10, 20 and 50 (Scotland also has a £1 bill). There are coins of 1, 2, 5, 10, 20 and 50p and £1 and £2. You can exchange dollars or traveler's checks at banks, main post offices, exchange offices and some travel agencies. Buy traveler's checks in pounds sterling, so you do not lose money every time you change them. Credit cards are widely accepted throughout Britain, and ATMs are very common in shopping areas. When sightseeing, it is a good idea to carry a mix of large and small denominations.
Exchange rate at press time: $1 = £0.69

TIPS AND GRATUITIES

Service	Tip
Restaurants (where service is not included)	10–15%
Cafés/bars	change
Taxis	10%
Porters	50p–75p
Hairdressers	10%
Tour guides	£1–£2
Chambermaids	change
Cloakroom attendants	10p–20p

COMMUNICATIONS

POST OFFICES

Buy stamps at post offices, gas stations, tobacconists and supermarkets. Out-of-town post offices often close 1–2 and Wednesday afternoon. Mailboxes ("pillar-boxes") are red, and are usually free-standing. Pillar-boxes show who was monarch at the time of their installation (ER II, for instance, stands for Elizabeth *Regina* II).

TELEPHONES

Public telephones are easy to find, although the traditional red booths are now rare in towns and cities. Use cash, a credit card or a prepaid telephone card; most phones accept coins and cards. Public telephones take 10p, 20p, 50p and £1 coins (20p is the minimum call charge), but if you put a higher-value coin in and do not use it all up the difference will not be refunded. Buy phone cards from tobacconists, post offices, stationery stores and anywhere displaying the phone card sign.

Phoning in Britain
All British numbers in this book include an area code: dial the number listed. To call the operator dial 100.

Phoning Britain from abroad
The country code for Britain is 44. Note that British numbers in this book do not include the country code; you will need to prefix it if you are phoning from another country. To phone Britain from the United States or Canada, omit the first zero from the British number, and add the prefix 011 44. Example: 011 2233 4455 becomes 011 44 11 2233 4455.

Phoning from Britain
To phone the United States or Canada from Britain, prefix the area code and number with 001. Example: (111) 222-3333 becomes 001 111 222-3333.

To call international information dial 153.

EMERGENCY TELEPHONE NUMBERS

Police	999
Fire service	999
Ambulance	999

Emergency calls are free from phone booths.

HOURS OF OPERATION

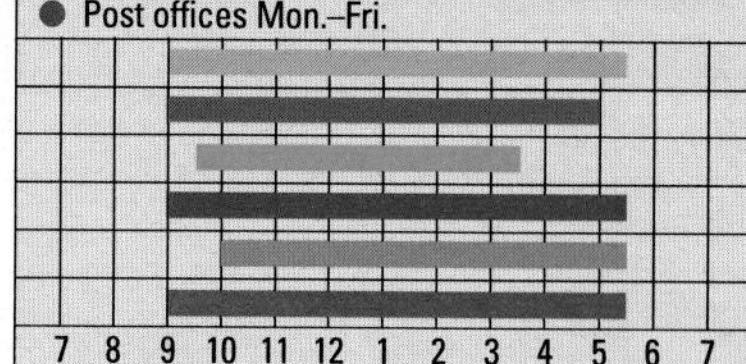

The times above are traditional hours of operation. Many malls and city-center stores open for longer hours and also on Sunday. Convenience grocery stores stay open until late in the evening.

Banks and post offices open on Saturday, but some out-of-town services have short hours.

Museum opening times vary. Some major sights close on Monday and open later one evening a week; more modest sights of interest may close off season, so it is advisable to check with the local tourist office.

Note that many restaurants do not open for dinner until around 6 or 7 p.m. Up to this time chain restaurants and fast-food outlets are usually the only places serving meals.

NATIONAL HOLIDAYS

Banks, businesses and smaller stores close on these days, although larger stores may remain open.

Jan. 1	**New Year's Day**
Mar./Apr.	**Good Friday**
Mar./Apr.	**Easter Monday**
1st Mon. of May	**May Bank Holiday**
Last Mon. of May	**Spring Bank Holiday**
Last Mon. of Aug.	**August Bank Holiday**
Dec. 25	**Christmas Day**
Dec. 26	**Boxing Day**

When Dec. 25 and 26 fall on a weekend, the preceding Friday or following Monday or Tuesday are public holidays. If Jan. 1 falls on a weekend, usually the first Monday in January is a public holiday.

PHOTOGRAPHY

British skies are unpredictable, so pack a range of film speeds. The countryside is very green, however, so landscape shots work well if the weather is good. Most museums will not allow you to take pictures; check first. Film and camera batteries are available from grocery stores, pharmacies and camera stores. Rapid-developing services are common and reasonably priced.

HEALTH

MEDICAL INSURANCE

Private insurance is recommended. Visitors can receive treatment in emergency rooms but are charged if admitted to a hospital. You can seek advice from a doctor at a surgery or health center; you must make an appointment, and a charge will be made. Doctors are listed in the yellow pages, or ask at your hotel or a tourist office.

DENTAL SERVICES

Dentists charge for consultations or treatment. Emergency treatment is available out of hours in towns and cities (see the yellow pages). Check if it is covered by your medical insurance.

SUN ADVICE

Although not renowned for warm weather, Britain does have its moments, and it is not unheard of for July and August to be as hot as the Mediterranean. Visiting historic sights can involve being outside for prolonged periods, so cover up, apply sunscreen and drink plenty of water.

DRUGS

Prescription and nonprescription medicines are available from pharmacies (chemists). Pharmacists can advise on medication for common ailments. Notices in all pharmacy windows give details of emergency facilities open outside regular hours.

SAFE WATER

Tap water is safe to drink, even in remote areas. Mineral water is widely available but is usually quite expensive, particularly in restaurants.

RESTROOMS

Public restrooms (toilets, lavatories, WCs, or, in everyday parlance, "loos") are generally easy to find and maintained to a high standard. Most are free, but a charge is made for those at major rail stations (about 20p).

ELECTRICITY

Britain has a 240-volt power supply. Electrical sockets take plugs with three square pins, so an adapter is needed for American appliances. A transformer is also required for appliances operating on 110 or 120 volts.

NATIONAL TRANSPORTATION

TRAIN

Rail services are good in Britain. First class is comfortable but more expensive than standard. Intercity (high-speed) trains connect cities. If you plan to use trains frequently, rail cards offer discounts: contact BritRail Travel, 1500 Broadway, New York, NY 10036; (212) 575-2542 or (800) 677-8585. Once you are in Britain, Rail Rover passes are good value for regional rail travel: ☎ 08457 484950.

BUS

Bus travel is half the cost of rail travel. The main operator for local (bus) and long-distance (coach) travel in Britain is National Express. For details phone 08705 808080. Euroline buses operate from Britain to the rest of Europe: ☎ 08705 143219.

FERRY

The busiest ferries run between south-east England and France (a high-speed train also shuttles passengers and cars through the Channel Tunnel). Service is frequent, especially in summer. Ferries serve the smaller British islands, Ireland, Spain, Belgium, Netherlands, Germany, Denmark, Sweden and Norway.

DRIVING

DRIVE ON THE LEFT

SPEED LIMITS

British speed limits are stringently enforced by police patrols and also by strategically positioned cameras that detect speeding motorists.

Limited-access highways (motorways); divided highways (dual carriageways)
70 m.p.h.

Main roads
50 or 60 m.p.h.

Urban areas
30 or 40 m.p.h.

SEAT BELTS

Must be worn in front and rear seats at all times.

BLOOD ALCOHOL

The legal blood alcohol limit is 0.08%. Random breath tests on drivers are carried out frequently, especially late at night, and the penalties for offenders are severe.

DRIVING continued

TOLLS

Limited-access highways are free. Some bridges levy a toll, usually minimal. The Severn Bridge, joining England and Wales, is expensive on the way into Wales, but there is no charge on the return trip.

CAR RENTAL

The leading rental firms have offices at airports, train stations and ferry terminals. Hertz offers discounted rates for AAA members (see page 15).
For reservations:

	UNITED STATES	BRITAIN
Alamo	(800) 327-9633	08706 000044
Avis	(800) 331-2112	08706 060100
Budget	(800) 527-0700	0800 181181
Hertz	(800) 654-3080	08708 448844

FUEL

Gasoline (petrol) and diesel are priced in liters and are expensive. There are two grades of unleaded gas: super (98 octane) and premium (97 octane). Most gas stations are self-service, and 24-hour facilities are common.

AAA AFFILIATED MOTORING CLUB

The Automobile Association (AA), Fanum House, Basingstoke, Hampshire RG21 4EA
☎ 08705 448866, fax 01256 493022 (administration). If you break down while driving, phone ☎ 0800 0289018 (AA breakdown service). Not all automobile clubs offer full services to AAA members.

BREAKDOWNS AND ACCIDENTS

There are emergency telephones at regular intervals on limited-access and divided highways.
If you are involved in an accident
☎ 999 for police, fire and ambulance assistance. Most car rental firms provide their own free rescue service; if your car is rented, follow the instructions in the documentation. Use of a car repair service other than those authorized by your rental firm may violate your rental agreement.

OTHER INFORMATION

The minimum age for driving a car is 17 (may be higher for some car rental firms).

An International Driving Permit (IDP) is recommended; some rental firms require them, and they can speed up formalities if you are involved in an accident.

A Green Card (international motor insurance certificate) is recommended if you are driving a private car; see page 16 for more information.

USEFUL WORDS AND PHRASES

Spotting the differences between American and British English is fun, especially as some regional accents are almost incomprehensible to the untrained ear! Britons have become familiar with Americanisms through imported American television shows, but it is still possible to make a blunder. Below are some illustrations of the "Atlantic divide."

American	British
1 lb	*0.45 kilogram*
ATM	*cashpoint*
ball-point pen	*biro*
to call collect	*to reverse the charges*
check	*cheque*
check (in a restaurant)	*bill*
elevator	*lift*
first/second floor (etc.)	*ground/first floor (etc.)*
movie theater	*cinema*
phone booth	*phone box*
reserve (reservation)	*book (reservation)*
restroom	*toilet/loo (colloquial)*
Scotch™ tape	*sticky tape/Sellotape™*
trash or garbage can	*dustbin or rubbish bin*
food and drink	
(soft hamburger) bun	*bap*
beer	*bitter (dark)/lager (light)*
candy	*sweets*
(potato) chips	*crisps*
cookies	*biscuits*
corn	*maize*
cotton candy	*candyfloss*
eggplant	*aubergine*
french fries	*chips*
grocery store	*supermarket*
Jell-O™	*jelly*
jelly	*jam*
liquor store	*off-licence*
oatmeal	*porridge*
Saranwrap™	*cling film*
zucchini	*courgette*
fashion	
bangs	*fringe*
pants	*trousers*
pantyhose	*tights*
suspenders	*braces*
undershirt	*vest*
vest	*waistcoat*
getting around	
hood (of a car)	*bonnet*
one-way trip	*single*
parking lot	*car park*
paved shoulder	*lay-by*
rotary/traffic circle	*roundabout*
round trip	*return ticket*
sidewalk	*pavement*
stick shift	*manual*
subway	*tube/underground*
truck	*lorry*
trunk (of a car)	*boot*

PRE-TRIP ESSENTIALS…

WHAT YOU NEED

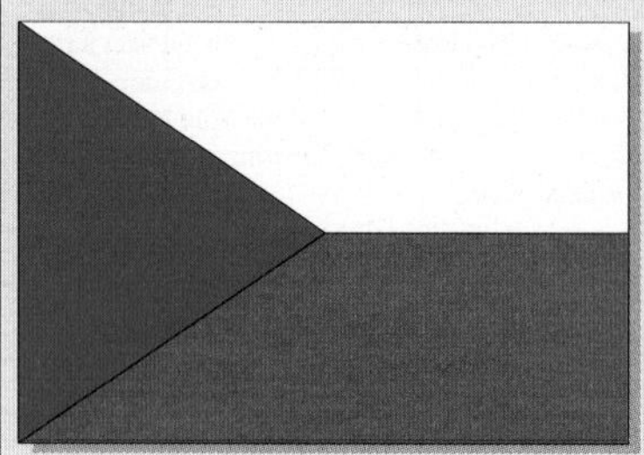

ESSENTIAL FOR TRAVELERS

● Required ● Recommended ● Not required

Passport
Visa*
Travel, medical insurance
Round-trip or onward airline ticket
Local currency
Traveler's checks
Credit cards
First-aid kit and medicines
Inoculations

*Canadian citizens may stay up to 180 days without a visa. U.S. citizens who wish to stay longer than 30 days must apply for a visitor permit (this can only be done in the Czech Republic; contact your hotel or a tourist office for details).

ESSENTIAL FOR DRIVERS*

Driver's license
International Driving Permit
Car insurance (for nonrental cars)
Car registration (for nonrental cars)

*see also DRIVING section

IMPORTANT ADDRESSES

Czech Tourist Authority
1109–1111 Madison Avenue,
New York, NY 10028
☎ (212) 288-0830
Fax (212) 288-0971; www.czechcenter.com

Česká Centrála Cestovního Ruchu (Czech Tourist Authority)
Vinohradská 46, PO Box 32,
120 41, Praha (Prague) 2, Czech Republic
☎ 02 2158 0111
Fax 02 2424 7516; www.visitczech.cz

American Embassy
Tržiště 15, Mala Strana,
118 01 Praha (Prague) 1, Czech Republic
☎ 02 5753 0663
Fax 02 5732 0583
Telephone inquiries Mon.–Fri. 9–4:30
Personal inquiries Mon.–Fri. 9–noon

COUNTRY ESSENTIALS…

CUSTOMS

YES

Duty-free limits on goods brought in: 200 cigarettes or 100 cigarillos or 50 cigars or 250 g. tobacco; 1 L alcohol over 22% volume; 2 L wine; 50 ml. perfume or 250 ml. toilet water; plus any other duty-free goods (including gifts) to the value of 6,000Kčs, (3,000Kčs for those under 15). Persons importing alcohol must be 18 and over, for cigarettes and tobacco products 16 and over. There is no restriction on the import or export of Czech or foreign currencies, but amounts in excess of 200,000Kčs (or its equivalent) must be declared.

NO

No unlicensed drugs, firearms, ammunition, offensive weapons, obscene material, unlicensed animals, counterfeit or copied goods, meat and poultry.

For customs limits for returning U.S. citizens see page16.

MONEY

The Czech Republic's currency is the Koruna česká (Kč) – or Czech crown – which is divided into 100 haléřů (h) – or hellers – although you won't find many of the latter around. The denominations of Koruna česká bills are 50, 100, 200, 500, 1,000, 2,000 and 5,000. There are coins of 10, 20 and 50 h and 1, 2, 5, 10, 20 and 50Kč. You can exchange dollars or traveler's checks *(cestovni sek)* at a bank *(banka)*, exchange office *(smenárna)*, post office *(posta)* or hotel; you will need ID. It is an offense to change money through black-market money dealers; in any case, they rarely offer an attractive rate. The Czech Republic is not part of the E.U.
Exchange rate at press time: $1 = 38Kč

TIPS AND GRATUITIES

Tips are welcomed in restaurants and cafés, although service is normally included.

Restaurants (even when service is included)	5–10%
Cafés/bars	5–10%
Taxis	10%
Porters	40Kč
Hairdressers	10%
Tour guides	20Kč

COMMUNICATIONS

POST OFFICES

Buy stamps *(známky)* at a post office *(posta)*, a newsstand/kiosk *(trafika/tabák)* or from a hotel.

The postal service is slow and erratic but not expensive. Mailboxes are orange and blue. Hours for out-of-town post offices may vary.

TELEPHONES

The Czech telephone system is generally modern and efficient. City booths take telephone cards *(telefonní karta)* worth 175 or 320Kč, which can be bought from newsstands, tobacconists, post offices, shops, hotels and travel agencies. Coin-operated telephones (increasingly hard to find and less reliable) use 1, 2, 5 and 10Kč. Gray booths have international dialing facilities. Older, orange ones are for national calls only. There are often instructions in English inside the booth.

Phoning inside the Czech Republic
All Czech telephone numbers in this book include an area code: dial the number that is listed.

To call the operator dial 120.

Phoning the Czech Republic from abroad
The country code for the Czech Republic is 420. Note that Czech numbers in this book do not include the country code; you will need to prefix this number if you are phoning from another country. To phone the Czech Republic from the United States or Canada, omit the first zero from the Czech number, and add the prefix 011 420. Example: 01 12 23 34 becomes 011 420 1 12 23 34.

Phoning from the Czech Republic
To phone the United States or Canada from the Czech Republic, prefix the number with 001. Example: (111) 222-3333 becomes 001 111 222-3333. To call international information dial 0149. For an international operator dial 0131, 0132, 0133, 0134 or 0135.

EMERGENCY TELEPHONE NUMBERS

Police *(policie)*	158
Fire *(pozar)*	150
Ambulance *(ambulance)*	155

Emergency calls are free from phone booths.

HOURS OF OPERATION

- Stores Mon.–Fri.
- Museums/monuments
- Offices Mon.–Fri.
- Pharmacies Mon.–Fri.
- Banks Mon.–Fri.
- Post offices Mon.–Fri.

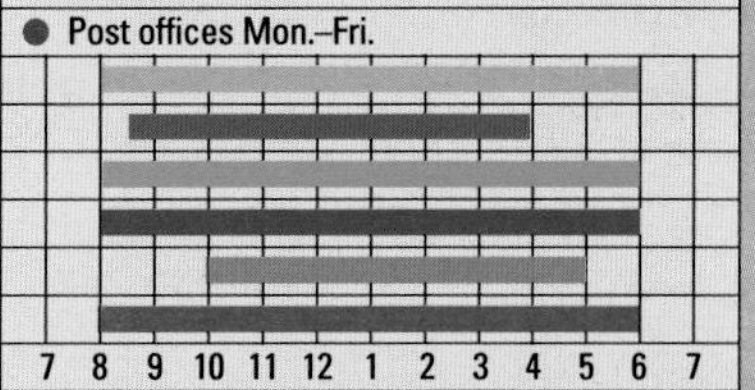

Saturday afternoon is early closing; many stores close at noon or 1. Some stores, especially in the country, close noon–1 for lunch.

Food stores in the large cities open at 6 a.m., and large stores and shopping centers stay open until 8 p.m. (4 p.m. on Saturday). Most stores are closed on Sunday, but increasing numbers are opening.

Some city banks and post offices open on Saturday morning. Some tourist resorts may have special opening times.

Museums often close on Monday and days following public holidays, and opening times may be reduced during the winter.

NATIONAL HOLIDAYS

Banks, businesses and most stores close on these days. Monuments, museums and galleries usually open on public holidays (except Jan. 1, Easter, and Dec. 25 and 26) but are closed the following day.

Jan. 1	**New Year's Day**
Mar./Apr.	**Easter Monday**
May 1	**May Day**
May 8	**Liberation Day**
Jul. 5	**SS Cyril and Methodius' Day**
Jul. 6	**Jan Huss Day**
Sep. 28	**Czech Statehood Day**
Oct. 28	**Independence Day**
Nov. 17	**Day of Fight for Freedom and Democracy**
Dec. 24	**Christmas Eve**
Dec. 25	**Christmas Day**
Dec. 26	**St. Stephen's Day**

PHOTOGRAPHY

After years of official photography restrictions, visitors are now free to photograph almost anywhere. You can buy film in the numerous small shops at Staré Město in the Old Town and Malá Strana in the Lesser Quarter. Avoid Czech brands of color film, as you may not be able to get them processed outside the country. Many stores in tourist areas offer developing services.

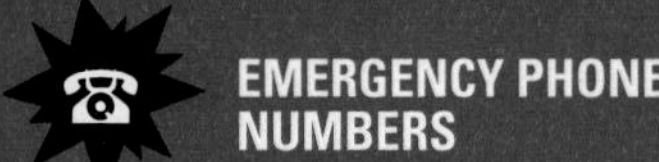

EMERGENCY PHONE NUMBERS

POLICE 158 *(Policie)*

HEALTH

MEDICAL INSURANCE
Private medical insurance is recommended. U.S. and Canadian visitors can receive treatment in a hospital emergency and accident unit, but you will be charged if you are admitted to a hospital (*nemocnice*). You may be asked to show your passport when seeking hospital treatment. The following clinics in Prague have English-speaking doctors: the American Medical Center, ☎ 02 80 77 56, and the Canadian Medical Center ☎ 02 316 5519.

DENTAL SERVICES
A dentist *(zubař)* will charge for any treatment given, so check if it is covered by your medical insurance. For an English-speaking dentist, ask at your hotel or embassy or at a tourist office.

SUN ADVICE
June through August is the sunniest period, when adequate sun protection should be applied.

DRUGS
A pharmacy *(lékárna)* is the only place you can buy over-the-counter medicines. Pharmacies also dispense many drugs normally available only on prescription in other Western countries. However, it is advisable to bring supplies of your own medicines with you. If you need a pharmacy outside regular hours, information about the nearest all-night facility is posted at all pharmacies.

SAFE WATER
It is not advisable to drink tap water. Bottled water is available everywhere; still table water *(Stolní pitní voda)* is the most common.

RESTROOMS

Public restrooms *(toaleta)* are not easy to find, and you will be charged for toilet tissue. It may be best to use a café or restaurant facility after buying a drink. Attendants appreciate small change – 2Kč or thereabouts – as this may be their only wage.

ELECTRICITY

The Czech Republic has a 220-volt power supply. Electrical sockets take plugs with two round pins; American appliances will need a plug adapter, and will require a transformer if they do not have a dual-voltage facility.

NATIONAL TRANSPORTATION

TRAIN *(vlak)*
The Czech national rail company, České Dráhy (CD), is extensive and inexpensive, but often crowded. The fast trains stop at major cities; local trains stop everywhere; but usually provide only second-class service. All long-distance trains have two classes; some have dining carriages and overnight services. Reserve seats on express trains; don't rely on international trains having air conditioning: ☎ 02 2422 4200.

BUS *(autobusy)*
Inexpensive and popular with the Czechs. Reserve for weekends, national holidays or early morning. Tickets are purchased from the bus station kiosk or the driver. Large items of luggage will be stowed for a small charge. Trams *(tramvaj)* and trolley buses *(trolejbus)* are the best way to get around town. Euroline buses connect to other countries: ☎ 02 2423 9318.

FERRY *(prévos)*
From April to September boats cruise the Vltava river as far as Troja Château to the north of Prague and Slapy Lake to the south ☎ 02 298 309 or 9000 0822

DRIVING

DRIVE ON THE RIGHT

SPEED LIMITS
Police can give on-the-spot fines of up to 2,000Kčs. If this should happen to you, ask for a receipt.

Limited-access highways *(dalnice)*
130 k.p.h. (80 m.p.h.)

Main roads
90 k.p.h. (55 m.p.h.)

Urban areas
50 k.p.h. (31 m.p.h.)

SEAT BELTS
Must be worn in front and back seats at all times. Children under 12 (or under 4 feet 10 inches) cannot travel in the front seat.

BLOOD ALCOHOL
The legal blood alcohol limit is zero. Random breath tests on drivers are carried out frequently, especially late at night, and the penalties for offenders are severe.

DRIVING continued

TOLLS

A tax is levied for use of highways and express roads. A sticker must be purchased and displayed, and failure to do so will result in a fine. The sticker can be bought at the Czech border, ÚAMK offices (see below), gas stations or post offices.

CAR RENTAL

The leading rental firms have offices at airports and train stations. Hertz offers discounted rates for AAA members (see page 15). For reservations:

	UNITED STATES	CZECH REPUBLIC
Alamo	(800) 327-9633	02 2481 0515 (Europcar)
Avis	(800) 331-2112	02 2185 1225
Budget	(800) 527-0700	02 316 5214
Hertz	(800) 654-3080	02 2223 1010

FUEL

Gas, sold in liters, is leaded (special: 90 octane and super: 96 octane), unleaded (natural: 91, 95 and 98 octane) or diesel. Some out-of-town stations *(benzinová pumpa)* close for lunch and after 6. There are 24-hour gas stations in cities and along highways.

AAA AFFILIATED MOTORING CLUB

Ústřední automotoklub Ceské republiky (ÚAMK; CR)
Na Strži 9, CZ-140 02 Prague 4
☎ 02 6110 4242, fax 02 6110 4235

Not all automobile clubs offer full services to AAA members.

BREAKDOWNS AND ACCIDENTS

There are 24-hour emergency phones at regular intervals on highways. Most car rental firms provide their own free rescue service; if your car is rented, follow the instructions given in the documentation. Use of a car repair service other than those authorized by your rental company may violate your agreement.

☎ 158 for police assistance.

OTHER INFORMATION

The minimum age for driving a car is 18 (may be higher for some car rental firms). An International Driving Permit (IDP) is recommended; some rental firms require them, and they can speed up formalities if you are involved in an accident. A Green Card (international motor insurance certificate) is recommended for a private car; see page 16 for more information. Visible damage to a car entering the country must be certified by border authorities. If damage occurs inside the country, a police report must be obtained at the scene of the accident. Damaged vehicles are allowed out of the country only upon presentation of this document.

USEFUL WORDS AND PHRASES

The official language of the Czech Republic is Czech *(Česky)* – a highly complex Slav tongue. Czech sounds and looks daunting, but apart from a few special letters, each letter and sound is pronounced as it is written – the key is to stress the first syllable of a word. If you have any knowledge of Polish or Russian you will be able to understand much.

Any attempt to speak Czech will be heartily appreciated, although English is spoken by many involved in the tourist trade. Below are a few words that may be helpful.

Do you speak English?	*Mluvíte anglicky?*
What is your name?	*Jak se jmenujete?*
hello	*ahoj*
good morning	*dobré jitro*
goodbye	*na shledanou*
good night	*dobrou noc*
How much?	*Kolik?*
excuse me	*promiňte*
I am American	*Jsem Američan(ka)*
I would like	*Chtěl(a) bych*
I don't understand	*Nerozumím*
no smoking	*kouření zakazano*
okay	*dobrá*
open	*otevřeno*
closed	*zavřeno*
please	*prosím*
thank you	*děkuji*
ticket	*lístek*
(one-way/round trip)	*(jednosměrnou/zpátečni)*
Where is...?	*Kde je...?*
yes/no	*ano/ne*
you're welcome	*není zač*
the hotel	***hotel***
breakfast	*snídaně*
reservation	*mám reservaci*
key	*klič*
single/double room	*jednolužkovy/ dvoulužkovy pokoj*
room	*pokoj*
Where is the toilet?	*Kde je záchod?*
shower	*sprcha*
bathroom	*koupelna*
the restaurant	***restaurace***
beef	*hovězi*
bread	*chleb*
chicken	*kuře*
the check	*účet*
coffee	*káva*
dish of the day	*nabídka dne*
dessert	*moučnik*
fish	*ryba*
lamb	*jehněčí*
pork	*vepřové maso*
seafood	*mořské ryby*
starter	*předkrm*
wine	*víno*

PRE-TRIP ESSENTIALS...

WHAT YOU NEED

ESSENTIAL FOR TRAVELERS

● Required ● Recommended ○ Not required

Passport	●
Visa	○
Travel, medical insurance	●
Round-trip or onward airline ticket	○
Local currency	●
Traveler's checks	●
Credit cards	●
First-aid kit and medicines*	●
Inoculations	○

*see also HEALTH section

ESSENTIAL FOR DRIVERS*

Driver's license	●
International Driving Permit	●
Car insurance (for nonrental cars)	●
Car registration (for nonrental cars)	●

*see also DRIVING section

IMPORTANT ADDRESSES

Danish & Swedish Tourist Boards
655 Third Avenue, 18th Floor
New York, NY 10017
☎ (212) 885-9700
Fax (212) 885-9726
www.visitdenmark.dk

Danmarks Turtistråd (Danish Tourist Board)
Vesterbrogade 6D
DK-1620 Copenhagen V, Denmark
☎ 33 11 14 15
Fax 33 11 14 16

American Embassy
Dag Hamarskjölds Allé 24
DK-2100 Copenhagen Ø, Denmark
☎ 35 55 31 44
Fax 35 38 96 16
Personal visits require an appointment.

COUNTRY ESSENTIALS...

CUSTOMS

YES

Duty-free limits on goods brought in from non-European Union countries: 200 cigarettes or 100 cigarillos or 50 cigars or 250 g. tobacco; 2 L. wine; 1 L. alcohol over 22% volume; 2 L. alcohol under 22% volume; 50 ml. perfume; 250 ml. toilet water; plus any other duty-free goods (including gifts) to the value of DKr1,350. There is no limit on the importation of tax-paid goods purchased within the European Union, provided they are for your own personal use. Limits for alcohol and tobacco products apply to visitors aged 17 or over. There are no currency regulations.

NO

No unlicensed drugs, weapons, ammunition, obscene material, pets or other animals, counterfeit money or copied goods, meat or poultry.

For customs limits for returning U.S. citizens see page 16.

MONEY

Denmark's currency is the krone (DKr), which is divided into 100 øre. The denominations of krone bills are 50, 100, 200, 500 and 1,000. There are coins of 25 and 50 øre and 1, 2, 5, 10 and 20DKr. Banks may not exchange foreign bank notes of high denominations. Denmark was one of the two Scandinavian countries that chose not to adopt the euro as its official currency on Jan 1, 1999. However, tourists coming from the euro zone may still use a euro credit card; the exchange rate does not fluctuate.
Senior citizens and holders of International Student Identity Cards (ISIC) can often obtain discounts on travel and entrance fees.
Exchange rate at press time: $1 = DKr8

TIPS AND GRATUITIES

Tips are not expected, but you may tip for outstanding service.

Restaurants (service is always included)	change
Cafés/bars	change
Taxis (tips included in fare)	change
Porters	change
Chambermaids	change
Cloakroom attendants	change

COMMUNICATIONS

POST OFFICES

Stamps *(frimerker)* can be bought at a post office *(postkontoret)*, newsstand *(aviskiosk)* or stationer *(papirhandel)*.

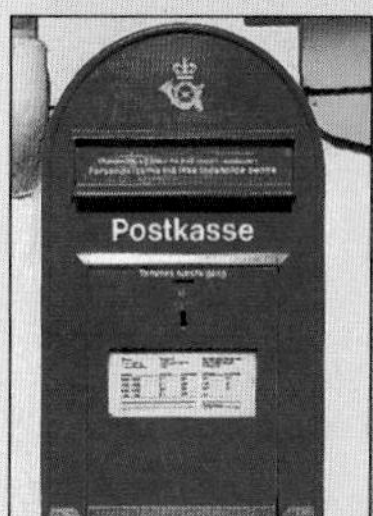

Mailboxes *(postkasse)* are red with a yellow horn and crown. Hours for out-of-town post offices may vary.

TELEPHONES

Danish public telephones *(telefon)* work efficiently for national and international calls, but some will not refund your money if the call is not answered. Some phones require coins to be inserted after dialing, when you hear ringing. Use, DKr1, DKr2, DKr5, DKr10 and DKr20 coins. Phone card booths are also available; buy the cards (DKr30, DKr50 or DKr100) from a post office, railroad station or newsstand.

Phoning inside Denmark
All telephone numbers are 8 digits and include the regional code. Dial all digits when making a call.

To call the operator dial 110; to call collect dial 115; for the long-distance operator dial 114.

Phoning Denmark from abroad
The country code for Denmark is 45. Note that Danish numbers in this book do not include the country code; you will need to prefix this number if you are phoning from another country. To phone Denmark from the United States or Canada add the prefix 011 45.
Example: 11 22 33 44 becomes 011 45 11 22 33 44.

Phoning from Denmark
To phone the United States or Canada from Denmark, prefix the area code and number with 001.
Example: (111) 222-3333 becomes 001 111 222-3333.
To call international information dial 113.

EMERGENCY TELEPHONE NUMBERS

Police *(politi)*	112
Fire *(brandvæsen)*	112
Ambulance *(sygevogn)*	112

Emergency calls are free from phone booths.

HOURS OF OPERATION

- Stores Mon.–Sat.
- Museums/monuments
- Offices Mon.–Fri.
- Pharmacies Mon.–Fri.
- Banks Mon.–Fri.
- Post offices Mon.–Fri.

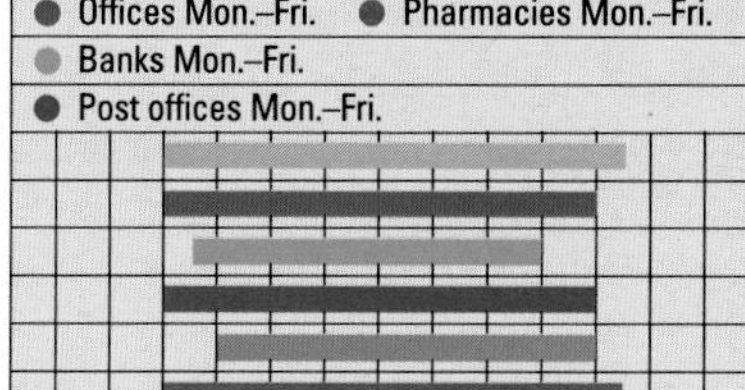

Although Sunday is the official closing day, souvenir shops in many towns and grocery stores in summer vacation areas stay open.

Many bakeries and *patisseries* also open on Sunday morning.

On Friday stores stay open until 7 or 8 p.m. Most shops close early on Saturday afternoon, but many shops in Copenhagen are open until 5 p.m.

Department stores and supermarkets often stay open later than 5:30 p.m.

Large gas stations sell convenience foods.

Banks in Copenhagen are open until 5 p.m. On Thursday all banks are open until 6 p.m. Some post offices open Saturday 9–noon.

NATIONAL HOLIDAYS

Banks, businesses and most stores close on these days.

Jan. 1	**New Year's Day**
Mar./Apr.	**Maundy Thursday**
Mar./Apr.	**Good Friday**
Mar./Apr.	**Easter Monday**
Apr. /May	**Great Prayer Day**
May/Jun.	**Ascension Day**
May/Jun.	**Pentecost Monday**
Jun. 5	**Constitution Day**
Dec. 24	**Christmas Eve**
Dec. 25	**Christmas Day**
Dec. 26	**St. Stephen's Day**
Dec. 31	**New Year's Eve**

PHOTOGRAPHY

Denmark is not renowned for bright sunshine and the winter months have short daylight hours, so pack plenty of 200 ASA-speed film. Check that photography is permitted before taking pictures in museums. Film and camera batteries are readily available from tourist stores, and rapid-developing services are widely available.

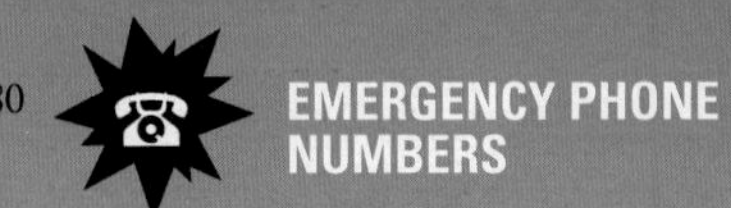

HEALTH

MEDICAL INSURANCE

Private medical insurance is recommended. In an emergency, visitors from the U.S. and Canada can receive free temporary treatment in a hospital *(hospitalet)*. You will be charged for more extensive treatment. Health offices *(kommunes social og sundhedforvaltning)* have lists of hospitals and doctors, or ask at your hotel.

DENTAL SERVICES

Dentists *(tandlægen)* will charge for any treatment given. They are listed in the telephone directory, and off-hours treatment is available in some clinics. Advice can be sought at tourist and health offices. Check that treatment is covered by your medical insurance.

SUN ADVICE

The warmest months are July and August. The sun in Denmark is not particularly fierce, but sun protection is still advised, especially on boats or near the water.

DRUGS

To obtain a prescription medicine at a pharmacy *(apotek)* it must be prescribed by a Scandinavian doctor, so make sure that your supply of prescribed medicines will last your stay. Additionally, some preparations available over the counter in the U.S. may be obtained in Denmark only with a prescription. Outside regular hours, the nearest all-night facility is posted at all pharmacies.

SAFE WATER

Tap water is safe to drink, and mineral water *(mineralvand)* is widely available.

RESTROOMS

Public restrooms *(toiletterne)* are easy to find, clean, well equipped and usually free. They are often indicated by a symbol, or marked WC or *Damer* (women) and *Herrer* (men).

ELECTRICITY

Denmark has a 220-volt power supply. Electrical sockets take plugs with two round pins; American appliances will need a plug adapter and will require a transformer if they do not have a dual-voltage facility.

NATIONAL TRANSPORTATION

TRAIN *(tog)*

Copenhagen is an important meeting point for trains between Europe and the rest of Scandinavia. The Danish State Railroad, Danske Statsbaner (DSB), runs an efficient service with trains linking to Germany and Sweden. Most domestic trains have refreshment facilities; seat reservations are recommended. For information, phone ☎ 33 14 17 01.

BUS *(bus)*

The domestic bus service is good; ask for details at local tourist offices. Eurolines services run between other European countries (☎ 99 34 44 88).

FERRY *(færge)*

There are numerous ferry services from Denmark, with year-round connections to many northern European countries. DFDS Seaways has an office in Denmark, ☎ 33 42 33 42, and in Florida, ☎ (954) 491-7909.

DRIVING

DRIVE ON THE RIGHT

SPEED LIMITS

Police can impose on-the-spot fines.

Limited-access highways *(motorvej)*
110 k.p.h. (68 m.p.h.)

Main roads
80 k.p.h. (49 m.p.h.)
Minimum speed **40 k.p.h. (24 m.p.h.)**

Urban areas
50 k.p.h. (31 m.p.h.)

SEAT BELTS

Must be worn in front and back seats at all times.

BLOOD ALCOHOL

The legal blood alcohol limit is 0.05%. Random breath tests on drivers are carried out frequently, especially late at night, and the penalties for offenders are severe.

DRIVING continued

TOLLS

There are no tolls on highways. However, the "Great Belt" *(Store Bælt)* tunnel and bridge from Korsør to Nyborg and the impressive 10-mile Øresund tunnel and bridge from Copenhagen to Malmö (Sweden) both levy a toll.

CAR RENTAL

The leading car rental companies have offices at airports, principal railroad stations and ferry terminals. Hertz offers discounted rates for AAA members (see page 15). For reservations:

	UNITED STATES	DENMARK
Alamo	(800) 327-9633	33 55 99 00 (Europcar)
Avis	(800) 331-2112	33 15 22 99
Budget	(800) 527-0700	33 11 12 34
Hertz	(800) 654-3080	33 17 90 20

FUEL

Gas (*benzin*) is sold in liters; unleaded gas *(blyfri)* comes in 95 and 98 octane ratings. Self-service gas stations *(tank selv* or *selvbetjening)* are common, except on limited-access highways. Most gas stations take credit cards, and some have automatic pumps for DKr100 and DKr50 bills.

AAA AFFILIATED MOTORING CLUB

Forenede Danske Motorejere (FDM)
Firskovvej 32, P.O. Box 500, 2800 Lyngby
☎ 45 27 07 07, fax 45 27 09 93

Not all automobile clubs offer full services to AAA members.

BREAKDOWNS AND ACCIDENTS

Report accidents to the Dansk Forening for International Motorkoretojsforsikring, Amaliegade 10, 1256 Copenhagen (☎ 33 13 75 55). Most car rental firms provide their own free rescue service; if your car is rented, follow the instructions given in the documentation. Use of a car repair service other than those authorized by your rental company may violate your agreement.

OTHER INFORMATION

The minimum legal age for driving a car is 18 (may be higher for some car rental firms).

An International Driving Permit (IDP) is recommended; some rental firms require them, and they can speed up formalities if you are involved in an accident.

A Green Card (international motor insurance certificate) is recommended if you are driving a private car; see page 16 for more information.

Use dimmed headlights at all times.

USEFUL WORDS AND PHRASES

Danish is a Germanic language, close to Swedish and Norwegian, but it is tricky to pronounce because some letters *(d, g)* are silent in the middle or at the end of words, *h* before a *v* becomes silent, and some specifically Scandinavian vowels *(å, ø,* and *æ)* are awkward to say correctly. But Danes are aware of this, and most of them speak very good English. In addition, menus are often in English or German.

In the Danish alphabet, the following letters come after *z: å, ø,* and *æ.* (Århus, for example, comes at the end of the alphabet.) *Å* is used in place of *aa,* although the city of Aalborg prefers to write the two vowels out in full.

The following words and phrases should help you:

Do you speak English?	*Taler de Engelsk?*
excuse me	*undskyld*
hello/goodbye	*hej/farvel*
how much is...?	*hvor meget koster det?*
I am American	*Jeg er Amerikaner*
I'd like...	*jeg vil gerne have...*
I don't understand	*jeg forstår det ikke*
open/closed	*åben/lukket*
please/thank you	*værså venlig/tak*
ticket (one-way/ round trip)	*billet (enkeltbillet/ en tur-retur)*
where is/are...?	*hvor er...?*
yes/no	*ja/nej*
the hotel	***hotel***
breakfast	*morgenmad*
key	*nøgle*
for one/two nights	*en nat/to nætter*
for one person/ two people	*enkeltværelse/ dobbeltværelse*
room	*værelse*
shower	*brusebad*
the restaurant	***restaurant***
Danish pastry	*Wienerbrød*
beef	*bøf*
bread	*brød*
butter	*smør*
cheese	*ost*
chicken	*kylling*
the check	*regningen*
coffee/tea	*kaffe/the*
dessert	*dessert*
fruit salad	*frugtsalat*
fish	*fisk*
shellfish	*skaldyr*
herring	*sild*
trout	*ørred*
cod	*torsk*
shrimps	*rejer*
pork	*svinkød*
potatoes	*kartofler*
starter	*forret*
vegetables	*grøntsager*
wine	*vin*

PRE-TRIP ESSENTIALS...

WHAT YOU NEED

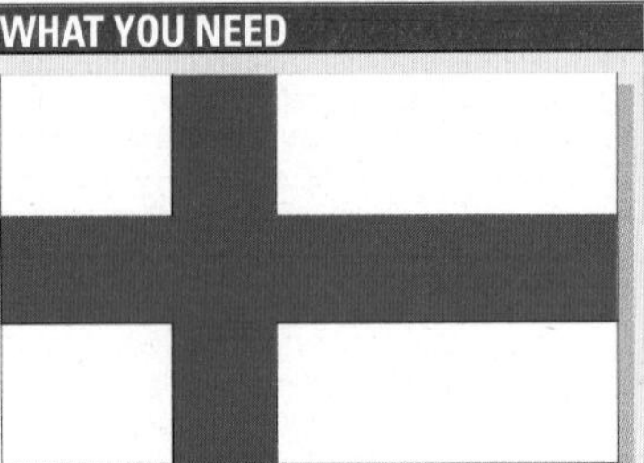

ESSENTIAL FOR TRAVELERS

● Required ● Recommended ● Not required

Passport	●
Visa	●
Travel, medical insurance	●
Round-trip or onward airline ticket	●
Local currency	●
Traveler's checks	●
Credit cards	●
First-aid kit and medicines	●
Inoculations	●

ESSENTIAL FOR DRIVERS*

Driver's license	●
International Driving Permit	●
Car insurance (for nonrental cars)	●
Car registration (for nonrental cars)	●

*see also DRIVING section

IMPORTANT ADDRESSES

Finnish Tourist Board
PO Box 4649
Grand Central Station
New York, NY 10163-4649
☎ (212) 885 9700 or (800) 346-4636
Fax (212) 885-9739
www.finland-tourism.com/us

Finnish Tourist Board
Töölönkatu 11
PO Box 625
FI-00101 Helsinki, Finland
☎ 09 417 6911
Fax 09 4176 9399 or 09 4176 9333
www.mek.fi

American Embassy
Itäinen Puistotie 14B
FI-00140 Helsinki, Finland
☎ 09 171 931
Fax 09 171 546
Personal appointments Mon.–Fri. 9–noon
Telephone inquiries Mon.–Fri. 2–4

COUNTRY ESSENTIALS...

CUSTOMS

YES

Duty-free limits on goods brought in from non-European Union countries: 200 cigarettes or 100 cigarillos or 50 cigars or 250 g. tobacco; 1 L. alcohol over 22% volume or 2 L. alcohol under 22% volume; 50 ml. perfume; 250 ml. toilet water; plus any other duty-free goods (including gifts) to the value of Fmk1,100. **Limits on tax-paid goods (tax-free goods in brackets) purchased within the European Union**: 300 (200) cigarettes or 150 (100) cigarillos or 75 (50) cigars or 400 g. (250 g.) tobacco; 1 (1) L. alcohol over 22% volume; 3 (2) L. alcohol under 22% volume or 5 (2) L. wine; 32 (32) L. beer; plus any other duty-free goods to the value of Fmk550. There are no currency regulations. Pets are allowed if vaccinated against rabies between one and 12 months prior to date of arrival.

NO

No unlicensed drugs, weapons, ammunition, obscene material, counterfeit money or copied goods, meat or poultry.

For customs limits for returning U.S. citizens see page 16.

MONEY

Finland's currency is the markka (Fmk, FIM or mk), which is divided into 100 pennia (p). The denominations of markka bills are 20, 50, 100, 500 and 1,000. There are coins of 10 and 50 pennia and 1, 5 and 10 Fmk. Exchange dollars and traveler's checks at a bank *(pankki)* or an exchange office, as the exchange rate in city hotels may be poor. On Jan. 1, 1999, the euro became the official currency of Finland and the markka became a denomination of the euro. Euro bills and coins were introduced on Jan. 1, 2002. Both euro bills and coins and the old national currency will be in use during a transitional period, after which time the euro will be the only currency accepted.
Exchange rate at press time: $1 = Fmk7

TIPS AND GRATUITIES

Tips are welcomed, but not expected.

Restaurants	change
Cafés/bars	change
Taxis; hairdressers	none
Porters; restroom attendants	change
Chambermaids	change
Cloakroom attendants; hotel/restaurant doormen	Fmk7

TIME ZONES

HELSINKI	NEW YORK	CHICAGO	DENVER	SAN FRANCISCO
12:00 noon	7 hours behind Finland	8 hours behind Finland	9 hours behind Finland	10 hours behind Finland

COMMUNICATIONS

POST OFFICES

Most post offices are open Mon.–Fri. 9–5. General delivery can be received from main post offices *(posti)*.

Hours for out-of-town post offices may vary. Stamps *(postimerkki)* can be bought at post offices, bookstores, newsstands (R-kiosks), railroad and bus stations, and some hotels. Mailboxes are usually yellow and set into walls.

TELEPHONES

The Finnish public telephone system is efficient and accepts mostly credit cards and prepaid telephone cards. Phone cards worth Fmk30, Fmk50 and Fmk100 are available from R-kiosks, telephone company (Sonera) shops and post offices. Most people use their own cell phone, and you can rent one for the length of your stay.

Phoning inside Finland
All Finnish telephone numbers in this book include an area code: dial the number listed.

To call the operator dial 115.

Phoning Finland from abroad
The country code for Finland is 358; to phone Finland from the United States or Canada, omit the first zero from the Finnish number and prefix with 011 358. (Finnish area codes have one or two digits.)
Example: 01 122 3344 becomes 011 358 1 122 3344.

Phoning from Finland
To phone the United States or Canada from Finland, prefix the area code and number with 001. (There are other numbers to dial out of the country depending on what telephone system you are using: 990, 994 or 999.) Example: (111) 222-3333 becomes 001 111 222-3333.
To make a long distance call, dial 02 0222.
For national information, dial 02 0208.

EMERGENCY TELEPHONE NUMBERS

Police *(poliisi)*	112
Fire *(palokunta)*	112
Ambulance *(ambulanssi)*	112

Emergency calls are free from phone booths.

HOURS OF OPERATION

- Stores Mon.–Sat.
- Pharmacies Mon.–Sat.
- Offices Mon.–Fri.
- Banks Mon.–Fri.
- Post offices Mon.–Fri.

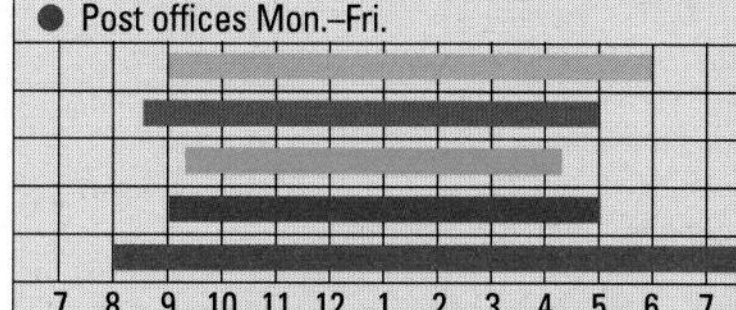

Many stores close at 3 on Saturday, but department stores and most shopping malls stay open until 6. During the week, large stores extend their hours to 8 or 9, and open on Sunday from June through August.

Grocery stores stay open until 8 or 9.

Some gas stations close on Sunday.

Out-of-town post offices and banks may have shorter hours, and some city post offices and banks stay open into the evening.

Museum and monument opening times vary; they may have shorter hours of operation in the winter, and close on Monday or Tuesday. Check opening times with the local tourist office.

Smaller pharmacies *(apteekki)* may close earlier on Saturday. In Helsinki, the pharmacy Yliopiston, Mannerheimintie 96, ☎ 0203 20 200, is open 24 hours.

NATIONAL HOLIDAYS

Banks, businesses and most stores close on these days.

Jan. 1	**New Year's Day**
Jan. 6	**Epiphany**
Mar./Apr.	**Good Friday**
Mar./Apr.	**Easter Monday**
May 1	**May Day**
May	**Ascension**
Jun. 21–22	**Midsummer's Day Eve and Midsummer's Day**
Nov.	**All Saints' Day**
Dec. 6	**Independence Day**
Dec. 24	**Christmas Eve**
Dec. 25	**Christmas Day**
Dec. 26	**St. Stephen's Day**

PHOTOGRAPHY

There is a contrast in seasonal light conditions: subarctic winter nights are long, while in the north the midnight sun shines throughout the summer. Bring a tripod if you hope to photograph the northern lights *(aurora borealis)*. Check whether photography is permitted in museums. Film and batteries can be purchased at tourist-oriented stores, and rapid-developing services are widely available.

HEALTH

MEDICAL INSURANCE

Private medical insurance is recommended. All treatment in a hospital *(sairaala)* has to be paid for. Foreign visitors can receive good service at a private hospital or health center *(lääkäriasema)*; for information, phone ☎ 10023.

DENTAL SERVICES

Dentists *(hammaslääkäri)* charge for treatment and can be expensive, so check that treatment is covered by your medical insurance. 24-hour clinics are available in city hospitals.

SUN ADVICE

Southeast Finland has the highest summer temperature in Scandinavia, so precautions are necessary. Use a suitable sunscreen and cover up sensitive skin.

DRUGS

Prescription and nonprescription medicines are available from pharmacies *(apteekki)*. If you need a pharmacy outside regular hours, information about the nearest all-night facility is posted at all pharmacies. Note that drugstores *(kemikaalikauppa)* sell only cosmetics.

SAFE WATER

Tap water is safe to drink, and mineral water *(kivennäisvesi)* is widely available.

RESTROOMS

Public restrooms are easy to find, immaculately clean and modern, and are designated by *Miehille/Miehet* (men) and *Naisille/Naiset* (women). There may be a small charge, but many are free. Attendants welcome loose change as a tip.

ELECTRICITY

Finland has a 220-volt power supply. Electrical sockets take plugs with two round pins; American appliances will need a plug adapter and will require a transformer if they do not have a dual-voltage facility.

NATIONAL TRANSPORTATION

TRAIN *(juna)*

The Finnish state railroad *(Valtion Rautatiet,* or *VR)* runs an efficient, modern service extending north to southern Lapland. Train fares are good value. For timetable *(Suomen kulkuneuvot)* information, phone ☎ 03 072 0900. If you are planning extensive rail travel, buy a Finnrailpass, which can be bought from a tourist office or sold in the US by Rail Europe ☎ (800) 848-7245.

BUS *(bussi)*

Bus lines run to even the most remote corners of Finland. Bus Holiday Tickets (discount cards) are available for those traveling long distances (valid 2 weeks). For information, phone ☎ 09 6136 8433 or 09 6136 8526.

FERRY *(laiva)*

There are many excursions exploring Finland's eastern lake system and the country's canal network. Trips into Russia, Estonia, Latvia and Lithuania are possible; check with the tour operator whether a short-term visa is required. These can be obtained through the country's embassy or a travel agent. Ferry companies: Finnjet-Silja Line: ☎ 09 180 41; Tallink: ☎ 09 2282 1211; and Viking Line: ☎ 09 123 577.

DRIVING

DRIVE ON THE RIGHT

SPEED LIMITS

Minor fines can be imposed on the spot, but not collected. Payment can be made at a post office.

Limited-access highways *(moottoritie)*
120 k.p.h. (74 m.p.h.) in summer
100 k.p.h. (62 m.p.h.) in winter
Divided highways
100 k.p.h. (62 m.p.h.)

Main roads
80 k.p.h. (49 m.p.h.)

Urban areas
40–60 k.p.h. (24–37 m.p.h.)

SEAT BELTS

Must be worn in front and back seats at all times.

BLOOD ALCOHOL

The legal blood alcohol limit is 0.05%. Random breath tests on drivers are carried out frequently, especially late at night, and the penalties for offenders are severe.

DRIVING continued

TOLLS

There are no highway tolls in Finland.

CAR RENTAL

The leading rental firms have offices at airports and train stations. Hertz offers discounted rates for AAA members (see page 15). For reservations:

	UNITED STATES	FINLAND
Alamo	(800) 327-9633	09 6122 0255
Avis	(800) 331-2112	09 859 8333
Budget	(800) 527-0700	09 870 0780
Hertz	(800) 654-3080	02 0555 2333

FUEL

There is no leaded gas in Finland. Unleaded 98 octane gas contains some additives, making it suitable for cars not yet converted to unleaded fuel. For cars fitted with a catalytic converter, use 95 octane gas.

AAA AFFILIATED MOTORING CLUB

Autoliitto (AL)
Hämeentie 105A, FI-00550 Helsinki
☎ 09 7258 4400, fax 09 7258 4460
If you break down while driving, phone ☎ 09 7747 6400 (24 hours) for the AL breakdown service.
Not all automobile clubs offer full services to AAA members.

BREAKDOWNS AND ACCIDENTS

There are 24-hour emergency phones at regular intervals on highways. If you are involved in an accident, phone ☎ 112 for police, fire or ambulance. Accidents should be reported without delay to: Finnish Motor Insurers' Center, Green Card Bureau and Guarantee Fund (Liikennevakuutuskeskus), Bulevardi 28, FIN-00120 Helsinki ☎ 09 680 401, fax 09 6804 0368.
Most car rental firms provide their own free rescue service; if your car is rented, follow the instructions given in the documentation. Use of a car repair service other than those authorized by your rental company may violate your agreement.

OTHER INFORMATION

The minimum age for driving a car is 18 (may be higher for some car rental firms). An International Driving Permit (IDP) is recommended; some rental firms require them, and they can speed up formalities if you are involved in an accident.
A Green Card (international motor insurance certificate) is recommended if you are driving a private car; see page 16 for more information.
Dimmed headlights must be used at all times. In winter, snow tires or chains are essential; you can buy or rent winter driving equipment from Autoliitto. Watch out for signs warning of elk and reindeer crossing roads – these animals are more active at dusk.

USEFUL WORDS AND PHRASES

Finnish is a complex and difficult language to learn, and bears little or no resemblance to neighboring languages. However, Swedish is Finland's second, more accessible, language, and most people speak some English.

Finnish uses compound words, which are pronounced exactly as they are written. The first syllable of a word is always stressed, and each letter is pronounced individually.

Do you speak English?	*Puhutteko englantia?*
excuse me	*anteeksi*
hello	*terve*
goodbye	*näkemiin*
how much?	*kuinka paljon?*
how are you?	*kuinka voitte?*
Is it near?	*Onko se lähellä?*
I'd like…	*Haluaisin…*
I don't understand	*en ymmärrä*
non-smoking	*tupakointi kielletty*
okay	*ja lyh*
open/closed	*avoinna/suljettu*
please/thank you	*olkaa hyvä/kiitos*
ticket (one-way/	*menolippu*
round trip)	*meno-paluulippu*
where is…?	*missä on…?*
yes/no	*kyllä or joo/ei*
the hotel	***hotelli***
breakfast	*aamiainen*
key	*avain*
room	*huone*
shower	*suihku*
it's too expensive	*se on liian kallis*
the restaurant	***ravintola***
beef	*nauta*
bread	*leipä*
chicken	*kana*
steak	*pihvl*
coffee	*kahvi*
milk	*maito*
dessert	*jälkiruoka*
main course	*pääruoka*
fish	*kala*
lamb	*karitsa*
pork	*sianliha*
seafood	*äyrläisiä*
soup	*keitto*
wine	*vini*

PRE-TRIP ESSENTIALS...

WHAT YOU NEED

ESSENTIAL FOR TRAVELERS

● Required ● Recommended ○ Not required

Passport	●
Visa	○
Travel, medical insurance	●
Round-trip or onward airline ticket	○
Local currency	●
Traveler's checks	●
Credit cards	●
First-aid kit and medicines	●
Inoculations	○

ESSENTIAL FOR DRIVERS*

Driver's license	●
International Driving Permit	●
Car insurance (for nonrental cars)	●
Car registration (for nonrental cars)	●

*see also DRIVING section

IMPORTANT ADDRESSES

French Government Tourist Office
16th Floor, 444 Madison Avenue
New York, NY 10022
☎ (212) 838-7800
Fax (212) 838-7855

Maison de la France
(French Government Tourist Office)
20 avenue de l'Opéra
75041 Paris Cedex 01, France
☎ 01 42 96 70 00
Fax 01 42 96 70 71
www.franceguide.com

American Embassy
2 avenue Gabriel
75008 Paris, France
☎ 01 43 12 22 22
Fax 01 42 66 97 83

American Embassy (Consular Section)
Office of American Services
2 rue St.-Florentin
75001 Paris, France
☎ 01 43 12 46 54 (passports)
American Citizens Services: Mon.–Fri. 9–3

COUNTRY ESSENTIALS...

CUSTOMS

YES

Duty-free limits on goods brought in from non-European Union countries: 200 cigarettes or 100 cigarillos or 50 cigars or 250 g. tobacco; 2 L. wine; 1 L. alcohol over 22% volume; 2 L. alcohol under 22%; 60 ml. perfume; 250 ml. toilet water; plus any other duty-free goods (including gifts) to the value of 300Fr. There is no limit on the importation of tax-paid goods purchased within the European Union, provided they are for your own personal use. Unlimited currency may be taken into France, but an amount of 50,000Fr or more must be declared if it is to be re-exported.

NO

No unlicensed drugs, weapons, ammunition, obscene material, pets or other animals, counterfeit money or copied goods, meat or poultry.

For customs limits for returning U.S. citizens see page 16.

MONEY

France's currency is the franc (Fr), which is divided into 100 centimes. The denominations of franc bills are 20, 50, 100, 200 and 500. There are coins of 5, 10, 20 and 50 centimes and 1, 2, 5, 10 and 20Fr. You can exchange dollars or traveler's checks *(chèques de voyage)* at a bank *(banque)* or an exchange office *(bureau de change)*. On Jan. 1, 1999, the euro became the official currency of France and the French franc became a denomination of the euro. Euro bills and coins were introduced on Jan. 1, 2002. Both euro bills and coins and the old national currency will be in use during a transitional period, after which time the euro will be the only currency accepted. Exchange rate at press time: $1 = 7Fr

TIPS AND GRATUITIES

Tips *(pourboires)* are welcomed, but not expected.

Restaurants (service is almost always included)	change
Cafés/bars (service is almost always included)	change
Taxis	5–10Fr
Porters	5–10Fr
Chambermaids	10–50Fr
Hairdressers	5–10Fr
Cloakroom attendants	2–5Fr

COMMUNICATIONS

POST OFFICES

Buy stamps *(timbres-poste)* at a post office *(poste)*, newsstand *(marchand de journaux)* or tobacconist (*Tabac*).

Hours of out-of-town post offices may vary. Mailboxes are yellow and wall mounted or free-standing; there are separate compartments for local mail (*départemental*), for elsewhere in France, and abroad *(autres départements/ destinations)*.

TELEPHONES

The telephone system in France is very efficient, and phone booths with instructions in English are easy to find. Nearly all phones are operated solely with a phone card *(télécarte)*, which can be bought from post offices, France Telecom offices, newsstands, many tobacconists and SNCF (railway) counters. You can use credit cards in some booths.

Phoning inside France
All telephone numbers are 10 digits, and include the regional code. Dial all digits when making a call.

Phoning France from abroad
The country code for France is 33. Note that French numbers in this book do not include the country code; you need to prefix this number if you are phoning from another country. To phone France from the United States or Canada, omit the first zero from the French number, and add the prefix 011 33.
Example: 01 22 33 44 55 becomes 011 33 1 22 33 44 55.

Phoning from France
To phone the United States or Canada from France, prefix the area code and number with 001.
Example: (111) 222-3333 becomes 001 111 222-3333.

For directory inquiries dial 12.

For the operator dial 13.

EMERGENCY TELEPHONE NUMBERS

Police *(police)*	17
Fire *(pompiers)*	18
Ambulance *(ambulance)*	15

Emergency calls are free from phone booths.

HOURS OF OPERATION

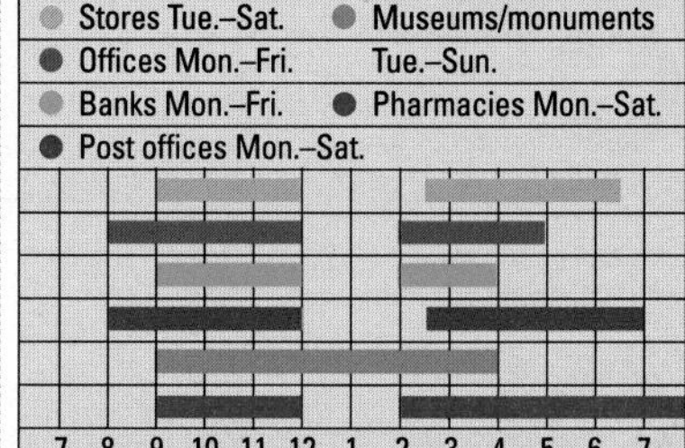

Many stores close on Sunday and all day or a half-day Monday, although some food establishments, especially bakeries, open Sunday mornings. Hypermarkets (large all-purpose stores) are open Mon.–Sat. 9 a.m.– 10 p.m., although many close Monday morning. Opening hours are longer in resort areas and major towns and cities.

Out-of-town banks may stay closed on Monday, while city banks may open on Saturday morning. Post offices close at noon on Saturday.

Museum times vary considerably, and it is best to check before a visit. Municipal museums close on Monday, while national museums close on Tuesday (except Versailles, Trianon Palace and Musée d'Orsay, which close on Monday). Many museums close on national holidays.

NATIONAL HOLIDAYS

Banks, businesses and most stores close on these days.

Jan. 1	**New Year's Day**
Mar./Apr.	**Easter Monday**
May 1	**May Day**
May 8	**VE Day**
May	**Ascension Day**
May/Jun.	**Pentecost Monday**
Jul. 14	**Bastille Day**
Aug. 15	**Assumption of the Virgin**
Nov. 1	**All Saints' Day**
Nov. 11	**Armistice Day**
Dec. 25	**Christmas Day**

PHOTOGRAPHY

The range of subjects to photograph in France is enormous, and the light is usually favorable in the summer months. Film is readily available from stores and photo labs, although development is rather expensive. Some museums and churches will allow you to photograph inside, but permission for flash photography is usually required.

HEALTH

MEDICAL INSURANCE

Private medical insurance is recommended. Visitors from non-E.U. countries have to pay for all medical treatment; keep all receipts and medicine labels to claim on your travel insurance. If you wish to see an English-speaking doctor *(médecin)* ask at your consulate or hotel.

DENTAL SERVICES

A dentist *(dentiste)* charges for treatment. Emergency help is available from dentists listed in the yellow pages *(pages jaunes)*. Check that your private medical insurance covers dental treatment.

SUN ADVICE

The yearly average for sunshine is high: 2,500 hours (3,000 hours along the coast). Summers, particularly July and August, can be dry and hot, especially in the south. When outside wear a hat and drink plenty of fluids. On the beach a high factor sunscreen is essential.

DRUGS

Prescription medicines and medical advice can be obtained from a pharmacy *(pharmacie)*, designated by a green cross sign. If you need medicines outside regular hours, information about the nearest 24-hour facility is posted on the door of all pharmacies.

SAFE WATER

It is safe to drink tap water, but never drink from a fountain marked *"eau non potable"* ("not drinking water"). Many French people prefer the taste of bottled mineral water *(eau minérale en bouteille)*, which is widely available. A less expensive alternative is *eau de source*, which is spring water.

RESTROOMS

It is not difficult to find a restroom (*toilettes* or WC, pronounced *vay-say* in French), although you may still find the old-fashioned "squat" variety. Hygiene is usually of a reasonable standard. There is a small fee to use facilities in train stations. If you need to use the restroom in a café or bar, buy a drink first.

ELECTRICITY

France has a 220-volt power supply. Electrical sockets take plugs with two round pins (occasionally with three round pins); American appliances will need a plug adapter and will require a transformer if they do not have a dual-voltage facility.

NATIONAL TRANSPORTATION

TRAIN *(train)*

The state rail company is the Société Nationale des Chemins de Fer Français (SNCF): ☎ 08 36 35 35 35 (toll call). Trains are fast, reliable and comfortable, with numerous discounts available. A "turn-up-and-go" car-carrying service from Calais (Le Shuttle) to Folkstone, England, and a Paris–London passenger train (Eurostar) both run through the tunnel under the English Channel.

BUS *(bus)*

Bus services in cities are excellent, but rural areas may be less well served. Long-distance bus stations are usually close to railroad stations, and major train and bus services usually co-ordinate (a long-distance bus is called a *car*). Bus services shown on train timetables are run by the SNCF, and rail tickets are often valid for them. The Eurolines international bus network operates in France: ☎ 08 36 69 52 52 (toll call).

FERRY *(ferry)*

There are frequent traditional and fast ferry sailings to Britain from ports along the English Channel. A car-carrying train service also operates – see TRAIN above. Some Mediterranean ferries operate in summer only and may need reservations in advance.

DRIVING

DRIVE ON THE RIGHT

SPEED LIMITS

Traffic police can impose severe on-the-spot fines.

Limited-access highways *(autoroutes)*
130 k.p.h. (80 m.p.h.)
Outer lane minimum **80 k.p.h. (49 m.p.h.)**
On wet roads **110 k.p.h. (68 m.p.h.)**
In fog with visibility less than 50 m (55 yards) **50 k.p.h. (31 m.p.h.)**
Divided highways **110 k.p.h. (68 m.p.h.)**

Main roads
90 k.p.h. (55 m.p.h.)
On wet roads **80 k.p.h. (49 m.p.h.)**

Urban areas
50 k.p.h. (31 m.p.h.)

SEAT BELTS

Must be worn in front and back seats at all times.

BLOOD ALCOHOL

The legal blood alcohol limit is 0.05%. Random breath tests on drivers are carried out frequently, and the penalties for offenders are severe.

DRIVING continued

TOLLS

There are tolls on many limited-access highways *(autoroutes à péage)*. Collect a ticket on entry and keep it in a safe place: you must show the ticket and pay when exiting. Cash and credit cards are accepted.

CAR RENTAL

The leading rental firms have offices at airports and train stations. Hertz offers discounted rates for AAA members (see page 15). For reservations:

	UNITED STATES	FRANCE
Alamo	(800) 327-9633	08 03 35 23 52 (Europcar)
Avis	(800) 331-2112	08 02 05 05 05
Budget	(800) 527-0700	08 00 10 00 01
Hertz	(800) 654-3080	08 01 34 73 47

FUEL

Gas stations are generally easy to find, and highway service areas are open 24 hours. Gas *(essence)* is unleaded *(sans plomb)* and sold in liters. Credit cards (though not all international credit cards) are widely accepted; many pumps read cards directly, so the customer does not have to pay at the counter. Gas stations are less common in rural areas, and some close on Sunday.

AAA AFFILIATED MOTORING CLUB

Fédération Française des Automobile-Clubes et des Usagers de la Route (FFAC)

8 place de la Concorde, F-75008 Paris
☎ 01 53 30 89 30, fax 01 53 30 89 29
Not all automobile clubs offer full services to AAA members.

BREAKDOWNS AND ACCIDENTS

If you are involved in an accident, phone ☎ 17 for police assistance. There are orange emergency telephones every 2 km (1.2 miles) on highways.

Most car rental firms provide their own free rescue service; if your car is rented, follow the instructions given in the documentation. Use of a car repair service other than those authorized by your rental company may violate your agreement.

OTHER INFORMATION

The minimum age for driving a car is 18 (may be higher, usually between 21 and 25, for some car rental firms).

An International Driving Permit (IDP) is recommended; some rental firms require them, and they can speed up formalities if you are involved in an accident.

A Green Card (international motor insurance certificate) is recommended if you are driving a private car; see page 16 for more information.

USEFUL WORDS AND PHRASES

You'll be well received if you try to pronounce words correctly. Don't worry too much about rolling your *r*'s, though; the French realize how difficult it can be.

Final consonants are seldom pronounced. For instance, the masculine adjective *ouvert* (open) is pronounced [oo-ver]; the feminine *ouverte* [oo-vert]. The final consonant in a word like *vin, bon* or *grand* alters the last vowel, making it nasal.

h is silent	*hôtel* [o-tel]
th is *t* (but *ch* is *sh*)	*thé* [tay]; *chaud* [show]
ou is full	*tout* [too]
u is tight, as in cupola	*tu* [tu], *menu* [meuh-nu]
c and g hard before a, o, u	*car* [car], *guide* [geed]
c and g soft before i or e	*cigarette, age* [arzh]
ç is soft (before an a)	*français* [frahn-say]
gn as in union	*agneau* [an-yo]

Do you speak English?	*Parlez-vous anglais?*
excuse me	*excusez-moi*
hello/goodbye	*bonjour/au revoir*
How much is this?	*C'est combien?*
I am American	*Je suis Américain/e*
I'd like...	*je voudrais...*
I don't understand	*Je ne comprends pas*
non-smoking	*non-fumeurs*
okay	*OK (informal)*
open/closed	*ouvert/fermé*
please/thank you	*s'il vous plaît/merci*
ticket	*billet*
(one-way/round trip)	*(simple/aller-retour)*
where is...?	*où est...?*
yes/no	*oui/non*
you're welcome	*de rien*
the hotel	***l'hôtel***
breakfast	*petit déjeuner*
I have a reservation	*j'ai réservé*
key	*clé*
for one/two nights	*pour une/deux nuit(s)*
one/two people	*une/deux personne(s)*
room	*une chambre*
shower	*une douche*
with en-suite bathroom	*avec salle de bains*
the restaurant	***le restaurant***
beef	*boeuf*
bread	*pain*
the check	*L'addition*
chicken	*poulet*
coffee	*café*
dessert	*dessert*
dish of the day	*plat du jour*
fish	*poisson*
lamb	*agneau*
main course	*plat principal*
pork	*porc*
seafood	*fruits de mer*
starter	*entrée*
wine	*vin*

PRE-TRIP ESSENTIALS...

WHAT YOU NEED

ESSENTIAL FOR TRAVELERS

● Required ● Recommended ● Not required

Passport	●
Visa	●
Travel, medical insurance	●
Round-trip or onward airline ticket	●
Local currency	●
Traveler's checks	●
Credit cards	●
First-aid kit and medicines	●
Inoculations	●

ESSENTIAL FOR DRIVERS*

Driver's license	●
International Driving Permit	●
Car insurance (for nonrental cars)	●
Car registration (for nonrental cars)	●

*see also DRIVING section

IMPORTANT ADDRESSES

German National Tourist Office
122 East 42nd Street
New York, NY 10168-0072
☎ (212) 661-7200
Fax (212) 661-7174
www.us.germany-tourism.de

German National Tourist Board
Beethovenstrasse 69
60325 Frankfurt am Main, Germany
☎ 069 974 64-0
Fax 069 751 903
www.deutschland-tourismus.de

American Embassy
Neustädtische Kirchstrasse 4–5
10117 Berlin, Germany
☎ 030 8305-0
Fax 030 8305-1215

COUNTRY ESSENTIALS...

CUSTOMS

YES

Duty-free limits on goods brought in from non-European Union countries: 200 cigarettes or 100 cigarillos or 50 cigars or 250 g. tobacco; 2 L. wine; 1 L. alcohol over 22% volume; 2 L. alcohol under 22%; 50 ml. perfume; 250 ml. toilet water; plus any other duty-free goods (including gifts) to the value of DM115. There is no limit on the importation of tax-paid goods purchased within the European Union, provided they are for your own personal use. There are no currency regulations.

NO

No unlicensed drugs, weapons, ammunition, obscene material, pets or other animals, counterfeit money or copied goods, meat or poultry.

For customs limits for returning U.S. citizens see page 16.

MONEY

Germany's currency is the Deutsche mark (DM), which is divided into 100 pfennigs (Pf). The denominations of Deutsche mark bills are 5, 10, 20, 50, 100, 200, 500 and 1,000. There are coins of 1, 2, 5, 10 and 50 Pf and 1, 2 and 5DM. You can exchange dollars or traveler's checks *(Reiseschecks)* at a bank *(Bank)* or an exchange office *(Wechselbüro)*. On Jan. 1, 1999, the euro became the official currency of Germany and the mark became a denomination of the euro. Euro bills and coins were introduced on Jan. 1, 2002. Both euro bills and coins and the old national currency will be in use during a transitional period, after which time the euro will be the only currency accepted. Exchange rate at press time: $1 = DM2

TIPS AND GRATUITIES

Restaurants (where service is not included)	10%
Cafés/bars (where service is not included)	10%
Taxis	10%
Porters	change
Chambermaids	change
Hairdressers	change
Restroom attendants	change
Cloakroom attendants	change

COMMUNICATIONS

POST OFFICES

Buy stamps *(Briefmarken)* at a post office *(Postamt)* or newsstand *(Informationsstand)*.

Hours for out-of-town post offices may vary. Mailboxes are bright yellow.

TELEPHONES

Black telephones have instructions in English, and most operators are bilingual. Increasingly fewer phones accept coins; most are operated by telephone cards (*Telefonkarten*), which can be bought at any post office. International calls can be made from any booth. If the telephone is not functioning properly, dial 11171.

Phoning inside Germany
German telephone numbers in this book include an area code: dial the number listed.

Operator: ☎ 01189.

Phoning Germany from abroad
The country code for Germany is 49. Note that German numbers in this book do not include the country code; you will need to prefix this number if you are phoning from another country. To phone Germany from the United States or Canada, omit the first zero from the German number, and add the prefix 011 49. (Note that the number of digits in German area codes varies.)
Example: 011 22 33 44 becomes 011 49 11 22 33 44.

Phoning from Germany
To phone the United States or Canada from Germany, prefix the area code and number with 001.
Example: 111 222-3333 becomes 001 111 222-3333.
To call international information dial 00118.

EMERGENCY TELEPHONE NUMBERS

Police *(Polizei)*	110
Fire *(Feuerwehr)*	112
Ambulance *(Krankenwagen)*	112

*In some states ambulance is 115
Emergency calls are free from phone booths.

HOURS OF OPERATION

● Stores Mon.–Sat. ● Museums/monuments Tue.–Sat.
● Offices Mon.–Fri.
● Banks Mon.–Fri. ● Pharmacies Mon.–Sat.
● Post offices Mon.–Sat.

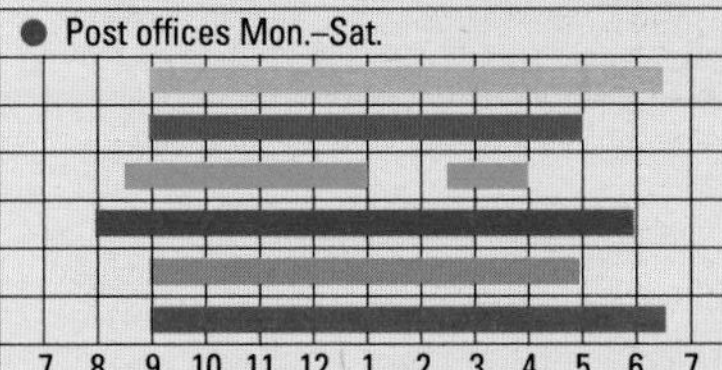

Store hours of operation vary considerably, so even within cities there is no standard rule. Stores, including pharmacies, tend to close at 4 on Saturday and are open until 10:30 p.m. on Thursday.

Banks stay open until 5:30 on Thursday. Post offices open 8–noon on Saturday. Post offices at airports and railway stations operate longer hours.

Government offices close promptly at 4, or at 2 on Friday.

Museums often close on Monday and open late on Thursday; some close for lunch.

NATIONAL HOLIDAYS

Banks, businesses and most stores close on these days.

Jan. 1	**New Year's Day**
Jan. 6	**Epiphany (Bavaria, Baden Württemberg and Saxony only)**
Mar./Apr.	**Good Friday**
Mar./Apr.	**Easter Monday**
May 1	**Labor Day**
May	**Ascension Day**
May/Jun.	**Pentecost Monday**
Aug. 15	**Assumption of the Virgin (Bavaria and Saarland only)**
Oct. 3	**Day of German Unity**
Nov. 1	**All Saints' Day (Baden- Württemberg, Bavaria, North Rhine-Westphalia, Rhineland-Palatinate and Saarland only)**
Dec. 25	**Christmas Day**
Dec. 26	**St. Stephen's Day**

PHOTOGRAPHY

The light is generally good. In addition to the glorious architecture of the big cities, there are many colorful, quaint street scenes to be snapped in provincial Germany, and the landscapes are equally appealing. Photography is generally forbidden in museums and churches. Quality brand film and batteries are easy to find, and there are many rapid-developing facilities.

HEALTH

MEDICAL INSURANCE

U.S. and Canadian visitors must pay for medical treatment from a doctor or at a hospital *(Krankenhaus)*. Keep all receipts to claim on your travel insurance. For details on emergency, weekend or English-speaking doctors, ask your hotel or consulate.

DENTAL SERVICES

A dentist *(Zahnarzt)* always charges for treatment. Emergency help is available from dentists listed in the local telephone directory. Check that your private medical insurance covers dental treatment.

SUN ADVICE

Germany's Continental climate brings cold, clear winters and warm summers, when sun protection is needed. Use sunscreen; children and those with fair skin should be vigilant.

DRUGS

Prescription medicines and advice can be obtained from a pharmacy *(Apotheke)*; cosmetics and toiletries at a *Drogerie*. If you need medicine outside regular hours, information about the nearest 24-hour facility is posted on the door of all pharmacies.

SAFE WATER

Water is safe to drink in Germany, but you may prefer to drink bottled mineral water *(Sprudelwasser)*, which is widely available.

RESTROOMS

Finding a restroom *(Toilette)* is not difficult; they are usually identified by symbols, or are designated *Herren* (men) and *Damen* or *Frauen* (women). Most are free, although some are operated by a 10Pf coin. If there is an attendant, small change is appreciated as a tip.

ELECTRICITY

Germany has a 220-volt power supply. Electrical sockets take plugs with two round pins or sometimes three pins in a vertical row; American appliances will need a plug adapter and will require a transformer if they do not have a dual-voltage facility.

NATIONAL TRANSPORTATION

TRAIN *(Zug)*

Germany's fast, efficient rail network is operated by Deutsche Bahn (DB). ICE is a modern service of long-distance, high-speed trains. Regional trains are modern and comfortable, and connect with long-distance services. Local services are called SE or S-Bahn. There are many fare reductions available; for bookings and information, phone ☎ 01805 996 633 (24 hours).

BUS *(Bus)*

Towns and villages not served by the rail network usually have bus links, with timetables and routes co-ordinating with trains. German towns have their own buses, and one ticket is often good for other types of city transportation. The Eurolines international bus service operates in Germany: ☎ 089 54 58 70-0.

FERRY *(Fähre)*

Ferries from the ports of Lubeck and Kiel in the north connect to Denmark and Sweden. Boats also offer a service on many German lakes, rivers and canals. Ask for details at your travel agency or a local tourist office, where reservations can often be made.

DRIVING

DRIVE ON THE RIGHT

SPEED LIMITS

Traffic police can impose severe on-the-spot fines.

Limited-access highways *(Autobahn)*: unless signposted there is no speed limit but the suggested limit is **130 k.p.h. (80 m.p.h.)**

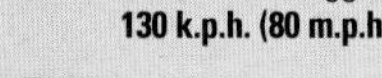

Main roads **100 k.p.h. (62 m.p.h.)**

Urban areas **50 k.p.h. (31 m.p.h.)**

SEAT BELTS

Must be worn in front and back seats at all times. Children under 12 must sit on child seat cushions to enable seat belts to fit properly.

BLOOD ALCOHOL

The legal blood alcohol limit is 0.05%. Random breath tests on drivers are carried out frequently, especially late at night, and the penalties for offenders are severe.

DRIVING continued

TOLLS

There are no highway tolls.

CAR RENTAL

The leading rental firms have offices at airports and train stations. Hertz offers discounted rates for AAA members (see page 15). For reservations:

	UNITED STATES	GERMANY
Alamo	(800) 327-9633	030 41 01 33 83
Avis	(800) 331-2112	0180 5 55 77 55
Budget	(800) 527-0700	0180 5 25 25 25
Hertz	(800) 654-3080	0180 5 33 35 35

FUEL

Gas *(Benzin)* and diesel fuel are sold in liters. Gas stations are easy to find, and most highway services are open 24 hours. Self-service stations are called *Selbstbedienung* or *SB-Tanken*, and credit cards are widely accepted.

AAA AFFILIATED MOTORING CLUB

Allgemeiner Deutscher Automobil-Club E.V. (ADAC)
Am Westpark 8, 81373 Munich
☎ 089 76 76-0, fax 089 76 76-25 00
If you break down while driving, phone ☎ 01802 22 22 22 (ADAC breakdown service).
Not all automobile clubs offer full services to AAA members.

BREAKDOWNS AND ACCIDENTS

Most car rental firms provide their own free rescue service; if your car is rented, follow the instructions given in the documentation. Use of a car repair service other than those authorized by your rental company may violate your agreement.

If you are involved in an accident, phone ☎ 110 for police.

OTHER INFORMATION

The minimum age for driving a car is 18 (may be higher for some car rental firms).

You must keep an official translation with your driver's license; your embassy or a tourist office can help. An International Driving Permit (IDP) is recommended; some rental firms require them, and they can speed up formalities if you are involved in an accident.

A Green Card (international motor insurance certificate) is recommended if you are driving a private car; see page 16 for more information.

On-the-spot fines can be imposed if you run out of gas on a highway.

USEFUL WORDS AND PHRASES

German has many dialects. Language in the north descended from Old Saxon, and in the south from Old High German. Their differences were resolved by Standard German (*Schriftdeutsch*), created by Martin Luther when he translated the Bible in the 16th century.

Germans are helpful to visitors who attempt to communicate in German, although English is widely spoken.

ü is like the *u* in cupola	*über* (over)
ie sounds like heat	*Sie* (you)
ei sounds like height	*Eingang* (entrance)
ch is a harsh rasp...	*J. S. Bach*
j is like the English *y*	*ja* (yes)
r is rolled, as in French	*Fräulein* (Miss)
w sounds like English *v*	*wo* (where)
z is like English *ts*	*Zeit* (time)

Do you speak English?	*Sprechen Sie Englisch?*
excuse me	*Verzeihung*
hello	*Guten Tag*
goodbye	*Auf Wiedersehen*
How much is...?	*Wieviel kostet...?*
I am American	*Ich bin Amerikaner (in)*
I'd like...	*Ich hätte gerne*
I don't understand	*Ich verstehe nicht*
non-smoking	*Nichtraucher*
okay	*OK*
open/closed	*offen/geschlossen*
please/thank you	*bitte/danke*
one-way ticket	*einfache Fahrkarte*
round trip ticket	*Rückfahrkarte*
where is...?	*wo ist...?*
yes/no	*ja/nein*
you're welcome	*bitte*

the hotel	***das Hotel***
breakfast	*Frühstück*
reservation	*Reservieren*
key	*Schlüssel*
for one/two nights	*für eine Nacht/ zwei Nächte*
for one/two people	*für eine Person/ zwei Personen*
room	*Zimmer*
shower	*Dusche*

the restaurant	**das Restaurant**
beefsteak	*Steak*
bread	*Brot*
chicken	*Hähnchen*
the check	*Rechnung*
coffee	*Kaffee*
dish of the day	*Tagesgericht*
dessert	*Desserts*
entree	*Hauptgericht*
fish	*Fisch*
lamb	*Lamm*
pork	*Schweinefleish*
seafood	*Meeresfrüchte*
first courses	*Vorspeisen*
wine	*Wein*

PRE-TRIP ESSENTIALS…

WHAT YOU NEED

ESSENTIAL FOR TRAVELERS

● Required ● Recommended ○ Not required

Passport	●
Visa	○
Travel, medical insurance	●
Round-trip or onward airline ticket	○
Local currency	●
Traveler's checks	●
Credit cards	●
First-aid kit and medicines*	●
Inoculations	●

*see also HEALTH section

ESSENTIAL FOR DRIVERS*

Driver's license	●
International Driving Permit	●
Car insurance (for nonrental cars)	●
Car registration (for nonrental cars)	●

*see also DRIVING section

IMPORTANT ADDRESSES

Greek National Tourism Organization
Olympic Tower
645 Fifth Avenue
New York, NY 10022
☎ (212) 421-5777
Fax (212) 826-6940
www.greektourism.com

Hellenic Tourism Organization
(Greek National Tourism Organization)
Ødos Amerikis 2
10564 Athens, Greece
☎ 01 331 0565 or 01 331 0692
Fax 01 325 2895
www.gnto.gr

American Embassy
91 Vassilissis Sophias Avenue
10160 Athens, Greece
☎ 01 721 2951
Fax 01 645 6282
Open Mon.–Fri. 8:30–5

COUNTRY ESSENTIALS…

CUSTOMS

YES

Duty-free limits on goods brought in from non-European Union countries: 200 cigarettes or 100 cigarillos or 50 cigars or 250 g. tobacco; 2 L. wine; 1 L. alcohol over 22% volume; 2 L. alcohol under 22% volume; 50 ml. perfume; 250 ml. toilet water; plus any other duty-free goods (including gifts) to the value of Dr50,000. There is no importation limit for tax-paid goods purchased within the European Union, provided they are for personal use. Any amount of foreign currency over $200 (U.S.) or the equivalent must by law be declared at the customs entry point. Up to Dr20,000, and $1,000 in foreign currency may be exported by visitors.

NO

No unlicensed drugs, weapons, ammunition, obscene material, pets or other animals, counterfeit money or copied goods, meat or poultry.

For customs limits for returning U.S. citizens see page 16.

MONEY

The Greek currency is the drachma (Dr). The denominations of drachma bills are 500, 1,000, 5,000 and 10,000, and coins of 5, 10, 20, 50 and 100Dr. Traveler's checks are widely accepted, and some gift stores accept dollars. Exchange dollars or traveler's checks *(taxithiotiki epitayi)* at a bank *(trapeza)* or an exchange office *(sarafiko)*. You can get cash at a bank with a credit card, but there is usually a charge. Euro bills and coins were introduced on Jan. 1, 2002. Both euro bills and coins and the old national currency will be in use during a transitional period, after which time the euro will be the only currency accepted. Exchange rate at press time: $1 = Dr381

TIPS AND GRATUITIES

Tips *(poorbwáar)* are welcomed, but not expected or obligatory.

Restaurants (where service is not included)	10–15%
Cafés/bars	change
Taxis	change
Porters	Dr500
Chambermaids	Dr100 per day
Cloakroom attendants	change

TIME ZONES

ATHENS	NEW YORK	CHICAGO	DENVER	SAN FRANCISCO
12:00 noon	6 hours behind Greece	7 hours behind Greece	8 hours behind Greece	9 hours behind Greece

COMMUNICATIONS

POST OFFICES

Buy stamps *(ghramatósima)* at a post office *(takhithromio)*, distinguished by a yellow "OTE" sign. City and town post offices often cash traveler's checks. Lines can be long at post office counters; if you simply need stamps, try a corner kiosk *(periptero)* selling postcards.

Hours for out-of-town post offices may vary.

TELEPHONES

Most public telephones take phone cards available from kiosks, local stores and OTE (Organismos Tilepikoinonion Ellados, pronounced O-tay) offices. If your calls are short and local, use a street kiosk *(periptero)* where you pay after the call. For an international call, you can also use a coin-operated telephone in a restaurant, bar or hotel lobby; they take Dr10, Dr20, Dr50 and Dr100 coins. You can be called back on these telephones, and they have instructions in English.

Phoning inside Greece
All Greek telephone numbers in this book include an area code: dial the number that is listed.

To call the operator dial 132 (or 131 in Athens).

Phoning Greece from abroad
The country code for Greece is 30. Note that Greek numbers in this book do not include the country code; you will need to prefix this number if you are phoning from another country. To call a Greek number from the United States or Canada, omit the first zero and add the prefix 011 30. (Note that Greek phone numbers vary in the number of digits.)
Example: 01 122 3344 becomes 011 30 1 122 3344.

Phoning from Greece
To phone the United States or Canada from Greece, prefix the area code and number with 001. Example: (111) 222-3333 becomes 001 111 222-3333. To call international information dial 161.

EMERGENCY TELEPHONE NUMBERS

Police *(astinomia)*, general emergencies	100
Tourist police (Athens only)	171
Fire *(fotyá)*	199
Ambulance *(asthenoforo)*	166

Emergency calls are free from phone booths.

HOURS OF OPERATION

- Stores Mon.–Sat.
- Museums/monuments
- Offices Mon.–Fri.
- Architectural sites
- Banks Mon.–Fri.
- Pharmacies Mon.–Fri.
- Post offices Mon.–Sat.

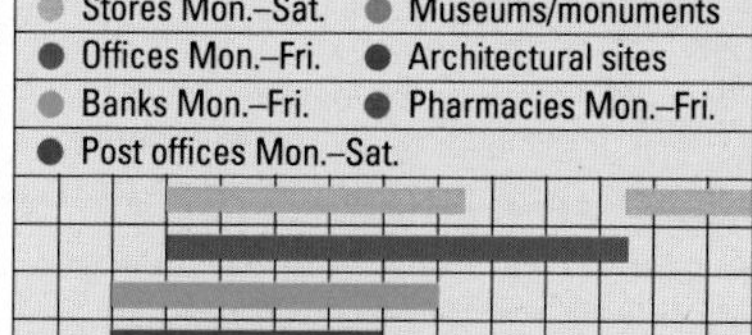

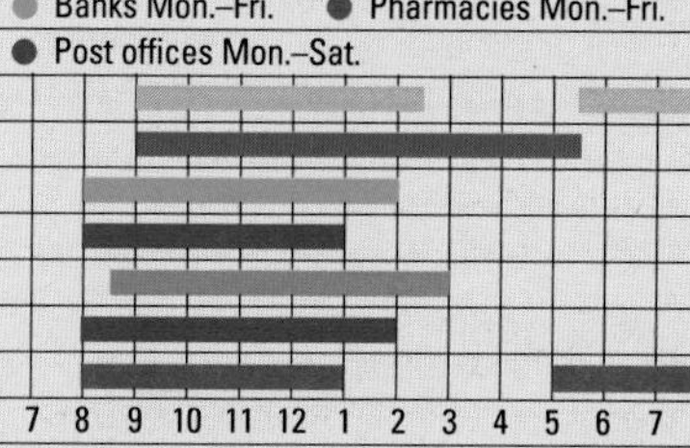

In tourist areas stores open at 8 a.m. and close late; they have shorter hours off-season, and some close completely in winter.

Banks close at 1:30 Fridays. They may stay open longer hours at peak season in resort areas.

Post offices close at noon on Saturday.

Architectural sites usually close in the afternoon; some reopen in the evening in the summer, but all sites vary their hours depending on the time of year. It is best to check locally. Many architectural sites, museums and monuments close on Monday.

Restaurants open all day in resort areas but may close off-season.

NATIONAL HOLIDAYS

Banks, businesses, and most stores and museums close on these days, but restaurants and some stores in tourist areas may stay open.

Jan. 1	**New Year's Day**
Jan. 6	**Epiphany**
Feb./Mar.	**Shrove Monday**
Mar. 25	**Independence Day**
***Mar./Apr.**	**Good Friday**
***Mar./Apr.**	**Easter Monday**
May 1	**Labor Day**
May/Jun.	**Pentecost Monday**
Aug. 15	**Assumption of the Virgin**
Oct. 28	**Óchi Day**
Dec. 25	**Christmas Day**
Dec. 26	**St. Stephen's Day**

* Greece observes the Orthodox calendar, and the date on which Easter falls may differ from that observed by Western nations.

PHOTOGRAPHY

The sun in Greece is strong, and slow film is ideal. Photograph the sights early in the morning, before the crowds mass and when the light is at its best. In rural areas deep blue seas and rustic villages make interesting subjects. Beware of taking shots near military bases, and ask first in museums and churches. Brand names of film and camera batteries are widely available.

HEALTH

MEDICAL INSURANCE

Private medical insurance is recommended. Visitors from non-E.U. countries can receive basic treatment at hospital emergency rooms. Admittance to a hospital *(nosokomío)* or consultation with a doctor *(iatrós)* will entail a fee. Ask your hotel, consulate or the tourist police for information on English-speaking doctors.

DENTAL SERVICES

Dentists *(odhondoyatrós)* always charge for treatment, so check that your medical insurance covers it; keep all receipts for insurance purposes. Treatment is available from English-speaking dentists listed in the telephone directory, or ask at your hotel.

SUN ADVICE

Summer, particularly July and August, can be oppressively hot and humid. Seek shelter inside a museum, or cover up, apply a sunscreen and drink plenty of fluids. Be especially careful on boats or near the water.

DRUGS

A pharmacy *(farmakío)*, distinguished by a green cross, has staff qualified to offer medical advice and provide a wide range of prescription medicines. Information about the nearest all-night facility is usually posted at pharmacies. Note that codeine is banned and you can be fined for carrying it.

SAFE WATER

Tap water is safe to drink but because of the high level of minerals it can cause upsets. Bottled water *(metaliko nero)* is available everywhere at a reasonable cost.

RESTROOMS

Finding a clean restroom *(toualéta)* away from tourist areas can be difficult. It is advisable to use facilities in cafés and restaurants after buying a drink. Restrooms are free. The Greek sewage system does not take toilet tissue, even in café and restaurant facilities; use the wastebin provided.

ELECTRICITY

Greece has a 220-volt power supply. Electrical sockets take plugs with two round pins; American appliances will need a plug adapter and will require a transformer if they do not have a dual-voltage facility.

NATIONAL TRANSPORTATION

TRAIN *(tréno)*

Greek trains are run by Organismos Sidirodromon Ellados (OSE), a service predominantly for the mainland. The network is limited, and a reservation is essential on most express trains. For rail information in Athens: ☎ 145 (domestic services) or 147 (international services).

BUS *(leoforío)*

Buses are popular and frequent; few villages or ferry ports are without a bus link. Buy city-to-city tickets from the bus station; in rural areas tickets *(isitirio)* are issued by a conductor on the bus. For bus information in Athens: ☎ 185.

FERRY *(féribot)*

Ferries serve all of the Greek islands, and boat excursions run from May to October. You can take a boat from the port of Piraeus to most islands, but check the length of the trip on the timetable – some ferries stop at every island. You can usually buy a ticket on the day of travel unless you are reserving a cabin or taking a car. You may need to reserve in advance in mid-August and over the Easter period; ask at a travel agency or tourist office.

DRIVING

DRIVE ON THE RIGHT

SPEED LIMITS

Police can impose on-the-spot fines but they cannot collect them.

Limited-access highways
120 k.p.h. (74 m.p.h.)
Divided highways
110 k.p.h. (68 m.p.h.)

Main roads
80 k.p.h. (55 m.p.h.)

Urban areas
50 k.p.h. (31 m.p.h.)

SEAT BELTS

Must be worn in the front seat at all times and in the rear seat where fitted. Children under 10 are not allowed to travel in the front seat.

BLOOD ALCOHOL

The legal blood alcohol limit is 0.05%. Random breath tests on drivers are carried out frequently, especially late at night, and the penalties for offenders are severe.

DRIVING continued

TOLLS

There are highway tolls in Greece.

CAR RENTAL

The leading rental firms have offices at airports, train stations and principal ferry terminals. Hertz offers discounted rates for AAA members (see page 15). For reservations:

	UNITED STATES	GREECE
Alamo	(800) 327-9633	01 921 5789 (InterRent/EuropeCar)
Avis	(800) 331-2112	01 322 4951
Budget	(800) 527-0700	01 922 6666
Hertz	(800) 654-3080	01 922 0102

FUEL

Gas *(venzini)* is sold in liters and usually comes in five grades: super *(sooper)*, regular *(apli)*, unleaded *(amolyvdhi)*, super unleaded *(sooper amolyvdhi)* and diesel *(petrelaio)*. There are few stations in remote areas; they are less likely to be open on weekends and may not take credit cards.

AAA AFFILIATED MOTORING CLUB

Automobile and Touring Club of Greece (ELPA)
395 Messogion Street, 153 43 Agia Paraskevi, Athens ☎ 01 606 8800, fax 01 606 8981
If you break down while driving, phone ☎ 104 (ELPA breakdown service).
Not all automobile clubs offer full services to AAA members.

BREAKDOWNS AND ACCIDENTS

There are emergency telephones at regular intervals on highways. If you are involved in an accident, phone ☎ 100 for police.
Most car rental firms provide their own free rescue service; if your car is rented, follow the instructions given in the documentation. Use of a car repair service other than those authorized by your rental company may violate your agreement.

OTHER INFORMATION

The minimum age for driving a car is 17 (may be higher for some car rental firms).

An International Driving Permit (IDP) is recommended; some rental firms require them, and they can speed up formalities if you are involved in an accident. A Green Card (international motor insurance certificate) is recommended if you are driving a private car; see page 16 for more information.

You can be fined for unnecessary use of the horn.

USEFUL WORDS AND PHRASES

The Greek language can be daunting to the visitor; it uses a different alphabet and is spoken with staccato rapidity. The way words and place names are converted into English varies considerably according to which transliteration system a translator happens to prefer.

With patience and a keen ear, you should be able to recognize what sounds these unfamiliar letters stand for. Learning the Greek alphabet may enable you to deduce the meaning of signs and notices. The easiest thing to do, however, is to learn a few basic courtesy phrases.

The Greeks realize how difficult their language appears to foreigners, and they appreciate visitors' attempts to speak it.

Do you speak English?	*milate angliká?*
excuse me	*signomi*
hello/goodbye	*yásou/chérete*
how much?	*póso?*
I'd like	*tha íthela*
I do not understand	*dhen katalavéno*
non-smoking	*khoros ya mi kapnízondes*
okay	*endáýsi*
open/closed	*aniktos/klistos*
please/you're welcome	*parakaló*
thank you	*efharistó*
ticket	*isitiro*
one-way/round trip	*apló/isitiro met epistrofis*
where is...?	*poo íne?*
yes/no	*né/óhi*

the hotel	***xenodochio***
breakfast	*proino*
key	*klidhí*
for one/two nights	*ya mía/dhýo vradhiés*
for one/two people	*yiá éna/dhýo átoma*
room	*éna dhomátio*
shower	*doos*

the restaurant	***estiatorio***
food	*fagitó*
starter	*proto piato*
olives	*eliés*
stuffed vine leaves	*dolmadakia*
beans	*fasólia*
bread	*psomi*
water	*neró*
beer	*bira*
wine	*krasí*
coffee	*kafé*
meat balls	*kefthédes*
chicken	*kotópoulo*
lamb	*arnáki*
pork	*hirino*
cod's roe paté	*taramosalata*
lobster	*astakós*
red mullet	*barboúnia*
squid	*kalamarákia*
dessert	*glikisma*
the check	*logariasmós*

PRE-TRIP ESSENTIALS…

WHAT YOU NEED

ESSENTIAL FOR TRAVELERS

● Required ● Recommended ○ Not required

Passport	●
Visa	○
Travel, medical insurance	●
Round-trip or onward airline ticket	○
Local currency	●
Traveler's checks	●
Credit cards	●
First-aid kit and medicines	●
Inoculations	○

ESSENTIAL FOR DRIVERS*

Driver's license	●
International Driving Permit	●
Car insurance (for nonrental cars)	●
Car registration (for nonrental cars)	●

*see also DRIVING section

IMPORTANT ADDRESSES

Hungarian National Tourist Office
150 East 58th Street, 33rd Floor
New York, NY 10155-3398
☎ (212) 355-0240
Fax (212) 207-4103
www.gotohungary.com

Hungarian National Tourist Office
H-1052 Budapest
Sütő utca 2
Hungary
☎ 1 317 9800
Fax 1 317 9656
www.hungarytourism.hu

American Embassy
H-1054 Budapest
Szabadság tér 12
Hungary
☎ 1 475 4400 (8 a.m.–5 p.m.); 1 475 4703 or 1 475 4924 (5 p.m.–8 a.m.)
Fax 1 475 4764

COUNTRY ESSENTIALS…

CUSTOMS

YES

Duty-free limits on goods brought in: You may bring in personal items for your stay. Persons over the age of 16 may also import: 250 cigarettes or 50 cigars or 250 g. tobacco; 1 L. alcohol over 22% volume or 2 L. alcohol under 22% volume; 100 ml. perfume; 250 ml. toilet water; plus any other duty-free goods to the value of Ft270,000. Hungary is not part of the European Union. You may bring in up to Ft350,000 in local currency. There is a restriction on exporting convertible currencies (including dollars): the equivalent of Ft100,000.

NO

No unlicensed drugs, weapons, ammunition, obscene material, pets or other animals, counterfeit money or copied goods, meat or poultry.

For customs limits for returning U.S. citizens see page 16.

MONEY

Hungary's currency is the forint (Ft or HUF), which is divided into 100 next-to-valueless fillérs. The denominations of forint bills are 200, 500, 1,000, 2,000, 5,000, 10,000 and 20,000. There are coins of 1, 2, 5, 10, 20, 50 and 100 forints. You can exchange dollars or traveler's checks *(utazasi csekket)* at a bank *(bank)*, exchange office *(penzvalto)*, post office *(posta)* and some hotels. Do not rely on being able to pay by credit card; although they are increasingly common, they are not accepted everywhere.

Exchange rate at press time: $1 = Ft285

TIPS AND GRATUITIES

Tips *(borravaló)* are welcomed, but not expected, where service is not included.

Restaurants	10–20%
Cafés/bars	10–20%
Taxis	10%
Porters	to reflect quality of service
Chambermaids	ro reflect quality of service
Hairdressers	10%
Gas station attendants	change
Cloakroom attendants	change

COMMUNICATIONS

POST OFFICES

Buy stamps *(bélyeg)* at a post office *(posta)*, newsstand/tobacconist *(dohanyaruda)* or from a hotel.

Hours for out-of-town post offices may vary. Mail boxes are wall-mounted and red with a calling-horn emblem.

TELEPHONES

You can use cash and prepaid phone cards to make a call in Hungary. For direct dialing for national and international calls, use Ft10, Ft20, Ft50 and Ft100 coins. International calls can be made from red phone booths. Phone cards of 50 and 100 units can be bought from newsstands/tobacconists, gas stations, post offices and hotels.

Phoning inside Hungary

Hungarian telephone numbers include an area code of one or two digits (there is no initial zero). For long-distance calls within Hungary precede the number with 06. Numbers in Budapest are seven digits, not including the area code; the area code is 1.
To call the operator dial 191.

Phoning Hungary from abroad

The country code for Hungary is 36. Note that Hungarian numbers in this book do not include the Hungarian country code; you will need to prefix this number if you are phoning from another country. To phone Hungary from the United States or Canada, add the prefix 011 36 before the area code and number. Example: 1 122 3344 becomes 011 36 1 122 3344.

Phoning from Hungary

To phone the United States or Canada from Hungary, prefix the area code and number with 001. Example: (111) 222-3333 becomes 001 111 222-3333. To call the international operator dial 190; for international directory inquiries dial 199.

EMERGENCY TELEPHONE NUMBERS

General emergency	112
Police *(rendörség)*	107
Fire *(tüzoltóság)*	105
Ambulance *(mentök)*	104

HOURS OF OPERATION

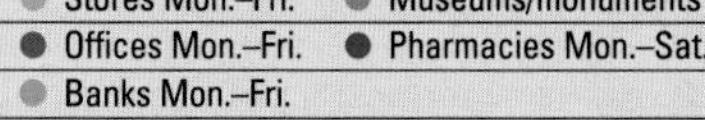

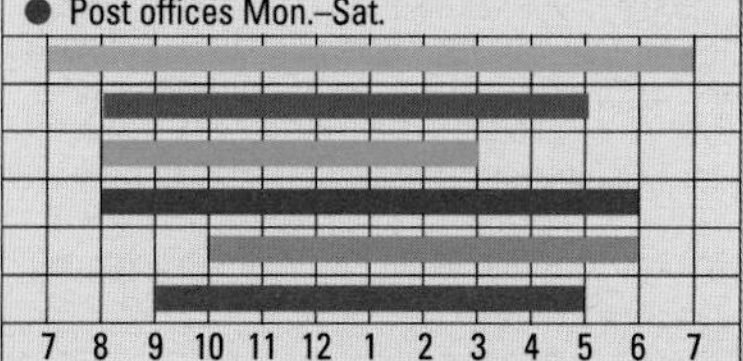

Department stores are open Mon.–Fri. 10–6, Sat. 9–1. Saturday afternoon is early closing, and few stores remain open after 1 or 2 p.m. Thursday is late-night shopping until 7 or 8 p.m. Grocery stores and other food stores have longer hours and also open on Sunday morning. In large cities, some stores stay open 24 hours. In smaller towns, stores close over lunchtime. Large shopping centers in cities are open Mon.–Sat. 10–9, Sun. 10–6.

Banks close at 1 p.m. on Friday.

Post offices close at 1 p.m. on Saturday.

Many museums close on Monday.

NATIONAL HOLIDAYS

Banks, businesses and most stores are closed on these days; if a public holiday falls on a Tuesday or a Thursday, the day between it and the weekend also becomes a holiday.

Jan. 1	**New Year's Day**
Mar. 15	**Day of the Nation (anniversary of 1848 revolution)**
Mar./Apr.	**Easter Monday**
May 1	**Labor Day**
May/Jun.	**Pentecost Monday**
Aug. 20	**Constitution Day**
Oct. 23	**Day of the Proclamation of the Republic**
Dec. 25	**Christmas Day**
Dec. 26	**St. Stephen's Day**

PHOTOGRAPHY

Hungary has spectacular landscapes, including the Danube bend north of Budapest, one of the most beautiful stretches of this great river, and romantic Lake Balaton, framed by vineyards. Vendors near historic sights sell overpriced 35mm color film; it is widely available, so buy it elsewhere. Batteries and developing services are available in towns and cities.

EMERGENCY PHONE NUMBERS

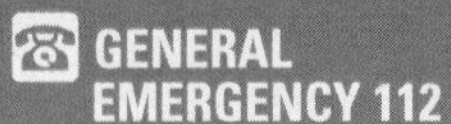

HEALTH

MEDICAL INSURANCE

Private medical insurance is recommended. U.S. and Canadian visitors can receive free transportation to a hospital *(kórház)* for emergency treatment. All further treatment and care has to be paid for. Fees for medical care are set by the individual hospital or practice. There is a 24-hour private medical care service with English-speaking doctors in Budapest: Falck SOS Hungary. It also has its own ambulance service ✉ Kapy utca 49B, Budapest II ☎ 1 200 0100.

DENTAL SERVICES

Dentists *(forgovos)* charge for treatment, but quality dental work is relatively inexpensive. Check that it is covered by your medical insurance. Dentists are listed in the yellow pages; ask for English-speaking dentists at your embassy or hotel, or at a tourist office. There is a 24-hour dental service in Budapest: SOS Dental Service, ✉ Király utca 14, Budapest VI ☎ 1 267 9602.

SUN ADVICE

Hungary has up to 2,500 hours of sun annually, one of the highest levels in Europe. In summer, 9 or 10 hours a day can be expected, so protection is essential.

DRUGS

A pharmacy *(gyógyszetár* or *patica)* sells both prescription and nonprescription medicines (bring your own medication if you need a specific product). Most are cheaper than similar U.S. products. Information about the nearest 24-hour facility is posted at all pharmacies.

SAFE WATER

Although tap water is safe, you may find it causes mild upsets. Bottled mineral water *(ásvány víz)* and soda water *(szoda víz)* are widely available and advised.

RESTROOMS

Public restrooms *(mosdó)* are fairly easy to find, and are usually indicated by a symbol or marked WC, and designated by *férfi* for men and *nöi* for women. A charge of between Ft50 and Ft200 may be made.

ELECTRICITY

Hungary has a 220-volt power supply. Electrical sockets take plugs with two round pins; American appliances will need a plug adapter and will require a transformer if they do not have a dual-voltage facility.

NATIONAL TRANSPORTATION

TRAIN *(vonat)*

The state railroad, Magyar Államvasutak (MÁV), serves most towns. The best trains are express, linking Budapest with provincial centers; when journeying cross-country it may be quicker to go via the capital. Fares are low, and MÁV offers many discounted fares, including rail cards good for unlimited travel; ☎ 1 461 5500 (24 hours).

BUS *(busz)*

Long-distance buses are expensive, but sometimes quicker than trains. The main Budapest terminal is at Erzsebét tér. The main operator is state-owned Volánbusz, whose yellow buses serve even very small communities. Volánbusz is a member of Eurolines, who operate an international bus service; ☎ 1 485 2100 (for domestic and international services; daily 6 a.m.–10 p.m.).

FERRY *(komp)*

Ferries run on Lake Balaton, the Danube between Budapest and Esztergom, and the Tisza river (serving Tokaj, Szolnok, Csongrád and Szeged). Ferries generally run spring to late autumn. Obtain Budapest information from the Vigadó tér landing stage; ☎ 1 318 1223.

DRIVING

DRIVE ON THE RIGHT

SPEED LIMITS

On-the-spot fines of up to Ft30,000 can be imposed by the police. Receipts must be issued.

Limited-access highways *(autópályára)*
120 k.p.h. (74 m.p.h.)
Divided highways **100 k.p.h. (62 m.p.h.)**

Main roads
80 k.p.h. (49 m.p.h.)

Urban areas
30–50 k.p.h. (18–31 m.p.h.)

Some limits increased in 2001; information boards near border crossing points display details.

SEAT BELTS

Must be worn in front and rear seats at all times.

BLOOD ALCOHOL

The legal blood alcohol limit is zero. Random breath tests on drivers are carried out frequently, especially at night.

TOLLS

There are tolls on the M1 and M5.

DRIVING continued

CAR RENTAL

The leading rental firms have offices at airports and railroad stations. Hertz offers discounted rates for AAA members (see page 15). For reservations:

	UNITED STATES	HUNGARY
Alamo	(800) 327-9633	1 477 1080 (Europcar)
Avis	(800) 331-2112	1 318 4158
Budget	(800) 527-0700	1 214 0420
Hertz	(800) 654-3080	1 296 0998

FUEL

Fuel *(benzin)* is sold in liters: unleaded *(ólommentes benzine)* is graded 91, 95 and 98 octane. Diesel can be bought along major routes and in cities. Many gas stations *(benzinkút)* are self-service, although you may not be able to use a credit card in smaller stations. A map of rural gas stations is available from MAK (see below).

AAA AFFILIATED MOTORING CLUB

Magyar Autóklub (MAK)
H-1024 Budapest, Rómer Flóris utca 4/a
☎ 1 345 1800, fax 1 345 1801

If you break down while driving, phone ☎ 1 212 2821 (MAK breakdown service). Not all automobile clubs offer full services to AAA members.

BREAKDOWNS AND ACCIDENTS

If you have an accident, phone ☎ 107 for police, and ask for an interpreter at the scene. You are legally required to report personal injury. Most car rental firms provide their own free rescue service; if your car is rented, follow the instructions given in the documentation. Use of a car repair service other than those authorized by your rental company may violate your agreement. Vehicles with damaged bodywork may only leave the country with an official certificate. If you have insurance queries after an accident, call the Hungarian Insurance Company (Hungária Biztosító Rt.), 1113 Budapest, Hamzsabégi út 60; ☎ 1 466 5023.

OTHER INFORMATION

The minimum age for driving a car is 18 (may be higher for some car rental firms).

An International Driving Permit (IDP) is recommended; some rental firms require them, and they can speed up formalities if you are involved in an accident. A Green Card (international motor insurance certificate) is needed if you are driving a private car; see page 16 for more information.

Dimmed headlights must be used at all times outside built-up areas.

USEFUL WORDS AND PHRASES

Hungarian, called Magyar by its speakers, is a difficult language, related to Finnish and Estonian. German is traditionally the second language, but English is gradually replacing it, especially among the younger generation.

Apart from a few international words *(posta, telefon)*, Hungarian offers few clues as to its meaning. However, pronunciation is regular – letters consistently stand for the same sounds.

By learning basic words, street signs, notices and labels will begin to make sense.

Do you speak English?	*Beszél angolul?*
What is your name?	*Hogy hívnak?*
excuse me	*elnézést*
hello	*jó napot kivanok*
goodbye	*viszontlátásra*
yes/no	*igen/nem*
how much?	*mennyibe kerul?*
I am American	*Amerikai vagyok*
I don't understand	*nem értem*
non-smoking	*nem domanyzo*
open	*nyitva*
closed	*zárva*
please	*kérem*
thank you	*köszönöm*
ticket	*jegy*
(one-way/round trip)	*(egyiranyu/retur)*
where is...?	*hol van...?*
the hotel	***szálloda***
you're welcome	*szívesen*
Where is the restroom?	*Hol a mosdó?*
breakfast	*reggeli*
reservation	*foglalás*
key	*kulcs*
room	*szoba*
shower	*zuhany*
the restaurant	***étterem/vendeglo/ etkezde***
beef	*marha*
beer	*sör*
bread	*kenyer*
the check	*szamla*
coffee/tea	*kávé/tea*
dessert	*édesség*
fish	*hal*
fruit	*gyümölcs*
ice cream	*fagylalt*
meat	*hús*
pork	*sertés*
potato	*burgonya*
poultry	*csirke*
starter	*elöételek*
vegetable	*zöldség*
wine	*bor*

PRE-TRIP ESSENTIALS...

WHAT YOU NEED

ESSENTIAL FOR TRAVELERS

● Required ● Recommended ○ Not required

Passport	●
Visa	○
Travel, medical insurance	●
Round-trip or onward airline ticket	○
Local currency	●
Traveler's checks	●
Credit cards	●
First-aid kit and medicines	●
Inoculations	○

ESSENTIAL FOR DRIVERS*

Driver's license	●
International Driving Permit	●
Car insurance (for nonrental cars)	●
Car registration (for nonrental cars)	●

*see also DRIVING section

IMPORTANT ADDRESSES

Irish Tourist Board
345 Park Avenue, New York, NY 10154
☎ (800) 223-6470, fax (212) 371-9052

Bord Fáilte – Irish Tourist Board
Baggot Street Bridge, Dublin 2, Republic of Ireland
☎ 1850 230 330, fax 01 602 4100
www.ireland.travel.ie

American Embassy (Republic of Ireland)
42 Elgin Road, Ballsbridge
Dublin 4, Republic of Ireland
☎ 01 668 8777, fax 01 668 9946
American Citizens Services: Mon.–Fri. 9–3

Northern Ireland Tourist Board
551 Fifth Avenue, Suite 701, New York, NY 10176
☎ (212) 922-0101, fax (212) 922-0099

Northern Ireland Tourist Board
59 North Street, Belfast BT1 1NB, County Antrim, Northern Ireland
☎ 028 9023 1221, fax 028 9024 0960
www.discovernorthernireland.com

American Consulate (Northern Ireland)
Queen's House, 14 Queen Street
Belfast BT1 6EQ, Northern Ireland
☎ 028 9032 8239; fax 028 9024 8482
Open Mon.–Fri. 8:30–5

COUNTRY ESSENTIALS...

CUSTOMS

YES

Duty-free limits on goods brought in from non-European Union countries: 200 cigarettes or 50 cigarillos/cigars or 250 g. tobacco; 2 L. wine; 1 L. alcohol over 22% volume or 2 L. alcohol under 22% volume; 50 ml. perfume; 250 ml. toilet water; plus any other duty-free goods (including gifts) to the value of £142. There is no limit on the importation of tax-paid goods purchased within the European Union, provided they are for your own personal use. There are no currency regulations.

NO

No unlicensed drugs, weapons, ammunition, obscene material, pets or other animals, counterfeit money or copied goods, meat or poultry.

For customs limits for returning U.S. citizens see page 16.

MONEY

The Republic of Ireland's currency is the Irish pound or punt (£), which is divided into 100 pence (p). The denominations of pound bills are 5, 10, 20 and 50. There are coins of 1, 2, 5, 10, 20 and 50p and £1. Credit cards are accepted in hotels, large stores and upscale restaurants; check first in small or rural establishments. Exchange dollars or traveler's checks at a bank, exchange office, post office or a large hotel. On Jan.1, 1999, the euro became the official currency of the Republic of Ireland and the pound became a denomination of the euro. Euro bills and coins were introduced on Jan. 1, 2002. Both euro bills and coins and the old national currency will be in use during a transitional period, after which time the euro will be the only currency accepted. Exchange rate at press time: $1 = £0.88. For information about currency in Northern Ireland, see page 470.

TIPS AND GRATUITIES

Restaurants (if service is not included)	10–15%
Cafés/bars (if service is not included)	10%
Taxis	10%
Porters	50p per bag
Hairdressers	50p–£1
Tour guides	50p–£1

COMMUNICATIONS

POST OFFICES

Buy stamps at post offices, newsstands/tobacconists, large grocery stores and hotels.

Hours for out-of-town post offices may vary. Mailboxes are green in the Republic of Ireland and red in Northern Ireland.

TELEPHONES

Public phone booths are blue and cream, and take cash (10p, 20p, 50p or £1 coins) or prepaid phone cards bought from newsstands, post offices and local stores. Some city phones take credit cards.

For calls made to or from Northern Ireland, follow the instructions for Britain on page 471.

Phoning inside Ireland
All Irish phone numbers in this book include the area code; dial the number listed.

To call the operator dial 10.

Phoning the Republic of Ireland from abroad
The country code for the Republic of Ireland is 353. Note that Irish numbers in this book do not include the country code; you will need to prefix this if you are phoning from another country. To phone Ireland from the United States or Canada, omit the first zero from the Irish number, and add the prefix 011 353. (Note that the number of digits in Irish area codes varies.)
Example: 01 122 3344 becomes 011 353 1 122 3344.

Phoning from Ireland
To phone the United States or Canada from Ireland, prefix the area code and number with 001.
Example: (111) 222-3333 becomes 001 111 222-3333.

To call international information dial 11818.

EMERGENCY TELEPHONE NUMBERS

Police *(gardaí)*	999
Fire Service	999
Ambulance	999

Emergency calls are free from phone booths.

HOURS OF OPERATION

- Stores Mon.–Sat.
- Museums/monuments
- Offices Mon.–Fri.
- Pharmacies Mon.–Sat.
- Banks Mon.–Fri.
- Post offices Mon.–Sat.

7 8 9 10 11 12 1 2 3 4 5 6 7

Hours in chart refer to the Republic of Ireland; hours for Northern Ireland may differ slightly.

Some stores stay open until 8 or 9 on Thursday or Friday. In smaller towns and rural areas stores close in the afternoon on one day of the week. Pharmacies may close earlier on Saturday.

Some banks in small towns close 12:30–1:30. Banks open until 5 p.m. one day a week (Thursdays in Dublin). Nearly all banks are closed on Saturday.

Post offices close for lunch (1–2:15) and open until 5 p.m. on Saturdays.

Hours for museums and tourist sights vary; always check with the local tourist office. Many places close from October to March, although most major sights are open all year.

NATIONAL HOLIDAYS

Banks, businesses and most stores close on these days. Museums also may have restricted hours.

Jan. 1	**New Year's Day**
Mar. 17	**St. Patrick's Day**
***Mar./Apr.**	**Good Friday**
Mar./Apr.	**Easter Monday**
1st Mon. in May	**May Holiday**
Last Mon. in May	**Spring Bank Holiday (NI only)**
1st Mon. in Jun.	**June Holiday**
Jul. 11	**Orangeman's Day (NI only)**
1st Mon. in Aug.	**August Holiday**
Last Mon. in Aug.	**Summer Bank Holiday (NI only)**
Last Mon. in Oct.	**October Holiday**
Dec. 25	**Christmas Day**
Dec. 26	**St. Stephen's Day**

* Good Friday, though not officially a public holiday, is observed in most of Ireland.

PHOTOGRAPHY

Irish skies are unpredictable, and the light frequently poor, so you may need fast film. However, the landscapes are justifiably a photographer's favorite, so you may wish to bring a tripod; the rugged nature of the island also lends itself to black and white work. Film and camera batteries are widely available in many stores and drugstores.

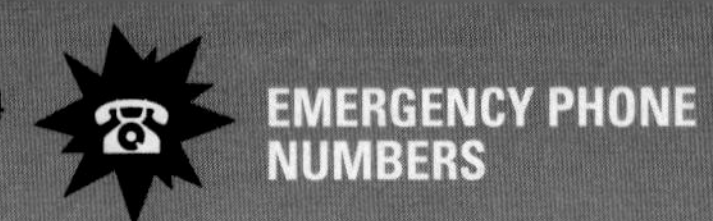

EMERGENCY PHONE NUMBERS

POLICE 999 (Gardaí)

HEALTH

MEDICAL INSURANCE
Private medical insurance is recommended. U.S. and Canadian visitors can receive treatment in emergency rooms, but are charged if admitted to a hospital bed. A general practitioner also will charge for services.

DENTAL SERVICES
Dentists charge for treatment. Dental work is expensive, so check to see if it is covered by your medical insurance. Dentists are listed in the yellow pages, or ask at your embassy, hotel or at a tourist office.

SUN ADVICE
The sunniest months are May and June, with 5–6½ hours of sun a day (the extreme southwest is the sunniest). July and August are the warmest. During these months you should take sensible precautions against the sun.

DRUGS
Pharmacies (also called chemists) sell a range of prescription and non-prescription medicines. If you need medicine outside regular hours, information about the nearest 24-hour facility should be posted on the door of all pharmacies.

SAFE WATER
Tap water is safe to drink throughout Ireland. If, however, you prefer mineral water you will find it widely available.

RESTROOMS

Identify restrooms by *Fir* (men) and *Mná* (women). A small charge is levied in restrooms at some railroad stations, but most other facilities are free. The standards of hygiene are moderate. You will be welcomed into any local pub if you need to use their facilities, but stop for a drink and a talk while you are there.

ELECTRICITY

Ireland has a 230-volt power supply. Electrical sockets either take plugs with two round pins or three square pins; American appliances will need a plug adapter and will require a transformer if they do not have a dual-voltage facility.

NATIONAL TRANSPORTATION

TRAIN
Ireland's rail company is Iarnród Éireann (IÉ). Trains are the fastest way of covering long distances and are generally reliable and comfortable, but the network is limited and one-way tickets cost almost as much as round-trip tickets. Midweek is less expensive than weekends, and there are many special offers on fares. For information: ☎ 01 836 6222.

BUS
Bus Éireann operates a network of express bus routes serving most of the country (some run summer only). For information: ☎ 01 836 6111.

FERRY
A car ferry runs between Ballyhack (County Wexford) and Passage East (County Waterford); ☎ 051 382 480, saving 60 miles on the road trip. Another serves Killimer (County Clare) and Tarbert (County Kerry); ☎ 065 905 3124. There also are ferries to several islands; ask for details at a local tourist office. There are regular ferries from Belfast, Larne, Dublin, Dun Laoghaire, Cork and Rosslare to ports on the mainland of Britain.

DRIVING

DRIVE ON THE LEFT

SPEED LIMITS
Traffic police can impose on-the-spot fines.

Limited-access highways (motorways)
112 k.p.h. (70 m.p.h.)

Main roads
100 k.p.h. (62 m.p.h.)

Urban areas
48/50 k.p.h. (29/30 m.p.h.)

SEAT BELTS
Must be worn in front and back seats at all times.

BLOOD ALCOHOL
The legal blood alcohol limit is 0.08%. Random breath tests on drivers are carried out frequently, especially late at night, and the penalties for offenders are severe.

DRIVING continued

TOLLS

Tolls are charged at two locations in the Dublin area: the M50 Ring Road between the N4 and N3 interchanges, and on the R131 East Link Bridge. There are no tolls on other highway or national routes.

CAR RENTAL

The leading rental firms have offices at airports, railroad stations and large ferry terminals. Hertz offers discounted rates for AAA members (see page 15).
For reservations:

	UNITED STATES	REPUBLIC OF IRELAND
Alamo	(800) 327-9633	01 844 4086
Avis	(800) 331-2112	01 605 7501
Budget	(800) 527-0700	01 844 5150
Hertz	(800) 654-3080	01 844 5466

FUEL

Gas is unleaded and sold in liters; diesel also is easily purchased. Gas stations in villages stay open until 8 or 9 p.m. and usually open after Mass on Sunday.

AAA AFFILIATED MOTORING CLUB

The Automobile Association Ireland (AA Ireland) 23 Suffolk Street, Dublin 2
☎ 01 617 9999, fax 01 617 9400
If you break down while driving, phone ☎ 1800 66 77 88 (AAI breakdown service).
Not all automobile clubs offer full services to AAA members.
Northern Ireland: see BRITAIN section (page 473).

BREAKDOWNS AND ACCIDENTS

There are 24-hour emergency phones at regular intervals on highways: ☎ 999 if involved in an accident.
Most car rental firms provide their own free rescue service; if your car is rented, follow the instructions given in the documentation. Use of a car repair service other than those authorized by your rental company may violate your agreement.

OTHER INFORMATION

The minimum age for driving a car is 17 (may be higher for some car rental firms).

An International Driving Permit (IDP) is recommended; some rental firms require it, and it can speed up formalities if you are involved in an accident.

A Green Card (international motor insurance certificate) is recommended if you are driving a private car; see page 16 for more information.

In the Republic of Ireland road signs are marked in kilometers, but you may still come across old direction signs in miles.

In some urban areas, parking is limited to certain times and periods. Where this is signed you must buy a disk from a newsstand and display it on the dashboard of your car.

USEFUL WORDS AND PHRASES

Although the Republic of Ireland is officially bilingual, and the Irish language (Gaelic or *Gaeilge*) is learned by all schoolchildren, English is more commonly spoken. There are around 80,000 native speakers of Irish, making it Europe's least widespread official language.

Because it often reflects expressions in Gaelic, Irish English is famed for its picturesque turns of phrase, much more poetic than American or British English.

The Gaelic language is enjoying a revival: radio, television and the Internet all stir up interest in the old language. There are Gaelic-speaking clubs as far away as the U.S. West Coast.

You are not likely to pick up very much Irish on a brief trip to Ireland; it is not related to English, and to an English speaker the spelling does not appear to reflect the pronunciation.

Following are pronunciations of words you may come across:

Bord Fáilte (Irish Tourist Board)	bord fawlty
Ceilidh (traditional dance night)	kaylee
Gaeilge (the Irish language)	gale-geh
Gaeltacht (Irish-speaking country)	gale-tackt
Garda (policeman)	gawrdah
Fleadh (traditional music evening)	flah
Taoiseach (prime minister)	teeschock

Numbers:

1	*a haon*	a hay-on
2	*a dó*	a doe
3	*a trí*	a tree
4	*a ceathair*	a ca-hir
5	*a cuíg*	a koo-ig
6	*a sé*	a shay
7	*a seacht*	a shocked
8	*a hocht*	a huct
9	*a naoi*	a neigh
10	*a deich*	a de

Other words:

good day	*lá maith*	law mah
goodbye	*slán*	slawn
goodnight	*oíche mhaith*	ee-ha vah
How are you?	*Conas taio?*	co-nus tee?
please	*más é do thoil é*	maws eh duh hull eh
thanks	*gura maith agat*	gurrah mah a-gut
pub	*tábhairne*	taw-er nay
water	*uisce*	ishkek
whiskey	*fuisci*	fwishgee
yes	*sea*	shah

PRE-TRIP ESSENTIALS...

WHAT YOU NEED

ESSENTIAL FOR TRAVELERS

● Required ● Recommended ● Not required

Passport	●
Visa	●
Travel, medical insurance	●
Round-trip or onward airline ticket	●
Local currency	●
Traveler's checks	●
Credit cards	●
First-aid kit and medicines	●
Health innoculations	●

ESSENTIAL FOR DRIVERS*

Driver's license	●
International Driving Permit	●
Car insurance (for private cars)	●
Car registration (for private cars)	●

*see also DRIVING section

IMPORTANT ADDRESSES

Italian Government Travel Office
630 Fifth Avenue
Suite 1565
New York, NY 10111
☎ (212) 245-5095 or (212) 245-4822
Fax (212) 586-9249
www.italiantourism.com

Ente Nazionale Italiano per il Turismo (Italian State Tourist Board)
Via Marghera 2
00185 Rome, Italy
☎ 06 49711
Fax 06 446 3379
www.enit.it

American Embassy
Via Vittorio Veneto 119a
00187 Rome, Italy
☎ 06 46741
Fax 06 488 2672
Open Mon.– Fri. 8:30–5:30

COUNTRY ESSENTIALS...

CUSTOMS

YES

Goods brought into Italy from non-European Union countries limited to: 200 cigarettes or 100 cigarillos or 50 cigars or 250 g. tobacco; 2 L wine; 1 L. alcohol over 22% volume or 2 L. alcohol under 22% volume; 50 ml. perfume; 250 ml. toilet water; plus any other duty-free goods (including gifts) to the value of L30,000. There is no limit on the importation of tax-paid goods purchased within the European Union, provided they are for your own personal use. Foreign or local currency in excess of L20,000,000 must be declared on arrival.

NO

No unlicensed drugs, weapons, ammunition, obscene material, pets or other animals, counterfeit money or copied goods, meat or poultry.

For customs limits for returning U.S. citizens see page 16.

MONEY

Italy's currency is the lira (L or Lit; plural lire). The denominations of lira bills are 1,000, 2,000, 5,000, 10,000, 20,000, 50,000, 100,000 and 500,000. There are coins of 50, 100, 200, 500 and L1,000. Exchange dollars or traveler's checks *(assegni touristici)* at a bank *(banca)* or exchange office *(ufficio di cambio)*. Hotels may exchange traveler's checks, but stores do not. ATMs *(sportello automatico)* are fairly common and accept major credit cards. On Jan. 1, 1999, the euro became the official currency and the Italian lira a denomination of the euro. Euro bills and coins were introduced on Jan. 1, 2002. Both euro bills and coins and the old national currency will be in use during a transitional period, after which the euro will be the only currency accepted. Exchange rate at press time: $1 = L2,165

TIPS AND GRATUITIES

Restaurants (service usually included but add L1,000 per person)	
Cafés/bars	L200
Taxis	15%
Porters	L2,000
Chambermaids	L3,000 weekly
Restrooms	L100 minimum
Cloakroom attendants	L1,000

COMMUNICATIONS

POST OFFICES

Buy stamps *(francobolli)* at a post office *(ufficio postale)* or at a tobacconist *(tabaccaio)*. Mailboxes (red) often have two slots, one for local mail *(per la città)*, the other for out-of-town mail *(tutte le altre destinazioni)*. Mail sent to and from Italy can take up to 3 weeks; to speed delivery send it express *(espresso)* or recorded *(raccomandata)*.

TELEPHONES

Pay phones are usually found in bars and other public places. Coin-operated phones take L100, L200 and L500 coins (minimum charge L200). Prepaid cards *(carta telefonica)* for card-operated phones are available in values of L5,000, L10,000 and L15,000 from tobacconists, bars, post offices, newsstands, railroad stations and dispensers showing a Telecom Italia (TI) logo. When making international calls use a prepaid card, tear the corner off before using it. Calls from hotel rooms always incur a surcharge.

Phoning inside Italy
All telephone numbers in Italy include an area code that must always be dialed.

To call the operator dial 10.

Phoning Italy from abroad
The country code for Italy is 39. Note that Italian numbers in this book do not include the country code; you will need to prefix this number if you are phoning from another country. To call Italy from the United States or Canada dial the prefix 011 39. Include the first zero of the regional code. There is no standard number of digits in Italian numbers. Example: 01 122 3344 becomes 011 39 01 122 3344.

Phoning from Italy
To phone the United States or Canada from Italy, prefix the area code and number with 001. Example: (111) 222-3333 becomes 001 111 222-3333.

To call international information dial 170.

EMERGENCY TELEPHONE NUMBERS

Police *(policia)*	113 (local), 112 (national)
Fire service *(pompieri)*	115
Ambulance *(ambulanza)*	118

Emergency calls are free from phone booths.

HOURS OF OPERATION

- Stores Mon.–Sat.
- Offices Mon.–Fri.
- Banks Mon.–Fri.
- Post offices Mon.–Fri.
- Museums/monuments
- Architectural sites
- Churches/pharmacies

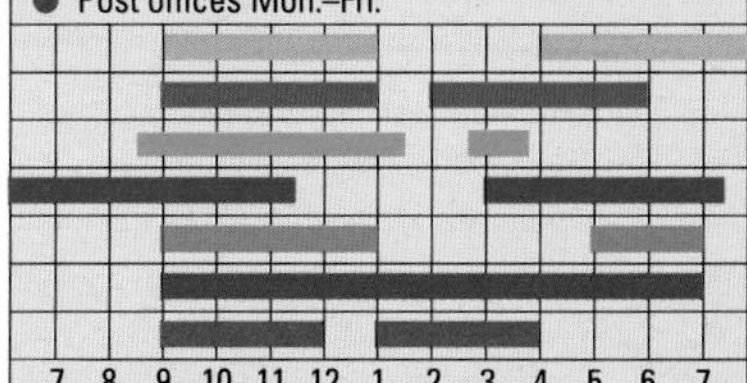

Department stores, some grocery stores and stores in tourist areas may not close at lunchtime, and sometimes stay open until later in the evening. Some stores close on Monday morning and may close on Saturday afternoon in summer; most stores close on Sunday.

Some banks close at 2 and do not reopen later in the afternoon.

Post office times may vary slightly; some may close at 2 p.m. and not reopen later in the afternoon and they may be open Saturday 8:30–noon.

Many museums are open in the afternoon (usually 5–7), others are open all day, and a few stay open late into the evening. Many museums close early on Sunday (around 1), and most are closed Monday.

NATIONAL HOLIDAYS

Banks, businesses, and most stores and museums close on these days. Most cities, towns and villages celebrate their patron saint's day, but generally most establishments remain open.

Jan. 1	**New Year's Day**
Jan. 6	**Epiphany**
Mar./Apr.	**Easter Monday**
Apr. 25	**Liberation Day 1945**
May 1	**Labor Day**
Aug. 15	**Assumption of the Virgin**
Nov. 1	**All Saints' Day**
Dec. 8	**Immaculate Conception**
Dec. 25	**Christmas Day**
Dec. 26	**St. Stephen's Day**

PHOTOGRAPHY

The light in Italy is usually very good, so you will probably be using film with a low ASA rating. Avoid taking shots around noon, when the shadows are harsh. Photography is banned in most museums and churches, but you may be allowed to shoot without a flash. Film *(pellicola)* and developing *(sviluppo)* are expensive, especially near popular tourist sights.

EMERGENCY PHONE NUMBERS

POLICE (*Policia*) 113 (local) 112 (national)

HEALTH

MEDICAL INSURANCE
Private medical insurance is strongly recommended. Visitors from non-European Union countries can receive treatment in a hospital accident and emergency room, but you will be charged if you are admitted to a bed. A general practitioner *(medico)* can deal with less urgent cases, but also will charge.

DENTAL SERVICES
Emergency dental treatment is available from English-speaking dentists listed in the yellow pages *(pagine gialle)*. A fee will be charged, so check that you are covered for treatment on your private medical insurance.

SUN ADVICE
In summer, particularly in July and August, it can be oppressively hot and humid in cities. On sunny days cover head and shoulders and use a sunscreen. Cathedrals and other stone buildings can be refreshingly cool. Take frequent breaks in the shade and drink plenty of fluids.

DRUGS
A pharmacy *(farmacia)* displays a green cross symbol and has staff who can provide prescription medicines and offer advice on minor ailments. Information about the address of the nearest 24-hour facility is normally posted at every pharmacy.

SAFE WATER
In isolated rural areas it is not advisable to drink tap water. However, across most of the country tap water is perfectly safe, although most Italians prefer to drink bottled mineral water *(acqua minerale)*, which is inexpensive and widely available.

RESTROOMS

Finding a restroom *(gabinetto/bagno/toletta)* can be difficult away from airports, rail and bus stations, highway service areas and museums. Leave a small tip (about L100) for the attendant. If using the facilities in a bar you will be expected to buy a drink. Some bars have separate restrooms for men *(signori)* and women *(signore)*.

ELECTRICITY

Italy has a 220-volt power supply (in some areas, 125 volts). Electrical sockets take plugs with two round pins or sometimes three pins in a vertical row. American appliances will need a plug adapter and will require a transformer if they do not have a dual-voltage facility.

NATIONAL TRANSPORTATION

TRAIN *(treno)*
Italian State Railways (*Ferrovie dello Stato*, or FS) provide an efficient range of services. Regionale, Diretto and Espresso trains are slow for long journeys; InterCity trains, which do not make stops at each station *(stazione)*, cost more but are faster; the Pendolino is the fastest and most expensive.

BUS *(autobus)*
There is no national bus company, but each major city has its own company for short-, medium- and some long-distance bus travel. International Eurolines buses run from the main Italian cities: ☎ 055 357 110.

FERRY *(tragheto)*
Genoa and Naples are the main Mediterranean ports, with regular services to Sicily and Sardinia. Naples also has services to Capri and other islands. Many services are reduced off-season, and some are cut altogether. Reserve well in advance for car ferries.

DRIVING

DRIVE ON THE RIGHT

SPEED LIMITS
Police can demand up to a quarter of an imposed fine to be paid on the spot.

Limited-access highways *(autostrada)*
130 k.p.h. (80 m.p.h.)

Main roads
90–110 k.p.h. (55–68 m.p.h.)

Urban areas
50 k.p.h. (31 m.p.h.)

SEAT BELTS
Must be worn in front and back seats at all times.

BLOOD ALCOHOL
The legal blood alcohol limit is 0.08%. Random breath tests are carried out frequently, especially late at night.

DRIVING continued

TOLLS
You will be issued a ticket on entering nearly every limited-access highway *(autostrada)*: pay on leaving. You can buy a prepaid card *(viacard)* at tollbooths, service areas, tourist offices and tobacconists.

CAR RENTAL
The leading rental firms have offices at airports, railroad stations and ferry terminals. Hertz offers discounted rates for AAA members. Also see page 15 for general information about renting a car in Europe. For reservations:

	UNITED STATES	ITALY
Avis	(800) 331-2112	02 715 123
Budget	(800) 527-0700	06 2293 5620
Dollar	(800) 252-897	055 318 609
Hertz	(800) 654-3080	055 307 370

FUEL
Gas *(benzina)* is unleaded *(senza piombo)* and sold in liters. Outside urban areas, stations open daily 7–12:30 and 3–7:30. Highway services are open 24 hours. Credit cards are not widely accepted away from highways.

AAA AFFILIATED MOTORING CLUB
Automobile Club D'Italia (ACI),
Via Marsala 8, 00185 Rome
☎ 06 49 981, fax 06 445 2702
If you break down while driving, phone ☎ 803000 and enter 1 (ACI breakdown service).
Not all automobile clubs offer full services to AAA members.

BREAKDOWNS AND ACCIDENTS
There are emergency phones at regular intervals on all highways. If you are involved in an accident, phone ☎ 113 for emergency medical help and police.
Most car rental firms provide their own free rescue service; if your car is rented, follow the instructions given in the documentation. Use of a car repair service other than those authorized by your rental company may violate your agreement.

OTHER INFORMATION
The minimum age for driving a car is 18 (may be higher for some car rental firms).

An International Driving Permit (IDP) is recommended; some rental firms require it, and it can speed up formalities if you are involved in an accident. A Green Card (international motor insurance certificate) is recommended if you are driving a private car; see page 16 for more information.

Dimmed headlights are required by law when passing through tunnels, even if they are well lit.

USEFUL WORDS AND PHRASES

Italian pronunciation is consistent with spelling, and vowels are always pronounced. The letter *h* is always silent, but can modify the sound of letters *c* and *g*. As a general rule, accentuate the next-to-last syllable.

c is hard before a, o, u, h	*medico; Chianti*
c is soft before i or e	*ciao* [chow]
g is hard before a, o, u, h	*Gucci, Lamborghini*
g is soft before i or e	*gelati* [jel-ah-tee]
gl as in Amelia	*figlia* [fee-lyah]
gn as in union	*gnocchi* [nyee-ok-kee]
sc before i or e is soft	*prosciutto* [pro-shoot-toh]

Where two consonants appear together, each belongs to a different syllable.

Do you speak English?	*Parla inglese?*
excuse me	*mi scusi*
goodbye	*arrivederci*
hello	*buongiorno*
How much is...?	*Quanto costa...?*
I am American	*sono Americano/-a*
I'd like...	*vorrei...*
I don't understand	*non capisco*
non-smoking	*per non fumatori*
okay	*va bene*
open/closed	*aperto/chiuso*
please/thank you	*per favore/grazie*
ticket (one-way/round trip)	*biglietto (andata sola/andata ritorno)*
where is...?	*dov'è...?*
yes/no	*sì/no*
you're welcome	*prego*
the hotel	***l'albergo***
breakfast	*prima colazione*
I have a reservation	*ho prenotato*
key	*una chiave*
for one/two nights	*per una/due notte/-i*
one/two people	*una/due persona/-e*
room	*una camera*
shower	*una doccia*
with en-suite bathroom	*con bagno privato*
the restaurant	***il ristorante***
starter	*l'antipasto*
entrée	*il secondo*
beef	*il manzo*
bread	*il pane*
chicken	*il pollo*
coffee	*il caffè*
dish of the day	*il piatto del giorno*
seafood	*i frutti di mare*
fish	*il pesce*
lamb	*l'agnello*
pork	*il maiale*
wine	*il vino*
dessert	*il dolce*
the check	*il conto*

PRE-TRIP ESSENTIALS...

WHAT YOU NEED

ESSENTIAL FOR TRAVELERS

● Required ● Recommended ● Not required

Passport	●
Visa	● (Not required)
Travel, medical insurance	●
Round-trip or onward airline ticket	● (Not required)
Local currency	●
Traveler's checks	●
Credit cards	●
First-aid kit and medicines	●
Inoculations	● (Not required)

ESSENTIAL FOR DRIVERS*

Driver's license	●
International Driving Permit	●
Car insurance (for nonrental cars)	●
Car registration (for nonrental cars)	●

*see also DRIVING section

IMPORTANT ADDRESSES

Luxembourg National Tourist Office
17 Beekman Place
New York, NY 10022
☎ (212) 935-8888
Fax (212) 935-5896
www.visitluxembourg.com

Office National du Tourisme
(Luxembourg National Tourist Office)
Boîte Postale. 1001
L-1010 Luxembourg
☎ 42 82 82-1
Fax 42 82 82-38
www.etat.lu/tourism

American Embassy
Chancellerie 22, boulevard Emmanuel Servais
L-2535 Luxembourg
☎ 46 01 23
Fax 46 14 01
Inquiries: Mon.–Tue. and Thu.–Fri. 8:30–11:30

COUNTRY ESSENTIALS...

CUSTOMS

YES

Duty-free limits on goods brought in from non-European Union countries:
200 cigarettes or 100 cigarillos or 50 cigars or 250 g. tobacco; 2L. wine; 1 L. alcohol over 22% volume or 2 L. alcohol under 22% volume; 50 ml. perfume; 250 ml. toilet water; plus any other duty-free goods (including gifts) to the value of 7,300F. There is no limit on the importation of tax-paid goods purchased within the European Union, provided they are for your own personal use. There are no currency regulations for francs or euros, but there is a limit of $10,000 in cash or traveler's checks entering or leaving Luxembourg.

NO

No unlicensed drugs, weapons, ammunition, obscene material, pets or other animals, counterfeit money or copied goods, meat or poultry.

For customs limits for returning U.S. citizens see page 16.

MONEY

Luxembourg's currency is the franc (F or Flux), which is divided into 100 centimes. The denominations of franc bills are 100, 500, 1,000, 5,000 and 10,000. There are coins of 50 centimes (rarely seen) and 1, 5, 20 and 50F. Belgian francs have the same value and can be used in Luxembourg, but the Luxembourg franc cannot be used in Belgium. Exchange dollars and traveler's checks *(cheques de voyage)* at a bank *(banque)* or an exchange office *(bureau de change)*. On Jan. 1, 1999, the euro became the official currency of Luxembourg and the franc became a denomination of the euro. Euro bills and coins were introduced on Jan. 1, 2002. Both euro bills and coins and the old national currency will be in use during a transitional period, after which time the euro will be the only currency accepted. Exchange rate at press time: $1 = 45F

TIPS AND GRATUITIES

Restaurants, cafés and bars (service usually included)	round up to nearest 50 or 100F
Taxis	100–200F
Porters, chambermaids	50–100F
Hairdressers	100F
Restroom attendants	10F
Cloakroom attendants	20F per coat

TIME ZONES

LUXEMBOURG	NEW YORK	CHICAGO	DENVER	SAN FRANCISCO
12:00 noon	6 hours behind Luxembourg	7 hours behind Luxembourg	8 hours behind Luxembourg	9 hours behind Luxembourg

COMMUNICATIONS

POST OFFICES

Buy stamps *(timbres-poste)* at a post office *(poste)*, newsstand/tobacconist *(tabac-journaux)*, or at a bookstore. Mailboxes are small, bright and yellow, and are attached to walls and post offices. Hours for out-of-town post offices may vary.

TELEPHONES

Finding a public telephone *(cabine téléphonique)* is easy. Phone booths usually have pictorial instructions, with French and German text. You can use most denominations of coins, or buy a prepaid phone card *(télécarte)* from a post office or railroad station. Public phones in restaurants are more expensive than those in post offices or on the street.

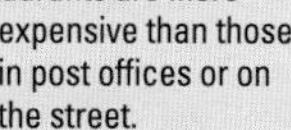

Phoning inside Luxembourg
There are no area codes in Luxembourg; dial the number that is listed.

To call the operator dial 017.

Phoning Luxembourg from abroad
The country code for Luxembourg is 352. Note that Luxembourg numbers in this book do not include the country code; you will need to prefix this number if you are phoning from another country. To phone Luxembourg from the United States or Canada, add the prefix 011 352.
Example: 11 22 33 becomes 011 352 11 22 33.

Phoning from Luxembourg
To phone the United States or Canada from Luxembourg, prefix the area code and number with 001.
Example: (111) 222-3333 becomes 001 111 222-3333.

EMERGENCY TELEPHONE NUMBERS

Police *(police)*	113
Fire *(pompiers)*	112
Ambulance *(ambulance)*	112

Emergency calls are free from phone booths.

HOURS OF OPERATION

- Stores Tue.–Sat.
- Pharmacies Tue.–Sat.
- Offices Mon.–Fri.
- Banks Mon.–Fri.
- Post offices Mon.–Fri.

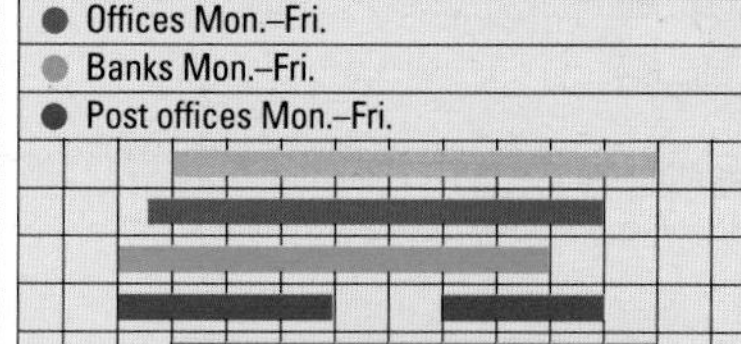

Many stores and pharmacies do not open until 1 or 2 on Monday afternoon, and most are closed on Sunday. Many establishments have long lunch breaks.

Provincial post offices and banks may have shorter hours, but some city post offices and banks stay open into the evening.

Opening times for museums and monuments vary, and they are frequently closed on Monday or Tuesday – check with the local tourist office.

NATIONAL HOLIDAYS

Banks, businesses and most stores close on these days.

Jan. 1	**New Year's Day**
Feb./Mar.	**Carnival Day**
Mar./Apr.	**Easter Monday**
May 1	**Labor Day**
May	**Ascension Day**
May/Jun.	**Pentecost Monday**
Jun. 23	**National Day**
Aug. 15	**Assumption of the Virgin**
Sep. 2	**Luxembourg City Fete**
Nov. 1	**All Saints' Day**
Dec. 25	**Christmas Day**
Dec. 26	**St. Stephen's Day**

PHOTOGRAPHY

Luxembourg enjoys a temperate climate, and the light is good. Check that photography is permitted before taking pictures in museums. Film and camera batteries are readily available from tourist stores, and rapid-developing services are widely available.

HEALTH

MEDICAL INSURANCE

Private medical insurance is recommended; U.S. and Canadian visitors can be treated in emergency rooms, but are charged if admitted to a hospital *(hôpital)*. Phone ☎ 112 for 24-hour information on hospitals and English-speaking doctors.

DENTAL SERVICES

A dentist *(dentiste)* will charge a fee for treatment, so check whether this is covered by your medical insurance. Emergency clinics are available in city hospitals. To find a dentist look in the yellow pages *(pages jaunes)* or ask at your hotel.

SUN ADVICE

You will not experience extremes of temperature in Luxembourg, but the sunshine during summer months can burn, so good sun protection is essential.

DRUGS

Prescription medicines and advice can be obtained from a pharmacy *(pharmacie)*, identified by a green cross. Information about the nearest 24-hour facility is posted at all pharmacies, or phone ☎ 112 for information.

SAFE WATER

Tap water is safe to drink, and bottled mineral water *(eau minérale)* is widely available.

RESTROOMS

Restrooms *(toilettes)* are usually clean, modern and easy to find. They may also be called *"WC"* (pronounced vay-say). Coin-operated facilities take 5F coins; those with an attendant usually charge 10F.

ELECTRICITY

Luxembourg has a 220-volt power supply. Electrical sockets take plugs with two round pins; American appliances will need a plug adapter and will require a transformer if they do not have a dual-voltage facility.

NATIONAL TRANSPORTATION

TRAIN *(train)*

The national rail company is Chemins de Fer Luxembourgeois (CFL). The network is limited, and because of the small size of the country most services run through the city of Luxembourg. Most CFL trains are comfortable, but standards can vary. Bus and train network cards are a good value and valid until 8 a.m. the following day. For information: ☎ 49 90 49 90.

BUS *(bus)*

Long-distance, CFL-operated buses complement the rail network (☎ 22 03 07 07). The Eurolines international bus network serves Brussels; from there you must catch a train to Luxembourg.

RIVER BOAT *(bateau-mouche)*

There are many excursions exploring Luxembourg's magnificent Moselle river, which stretches the entire eastern length of the country. For details, contact the regional tourist office: Entente des Communes et des Syndicats d'Initiative de la Moselle Luxembourgeoise, 32 route de Thionville, L-6701 Grevenmacher, ☎ 75 82 75.

DRIVING

DRIVE ON THE RIGHT

SPEED LIMITS

Police impose minor on-the-spot fines, but cannot collect them.

Limited access highways *(autoroutes)*
120 k.p.h. (74 m.p.h.)
minimum speed **40 k.p.h. (24 m.p.h.)**

Main roads
90 k.p.h. (55 m.p.h.)

Urban areas
50 k.p.h. (31 m.p.h.)

SEAT BELTS

Must be worn in front and back seats at all times. Children under 12 and/or under 59 inches in height are not permitted to sit in the front seat.

BLOOD ALCOHOL

The legal blood alcohol limit is 0.08%. Random breath tests on drivers are carried out frequently, especially late at night, and the penalties for offenders are severe.

DRIVING continued

TOLLS
There are no highway tolls in Luxembourg.

CAR RENTAL
The leading rental firms have offices at airports and train stations. Hertz offers discounted rates for AAA members (see page 15). For reservations:

	UNITED STATES	LUXEMBOURG
Alamo	(800) 327-9633	40 42 28 (Europcar)
Avis	(800) 331-2112	48 95 95
Budget	(800) 527-0700	44 19 38
Hertz	(800) 654-3080	43 46 45

FUEL
Many gas stations *(station de service)* are self-service, and 24-hour facilities are common. Stations on highways often have café facilities. The price of gas is fixed by the government, but self-service stations often offer discounts. Major credit cards are accepted.

AAA AFFILIATED MOTORING CLUB
Automobile Club du Grand-Duché de Luxembourg (ACL)
54 route de Longwy, L-8007 Bertrange,
☎ 45 00 45-1, fax 45 04 55
If you break down while driving, phone ☎ 45 00 45-1 (ACL 24-hour breakdown service).
Not all automobile clubs offer full services to AAA members.

BREAKDOWNS AND ACCIDENTS
There are emegency phones at regular intervals on highways. If you are involved in an accident, phone for emergency assistance (☎ 113 for police or ☎ 112 for fire or ambulance).
Most car rental firms provide their own free rescue service; if your car is rented, follow the instructions given in the documentation. Use of a car repair service other than those authorized by your rental company may violate your agreement.

OTHER INFORMATION
The minimum age for driving a car is 17 (may be higher for some car rental firms).

An International Driving Permit (IDP) is recommended; some rental firms require them, and they can speed up formalities if you are involved in an accident.

A Green Card (international motor insurance certificate) is recommended if you are driving a private car; see page 16 for more information.

USEFUL WORDS AND PHRASES

Because the Grand Duchy of Luxembourg is tucked between Belgium, France and Germany, Luxembourgers often slip unconsciously between different languages.

The official language (and, unofficially, the language of the elite) is French, but German is used for many situations. In addition to this, there is a third, everyday language: Lëtzebuergesch, a symbol of both national identity and Luxembourg's ability to assimilate other cultures.

The roots of Luxembourg's own language are Germanic, but it has evolved into a dialect that Germans no longer understand. The use of Lëtzebuergesch is primarily an oral tradition. It was only in 1984 that its spelling was decreed by law; up until then Luxembourgers spelled words more or less as they pleased.

French, German and Lëtzebuergesch are taught in schools, and English also is widely spoken, especially among the young and those working in the tourist trade. Don't expect Luxembourgers in rural areas to have mastered a fourth language, however!

Lëtzebuergesch is resilient enough to exist side-by-side with such widely spoken languages as French and German; but as the patois of a tiny, landlocked duchy it's evidently not very exportable. So if you have the opportunity to speak a word or two of this country's uniting language you'll raise a smile and a welcome.

good morning/hello	*moien*
goodbye	*addi*
thank you (very much)	*merci (villmols)*
sorry	*pardon*
excuse me	*entschellest*
please	*wanneschglift*
I don't understand	*ech verstin*

Food and drink

coffee	*Kaffi*
green bean soup	*Bou'neschlupp*
nettle soup	*Brennesselszopp*
potato soup	*Gromperenzopp*
potato dumplings	*Gromperekniddeln*
trout in Riesling sauce	*F'rell am Rèisleck*
pike in green liquor	*Hiecht mat Kraïderzooss*
crayfish	*Kriibsen*
blood sausage	*Trèipen*
pork in aspic	*Jhelli*
chicken in Riesling sauce	*Hong am Rèisleck*
tripe	*Kuddelfleck*
cheesecake	*Kéiskuch*
apple cake	*Äppelkuch*

For useful phrases in French, see page 489; for phrases in German see page 493.

NETHERLANDS – ESSENTIAL INFORMATION

PRE-TRIP ESSENTIALS…

WHAT YOU NEED

ESSENTIAL FOR TRAVELERS

● Required ● Recommended ● Not required

Passport	●
Visa	● (not required)
Travel, medical insurance	●
Round-trip or onward airline ticket	● (not required)
Local currency	●
Traveler's checks	●
Credit cards	●
First-aid kit and medicines	●
Inoculations	● (not required)

ESSENTIAL FOR DRIVERS*

Driver's license	●
International Driving Permit	●
Car insurance (for nonrental cars)	●
Car registration (for nonrental cars)	●

*see also DRIVING section

IMPORTANT ADDRESSES

Netherlands Board of Tourism
355 Lexington Avenue, 19th floor
New York, NY 10017
☎ (212) 370-7360; fax (212) 370-9507
www.goholland.com

Netherlands Board of Tourism
25 Adelaide Street East, Suite 710
Toronto, Ontario, M5C 1Y2
☎ (888) 246-5526; fax (416) 363-1470
www.holland.com

Nederlands Bureau voor Toerisme (Netherlands Board of Tourism)
Postbus 458, 2260 MG Leidschendam
The Netherlands
☎ 070 370 5705; fax 070 320 1654
www.holland.com

American Embassy
Lange Voorhout 102
2514 EJ The Hague, The Netherlands
☎ 070 310 9209; fax 070 361 4688
Hours: Mon.–Fri. 8:15–5; personal callers should phone for an appointment.

COUNTRY ESSENTIALS…

CUSTOMS

YES

Duty-free limits on goods brought in from non-European Union countries:
200 cigarettes or 100 cigarillos or 50 cigars or 250 g. tobacco; 2 L wine; 1 L alcohol over 22% volume or 2 L alcohol under 22% volume; 50 ml. perfume; 250 ml. toilet water; plus any other duty-free goods (including gifts) to the value of 225f. There is no limit on the importation of tax-paid goods purchased within the European Union, provided they are for your own personal use. There are no currency regulations.

NO

No unlicensed drugs, weapons, ammunition, obscene material, pets or other animals, counterfeit money or copied goods, meat or poultry.

For customs limits for returning U.S. citizens see page 16.

MONEY

The Dutch currency is the guilder, or florin (variously denoted as f, Dfl, fl, Hfl or Gld), which is divided into 100 cents (c). The denominations of guilder bills are 10, 25, 50, 100, 250 and 1,000. There are coins of 5, 10 and 25c and 1, 2.5 and 5f. You can change dollars and traveler's checks *(reischeques)* at a bank, an exchange office or the larger VVV (tourist office) bureaus. On Jan. 1, 1999, the euro became the official currency in the Netherlands and the guilder became a denomination of the euro. Euro bills and coins were introduced on Jan. 1, 2002. Both euro bills and coins and the old national currency will be in use during a transitional period, after which time the euro will be the only currency accepted.
Exchange rate at press time: $1 = 2.5f

TIPS AND GRATUITIES

Restaurants (service is always included)	change
Cafés/bars (service is always included)	change
Taxis (service is always included)	change
Porters	change
Hairdressers	change
Chambermaids	change
Restroom attendants	25c
Cloakroom attendants	none

TIME ZONES

THE HAGUE	NEW YORK	CHICAGO	DENVER	SAN FRANCISCO
12:00 noon	6 hours behind Netherlands	7 hours behind Netherlands	8 hours behind Netherlands	9 hours behind Netherlands

COMMUNICATIONS

POST OFFICES

Buy stamps *(postzegels)* at a post office *(postkantoor* or *PTT),* newsstand or souvenir shop. There are stamp vending machines in post offices, but if you are buying from a counter make sure you are in a line for stamps. Mailboxes have two slots; foreign mail should be dropped into the slot marked *Overige.* Hours for out-of-town post offices may vary.

TELEPHONES

You can use cash, credit cards and prepaid phone cards *(kaarttelephoon)* to make a call in the Netherlands. Coin-operated phones take 25c, 1f and 2.5f; cards can be bought from post offices, Primafoon (Dutch Telecom) shops, newsstands and tobacconists for 10, 25 and 50f. Calls also can be made from post offices and *Telehouse* booths, where you make your call and pay afterwards; most have the same hours as post offices, although some stay open later.

Phoning inside the Netherlands
All Dutch telephone numbers in this book include an area code; dial the number listed.

To call the operator dial 118.

Phoning the Netherlands from abroad
The country code for the Netherlands is 31. Note that Dutch numbers in this book do not include the country code; you will need to prefix this number if you are phoning from another country. To phone the Netherlands from the United States or Canada, omit the first zero from the Dutch number and dial the prefix 011 31. Example: 011 223 3445 becomes 011 31 11 223 3445.

Phoning from the Netherlands
To phone the United States or Canada, prefix the area code and number with 001. Example: (111) 222-3333 becomes 001 111 222-3333.

To call international information dial 0900 8418 (toll call).

EMERGENCY TELEPHONE NUMBERS

Police *(politie)*	112
Fire *(brandweer)*	112
Ambulance *(ziegenwagen)*	112

Emergency calls are free from phone booths.

HOURS OF OPERATION

Stores close at 5 on Saturday. In Amsterdam many stores open Sunday 1–5 and in Rotterdam noon–5. In most other Dutch cities stores open one Sunday a month. Larger city stores stay open until 9 p.m. on Thursday or Friday. In tourist areas many shops open daily from early morning until late evening. In rural areas many stores close for lunch.

Most post offices also are open 8:30–noon on Saturday. Out-of-town post offices and banks may have shorter hours. Some city post offices and banks stay open into the evening.

Museums and monuments usually are open 1–5 on Sunday; some may close on Monday, while in rural areas they may be closed October through March.

NATIONAL HOLIDAYS

Banks, businesses and most stores close on these days, except for Good Friday, when most shops remain open.

Jan. 1	**New Year's Day**
Mar./Apr.	**Good Friday**
Mar./Apr.	**Easter Monday**
Apr. 30	**Queen's Birthday**
May 5	**Liberation Day**
May/Jun.	**Ascension Day**
May/Jun.	**Pentecost Monday**
Dec. 25	**Christmas Day**
Dec. 26	**St. Stephen's Day**

PHOTOGRAPHY

The Dutch climate is essentially maritime; conditions for outdoor photography are gentle but changeable. Some museums do not allow photography; check before taking pictures. Film and camera batteries are readily available from stores catering to tourists; rapid-developing services also are widely available.

HEALTH

MEDICAL INSURANCE

Private medical insurance is recommended. U.S. and Canadian visitors can receive emergency treatment, but are charged if admitted to a hospital *(ziekenhuis)*. Doctors *(dokter)* are listed at the beginning of the telephone directory; English is widely spoken throughout the medical profession. Tourist Medical Service: doctor, ☎ 020 592 3355; dentist, ☎ 020 570 9595.

DENTAL SERVICES

Dentists charge for treatment and can be expensive. Look in the telephone directory, or ask about local dentists at your hotel or embassy, or at a tourist office (see also Medical Insurance above).

SUN ADVICE

The Netherlands' maritime climate is not one of extremes, but precautions against sunburn should be taken from June through August.

DRUGS

For nonprescription medicines go to a pharmacy *(drogisterij)*. If you need prescription medicines you will have to go to an *apotheek*, where staff also are trained to treat minor ailments. If you need medicine outside regular hours, information about the nearest all-night facility is posted at all pharmacies.

SAFE WATER

Tap water is safe to drink throughout the Netherlands. Mineral water is widely available.

RESTROOMS

There are not many public restrooms, although you will usually find adequate and clean facilities in museums, department stores and roadside service areas. Cafés provide restrooms for the use of customers; buy a drink if you need to use them.

ELECTRICITY

The Netherlands has a 220-volt power supply. Electrical sockets take plugs with two round pins; American appliances will need a plug adapter and will require a transformer if they do not have a dual-voltage facility.

NATIONAL TRANSPORTATION

TRAIN *(trein)*

Netherlands Railways, or Nederlandse Spoorwegen (NS), network is fast, clean, modern, punctual and fairly inexpensive. Information in English is widely available from stations; ☎ 09009296 (toll call) for international train service, ☎ 0900 9292 (toll call) for domestic train and bus service.

BUS *(bus)*

Bus travel is well-organized, with many connections to trains (bus and railroad stations are usually next to each other). If you're planning several trips ask for the Nationale Buswijer, which provides maps and full route details; ☎ 0900 9292 (toll call) for information. The Eurolines European bus network operates in the Netherlands; ☎ 020 560 8787.

FERRY *(veerboot)*

Several ports on the North Sea coast connect the Netherlands with other European countries (including Britain). Companies offer one-way fares, so it is possible to leave and return from different ports (ask a travel agent for details). Canal trips are a good way to explore the Netherlands; details from VVV tourist information offices.

DRIVING

DRIVE ON THE RIGHT

SPEED LIMITS

Police can impose on-the-spot fines.

Limited-access highways *(autoweg)*
100 k.p.h. (62 m.p.h.) or **120 k.p.h. (74 m.p.h.)**

Main roads
80 k.p.h. (49 m.p.h.)

Urban areas
50 k.p.h. (31 m.p.h.)

SEAT BELTS

Must be worn in front and back seats at all times.

BLOOD ALCOHOL

The legal blood alcohol limit is 0.05%. Random breath tests on drivers are carried out frequently, especially late at night, and the penalties for offenders are severe.

DRIVING continued

TOLLS
There are no highway tolls in the Netherlands, but there is a toll for the Kiltunnel near Dordrecht (7f round trip).

CAR RENTAL
The leading rental firms have offices at airports and train stations. Hertz offers discounted rates for AAA members (see page 15). For reservations:

	UNITED STATES	NETHERLANDS
Alamo	(800) 327-9633	020 600 0531 (Europcar)
Avis	(800) 331-2112	020 430 9611
Budget	(800) 527-0700	023 567 1222
Hertz	(800) 654-3080	023 562 0028

FUEL
Many gas stations are self-service and 24-hour facilities are common. Unleaded gas *(Super-Plus* and *Euro-Super)*, lead-replacement fuel and diesel are available, and credit cards are accepted at most garages.

AAA AFFILIATED MOTORING CLUB
Koninklijke Nederlandse Toeristenbond (ANWB – Royal Dutch Touring Club)
Wassenaarseweg 220, 2596 EC, The Hague ☎ 070 314 7147, fax 070 314 6969
If you break down while driving, phone ☎ 0800 0888 (ANWB breakdown service).
Not all automobile clubs offer full services to AAA members.

BREAKDOWNS AND ACCIDENTS
There are yellow 24-hour emergency phones at regular intervals on highways. All accidents involving personal injury must be reported to the police; ☎ 112.
Most car rental firms provide their own free rescue service; if your car is rented, follow the instructions given in the documentation. Use of a car repair service other than those authorized by your rental company may violate your agreement.

OTHER INFORMATION
The minimum age for driving a car is 18 (usually between 21 and 25 for car rental firms).

An International Driving Permit (IDP) is recommended; some rental firms require them, and they can speed up formalities if you are involved in an accident.

A Green Card (international motor insurance certificate) is recommended if you are driving a private car; see page 16 for more information.

Drivers should yield to vehicles approaching from the right. In built-up areas, trams and buses have the right of way when leaving bus stops. Also beware of cyclists and skaters.

USEFUL WORDS AND PHRASES

It is not easy to reproduce the guttural sounds that make up the Dutch language. There are many similarities between German and Dutch, although the Dutch go to great lengths to point out the differences.

English is spoken fluently by a large proportion of the population, who learn foreign languages from an early age.

Dutch pronunciation is similar to English, with some variations:

j as in *y*ellow
v like an *f* as in *f*ar
w like a *v* as in *v*at
ng as in bri*ng*
nj as in o*ni*on

Double consonants keep their separate sounds: for instance, *k* and *n* together are never pronounced as in the English "know."

Some letters and diphthongs are tricky. If the letter is doubled, the vowel sound is lengthened. For example:

a as in sap, aa as in art
e as in let, ee as in fate
o as in mop, oo as in mope
oe as in food
au, ou and ui as in how
ei and ij as in line
ch as in Bach
tje as in church
tie as in tee

Do you speak English?	*Spreekt u Engels?*
excuse me	*pardon*
hello	*hallo* or *dag*
goodbye	*tot ziens*
yes/no	*ja/nee*
how much is?	*wat kost?*
I want…	*ik wil…*
I don't understand	*Ik begrijp het niet*
open/closed	*open/gesloten*
please	*alstublieft*
thank you	*bedankt*
ticket (one-way/	*enkele reis*
round trip)	*retour*
where's the…?	*waar is het…?*
airport	*vliegveld*
room	*kamer*
breakfast	*ontbijt*
dinner	*diner*
May I order?	*Mag ik even bestellen?*
steak	*biefstuk*
bread	*brood*
chicken	*kip*
coffee/tea	*koffie/thee*
sandwich	*broodje*
dish of the day	*daschotel*
lamb	*lamsvlees*
pork	*fricandeau*
wine	*wijn*

PRE-TRIP ESSENTIALS…

WHAT YOU NEED

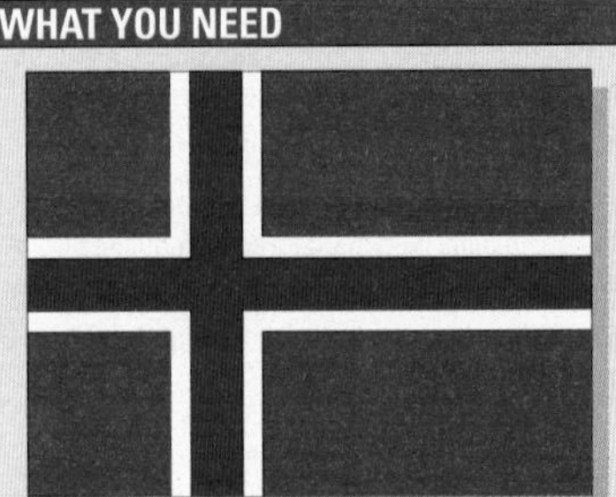

ESSENTIAL FOR TRAVELERS

● Required ● Recommended ● Not required

Passport	●
Visa	Not required
Travel, medical insurance	●
Round-trip or onward airline ticket	Not required
Local currency	●
Traveler's checks	●
Credit cards	●
First-aid kit and medicines	●
Inoculations	Not required

ESSENTIAL FOR DRIVERS*

Driver's license	●
International Driving Permit	●
Car insurance (for nonrental cars)	●
Car registration (for nonrental cars)	●

*see also DRIVING section

IMPORTANT ADDRESSES

Norwegian Tourist Board
655 Third Avenue, Suite 1810,
New York, NY 10017
☎ (212) 885-9700; fax (212) 885-9710
www.visitnorway.com

Oslo Promotion (Oslo Visitors and Convention Bureau)
Brynjulf Bullsplass 1
N-0250 Oslo (Vestbanen)
☎ 23 11 78 80 (Mon.–Fri. 9–4)
Fax 22 83 81 50
www.visitoslo.com

Norges Turistråd (Norwegian Tourist Board)
Postboks 2893 Solli
Drammensveien 40
N-0230 Oslo, Norway
☎ 22 92 52 00; fax 22 56 05 05
www.ntr.com

American Embassy
Drammensveien 18
N-0244 Oslo, Norway
☎ 22 44 85 50; fax 22 56 27 51
Mon.–Fri. 9–5

COUNTRY ESSENTIALS…

CUSTOMS

YES

Limits on goods brought in regardless of duty paid:

200 cigarettes or 250 g. tobacco and 200 cigarette papers; 1 L. alcohol 22–60%; 1 L. alcohol under 22%; 2 L. beer. You must be over 19 to bring in spirits and over 17 to bring in wine, beer and tobacco products.

Notify customs if you leave Norway with more than KR25,000 (in bills and coins of any currency).

NO

No unlicensed drugs, weapons, ammunition, obscene material, pets or other animals, counterfeit money or copied goods, meat or poultry.

For customs limits for returning U.S. citizens see page 16.

MONEY

Norway's currency is the krone (KR), which is divided into 100 øre. The denominations of krone bills are 50, 100, 500 and 1,000. There are coins of 10 and 50 øre and KR1, KR5, KR10 and KR20. You can exchange dollars or traveler's checks *(reisesjekk)* at a bank *(bank)*, exchange office *(vekslekontor)*, post office *(postkontor)* or hotel; you will need ID. Credit cards *(kredittkort)* are widely accepted in hotels, main stores and more expensive restaurants.
Exchange rate at press time: $1 = KR9

TIPS AND GRATUITIES

Restaurants (service is usually included)	5–10%
Cafés/bars (service is usually included)	5–10%
Taxis	10% (optional)
Porters	KR5 per bag
Hairdressers	change
Chambermaids	KR5
Restroom attendants	KR3
Cloakroom attendants	change

COMMUNICATIONS

POST OFFICES

Buy stamps *(frimerker)* at a post office *(postkontor)*, a newsstand/tobacconist *(narvesen)* or from a hotel.

Hours for out-of-town post offices may vary. Mailboxes are red.

TELEPHONES

You can use cash or a telephone card to make a call in Norway. Most phone booths have direct dialing for international calls. Use KR1, KR5, KR10 and KR20 coins (there is a minimum charge of KR2). Greencard phones accept phone cards (KR40, KR90 and KR140), available from Narvesen and MIX kiosks and from post offices. In cities and large towns, phone company offices are open late and offer many services. English-speaking operators are normally available.

Phoning inside Norway
There are no area codes in Norway; all numbers are eight digits: dial the number that is listed. To call the operator dial 117; for directory inquiry information (national plus Sweden and Denmark) dial 180.

Phoning Norway from abroad
The country code for Norway is 47. Note that Norwegian numbers in this book do not include the country code; you will need to prefix this number if you are phoning from another country. To phone Norway from the United States or Canada, simply add the prefix 011 47.
Example: 11 22 33 44 becomes 011 47 11 22 33 44.

Phoning from Norway
To phone the United States or Canada from Norway, prefix the area code and number with 001.
Example: (111) 222-3333 becomes 001 111 222-3333.

To call international information dial 181.
For the international operator dial 115.

EMERGENCY TELEPHONE NUMBERS

Police *(politi)*	112
Fire *(brannvesen)*	110
Ambulance *(ambulanse)*	113

Emergency calls are free from phone booths.

HOURS OF OPERATION

- Stores Mon.–Fri.
- Museums/monuments
- Offices Mon.–Fri.
- Pharmacies Mon.–Fri.
- Banks Mon.–Fri.

- Post offices Mon.–Fri.

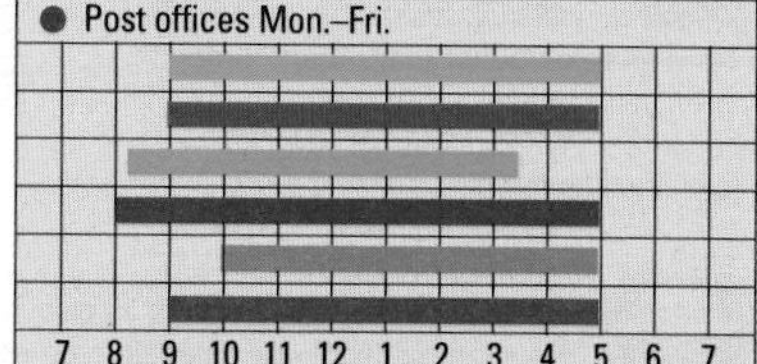

Some stores close at 4. On Thursdays most stores close between 6 and 8. On Saturdays most close between 1 and 3. City grocery stores may stay open longer. Most stores are closed on Sunday. Stores around tourist attractions may have special hours.

Banks generally close half an hour earlier in summer, but stay open until 5 on Thursday all year.

Post offices are open 8–1 on Saturday.

Museums often close on Monday, and hours of operation may be reduced during the winter.

NATIONAL HOLIDAYS

Banks, businesses and most stores close on these days.

Jan. 1	**New Year's Day**
Mar./Apr.	**Maundy Thursday**
Mar./Apr.	**Good Friday**
Mar./Apr.	**Easter Monday**
May 1	**Labor Day**
May 17	**Constitution Day**
May	**Ascension Day**
May/Jun.	**Pentecost Monday**
Dec. 25	**Christmas Day**
Dec. 26	**St. Stephen's Day**

PHOTOGRAPHY

Spectacular shots are possible in fjord country if the weather is right (bear in mind that Norway is susceptible to poor light, especially during the winter). Photography is not permitted in some museums and places of historic interest – check before taking pictures. Film and camera batteries are readily available in towns.

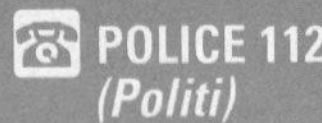

HEALTH

MEDICAL INSURANCE
U.S. and Canadian visitors will be charged for medical assistance, including treatment in a hospital *(sykehus)* emergency room. Many general practitioners speak English; your hotel can find one for you, or look under *Lege* in the telephone directory.

DENTAL SERVICES
A dentist *(tannlege)* will charge you for treatment, so check your medical insurance for this coverage. Many dentists speak English; ask a tourist office or your hotel to find one for you. Emergency treatment can be sought after hours in city clinics and practices.

SUN ADVICE
Despite its northerly location, Norway is affected by the Gulf Stream, which means warm weather during the summer months. Use an appropriate sunscreen.

DRUGS
A pharmacy *(apotek)* sells prescription medicines, and many pharmacists speak English. Information about the nearest late-night or 24-hour facility is posted at all pharmacies. If you need perfume or cosmetics, go to a *parfymeri.*

SAFE WATER
Tap water is safe to drink throughout Norway. Mineral water *(mineralvann)* is widely available.

RESTROOMS

Public restrooms *(toaletter)* are easy to find. Facilities are separate for men *(herrer)* and women *(damer)*, and are identified by symbols or a "WC" sign. They are invariably clean and modern, and a small charge (usually KR3) may be made.

ELECTRICITY

Norway has a 220-volt power supply. Electrical sockets take plugs with two round pins; American appliances will need a plug adapter and will require a transformer if they do not have a dual-voltage facility.

NATIONAL TRANSPORTATION

TRAIN *(tog)*
The Norges Statsbaner (NSB) network operates south of the Arctic Circle. Travel is comfortable and efficient but not cheap. Long distance and overnight trains require reservations. Inquire about discounts when reserving your seat (☎ 81 50 08 88; dial 4 for an English-speaking operator).

BUS *(buss)*
Buses are an excellent, inexpensive way to explore regions that are less well-served by train. Buy your ticket on board (for popular routes it may be best to reserve through a travel agent). Eurolines international buses operate in Norway; ☎ 81 54 44 44.

FERRY *(ferje)*
Norway relies heavily on ferries, especially in the fjords. They often connect with trains and buses. Car ferries operate on a first-come, first-served system; payment is made on board. Some waterways, such as Lake Mjosa and the Telemark Canal, have ferry services. *Hurtigruten*, a grand coastal steamer, links Bergen with Kirkenes, in far northern Norway, calling at 34 ports en route.

DRIVING

DRIVE ON THE RIGHT

SPEED LIMITS
Police can impose on-the-spot fines.

Limited-access highways *(motorvei)*
90 k.p.h. (55 m.p.h.)

Main roads
80 k.p.h. (49 m.p.h.)

Urban areas
50 k.p.h. (31 m.p.h.); usually **30 k.p.h. (18 m.p.h.)** in residential areas

SEAT BELTS
Must be worn in front and back seats at all times. Children under four may not travel in the front (unless in a rear-facing child seat in a vehicle not equipped with an air bag).

BLOOD ALCOHOL
The legal blood alcohol limit is 0.02%. Random breath tests on drivers are carried out frequently, especially late at night, and the penalties for offenders are severe.

DRIVING continued

TOLLS
There are tolls to enter Bergen, Oslo and Trondheim. There also are tolls for some highways, bridges and tunnels.

CAR RENTAL
The leading rental firms have offices at airports and train stations. Hertz offers discounted rates for AAA members (see page 15). For reservations:

	UNITED STATES	NORWAY
Alamo	(800) 327-9633	22 60 70 22 (Europcar)
Avis	(800) 331-2112	66 77 11 11
Budget	(800) 527-0700	73 53 82 80
Hertz	(800) 654-3080	67 16 80 00

FUEL *(olje)*
Gas and diesel are sold in liters, and many stations *(bensinstasjon)* are self-service. Gas stations are not as common in the more remote northern areas, and credit cards are not always accepted.

AAA AFFILIATED MOTORING CLUB
Norges Automobilforbund (NAF)
Storgaten 2, N-0155 Oslo
☎ 22 34 14 00, fax 22 33 13 72
If you break down while driving, phone ☎ 81 00 05 05 (NAF breakdown service). A fee is charged for breakdown service. Not all automobile clubs offer full services to AAA members.

BREAKDOWNS AND ACCIDENTS
There are 24-hour emergency phones at regular intervals on highways and along mountain passes. All accidents involving personal injury must be reported to the police (☎ 112).
Most car rental firms provide their own free rescue service; if your car is rented, follow the instructions given in the documentation. Use of a car repair service other than those authorized by your rental company may violate your agreement.

OTHER INFORMATION
The minimum age for driving a car is 18 (may be higher for some car rental firms).

An International Driving Permit (IDP) is recommended; some rental firms require them, and they can speed up formalities if you are involved in an accident. A Green Card (international motor insurance certificate) is recommended if you are driving a private car; see page 16 for more information.

You are required by law to use dimmed headlights at all times when driving. Snow tires and chains are advised from Nov. 1 until Easter; rent tires and chains from NAF or at border crossings.

USEFUL WORDS AND PHRASES

There are two official, and similar forms of Norwegian. Riksmal, or Bokmal ("book language"), is an old form of Norwegian. Athough many bureaucrats speak in Bokmal, it is mostly used in its written form. Landsmal, or Nynorsk, has its roots in Old Norse dialects but developed out of the wave of Norwegian nationalism in the 19th century. You will encounter both during your stay; it is not uncommon for speakers to use a combination of both, but writing rarely mixes styles.

Most people, especially the young, speak some English; alternatively, a knowledge of German will help. The phrases below are translated into Bokmal.

Do you speak English?	*Snakker du engelsk?*
excuse me	*unnskyld*
hello	*god dag*
goodbye	*ha det bra*
how much?	*hvor mye?*
I would like	*Jeg vil gjerne*
I don't understand	*Jeg forstår ikke*
non-smoking	*røyking forbudt*
open/closed	*åpen/stengt*
please	*vaer så shill*
thank you	*takk*
ticket (one-way/ round trip)	*enkeltbillett/ tur-returbillett*
Where is...?	*Hvor er...?*
yes/no	*ja/nei*
early/late	*tidlig/sent*
hot/cold	*varm/kald*
big/small	*stor/liten*
good/bad	*god/dårlig*
airport	flyplass
you're welcome	*vaer så god*
the restaurant	***restaurant***
beef	*oksekjøtt*
bread	*brød*
breakfast	*frokost*
biscuits	*kjeks*
chicken	*kylling*
coffee/tea	*kaffe/te*
salad	*salat*
dessert	*dessert*
entree	*hovedrett*
fish	*fisk*
lamb	*lammekjøtt*
pork	*svinekjøtt*
sandwich	*smørbrød*
hot-dog	*pølse*
seafood	sjø*mat*
lobster	*hummer*
herring	*sild*
starter	*forrett*
waffles	*vafler*
cranberries	*tranebær*
ice cream	*is*
wine	*vin*
the check	*regningen*

PRE-TRIP ESSENTIALS...

WHAT YOU NEED

ESSENTIAL FOR TRAVELERS

● Required ● Recommended ● Not required

Passport	●
Visa	●
Travel, medical insurance	●
Return or onward ticket	●
Local currency	●
Traveler's checks	●
Credit cards	●
First-aid kit and medicines	●
Inoculations	●

ESSENTIAL FOR DRIVERS*

Driver's license	●
International Driving Permit	●
Car insurance (for nonrental cars)	●
Car registration (for nonrental cars)	●

*see also DRIVING section

IMPORTANT ADDRESSES

Portuguese National Tourist Office
590 Fifth Avenue
New York, NY 10036-4785
☎ (212) 719 3985
Fax (212) 764-6137
www.portugal.org

Portuguese Trade and Tourism Office
Avenida 5 de Outubro 101
1050 Lisbon, Portugal
☎ 21 793 0103
Fax 21 795 0965
www.portugalinsite.pt

American Embassy
Avenida Forças Armadas
1600 Lisbon, Portugal
☎ 21 727 3300
Fax 21 726 9109
Mon.–Fri. 8–5

COUNTRY ESSENTIALS...

CUSTOMS

YES

Duty-free limits on goods brought in from non-European Union countries: 200 cigarettes or 100 cigarillos or 50 cigars or 250 g. tobacco; 2 L. wine; 1 L. alcohol over 22% volume or 2 L. alcohol under 22% volume; 50 ml. perfume; 250 ml. toilet water; plus any other duty-free goods (including gifts) to the value of 7,500Esc. Local or foreign currency exceeding 2,500,000Esc must be declared on arrival. Foreign currency may be exported if it was declared on entry, but no more than 1,000,000Esc may be exported. There is no limit on the importation of tax-paid goods purchased within the European Union if they are for personal use.

NO

No unlicensed drugs, weapons, ammunition, obscene material, pets or other animals, counterfeit money or copied goods, meat or poultry.

For customs limits for returning U.S. citizens see page 16.

MONEY

Portugal's currency is the escudo (Esc), which is divided into 100 centavos. The denominations of escudo bills are 500, 1,000, 2,000, 5,000 and 10,000. There are coins of 1, 2, 5, 10, 20 and 50 centavos and 1, 5, 10, 20, 50, 100 and 200Esc. You can change dollars or traveler's checks *(traveller cheques)* at a bank *(banco)* or an exchange office *(casa de cambio)*. On Jan. 1 1999, the euro became the official currency of Portugal and the escudo became a denomination of the euro. Euro bills and coins were introduced on Jan. 1, 2002. Both euro bills and coins and the old national currency will be in use during a transitional period, after which time the euro will be the only currency accepted. Exchange rate at press time: $1 = 224Esc

TIPS AND GRATUITIES

Service	Tip
Restaurants (where service is not included)	10%
Cafés/bars (where service is not included)	change
Taxis	10%
Porters	100–200Esc
Hairdressers	200Esc
Chambermaids	500Esc
Restroom attendants	100Esc
Cloakroom attendants	100Esc

COMMUNICATIONS

POST OFFICES

Buy stamps *(selos)* at a post office *(correio)* or anywhere that has the sign of a red horse on a white circle over a green background. You may also see the words "Correio de Portugal."

Hours for out-of-town post offices may vary.

TELEPHONES

You can use 10Esc, 20Esc and 50Esc coins in a phone booth *(telefonar)*. Public phones are easily found on the street and in cafés, main post offices, and at some newsstands and tourist offices. You can make an international call direct from a phone booth, but it is more convenient to find a post office where you can use a private booth and pay after the call. Phone cards are available from post offices for 750Esc and 1,800Esc.

Phoning inside Portugal
All Portuguese telephone numbers in this book include an area code; dial the number listed.

To call the operator dial 099. To call information dial 118.

Phoning Portugal from abroad
The country code for Portugal is 351. Note that Portuguese numbers in this book do not include the country code; you will need to prefix this number if you are phoning from another country. To phone Portugal from the United States or Canada dial the prefix 011 351.
Example: 11 122 3344 becomes 011 351 11 122 3344.

Phoning from Portugal
To phone the United States or Canada from Portugal, prefix the area code and number with 001.
Example: (111) 222-3333 becomes 001 111 222-3333.
For international operator outside Europe dial 098.
To call international information dial 179.

EMERGENCY TELEPHONE NUMBERS

Police *(polícia)*	112 or 115
Fire *(serviço do fogo)*	112 or 115
Ambulance *(ambulância)*	112 or 115

Emergency calls are free from phone booths.

HOURS OF OPERATION

- Stores Mon.–Sat.
- Museums/monuments
- Offices Mon.–Fri.
- Pharmacies Mon.–Sat.
- Banks Mon.–Fri.
- Post offices Mon.–Fri.

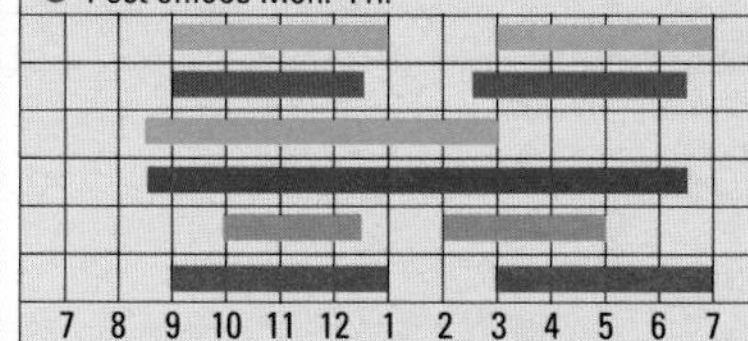

Most stores and pharmacies close at 1 on Saturday and are not open on Sunday. Stores in large towns or tourist areas are open Mon.–Sat. until midnight; some also open on Sunday. Grocery stores are usually open until 9 p.m.

Post offices and banks in rural areas often close for lunch. Some banks in Lisbon stay open until 6.

Museums generally close on Monday (some also close on Wednesday), and the smaller sights may have shorter hours of operation off-season.

NATIONAL HOLIDAYS

Banks, businesses and most stores close on these days. Additionally, there are many local festivals when everything comes to a halt and a whole town takes part in events.

Jan. 1	**New Year's Day**
Feb./Mar.	**Shrove Tuesday**
Mar./Apr.	**Good Friday**
Apr. 25	**Liberty Day**
May 1	**Labor Day**
May/Jun.	**Corpus Christi**
Jun. 10	**Portugal Day**
Aug. 15	**Assumption of the Virgin**
Oct. 5	**Republic Day**
Nov. 1	**All Saints' Day**
Dec. 1	**Independence Day**
Dec. 8	**Immaculate Conception**
Dec. 25	**Christmas Day**

PHOTOGRAPHY

Finding adequate light is rarely a problem in Portugal; rise early for atmospheric shots of fishing ports, villages, castles and the mountains. You will not be permitted to photograph at airports or military areas, and ask permission before taking pictures in museums and churches. Popular brands of film and batteries are widely available.

EMERGENCY PHONE NUMBERS

POLICE 112 or 115 *(Polícia)*

HEALTH

MEDICAL INSURANCE

U.S. and Canadian visitors will be charged for emergency medical treatment, consultation with a doctor and/or admittance to a hospital *(hospital)*. Ask at a tourist office or your hotel to find an English-speaking doctor.

DENTAL SERVICES

Dental treatment is charged for in Portugal. Ask at a tourist office or your hotel for a list of English-speaking dentists. Check that dental treatment is covered by your medical insurance.

SUN ADVICE

The sun is strong during summer, particularly in the south. Do not be deceived by the cooling breeze off the Atlantic. Avoid prolonged exposure and protect yourself with a sunscreen or cover up.

DRUGS

Prescription medicines are available from a pharmacy *(fármacia)*, distinguished by a large green cross. Pharmacists can prescribe remedies for minor ailments, and many speak English. Information about the nearest late-night or 24-hour facility is posted at all pharmacies.

SAFE WATER

Tap water is generally safe, but does not always taste too pleasant. It is advisable to drink bottled water *(agua mineral)*, especially in rural areas; *sem gas* means noncarbonated, *com gas* means carbonated.

RESTROOMS

Public restrooms *(retretes* or *lavabos)* are easy to find. Ladies' *(senhoras)* restrooms usually have a minimal charge and are generally clean. Men's *(homens)* restrooms are usually free.

ELECTRICITY

Most of Portugal has a 220-volt power supply, but in some rural areas the supply is 125 volts. Electrical sockets take plugs with two round pins; American appliances will need a plug adapter and a transformer if they do not have a dual-voltage facility.

NATIONAL TRANSPORTATION

TRAIN *(comboios)*

The Caminhos de Ferro Portugueses (CP) operates three types of service: *Inter-regional* and *Intercidade* (which both stop at most stations) and *Rapido* (express between Lisbon and Porto). Fares are reasonable, with many discount offers; ☎ 21 888 4025.

BUS *(autocarros)*

The state-owned Rodoviária National (RN) covers most of the country, and buses are generally comfortable (☎ 21 354 5775). Several private companies also maintain an extensive network. The Eurolines international bus network operates in Portugal; ☎ 21 315 2644.

FERRY *(barcos)*

Ferries cross the Rio Tejo from Lisbon to the suburb of Cacilhas from Cais da Alfândega (Terreiro do Paço) or from Cais de Sodré. From Setúbal ferries cross the Rio Sado to the Tróia peninsula. Tickets can be bought at the boat stations' ticket offices.

DRIVING

DRIVE ON THE RIGHT

SPEED LIMITS

Police can impose on-the-spot fines.

Limited-access highways *(autoestrada)*
120 k.p.h. (74 m.p.h.)
Divided highways
100 k.p.h. (62 m.p.h.)

Main roads
90 k.p.h. (55 m.p.h.)

Urban areas
50 k.p.h. (31 m.p.h.)

SEAT BELTS

Must be worn in front and back seats at all times.

BLOOD ALCOHOL

The legal blood alcohol limit is 0.05%. Random breath tests on drivers are carried out frequently, especially late at night, and the penalties for offenders are severe.

DRIVING continued

TOLLS
There are tolls on highways (*auto-estradas*) in Portugal. Highway numbers are prefixed by AE.

CAR RENTAL
The leading rental firms have offices at airports and train stations. Hertz offers discounted rates for AAA members (see page 15). For reservations:

	UNITED STATES	PORTUGAL
Alamo	(800) 327-9633	21 848 6191
Avis	(800) 331-2112	21 843 5550
Budget	(800) 527-0700	21 319 5555
Hertz	(800) 654-3080	0800 238 238 (toll-free)

FUEL *(gasolina)*
Gas and diesel are sold in liters, and many stations *(posto de gasolina)* are self-service. Gas stations, generally open daily 7 a.m.–8 p.m. (some 24 hours), are not as common in the more remote northern areas, and credit cards are not always accepted or incur an additional charge.

AAA AFFILIATED MOTORING CLUB
Automóvel Club de Portugal (ACP)
Rua Rosa Araújo 24–26, 1250–195
Lisbon ☎ 21 318 0100, fax 22 205 6698
Not all automobile clubs offer full services to AAA members.

BREAKDOWNS AND ACCIDENTS
There are 24-hour emergency phones at regular intervals on highways. If you are involved in an accident ☎ 112 or 115 for police assistance.
Most car rental firms provide their own free rescue service; if your car is rented, follow the instructions given in the documentation. Use of a car repair service other than those authorized by your rental company may violate your agreement.

OTHER INFORMATION
The minimum age for car rental is 21 (some rental firms stipulate 23).

An International Driving Permit (IDP) is essential; some rental firms require them, and they can speed up formalities if you are involved in an accident.

A Green Card (international motor insurance certificate) is essential if you are driving a private car; see page 16 for more information.

You are required by law to carry ID at all times.

USEFUL WORDS AND PHRASES

Portuguese is a Latin language, so an acquaintance with French, Spanish or Italian makes written Portuguese quite easy to understand. Understanding spoken Portuguese, however, is more difficult. Although on paper Portuguese words look similar to Spanish, they actually sound very different. Consonants are slurred, and vowels are flat and truncated, nasal or sometimes disregarded completely.

Although English is widely spoken in tourist areas, knowing a few Portuguese words will make your trip more rewarding.

Do you speak English?	*Fala Inglês?*
I'm sorry	*desculpe*
hello/goodbye	*olá/adeus*
yes/no	*sim/não*
how much?	*quanto?*
I am American	*sou Americano*
I would like	*queria um*
I don't understand	*não entendo*
non-smoking	*não fumadores*
okay	*está bem*
today/tomorrow	*hoje/amanhã*
open/closed	*aberto/fechado*
right/left	*direita/esquerda*
near/far	*perto/longe*
big/little	*grande/pequeno*
cheap/expensive	*barato/caro*
please	*se faz favor*
thank you	*obrigado (m.)/obrigada (f.)*
ticket	*bilhete*
one way/return	*ida/ida e volta*
where is...?	*onde é...?*
the hotel	***hotel***
breakfast	*pequeno almoço*
lunch	*almoço*
dinner	*jantar*
I have a reservation	*tenho uma marcacao*
key	*chave*
for one night	*para uma noite*
room	*quarto*
shower	*duche*
with bathroom	*com casa de banho*
the restaurant	***restaurante***
beef	*bife*
bread	*pão*
cheese	*queijo*
chicken	*frango*
the check	*a conta*
Is the service included?	*O serviço está incluido?*
coffee/tea	*café/chà*
dish of the day	*prato do dia*
dessert	*sobremesa*
fish	*peixe*
ham	*fiambre*
lamb	*carneiro*
pork	*porco*
starter	*entrada*
veal	*vitela*
wine	*vinho*

PRE-TRIP ESSENTIALS...

WHAT YOU NEED

ESSENTIAL FOR TRAVELERS

● Required ● Recommended ● Not required

Passport	●
Visa	○
Travel, medical insurance	●
Round-trip or onward airline ticket	○
Local currency	●
Traveler's checks	●
Credit cards	●
First-aid kit and medicines	●
Inoculations	○

ESSENTIAL FOR DRIVERS*

Driver's license	●
International Driving Permit	●
Car insurance (for nonrental cars)	●
Car registration (for nonrental cars)	●

*see also DRIVING section

IMPORTANT ADDRESSES

Tourist Office of Spain
666 Fifth Avenue, 35th floor
New York, NY 10103
☎ (212) 265-8822
Fax (212) 265-8864
www.okspain.org

Turespaña (Tourist Office of Spain)
Calle José Lázaro Galdiano 6
28071 Madrid, Spain
☎ 91 343 3500
Fax 91 343 3446
www.tourspain.es

American Embassy
Serrano 75
28006 Madrid, Spain
☎ 91 587 2200
Fax 91 587 2303
Personal inquiries: Mon.–Fri. 9–1

COUNTRY ESSENTIALS...

CUSTOMS

YES

Duty-free limits on goods brought in from non-European Union countries:
200 cigarettes or 100 cigarillos or 50 cigars or 250 g. tobacco; 2 L. wine; 1 L. alcohol over 22% volume; 2 L. alcohol under 22% volume; 60 ml. perfume; 250 ml. toilet water; plus any other duty-free goods (including gifts) to the value of 33,500PTA. The import of currency of any denomination exceeding 1,000,000PTA must be declared on arrival in Spain. There is no limit on the importation of tax-paid goods purchased within the European Union if they are for personal use.

NO

No unlicensed drugs, weapons, ammunition, obscene material, pets or other animals, counterfeit money or copied goods, meat or poultry.

For customs limits for returning U.S. citizens see page 16.

MONEY

Spain's currency is the peseta (PTA). The denominations of peseta bills are 1,000, 2,000, 5,000 and 10,000. There are coins of 5, 10, 25, 50, 100, 200 and 500PTA. A near-valueless one peseta coin exists, but sums are usually rounded down to the nearest five pesetas. Exchange dollars or traveler's checks *(cheques de viaje)* at a bank *(banco)* or exchange office *(oficina de canvi)*. On Jan. 1, 1999, the euro became the official currency of Spain and the peseta became a denomination of the euro. Euro bills and coins were introduced on Jan. 1, 2002. Both euro bills and coins and the old national currency will be in use during a transitional period, after which time the euro will be the only currency accepted. Exchange rate at press time: $1 = 186PTA

TIPS AND GRATUITIES

Tips are welcomed as a sign of good service. Most hotel, restaurant and café checks will include a service charge.

Restaurants (service is normally included)	5–10%
Cafés/bars (service is normally included)	change
Taxis	10%
Porters, chambermaids	100PTA
Cloakroom attendants	change

COMMUNICATIONS

POST OFFICES

Buy stamps *(sellos)* at a post office *(correos)*, a tobacconist *(estancos)* denoted by a "T" or at some hotels. Hours for out-of-town post offices may vary.

TELEPHONES

A public telephone *(teléfono)* takes 5PTA, 25PTA, 50PTA, 100PTA, 200PTA and 500PTA coins (minimum 20PTA). A phone card *(teletarjeta)* issued by Telefónica is available from post offices, tobacconists, newsstands and authorized retailers for 1,000PTA or 2,000PTA. Many public phone booths are thoroughly modern, with instructions in English and lists of national and international dialing codes posted inside them. In major cities, telecommunications stores offer facilities such as faxing and e-mail.

Phoning inside Spain
All Spanish phone numbers in this book include an area code; dial the number that is listed.
To call the operator dial 003.

Phoning Spain from abroad
The country code for Spain is 34. Note that Spanish numbers in this book do not include the Spanish country code; you will need to prefix this number if you are phoning from another country. To phone Spain from the United States or Canada dial the prefix 011 34. (Note that the number of digits in Spanish area codes varies.)
Example: 11 122 3344 becomes 011 34 11 122 3344.

Phoning from Spain
To phone the United States or Canada from Spain, prefix the area code and number with 001.
Example: (111) 222-3333 becomes 001 111 222-3333.
To call international information dial 025.

EMERGENCY TELEPHONE NUMBERS

Police *(policía)*	091
Fire *(bomberos)*	080
Ambulance *(ambulancia)*	061
General emergencies	112

Emergency calls are free from phone booths.

HOURS OF OPERATION

- Stores Mon.–Sat.
- Museums/monuments Tue.–Sat.
- Offices Mon.–Fri.
- Banks Mon.–Fri.
- Pharmacies Mon.–Sat.
- Post offices Mon.–Sat.

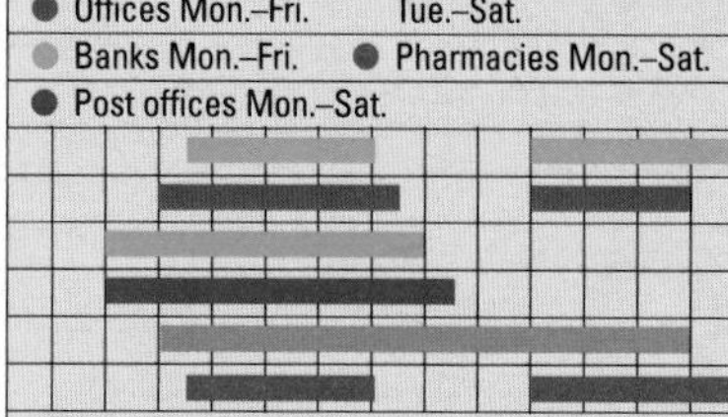

7 8 9 10 11 12 1 2 3 4 5 6 7

Department stores and grocery stores may operate the hours shown, especially in summer. In Madrid department stores open Mon.–Sat. 10–10, and also open the first Sun. of each month.

Business hours vary depending on season; many companies work *horas intensivas* (shorter, more intensive hours) from 8–3 in summer.

Banks are open Saturdays 9–1 in winter.

Most museums and monuments are closed on Monday, but many are open 9–2 on Sunday.

NATIONAL HOLIDAYS

Banks, businesses and most stores close on these days. Days marked (*) are not national holidays but are celebrated in Catalonia, when shops and offices may close.

Jan. 1	**New Year's Day**
Jan. 6	**Epiphany**
***Mar. 19**	**St. Joseph's Day**
Mar./Apr.	**Good Friday**
***Mar./Apr.**	**Easter Monday**
May 1	**Labor Day**
***May/Jun.**	**Pentecost Monday**
***Jun. 24**	**St. John's Day**
Aug. 15	**Assumption of the Virgin**
***Sep. 11**	**National Day (Catalonia)**
***Sep. 24**	**Our Lady of Mercy Day**
Oct. 12	**National Day**
Nov. 1	**All Saints' Day**
Dec. 6	**Constitution Day**
Dec. 8	**Immaculate Conception**
Dec. 25	**Christmas Day**
***Dec. 26**	**St. Stephen's Day**

PHOTOGRAPHY

The Spanish summer sun can be powerful at noon, making photos appear flat; take your pictures early in the morning or late in the evening. Ask permission before taking pictures in museums and churches. Film and camera batteries are readily available from specialist stores and *drouguerias* (drugstores).

HEALTH

MEDICAL INSURANCE

U.S. and Canadian visitors can receive treatment in a hospital emergency room, but are charged if admitted to a bed. There is an Anglo-American clinic in Madrid; ☎ 91 435 1823.

DENTAL SERVICES

You will be charged for dental treatment, so check whether it is covered by your medical insurance. Dentists *(dentista)* are listed in the yellow pages.

SUN ADVICE

The sun is strong during summer, particularly in the south. Dress sensibly, avoid prolonged exposure and protect yourself with a sunscreen.

DRUGS

Prescription medicines are available from pharmacies *(farmacias)*, designated by a green cross. Information about the nearest late-night or 24-hour facility is posted at all pharmacies.

SAFE WATER

Tap water is generally safe, although it can be heavily chlorinated. Mineral water *(agua mineral)* is inexpensive and is sold *con gaz* (carbonated) and *sin gaz* (noncarbonated). Drink plenty of water during hot weather.

RESTROOMS

Public restrooms *(servicios)* can usually be found in large department stores, museums and other places of interest to visitors. Elsewhere, restrooms may not be easy to find, but there is no charge. If you use the facilities in a bar you will be expected to buy a drink. Spanish words are *señores* for men and *señoras* for women.

ELECTRICITY

Most of Spain has a 220-volt power supply, but in some rural areas the supply is 110 or 125 volts. Electrical sockets take plugs with two round pins; American appliances will need a plug adapter, and either a dual voltage facility or a transformer.

NATIONAL TRANSPORTATION

TRAIN *(tren)*

The Red Nacional de los Ferrocarriles Españoles (RENFE) rail network is inexpensive to use. Take advantage of "blue days" *(dias azules)*, when lower fares prevail. There are express services for long-distance travel: Alaris, Talgo 200 and AVE (reservations required/advisable for all three). Information and reservations: ☎ 902 24 02 02 (24 hours).

BUS *(autobus)*

Spain has a good bus system, and the Spanish Tourist Board publishes a guide to domestic services. Ask at a tourist office for details. The Eurolines international bus service operates in Spain: ☎ 91 506 3360.

FERRY *(transbordador)*

Barcelona is the Mediterranean's biggest port and offers regular ferry service to the Balearic islands. One of the largest ferry operators is Trasmediterránea: ☎ 902 45 46 45. "Mini-cruises" of two or three days operate from northern Spain to and from Britain; obtain details from a travel agent.

DRIVING

DRIVE ON THE RIGHT

SPEED LIMITS

Police can impose on-the-spot fines.

Limited-access highways *(autopistas)*
120 k.p.h. (75 m.p.h.)
Divided highways
100 k.p.h. (62 m.p.h.)

Main roads
90 k.p.h. (56 m.p.h.)

Urban areas
50 k.p.h. (31 m.p.h.)

SEAT BELTS

Must be worn in front and back seats at all times.

BLOOD ALCOHOL

The legal blood alcohol limit is 0.05%. Random breath tests on drivers are carried out frequently, especially late at night, and the penalties for offenders are severe.

DRIVING continued

TOLLS

A toll *(pedaggi autostradalia)* is levied on limited-access highways. Take a ticket when you enter and pay when exiting.

CAR RENTAL

The leading rental firms have offices at airports and train stations. Hertz offers discounted rates for AAA members (see page 15). For reservations:

	UNITED STATES	SPAIN
Alamo	(800) 327-9633	902 10 50 30 (Europcar)
Avis	(800) 331-2112	902 13 55 31
Budget	(800) 527-0700	901 20 12 12
Hertz	(800) 654-3080	91 509 7300

FUEL

Gas *(gasolina)* and diesel are sold in liters. Many gas stations *(gasolineras)* in towns and cities and on highways are open 24 hours.

AAA AFFILIATED MOTORING CLUB

Real Automóvil Club de España (RACE)

José Abascal 10, 28003 Madrid

☎ 91 594 9347, fax 91 448 3561

If you break down while driving, phone ☎ 91 593 3333 (RACE breakdown service). Not all automobile clubs offer full services to AAA members.

BREAKDOWNS AND ACCIDENTS

There are 24-hour emergency phones at regular intervals on highways. If you are involved in an accident, phone ☎ 091 for police.

Most car rental firms provide their own free rescue service; if your car is rented, follow the instructions given in the documentation. Use of a car repair service other than those authorized by your rental company may violate your agreement.

OTHER INFORMATION

The minimum age for driving a car is 18 (may be higher for some car rental firms).

An International Driving Permit (IDP) is recommended; some rental firms require them, and they can speed up formalities if you are involved in an accident.

A Green Card (international motor insurance certificate) is recommended if you are driving a private car. See page 16 for more information. The police may impound your car if you fail to produce a Green Card after an accident.

It is advisable to obtain a bail bond from your automobile insurer. This will facilitate your release if you commit a traffic offense or are involved in an accident. A bail bond is usually included when you rent a car in Spain; if you rent a car in another country and intend to drive to Spain, advise your rental company.

USEFUL WORDS AND PHRASES

Castilian is the main language in Spain, with three important regional languages: Catalan, spoken in Catalonia and Valencia; Basque, the official language of the Basque north; and Galician, spoken in the northwest.

Catalan is closely related to Occitan (or Provençal), and Galician has noticeable links with Portuguese. The Basque tongue is unique, having no connection with any language in Europe.

The following words and phrases are in Castilian:

Do you speak English?	*¿Habla usted inglés?*
excuse me	*perdone*
hello	*hola*
goodbye	*adiós*
yes/no	*sí/no*
how much?	*¿cuánto?*
I would like	*me gustaría*
I don't understand	*no entiendo*
no smoking	*no fumadores*
okay	*vale*
open/closed	*abierto/cerrado*
today/tomorrow	*hoy/mañana*
here/there	*aquí/allí*
more/less	*más/menos*
please	*por favor*
thank you	*gracias*
you're welcome	*de nada*
how/what	*cómo/qué*
left/right	*izquierda/derecha*
What time is it?	*¿Qué hora es?*
travel ticket	*el billete*
one way/return	*ida/ida y vuelta*
where is...?	*¿donde está...?*
the hotel	***el hotel***
breakfast	*desayuno*
lunch	*la comida*
dinner	*la cena*
I have a reservation	*Tengo una reserva*
key	*llave*
room	*habitación*
shower	*ducha*
the restaurant	***restaurante***
beef	*la carne de vaca*
bread	*el pan*
cheese	*queso*
chicken	*el pollo*
coffee	*el café*
dish of the day	*el plato del día*
dessert	*el postre*
fish	*el pescado*
pork	*la carne de cerdo*
starter	*primer plato*
wine, red/white	*el vino tinto/blanco*
the check	*la cuenta*

PRE-TRIP ESSENTIALS...

WHAT YOU NEED

ESSENTIAL FOR TRAVELERS

● Required ● Recommended ○ Not required

Passport	●
Visa	○
Travel, medical insurance	●
Round-trip or onward airline ticket	○
Local currency	●
Traveler's checks	●
Credit cards	●
First-aid kit and medicines	●
Inoculations	○

ESSENTIAL FOR DRIVERS*

Driver's license	●
International Driving Permit	●
Car insurance (for nonrental cars)	●
Car registration (for nonrental cars)	●

*see also DRIVING section

IMPORTANT ADDRESSES

Danish and Swedish Tourist Boards
PO Box 4649, Grand Central Station
New York, NY 10163-4649
☎ (212) 885-9700
Fax (212) 885-9764
www.gosweden.org

Sveriges Rese– och Turistråd AB (Swedish Travel and Tourism Council)
P.O.Box 3030, Kungsgatan 36
SE-103 61 Stockholm, Sweden
☎ 08 725 55 00
Fax 08 725 55 31
www.visit-sweden.com

American Embassy
Dag Hammarskjölds Väg 31
SE-115 89 Stockholm, Sweden
☎ 08 783 53 00
Fax 08 661 19 64
Open Mon.–Fri. 8–4:30

COUNTRY ESSENTIALS...

CUSTOMS

YES

Duty-free limits on goods brought in from non-European Union countries:
200 cigarettes or 100 cigarillos or 50 cigars or 250 g. tobacco; 2 L. wine; 2 L. alcohol under 22% volume or 1 L. alcohol over 22% volume; 15 L. beer; 50 ml. perfume; 250 ml. toilet water; plus any other duty-free goods (including gifts) to the value of 700SKr. There are no currency regulations. There is no limit on the importation of tax-paid goods purchased within the European Union if they are for personal use.

NO

No unlicensed drugs, weapons, ammunition, obscene material, pets or other animals, counterfeit money or copied goods, meat or poultry.

For customs limits for returning U.S. citizens see page 16.

MONEY

Sweden's currency is the krona (SKr or KR; plural kronor), which is divided into 100 öre. The denominations of krona bills are 20, 50, 100, 500, 1,000 and 10,000. There are coins of 50 öre, and 1, 5 and 10SKr. Exchange dollars and traveler's checks *(resechecker)* at a bank or an exchange office. "Forex" exchange offices have distinctive yellow signs. Although a member of the European Union, Sweden chose not to adopt the euro as its official currency on Jan. 1, 1999. However, it is possible for tourists coming from the euro zone to pay with a euro credit card; the exchange rate does not fluctuate.
Exchange rate at press time: $1 = 10SKr

TIPS AND GRATUITIES

Tips are welcomed but not expected or obligatory. In restaurants it is usual to round off the check to the nearest 10SKr; service is usually included.

Restaurants, cafés/bars (service is included)	change
Taxis	10%
Hairdressers, chambermaids	none
Porters, restroom attendants	change
Cloakroom attendants	7SKr

COMMUNICATIONS

POST OFFICES

Buy stamps *(frimarken)* at a post office *(postkontoret)*, newsstand *(nyhets-byra)* or stationer *(handel)*.

Hours for out-of-town post offices may vary.

TELEPHONES

You can use cash, credit cards and prepaid phone cards to make a phone call in Sweden. A public phone (*telefon*) takes 1SKr or 5SKr coins. Phone cards can be bought from newsstands or magazine kiosks (for example *Pressbyrån*). Credit card phones are indicated by a "CCC" or Tele2 sign. Operators speak English. You can make a half-price call from a Turist Telefon (only found in cities) from mid-June to mid-August; these phones are clearly marked.

Phoning inside Sweden
All Swedish numbers in this book include an area code; dial the number that is listed. To call the operator dial 90130.

Phoning Sweden from abroad
The country code for Sweden is 46. Note that Swedish numbers in this book do not include the Swedish country code; you will need to prefix this number if you are phoning from another country. To phone Sweden from the United States or Canada, omit the first zero from the Swedish number and add the prefix 011 46.
Example: 01 122 33 44 becomes 011 46 1 122 33 44.

Phoning from Sweden
To phone the United States or Canada from Sweden, prefix the area code and number with 001.
Example: (111) 222-3333 becomes 001 111 222-3333.

To call international information dial 07977.

EMERGENCY TELEPHONE NUMBERS

Police *(polis)*	112
Fire *(brandkår)*	112
Ambulance *(ambulans)*	112

Emergency calls are free from phone booths.

HOURS OF OPERATION

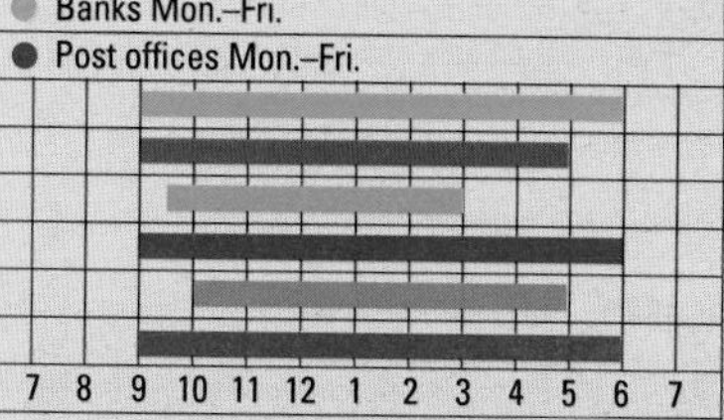

In large towns, department stores stay open until 8 or 10 p.m., and some also are open Sunday noon–4. Stores often close on Saturday afternoon, and usually close early the day before a public holiday. Some smaller stores may close for lunch.

Post offices may stay open later in main cities. They are open Sat. 10–1.

Banks also open on Thursday between 4 and 5:30 and in some cities until 5:30 Mon.–Fri.

Some museums close on Monday and stay open late one or two nights a week.

Some pharmacies (*apotek*) in major cities are open 24 hours.

NATIONAL HOLIDAYS

Banks, businesses and most stores close on these days; they may also be closed or close earlier the day before a holiday.

Jan. 1	**New Year's Day**
Jan. 6	**Epiphany**
Mar./Apr.	**Good Friday**
Mar./Apr.	**Easter Monday**
May 1	**Labor Day**
May	**Ascension Day**
May/Jun.	**Pentecost Monday**
Jun. 24	**Midsummer's Day**
Nov. 1	**All Saints' Day**
Dec. 24	**Christmas Eve**
Dec. 25	**Christmas Day**
Dec. 26	**St. Stephen's Day**
Dec. 31	**New Year's Eve**

PHOTOGRAPHY

Make sure you pack film for poor light at certain times in the winter. If you have the right equipment, photographs of the northern lights *(aurora borealis)* are possible. Check first before taking photographs in museums; it may be forbidden or you may have to ask permission. Film and camera batteries are readily available from tourist stores. Rapid-developing services also are widely available.

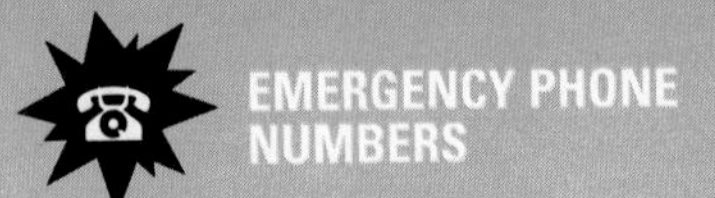

HEALTH

MEDICAL INSURANCE

Private medical insurance is recommended. Visitors can receive treatment at a hospital accident and emergency room, but you will be charged if you are admitted to a hospital bed. There are no general practitioners; go straight to a hospital clinic *(akutmottagning* or *vårdcentral)*.

DENTAL SERVICES

Dentists *(tandläkeren)* always charge for treatment. Emergency treatment is available after hours in major cities. Clinics are indicated by *"Tandläkare"* or *"Folktandvård"* signs.

SUN ADVICE

The Gulf Stream dictates Sweden's temperate climate of warm sunshine during July and August. Although the sun is not fierce, good sun protection is necessary. Take precautions near the water.

DRUGS

Prescription and nonprescription drugs and medicines are available from a pharmacy *(apotek)*. If you need a pharmacy outside regular hours, information about the nearest all-night facility is posted at all pharmacies.

SAFE WATER

Tap water is safe to drink, and mineral water *(mineralvatten)* is widely available.

RESTROOMS

Public restrooms *(toalett)* are easy to find. Charges of between 1SKr and 5SKr may be made in some restrooms. Separate facilities for men (*Herrar*) and women (*Damer*) are always clean and modern.

ELECTRICITY

Sweden has a 220-volt power supply. Electrical sockets take plugs with two round pins; American appliances will need a plug adapter and will require a transformer if they do not have a dual-voltage facility.

NATIONAL TRANSPORTATION

TRAIN *(tåg)*

The Swedish National Railways (Statens Järnvägar) runs an efficient and extensive system, extending above the Arctic Circle. The trains are fast and modern. On some trains reservations are required; it is usually advisable to make them. For information: ☎ 0498 20 33 80 . A free timetable is available from any station *(järnvägsstation)*.

BUS *(buss)*

Swedish bus travel is straightforward and inexpensive. Express services run between cities and into Norway, Finland and Denmark. A good, frequent domestic service runs to northern Sweden. The largest bus operator is Swebus Express. For long-distance bus service information: ☎ 08 655 00 90. International Euroline buses operate in Sweden; ☎ 08 440 85 70.

FERRY *(farja)*

Ferry services in Sweden are not as extensive as those in Finland and Denmark, but you can get various island-hopping boat passes or coupons. Most start from Stockholm; passes are available from Waxholmbolaget, Stromkajen, Stockholm, ☎ 08 679 58 30.

DRIVING

DRIVE ON THE RIGHT

SPEED LIMITS

Police can impose on-the-spot fines, but cannot collect them.

Limited-access highways
110 k.p.h. (68 m.p.h.)
Divided highways
90 k.p.h. (55 m.p.h.)

Main roads
70 k.p.h. (43 m.p.h.)

Urban areas
50 k.p.h. (31 m.p.h.)

SEAT BELTS

Must be worn in front and rear seats at all times.

BLOOD ALCOHOL

The legal blood alcohol limit is 0.02% so alcohol should be avoided completely. Random breath tests on drivers are carried out frequently, especially late at night, and the penalties for offenders are severe.

DRIVING continued

TOLLS

There are no highway tolls in Sweden.

CAR RENTAL

The leading rental firms have offices at airports and train stations. Hertz offers discounted rates for AAA members (see page 15). For reservations:

	UNITED STATES	SWEDEN
Alamo	(800) 327-9633	020 78 11 80 (Europcar; (toll-free)
Avis	(800) 331-2112	020 78 82 00 (toll-free)
Budget	(800) 527-0700	020 78 77 87 (toll-free)
Hertz	(800) 654-3080	020 21 12 11 (toll-free)

FUEL

Gas (*själva*) is sold in liters. Major credit cards are usually accepted. Self-service *(tanka själv)* stations require 20SKr, 50Skr or 100SKr bills in their automated machines *(sedel automat)*; service not available for diesel. Many gas stations on highways and in main towns are open 24 hours.

AAA AFFILIATED MOTORING CLUB

Motormännens Riksförbund (M)
Sveavägen 159, Stockholm
☎ 08 690 38 00, fax 08 690 38 24

Not all automobile clubs offer full services to AAA members.

BREAKDOWNS AND ACCIDENTS

There are 24-hour emergency phones at regular intervals on highways. If you are involved in an accident, phone ☎ 112 for police.

If you break down while driving, contact the Larmtjänst service: ☎ 020 91 00 40 (toll-free). Most car rental firms provide their own free rescue service; if your car is rented, follow the instructions given in the documentation. Use of a car repair service other than those authorized by your rental company may violate your agreement.

OTHER INFORMATION

The minimum age for driving a car is 18 (may be higher for some car rental firms).

An International Driving Permit (IDP) is recommended; some rental firms require them, and they can speed up formalities if you are involved in an accident.

A Green Card (international motor insurance certificate) is recommended if you are driving a private car; see page 16 for more information.

Dimmed headlights must be turned on year-round, even during daylight hours.

USEFUL WORDS & PHRASES

Swedes are not used to foreigners speaking their language, although efforts to speak Swedish are appreciated; most Swedes also speak English. German, Danish and Norwegian are often understood.

In Swedish, a vowel sound is usually long when it is the final syllable, and verbs are the same regardless of person. Definite articles are determined by the ending of the noun: -en and -et for singular nouns and -na or -n for plural. There are an additional three letters in the Swedish alphabet - å, ä and ö - which always appear at the end in alphabetical lists.

There are two words for "you": *du* and *ni*. *Ni* is the polite form, *du* is the familiar form. Unlike some other European countries, it is not necessarily impolite to address a complete stranger with the familiar form. In fact, many Swedes consider the polite form to be old-fashioned.

Do you speak English?	*Talar ni Engelska?*
excuse me	*ursäkta mig*
hello	*hej*
goodbye	*adjö/hej då*
yes/no	*ja/nej*
how much is it?	*hur mycket kostar den?*
I am American	*Jag är från U.S.A.*
I'd like	*Jag skulle vilja ha*
I don't understand	*Jag förstår inte*
non-smoking	*rökning förbjuden*
open	*öppen/öppet*
closed	*stängt*
please	*snälla, vänligen*
thank you	*tack*
ticket (one-way/round trip)	*en enkelbiljett*
What is your name?	*Vad heter du?*
the hotel	***hotell***
breakfast	*frukost*
lunch	*lunch*
dinner	*middag*
key	*nyckel*
room	*rum*
shower	*dusch*
the restaurant	***restaurang***
bread	*bröd*
coffee/tea	*kaffe/te*
beef	*nötkött, oxkött*
chicken	*kyckling*
fish	*fisk*
lamb	*lammkött*
pork	*fläsk*
poultry	*fågel*
beer	*öl*
wine	*vin*
dessert	*efterrätt*
ice cream	*glass*
please bring the check	*notan tack*

SWITZERLAND – ESSENTIAL INFORMATION

PRE-TRIP ESSENTIALS...

WHAT YOU NEED

ESSENTIAL FOR TRAVELERS

● Required ● Recommended ○ Not required

Passport	●
Visa	○
Travel, medical insurance	●
Round-trip or onward airline ticket	○
Local currency	●
Traveler's checks	●
Credit cards	●
First-aid kit and medicines	●
Inoculations	○

ESSENTIAL FOR DRIVERS*

Driver's license	●
International Driving Permit	●
Car insurance (for nonrental cars)	●
Car registration (for nonrental cars)	●

*see also DRIVING section

IMPORTANT ADDRESSES

Switzerland Tourism
Swiss Center, 608 Fifth Avenue
New York, NY 10020
☎ (212) 757-5944
Fax (212) 262-6116
www.myswitzerland.com

Switzerland Tourism
Tödistrasse 7
CH-8027 Zürich, Switzerland
☎ 01 288 1111
Fax 01 288 1205
www.switzerlandtourism.com

American Embassy
Jubiläumsstrasse 93
CH-3001 Bern, Switzerland
☎ 031 357 7011
Fax 031 357 7344
Open Mon.–Fri. 8:30–12:30 and 1:30–5:30

COUNTRY ESSENTIALS...

CUSTOMS

YES

Duty-free limits on goods brought in from non-European countries:
400 cigarettes or 100 cigarillos or cigars or 500 g. tobacco; 2 L. alcohol under 15% volume or 1 L. alcohol over 15% volume; plus any other duty-free goods (including gifts) to the value of SF100. These limits apply to visitors aged 17 and over. There are no currency regulations. There is no limit on the importation of tax-paid goods purchased within the European Union if they are for personal use.

NO

No unlicensed drugs, weapons, ammunition, obscene material, pets or other animals, counterfeit money or copied goods, meat or poultry.

For customs limits for returning U.S. citizens see page 16.

MONEY

Switzerland's currency is the Swiss franc (SF), which is divided into 100 centimes or "Rappen." The denominations of franc bills are 10, 20, 50, 100, 200, 500 and 1,000. There are coins of 5, 10, 20 and 50 centimes and 1, 2 and 5SF. Exchange dollars or traveler's checks *(Reiseschecks)* at a bank *(Bank)*, exchange office *(Wechselbüro)*, post office *(Postamt)* or hotel. Swiss Bankers traveler's checks (in Swiss francs) can be obtained from various overseas branches of most Swiss banks as well as branches of American Express and are accepted in Switzerland at their face value and without a commission fee. Exchange rate at press time: $1 = 1.7SF

TIPS AND GRATUITIES

Tips are welcomed but not expected, as a service charge is always included. A small tip is accepted for exceptional service.

Restaurants, cafés/bars (service included)	change
Taxis (usually includes service)	change
Porters, chambermaids	change
Hairdressers	change
Restroom/cloakroom attendants	change

COMMUNICATIONS

POST OFFICES

Buy stamps *(Briefmarken)* at a post office *(Postamt)*, newsstand *(Informationsstand)* or from a hotel.

Hours for out-of-town post offices may vary.

TELEPHONES

You can use cash or a prepaid phone card *(Kartentelefon)* to make a call in Switzerland. Most telephones have direct dialing for international calls; if you need to go through an operator dial 114. A Taxcard (phone card) can be bought from newsstands, gas stations, railroad stations and post offices for 5, 10, 20, 50 and 100SF. Check that the phone booth is equipped with a Taxcard reader. You can also make a call with 1 and 5SF coins.

Phoning inside Switzerland
All Swiss telephone numbers in this book include an area code; dial the number that is listed. To call national information dial 111.

Phoning Switzerland from abroad
The country code for Switzerland is 41. Note that Swiss numbers in this book do not include the country code; you will need to prefix this number if you are phoning from another country. To phone Switzerland from the United States or Canada, omit the first zero from the Swiss number and add the prefix 011 41. (Note that Swiss area codes are either one or two digits.) Example: 01 122 33 44 becomes 011 41 1 122 33 44.

Phoning from Switzerland
To phone the United States or Canada from Switzerland, prefix the area code and number with 001.
Example: (111) 222-3333 becomes 001 111 222-3333.
To call the international operator dial 114.
To call international information dial 1159.

EMERGENCY PHONE NUMBERS

Police *(Polizei)*	117
Fire *(Feuerwehr)*	118
Ambulance *(Krankenwagen)*	117 or 144

Emergency calls are free from phone booths.

HOURS OF OPERATION

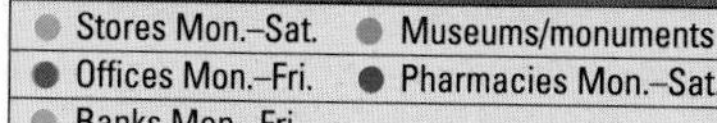

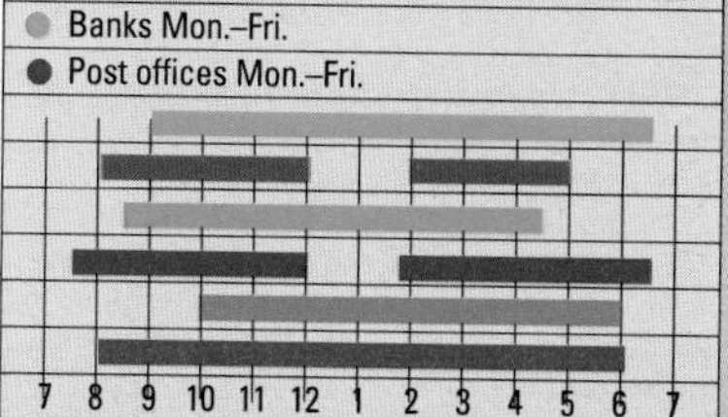

Stores close on Saturday afternoon at 4 or 5. In large towns stores may close on Monday morning, while out-of-town stores often close on a Wednesday or Thursday afternoon; some also may close for lunch (noon–1:30).

The hours of operation for banks are varied and complicated depending on the town; inquire at your hotel or a tourist office.

Post offices close at 11 on Saturday morning except for some major offices in cities, which close later; small offices have briefer hours of operation.

Museums often close on Monday and hours vary, so check locally.

NATIONAL HOLIDAYS

Banks, businesses and most stores close on these days. Various cantons observe other national holidays such as Jan. 2, May 1, Corpus Christi and All Saints' Day.

Jan. 1	**New Year**
Mar./Apr.	**Good Friday**
Mar./Apr.	**Easter Monday**
May	**Ascension Day**
May/Jun.	**Pentecost Monday**
Aug. 1	**National Day**
Dec. 25	**Christmas Day**
Dec. 26	**St. Stephen's Day**

PHOTOGRAPHY

The conditions for taking photographs vary, although generally the light is bright. Check first before taking photographs in churches and museums; it may be forbidden or you may have to ask for permission. Film and camera batteries are readily available around tourist areas, but prices may be high. Rapid-developing services also are widely available.

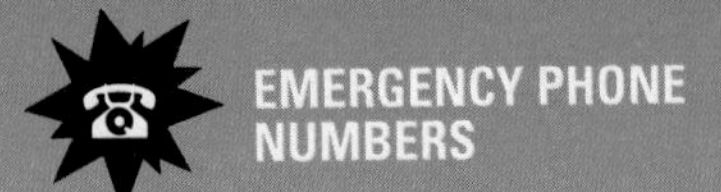

EMERGENCY PHONE NUMBERS

POLICE 117 *(Polizei)*

HEALTH

MEDICAL INSURANCE

Private medical insurance is recommended. U.S. and Canadian visitors will have to pay for all medical treatment, including emergency assistance, consultation or admittance to a hospital *(Krankenhaus)*. If you are planning to take part in winter sports, special sports policies are widely available. For information on medical issues dial Anglo-Phone, 157 5014 (toll call), from anywhere in Switzerland.

DENTAL SERVICES

A dentist *(Zahnarzt)* will charge for any treatment; dental work is expensive, so check whether it is covered by your medical insurance. Dentists are listed in the telephone directory, or ask for English-speaking dentists at your embassy or hotel, or at a tourist office.

SUN ADVICE

Conditions vary considerably; no country in Europe combines within so small an area such marked climatic contrasts. The sun can be deceptively strong in the mountains; protection is essential. The warmest part of Switzerland is south of the Alps, which is under the influence of the Mediterranean. Sun protection is needed; it is advisable to wear a hat and apply a sunscreen.

DRUGS

Pharmacies sell a range of medicines and drugs and dispense prescriptions. Many pharmacists speak English. At least one pharmacy in every town stays open late; information is displayed on store doors.

SAFE WATER

Tap water is safe to drink throughout Switzerland. Mineral water *(Sprudelwasser)* is widely available.

RESTROOMS

Most toilets *(Toiletten)* are clean and well maintained. They are indicated by a variety of signs, such as "WC" or Toiletten. Women's restrooms are designated *Damen, Frauen, Femmes, Dames, Signore* or *Donne;* men's as *Herren, Männer, Hommes, Messieurs, Signori* or *Uomini.*

ELECTRICITY

Switzerland has a 220-volt power supply. Electrical sockets take plugs with two round pins; American appliances will need a plug adapter and will require a transformer if they do not have a dual-voltage facility.

NATIONAL TRANSPORTATION

TRAIN *(Zug)*

Swiss Federal Railways is Chemins de Fer Fédéreaux (CFF) in French, Schweizerische Bundesbahnen (SBB) in German, and Ferrovie Federali Svizzere (FFS) in Italian. It runs a fast, clean and efficient service. Express trains only stop at major cities. Regionalzuge are slow trains usually running the same routes. To reach an English-speaking operator, ☎ 0900 300300. There are various good-value rail passes available. Inquire at tourist offices or any large railroad station.

BUS *(Bus)*

The bus service takes passengers to mountainous regions where railroads are unable to go. Mail bus routes encounter magnificent scenery joining villages and towns, occasionally even delivering the mail. There are many special offers; passes and cards that combine train, bus and boat travel are available at reduced rates. Eurolines operates in Switzerland; ☎ 0900 573747.

FERRY *(Fähre)*

There are many excursions on Switzerland's lakes. Regional tourist offices in different cantons can offer information, and some take reservations.

DRIVING

DRIVE ON THE RIGHT

SPEED LIMITS

Police can impose on-the-spot fines, for which a receipt is issued.

Limited-access highways *(Autobahn)*
120 k.p.h. (74 m.p.h.)
Divided highways
100 k.p.h. (62 m.p.h.)

Main roads
80 k.p.h. (49 m.p.h.)

Urban areas
50 k.p.h. (31 m.p.h.)

SEAT BELTS

Must be worn in front and back seats at all times. Children under 12 are not allowed in a front seat.

BLOOD ALCOHOL

The legal blood alcohol limit is 0.08%. Random breath tests on drivers are carried out frequently, especially late at night, and the penalties for offenders are severe.

DRIVING continued

TOLLS

An annual road tax of SF40 is levied on all cars and motorcycles using Swiss highways. Permits *(Vignettes)* are available at border crossings, post offices and service areas in Switzerland and are valid for multiple re-entry into Switzerland within the duration of the license period. To avoid delay at the border it is advisable to buy the permit in advance from a Swiss tourist office.

CAR RENTAL

The leading rental firms have offices at airports and train stations. Hertz offers discounted rates for AAA members (see page 15). For reservations:

	UNITED STATES	SWITZERLAND
Alamo	(800) 327-9633	022 788 2434
Avis	(800) 331-2112	022 732 2606
Budget	(800) 527-0700	022 900 2400
Hertz	(800) 654-3080	022 731 1200

FUEL

Gas and diesel are sold in liters. There are 24-hour gas stations on highways and in cities; many have refreshment facilities and stores. Credit cards are accepted.

AAA AFFILIATED MOTORING CLUB

Touring Club Suisse (TCS)
Chemin de Blandonnet 4, CH-1214
Vernier/Geneva, Switzerland
☎ 022 417 2727, fax 022 417 2702
If you break down while driving, phone ☎ 140 (TCS breakdown service). Not all automobile clubs offer full services to AAA members.

BREAKDOWNS AND ACCIDENTS

There are 24-hour emergency phones at regular intervals on highways. If you are involved in an accident, phone ☎ 117 for police. Most car rental firms provide their own free rescue service; if your car is rented, follow the instructions given in the documentation. Use of a car repair service other than those authorized by your rental company may violate your agreement.

OTHER INFORMATION

The minimum age for driving a car is 18 (may be higher for some car rental firms). An International Driving Permit (IDP) is recommended; some rental firms require them, and they can speed up formalities if you are involved in an accident. A Green Card (international motor insurance certificate) is recommended if you are driving a private car; see page 16 for more information. Dimmed headlights must be used when passing through tunnels. Yellow mail buses have priority at all times, as do vehicles ascending mountain roads. Many mountain pass roads are closed from October through June. For traffic conditions and weather reports: ☎ 163.

USEFUL WORDS AND PHRASES

There are four official languages spoken in Switzerland: German, French, Italian and Romansch. About 18% of the population in southwest Switzerland speak French. South of the Alps, Italian (12%) is predominant throughout Ticino and parts of the Grisons (also known as the Graubunden). Most Swiss (65%) speak German. A Swiss-German dialect with a variety of local variations is used in everyday conversation; traditional German is used for business purposes.

The fourth language is Romansch, an ancient hybrid of Celtic and Latin tongues spoken by about 40,000 people in the Surselva region of southeastern Switzerland.

This coexistence of distinct languages results in a true "European" nation. The Romansch area is probably the most "Swiss" part of the country. French influence is evident in Lausanne, while Lugano exhibits both Italian and Swiss influences.

Every Swiss child learns two or three languages. English is spoken throughout the country, but an attempt to say a few words in any of Switzerland's languages will always be appreciated.

See page 489 for French words, page 493 for German and page 509 for Italian.

The hotels and restaurants in this book were selected by on-site contributing authors and include establishments in several price ranges. Since price is often the best indication of the level of facilities and quality of service guests can expect, a three-tiered price guide appears at the beginning of the listings for each featured city. Keep in mind that prices vary widely depending on the country; dinner in Helsinki, for example, can cost up to three times as much as a similar dinner in Athens or Prague. Because variable rates will affect the amount of foreign currency that can be exchanged for dollars (and thus affect the cost of a room or a meal), price ranges are given in the local currency.

Although price ranges and any given days/times restaurants are closed were accurate at press time, this information is always subject to change without notice. If there is a certain establishment in which you're interested, it is always advisable to call ahead and verify specific amenities or hours of operation. The larger and more expensive hotels, and the better-known restaurants, are more likely to have someone who speaks English on staff; smaller establishments, particularly in southern Europe, may not. In such cases it may be more productive to inquire by fax rather than phone.

Map coordinates given in each listing relate to the city maps and give an idea of the approximate area in which each establishment is located. Although you may be able to find some of the street locations on these maps, pick up a more detailed city map from the local tourist office to help you find places.

Facilities suitable for travelers with disabilities vary greatly, and you are strongly advised to contact an establishment directly to determine whether it will be able to meet your needs. Buildings in the old sections of city centers may not be adequately designed or equipped for visitors with limited or impaired mobility.

Accommodations

Accommodations have been selected with two considerations in mind: a particularly attractive character or sense of local flavor, or a central location that is convenient for sightseeing. Establishments in different price ranges are included for each city.

Centrally located hotels fill up quickly, especially during busy summer vacation periods; make reservations well in advance. Many international hotel chains have Internet sites that either

HOTELS AND RESTAURANTS

"*NOTHING helps scenery like ham and eggs.*"

From *A Tramp Abroad*, by Mark Twain

allow you to make online reservations or provide a central reservation phone number. In-room bathrooms (usually referred to as "en-suite facilities") may not be available in smaller budget hotels.

European hotels normally provide a light breakfast of rolls or croissants and coffee (where this is not the case, the listing description notes that the rate is for "room only"). Breakfast in British and Irish hotels, however, is likely to be a full meal of bacon, sausage, eggs, fried potatoes and toast that should leave you feeling well-fed most of the day.

Some hotels offer a price for overnight accommodations that includes an evening meal (known as "half-board" in Great Britain and Ireland and *demi-pension* in French-speaking countries).

Eating Out

Listed restaurants range from upscale places suitable for an elegant evening out to small cafés where you can stop and take a leisurely break from a busy day of sightseeing. Some are close to attractions; where this is the case, there is a cross-reference under the attraction listing. Other possibilities for getting a bite to eat are the cafeterias and restaurants on the premises of museums and galleries.

For the homesick, many U.S. fast-food chains have found their way to Europe. But be sure to sample the amazing variety of indigenous European fast food: *crêpes* (filled pancakes) in France; tasty hot *Wurst* (sausages) in Germany and Austria; fish and chips (fish fillets and french fries) in Britain; the savory *tapas* appetizers served in Spanish bars; and the wonderful pizzas in Italy – served crusty and piping hot from charcoal ovens or *al taglio* (sliced to go) on street corners.

For a more civilized break, many European hotels, especially the larger ones in big cities, are not only options for an overnight stay but also for a meal. Their lounges and bars often are comfortable, quiet places to stop and relax over morning coffee, afternoon tea with cakes and sandwiches, or an evening drink. A stop also provides an opportunity to use the hotel's restroom. Top-flight hotels often serve fairly reasonably priced snacks, but inquire about prices before ordering if you're traveling on a budget.

Alcoholic beverages have a rich European heritage. France, Germany and Spain produce memorable wines; beers in the Czech Republic, Belgium and Britain are justly famed; and Guinness, of course, is an Irish institution. And the nonalcoholic fruit juices (*portokalada freska*) served in Greece – orange, lemon, watermelon, peach – are wonderfully fresh and a perfect antidote to the hot Greek summer sun.

KEY TO SYMBOLS

- map page number and coordinates
- address
- telephone number
- days/times closed
- nearest subway station
- nearest bus/trolley bus/tram/funicular route
- ferry
- $$$ expensive
- $$ moderate
- $ inexpensive
- AX American Express
- DC Diners Club
- MC MasterCard
- VI VISA

VIENNA HOTELS

Price guide: (double room with breakfast for two people)
$ S700–1,000
$$ S1,000–2,000
$$$ over S2,000

Ana Grand Hotel Wien $$$
This is the ultimate in luxury, combining the style and service of a majestic old European hotel with modern comforts. Ask about the Grand Opera package, which includes a champagne buffet breakfast, the best seats at the opera (book 2 weeks in advance) and a two-course meal afterward in the hotel's smart restaurant, Le Ciel.
26 D2 Kärtner Ring 9
01 51 58 00; fax 01 51 51 313
Tram 1, 2, D, J AX, DC, MC, VI

Kärtnerhof $$
The Kärtnerhof, situated in the city center, is convenient for sightseeing. It occupies a 19th-century building with a roof garden and sits quietly on a cul-de-sac, where a gate leads to the beautiful courtyard of Heiligenkreuzerhof.
26 D3 Grashofgasse 4
01 51 21 923; fax 01 513 22 28 33
Stephansplatz, Schwedenplatz
AX, DC, MC, VI

König von Ungarn $$$
This 18th-century building has rooms set around a covered central courtyard, which has been converted into an elegant bar/sitting room. The restaurant serves traditional Viennese meals in the vaulted dining rooms. It's very close to St. Stephen's Cathedral and next to the Figarohaus (Figaro House), so named because Mozart composed his opera *The Marriage of Figaro* while living in an apartment there.
26 D2 Schulerstrasse 10
01 51 58 40; fax 01 51 58 48
Stephansplatz 1A AX, DC, MC, VI

Pension Felicitas $
Hidden away on a quiet side street in Josefstadt, just behind the parliament building, this accommodation is for those who like a personal hotel touch: It feels a little like you're staying in somebody's home, perfect after a day's sightseeing.
26 C3 Josefsgasse 7
01 40 57 212-0 Rathaus
No credit cards

Römischer Kaiser $$
Originally a small baroque palace in the Old City, this is now an exotically furnished hotel with crimson fabrics and sparkling chandeliers. The hotel makes special arrangements such as a casino package, called "Rouge et Noir." There's no restaurant on the premises.
26 D2 Annagasse 16 01 5127 751-0; fax 01 512 77 51-13
Stephansplatz 1, 4
AX, DC, MC, VI

VIENNA RESTAURANTS

Price guide: (dinner per person, excluding drinks)
$ S150–200
$$ S200–300
$$$ over S300

Augustinerkeller $$
A range of good Austrian- and Viennese-style dishes are served with locally produced wines. It's popular with foreign visitors.
26 D2 Augustinerstrasse 1
01 53 31 026 Closed Sun.
U1, U2, U4 to Oper AX, DC, VI

Café Dreschler $$
The first café that opens its doors in the mornings has an interesting mix of customers, including people on their way home from a late night out and stall owners on their way to an early start at the market. Expect a quiet, smoky atmosphere and billiard tables. Hot dishes are served throughout the day.
26 C2 Linke Wien Zeile 22
Closed Sun. U1, U2, U4
4A, 59A; trams 62, 65
No credit cards

Do & Co Im Haas-Haus $$$
Shellfish, Thai and Japanese dishes are specialties at this trendy top-floor restaurant in the glass-fronted Haas-Haus building. You'll get good views of the cathedral.
26 D3 7th floor, Haas-Haus, Stephansplatz 12 01 53 53 969
U1, U3 AX, DC, MC, VI

Im Palais Schwarzenberg $$$
For excellent views of the Belvedere gardens come to this classy restaurant, which serves wonderful game dishes like stuffed guinea fowl in white port sauce and medallions of delicious venison.
26 D2 Schwarzenberger-

Eating in Innsbruck

Most of Innsbruck's best – and most expensive – restaurants are located in a tiny area of Old Town, along with some excellent cafés and coffeehouses. Many serve meals all day, so you can eat when you feel like it, a bonus if you've been skiing or hiking. Maria-Theresien-Strasse has a number of self-service and fast-food restaurants if you're looking for a quick lunchtime snack. For lunch with a view, take the Hungerburgbahn to Hoch-Innsbruck, where there are several restaurants with pretty terraces, or ride the cable car up to Seegrube mountain and eat on the terrace while enjoying a superb mountain panorama. The daily market, held in the Markthalle building beside the river, is an excellent place to buy provisions for a picnic.

platz 9 ☎ 01 79 84 515 Trams D, 1, 2 AX, DC, MC, VI

Stadtbeisel $$
Original Viennese dishes are served in the oldest part of the Old Town. Typical items include *Wiener Tafelspitz* (boiled rump of beef with apple and horseradish sauce) and delicious sautéed pike or perch with garlic butter and venison in brandy sauce.
26 D3 ✉ Naglergasse 21 ☎ 01 53 33 507 U3 VI

Steirereck $$$
Tables set out in the green conservatory, and in summer on a veranda, make this a great spot for a special occasion or a relaxing lunch. The food is a mix of traditional, new and regional, and there is an outstanding wine list from the richly stocked, vaulted cellars.
26 E2 ✉ Rasumofskygasse 2 ☎ 01 71 33 168 Closed Sat.–Sun. U3 to Rochusgasse AX, DC, MC, VI

INNSBRUCK HOTELS

Price guide: (double room with breakfast for two people)
$ S700–1,000
$$ S1,000–2,000
$$$ over S2,000

Central $$$
This centrally located hotel is big on comfort and service and has a wide range of facilities, including a sunning terrace.
35 A1 ✉ Gilmstrasse 5 ☎ 0512 5920; fax 0512 580310 4, 0 AX, DC, MC, VI

Europa Tyrol $$$
Innsbruck's top hotel has a wide range of rooms at varying prices, some elegant public areas, and a friendly and welcoming staff.
35 B1 ✉ Südtirolerplatz 2 ☎ 0512 5931; fax 0512 587800 1, 3, 6 AX, DC, MC, VI

Goldener Adler $$$
A truly charming and historic hotel in the heart of old Innsbruck, where modern comfort goes hand-in-hand with Tyrolean character. There also are two excellent restaurants.
35 A2 ✉ Herzog-Friedrichstrasse 6 ☎ 0512 571111; fax 0512 584409 A, 0; tram 1 AX, DC, MC, VI

Maximilian $$
On the edge of Old Town, this modern hotel combines comfort with traditional service and atmosphere.
35 A2 ✉ Marktgraben 7–9 ☎ 0512 59967; fax 0512 577450 A, 0; tram 1 AX, DC, MC, VI

Weisses Kreuz $$
Mozart once stayed at this 15th-century Old Town hotel, which combines Tyrolean charm with modern comfort. Restaurants are on the premises.
35 A2 ✉ Herzog-Friedrichstrasse 31 ☎ 0512 59479; fax 0512 5947990 A, 0; tram 1 AX, DC, MC, VI

INNSBRUCK RESTAURANTS

Price guide: (dinner per person, excluding drinks)
$ S150–200
$$ S200–300
$$$ over S300

Altstadtstüberl $$
Known for its contemporary cooking, this Old Town restaurant offers good vegetarian dishes.
35 A2 ✉ Riesengasse 13 ☎ 0512 582347 Closed Sun. A, 0; tram 1 DC, VI

Gasthof-Hotel Weisses Kreuz $$
One of Innsbruck's oldest and best restaurants serves Tyrolean and Austrian specialties in charming dining rooms.
35 A2 ✉ Herzog-Friedrichstrasse 31 ☎ 0512 573880 A, 0; tram 1 AX, DC, MC, VI

Hirschenstuben $$
This Old Town restaurant offers fish and international dishes, as well as traditional favorites.
35 A2 ✉ Kiebachgasse 5 ☎ 0512 582979 Closed Mon. lunch and Sun. A, 0; tram 1 AX, DC, MC, VI

Ottoburg $
This cozy restaurant, a good value, serves a wide range of Austrian and vegetarian dishes.
35 A2 ✉ Herzog-Friedrichstrasse 1 ☎ 0512 584338 Closed Sun. A, 0; tram 1 AX, MC, VI

Restaurant Goldener Adler $$
Its decor and friendly staff make this traditional restaurant popular with locals and tourists alike.
35 A2 ✉ Herzog-Friedrichstrasse 6 ☎ 0512 571111-0 A, 0; tram 1 AX, DC, MC, VI

SALZBURG HOTELS

Price guide: (double room with breakfast for two people)
$ S700–1,000
$$ S1,000–2,000
$$$ over S2,000

Altstadthotel Wolf-Dietrich $$$
This comfortable family-run hotel on the edge of the city's historic center has a good restaurant and an indoor swimming pool.
40 C4 ✉ Wolf-Dietrich-Strasse 7 ☎ 0662 871 275; fax 0662 882 320 29 AX, DC, MC, VI

Altstadt Radisson $$$
This renovated luxury hotel, in one of Salzburg's oldest buildings in the heart of the Old Town, has lovely rooms and an excellent restaurant.
40 C2 ✉ Rudolfskai 28/Judengasse 15 ☎ 0662 848 571-0; fax 0662 848 571-6 5, 6, 49, 51, 55, 95 AX, DC, MC, VI

Am Dom $$
Book ahead to ensure a room at this good, reasonably priced choice in the heart of the historic center.
40 C2 ✉ Goldgasse 17 ☎ 0662 842 765; fax 0662 842 765-55 5, 6, 49, 51, 55, 95 AX, DC, MC, VI

Goldener Hirsch $$$
This luxurious, baronial-style hotel is one of Salzburg's oldest and most famous accommodations, and provides service to match.
40 B3 ✉ Getreidegasse 37 ☎ 0662 80 84-0; fax 0662 843 349 1, 2, 5, 6, 15, 29, 51, 55 AX, DC, MC, VI

Schloss Mönstein $$$
This luxury-class hotel is beautifully situated in wooded grounds high above the old center of Salzburg.
40 A3 ✉ Am Mönchsberg 26 ☎ 0662 848 555-0; fax 0662 848 559 1, 2, 15, 27, 29, 49, 60, 80, 81, 95 AX, DC, MC, VI

SALZBURG RESTAURANTS

Price guide: (dinner per person, excluding drinks)
$ S150–200
$$ S200–300
$$$ over S300

KEY TO SYMBOLS

- map page number and coordinates
- address
- telephone number
- days/times closed
- nearest subway station
- nearest bus/trolley bus/tram/funicular route
- ferry
- $$$ expensive
- $$ moderate
- $ inexpensive
- AX American Express
- DC Diners Club
- MC MasterCard
- VI VISA

Chocolates Galore

Bruges' largest chocolate shop is Pralinette at Wollestraat 31B. Here you can see the daily production of fresh chocolate in a workshop where traditional methods are used, from the preparation of the chocolate in melting cauldrons to the hand-making process, in which white, milk and dark chocolate is fashioned into a variety of forms. The aroma of chocolate alone is mouthwatering. Pralinette has its own recipe using butter and fresh cream to produce 78 different types of chocolate, including delicious coffee chocolates known as *Pralinettes de Brugge*.

Augustiner Bräu $
This huge restaurant and summer beer garden serves beer, wurst and simple Austrian fare in wood-paneled halls and is very popular with tourists.
40 A4 Augustinergasse 4 0662 431 246 27, 60, 80, 81 No credit cards

Bei Bruno $$$
This smart restaurant features dishes from the Tyrol, along with local specialties and an interesting wine list.
40 B3 Makartplatz 4 0662 878 417 Closed Sun. 2, 6, 51 AX, DC, MC, VI

Festungsrestaurant $$
Located in the Hohensalzburg Fortress (see page 43), this restaurant has panoramic views of the Salzburg area combined with old-fashioned Austrian cooking (reservations required Jul.–Aug.).
40 C1 Hohensalzburg, Mönchsberg 34 0662 841 780 Closed Mon.–Tue., Sep.–May; dinner Wed.–Sun., Nov.–Mar. Festungbahn funicular MC, VI

Stiftskeller St. Peter $$
Said to be Europe's oldest restaurant, Stiftskeller is a popular beer cellar serving reasonably priced beer, wine and local dishes.
40 B2 Stiftsbezirk 1/4 0662 841 268-0 1, 2, 5, 6, 15, 29, 49, 51, 55, 95 AX, DC, MC, VI

BRUSSELS HOTELS

Price guide: (double room with breakfast for two people)
$ up to 3,000BF
$$ 3,000–7,000BF
$$$ over 7,000BF

Amigo $$$
This charming hotel is located near the heart of old Brussels, just behind Grand-Place. It has modern amenities, but with luxurious style and elegance; there's a good chance you may bump into media stars over sumptuous breakfasts.
56 B2 rue de l'Amigo 1–3 02 547 4747; fax 02 513 5277 Gare Centrale 34, 48, 94; tram 23, 52, 55, 56 AX, DC, MC, VI

Conrad International $$$
Located on avenue Louise, in Brussels' fashionable shopping quarter, this luxurious, modern hotel is close to tram and subway connections to the rest of the city.
56 B1 avenue Louise 71 02 542 4242; fax 02 542 4200 Tram 93, 94 AX, DC, MC, VI

Le Dixseptième $$$
Seventeenth-century ambience and quality service typify this very stylish central hotel, not far from Grand-Place.
56 B2 rue de la Madeleine 25 02 502 5744; fax 02 502 6424 Gare Centrale AX, DC, MC, VI

Metropole $$$
This expensive but very luxurious hotel has a long pedigree; it opened in the 1890s and still reflects *fin de siècle* elegance. The in-house restaurant, L'Alban Chambon, has top cuisine to match.
56 B3 place de Brouckère 31 02 217 2300; fax 02 218 0220 De Brouckère Tram 23, 52, 55, 81 AX, DC, MC, VI

Noga $
Although this small, charming hotel with modern rooms has a cozy "old" Brussels style (and ample breakfasts), it doesn't have good views from bedroom windows. It's located in the convenient and attractive St. Catherine district.
56 B4 rue du Béguinage 38 02 218 6763; fax 02 218 1603 St. Catherine 47 AX, DC, MC, VI

BRUSSELS RESTAURANTS

Price guide: (dinner per person, excluding drinks)
$ 400–500BF
$$ 500–1,000BF
$$$ over 1,000BF

Aux Armes de Bruxelles $$$
Good Belgian cuisine, either in a traditional restaurant setting or in the more relaxed bistro, is offered at this art deco-style restaurant in the rue des Bouchers district.
56 B2–B3 rue des Bouchers 13 02 511 5598 Closed Mon., mid-Jun. to mid-Jul. Bourse Tram 23, 52, 56, 81 MC, VI

La Belle Maraîchère $$$
Fish and lobster are the specialties at this restaurant, considered one of Brussels' best, in what was

once the dockside district of St. Catherine.
56 A3 place St.-Catherine 11A 02 512 9759 Closed Wed.–Thu. St.-Catherine 47 AX, DC, VI

Comme Chez Soi $$$
Brussels' top gastronomic experience can be savored at this celebrated restaurant. New Belgian cuisine with traditional specialties is featured; reserve well in advance.
56 A2 place Rouppe 23 02 512 2921 Closed Sun. and Mon. in Jul. Tram 23, 52, 55, 56 AX, DC, MC, VI

La Maison du Cygne $$$
This stylish restaurant in one of the guild house buildings in Grand-Place was originally a medieval tavern, and then headquarters of the Guild of Butchers. Enjoy truffles and braised turbot while contemplating the fact that Karl Marx wrote part of the *Communist Manifesto* here.
56 B2 Grand-Place 9 02 511 8244 Closed Sat. lunch and Sun. Gare Centrale Tram 23, 52, 56, 81 AX, DC, MC, VI

La Rose Blanche $$–$$$
Belgian cuisine is cooked in beer at this tavern serving 50 traditional and special beers.
56 B2 Grand-Place 11 02 513 6479 Gare Centrale Tram 23, 52, 56, 81 AX, DC, MC, VI

La Truffe Noire $$$
This top award-winning French restaurant serves truffles with just about everything, in luxurious surroundings.
56 Off the map boulevard de la Cambre 12 02 640 4422 Closed Sat. lunch and Sun. last 3 weeks in Aug. Tram 23, 90 AX, DC, MC, VI

BRUGES HOTELS
Price guide: (double room with breakfast for two people)
$ up to 3,000BF
$$ 3,000–7,000BF
$$$ over 7,000BF

Bourgoensche Cruyce $$
This small, comfortable quality hotel sits within a courtyard and overlooks a lovely stretch of canal. The Dijver and the Markt are nearby.
62 B2 Wollestraat 41–43 050 337 926; fax 050 341 968 1, 6, 11, 16 AX, MC, VI

De Orangerie $$$
One of Bruges' most lauded hotels is within this 17th-century, ivy-clad building, with a superb canal-side location and views of the Dijver. Guests can have breakfast in the paneled dining room or on the canal-side terrace; they can also use the pool and sauna of the nearby De Tuilerieën Hotel.
62 B2 Kartuizerinnensstraat 10 050 341 649; fax 050 333 016 1, 6, 11, 16 AX, MC, VI

Die Swaene $$$
This beautifully furnished hotel is in a central but quiet location; its restaurant is noted for good food and service.
62 C2 Steenhouwersdijk 1 050 342 798; fax 050 336 674 1, 6, 11, 16 AX, MC, VI

Prinsenhof $$
A few streets east of the Markt is this pleasant, family-run hotel with friendly service and charming touches, including old clocks, chandeliers and antiques. It's known for its large breakfasts.
62 C2 Ontvangersstraat 9 050 342 690; fax 050 342 321 All buses AX, MC, VI

Ter Brughe $–$$
Located a few minutes' walk north of the Markt is this canal-side hotel, housed in a handsome building dating from the 16th century that is one of the oldest buildings in Bruges. Enjoy hearty breakfasts in the attractive vaulted cellar.
62 B3 Oost-Gistelhof 2 050 340 324; fax 050 338 873 All buses AX, MC, VI

BRUGES RESTAURANTS
Price guide: (dinner per person, excluding drinks)
$ 400–500BF
$$ 500–1,000BF
$$$ over 1,000BF

Brasserie Erasmus $$
With around 100 brands to choose from, it's obvious that this genuine Belgian eatery specializes in beers; among its specialties is *waterzooi*, rabbit stewed in beer.
62 B2 Wollestraat 35 050 335 781 Closed Mon. and late Jan.–early Feb. 1, 6, 11, 16 MC, VI

Den Gouden Harynck $$$
This popular and expensive restaurant has a stylish interior and serves fine Belgian and international cuisine. Seafood dishes from caviar to lobster are the specialty; make reservations in advance.
62 B1–B2 Groeninge 25 050 337 637 Closed Sun. and Mon.; the week after Easter; mid-Jul. to the first week of Aug.; last week of Dec. 1 MC, VI

Marieke van Brughe $$$
Belgian cuisine is at its finest in this traditional, art nouveau-style restaurant, popular with Brugeans (reserve ahead). Try the North Sea bouillabaisse or the *kalfs blanket*, veal ragout.
62 B1–B2 Mariastraat 17 050 343 366 1 MC, VI

Ristorante le due Venezie $–$$
Arrive early at this trattoria in the heart of Bruges for the best Italian cuisine around. Service is friendly.
62 B2 Kleine Sint Amandsstraat 2 050 332 326 Closed Tue. 1 MC, VI

Tom Pouce $–$$
This popular and conveniently located café-restaurant on the Burg serves traditional Belgian dishes and delicious waffles, pancakes and home-made ice cream.
62 B2 Burg 17 050 330 336 All buses MC, VI

GHENT HOTELS
Price guide: (double room with breakfast for two people)
$ up to 3,000BF
$$ 3,000–7,000BF
$$$ over 7,000BF

Chamade $$
Located just north of the railroad station but with quick access to trams for the city center, this modern hotel lacks architectural style but offers excellent service and superb views from the top-floor breakfast room.
70 Off the map Blankenbergestraat 2 09 220 1515; fax 09 220 9766 14, 15, 65, 69; tram 1, 10, 12, 40 AX, DC, MC, VI

KEY TO SYMBOLS

- map page number and coordinates
- address
- telephone number
- days/times closed
- nearest subway station
- nearest bus/trolley bus/tram/funicular route
- ferry
- $$$ expensive
- $$ moderate
- $ inexpensive
- AX American Express
- DC Diners Club
- MC Mastercard
- VI VISA

Banquets for All

You can go back through history while enjoying a hearty meal in Ghent. Various traditional banquets are staged in such fascinating venues as a 13th-century monastery, a medieval crypt or the hall of a castle. The Medieval Banquet is accompanied by troubadours, dancers and a court jester. The Belle Époque Cabaret Banquet features song and dance, tap dancers, a ventriloquist and other acts with themes from the 1870s to the 1930s. The Renaissance Banquet features court dances by dancers in period costume. The Mississipi Jazz evening features Cajun food and an accompaniment of Dixieland and blues music. For information and reservations, 09 233 8660.

Erasmus $$

This cozy, old-fashioned hotel with personal touches and antique furnishings is located near historic Kornlei; breakfasts are ample and very good.
70 A3 Poel 25 09 224 2195; fax 09 233 4241 Closed early Dec.–early Jan. 16, 18, 38 AX, MC, VI

Gravensteen $$

Housed in a 19th-century mansion, this comfortable hotel is conveniently located close to the Castle of the Counts and other city attractions. Try to get a reservation in the tower room, which has one of the best views over Ghent.
70 A4 Jan Breydelstraat 35 09 225 1150; fax 09 225 1850 Tram 1, 10, 11, 13 AX, DC, MC, VI

Novotel Gent Centrum $$

With an outdoor swimming pool, restaurant and good location, this large, comfortable hotel in the center of Ghent has quiet rooms overlooking a central courtyard.
70 B3 Goudenleeuwplein 5 09 224 2230; fax 09 224 3295 16, 17, 18, 19, 38; tram 12, 41 AX, DC, MC, VI

Sofitel Gent Belfort $$–$$$

This is a large luxury hotel in the historic heart of the city, opposite the Town Hall. Its many amenities, including a restaurant and fitness room, make it a decent value.
70 B3 Hoogpoort 63 09 233 3331; fax 09 233 1102 16, 17, 18, 19, 38; tram 12, 41 AX, DC, MC, VI

GHENT RESTAURANTS

Price guide: (dinner per person, excluding drinks)
- $ 400–500BF
- $$ 500–1,000BF
- $$$ over 1,000BF

De Hel $$$

This is a small restaurant in one of the Kraanlei's most delightful buildings, "The Flying Deer." French and Belgian cuisine are at their best in the candlelit dining room, with fine music playing in the background. Reservations are advised.
70 A4–B4 Kraanlei 81 09 224 3240 Closed Mon.–Tue. Tram 1, 11, 12, 40, 42 AX, DC, MC, VI

Graaf van Egmond $$–$$$

Long-established city restaurant with elegant furnishings and a view of the "Towers of Ghent," churches and civic buildings. Traditional Flemish and French cuisine.
70 A3 Sint-Michielsplein 21 09 225 0727 Closed first half of Nov. 16, 17, 18, 19, 38; tram 12, 41 AX, DC, MC, VI

Jan Breydal $$$

This expensive but very chic canal-side restaurant is a good place to come after a visit to the nearby Museum of Decorative Arts and Design. Fish dishes are a specialty of the French cuisine.
70 A4 Jan Breydelstraat 10 09 225 6287 Closed Mon. lunch and Sun. Tram 1, 11, 12 AX, DC, MC, VI

La Petite Provence $$–$$$

As the name implies, this cozy restaurant at the heart of Ghent offers good French cuisine as well as traditional local specialties. Reservations are advised.
70 B3 Donkersteeg 4 09 225 6501 Tram 1, 11, 12 AX, DC, MC, VI

St.-Jorishof–Cour St.-Georges $$$

This long-established, very popular and busy eatery in the heart of Ghent has good fish dishes and Belgian specialties. Reservations are advised.
70 B2–B3 Botermarkt 2 09 224 2424 Closed Sun. evening Tram 1, 21, 40 AX, DC, MC, VI

LONDON HOTELS

Price guide: (double room with breakfast for two people)
- $ £30–60
- $$ £60–100
- $$$ over £100

Central Park $$$

Popular, modern hotel, close to Kensington Gardens and within walking distance of Oxford Street.
86 A3 Queensborough Terrace 020 7229 2424, fax 020 7229 2904 Queensway AX, DC, MC, VI

The Dorchester $$$

This world-class hotel and its Park Lane address says everything about

the very best in luxury accommodations.
86 B2 Park Lane 020 7629 8888; fax 020 7409 0114 Hyde Park Corner AX, DC, MC, VI

London Marriott County Hall $$$
The large London Marriott occupies the majority of the historic County Hall building. It's located on the south bank of the River Thames but is close to the Hungerford Bridge pedestrian walkway, which goes into central London.
86 D2 County Hall 020 7028 5200; fax 020 7028 5300 Waterloo AX, DC, MC, VI

The Ritz $$$
Luxurious Louis XVI interiors and all the expense and style that goes with the name are the details you can expect at this hotel.
86 C2 150 Piccadilly 020 7493 8181; fax 020 7493 2687 Green Park AX, DC, MC, VI

St. George's $$$
Unique hotel within Henry Wood House, shared by the BBC. Rooms begin on the 15th floor and have superb city views.
86 C4 Langham Place, Regent Street 020 7580 0111; fax 020 7436 7997 Oxford Circus AX, DC, MC, VI

LONDON RESTAURANTS

Price guide: (dinner per person, excluding drinks)
$ £10–15
$$ £15–30
$$$ over £30

Café in the Crypt $
This inexpensive eatery, in the heart of London on Trafalgar Square (located in the crypt of St.-Martin-in-the-Fields Church), is well known and offers first-class soups, sandwiches and light meals.
86 D3 2b Duncannon Street 020 7839 4342 Charing Cross No credit cards

Chez Nico $$$
Outstanding French cuisine from one of Europe's top chefs is served here.
86 B3 90 Park Lane 020 7409 1290 Closed Sun. Hyde Park Corner AX, DC, MC, VI

The Connaught $$$
Old English and top French cuisine are available at this restaurant in the heart of fashionable Mayfair. Reservations are advised.
86 B3 Carlos Place 020 7499 7070 Grill room closed Sat. lunch Bond Street AX, MC, VI

Joe Allen $$
Celebrities dine at this excellent California-style restaurant, located on the edge of Covent Garden.
86 D3 13 Exeter Street 020 7836 0651 Covent Garden AX, MC, VI

Quaglino's $$
Located in an old ballroom, superbly designed and stylish Quaglino's is one of London's trendiest eateries. Modern Continental cuisine is served; reservations are advised.
86 C3 16 Bury Street 020 7930 6767 Green Park AX, DC, MC, VI

Rock and Sole Plaice $
This is one of the city's best places to sample fish and chips, the national dish. Take out in traditional style, or have a sit-down meal.
86 D3 47 Endell Street 020 7836 3785 Covent Garden No credit cards

EDINBURGH HOTELS

Price guide: (double room with breakfast for two people)
$ £30–60
$$ £60–100
$$$ over £100

Balmoral $$$
This classic Edwardian building dominates the east end of Princes Street. Traditional afternoon tea is served in the Palm Court.
98 B2 1 Princes Street 0131 566 2414; fax 0131 557 8740 17, 21, 26 AX, DC, MC, VI

Brodies Guest House $–$$
This is a typical Scottish bed-and-breakfast with comfortable rooms and very friendly service.
98 Off the map 22 East Claremont Street 0131 556 4032; fax 0131 556 9739 7, 8, 9, 19 MC, VI

Greenside Hotel $–$$
Quietly situated on the north side of Calton Hill, this pleasant, small hotel offers good views to the Firth of Forth from the top floors and has an in-house bar.
98 E3 9 Royal Terrace 0131 557 0022; fax 0131 557 0022 1, 4, 5, 26, 44, 63 AX, DC, MC, VI

Old Waverley $$–$$$
This long-established hotel, in the heart of the city on Princes Street, enjoys fine views of Edinburgh Castle and the Castle Monument.
98 B2 43 Princes Street 0131 556 4648; fax 0131 557 6316 17, 21, 26 AX, DC, MC, VI

Roxburghe Hotel $$$
Traditional Scottish hospitality prevails at this upscale hotel in the heart of Georgian Edinburgh, with amenities and extras to match its status.
98 B2 38 Charlotte Square 0131 240 5500; fax 0131 240 5555 34, 35 AX, DC, MC, VI

EDINBURGH RESTAURANTS

Price guide: (dinner per person, excluding drinks)
$ £10–15
$$ £15–30
$$$ over £30

Creelers $$
This restaurant and bistro just off the Royal Mile specializes in superb seafood, much of it delivered from the owner's fishing business on Scotland's west coast. Start with oysters and mussels, then go on to a main dish of turbot, cod, hake, monkfish or shellfish. Reservations are advised.
98 C2 3 Hunter Square 0131 220 4447 Closed Sun. 1, 6 MC, VI

The Deacon's House $
A life-size figure of the infamous Deacon Brodie (an 18th-century town councilor, socialite and part-time burglar) invites you down Lawnmarket to this popular café-restaurant. Good Scots broth, light snacks, and afternoon tea and scones are among the menu items.
98 C2 3 Brodies Close, Lawnmarket 0131 226 1894 1, 6 No credit cards

Duck's at Le Marché Noir $$
The unusual name of this restaurant is derived from the proprietor's last name. Expect excellent Scottish-

KEY TO SYMBOLS

- map page number and coordinates
- address
- telephone number
- days/times closed
- nearest subway station
- nearest bus/trolley bus/tram/funicular route
- ferry
- $$$ expensive
- $$ moderate
- $ inexpensive
- AX American Express
- DC Diners Club
- MC MasterCard
- VI VISA

English Pubs

The traditional English pub, from the term "public house," is another of those treasured institutions by which an entire culture is measured. The great thing about traditional pubs is their spirit of easygoing informality. Pubs were always the focus of local life, places where people exchanged views and took their hard-earned leisure. It is no coincidence that village pub and village church often stand cheek by jowl. In medieval times, churches and monasteries often owned the local pub, or "hostelry." In and around Oxford you will find traditional pubs that have not compromised with modern fashion, while still maintaining the highest standards of comfort and service. Try The Chequers, off High Street; the King's Arms, on the corner of Parks Road and Holywell Street; the Turf Tavern in Bath Place; the Isis Tavern at Iffley Lock; or The Perch at Binsey, located by the River Thames.

French cuisine – everything from quail eggs to venison – and some exquisite desserts. There's also a good wine list.
98 Off the map 2–4 Eyre Place Closed Sat. lunch and Sun. lunch 0131 558 1608 7, 8, 9, 19, 35 AX, DC, MC, VI

Stac Polly $$$
The very best in Scottish cuisine is provided in the most stylish of surroundings. Try haggis in filo pastry with plum sauce. You'll be very pleased with any of the beef, game and salmon dishes. It is advisable to make reservations.
98 Off the map 29–33 Dublin Street 0131 556 2231 Closed Sun. lunch 8, 9, 19, 39 AX, MC, VI

Witchery by the Castle $$
This restaurant is located by Edinburgh Castle Esplanade and made even more atmospheric by hundreds of candles reflected off gothic furnishings, tapestries and hand-painted timber ceilings. The Scottish menu has international influences, with the focus on seafood. Reservations are advised.
98 C1 352 Castle Hill 0131 225 5613 1, 6 AX, DC, MC, VI

OXFORD HOTELS

Price guide: (double room with breakfast for two people)
$ £30–60
$$ £60–100
$$$ over £100

The Balkan Lodge Hotel $–$$
Located east of Oxford but with easy access to the city center. One of the bright, attractive bedrooms is furnished with a four-poster bed and jacuzzi.
107 C1 315 Iffley Road 01865 244524; fax 01865 251090 4, 4A MC, VI

Eastgate Hotel $$$
A charming mid-size hotel near Magdalen Bridge and a short distance from river walks. All rooms are en-suite, and the Café Boheme restaurant is attached.
107 C1 The High, Merton Street 0870 400 8201; fax 01865 791681 Bus 2, 4, 13, 15, 51 AX, DC, MC, VI

Old Bank $$$
A skillfully restored former bank, a place of tranquility away from the bustle of High Street. The Quod Brasserie serves all-day meals.
107 C1 92–94 High Street 01865 799599; fax 01865 799598 All buses via High Street AX, DC, MC, VI

Palace $$
A small family hotel 1 mile from the city center. There is a comfortable lounge, as well as a bar and dining facilities.
107 C1 250 Iffley Road 01865 727627; fax 01865 200478 4, 4A, AX, MC, VI

The Randolph $$$
Top-of-the-line hotel with elegant interiors, extremely comfortable rooms and luxury service. Located near Baliol College and close to the city center.
107 A2 Beaumont Street 0870 400 8200; fax 01865 791678 All buses to Oxford bus station AX, DC, MC, VI

OXFORD RESTAURANTS

Price guide: (dinner per person, excluding drinks)
$ £10–15
$$ £15–30
$$$ over £30

Brown's $$$
If you want to mix in with the student crowd, Brown's is the place to do it. You can count on such excellent British dishes as steak, mushroom and Guinness pie. You may have to stand in line at this very busy restaurant.
107 A3 5–9 Woodstock Road, St. Giles 01865 511995 AX, DC, MC, VI

Cherwell Boathouse $$
Eat by the river at this charming and popular restaurant. You can rent a punt from a nearby boat concession if you want a genuine Oxford experience. Reservations are advised.
107 Off the map Bardwell Road 01865 552746 2, 7 AX, DC, MC, VI

Le Petit Blanc $$
This friendly, popular brasserie includes a special childen's menu, featuring Oxford sausage with mashed potatoes.

107 Off the map 71–72 Walton Street 01865 510999 AX, DC, MC, VI

Restaurant Elizabeth $$$
Fine French cuisine is served at this expensive restaurant opposite Christ Church College. There's a good selection of wines.
107 A1 82 St. Aldate's 01865 242230 Closed Mon. 2, 4, 13, 22, 51 AX, DC, MC, VI

Turf Tavern $
At this very traditional English pub-restaurant, in the heart of the university area near Radcliffe Square, you can experience British dishes like pork in cider, beef and beer pie or minted lamb, all at reasonable prices.
107 B2 4 Bath Place 01865 243235 All buses via High Street Credit cards for food only MC, VI

YORK HOTELS

Price guide: (double room with breakfast for two people)
$ £30–60
$$ £60–100
$$$ over £100

Alhambra Court $–$$
This attractive Georgian building is on a quiet side road within walking distance of central York. Pleasantly furnished, with good home cooking.
113 Off the map 31 St. Mary's, Bootham 01904 628474; fax 01904 610690 AX, MC, VI

Dean Court Hotel $$$
A handsome Victorian building in an unsurpassed location close to York Minster, with views of the Minster from upper front rooms. Very stylish, first-class facilities, including an award-winning restaurant.
113 B3 Duncombe Place 01904 625082; fax 01904 620305 AX, DC, MC, VI

The Judges Lodging $$$
Style, history and atmosphere combine to make a stay in this 18th-century Georgian house a rare experience. Built by a prominent physician, it was the residence of local judges from 1806 to 1976. There's an à la carte restaurant and brasserie, and it is conveniently close to the city center.
113 B2 9 Lendal Street 01904 638733; fax 01904 679947 AX, DC, MC, VI

Royal York Hotel $$$
This expensive but top-quality hotel near the railroad station offers easy access to the city center and provides excellent service.
113 A2 Station Road 01904 653681; fax 01904 653271 AX, DC, MC, VI

Savages $–$$
Savages, a few minutes' walk from central York, is in a quiet tree-lined area. It offers a good standard of accommodation and service as well as excellent home cooking.
113 Off the map 15 St. Peters Grove, Clifton 01904 610818; fax 01904 627729 AX, DC, MC, VI

YORK RESTAURANTS

Price guide: (dinner per person, excluding drinks)
$ £10–15
$$ £15–30
$$$ over £30

19 Grape Lane $$
This fine restaurant just off Petergate offers excellent modern British cuisine with an emphasis on fresh local produce. Reservations are advised for an evening meal.
113 B3 19 Grape Lane 01904 636366 Closed Sun.–Mon. AX, MC, VI

Blue Bicycle $$
Lively and attractive restaurant with distinctive decor, scrubbed wood tables, and walls sporting mirrors and pictures. Good fish dishes and fine wines. Reservations required.
113 C2 34 Fossgate 01904 673990 AX, DC, MC, VI

Ivy Restaurant $$
This award-winning restaurant in the Grange Hotel offers fine British cuisine. The same venue has a less expensive brasserie.
113 Off the map 1 Clifton 01904 644744 Closed Sat. lunch and Sun. lunch AX, DC, MC, VI

Old Orleans $$
This American-style eatery serves very good Cajun and Creole specialties, complemented by live jazz on some evenings.
113 B2 9–11 Low Ousegate 01904 620158 AX, DC, MC, VI

St. William's Restaurant $
The unbeatable setting of St. William's College, in the shadow of York Minster, enhances outdoor dining in the atmospheric cobbled courtyard (in good weather). Live jazz and good British food make this a delightful way to spend an evening. During the day, for a small fee, you can view the college's elegant medieval rooms.
113 C3 5 College Street 01904 634830 AX, DC, MC, VI

PRAGUE HOTELS

Price guide: (double room with breakfast for two people)
$ 1,000–2,500Kč
$$ 2,500–4,500Kč
$$$ over 4,500Kč

Evropa $–$$
This landmark art nouveau hotel on Wenceslas Square, rebuilt 1903–05, is complete with sculptures, wrought-iron balconies and a glass mosaic. The best rooms overlook the square but can be noisy. The restaurant has even more art nouveau embellishments to admire.
124 E2 Václavské náměstí 25 02 2422 8117; fax 02 2422 4541 Václavské náměstí AX, DC, MC, VI

Penzion U Medvídků $$
The name of this 15th-century former brewery tavern means "The Bears." There are 17 rooms in two categories: all have bathrooms, but those with extra facilities are double the price. There's a breakfast buffet.
124 C3 Na Perštýně 7 02 2421 1916; fax 02 2422 0930 Národní trída AX, DC, MC, VI

Savoy $$$
A relaxed atmosphere prevails at this top Prague hotel, located down the hill from Prague Castle. Rooms are well designed and modernized, making a perfect vacation base.
124 Off the map Keplerova 6 02 2430 2430; fax 02 2430 2128 Tram 22 AX, DC, MC, VI

Sax $$
On the steep hill leading to Prague Castle (just off Nerudova, near Charles Bridge), this hotel has an attractive interior and well-equipped, comfortable rooms.

KEY TO SYMBOLS

- map page number and coordinates
- address
- telephone number
- days/times closed
- nearest subway station
- nearest bus/trolley bus/tram/funicular route
- ferry
- $$$ expensive
- $$ moderate
- $ inexpensive
- AX American Express
- DC Diners Club
- MC MasterCard
- VI VISA

124 A4 Jánský vršek 328/3 02 53 84 22; fax 02 53 84 98 Malostranská Tram 12, 22 AX, MC, VI

U tří pštrosů $$$

"The House of the Three Ostriches" was built in 1606 by a feather trader: He sold ostrich feathers to nobles, who wore them in their hats. The painted Renaissance ceilings survive, and the hotel is just a step from Charles Bridge.
124 B3 Dražického náměstí 12/76 02 5732 0565; fax 02 5732 0611 Tram 12, 22 AX, DC, MC, VI

PRAGUE RESTAURANTS

Price guide: (dinner per person, excluding drinks)
$ 100–200Kč
$$ 200–600Kč
$$$ over 600Kč

David $$$

This small, family-run wine bar near the U.S. Embassy specializes in German-imported food, including duck, boar and rabbit. There's also a small vegetarian menu and good salads. It's very popular, so make reservations well in advance.
124 B3 Tržiště 21/611 02 5753 3109 Tram 12, 22 AX, MC, VI

Kosher Restaurace Shalom $$

Kosher lunches are served in the high-ceilinged hall that was formerly the setting for meetings in the Jewish Town Hall, in the heart of the Jewish Quarter. The menu is simple but ample; advance reservations are essential.
124 C4 Maielova 18, Staré Město 02 2481 0929 Closed Sat. and for dinner (daily) Staroměstská No credit cards

Reykavík $$

Located between Prague's historic Old Town Square and Charles Bridge, Reykavík serves Icelandic specialties and excellent fish dishes. Ingredients, flown in from the North Atlantic, include salmon, cod and haddock; try the delicious fish soup.
124 C3 Karlova 20, Staré Město 02 2422 9251 Staroměstská AX, DC, MC, VI

U Ševce Matouše $–$$

The name means "Matthew the Cobbler," and this is indeed a former cobbler's workshop under the arcades in Loreta Square. Generous portions of steak, ham, duck and beef *stroganoff* are served.
124 Off the map Loretánské náměstí 4 02 2051 4536 Tram 22 MC, VI

U Zlaté Hrušky $$$

Excellent Czech specialties, including pâté, duck and venison, and good wines are served in an attractive house with carved, rustic furniture. The name means "The Golden Pear."
124 Off the map Nový svět 3/77, Hradčany 02 2051 5356 Tram 22 AX, DC, MC, VI

COPENHAGEN HOTELS

Price guide: (double room with breakfast for two people)
$ DKr400–700
$$ DKr700–1,200
$$$ over DKr1,200

Admiral Hotel $$$

This big waterfront hotel, in a superbly renovated, 18th-century redbrick granary warehouse, is located close to Amalienborg Plads square. Regular rooms and family suites are available; a restaurant (breakfast is extra) and sauna are on the premises.
140 D3 Toldbodgade 24–28 33 74 14 14; fax 33 74 14 16 28 AX, MC, VI

Hotel d'Angleterre $$$

Famous, and famously expensive, this luxury hotel is on Kongens Nytorv Square. An 18th-century building reconstructed from the 1630 original features sumptuous furnishings, making it a favorite with visiting celebrities.
140 C2–C3 Kongens Nytorv 34 33 12 00 95; fax 33 12 11 18 10, 28 AX, MC, VI

City $$

This attractive, comfortable, modernized hotel in an old Copenhagen townhouse is near the center of things, but in a quiet location. Only breakfast is served.
140 D2 Peder Skrams Gade 24 33 13 06 66; fax 33 13 06 67 27 AX, MC, VI

Plaza $$$

Located in the heart of the city across from Tivoli, the luxurious, modern Plaza has superbly furnished

Danish Smørrebrød

Like their fellow Scandinavians, Danes are great believers in hearty lunches – and nothing is more filling or mouthwatering than *smørrebrød*, which translates simply as "buttered bread." If it sounds like "smothering," then that's exactly what happens to the large slice of rye bread that is the basis of *smørrebrød* when it is piled high with a tasty mix of salads and garnishes, shrimps and chunks of fish, beef or pork. You can accompany this mini-banquet with a Danish lager and a small glass of chilled *akvavit* (aquavit). You also can enjoy the Danish *kolt bord*, or cold table, a fantastic array of meat and fish dishes, salads and savory dips, hot dishes, and a selection of bread and rolls.

rooms. The Library Bar encourages literary browsing over drinks, and there's a good restaurant.
140 B1 Bernstorffsgade 4
33 14 92 62; fax 33 93 93 62
8, 250S AX, MC, VI

Top Hotel Hebron $$
This is a friendly family hotel close to the railroad station and Tivoli. Comfortable rooms have many amenities, and breakfast is available.
140 A1 Helgolandsgade 4
33 31 69 06; fax 33 31 90 67
6, 10, 16, 27, 28 AX, MC, VI

COPENHAGEN RESTAURANTS

Price guide: (dinner per person, excluding drinks)
$ DKr100–250
$$ DKr250–300
$$$ over DKr300

Nyhavns Færgekro $
One of the best restaurants on canal-side Nyhavn is this one, with a nautical theme that includes model boats hanging from the ceiling. Superb lunchtime buffets featuring a variety of herring dishes are a great deal; the Danish and French cuisine offered in the evenings is more expensive.
140 D2 Nyhavn 5 33 15 15 88 MC, VI

Peder Oxe $$
Built on the foundation of an old monastery, this noted restaurant/cellar bar is on Grey Brothers Square. Traditional Danish cuisine emphasizes hearty helpings of meat; the lunchtime *smørrebrød* is very good.
140 C2 Gråbrødretorv 11
33 11 00 77 DC, MC, VI

Restaurant Els $$$
Original painted wall panels from the 1850s add style to this popular Nyhavn restaurant, situated on a street leading off Kongens Nytorv Square. Excellent fish specialties and fine wines are served. Reservations are advised.
140 D2–D3 Store Strandstræde 3 33 14 13 41
AX, DC, MC, VI

Riz Raz $
This popular buffet restaurant serves Mediterranean-style hot and cold vegetarian dishes and salads, as well as Greek lamb and fish dishes. In good weather the garden is open.
140 C2 Kompagnistræde 20
33 15 05 75 DC, MC, VI

Skt. Gertruds Kloster $$$
Housed in an old monastery building, this smart, candlelit restaurant has a vaulted cellar and atmospheric dining rooms. Fish dishes are the specialty, with everything from mussels to lobster, and there's a big selection of wines. Reservations are advised.
140 C3 Hauser Plads 32
Closed for lunch 33 14 66 30 AX, DC, MC, VI

ODENSE HOTELS

Price guide: (double room with breakfast for two people)
$ DKr400–700
$$ DKr700–1,200
$$$ over DKr1,200

City Hotel $$
This is a comfortable, modern hotel near the Hans Christian Andersen House in the heart of the Old Town.
146 C2 Hans Mulesgade 5
66 12 12 58; fax 66 12 93 64
AX, MC, VI

Domir $
This friendly, medium-size hotel with comfortable rooms and plenty of amenities is located in the city center, within minutes of the railroad station and within easy walking distance of the Town Hall.
146 Off the map Hans Tausensgade 19 66 12 14 27; fax 66 12 17 82 AX, MC, VI

First Grand Hotel $$–$$$
One of Odense's most expensive hotels is situated in a handsome old building in a pleasant location across from the Fyns Kunstmuseum (Art Museum of Funen), close to the city center.
146 B2–B3 Jernbanegade 18 66 11 71 71; fax 66 14 11 71
AX, MC, VI

Pjentehus $
Just outside the city center, Pjentehus is a small, reasonably priced and comfortable bed and breakfast in a pleasant villa near the Hans Christian Andersen House.
146 C2 Pjentedamsgade 14
66 12 15 55; fax 66 17 82 08
No credit cards

Radisson SAS Hans Christian Andersen Hotel $$$
A very luxurious, modern hotel located close to Hans Christian Andersen House and next door to the Concert Hall and the Carl Nielsen Museum, the Radisson has its own restaurant, sauna, solarium, billiards room and casino.
146 C2 Claus Bergs Gade 7
66 14 78 00; fax 66 14 78 90
AX, MC, VI

ODENSE RESTAURANTS

Price guide: (dinner per person, excluding drinks)
$ DKr100–250
$$ DKr250–300
$$$ over DKr300

Den Gamle Kro $$$
This restaurant occupies a magnificent old building dating from 1683. Meals are served in several rooms, including the brick-vaulted cellar. Expect excellent Danish cuisine and other dishes.
146 B2–C2 Overgade 23
66 12 14 33 AX, MC, VI

Den Grimme Ælling $
This charming little restaurant on a cobbled lane just across the main road from the Hans Christian Andersen House is noted especially for its extravagant buffets.
146 B2 Hans Jensens Stræde 1 65 91 70 30 AX, MC, VI

Jensens Bøfhus $
This popular lunchtime grill and evening favorite serves steaks with lavish salads.
146 A2 Kongensgade 10
66 14 59 59 AX, MC, VI

Marie Louise $$$
This very stylish French restaurant is located in a charming courtyard complex and is surrounded by old houses.
146 B2 Lottrupsgård 9
66 17 92 95 AX, MC, VI

Restaurant Air Pub $$
This pub and restaurant offers a good atmosphere to go along with hearty Danish cooking and a decent selection of beers.
146 A2 Kongensgade 41
66 14 66 08 Closed Sun. AX, MC, VI

KEY TO SYMBOLS

- map page number and coordinates
- address
- telephone number
- days/times closed
- nearest subway station
- nearest bus/trolley bus/tram/funicular route
- ferry
- $$$ expensive
- $$ moderate
- $ inexpensive
- AX American Express
- DC Diners Club
- MC MasterCard
- VI VISA

Russian Restaurants

You can sample authentic Russian cuisine in Helsinki at one of the city's several Russian restaurants. Russian food is not noted for its lightness of touch, but it can be adventurous and is extremely filling. You can even start with caviar and sour cream if you want, before plunging into hearty meat dishes – lamb is a specialty, with cakes, fruit pies and ice cream for dessert. Two notable choices to try are Kasakka at Meritullinkatu 13, (09 135 6288), and Galleria Hariton at Kasarmikatu 44, (09 622 1717).

HELSINKI HOTELS

Price guide: (double room with breakfast for two people)
$ Fmk400–600
$$ Fmk600–800
$$$ over Fmk800

Anna $–$$
This well-appointed hotel is conveniently located on one of the quiet streets of the city center, within walking distance of the Esplanade. Its moderate size contributes to a friendly and relaxed atmosphere.
158 C3 Annankatu 1 09 616 621; fax 09 602 664 14, 14B, 17; tram 3B, 10 AX, MC, VI

Helka $
Located in the heart of the city, this recently renovated hotel offers good service, good value and a sauna.
158 B4 Pohjoinen Rautatiekatu 23a 09 613 580; fax 09 441 087 14, 14B, 32, 39, 45, 47 AX, MC, VI

Lord Hotel $$–$$$
This well-appointed hotel in a handsome art nouveau building provides a good restaurant, bars and a relaxing terrace.
158 C4 Lönnrotinkatu 29 09 615 815; fax 09 680 1315 20, 20N; tram 10 AX, MC, VI

Scandic Hotel Grand Marina $$$
Step from ferry to foyer, if you travel by Viking Line, and stay in this large hotel on the western side of the harbor. Rooms are elegant and comfortable; also here are bars, a bistro and the Grand Café.
158 D4 Katajanokanlaituri 7 09 16661; fax 09 664 764 52; tram 4 AX, MC, VI

Scandic Hotel Marski $$$
This large hotel, right at the heart of things on Mannerheimintie street, was recently enlarged and renovated.
158 C4 Mannerheimintie 10 09 68061; fax 09 642 377 20N, 24, 42; tram 10 AX, MC, VI

HELSINKI RESTAURANTS

Price guide: (dinner per person, excluding drinks)
$ Fmk50–150
$$ Fmk150–200
$$$ over Fmk200

Alexander Nevski $$$
The mix of French and Russian design goes well with Russian cuisine in this long-established restaurant. There are lots of appetizers, including sour cream with caviar.
158 C4 Pohjoisesplanadi 17 09 639 610 13, 64S, 77S; tram 1, 1A AX, MC, VI

Amadeus $$$
This top-quality restaurant in the "Street Museum" serves Finnish cuisine enjoyed in comfortable surroundings. Game specialties are offered when in season.
158 C4 Sofiankatu 4 09 626 6676 Closed Sun. Tram 1, 2, 4, 7, 3B, 3T AX, MC, VI

George $$
Try pigeon stuffed with spinach in herb sauce at this small restaurant, where Finnish cuisine is tempered with French and Italian flair.
158 C4 Kalevankatu 17 09 647 66 Closed Sun. 20N, 24, 42 AX, MC, VI

Kappeli $$
This is a stylish restaurant and café, with outside terraces on the Esplanade, in a pavilion of cast iron and glass dating from 1867. Good Finnish and Scandinavian dishes are offered, and the fish soup is recommended. The restaurant has its own brewery, and in summer there are concerts at the nearby bandstand.
158 C4 Eteläesplanadi 1 09 179 242 13, 64S, 77S; tram 1, 1A AX, MC, VI

Lyon $$
Good-quality French cuisine is presented in this unassuming and friendly restaurant opposite the Helsinki Opera House. The roasted breast of goose is a favorite.
158 C5 Mannerheimintie 56 09 408 131 Closed Sun. 16, 13, 21v; tram 4, 10 AX, DC, MC, VI

PARIS HOTELS

Price guide: (double room with breakfast for two people)
$ 400–600Fr
$$ 600–1,000Fr
$$$ over 1,000Fr

Bristol Paris $$$
The Louis XV-style rooms affirm the elegance at this hotel, which has a

rooftop pool and superb restaurant. 174 B3 112 rue du Faubourg-St.-Honoré 01 53 43 43 00; fax 01 53 43 43 01 Miromesnil AX, DC, MC, VI

Hôtel des Deux-Îles $$
This peaceful hotel, beautifully housed in a 17th-century house, has understated charm and elegance. 174 D2 59 rue St.-Louis-en-l'Île 01 43 26 13 35; fax 01 43 29 60 25 Pont-Marie AX, MC, VI

Hôtel des Grandes Écoles $$
This typically French hotel has pretty bedrooms and is set in a garden on a narrow street in the Latin Quarter. It's an excellent value. 174 D2 75 rue Cardinal-Lemoine 01 43 26 79 23; fax 01 43 25 28 15 Cardinal-Lemoine MC, VI

Istria $$
This small and comfortable hotel in the heart of Montparnasse once hosted Ernest Hemingway. 174 C1 29 rue Campagne-Première 01 43 20 91 82; fax 01 43 22 48 45 Raspail AX, DC, MC, VI

Pavillon de la Reine $$$
This romantic and luxurious hotel, complete with four-poster beds, is set in a garden on the beautiful place des Vosges. 174 E2 28 place des Vosges 01 42 77 96 40; fax 01 42 77 63 06 Bastille AX, DC, MC, VI

PARIS RESTAURANTS

Price guide: (dinner per person, excluding drinks)
$ 150–200Fr
$$ 200–300Fr
$$$ over 300Fr

La Coupole $$
This sprawling art deco brasserie, renowned in the 1920s, serves seafood, fish and steaks. 174 C1 102 boulevard du Montparnasse 01 43 20 14 20 Vavin AX, DC, MC, VI

Le Dôme $$$
The specialties at this famous Montparnasse brasserie are seafood and fish. Service is efficient. 174 C1 108 boulevard du Montparnasse 01 43 35 25 81 Vavin AX, MC, VI

Le Grizzli $$
Situated in the heart of Marais, this old-fashioned bistro serves dishes from central and southwest France. 174 D3 7 rue St.-Martin 01 48 87 77 56 Closed Sun. Hôtel-de-Ville AX, MC, VI

Le Poulbot Gourmet $$
This cozy restaurant is decorated with pictures of Montmartre. The owner-chef's cuisine is refined (veal kidneys in wine sauce are a specialty). *Prix-fixe* menu available. 174 Off the map 39 rue Lamarck 01 46 06 86 00 Closed Sun. Lamarck-Caulaincourt AX, DC, MC, VI

Nos Ancêtres les Gaulois $
This picturesque island restaurant offers a *prix-fixe* menu in convivial 17th-century surroundings. 174 D2 39 rue St.-Louis-en-l'Île 01 46 33 66 07 Closed Mon.–Fri. lunch Pont-Marie AX, DC, MC, VI

Saint Amarante $
Hearty country cooking is the specialty at this friendly and relaxed bistro near the Bastille. 174 E2 4 rue Biscornet 01 43 43 00 08 Closed Sat. lunch, Sun.–Mon. and Aug. Bastille MC, VI

LYON HOTELS

Price guide: (double room with breakfast for two people)
$ 400–600Fr
$$ 600–1,000Fr
$$$ over 1,000Fr

Grand Hôtel des Terreaux $$
This comfortable, medium-size hotel is beautifully situated just behind a lovely central square. 186 B3 16 rue Lanterne 04 78 27 04 10; fax 04 78 27 97 75 Hôtel de Ville AX, DC, MC, VI

Libertel Beaux-Arts $$
A turn-of-the-20th-century building houses this comfortable hotel in the center of the Presqu'Île. 186 B3 75 rue President Edouard-Herriot 04 78 38 09 50; fax 04 78 42 19 19 Cordeliers or Bellecour AX, DC, MC, VI

Hotel Sofitel Lyon Bellecour $$$
This deluxe hotel, centrally located on the Rhône river, is a good choice. 186 B2 20 quai Gailleton 04 72 41 20 20; fax 04 72 40 05 50 Bellecour AX, DC, MC, VI

Le Terminus St.-Paul $
Consider staying at this excellent budget choice in the middle of the Old Town. It has clean, simple and airy rooms. 186 A3 6 rue Lainrerie 04 78 28 13 29; fax 04 72 00 97 27 AX, DC, MC, VI

La Villa Florentine $$$
This deluxe hotel with many amenities – including a pretty garden – stands above the Old Town, on the slopes of Fourvière. 186 A2 25–27 montée St.-Barthélémy 04 72 56 56 56; fax 04 72 40 90 56 AX, DC, MC, VI

LYON RESTAURANTS

Price guide: (dinner per person, excluding drinks)
$ 150–200Fr
$$ 200–300Fr
$$$ over 300Fr

Le Café du Soleil $
One of the oldest *bouchons* in Lyon serves huge portions of French and Lyonnais fare in a friendly atmosphere. 186 A2 2 rue St.-Georges, place de la Trinité 04 78 37 60 02 Closed Sun. Vieux Lyon AX, DC, MC, VI

Chabert et Fils $
Sophisticated Lyonnais specialties served here include a chicken-liver *gâteau* and delicate soups. 186 B2 11 rue des Marronniers 04 78 37 01 94 Bellecour AX, DC, MC, VI

Christian Têtedoie $$–$$$
Rich but light specialties are on the menu at this elegant and professionally staffed restaurant. 186 A3 54 quai Pierre-Scize 04 78 29 40 10 Closed Sat. lunch, Sun. and first 3 weeks in Aug. AX, DC, MC, VI

Le Comptoir du Bœuf $
You can try Lyonnais specialties in this cozy, late-night restaurant next to the cathedral. 186 A2 3 place Neuve St.-Jean 04 78 92 82 35 Vieux Lyon AX, DC, MC, VI

KEY TO SYMBOLS

- map page number and coordinates
- address
- telephone number
- days/times closed
- nearest subway station
- nearest bus/trolley bus/tram/funicular route
- ferry
- $$$ expensive
- $$ moderate
- $ inexpensive
- AX American Express
- DC Diners Club
- MC MasterCard
- VI VISA

The *Belle Époque* in Nice

The *belle époque*, or "beautiful era," was the name the French gave to the early 20th century. During this period Nice's fame soared with the influx of up to 150,000 wealthy English and Russians who came here to while away northern winters in elegance. They expected luxury, and it was for them that sumptuous and grandiose hotels and villas were built. Some buildings survive today along the promenade des Anglais. The Hôtel Négresco is the most famous; enjoy a drink there in Edwardian style.

Les Eaux Vives $$$

This wonderful restaurant, in one of Lyon's smartest hotels, uses fine ingredients such as lobster and foie gras in balanced dishes. This is a popular choice; reservations are advised.

186 Off the map Hotel Metropole, 85 quai Joseph-Gillet 04 72 10 44 45 Closed first 3 weeks of Aug. 40, 43, 90E
AX, DC, MC, VI

NICE HOTELS

Price guide: (double room with breakfast for two people)
$ 400–600Fr
$$ 600–1,000Fr
$$$ over 1,000Fr

Elysée Palace $$$

There are excellent facilities, including a rooftop pool, at this modern luxury hotel.

194 B1 59 promenade des Anglais 04 93 97 90 90; fax 04 93 44 50 40 6, 9, 10, 12
AX, DC, MC, VI

Gounod $$

Just a 10-minute walk from the sea is this decent, moderately priced *belle époque* choice, with a quiet, central location.

194 C2 3 rue Gounod
04 93 16 42 00; fax 04 93 88 23 84
Closed late Nov.–late Dec.
9, 10, 12 AX, DC, MC, VI

Négresco $$$

One of the world's great hotels in the flamboyant *belle époque* style, with a superlative level of comfort, service and facilities.

194 B1 37 promenade des Anglais 04 93 16 64 00; fax 04 93 88 35 68 6, 9, 10, 12
AX, DC, MC, VI

Vendôme $$

This hotel has pretty rooms, air-conditioning, a peaceful garden and an Old Town location.

194 D1 26 rue Pastorelli
04 93 62 00 77; fax 04 93 13 40 78
6, 9, 12 AX, DC, MC, VI

Windsor $$

This famous hotel is centrally located and has a garden pool and beautifully frescoed rooms.

194 B1 11 rue Dalpozzo
04 93 88 59 35; fax 04 93 88 94 57
6, 9, 10, 12 AX, DC, MC, VI

NICE RESTAURANTS

Price guide: (dinner per person, excluding drinks)
$ up to 200Fr
$$ 200–300Fr
$$$ over 300Fr

Boccaccio $$–$$$

Located in the city center, this restaurant offers mouthwatering seafood specialties; in summer it offers the cool setting of its terrace. Reservations are advised.

194 C1 7 rue Masséna
04 93 87 71 76 3, 7, 10
AX, DC, MC, VI

Brasserie Flo $–$$

The food in this lively open-kitchen brasserie, housed in an old theater, is fine, but the decor and ambience are what make it worth a visit. It's also open late.

194 D1 2–4 rue Sacha Guitry
04 93 13 38 38 1, 4, 10, 22
AX, DC, VI

Chantecler $$$

Nice's finest restaurant, and one of the best in France, is housed in the opulent Hôtel Négresco and serves traditional French food. Reservations are advised.

194 B1 Hôtel Négresco, 37 promenade des Anglais 04 93 16 64 00 Closed mid-Nov. to mid-Dec. 6, 12 AX, DC, MC, VI

Nissa La Bella $

Locals flock to this Old Town restaurant, which serves a good range of Niçoise specialties, including *socca*, a chickpea pancake.

194 D1 6 rue Ste.-Réparate
04 93 62 10 20 Closed Sun. lunch 6, 9, 10 AX, DC, MC, VI

La Petite Maison $$–$$$

Join the regulars who enjoy good home cooking from a menu that features seasonal specialties and a fantastic range of hors d'oeuvres. Reservations are advised.

194 D1 11 rue St.-François-de-Paule 04 93 92 59 59
Closed Sun. 9, 10, 12, 22
AX, DC, MC, VI

STRASBOURG HOTELS

Price guide: (double room with breakfast for two people)
$ 400–600Fr
$$ 600–1,000Fr
$$$ over 1,000Fr

Baumann $$
Situated opposite the cathedral, this comfortable, traditional hotel has a lovely terrace and good restaurant; an excellent vacation choice.
200 B1–B2 16 place de la Cathédrale 03 88 32 42 14; fax 03 88 23 03 92 A, D AX, DC, MC, VI

Cathédrale $$
This excellent cathedral square hotel is close to Strasbourg's main sights and some of the city's best restaurants.
200 B1–B2 12–13 place de la Cathédrale 03 88 22 12 12; fax 03 88 23 28 00 A, D AX, DC, MC, VI

Comfort Hotel Center $–$$
This good-value budget hotel overlooks the water on the northern side of the old city center.
200 A2 1 quai de Paris 03 88 15 17 17; fax 03 88 15 17 15 AX, VI

Hôtel des Rohan $$
This pretty hotel on one of Strasbourg's most picturesque and historic streets is an easy stroll from the main sights.
200 B1 17–19 rue du Maroquin 03 88 32 85 11; fax 03 88 75 65 37 A, D AX, DC, VI

Mercure Centre $$
This convenient and comfortable hotel is located in the historic center, has large, soundproof rooms and offers very good facilities.
200 B2 25 rue Thomann 03 90 22 70 70; fax 03 90 22 70 71 A, D AX, DC, MC, VI

STRASBOURG RESTAURANTS

Price guide: (dinner per person, excluding drinks)
$ up to 200Fr
$$ 200–300Fr
$$$ over 300Fr

Aux Armes de Strasbourg $
Interesting local dishes and a huge variety of beers are served at this wonderfully atmospheric, wood-paneled restaurant.
200 B1 9 place Gutenberg 03 88 32 85 62 A, D AX, DC, MC, VI

Au Bon Vivant $
One of the few remaining traditional family-run restaurants in the city center is this winner, serving local specialties in a relaxed atmosphere.
200 B1 7 rue du Maroquin 03 88 32 77 81 Closed Thu. dinner and Fri. A, D AX, MC, VI

Au Petit Tonnelier $
This family-run restaurant, on one of the Old Town's prettiest streets, serves seasonal and regional dishes.
200 B1 16 rue des Tonneliers 03 88 32 53 54 Closed Sun. lunch A, D AX, MC, VI

Le Baeckeoffe d'Alsace $
An old timbered building in the loveliest part of the Old Town is the setting for this traditional, family-run *winstub* (there is another at 24 rue des Hallebardes).
200 A1 14 rue des Moulins 03 88 23 05 40 A, D AX, MC, VI

La Taverne de Maître Kanter $–$$
This big, busy brasserie serves generous portions of Strasbourg specialties such as *choucroute* (sauerkraut) and *tarte flambée* (onion tart), as well as seafood.
200 B2 11–13 rue des Grandes Arcades 03 88 32 18 19 A, D AX, DC, MC, VI

BERLIN HOTELS

Price guide: (double room with breakfast for two people)
$ up to DM150
$$ DM150–300
$$$ over DM300

Alsterhof $$–$$$
This is a small 1960s hotel located behind the KaDeWe department store. Despite the plain exterior, it is stylish inside, with 200 rooms, a smart restaurant and an annex conservatory.
216 B2 Augsburger Strasse 5 030 212 420; fax 030 218 3949 U-Bahn to Augsburger Strasse; S-Bahn to Zoologischer Garten AX, DC, VI

Golden Tulip Hotel Kronprinz $$–$$$
This elegant, privately owned and managed hotel, in a 66-room late 19th-century house, is only a few steps from the Ku'damm and has an attractive terraced beer garden.
216 A2 Kronprinzendamm 1 030 896 030; fax 030 893 1215 U-Bahn to Adenauerplatz; S-Bahn to Halensee AX, DC, MC, VI

Kempinski Hotel Bristol $$$
This hotel, once on Unter den Linden but now in the Ku'damm, has a famous name and a traditional style, with formal furnishings, chandeliers and deep-pile carpets. There are 301 rooms and 44 suites, and an elaborate menu in the restaurant.
216 B2 Kurfürstendamm 27 030 884 340; fax 030 883 6075 U-Bahn to Uhlandstrasse AX, DC, MC, VI

Transit $
Once a factory, this hotel has been converted into a pleasant, airy accommodation. It's basic but clean, in an attractive part of the Kreuzberg quarter, and the English-speaking staff are welcoming.
216 D1 Hagelberger Strasse 53–4 030 789 0470; fax 030 78 90 47 77 U-Bahn to Mehringdamm; S-Bahn to Yorckstrasse AX, MC, VI

Hotel-Pension Wittelsbach $$
The Wittelsbach caters to children, with a family floor including fully equipped playhouses, strollers and high chairs.
216 B1 Wittelsbacherstrasse 22 030 864 9840; fax 030 862 1532 U-Bahn to Konstanzer Strasse; S-Bahn to Charlottenburg AX, MC, VI

BERLIN RESTAURANTS

Price guide: (dinner per person, excluding drinks)
$ up to DM25
$$ DM25–50
$$$ over DM50

Alte Luxemburg $$$
What you get at one of the city's best restaurants is German food by chef Karl Wannemacher, who adds his inventive touch with herbs.
216 A2 Windscheidstrasse 31 030 323 8730 Closed for lunch and Sun. U-Bahn to Sophie-Charlotten-Platz AX, DC, VI

Bamberger Reiter $$$
This well-known restaurant, owned by Austrian-born Franz Raneburger, features Austro-Prussian cooking

KEY TO SYMBOLS

- map page number and coordinates
- address
- telephone number
- days/times closed
- nearest subway station
- nearest bus/trolley bus/tram/funicular route
- ferry
- **$$$** expensive
- **$$** moderate
- **$** inexpensive
- AX American Express
- DC Diners Club
- MC MasterCard
- VI VISA

Strasbourg Specials

Visualize French flair and imagination combined with high-quality ingredients and German influences, and you'll begin to understand the gastronomic delights that await you in Strasbourg. This is the home of foie gras, fatted goose liver eaten whole or made into pâté; *choucroute* (sauerkraut), assorted meats and spicy sausages served with mounds of pickled cabbage; and *kougelhupf*, yeast cake traditionally eaten for breakfast. There are other, less well-known regional dishes; look for *baeckeoffe*, a slow-cooked casserole featuring three different meats, and *tarte flambée*, an unctuous hot onion tart. The smooth, pungently aromatic Munster is Strasbourg's local cheese.

and other national styles. Try the goose-liver tarts.
216 B1 Regensburger Strasse 7 030 218 4282 Closed Sun.–Mon. Spichernstrasse AX, DC, MC, VI

Berliner Stube $$
Berliner Leber (liver) is the specialty at this large restaurant near the Ku'damm; international dishes are served, too.
216 B2 Los Angeles Platz 1 030 212 7750 Kurfürstendamm AX, DC, MC, VI

Borchardt $$$
Trendy Berliners love this attractive, 1920s-style bistro, where international and "new" cuisine is featured. Brunch is served here on Sundays.
216 D2 Französische Strasse 47 030 2038 7110 Französische Strasse AX, VI

Lutter & Wegner $$$
Austrian and German dishes are served in a historic 19th-century restaurant/wine bar on the Gendarmenmarkt, where the world-famous Berlin Symphony Orchestra has its home.
216 D2 Charlottenstrasse 56 030 20 29 54 10 Hausvogteiplatz AX

Zum Nussbaum $
The name of this traditional Berlin pub-style restaurant, or *Gasthaus*, means "The Nut Tree." It's pleasant location is in the old area called Nikolaiviertal which has been extensively renovated.
216 E3 Probstrasse 030 242 3095 Alexanderplatz

COLOGNE HOTELS

Price guide: (double room with breakfast for two people)
$ up to DM150
$$ DM150–300
$$$ over DM300

Buchholz $$
This private, family-run hotel with a friendly staff has 27 bedrooms. The central but quiet location is an added bonus. A shuttle service to the airport can be provided for customers on request.
225 C4 Kunibertsgasse 5 0221 16083-0; fax 0221 16083-41 Dom/Hbf AX, DC, MC, VI

Europa am Dom $$
Conveniently located directly opposite the cathedral, this elegant hotel is close to most museums. Nonsmoking rooms are available.
225 B3 Am Hof 38–46 0221 2058-0; fax 0221 258 2032 Dom/Hbf AX, DC, MC, VI

Das Kleine Stapelhäuschen $
Two adjacent town houses, in historically interesting buildings on the Rhine promenade, house a friendly hotel with a comfortable wine bar that's just a short walk from the cathedral.
225 C3 Fischmarkt 1–3 0221 257 7862; fax 0221 257 4232 Tram 1, 7, 9 MC, VI

Sofitel Mondial am Dom $$$
Despite its dull exterior, this is a comfortable, stylish hotel, situated between the cathedral and the river – ideal for exploring the Old Town. There's also a restaurant serving international and regional cuisine.
225 B3 Kurt-Hackenberg-Platz 1 0221 20630; fax 0221 206 3522 Dom/Hbf AX, DC, MC, VI

Viktoria $$
This turn-of-the-20th-century *Jugendstil* building by the Rhine offers some rooms with river views and a generous breakfast buffet.
225 Off the map Worringer Strasse 23 0221 441 071; fax 0221 441 073 Reichensperger Platz AX, DC, MC, VI

COLOGNE RESTAURANTS

Price guide: (dinner per person, excluding drinks)
$ up to DM25
$$ DM25–50
$$$ over DM50

Bosporus $$
Located in the multicultural quarter of Weidengasse, Bosporus has four set menus offering a wide range of Turkish dishes. The nearby Eigelstein quarter is equally lively.
225 B4 Weidengasse 36 0221 125 265 Tram 6, 15, 17 AX, DC, MC, VI

Braunhaus Sion $$
This busy side-street brewery-tavern, near the cathedral, is especially popular for lunch and coffee, and for strong *Kölsch* beer.

Traditionally dressed waiters roll out the barrels.
225 B3 Unter Taschenmacher 5–7 0221 257 8540 Tram 1, 7, 9 No credit cards

Kintaro $$
Japanese dishes are served in this popular sushi restaurant, where particularly good entrees include seaweed *(hijiki)* and octopus, cucumber and seaweed in vinegar *(tako su)*. Reservations are advised.
225 A3 Friesenstrasse 16 0221 135 255 Friesenplatz No credit cards

Päffgen in der Altstadt $$
This pub-cum-restaurant, belonging to Cologne's smallest brewery, is centrally located and convenient to the city's main attractions. Tasty regional dishes and *Kölsch* beer are served in a congenial atmosphere.
225 B2 Heumarkt 62 0221 257 7765 Closed Mon. Tram 1, 7, 9 No credit cards

Paul's Restaurant $$$
Located in a former pub in a typical quarter of Cologne, Paul's serves traditional and modern cuisine. Choose a bottle of wine, and you will only be charged for what you drink.
225 B3 Bülowstrasse 2 0221 766 839 Tram 12, 18 AX, MC

MUNICH HOTELS

Price guide: (double room with breakfast for two people)
$ up to DM150
$$ DM150–300
$$$ over DM300

Englischer Garten $$
This hotel, at the edge of the English Garden in Schwabing, is housed in a converted water mill. You'll really feel like you're in the heart of the country, especially when eating the breakfast buffet, served in the garden in summer.
230 Off the map Liebergesellstrasse 8 089 383 9410; fax 089 38 39 41 33 Münchener Freiheit No credit cards

Mandarin Oriental Munich $$$
Celebrity guests including Madonna and Prince Charles have stayed at the city's newest luxury hotel, with 73 rooms including luxurious suites.
230 D2 Neuturmstrasse 1 089 29 09 80; fax 089 22 25 39 Marienplatz Tram 19 AX, DC, MC, VI

Opera $$$
This 56-bed hotel, set in an old mansion with elegant arcades and a Renaissance courtyard, is convenient to upscale shopping.
230 D2 St. Anna-Strasse 10 089 22 55 33; fax 089 22 55 38 Lehel Tram 19 AX, DC, MC, VI

Splendid $$
Rooms at this small bed-and-breakfast in the city center are decorated in a range of styles, from baroque to Bavarian.
230 D2 Maximilianstrasse 54 089 29 66 06; fax 089 291 31 76 Lehel AX, DC, MC, VI

Torbräu $$$
Munich's oldest hotel has been in the heart of the Old Town for more than five centuries. On the premises are an Italian restaurant, café and 86 quiet, individually styled rooms.
230 C2 Tal 41 089 24 23 40; fax 089 24 23 42 35 Marienplatz or Isartor AX, MC, VI

MUNICH RESTAURANTS

Price guide: (dinner per person, excluding drinks)
$ up to DM25
$$ DM25–50
$$$ over DM50

Augustiner Bräu $$
Munich's oldest surviving brewery was producing its own beer until 1897, and now serves Bavarian dishes in its large hall. There's a beer garden in the courtyard.
230 B2 Neuhauser Strasse 27 089 23 18 32 57 Marienplatz or Karlsplatz AX, DC, MC, VI

Halali $$$
Unpretentious regional cooking, focusing on game dishes such as venison, is served with special touches like cranberry or wild mushroom sauce.
230 D3 Schönfeldstrasse 22 089 28 59 09 Closed Sun. Odeonsplatz AX, MC, VI

Ratskeller $$
Hearty local dishes are served in the New Town Hall's impressive vaulted cellars.
230 C2 Marienplatz 8 089 21 99 89-0 Marienplatz AX, MC, VI

Schlosscafé Palmenhaus $$
This elegant café is set in the palm house of Nymphenburg Palace.
230 Off the map Schloss Nymphenburg 089 17 53 09 Tram 12, 17 AX, MC, VI

Spatenhausan der Opera $$
The atmosphere is relaxed and the service good at this favored after-theater restaurant, which serves a Bavarian menu on the first floor, and other regional and international dishes on the second.
230 C3 Residenzstrasse 12 089 290 7060 Marienplatz DC, MC, VI

ATHENS HOTELS

Price guide: (double room with breakfast for two people)
$ Dr14,000–20,000
$$ Dr20,000–40,000
$$$ over Dr40,000

Acropolis House $
This clean and simple family-run hotel on the edge of the Plaka is an excellent budget choice, although not all rooms have baths.
244 B2 6–8 Kodrou Plaka 01 322 2344; fax 01 324 4143 11, 18 AX, DC, VI

Athenian Inn $$
Quietly situated near Kolonaki's smart shops, this hotel has a lot of Greek charm and atmosphere; make reservations in advance.
244 D3 22 Haritos Kolonaki 01 723 8097; fax 01 724 2268 3, 13 AX, DC, MC, VI

Grande Bretagne $$$
Athens' most historic, grandest and very traditional hotel, offering the highest level of service and amenities, is located on Sindagma Square.
244 C2 Syntagmatos 01 333 0000; fax 01 322 0211 1, 18, 15 AX, DC, MC, VI

Plaka $$
This conveniently located, renovated hotel has air-conditioning and a charming rooftop terrace that overlooks the Acropolis.

KEY TO SYMBOLS

- map page number and coordinates
- address
- telephone number
- days/times closed
- nearest subway station
- nearest bus/trolley bus/tram/funicular route
- ferry

$$$ expensive
$$ moderate
$ inexpensive
AX American Express
DC Diners Club
MC MasterCard
VI VISA

Water in Greece

It's important not to waste water in arid Greece, especially on the islands, where it often has to be shipped in by tankers. Although Athens' tap water is drinkable, bottled water is cheap and tastes better. Greeks are water connoisseurs, discussing the flavor and mineral properties of favorite spring varieties. Glasses of water are served alongside every drink you order in cafés: Drink it, or pour it in your ouzo and watch the clear spirit turn milky white. Since it's often hot and most places are not air-conditioned, it's important to drink plenty of water.

244 B2 Metropoleos and 7–8 Kapnikareas 01 322 2096; fax 01 322 412 12 AX, DC, MC, VI

Saint George Lycabettus $$$
Beautifully situated on the quiet, shady slopes of Lycabettus, this first-class hotel offers lovely views from its rooftop restaurant.
244 D3 2 Kleomenous Dexamini 01 729 0711; fax 01 729 0439 3, 8, 13 AX, DC, MC, VI

ATHENS RESTAURANTS

Price guide: (dinner per person, excluding drinks)
$ Dr250–350
$$ Dr350–700
$$$ over Dr700

Achillion $$
This pleasant restaurant near the Acropolis serves traditional dishes and has a pretty courtyard; live music is presented in the evenings.
244 B2 5 Dionissiou Areopagitou 01 921 8173 1, 9, 11, 18 AX, DC, VI

O Platanos $
This friendly Plaka *taverna* serves simple and delicious food at both indoor and outdoor tables.
244 B2 4 Diogenous, Plaka 01 322 0666 1, 9, 11, 18 No credit cards

Psaras $$
Tucked below the Acropolis on one of Plaka's prettiest streets is this 100-year-old *taverna*, serving home-cooked traditional dishes.
244 B2 16 Erekteos and Erotokritou Plaka 01 321 8733 Thission 1, 9, 11, 18 AX, VI

Saita $
This basement restaurant in the Plaka is usually packed with Greeks and foreigners who come for the good food and friendly service.
244 B2 21 Kidathineon 01 322 6671 1, 5, 9, 18 No credit cards

Vassilenas $$
Winston Churchill and Aristotle Onassis were among the customers of this family-run *taverna*, serving 16-course meals and many traditional specialties.
244 Off the map 72 Etolikou, Ayia Sophia, Piraeus 01 461 2457 Closed Sun. and in Aug. Piraeus No credit cards

BUDAPEST HOTELS

Price guide: (double room with breakfast for two people)
$ up to Ft17,500
$$ Ft17,500–44,500
$$$ over Ft44,500

Astoria $$
Set on a busy intersection in the center of Pest, this is a splendid hotel in an old building with a relaxing atmosphere. It was the headquarters of the Soviet army during the 1956 revolution.
258 C2 Kossuth Lajos utca 19–21 1 317 3411; fax 1 318 6798 Astoria AX, DC, MC, VI

Carlton $$
This is a spacious and simple hotel at the foot of Castle Hill. Of the 95 rooms – all with excellent facilities – only those on the upper floor have good views.
258 B3 Apor Péter utca 3 1 224 0990 and 1 224 0998; fax 1 224 0990 Battyány tér AX, DC, MC, VI

Hilton $$$
This modern building is in a prime position on Castle Hill, incorporating the ruins of a 13th-century Dominican cloister and a 17th-century Jesuit cloister. You'll get spectacular views over the Danube. Facilities include salons, cafés, shops and a courtyard concert area.
258 A3 Hess András tér 1–3 1 488 6600; fax 1 488 6644 Moszkva tér, then Várbusz (Castle Bus) AX, DC, MC, VI

Kempinski Hotel Corvinus $$$
This luxury hotel with an unusual post-modern design includes two presidential apartments. It's popular with business travelers.
258 C2 Erzsébet tér 7–8 1 429 3777; fax 1 429 4777 Deák tér AX, DC, MC, VI

Victoria $$
Marvelous views across to the Pest bank are a feature at this small and comfortable 27-room hotel on the Buda bank, overlooking Chain Bridge and convenient to many major tourist sights.
258 B3 Bem rakpart 11 1 457 8080; fax 1 457 8088 Battyány tér 16; tram 19 AX, DC, VI

BUDAPEST RESTAURANTS

Price guide: (dinner per person, excluding drinks)
$ up to Ft3,000
$$ Ft3,000–6,000
$$$ over Ft6,000

Alabárdos $$$
This smart, formal restaurant serves Hungarian dishes in ancient vaulted dining rooms. You'll get beautiful presentations and an attentive staff. There are only a few tables, so reserve well in advance.
258 A3 Országház utca 2
1 356 0851 Closed Sun.
Moszkva tér, then Várbusz (Castle Bus) AX, DC, MC, VI

Duna $$
Located in the art nouveau Gellért Hotel, this well-known restaurant rests over a thermal spring at the foot of Gellért Hill. Expect fine views of the river and specialties including pike, perch and veal.
258 C1 Gellért tér 1
1 385 2200 Trams 18, 19, 47, 49 AX, DC, MC, VI

Empire $$
The grand restaurant in the impressive turn-of-the-20th-century Astoria Hotel serves first-class Hungarian and international dishes and good wines in elegant surroundings. Gypsy bands serenade evening diners, and there also is an atmospheric café.
258 C2 Kossuth Lajos utca 19–21 1 317 3411 Astoria AX, MC, VI

Gundel $$$
Hungarian meals are served in a 100-year-old restaurant in City Park. The owner, George Lang, also owns the Café des Artistes in New York.
258 E4 Állatkerti út 2
1 321 3550 Hösök tere
AX, DC, MC, VI

Művész $
It's worth having refreshments at this coffeehouse, which has retained the ambience of Budapest's golden era of café society.
258 C3 Andrássy út 29 1 352 1337 Opera No credit cards

DUBLIN HOTELS

Price guide: (double room with breakfast for two people)
$ £30–60
$$ £60–100
$$$ over £100

Burlington $$$
This very large, top-quality hotel is located southeast of St. Stephen's Green, on the south side of the Royal Canal and about a 10-minute walk from the city center. It's best known for its stylish restaurant and bar.
Upper Leeson Street
01 660 5222; fax 01 660 3172
Dublin City 11, 13, 46
AX, DC, MC, VI

Clarion Stephen's Hall All-Suite Hotel $$$
Adjacent to St. Stephen's Green, this hotel offers a variety of accommodations, including penthouses, town houses, suites and studios.
The Earlsfort Centre, Lower Lesson Street
01 638 1111; fax 01 638 1122
Dublin City 11,13, 44, 46, 48
AX, DC, MC, VI

The Fitzwilliam $$
This small, pleasant family-run hotel on a famous Dublin Georgian street is close to the heart of things.
41 Upper Fitzwilliam Street
01 660 0448; fax 01 676 7488
Dublin City 10, 18
AX, DC, MC, VI

Longfield's Hotel $$$
This town house close to the city center has a relaxed atmosphere, with an emphasis on good service and hospitality.
Fitzwilliam Street 01 676 1367; fax 01 676 1542
Dublin City 10, 18
AX, DC, MC, VI

Shelbourne Méridien $$$
This famous central Dublin hotel, opened in 1824 (although the present building dates from 1867), is Dublin's oldest. It is beautifully appointed and has a good restaurant and bar. It's popular for fashionable – and expensive – afternoon tea overlooking St. Stephen's Green.
27 St. Stephen's Green
01 663 4500; fax 01 661 6006
Connolly or Heuston 11, 13, 44, 46, 48 AX, DC, MC, VI

DUBLIN RESTAURANTS

Price guide: (dinner per person, excluding drinks)
$ £10–15
$$ £15–30
$$$ over £30

Bewleys $$
The flagship Bewleys on Grafton Street is a legendary place, with a great feeling of being at the heart of Dublin. You can have breakfast, lunch and dinner here.
78 Grafton Street
01 677 6761 11, 13, 144
AX, DC, MC, VI

Chapter One $$
This literary-themed restaurant, in the Writers' Museum on North Dublin's Parnell Square, has fine Irish cuisine. Discuss Shaw over salmon or Joyce over venison.
18–19 Parnell Square
01 873 2266 or 01 873 2281
Closed Sun.–Mon. 3, 10, 11, 13, 16, 19 AX, DC, MC, VI

Cornucopia $
This good-value restaurant serves imaginative vegetarian food.
19 Wicklow Street
01 677 7583 Closed Sun.
All city center buses MC, VI

Gallagher's Boxty House $$
Good Irish cooking is found at this restaurant, whose name refers to *boxty*, a traditional potato pancake. If you want straightforward food with an Irish accent, this is the place.
20–21 Temple Bar
01 677 2762 11, 13, 46
AX, MC, VI

Restaurant Patrick Guilbaud $$$
This highly regarded French restaurant has a reputation for outstanding nouvelle cuisine. It's superbly understated, stylish and very expensive. There's a wonderful collection of Irish art.
21 Upper Merrion Street
01 676 4192 Closed Sun.–Mon. 11, 13, 46
AX, DC, MC, VI

ROME HOTELS

Price guide: (double room with breakfast for two people)
$ up to L200,000
$$ L200,000–400,000
$$$ over L400,000

Campo di' Fiore $$
You'll find comfortable rooms and a roof garden at this pretty, moderately

KEY TO SYMBOLS

- map page number and coordinates
- address
- telephone number
- days/times closed
- nearest subway station
- nearest bus/trolley bus/tram/funicular route
- ferry
- $$$ expensive
- $$ moderate
- $ inexpensive
- AX American Express
- DC Diners Club
- MC MasterCard
- VI VISA

Bread, Cakes and Cookies

In Italy, bread comes from a *panificio* or *forno*, cakes and cookies from a *pasticceria*. In Tuscany there is no salt in bread, a legacy of an age when baking was done once a week and saltless bread didn't get moldy. Once you're accustomed to it, it goes well with the strong, salty flavors of prosciutto or salami. Italian cakes are outstanding: luscious creations piled with fruit, filled with cream, oozing chocolate and soaked with liqueur. Italians often buy a large cake or selection of smaller ones to eat for Sunday dessert, or a piece of *panforte*, a traditional spiced fruit confection from Siena. It's acceptable to buy a single pastry or cake and eat it on the spot in the shop.

priced hotel near one of Rome's liveliest squares. Good value option.
292 B3 Via del Biscione 6 06 6880 6865; fax 06 687 6003 46, 62, 64 AX, DC, VI

Columbus $$
This historic hotel (a favorite of visiting prelates) is housed in a former Renaissance palace a stone's throw from St. Peter's, and has many original decorative features.
292 B3 Via delle Conciliazione 33 06 686 5435; fax 06 686 4874 23, 64 AX, DC, VI

Excelsior $$$
A stay at this world-class luxury hotel, with its opulent decor and high standard of service and elegance, is among Rome's most sybaritic experiences.
292 C4 Via Vittorio Veneto 125 06 47081; fax 06 482 6205 Barbarini 52, 53, 95 AX, DC, VI

Hotel d'Inghilterra $$$
Located a few minutes from the Spanish Steps, this historic hotel has antique furniture and discreet and excellent service.
292 C4 Via Bocca di Leone 14 06 69981; fax 06 679 8601 Spagna 119, 52, 61 AX, DC, VI

Navona $
This comfortable, simple and friendly hotel is a few minutes' stroll from the lovely piazza Navona. Be sure to make reservations ahead of time.
292 B3 Via dei Sediari 8 06 686 4203; fax 06 880 3802 70, 81, 90 AX, VI

ROME RESTAURANTS

Price guide: (dinner per person, excluding drinks)
$ L15,000–30,000
$$ L30,000–50,000
$$$ over L50,000

Alberto Ciarla $$$
One of Rome's finest restaurants, this winner has an elegant atmosphere, an outstanding wine list and good fish specials.
292 B2 Piazza San Cosimato 40 06 581 8668 Closed Sun. evening and for 15 days during Jan. and Aug. 44, 75, 170 AX, DC, MC, VI

Baffetto $
For a quintessential Roman experience and the best pizza in town, stand in line to get a table at this tiny pizzeria.
292 B3 Via del Governo Vecchio 114 06 686 1617 Closed Sun. lunch 46, 62, 64 No credit cards

Checchino dal 1887 $$$
This long-established restaurant specializes in the traditional Roman dishes of tripe, brains and offal. Reservations essential.
292 B1 Via Monte Testaccio 30 06 574 3816 Closed Sun.–Mon. and in Aug. 13, 23, 57 AX, DC, MC, VI

Da Lucia $
A tiny, typical Trastevere trattoria, Da Lucia has a friendly family atmosphere and great pasta.
292 B2 Vicolo del Mattonato 2b 06 580 3601 Closed Mon. and 2 weeks in Aug. 23, 65, 56 No credit cards

Da Paris $$
You can eat outside in summer at this very popular Trastevere restaurant serving fine pasta and fish dishes.
292 B2 Piazza San Calisto 7a 06 581 5378 Closed Sun. evening, Mon. and 3 weeks in Aug. 44, 56, 60 AX, DC, VI

Papà Giovanni $$$
Reservations are advised to enjoy this restaurant's light and innovative cooking and excellent wine list.
292 B3 Via dei Sediari 4 06 6880 4807 Closed Sun. and throughout Aug. 70, 81, 90 MC, VI

FLORENCE HOTELS

Price guide: (double room with breakfast for two people)
$ up to L200,000
$$ L200,000–400,000
$$$ over L400,000

Brunelleschi $$$
Book ahead to stay in this comfortable hotel filled with character, situated around a medieval tower in the heart of Florence.
302 C2 Piazza Santa Elisabetta 3 055 27370; fax 055 219 653 In the pedestrian zone AX, DC, MC, VI

Excelsior $$$
This is Florence's smartest hotel, with every comfort, exceptional

service and a rooftop terrace.
302 B3 Piazza Ognissanti 3 055 2715; fax 055 210 278 C AX, DC, MC, VI

Firenze $
This good budget choice, located close to the center of Florence, is popular with younger travelers.
302 C2 Piazza dei Donati 4 055 214 203; fax 055 212 370 In the pedestrian zone DC, VI

Monna Lisa $$$
Housed in a 15th-century palace, this hotel has grand public rooms and a tranquil garden; be sure to request a quiet bedroom.
302 E3 Borgo Pinti 27 055 247 9751; fax 055 247 9755 6, 31 AX, DC, MC, VI

Porta Rossa $$
This elegant, moderately priced hotel, housed in a 14th-century building near the Old Bridge, has wonderfully atmospheric public areas and is a good value.
302 C2 Via Porta Rossa 19 055 287 551; fax 055 282 179 In the pedestrian zone AX, DC, VI

FLORENCE RESTAURANTS

Price guide: (dinner per person, excluding drinks)
$ L15,000–30,000
$$ L30,000–50,000
$$$ over L50,000

Cantinetta Antinori $$
Enjoy Tuscan food with superb wine in a restaurant housed within the 15th-century Palazzo Antinori and belonging to this great wine-producing family. Dress up to feel in place.
302 B3 Piazza Antinori 3r 055 292 234 Closed Sat.–Sun. In the pedestrian zone AX, DC, MC, VI

Il Carmine $
This family-run restaurant serves good traditional Tuscan food in a friendly atmosphere.
302 B2 Piazza del Carmine 18r 055 218 601 Closed Sun. B AX, DC, VI

Dino $$
This uncluttered and airy restaurant serves simple yet elegant food and is popular with locals and tourists alike.
302 D2 Via Ghibellina 51r 055 241 452 Closed Sun. and Mon. 14 AX, DC, VI

Gauguin $$
One of Florence's rare vegetarian restaurants serves imaginative dishes and is very popular with the university crowd.
302 D4 Via degli Alfani 24a 055 234 0616 6 AX, DC, VI

Ponte Vecchio $$
Head to this restaurant in the heart of Florence for some real local cooking; it's popular with tourists, but none the worse because of it.
302 C2 Lungarno Archibusieri 8r 055 292 289 Closed Mon. In the pedestrian zone AX, DC, VI

NAPLES HOTELS

Price guide: (double room with breakfast for two people)
$ up to L200,000
$$ L200,000–400,000
$$$ over L400,000

Britannique $$
This quietly situated and comfortable hotel has a secluded garden and lovely views over the Bay of Naples.
309 B2 Corso Vittorio Emanuele 133 081 761 4145; fax 081 669 760 V1 AX, DC, VI

Canada $$
You'll have to reserve well in advance to get one of the sea-view rooms at this small and friendly hotel, near the harbor at Mergellina.
309 Off the map Via Mergellina 43 081 680 952; fax 081 680 952 R3 AX, DC

Excelsior $$$
One of Naples' grandest hotels is the Excelsior, in the elegant Chiaia district; it has period rooms and views of Capri.
309 A1 Via Partenope 48 081 764 0111; fax 081 764 9743 R3 AX, DC, VI

Mediterraneo $$
This large, modern hotel is conveniently located near the waterfront, and has good facilities and a lovely rooftop breakfast terrace.
309 B2 Via Nuovo Ponte di Tappia 25 081 551 2240; fax 081 552 5868 R2, R3 AX, DC, VI

Santa Lucia $$
This elegant and prestigious waterfront hotel near the Castel del'Ovo has spacious and well-furnished rooms.
309 A1 Via Partenope 46 081 764 0666; fax 081 764 8580 R3 AX, DC, VI

NAPLES RESTAURANTS

Price guide: (dinner per person, excluding drinks)
$ L15,000–30,000
$$ L30,000–50,000
$$$ over L50,000

Al 53 $$
Naples' oldest restaurant, complete with 17th-century furnishings and original mosaic pavement, serves great hors d'oeuvres, seafood pasta and Neapolitan desserts.
309 B3 Piazza Dante 53 081 549 9372 Closed Mon. R1, 24 No credit cards

Amici Miei $$
This elegant, friendly restaurant serves excellent antipasti, risotto and pasta dishes.
309 B2 Via Monte di Dio 78 081 764 6063 Closed Mon. R1, R3 AX, DC, VI

La Cantinella $$$
This seafront restaurant specializes in creative fish cooking, which you can enjoy on the terrace. The wine list is outstanding.
309 B1 Via Cuma 42 081 764 8838 Closed Wed. R3 AX, DC, VI

Trattoria Medina $$
This cheerful restaurant, packed with locals, serves authentic Neapolitan dishes, seafood and pizzas accompanied by live music.
309 B2 Via Medina 32 081 551 5233 Closed Thu. R3 AX, DC, MC, VI

Trianon $
Naples' finest and most popular pizzeria, offering numerous combinations, has been in business for more than 60 years.
309 B3 Via P Colletta 46 081 553 9426 R2, 14, 110 No credit cards

VENICE HOTELS

Price guide: (double room with breakfast for two people)

KEY TO SYMBOLS

- map page number and coordinates
- address
- telephone number
- days/times closed
- nearest subway station
- nearest bus/trolley bus/tram/funicular route
- ferry

$$$ expensive
$$ moderate
$ inexpensive
AX American Express
DC Diners Club
MC MasterCard
VI VISA

$ up to L200,000
$$ L200,000–400,000
$$$ over L400,000

Hotel agli Alboretti $$
Book well in advance to stay at this pleasant hotel, ideally situated on a tree-lined street between the Accademia and the Záttere.
314 C1 Rio Terrà Sant'Agnese, Dorsoduro 884 041 523 0058; fax 041 521 0158 1, 82 AX, DC, MC, VI

Canada $–$$
This is one of the best budget bets in Venice, with a good location near the Rialto; reserve in advance.
314 D2 Campo San Lio, Castello 5659 041 522 9912; fax 041 523 5852 1, 82 AX, DC, VI

Cipriani $$$
One of the world's most famous luxury hotels, with every comfort and impeccable service, is located amid beautiful gardens on the Giudecca (a chain of islets a short boat ride from central Venice).
314 Off the map Giudecca 10 041 520 7744; fax 041 520 3930 82, or use hotel's private launch service AX, DC, MC, VI

Danieli $$$
Considered to be Venice's finest hotel, the Danieli has style, elegance and class. Book a room in the older part, not in the modern annex.
314 D2 Riva degli Schiavoni, Castello 4196 041 522 6480; fax 041 522 0208 1 AX, DC, MC, VI

Pensione Seguso $$
This is a wonderfully atmospheric, old-fashioned *pension* overlooking the Giudecca Canal. Antique furniture and painted ceilings enhance many of the rooms, most of which have water views.
314 B1 Fondamenta ai Gesuati, Dorsoduro 779 041 528 6858; fax 041 522 2340 52, 82 AX, DC, VI

Plan Ahead for Venice

To enjoy a stress-free visit in Venice it is absolutely necessary to make hotel reservations ahead of time. Reservations for June to September should be made during the previous fall, as should those for the two weeks in February in which Carnival falls (although you may be able to get something closer to the time of your visit if you hunt around). Three months ahead should be enough time for other months. If you want to eat at a specific restaurant it's also advisable to make reservations; your hotel concierge will be happy to call and set them up.

VENICE RESTAURANTS

Price guide: (dinner per person, excluding drinks)
$ L15,000–30,000
$$ L30,000–50,000
$$$ over L50,000

Alla Madonna $$
This big, noisy fish restaurant, one of the most traditional in Venice, is hugely popular with locals, business people and tourists.
314 D2 Calle della Madonna, San Polo 594 041 522 3824 Closed Wed. and 2 weeks in Aug. 1, 82 AX, DC, MC, VI

Da Franz $$$
Situated near the Giardini Pubblici, this excellent fish and seafood restaurant has a summer terrace.
314 Off the map Fondamenta San Giuseppe, Castello 745 041 522 0861 Closed Tue. 1, 52 AX, DC, MC, VI

Dona Onesta $
The decor is simple and the Venetian dishes straightforward at this friendly local restaurant; reservations are advised. Good quality food at budget prices.
314 B2 Calle della Dona Onesta, Dorsoduro 041 522 9586 Closed Sun. 1 AX, VI

Harry's Dolci $$$
This offshoot of the famous Harry's Bar offers equally good food and service with the bonus of a waterfront terrace for summer dining; reserve in advance.
314 Off the map Fondamenta San Biagio, Giudecca 773 041 522 4844 Closed Tue., Nov.–Mar. 82 AX, DC, MC, VI

Taverna San Trovaso $
This lively neighborhood restaurant and pizzeria is always busy serving Venetian families and tourists.
314 B1 Fondamenta Priuli, Dorsoduro 1016 041 520 3703 Closed Mon. 1 AX, DC, MC, VI

LUXEMBOURG HOTELS

Price guide: (double room with breakfast for two people)
$ 2,000–3,000F
$$ 3,000–5,000F
$$$ over 5,000F

Central Molitor $$–$$$
This completely modernized business and tourist hotel is conveniently located between the tourist attractions and the railway station. Part of the Golden Tulip chain; special weekend rates.
329 B2 28 avenue de la Liberté 48 99 11; fax 48 33 82 9 AX, MC, VI

Français $$
Ideally located for easy strolls to the Old Town, this small hotel is at the heart of the city.
329 B3 14 place d'Armes 47 45 34; fax 46 42 74 All buses AX, MC, VI

Grand Hotel Cravat $$$
Place d'Armes is a few steps away from this stylish hotel overlooking the Pétrusse valley. The property is part of the well-known restaurant association Luxembourg à la Carte, and its own restaurant offers the very best French and traditional Luxembourg cuisine.
329 B3 29 boulevarde F. D. Roosevelt 22 19 75; fax 22 67 11 All buses AX, MC, VI

Italia $–$$
Located just off the place de Paris on rue d'Anvers, this pleasant, comfortable, small hotel is just a quick bus ride from the city center. Its restaurant specializes in Italian cuisine.
329 B2 15–17 rue d'Anvers 48 66 26-1; fax 48 08 07 9 AX, MC, VI

Sofitel $$$
This hotel is very modern, very luxurious and very expensive. It is located on the Kirchberg Plateau, next to the Centre Européen.
329 Off the map 6 rue du Fort Niedergrünewald 43 77 61; fax 42 50 91 All buses to Centre Européen AX, MC, VI

LUXEMBOURG RESTAURANTS
Price guide: (dinner per person, excluding drinks)
$ 400–600F
$$ 600–1,000F
$$$ over 1,000F

Caves Gourmandes $$–$$$
This popular and atmospheric restaurant in the Ilot Gastronomique complex is within part of the Old Town wall. The superb French cuisine features breast of duck with figs, and *crème brûlée* for dessert.
329 C3 32 rue de l'Eau 46 11 24 Closed Sat. lunch and Sun. All buses MC, VI

La Lorraine $$
Located on place d'Armes, this bright, attractive restaurant offers French cuisine with excellent fish dishes. You can choose your lobster from a tank by the door.
329 B3 7 place d'Armes 47 14 36 All buses MC, VI

Maison Des Brasseurs $$
This popular restaurant in Grand Rue serves classic country cooking and offers local dishes such as *Judd mat Gaardebounen* (roast and smoked pork) and vegetarian dishes.
329 B3 48 Grand Rue 47 13 71 Closed Sun. All buses MC, VI

Restaurant Speltz $$$
This beautifully appointed restaurant has a pleasant outdoor eating area in good weather and an excellent wine collection to accompany the top-quality French and Luxembourg cuisine, such as turbot or scorpion fish with tomatoes, olives and basil. There is a very good cheese selection. Reservations are advised.
329 B3 8 rue Chimay 47 49 50 Closed Sat. lunch and Sun. All buses MC, VI

Via Sud $$
French cuisine is offered at this popular restaurant, where you can eat outside on nice evenings. Try the red mullet in olive oil.
329 B3 22–24 rue du Curé 22 82 50 Closed Sun. All buses MC, VI

AMSTERDAM HOTELS
Price guide: (double room with breakfast for two people)
$ 150–300f
$$ 300–600f
$$$ over 600f

Ambassade Hotel $$
Located on the splendid Herengracht, the city's most elegant canal, this beautifully furnished hotel offers a good breakfast.
342 B2 Herengracht 335–353 020 555 0222; fax 020 555 0277 Tram 1, 2, 5, AX, MC, VI

Amstel Botel $
For a different experience, and waterside views from some rooms, stay in this permanently moored hotel boat near Centraal Station.
342 D3 Oosterdokskade 2–4 020 626 4247; fax 020 639 1952 22 AX, MC, VI

Hotel de L'Europe $$$
The private boat landing at this expensive luxury hotel overlooking the Amstel river says it all. A Victorian exterior welcomes the traveler into the renovated interior, where there is every modern amenity – including the finest *haute cuisine* and wine list at the hotel's Excelsior Restaurant.
342 C2 Nieuwe Doelenstraat 2–8 020 531 1777; fax 020 531 1778 Tram 4, 6, 9, 14 AX, MC, VI

Nova $
This modern hotel has a central location but is sheltered from street noise. Spotless en-suite rooms; friendly, efficient service.
342 C3 Nieuwezijds Voorburgwal 276 020 623 0066; fax 020 627 2026 Tram 1, 2, 5, 13, 17 AX, MC, VI

Pulitzer $$$
This stylish luxury hotel recaptures some of the spirit of old Amsterdam within its unified complex of 17th-century canal houses on the handsome Prinsengracht. Relax in the art nouveau Garden Room and the 17th-century Saxenburg Room.
342 B2 Prinsengracht 315–331 020 523 5277; fax 020 626 2646 Tram 6, 9, 14, 16, 24 AX, MC, VI

AMSTERDAM RESTAURANTS
Price guide: (dinner per person, excluding drinks)
$ 15–30f
$$ 30–45f
$$$ over 45f

Claes Claesz $$
This relaxed and friendly restaurant is situated on the banks of the Egelantiergracht, in the attractive Jordaan district. Good Dutch food is served, often to the accompaniment of background music.
342 B3 Egelantiersstraat 24 020 625 5306 Closed Mon. 10; tram 13, 14, 17 AX, MC, VI

Dorrius $$$
For a taste of real Dutch cuisine with a dash of French flair, this is the place. Try delicious oysters and eel or salted cod, cheese soufflé, and Dutch wines and liqueurs. Only dinner is served regularly, but

KEY TO SYMBOLS

- map page number and coordinates
- address
- telephone number
- days/times closed
- nearest subway station
- nearest bus/trolley bus/tram/funicular route
- ferry

$$$ expensive
$$ moderate
$ inexpensive
AX American Express
DC Diners Club
MC MasterCard
VI VISA

Weekend Treats

As in other Scandinavian cities, Oslo hotels cater to business people on weekdays. This makes room rates some of the most expensive in Europe. On weekends and during the holiday summer months fewer reservations are made, and hotels often offer discounts. You can stay in a luxury hotel from Friday night through Monday morning for a substantially reduced rate. Outside the height of summer this can also mean that there are few fellow guests, making your weekend stay seem even more exclusive. The high standard of service does not diminish with the price. Reduced rates on weekends and during holiday periods are common in many major European cities – it's always worth asking at the hotel you are interested in.

lunch is available through advance reservations.
342 C3 Nieuwezijds Voorburgwal 5 020 420 2224 Tram 1, 2, 5,13,17 AX, DC, MC, VI

In de Waag $$
For late-night international cuisine among the light of hundreds of candles, come to this fine, friendly French restaurant. A generous three-course lunch and special early evening menus are good values.
342 C3 Nieuwmarkt 4 020 422 7772 Waterlooplein MC, VI

De Silveren Spiegel $$$
Located in a restored redbrick 1614 building with yellow trimmings and shuttered windows, this restaurant has an exceptional menu ranging from traditional Dutch cuisine to fish specialties.
342 C4 Kattengat 4–6 020 624 6589 Tram 2, 5, 17 MC, VI

Toscanini $$
This stylish Jordaan district restaurant features excellent Italian food. The homemade *biscotti* is a specialty.
342 B4 Lindengracht 75 020 623 2813 Tram 18 MC, VI

THE HAGUE HOTELS

Price guide: (double room with breakfast for two people)
$ 200–300f
$$ 300–600f
$$$ over 600f

Carlton Ambassador Hotel $$
This luxury hotel in an elegant neighborhood is within easy walking distance of the city center.
350 B2 Sophialaan 2 070 363 0363; fax 070 360 0535 Tram 7, 8 AX, MC, VI

Delft Museum Hotel and Residence $$
When in Delft, spend at least one night in this luxuriously furnished hotel, attractively located on Oude Delft overlooking a tranquil canal.
350 Off the map Oude Delft 189 015 214 0930; fax 015 214 0935 Delft Railroad station Tram 1 AX, DC, MC, VI

Hotel Cattenburch $$
This comfortable small hotel with traditional service is located some distance from the city center, but it's near a tram connection. There's a restaurant on the premises.
350 B2 Laan Copes van Cattenburch 38 070 352 2335; fax 070 354 3119 Tram 1, 9 AX, MC, VI

Mercure $–$$
This modern hotel is located near the railroad station and city center. It also has a restaurant.
350 C1 Spui 180 070 363 6700; fax 070 363 9398 Tram 2, 3, 6, 7, 10, 16 AX, MC, VI

Steigenberger Kurhaus Hotel $$–$$$
If you base yourself at Scheveningen and want to overlook the beach, consider staying at this Old European-style hotel, built in the 1880s.
350 A4 Gevers Deynootplein 30, Scheveningen 070 416 2636; fax 070 416 2646 Tram 1, 8, 9 AX, MC, VI

THE HAGUE RESTAURANTS

Price guide: (dinner per person, excluding drinks)
$ 15–30f
$$ 30–45f
$$$ over 45f

Bodega De Posthoorn $$
This restaurant is housed in an attractive building in the stylish Lange Voorhout; reservations are strongly advised.
350 C2 Lange Voorhout 39a 070 360 4906 Tram 7, 8 AX, MC, VI

't Goude Hooft $$$
This is a very popular inn that was demolished and rebuilt in the 17th century. The decor is handsome and the food is good.
350 B1 Dag Groenmarkt 13 070 346 9713 Closed Sun. in winter Tram 2, 3, 6, 10 AX, DC, MC, VI

It Rains Fishes $$$
High-quality, expensive seafood is served in this intimate restaurant on one of The Hague's finest streets. Reservations are advised.
350 B2 Noordeinde 123 070 365 2598 Closed Mon. Tram 7, 8 AX, MC, VI

Les Ombrelles $$
Located in the attractive Denneweg area, this restaurant serves excellent fish dishes, including lobster and mussels.
350 C2 Hooistraat 4a
070 365 8789 Tram 2, 6, 8, 16
AX, DC, VI

Ristorante Roma $$
You'll find fine Italian cuisine here at the heart of The Hague's old quarter, north of the Kerkplein.
350 B1 Papestraat 22
070 346 2345 Closed Tue.
Tram 2, 6, 8, 16 AX, MC, VI

OSLO HOTELS

Price guide: (double room with breakfast for two people)
$ KR800–1,000
$$ KR1,000–1,400
$$$ over KR1,400

Ambassadeur Hotel Best Western $$
This stylish, comfortable hotel offers excellent service and a convenient location, in a peaceful area behind the Royal Palace. It's within easy reach of the city center.
365 B2 Camilla Colletts vei 15 22 44 18 35; fax 22 44 47 91
21 AX, MC, VI

Bristol $$$
This elegant hotel in the heart of Oslo has superb furnishings and decorations, as well as several bars and restaurants on the premises.
365 B1–B2 Kristian IV's gate 7 22 82 60 00; fax 22 82 60 01
33, 45; tram 3, 17, 18 AX, MC, VI

Continental $$$
This top-quality, very expensive hotel offers a prime location between the Royal Palace and City Hall. A member of "Leading Hotels of the World," it has two restaurants.
365 B1 Stortingsgata 24–26
22 82 40 00; fax 22 42 96 89
30, 31, 32, 83, 84; tram 12, 13, 19
AX, MC, VI

Grand $$$
One of Oslo's most prestigious and luxurious hotels is this handsome 19th-century accommodation right in the heart of the city. It has well-appointed rooms, good restaurants (including the Grand Café), bars, and an inviting rooftop sauna and swimming pool.
365 B1 Karl Johans gate 31
23 21 20 00; fax 23 21 20 01
Stortinget 33, 45 AX, MC, VI

Ritz $$
Within easy reach of the city's main attractions, this pleasant hotel is nestled in a quiet area on the outskirts of the center. The service is attentive and rooms are attractive.
365 B2 Frederik Stangs gate 3 22 92 61 00; fax 22 92 61 60 30, 32, 45, 83; tram 10, 15
AX, MC, VI

OSLO RESTAURANTS

Price guide: (dinner per person, excluding drinks)
$ KR50–80
$$ KR80–200
$$$ over KR200

Blom-Kunsterernes Restaurant $$$
Excellent Norwegian food is offered at this well-established restaurant. Try *lefse*, savory pastry wrapped around reindeer meat or other fillings. Reservations are advised.
365 B1 Karl Johans gate 41
23 13 95 00 Closed Sun.
Stortinget AX, DC, MC, VI

D/S Louise Restaurant and Bar $$
Located in the Aker Brygge complex, where there are good views across the harbor to Akershus Castle, this restaurant serves traditional and international specialties.
365 A1 Stranden 3
22 83 00 60 Tram 10, 15
AX, DC, MC, VI

Engebret Café $$
Founded in 1857 by Engebret Christoffersen, this restaurant still maintains a strong tradition. Try Norwegian and international cuisine, including traditional fish dishes. There's also an excellent lunch buffet.
365 B1 Bankplassen 1
22 82 25 25 Closed Sun.
60 AX, DC, MC, VI

Grand Café $$
Great tradition, including visits by Henrik Ibsen in his day, makes this Grand Hotel restaurant a favorite with locals. You can sample Norwegian cuisine from elk stew to *lutefisk* (marinated dried fish).
365 B1 Karl Johans gate 31
23 21 20 00 Tram 11, 13, 17, 18 AX, DC, MC, VI

Restaurant Det Gamle Raadhus $$
Located in the 17th-century building next to Akershus Castle, this restaurant is billed as Oslo's oldest eating establishment. International cuisine and fish specialties are served in a charming atmosphere. Reservations are strongly advised.
365 B1 Nedre Slottsgate 1
22 42 01 07 Closed Sun.
Tram 10, 15 AX, DC, MC, VI

LISBON HOTELS

Price guide: (double room with breakfast for two people)
$ up to 15,000Esc
$$ 15,000–30,000Esc
$$$ over 30,000Esc

As Janelas Verdes $$$
This small hotel, housed in an 18th-century townhouse, has large and luxurious rooms. Its location, well west of the city center, is the only drawback.
378 Off the map Rua das Janelas Verdes 47 21 396 8143; fax 21 396 8144 40, 49, 60
AX, DC, MC, VI

Britânia $$
Just east of Avenida da Liberdade, this small, friendly, comfortable, Art Deco-style hotel was refurbished in the 1990s.
378 A5 Rua Rodrigues Sampaio 17 21 315 5016; fax 21 315 5021 Avenida 9, 11, 31
AX, DC, MC, VI

Duas Nações $
Although only some rooms have private bathrooms, this hotel, housed in a 19th-century building, is a superb budget choice, located in the heart of the historic Baixa district.
378 B2–C2 Rua da Vitória 41
21 346 0710; fax 21 347 0206
Rossio AX, MC, VI

Metrópole $$
The elegant Metrópole is located on Rossio, Lisbon's busiest square; ask for a room at the back to avoid the noise.
378 B3 Praça do Rossio 30
21 321 9030; fax 21 346 9166
Rossio AX, DC, VI

Portugal

KEY TO SYMBOLS

- map page number and coordinates
- address
- telephone number
- days/times closed
- nearest subway station
- nearest bus/trolley bus/tram/funicular route
- ferry
- **$$$** expensive
- **$$** moderate
- **$** inexpensive
- AX American Express
- DC Diners Club
- MC MasterCard
- VI VISA

Eating in Portugal

The Portuguese do not eat at the same hours as their Spanish neighbors, so you won't have to wait until 10 p.m. for dinner. Many people eat dinner as early as 7:30, and restaurants remain open until about 10:30; they tend to close all day on Sunday. Breakfast is usually a light meal, and the lunch hour starts around 12:30. The daily menu (*ementa turística)* is an excellent value and normally offers a decent variety. Meals often start with a selection of appetizers, which arrive automatically and are added to your bill if you eat them. Portuguese helpings are big, but you can ask for a half portion.

Ritz Four Seasons $$$

Lisbon's most luxurious hotel opened in the 1950s. Sumptuously decorated, it has large rooms and suites and exceptional service.
378 Off the map Rua Rodrigo da Fonseca 88 21 383 2020; fax 21 383 1783 Rotonda 1, 9, 11 AX, DC, MC, VI

LISBON RESTAURANTS

Price guide: (dinner per person, excluding drinks)
$ 1,500–2,000Esc
$$ 2,000–4,000Esc
$$$ over 4,000Esc

Bota Alta $

For large portions of authentic Portuguese food, go to this very popular and traditional restaurant in the Upper Town, which has an attractive, rustic ambience.
378 B2 Travessa da Queimada 35/37 21 342 7959 Closed Sat. lunch and Sun. Restauradores AX, VI

Fidalgo $

This welcoming restaurant in the Upper Town serves fish and seafood. It has a trendy clientele.
378 B2 Rua da Barroca 27/31 21 342 2900 Closed Sun. Rossio 1, 11; tram 28 AX, DC, VI

Gambrinus $$$

There's an old-fashioned ambience at this deluxe, formal restaurant, where fish and seafood are the specialties; reservations advised.
378 A4 Rua das Portas de Santo Antão 23 21 342 1466 Rossio AX, DC, MC, VI

São Jerónimo $$

If you're sightseeing in Belém stop at this modern restaurant, close to the Jerónimo monastery, for fish and seafood.
378 Map inset Rua dos Jerónimo 12 21 364 8797 Closed Sat. lunch and Sun. 28, 49, 51; tram 15 AX, DC, VI

Tágide $$$

Great views, atmosphere and excellent food are what make this one of Lisbon's classiest restaurants.
378 C3 Largo da Academia Nacional de Belas Artes 12/20 21 342 0720 Rossio 58, 100 AX, DC, MC, VI

Via Graça $$

You'll find traditional Portuguese cooking and great views of the city at this candlelit restaurant.
378 D5 Rua Damasceno Monteiro 9b 21 887 0830 Closed Sat. lunch and Sun. Intendente Tram 28 AX, DC, MC, VI

PORTO HOTELS

Price guide: (double room with breakfast for two people)
$ up to 15,000Esc
$$ 15,000–30,000Esc
$$$ over 30,000Esc

Boavista $$

This peaceful, quiet hotel in the suburb of Foz is very comfortable and has great ocean views.
387 Off the map Esplanada do Castelo 58 22 618 0083; fax 22 617 3818 24; tram 18 AX, DC, MC, VI

Hotel da Bolsa $$

Friendly service and spacious rooms are the prevailing characteristics at this comfortable hotel. Excellent location in the heart of the historic center.
387 B2 Rua Ferreira Borges 101 22 202 6768; fax 22 205 8888 21, 22 AX, DC, VI

Infante Sagres $$$

Porto's best and classiest hotel is centrally located and has elegant public rooms filled with antiques, a pretty terrace and lovely bedrooms.
387 B3 Praça Filipa de Lencastre 62 22 339 8599; fax 22 205 4937 20, 21, 22 AX, DC, MC, VI

Internacional $$

Located just off the Praça de Liberdade, this friendly hotel has been recently refurbished.
387 B3 Rua do Almada 131 22 200 5032; fax 22 200 9063 20, 21, 22 AX, DC, MC, VI

Le Meridien Park Atlantic $$$

This big, international-style hotel has a restaurant and delivers excellent service.
387 Off the map Aveneda Boavista 1446 22 607 2500; fax 22 600 2031 22 AX, DC, MC, VI

PORTO RESTAURANTS

Price guide: (dinner per person,

excluding drinks)
$ 1,500–2,000Esc
$$ 2,000–4,000Esc
$$$ over 4,000Esc

Dona Filipa $$$
The restaurant at the Hotel Infante Sagres is one of Porto's best, serving Portuguese and international dishes in elegant surroundings.
387 B3 Praça Filipa de Lencastre 62 22 339 8500 21, 22 AX, DC, MC, VI

Filha da Mãe Preta $
There are lovely river views from this restaurant specializing in regional dishes such as squid, octopus, eel and *bacalhau* (dried, salted cod).
387 B1 Cais de Ribeira 13 22 208 6066 Closed Sun. AX, DC, MC, VI

Mercearia $
This traditional restaurant on the riverbank in Old Porto specializes in fish, seafood, soup and *bacalhau* recipes.
387 B1 Cais da Ribeira 32 22 200 4389 AX, VI

Porto Ibérico $$
If you're visiting the port warehouses across the river, this restaurant – serving a range of northern Portuguese and Spanish dishes – is a good choice.
387 B1 Rua do Rei Ramiro 697 22 370 6674 Closed Wed. 57, 91 AX, DC, MC, VI

Taberna de Bebóbos $$
Traditional Porto dishes are served at this atmospheric, historic tavern on the waterfront, in the oldest part of town.
387 B1 Cais da Ribeira 24 22 313 565 Closed Sun. AX, MC, VI

MADRID HOTELS

Price guide: (double room with breakfast for two people)
$ 6,000–15,000PTA
$$ 15,000–25,000PTA
$$$ over 25,000PTA

Asturias $
This conveniently located budget choice has a friendly staff and pleasant, clean rooms.
402 C2 Sevilla 2 91 429 6676; fax 91 429 4036 Sevilla AX, DC, VI

Carlos y Best Western $$
To be sure of a room, you'll want to reserve in advance at this good-value hotel in an excellent location near the Puerta del Sol.
402 B2 Maestro Vitoria 5 91 531 4100; fax 91 531 3761 Sol AX, MC, VI

Palace $$$
Recently refurbished and now owned by the Sheraton chain, this grand hotel is ideally situated within walking distance of Madrid's main attractions.
402 C2 Plaza Cortes 7 91 360 8000; fax 91 360 8100 Banco de España AX, MC, VI

Ritz $$$
Madrid's Ritz opened in 1910 and offers a level of luxury, service and facilities associated with this chain's stature.
402 D2 Plaza de la Lealtad 5 91 521 2856; fax 91 532 8776 Banco de España AX, MC, VI

Suecia $$
This quiet hotel is located between the Prado Museum and Puerta del Sol square.
402 C2 Marqués de Casa Riera 4 91 531 6900; fax 91 521 7141 Sevilla AX, MC, VI

MADRID RESTAURANTS

Price guide: (dinner per person, excluding drinks)
$ 2,000–4,500PTA
$$ 4,500–9,000PTA
$$$ over 9,000PTA

El Bodegon $$$
Many people think this is Madrid's best restaurant. El Bodegon offers a set menu at dinner and an à la carte lunch menu, with superb service.
402 C4 Pinar 15 91 562 3137 Closed Sun. and in Aug. Gregorio Marañón AX, MC, VI

La Bola $$
This long-established restaurant specializes in Madrid *cocido*, different stews cooked slowly in traditional pots. It also offers friendly service.
402 B2 Bola 5 91 547 6930 Closed Jul. Santo Domingo AX, MC, VI

Botín $$
Immensely popular with visitors, this restaurant, founded in 1725, serves good traditional grills and other meat dishes.
402 B2 Cuchilleros 17 91 366 3026 Sol AX, MC, VI

Los Galayos $$$
Located on the Plaza Mayor, this elegant restaurant, with a terrace and bar, serves Castilian dishes cooked in wood-fired ovens.
402 B2 Botoneras 5 (Plaza Mayor) 91 366 3028 Sol AX, DC, MC, VI

Hogar Gallego $$
This popular restaurant, just off the Plaza Mayor, serves Galician dishes; in summer you can eat on the terrace.
402 B2 Comandante Morenas 3 91 542 4826 Closed Aug. Sol AX, MC, VI

Hylogui $
This traditional restaurant, popular with locals, offers straightforward home cooking and a huge menu.
402 C2 Ventura de la Vega 3 91 429 7357 Closed Aug. Sevilla AX, MC, VI

BARCELONA HOTELS

Price guide: (double room with breakfast for two people)
$ 6,000–15,000PTA
$$ 15,000–25,000PTA
$$$ over 25,000PTA

Arts $$$
This 44-story waterfront hotel, with superb views across the city, epitomizes modern Barcelona. It has a high level of luxury.
411 Off the map Carrer de la Marina 19–21 93 221 1000; fax 93 221 1070 Ciutadella/Vila Olímpica AX, MC

Colón $$
Situated opposite the cathedral, this refurbished hotel combines a friendly and old-fashioned atmosphere with lots of comfort.
411 C2 Avenida de la Catedral 7 93 301 1404; fax 93 317 2915 Jaume I AX, VI

Husa Internacional $
A good budget choice, this hotel is located on La Rambla and has simple rooms (but not all with bath).
411 B2 La Rambla 78–80 93 302 2566; fax 93 317 6190 Liceu AX, MC, VI

KEY TO SYMBOLS

- map page number and coordinates
- address
- telephone number
- days/times closed
- nearest subway station
- nearest bus/trolley bus/tram/funicular route
- ferry

$$$ expensive
$$ moderate
$ inexpensive
AX American Express
DC Diners Club
MC MasterCard
VI VISA

Rivoli Ramblas $$$
This popular hotel with excellent facilities is housed in a restored Art Deco building on La Rambla.
411 B2 La Rambla 128
93 302 6643; fax 93 317 5053
Catalunya AX, MC, VI

Hotel Suizo $$
This comfortable and old-fashioned hotel is a five-minute walk from the cathedral and the historic Gothic Quarter.
411 C2 Plaza de l'Angel 12
93 310 6108; fax 93 315 0461
Jaume I 17, 19, 45 AX, DC, MC, VI

BARCELONA RESTAURANTS

Price guide: (dinner per person, excluding drinks)
$ 2,000–4,500PTA
$$ 4,500–9,000PTA
$$$ over 9,000PTA

Ca la Lluisa $$
This waterfront restaurant serves excellent *fideua* (a dish similar to paella) and delicious changing daily specials.
411 C2 Passeig Joan de Borbó 12, La Barceloneta 93 225 0695 Barceloneta

Conducta Ejemplar Le Rodizio $$
This very popular restaurant features Brazilian-style meat dishes and also offers a huge self-service buffet at good prices.
411 B3 Carrer Consell de Cent 403 93 265 5112
Closed Fri.–Sat. and Sun. evening
Girona AX, VI

Neichel $$$
Locally considered the finest restaurant in Barcelona, Neichel is noted for its daily specials, cheeses and desserts, and high level of service.
411 Off the map Beltran i Rózpide 16 93 203 8408
Closed Sat. lunch, Sun. and Aug. 1 to first week in Sep.
Palau Reial AX, MC, VI

Nou Celler $
This friendly and unpretentious neighborhood restaurant serves good traditional Catalan dishes at reasonable prices.
411 C2 Carrer de la Princessa 16 93 310 4773
Jaume I AX, VI

Set Portes $$$
One of Barcelona's best and most historic restaurants serves a wide range of excellent Catalan food and fine wines.
411 C2 Passeig de Isabel II 14 93 319 3033 Barceloneta
AX, MC, VI

SANTIAGO HOTELS

Price guide: (double room with breakfast for two people)
$ 6,000–15,000PTA
$$ 15,000–25,000PTA
$$$ over 25,000PTA

Hogar San Francisco $
This is a simple and peaceful hotel, housed in the old convent of St. Francis in the historic center, only a five-minute stroll from the cathedral.
418 A2 Campillo del Convento de San Francisco 981 572 463; fax 981 571 916 AX, MC, VI

Hostal El Rapido $
An example of a simple, clean pilgrim hostel, El Rapido is on one of the historic center's main streets.
418 A1 Rua do Franco 22
981 584 983 AX, VI

Compostela $$
This comfortable and spacious hotel outside the historic center offers superb views of the heart of the city.
418 Off the map Hórreo 1
981 585 700; fax 981 563 269
AX, MC, VI

Parador Hostal dos Reyes Católicos $$$
Considered by many to be the finest deluxe hotel in Spain, this *parador* is magnificently located on the cathedral square and housed in a superb 15th-century cloistered building.
418 A2 Plaza del Obradoiro 1
981 582 200; fax 981 563 094
AX, DC, MC, VI

San Carlos $$
This first-class hotel, facing the Galician parliament buildings, is conveniently located only a few minutes' walk from the town center.
418 Off the map Hórreo 106
981 560 505; fax 981 560 506
AX, VI

Andalucian Cuisine

Simplicity is all in Andalucian cooking, in which the superb quality of the ingredients, combined with a Moorish legacy of spices, almonds and oranges, has created one of Spain's most enjoyable cuisines. *Tapas* originated here, as did *gazpacho*, the cold summer soup, and sherry, a fortified wine that is drunk and used in cooking. There are tasty stews and soups, both thickened with lentils and potatoes, and every dish is redolent with olive oil, garlic and tomatoes. Excellent bread and rich Arab-inspired pastries and desserts complete the picture.

SANTIAGO RESTAURANTS

Price guide: (dinner per person, excluding drinks)
$ 2,000–4,500PTA
$$ 4,500–9,000PTA
$$$ over 9,000PTA

Botafumeiro $
This simple, unpretentious local restaurant just behind the cathedral serves inexpensive shellfish and other Galician specialties.
418 A2 Azabachería 16 981 584 439

Don Gaiferos $$
In the heart of the old center, this smart restaurant has a wonderful range of shellfish and seafood, in addition to other typically Galician dishes.
418 A1 Rua Nueva 23 981 583 894 AX, DC, MC, VI

El Estanco del Hórreo $$
Located just outside the historic center, this spacious restaurant is a good place to try local shellfish and the freshest of fish dishes.
418 Off the map Hórreo 26 981 563 808 Closed Sun. evenings AX, VI

Toñi Vicente $$$
Probably Santiago's most famous and elegant restaurant, Toñi Vicente specializes in the imaginative use of local ingredients.
418 Off the map Rosalía de Castro 24 981 594 100 AX, VI

SEVILLE HOTELS

Price guide: (double room with breakfast for two people)
$ 6,000–15,000PTA
$$ 15,000–25,000PTA
$$$ over 25,000PTA

Alfonso XIII $$$
Seville's top hotel, set in an attractive palm-shaded garden, has every comfort and an exceptional level of service.
425 B2 San Fernando 2 95 422 2850; fax 95 421 6033 21, 23, C3, C4 AX, DC, MC, VI

Bécquer $$
This modernized hotel is conveniently located between the river and the center of town and offers excellent service.
425 A3 Reyes Católicos 4 95 422 8900; fax 95 421 4400 43 AX, MC, VI

Casas de la Judería $$–$$$
This atmospheric hotel, located in the heart of Santa Cruz, features peaceful and shady courtyards with fountains, antique furniture and comfortable rooms.
425 B3 Callejón de Dos Hermanas 7 95 441 5150; fax 95 442 2170 5, C3, C4 AX, MC, VI

Melià Sevilla $$–$$$
This big and efficient modern hotel, conveniently located near lovely Maria Luisa Park, has many facilities, including a pool.
425 B2 Dr Pedro de Castro 1 95 442 1511; fax 95 442 1608 30, 31, 33 AX, MC, VI

San Gil $$–$$$
This attractive and spacious hotel is in a lovely old building complete with interior courtyards that feature fountains and palm trees.
425 B4 Parras 28 95 490 6811; fax 95 490 6939 C1, 14 AX, MC, VI

SEVILLE RESTAURANTS

Price guide: (dinner per person, excluding drinks)
$ 2,000–4,500PTA
$$ 4,500–9,000PTA
$$$ over 9,000PTA

Becerrita $$
This long-established restaurant serves traditional Andalucian recipes and prides itself on its homemade desserts.
425 B3 Recaredo 9 95 441 2057 10, 11, C1, C2 AX, VI

Bodegón Torre del Oro $$
A traditional restaurant serving fish and meat dishes, in a lovely 16th-century building near the river.
425 B2 Santander 15 95 421 4241 C4, 40, 41 AX, MC, VI

Enrique Becerra $$$
This pretty, elegant and friendly restaurant serves carefully prepared Andalucian dishes and has long been a favorite with American visitors.
425 B2 Gamazo 2 95 421 3049 10, 11, 12 AX, MC, VI

El Giraldillo $$
A pretty, tiled restaurant opposite the cathedral, El Giraldillo serves fresh fish and local specialties.
425 B2 Virgen de los Reyes 2 95 421 4525 41, 40, 42 AX, VI

El 3 de Oro $$
This lively and friendly restaurant in Santa Cruz is always packed with locals. The menu consists of straightforward, traditional but delicious Andalucian dishes.
425 B3 Santa María la Blanca 34 95 442 6820 1, C3, C4 AX, VI

STOCKHOLM HOTELS

Price guide: (double room with breakfast for two people)
$ 800–1,500SKr
$$ 1,500–2,200SKr
$$$ over 2,200SKr

Diplomat $$–$$$
This comfortable hotel in a handsome early 20th-century building overlooks the waterfront on the road to Djurgården. The Diplomat Tea House is a delightful place to stop for afternoon tea with tasty treats.
437 C2 Strandvägen 7C 08 459 68 00; fax 08 459 68 20 Closed Dec. 25 47, 69 AX, MC, VI

First Hotel Reisen $$$
A popular and well-appointed hotel on the east side of the Old Town, within easy walking distance of the city center.
437 B2–C2 Skeppsbron 12–14 08 22 32 60; fax 08 20 15 59 46, 55 AX, MC, VI

Grand Hôtel $$$
The handsome facade of this top-quality hotel faces across the Norrström to the Royal Palace. Facilities are luxurious; restaurants serve international as well as local cuisine, and the hotel is famous for its *smörgåsbord.*
437 C2 Sodra Blasieholmshamnen 8 08 679 35 00; fax 08 611 86 86 65 AX, MC, VI

Mälardrottningen Hotel $
Once owned by American Woolworth heiress Barbara Hutton, this 1920s converted luxury yacht is a hotel with a difference. It's moored on the west side of the Old Town. The restaurant serves excellent international and Swedish cuisine.
437 B2 Riddarholmen 111 08 545 187 80; fax 08 24 36 76 Gamla Stan 53 AX, MC, VI

KEY TO SYMBOLS

- map page number and coordinates
- address
- telephone number
- days/times closed
- nearest subway station
- nearest bus/trolley bus/tram/funicular route
- ferry
- $$$ expensive
- $$ moderate
- $ inexpensive
- AX American Express
- DC Diners Club
- MC MasterCard
- VI VISA

Sports events in Stockholm

Two major events take place in June. The Archipelago Boat Day is a traditional parade of old-time steamboats from Stockholm to the islands of Vaxholm and back again, finishing at Strömkajen in the heart of the city (for information 08 662 89 02). The Stockholm Marathon is an international race starting and finishing in Stockholm Stadium, with participants from 40 nations running through the city center (for information 08 667 19 30).

Radisson SAS Strand Hotel $$$
This comfortable hotel with modern facilities is in a fine old building on the southwest side of Nybroviken inlet. Enjoy views across the water from the top-floor restaurant.
437 B2 Nybrokajen 9
08 506 640 00; fax 08 506 640 01
Kungsträdgården 65 AX, MC, VI

STOCKHOLM RESTAURANTS

Price guide: (dinner per person, excluding drinks)
$ 50–150SKr
$$ 150–250SKr
$$$ 250–300SKr

Den Gyldene Freden $$$
Established in 1722, this famous Old Town restaurant has long attracted the rich and famous, including Nobel Prize selection committee members. Even the restroom has 18th-century poetry on the wall. The international and Swedish cuisine is outstanding, but you'll need reservations.
437 B2 Österlånggatan 51
08 24 97 60 Closed Sun.
46, 55 AX, DC, MC, VI

KB $$
Near the Royal Drama Theater and traditionally the haunt of writers and artists, this excellent restaurant serves Swedish and French cuisine. It can be pricey, but a special menu often lists less expensive dishes. It's very busy and reservations are strongly advised, even for lunch.
437 C2 Smålandsgaten 7
08 679 60 32 Closed Sun. and late Jun.–early Aug. Östermalmstorg
46, 47, 62, 69 AX, DC, MC, VI

Kungshallens Restauranger $
This big food outlet, arranged on several levels in the heart of modern Stockholm, offers every kind of fast food from kebabs to pizzas, salads, sandwiches and hot dogs.
437 B3 Kungsgaten 44
08 20 94 44 Hötorget 41, 53 No credit cards

Pontus in the Green House $$$
Another Old Town institution, Pontus in the Green House is expensive and always busy, but superb fish dishes, specialty sauces and great service make it worth the money. Reservations are advised.
437 B2 Österlånggatan 17
08 23 85 00 Closed Sun.
46, 55 MC, VI

Zum Franziskaner $$
Located in Gamla Stan, this is the oldest restaurant in Stockholm, founded in 1421. Swedish and German home cooking is served in authentic *Jugendstil* surroundings.
437 C2 Skeppsbron 44
08 411 88 30 Closed Sun.
Gamla Stan MC, VI

GENEVA HOTELS

Price guide: (double room with breakfast for two people)
$ SF100–250
$$ SF250–400
$$$ over SF400

Hôtel des Bergues $$$
For ultimate Swiss style, stay at Switzerland's oldest grand hotel, with lovely lake and mountain views.
451 B3 quai des Bergues 33
022 908 7000; fax 022 908 7090
1, 4, 9, 10 AX, DC, MC, VI

Edelweiss Manotel $
A popular choice with tourists, this chalet-style hotel near the lakeside has attractive, comfortable rooms and stages frequent folklore evenings.
451 B3 place de la Navigation 2 022 544 5151; fax 022 544 5199 1 AX, DC, MC, VI

Eden $–$$
In a quiet area near Mon Repos park and the lake, this comfortable hotel has a good restaurant and a friendly, relaxed atmosphere.
451 Off the map rue de Lausanne 135 022 716 3700; fax 022 731 5260 4, 18 AX, DC, MC, VI

Luserna $
If you're looking for quiet surroundings choose this friendly, good-value suburban hotel, with a large garden, and easily accessible by bus.
451 A3 avenue de Luserna 12
022 345 4676; fax 022 949 5636
10, 11; tram12 AX, DC, MC, VI

Rio $
This traditional, centrally located hotel, housed in a turn-of-the-20th-century building, is an excellent budget choice.
451 A3 place Isaac-Mercier 1
022 732 3264; fax 022 732 8264
7 DC, MC, VI

Tiffany $$
This newly renovated hotel in the heart of Geneva is furnished in belle

époque style, with comfortable rooms, a bar and a restaurant.
451 A2 rue des Marbriers 1
022 708 1616: fax 022 708 1617
13 AX, DC, MC, VI

GENEVA RESTAURANTS

Price guide: (dinner per person, excluding drinks)
$ SF25–45
$$ SF45–60
$$$ over SF60

Auberge de Coutance $$$
This elegant French restaurant with exceptional service offers dishes such as foie gras and duck specialties.
451 A3 rue Coutance 25
022 732 7919 Closed Sun. evening 13, 16 AX, DC, MC, VI

Auberge de Savièse $$
Enjoy a selection of Swiss specialties in this friendly restaurant, which features different types of fondue.
451 B3 rue des Pâquis 20
022 732 8330 1 AX, DC, MC, VI

Cuccagna $$
A good choice when Swiss cheese begins to pall, this cheery Italian restaurant features pizzas.
451 B1 rue de St.-Joseph 3
022 342 0882 12, 13 AX, DC, MC, VI

Restaurant Hung Wan $$
Geneva's best Chinese restaurant is conveniently located near the lake and features Szechuan, Cantonese and Hong Kong dishes.
451 B3 quai de Mont-Blanc 7
022 731 7330 1 AX, DC, VI

Restaurant des Vieux Grenadiers $$
This typical Genevan restaurant specializes in regional dishes and fondues. It has a pretty summer terrace and occasional live jazz. Pleasant after a day's sightseeing.
451 B3 rue de Carouge 92
022 320 1327 Closed Sun. and Thu. evenings 12, 13 AX, MC, VI

Swiss Cottage $$
Tourists flock to this chalet-style restaurant serving dishes incorporating Swiss cheese. Open evenings only. An Alpine floor show is featured.
451 Off the map rue Barton 6
022 732 4000 1 AX, DC, MC, VI

ZURICH HOTELS

Price guide: (double room with breakfast for two people)
$ SF150–250
$$ SF250–400
$$$ over SF400

Dolder Grand Hotel $$$
Situated high above Zurich, with wide views from the terraces, this luxury hotel offers every comfort as well as excellent service.
456 Off the map
Kurhausstrasse 65 01 269 3000; fax 01 269 3001 3, 8, 15 AX, DC, MC, VI

Bristol $
This is a friendly and comfortable hotel near the railroad station, with modern and functional rooms.
456 B4
Stampfenbachstrasse 34 01 261 8400; fax 01 251 1951 3, 31, 46 AX, DC, MC, VI

Eden au Lac $$$
Stay at this elegant lakeside hotel, built in 1909, for the ultimate in comfort, luxury and service.
456 B1 Utoquai 45 01 266 2525; fax 01 266 2500 4 AX, DC, MC, VI

Franziskaner $
This reasonably priced hotel, overlooking a pretty square, has comfortable rooms and a restaurant.
456 B2 Niederdorferstrasse 1
01 250 5300; fax 01 250 5301
4, 15 AX, DC, MC, VI

Krone Unterstrass $$
This well-equipped, comfortable hotel caters to business travelers and is located in a quiet residential area 10 minutes fom the city center.
456 Off the map
Schaffhauserstrasse 1 01 360 5656; fax 01 360 5600 7, 15 AX, DC, MC, VI

Rössli $–$$
The inconspicuous exterior of the Rössli hides a comfortable and imaginatively designed hotel with well-equipped rooms.
456 B2 Rössligasse 7
01 256 7050; fax 01 256 7051
4, 15 AX, DC, MC, VI

ZURICH RESTAURANTS

Price guide: (dinner per person, excluding drinks)
$ SF25–45
$$ SF45–60
$$$ over SF60

Adler's Swiss Chuchi $
This friendly restaurant in the Hotel Adler is a good bet if you want to sample meat or cheese fondue or local veal specialties.
456 B2 Rosengasse 10
01 266 9666 4, 15 AX, DC, MC, VI

Bierhalle Kropf $$
This cheerful restaurant with sumptuously decorated rooms has been serving local dishes since 1888.
456 A2 In Gassen 16 01 221 1805 Closed Sun. 2, 8, 9, 11 MC , VI

Haus Zum Rüden $$$
Overlooking the Limmat River, this historic restaurant serves the best of Swiss specialties in an elegant atmosphere.
456 B2 Limmatquai 42
01 261 9566 Closed Sat.–Sun. 4, 15 AX, DC, MC, VI

Kronenhalle $$–$$$
This long-established restaurant offers traditional dishes beneath artworks by Picasso and Matisse.
456 B2 Rämistrasse 4 01 251 6669 2, 4, 5, 9, 11, 15 AX, DC, MC, VI

Mère Cathérine $
This centrally located garden restaurant serves fish and seafood, with an accent on Mediterranean and Provençal dishes.
456 B2 Nägelihof 3 01 250 5940 4, 15 AX, MC, VI

Münsterhof $$
Historic Münsterhof serves traditional Swiss specialties at good prices and also has a garden.
456 A2 Münsterhof 6
01 211 4340 4, 15 AX, DC, MC, VI

Walliser Kanne $$
This friendly restaurant features every imaginable type of fondue – meat, cheese, *chinoise* – as well as raclette and Swiss specialties such as *rösti* (a potato pancake).
456 A3 Lintheschergasse 21
01 211 3133 10, 11, 13 AX, DC, MC, VI

EUROPEAN DISTANCE CHART

Road distances, in kilometers (km), are calculated by the shortest or quickest routes (highways, main roads) from center to center and do not take into account seasonal weather conditions.

Miles	Km
1	1.6
10	16
20	32
30	48
40	64
50	80
100	160
200	320
300	480
400	640
500	800
1000	1600

Amsterdam (NL)	Athína (Athens) (GR)	Barcelona (E)	Berlin (D)	Brugge/Bruges (B)	Brussel/Bruxelles (Brussels) (B)	Budapest (H)	Den Haag (The Hague) (NL)	Dublin (IRL)	Edinburgh (GB)	Firenze (Florence) (I)	Genève (Geneva) (CH)	Gent (Ghent) (B)	Helsinki (FIN)	Innsbruck (A)	København (Copenhagen) (DK)	Köln (Cologne) (D)	Lisboa (Lisbon) (P)	London (GB)	Luxembourg (L)	Lyon (F)	Madrid (E)	München (Munich) (D)	Nápoli (Naples) (I)	Nice (F)	Odense (DK)	Oslo (N)
1736																										
1600	1591																									
653	1577	1889																								
269	1680	1372	832																							
210	1568	1403	773	101																						
1413	1521	2085	874	1473	1368																					
64	1755	1574	697	211	180	1432																				
959	2350	1958	1522	704	791	2163	930																			
1092	2483	2091	1655	837	924	2296	1063	538																		
1387	544	1103	1228	1331	1219	1085	1406	2001	2134																	
1004	973	809	1119	769	724	1276	896	1355	1488	606																
221	1635	1367	783	52	56	1423	191	742	875	1286	764															
1542	2864	2929	1013	1748	1689	2449	1586	2438	2571	2515	2159	1700														
1001	832	1381	750	1061	956	731	1021	1751	1884	483	574	1011	2037													
926	2248	2313	397	1132	1073	1833	970	1822	1955	1899	1543	1084	620	1421												
262	1481	1419	569	315	210	1158	282	1005	1138	1132	749	265	1502	747	886											
2370	2847	1258	2908	2161	2168	3340	2341	2747	2880	2359	2065	2156	3841	2637	3225	2345										
482	1873	1481	1045	227	314	1686	453	463	665	1524	878	265	1961	1274	1345	528	2270									
410	1356	1190	759	324	212	1193	384	1014	1147	1007	512	279	1697	677	1081	230	2222	537								
932	1069	652	1233	779	734	1429	906	1365	1498	693	153	774	2272	727	1656	751	1908	888	522							
1809	2188	630	2347	1600	1607	2681	1779	2186	2319	1700	1406	1595	3279	1978	2663	1784	625	1709	1660	1249						
834	990	1396	583	894	789	690	854	1584	1717	641	587	844	1870	163	1254	580	2677	1107	566	740	1993					
1859	594	1577	1700	1803	1691	1557	1878	2473	2606	474	1080	1758	2987	955	2371	1604	2833	1996	1479	1167	2174	1113				
1396	910	681	1347	1268	1223	1403	1394	1853	1986	421	541	1263	2551	700	1935	1142	1937	1376	1011	472	1278	858	895			
765	2086	2151	599	971	911	1671	809	1660	1793	1737	1381	922	781	1260	165	724	3063	1183	919	1495	2502	1093	2209	1774		
1510	2832	2897	981	1716	1657	2417	1554	2406	2539	2483	2127	1668	530	2005	588	1470	3809	1929	1665	2241	3247	1838	2954	2519	749	
589	1980	1588	1152	334	421	1793	560	396	598	1631	985	372	2068	1381	1452	635	2377	90	644	995	1816	1214	2103	1483	1290	2036
509	1508	1067	1047	300	307	1494	480	888	1021	1141	542	295	1980	953	1364	484	1856	411	376	466	1295	831	1614	954	1202	1948
2170	2647	1213	2708	1961	1968	3140	2141	2547	2680	2159	1865	1956	3641	2437	3025	2145	318	2070	2022	1708	564	2477	2632	1737	2863	3609
967	1375	1754	343	1027	922	531	987	1717	1850	1026	984	977	1377	549	761	713	2895	1240	747	1098	2333	382	1498	1243	957	1345
1663	521	1381	1504	1607	1495	1362	1683	2277	2410	278	885	1562	2791	759	2175	1409	2637	1800	1283	971	1978	917	219	700	2014	2759
977	1007	1535	726	1037	932	553	997	1727	1860	658	725	987	2013	180	1397	723	2791	1250	722	879	2132	139	1129	875	1236	1981
2078	2555	1166	2616	1869	1876	3048	2049	2454	2587	2067	1773	1864	3549	2345	2933	2053	549	1977	1930	1616	646	2385	2540	1645	2771	3517
2354	2599	1041	2892	2145	2152	3092	2325	2733	2866	2111	1817	2140	3825	2389	3209	2329	408	2256	2206	1660	543	2404	2584	1689	3047	3793
1542	2864	2929	1013	1748	1689	2449	1586	2438	2571	2515	2159	1700	1800	2037	620	1502	3841	1961	1697	2273	3279	1870	2986	2551	781	530
628	1133	1147	753	543	431	1063	602	1213	1346	784	401	498	1793	471	1177	354	2335	736	219	491	1744	360	1256	794	1015	1761
1345	537	1256	1126	1289	1177	847	1364	1959	2092	256	584	1244	2413	381	1797	1090	2512	1482	965	701	1853	539	728	574	1636	2381
1157	1124	1843	637	1217	1112	244	1176	1907	2040	843	1020	1167	2193	475	1577	902	3084	1430	937	1174	2440	434	1315	1161	1415	2161
805	2196	1804	1368	550	637	2009	776	322	311	1847	1201	588	2284	1597	1668	851	2593	339	860	1211	2032	1430	2319	1699	1506	2252
831	940	1095	844	775	663	996	851	1446	1579	591	285	730	1986	284	1370	577	2351	969	451	439	1692	306	1062	600	1209	1954

	Oxford (GB)	Paris (F)	Porto (P)	Praha (Prague) (CZ)	Roma (Rome) (I)	Salzburg (A)	Santiago de Compostela (E)	Sevilla (Seville) (E)	Stockholm (S)	Strasbourg (F)	Venézia (Venice) (I)	Wien (Vienna) (A)	York (GB)
Paris (F)	518												
Porto (P)	2177	1656											
Praha (Prague) (CZ)	1347	1049	2695										
Roma (Rome) (I)	1907	1419	2437	1303									
Salzburg (A)	1347	987	2591	377	934								
Santiago de Compostela (E)	2084	1564	231	2603	2345	2499							
Sevilla (Seville) (E)	2363	1840	679	2762	2389	2543	910						
Stockholm (S)	2068	1982	3641	1377	2791	2013	3548	3827					
Strasbourg (F)	843	489	2135	618	1060	516	2042	2157	1793				
Venézia (Venice) (I)	1589	1119	2312	816	532	436	2219	2266	2413	742			
Wien (Vienna) (A)	1537	1238	2884	294	1119	297	2791	2853	2193	807	605		
York (GB)	295	734	2393	1563	2123	1573	2300	2579	2284	1059	1805	1753	
Zürich (CH)	1076	664	2151	712	867	445	2058	2105	1986	229	548	740	1292

Index

Index

Acknowledgements

Abbreviations for terms appearing below: (t) top; (b) bottom; (l) left; (r) right; (c) centre

The Automobile Assocation wishes to thank the following photographers and libraries for their assistance in the preparation of this book. Mary Evans Picture Library 45(t), 278(t); Ghent Altarpiece, Central Panel, 1432: Lord in Majesty between Virgin Mary and St. John the Baptist; below – Adoration of the Lamb by Jan van Eyck (c.1390–1441) St. Bavo Cathedral, Ghent, Belgium/Bridgeman Art Library 75; Bruce Coleman Collection 193; Corbis/Layne Kennedy 152; Des Hannigan 71, 163(c), 439, 440, 441, 467(t), 479(b), 483(t), 483(b), 511(t), 515(t), 515(b), 519(t), 519(b), 531(t), 531(b); John Heseltine Archive 308, 312, 313; Innsbruck Tourism 39; The J Allan Cash Photolibrary 229, 455; Mri Bankers Guide To Foreign Currency 462, 466, 470, 474, 478, 482, 486, 490, 494, 498, 502, 506, 510, 514, 518, 522, 526, 530, 534; Pictures Colour Library 47(c), 157, 189, 192, 364, 456(t); Rex Features Ltd 121; Spanish Tourist Office 526; Spectrum Colour Library 73, 154, 197, 201, 331, 351, 463(t), 491(t); World Pictures 38, 43, 44, 45(b), 47(b), 48, 55, 61, 69, 74, 155, 162, 163(t), 169, 187, 191(t), 199, 202, 203(t), 203(c), 205, 224, 322, 324, 327, 332, 333, 341(b), 353, 354, 355, 356, 360, 361, 368, 369, 375, 391(t), 418, 420, 421, 422, 423, 435, 438, 443, 450, 452, 454, 456(b), 458, 460; Carol Weitz 463(b), 535(t), 535(b)

The remaining photographs are held in the Association's own library (AA Photo Library) and were taken by the following photographers: AA Photo Library 57, 83, 93, 109, 110, 117, 281(b), 363, 390; Adrian Baker 34, 211, 449, 538; Peter Baker 18, 22, 32, 37, 97(t); M Birkitt 471(t); Liam Blake 270; Jamie Blandford 266; Jim Carnie 82; Michelle Chaplow 399, 417(b), 527(t), 527(b); Douglas Corrance 101, 102; Steve Day 274, 401(t), 413, 414, 415, 444; J Edmanson 168, 307(t), 406(b); Richard Elliott 105; Philip Enticknap 409; Derek Forss 76, 132, 137, 139, 145, 148, 150; Terry Harris 246, 247, 249; A Hemmison 227; Stephen Hill 503(b); Jim Holmes 5, 507(t); JW Jorgensen 135, 144, 151(tl), 151(tr), 479(t); Alex Kouprianoff 52, 53, 58, 59(t), 59(b), 63, 64, 65, 66, 67, 68, 374, 377, 381, 383(t), 383(b), 384, 385, 388, 391(b), 467(b), 511(b), 523(t); Andrew Lawson 106; S McBride 269; S&O Mathews 471(b), 495(t), 495(b); Eric Meacher 81, 191(b), 262, 417(t); Dario Miterdiri 294, 299(c), 300; Andrew Molyneux 392, 397, 424, 427; Rob Moore 487(t), 487(b); George Munday 271; Kim Naylor 430; Rich Newton 112, 115; D Noble 23, 25, 30, 33, 181(t); Ken Paterson 98, 104, 170, 176, 178, 179, 185, 238, 257, 261, 263, 264, 265, 287, 334, 338/339, 339, 341(t), 345, 346, 347, 348, 499(t); Bertrand Rieger 181(c); Douglas Robertson 396; Clive Sawyer 29, 126, 130, 164, 212, 215, 219, 220, 222, 234, 235(t), 237(b), 282, 289, 291, 296, 297, 298, 299(t), 301, 305, 307(b), 317, 319, 320, 321(t), 321(b); Michael Short 273, 278; M Siebert 31(t), 31(c); Slide File 277, 280; Barrie Smith 90, 94, 97(b), 507(b); Antony Souter 118, 171(b), 173, 180, 182, 183, 221(t), 221(c), 223, 233, 235(b), 236, 237(t), 491(b); Rick Strange 171(t), 198, 401(b), 405(t), 405(b), 406(t), 407, 408; R Surman 251; JA Tims 2, 96, 429; D Traverso 206; Jonathon Welsh 111; Stephen Whitehorn 276, 279, 281(t), 503(t); Peter Wilson 116/117, 243, 248, 250, 252, 260, 370, 412, 416, 523(b); TimWoodcock 85; Gregory Wrona 499(b); John Wyand 123, 127, 128, 129(t), 129(c), 131(t), 131(b), 475(t), 475(b); Wyn Voysey 95